Audi
Owners
Workshop
Manual

by Alec J Jones
BSc Eng, C Eng

Models covered

UK: Audi 100: LS, GLS, L5S, GL5S, GL5E, & CD5E
Audi 100 Avant; L, GL5S, & CD5E
1588 & 1984 cc four-cylinder and 2144 cc five-cylinder petrol engines
USA: Audi 5000 Sedan, 131 cu in (2144 cc) five-cylinder gasoline engine

Covers manual and automatic transmission versions. Does not cover diesel engined models

ISBN 0 85696 428 X

HAYNES PUBLISHING GROUP
SPARKFORD YEOVIL SOMERSET ENGLAND
distributed in the USA by
HAYNES PUBLICATIONS INC
861 LAWRENCE DRIVE
NEWBURY PARK
CALIFORNIA 91320
USA

Acknowledgements

Thanks are due to Volkswagenwerk AG for the supply of technical information and certain illustrations, to Castrol Limited who supplied lubrication data, and to the Champion Sparking Plug Company who supplied the illustrations showing the various spark plug conditions. The bodywork repair photographs used in this manual were provided by Lloyds Industries Limited who supply 'Turtle Wax', 'Dupli-color Holts', and other Holts range products.

Lastly, special thanks are due to all those people at Sparkford who helped in the production of this manual. Particularly Martin Penny and Les Brazier who carried out the mechanical work and took the photographs, respectively, Hugh Mayes who edited the text and Stanley Randolph who planned the layout of each page.

About this manual

Its aims

The aim of this manual is to help you get the best value from your vehicle. It can do so in several ways. It can help you decide what work must be done (even should you choose to get it done by a garage), provide information on routine maintenance and servicing, and give a logical course of action and diagnosis when random faults occur. However, it is hoped that you will use the manual by tackling the work yourself. On simpler jobs it may be even quicker than booking the vehicle into a garage, and going there twice to leave and collect it. Perhaps most important, a lot of money can be saved by avoiding the costs the garage must charge to cover its labour and overheads.

The manual has drawings and descriptions to show the function of the various components so that their layout can be understood. Then the tasks are described and photographed in a step-by-step sequence so that even a novice can do the work.

Its arrangement

The manual is divided into twelve Chapters, each covering a logical sub-division of the vehicle. The Chapters are each divided into Sections, numbered with single figures, eg 5; and Sections into paragraphs (or sub-sections), with decimal numbers following on from the Section they are in, eg 5.1, 5.2, 5.3 etc.

It is freely illustrated, especially in those parts where there is a detailed sequence of operations to be carried out. There are two forms of illustration: figures and photographs. The figures are numbered in sequence with decimal numbers, according to their position in the Chapter: eg Fig. 6.4 is the 4th drawing/illustration in Chapter 6. Photographs are numbered (either individually or in related groups) the same as the Section or sub-section of the text where the operation they show is described.

There is an alphabetical index at the back of the manual as well as a contents list at the front.

References to the 'left' or 'right' of the vehicle are in the sense of a person in the driver's seat facing forwards.

Unless otherwise stated, nuts and bolts are removed by turning anti-clockwise, and tightened by turning clockwise.

Whilst every care is taken to ensure that the information in this manual is correct no liability can be accepted by the authors or publishers for loss, damage or injury caused by any errors in, or omissions from the information given.

Introduction to the Audi 100/5000

The new Audi 100 was introduced into the UK in 1976 but bears little resemblance to the earlier model given the same designation. The body and front suspension are completely new and the rear suspension has been rearranged. The car is exceptionally roomy for its size and has a luxury standard of trim and equipment. During the summer of 1977, a similar vehicle, the Audi 5000, was introduced in the USA.

A range of models has been produced, comprising saloons with two, or four-doors, as well as a five-door hatchback version known as the Avant. There is the choice of a four-cylinder engine of 1.6 litre, or 2.0 litre capacity, as well as a five-cylinder 2.2 litre engine which has been developed by adding a further cylinder to the smaller engine. This latter engine is the only one available in the USA but, according to the intended market worldwide, it is produced in carburettor or fuel injection form. The transmission is either a four-speed manual gearbox, or a three-speed automatic transmission.

For each combination of engine and body style there is also a choice of two or more different standards of trim, but only part of the overall range of body, engine and trim options is available in any given market.

Contents

Audi 100 GL5S Saloon

Audi 100 GL5S Fastback

General dimensions, weights and capacities

Dimensions

	Audi 100	Audi 100 Avant	Audi 5000
Overall length	4660/4680 mm * (183.5/184.3 in) *	4567/4587 mm * (179.8/180.6 in) *	4814 mm (189.5 in)
Overall width	1768 mm (69.6 in)	1768 mm (69.6 in)	1768 mm (69.6 in)
Track, front/rear	1470/1445 mm (57.9/56.9 in)	1470/1445 mm (57.9/56.9 in)	1470 mm (57.9 in)
Ground clearance	128 mm (5.04 in)	128 mm (5.04 in)	112 mm (4.4 in)
Wheelbase	2688 mm (105.8 in)	2688 mm (105.8 in)	2677 mm (105.4 in)
Turning circle	1134 mm (44.6 in)	1134 mm (44.6 in)	1134 mm (44.6 in)

* With overriders

Weights

	Audi 100/Audi 100 Avant	Audi 5000
Kerb weight:		
1.6 litre	1110 kg (2447 lb)	–
2.0 litre	1150 kg (2535 lb)	–
2.2 litre	1170 kg (2579 lb)	1222 kg (2694 lb)
Trailer weights:		
Trailer without brakes:		
1.6 litre	590 kg (1301 lb)	–
2.0 litre	610 kg (1345 lb)	–
2.2 litre carburettor	610 kg (1345 lb)	–
2.2 litre fuel injection	620 kg (1368 lb)	600 kg (1323 lb)
Trailer with brakes (manual transmission):		
1.6 litre	1000 kg (2205 lb)	–
2.0 litre	1200 kg (2645 lb)	–
2.2 litre carburettor	1350 kg (2755 lb)	–
2.2 litre fuel injection	1500 kg (3307 lb)	1050 kg (2315 lb)
Trailer with brakes (automatic transmission):		
1.6 litre	1000 kg (2205 lb)	–
2.0 litre	1350 kg (2755 lb)	–
2.2 litre carburettor	1400 kg (3085 lb)	–
2.2 litre fuel injection	1600 kg (3525 lb)	1050 kg (2315 lb)

Capacities

Fuel tank total capacity	13.2 Imp gal, 15.9 US gal, 60 litres
Fuel tank reserve (included in total capacity)	1.8 Imp gal, 2.1 US gal, 8 litres
Engine oil capacity (with filter change):	
1.6 litre engine	7.0 Imp pt, 8.4 US pt, 4.0 litres
Other engines	8.8 Imp pt, 10.6 US pt, 5.0 litres
Engine oil capacity (without filter change):	
1.6 litre engine	6.2 Imp pt, 7.4 US pt, 3.5 litres
Other engines	7.9 Imp pt, 9.5 US pt, 4.5 litres
Oil capacity between MAX and MIN marks on dipstick	1.75 Imp pt, 2.1 US pt, 1.0 litre
Cooling system (including heater):	
1.6 litre engne	12.3 Imp pt, 14.8 US pt, 7.0 litres
2.0 litre engine	13.2 Imp pt, 15.8 US pt, 7.5 litres
2.2 litre engine and 2.0 litre engine with side mounted radiator	14.1 Imp pt, 16.9 US pt, 8.1 litres
Manual gearbox/final drive:	
1.6 and 2.0 litre engines	3.0 Imp pt, 3.6 US pt, 1.7 litres
2.2 litre engine	4.6 Imp pt, 5.5 US pt, 2.6 litres
Automatic transmission:	
Total	10.6 Imp pt, 12.7 US pt, 6.0 litres
Fluid change	5.3 Imp pt, 6.4 US pt, 3.0 litres
Final drive	1.76 Imp pt, 2.1 US pt, 1.0 litre

Use of English

As this book has been written in England, it uses the appropriate English component names, phrases, and spelling. Some of these differ from those used in America. Normally, these cause no difficulty, but to make sure, a glossary is printed below. In ordering spare parts remember the parts list will probably use these words:

English	American	English	American
Aerial	Antenna	Layshaft (of gearbox)	Countershaft
Accelerator	Gas pedal	Leading shoe (of brake)	Primary shoe
Alternator	Generator (AC)	Locks	Latches
Anti-roll bar	Stabiliser or sway bar	Motorway	Freeway, turnpike etc
Battery	Energizer	Number plate	License plate
Bodywork	Sheet metal	Paraffin	Kerosene
Bonnet (engine cover)	Hood	Petrol	Gasoline
Boot lid	Trunk lid	Petrol tank	Gas tank
Boot (luggage compartment)	Trunk	'Pinking'	'Pinging'
Bottom gear	1st gear	Propeller shaft	Driveshaft
Bulkhead	Firewall	Quarter light	Quarter window
Cam follower or tappet	Valve lifter or tappet	Retread	Recap
Carburettor	Carburetor	Reverse	Back-up
Catch	Latch	Rocker cover	Valve cover
Choke/venturi	Barrel	Roof rack	Car-top carrier
Circlip	Snap-ring	Saloon	Sedan
Clearance	Lash	Seized	Frozen
Crownwheel	Ring gear (of differential)	Side indicator lights	Side marker lights
Disc (brake)	Rotor/disk	Side light	Parking light
Drop arm	Pitman arm	Silencer	Muffler
Drop head coupe	Convertible	Spanner	Wrench
Dynamo	Generator (DC)	Sill panel (beneath doors)	Rocker panel
Earth (electrical)	Ground	Split cotter (for valve spring cap)	Lock (for valve spring retainer)
Engineer's blue	Prussian blue	Split pin	Cotter pin
Estate car	Station wagon	Steering arm	Spindle arm
Exhaust manifold	Header	Sump	Oil pan
Fast back (Coupe)	Hard top	Tab washer	Tang; lock
Fault finding/diagnosis	Trouble shooting	Tailgate	Liftgate
Float chamber	Float bowl	Tappet	Valve lifter
Free-play	Lash	Thrust bearing	Throw-out bearing
Freewheel	Coast	Top gear	High
Gudgeon pin	Piston pin or wrist pin	Trackrod (of steering)	Tie-rod (or connecting rod)
Gearchange	Shift	Trailing shoe (of brake)	Secondary shoe
Gearbox	Transmission	Transmission	Whole drive line
Halfshaft	Axleshaft	Tyre	Tire
Handbrake	Parking brake	Van	Panel wagon/van
Hood	Soft top	Vice	Vise
Hot spot	Heat riser	Wheel nut	Lug nut
Indicator	Turn signal	Windscreen	Windshield
Interior light	Dome lamp	Wing/mudguard	Fender

Miscellaneous points

An 'oil seal' is fitted to components lubricated by grease!

A 'damper' is a 'shock absorber', it damps out bouncing, and absorbs shocks of bump impact. Both names are correct, and both are used haphazardly.

Note that British drum brakes are different from the Bendix type that is common in America, so different descriptive names result. The shoe end furthest from the hydraulic wheel cylinder is on a pivot; interconnection between the shoes as on Bendix brakes is most uncommon. Therefore the phrase 'Primary' or 'Secondary' shoe does not apply. A shoe is said to be 'Leading' or 'Trailing'. A 'Leading' shoe is one on which a point on the drum, as it rotates forward, reaches the shoe at the end worked by the hydraulic cylinder before the anchor end. The opposite is a 'Trailing' shoe, and this one has no self servo from the wrapping effect of the rotating drum.

Buying spare parts
and vehicle identification numbers

Buying spare parts

Spare parts are available from many sources. VW/Audi have many dealers throughout the UK, and other dealers, accessory stores and motor factors will also stock VW/Audi spare parts.

Our advice regarding spare part sources is as follows:

Officially appointed vehicle main dealers – This is the best source of parts which are peculiar to your vehicle and are otherwise not generally available (eg complete cylinder heads, internal transmission components, badges, interior trim etc). It is also the only place at which you should buy parts if your vehicle is still under warranty. To be sure of obtaining the correct parts it will always be necessary to give the storeman your vehicle's engine and chassis number, and if possible, to take the 'old' part along for positive identification. Remember that many parts are available on a factory exchange scheme – any parts returned should always be clean! It obviously makes good sense to go straight to the specialists on your vehicle for this type of part, for they are best equipped to supply you.

Other dealers and auto accessory stores – These are often very good places to buy materials and components needed for the maintenance of your vehicle (eg oil filters, spark plugs, bulbs, fan belts, oils and greases, touch-up paint, filler paste etc). They also sell general accessories, usually have convenient opening hours, charge lower prices and can often be found not far from home.

Motor factors – Good factors will stock all of the more important components which wear out relatively quickly (eg clutch components, pistons, valves, exhaust systems, brake cylinders/pipes/hoses/seals/shoes and pads etc). Motor factors will often provide new or reconditioned components on a part exchange basis – this can save a considerable amount of money.

Vehicle identification numbers

Modifications are a continuing and unpublicised process in vehicle manufacture. Spare parts manuals and lists are compiled on a numerical basis, the individual vehicle numbers being essential to identify correctly the component required.

Identification plate: Some, but not all vehicles have an identification plate on the front panel, next to the bonnet latch (Fig. 1) and this plate includes the chassis number.

Chassis number: The chassis number is also stamped on the rear panel of the engine compartment. It will be found near the ignition coil mounting and behind the power steering reservoir on power steering models (photo).

Engine number: On the 1·6 and 2·2 litre engines the engine number is stamped on the left-hand side of the engine on the cylinder block between numbers two and three spark plugs (photo). On the 2·0 litre engine the number is on the rear mounting plate (Fig. 2).

Position of identification plate on front panel (when fitted)

Chassis number

Engine number (1.6 and 2.2 litre)

Engine number 2.0 litre

Tools and working facilities

Introduction

A selection of good tools is a fundamental requirement for anyone contemplating the maintenance and repair of a motor vehicle. For the owner who does not possess any, their purchase will prove a considerable expense, offsetting some of the savings made by doing-it-yourself. However, provided that the tools purchased are of good quality, they will last for many years and prove an extremely worthwhile investment.

To help the average owner to decide which tools are needed to carry out the various tasks detailed in this manual, we have compiled three lists of tools under the following headings: *Maintenance and minor repair*, *Repair and overhaul*, and *Special*. The newcomer to practical mechanics should start off with the *Maintenance and minor repair* tool kit and confine himself to the simpler jobs around the vehicle. Then, as his confidence and experience grows, he can undertake more difficult tasks, buying extra tools as, and when, they are needed. In this way, a *Maintenance and minor repair* tool kit can be built-up into a *Repair and overhaul* tool kit over a considerable period of time without any major cash outlays. The experienced do-it-yourselfer will have a tool kit good enough for most repair and overhaul procedures and will add tools from the *Special* category when he feels the expense is justified by the amount of use to which these tools will be put.

It is obviously not possible to cover the subject of tools fully here. For those who wish to learn more about tools and their use there is a book entitled *How to Choose and Use Car Tools* available from the publishers of this manual.

Maintenance and minor repair tool kit

The tools given in this list should be considered as a minimum requirement if routine maintenance, servicing and minor repair operations are to be undertaken. We recommend the purchase of combination spanners (ring one end, open-ended the other); although more expensive than open-ended ones, they do give the advantages of both types of spanner.

Combination spanners - 10, 11, 12, 13, 14 and 17 mm
Adjustable spanner - 9 inch
Engine sump/gearbox/rear axle drain plug key (where applicable)
Spark plug spanner (with rubber insert)
Spark plug gap adjustment tool
Set of feeler gauges
Brake adjuster spanner (where applicable)
Brake bleed nipple spanner
Screwdriver - 4 in long x $\frac{1}{4}$ in dia (flat blade)
Screwdriver - 4 in long x $\frac{1}{4}$ in dia (cross blade)
Combination pliers - 6 inch
Hacksaw, junior
Tyre pump
Tyre pressure gauge
Grease gun (where applicable)
Oil can
Fine emery cloth (1 sheet)
Wire brush (small)
Funnel (medium size)

Repair and overhaul tool kit

These tools are virtually essential for anyone undertaking any major repairs to a motor vehicle, and are additional to those given in the *Maintenance and minor repair* list. Included in this list is a comprehensive set of sockets. Although these are expensive they will be found invaluable as they are so versatile - particularly if various drives are included in the set. We recommend the $\frac{1}{2}$ in square-drive type, as this can be used with most proprietary torque wrenches. If you cannot afford a socket set, even bought piecemeal, then inexpensive tubular box spanners are a useful alternative.

The tools in this list will occasionally need to be supplemented by tools from the *Special* list.

Sockets (or box spanners) to cover range in previous list
Reversible ratchet drive (for use with sockets)
Extension piece, 10 inch (for use with sockets)
Universal joint (for use with sockets)
Torque wrench (for use with sockets)
'Mole' wrench - 8 inch
Ball pein hammer
Soft-faced hammer, plastic or rubber
Screwdriver - 6 in long x $\frac{5}{16}$ in dia (flat blade)
Screwdriver - 2 in long x $\frac{5}{16}$ in square (flat blade)
Screwdriver - 1$\frac{1}{2}$ in long x $\frac{1}{4}$ in dia (cross blade)
Screwdriver - 3 in long x $\frac{1}{8}$ in dia (electricians)
Pliers - electricians side cutters
Pliers - needle nosed
Pliers - circlip (internal and external)
Cold chisel - $\frac{1}{2}$ inch
Scriber (this can be made by grinding the end of a broken hacksaw blade)
Scraper (this can be made by flattening and sharpening one end of a piece of copper pipe)
Centre punch
Pin punch
Hacksaw
Valve grinding tool
Steel rule/straight edge
Allen keys
Selection of files
Wire brush (large)
Axle-stands
Jack (strong scissor or hydraulic type)

Special tools

The tools in this list are those which are not used regularly, are expensive to buy, or which need to be used in accordance with their manufacturers' instructions. Unless relatively difficult mechanical jobs are undertaken frequently, it will not be economic to buy many of these tools. Where this is the case, you could consider clubbing together with friends (or a motorists' club) to make a joint purchase, or borrowing the tools against a deposit from a local garage or tool hire specialist.

The following list contains only those tools and instruments freely available to the public, and not those special tools produced by the vehicle manufacturer specifically for its dealer network. You will find occasional references to these manufacturers' special tools in the text of this manual. Generally, an alternative method of doing the job without the vehicle manufacturer's special tool is given. However, sometimes, there is no alternative to using them. Where this is the case and the relevant tool cannot be bought or borrowed you will have to entrust the work to a franchised garage.

Valve spring compressor
Piston ring compressor
Balljoint separator
Universal hub/bearing puller
Impact screwdriver
Micrometer and/or vernier gauge
Carburettor flow balancing device (where applicable)
Dial gauge
Stroboscopic timing light
Dwell angle meter/tachometer
Universal electrical multi-meter
Cylinder compression gauge
Lifting tackle
Trolley jack
Light with extension lead

The bolts of the driveshaft mounting flanges and those of the cylinder head may have multi-point (polygon) socket-heads which require the use of the appropriate special socket adaptor tool (photo).

Multi-point (polygon) socket headed bolt and tool

Buying tools

For practically all tools, a tool factor is the best source since he will have a very comprehensive range compared with the average garage or accessory shop. Having said that, accessory shops often offer excellent quality tools at discount prices, so it pays to shop around.

Remember, you don't have to buy the most expensive items on the shelf, but it is always advisable to steer clear of the very cheap tools. There are plenty of good tools around at reasonable prices, so ask the proprietor or manager of the shop for advice before making a purchase.

Care and maintenance of tools

Having purchased a reasonable tool kit, it is necessary to keep the tools in a clean serviceable condition. After use, always wipe off any dirt, grease and metal particles using a clean, dry cloth, before putting the tools away. Never leave them lying around after they have been used. A simple tool rack on the garage or workshop wall, for items such as screwdrivers and pliers is a good idea. Store all normal spanners and sockets in a metal box. Any measuring instruments, gauges, meters, etc, must be carefully stored where they cannot be damaged or become rusty.

Take a little care when tools are used. Hammer heads inevitably become marked and screwdrivers lose the keen edge on their blades fom time to time. A little timely attention with emery cloth or a file will soon restore items like this to a good serviceable finish.

Working facilities

Not to be forgotten when discussing tools, is the workshop itself. If anything more than routine maintenance is to be carried out, some form of suitable working area becomes essential.

It is appreciated that many an owner mechanic is forced by circumstances to remove an engine or similar item, without the benefit of a garage or workshop. Having done this, any repairs should always be done under the cover of a roof.

Wherever possible, any dismantling should be done on a clean flat workbench or table at a suitable working height.

Any workbench needs a vice: one with a jaw opening of 4 in (100 mm) is suitable for most jobs. As mentioned previously, some clean dry storage space is also required for tools, as well as the lubricants, cleaning fluids, touch-up paints and so on which become necessary.

Another item which may be required, and which has a much more general usage, is an electric drill with a chuck capacity of at least $\frac{5}{16}$ in (8 mm). This, together with a good range of twist drills, is virtually essential for fitting accessories such as wing mirrors and reversing lights.

Last, but not least, always keep a supply of old newspapers and clean, lint-free rags available, and try to keep any working area as clean as possible.

Spanner jaw gap comparison table

Jaw gap (in)	Spanner size
0·250	$\frac{1}{4}$ in AF
0·277	7 mm
0·313	$\frac{5}{16}$ in AF
0·315	8 mm
0·344	$\frac{11}{32}$ in AF; $\frac{1}{8}$ in Whitworth
0·354	9 mm
0·375	$\frac{3}{8}$ in AF
0·394	10 mm
0·433	11 mm
0·438	$\frac{7}{16}$ in AF
0·445	$\frac{3}{16}$ in Whitworth; $\frac{1}{4}$ in BSF
0·472	12 mm
0·500	$\frac{1}{2}$ in AF
0·512	13 mm
0·525	$\frac{1}{4}$ in Whitworth; $\frac{5}{16}$ in BSF
0·551	14 mm
0·563	$\frac{9}{16}$ in AF
0·591	15 mm
0·600	$\frac{5}{16}$ in Whitworth; $\frac{3}{8}$ in BSF
0·625	$\frac{5}{8}$ in AF
0·630	16 mm
0·669	17 mm
0·686	$\frac{11}{16}$ in AF
0·709	18 mm
0·710	$\frac{3}{8}$ in Whitworth; $\frac{7}{16}$ in BSF
0·748	19 mm
0·750	$\frac{3}{4}$ in AF
0·813	$\frac{13}{16}$ in AF
0·820	$\frac{7}{16}$ in Whitworth; $\frac{1}{2}$ in BSF
0·866	22 mm
0·875	$\frac{7}{8}$ in AF
0·920	$\frac{1}{2}$ in Whitworth; $\frac{9}{16}$ in BSF
0·938	$\frac{15}{16}$ in AF
0·945	24 mm
1·000	1 in AF
1·010	$\frac{9}{16}$ in Whitworth; $\frac{5}{8}$ in BSF
1·024	26 mm
1·063	$1\frac{1}{16}$ in AF; 27 mm
1·100	$\frac{5}{8}$ in Whitworth; $\frac{11}{16}$ in BSF
1·125	$1\frac{1}{8}$ in AF
1·181	30 mm
1·200	$\frac{11}{16}$ in Whitworth; $\frac{3}{4}$ in BSF
1·250	$1\frac{1}{4}$ in AF
1·260	32 mm
1·300	$\frac{3}{4}$ in Whitworth; $\frac{7}{8}$ in BSF
1·313	$1\frac{5}{16}$ in AF
1·390	$\frac{13}{16}$ in Whitworth; $\frac{15}{16}$ in BSF

A Haltrac hoist and gantry in use during a typical engine removal sequence

Jacking, towing and emergency starting

Jacking

It is important that the vehicle is only lifted at the marked jacking points, regardless of the type of jack being used. On no account should the vehicle be lifted by placing any type of jack under the sump, gearbox, or rear axle because this can cause serious damage.

There are two jacking points on each side (Fig. 3) and their position is marked by an arrowhead pressed in the sill panel (photo). If using any jack other than the car's own body jack, place a block of wood between the jack and the car sill. Always supplement the jack with axle-stands.

Body jack and rear lifting point (arrowed)

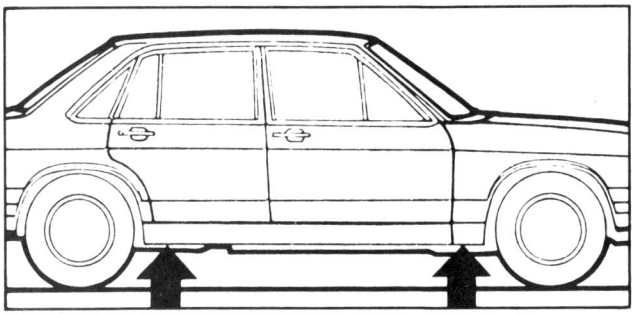

Position of jacking points

Front reinforced lifting/jacking point (arrowed)

Rear reinforced lifting/jacking point (arrowed)

Front towing point

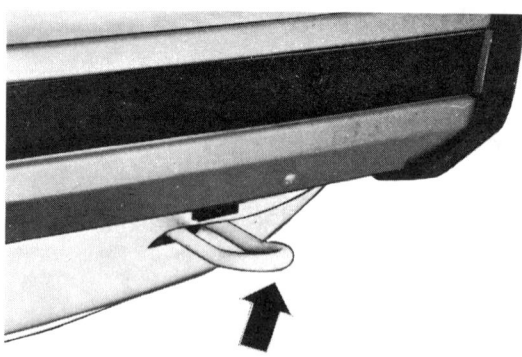

Rear towing point

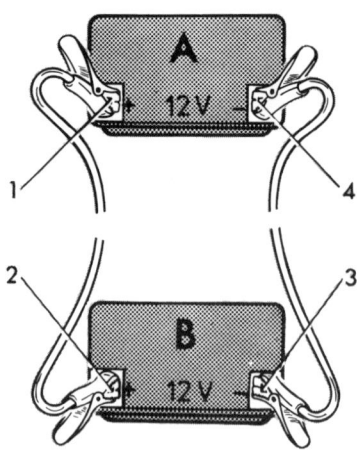

Order of making battery connections for emergency starting

A   **Discharged battery**   B   **Booster battery**

Towing

Towing anchorages are fitted to the front and the rear of the vehicle and a tow line should not be attached to any other points. It is preferable to use a slightly elastic towline, to reduce the strain on both vehicles, either by having a towline manufactured from synthetic fibre, or one which is fitted with an elastic link.

Precautions when towing

1   Turn the ignition key of the vehicle being towed, so that the steering wheel is free (unlocked).

2   Remember that when the engine is not running the brake servo will not operate, so that additional pressure will be required on the brake pedal after the first few applications.

3   *Vehicles with automatic transmission:* Ensure that the gear selector lever is at "N". Do not tow faster than 30 mph (50 kph), or further than 30 miles (50 km) unless the front wheels are lifted clear of the ground.

Emergency starting

1   If the engine should fail to start because the battery is discharged,

it is possible to use jumper leads to the battery in another vehicle. In vehicles with automatic transmission this method is the only means of emergency starting, because they cannot be started by towing.

2   Check that the booster battery is also a 12 volt one and its ampere hour capacity is similar to the one in the vehicle to be started.

3   The jumper cables must be of an adequate cross-section to carry the heavy current involved (similar in size to the starter motor cable). It is also important that the clips at the end of the cables are capable of making a good electrical connection.

4   If the vehicle to be started has been left out in very cold weather, check that the electrolyte in its battery has not frozen. If necessary remove the battery and thaw it before attempting to start the vehicle.

5   Make sure that there is no metal to metal contact between any part of the two vehicles.

6   Unscrew the cell plugs of both batteries, but leave them in place over the filler openings. This is because large volumes of gas are generated when the battery passes a heavy current and the normal venting allowed by the filler caps may not be adequate.

7   Start the engine of the vehicle from which current is to be taken. Leave the engine running and connect one of the jumper leads to the positive (+) terminal of the battery of the car to be started, then connect the other end to the positive (+) pole of the battery of the booster vehicle.

8   Connect one end of the second jumper lead to the negative (−) terminal of the booster battery and finally connect the other end of this jumper lead to the negative (−) terminal of the battery in the vehicle to be started. Take particular care that the ends of the jumper leads cannot touch any metal except the particular battery terminal to which they are connected. It is important to ensure that the clips at the end of the jumper leads cannot fall over and touch the battery clamp, or any other metal.

9   Start the engine of the stranded vehicle in the normal way and when its engine is running, disconnect the jumper leads in exactly the reverse order to the way in which they were connected.

10 Screw in the cell plugs of both batteries.

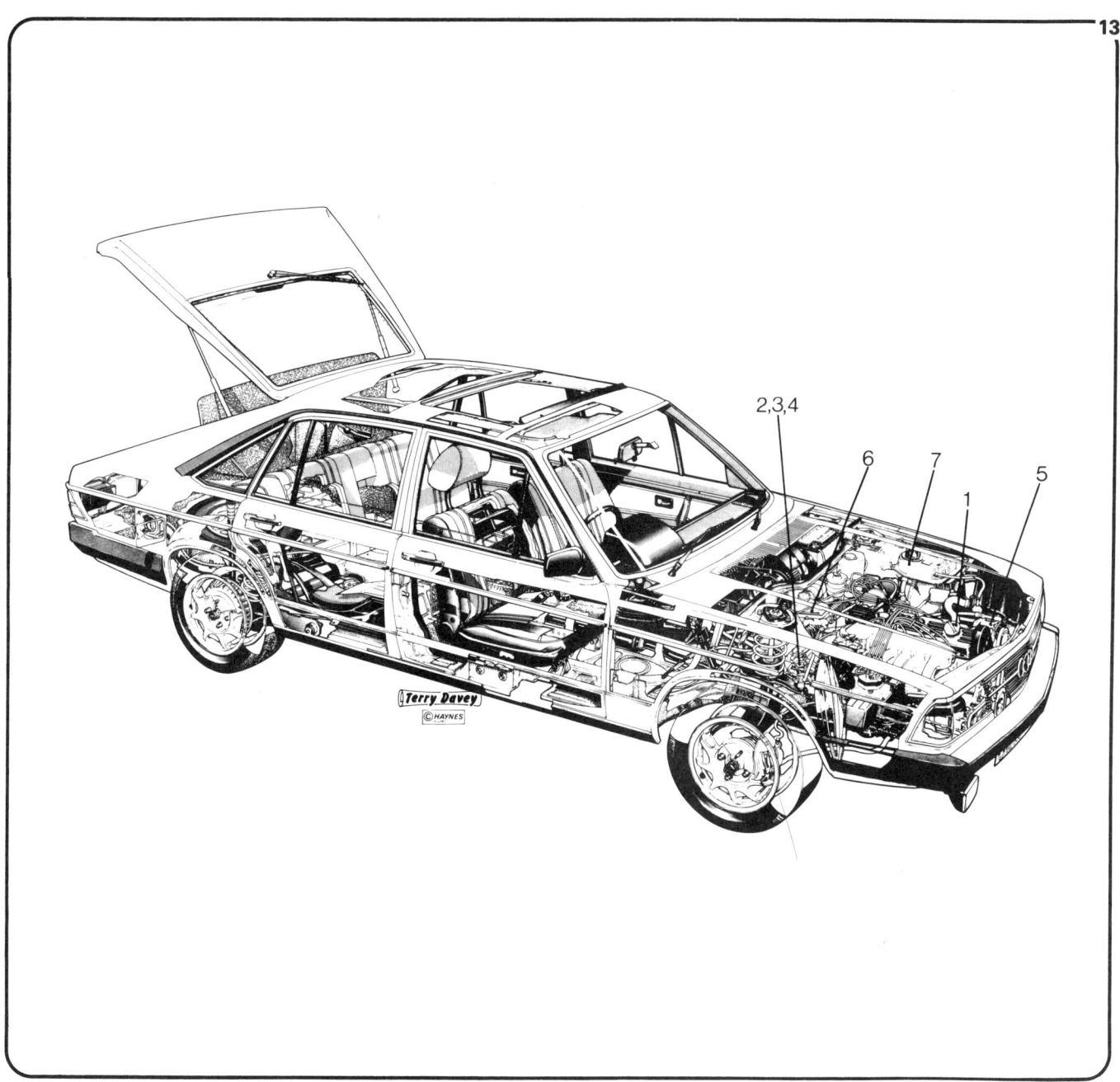

Recommended lubricants and fluids

Component or system	Lubricant type or specification
Engine (1)	20W/50 multigrade oil
Manual transmission/final drive (2)	SAE 80W hypoid gear oil
Final drive (automatic transmission fitted) (3)	SAE 90 hypoid gear oil
Automatic transmission (4) and power steering fluid (5)	Dexron automatic transmission fluid
Clutch and brake system reservoir (6)	SAE J1703E (US FMVSS 116 DOT 3)
Cooling system (7)	Ethylene glycol antifreeze
Hinges and locks	Light mineral oil

Note: *The above are general recommendations only. Lubrication requirements vary from territory to territory and depend on vehicle usage. If in doubt, consult the operator's handbook supplied with the vehicle, or your nearest dealer.*

Routine maintenance

Introduction

Regular maintenance ensures that a car is safe, reliable and economical. It is important to make regular checks so that problems are spotted before they lead to a breakdown and it is also necessary that certain jobs are done at specified intervals of time or after specified mileages.

1 Daily maintenance

The fuel level
Operation of the lights and turn indicators
Operation of the brakes
Operation and fluid level of the windscreen washer and headlamp washers (photos). Also rear window washer on Avant

2 Weekly maintenance

Check the engine oil (photos)
Check the radiator coolant level
Check the levels in the brake and clutch fluid reservoir and the power steering reservoir – when fitted (photos)
If any of the above items require topping-up frequently, it is necessary to find the cause and rectify it
Check the battery electrolyte level (photo)
Examine the tyres for cuts, or uneven wear
Look for leaks, signs of wear and damage to hoses, drivebelts, electrical wiring, or anything else which looks abnormal

Windscreen washer reservoir

Headlamp washer reservoir

Engine oil dipstick

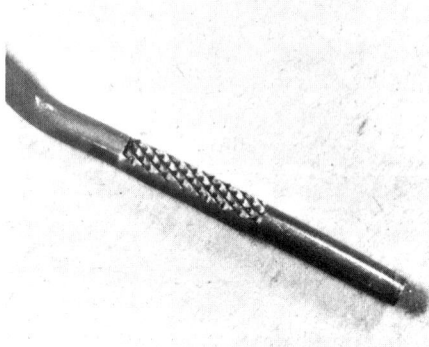

Oil level should be on patterned part

Topping-up the engine oil

Checking the coolant reservoir level

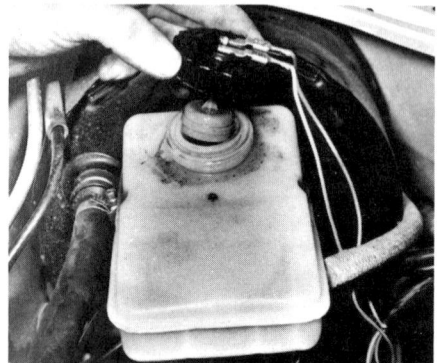

Brake and clutch fluid reservoir

Power steering fluid reservoir

Checking the battery electrolyte level

3   Every 6 months or 5000 miles (8000 km)

Renew engine oil (not filter)
Check brake disc pad wear
Lubricate controls, hinges etc.

4   Every 12 months or 10 000 miles (16 000 km)

Change engine oil and renew filter
Check clutch adjustment
Check for wear in steering system and condition of flexible bellows
Check drivebelt tension and adjust
Check automatic transmission or manual transmission fluid level
Check condition of brake flexible hoses and pipelines
Check exhaust system for condition
Renew spark plugs
Renew distributor contact points
Check rear brake linings and adjust
Check wear of tyre tread
Check CV joint flexible boots for splits
Top-up final drive oil level (automatic transmission fitted)
Top-up power steering oil level (when fitted)
Top-up fluid in self-levelling suspension system
* Final drive is 'filled for life' and an oil change is not specified although drain and filler/level plugs are fitted

Sweden only
Adjust tappet clearances
Renew fuel filter (K-Jetronic)
Check EGR (emission control) system

5   Every 24 months or 20 000 miles (32 000 km)

Adjust tappet clearances
Renew fuel filter
Renew air cleaner element
Renew hydraulic brake fluid

Sweden only
Renew automatic transmission fluid

6   Every 3 years or 30 000 miles (48 000 km)

Renew automatic transmission fluid *

7   Every 80 000 miles (128 000 km)

Renew camshaft drivebelt and idler pulley
Recondition fuel injectors (where fitted) and adjust (dealer operation)
* Manual transmission is 'filled for life' and an oil change is not specified although drain and filler/level plugs are fitted

Chapter 1 Engine

Contents

Specifications

1.6 litre – Part A

General

Code letters	YV (96.9 cu in)
Capacity	1588 cc
Output	63 kW (85 bhp) at 5600 rpm
Torque	91 lbf/ft (124 Nm) at 3200 rpm
Bore	79.5 mm (3.12 in)
Stroke	80 mm (3.150 in)
Compression ratio	8.2:1
Valve timing:	
Inlet open	4° BTDC
Inlet closes	46° ABDC
Exhaust opens	44° BBDC
Exhaust closes	6° ATDC
Firing order	1-3-4-2
Fuel octane rating	91 RON minimum
Oil capacity:	
Including filter	4 litres, 7.04 Imp pt, 8.4 US pt
Excluding filter	3.5 litres, 6.2 Imp pt, 7.4 US pt
Oil pressure (minimum)	2.0 kgf/cm² (28 lbf/in²)
Idle speed	950 ± 50 rpm
Compression pressure (engine at at least 30°C and throttle open):	
New	9 to 13 kg/cm² (128 to 185 lbf/in²)
Wear limit	7 kg/cm² (99.6 lbf/in²)
Max difference between cylinders	2 kg/cm² (28.5 lbf/in²)

Intermediate shaft
Axial play . . . .   0.25 mm (0.009 in)

Crankshaft
Needle bearing depth . . . .   1.5 mm (0.059 in)
End play:
   New . . . .   0.07 to 0.17 mm (0.003 to 0.007 in)
   Wear limit . . . .   0.25 mm (0.009 in)
Journal diameters
Main bearing:
   Original size . . . .   54.00 −0.022 to −0.042 mm (2.126 −0.0009 to −0.0016 in)
   1st undersize . . . .   53.75 −0.022 to −0.042 mm (2.116 −0.0009 to −0.0016 in)
   2nd undersize . . . .   53.50 −0.022 to −0.042 mm (2.102 −0.0009 to −0.0016 in)
   3rd undersize . . . .   53.25 −0.022 to −0.042 mm (2.097 −0.0009 to −0.0016 in)
Big-end bearing:
   Original size . . . .   46.00 −0.022 to −0.042 mm (1.811 −0.0009 to −0.0016 in)
   1st undersize . . . .   45.75 −0.022 to −0.042 mm (1.802 −0.0009 to −0.0016 in)
   2nd undersize . . . .   45.50 −0.022 to −0.042 mm (1.792 −0.0009 to −0.0016 in)
   3rd undersize . . . .   45.25 −0.022 to −0.042 mm (1.782 −0.0009 to −0.0016 in)

Pistons
Piston-to-bore clearance:
   New . . . .   0.03 mm (0.0012 in)
   Wear limit . . . .   0.07 mm (0.0028 in)
Groove-to-ring clearance:
   New . . . .   0.02 to 0.05 mm (0.0008 to 0.0020 in)
   Wear limit . . . .   0.15 mm (0.0059 in)

Piston oversizes:

	Piston diameter	Bore diameter
Standard	79.48 mm (3.129 in)	79.51 mm (3.130 in)
1st oversize	79.73 mm (3.139 in)	79.76 mm (3.140 in)
2nd oversize	79.98 mm (3.149 in)	80.01 mm (3.150 in)
3rd oversize	80.48 mm (3.169 in)	80.51 mm (3.170 in)

Piston wear limit:
   Difference between skirt diameter and nominal
   dimension of crown . . . .   0.04 mm (0.002 in)

Piston rings
Endgap clearance (ring 15 mm from bottom of bore):
   New . . . .   0.30 to 0.45 mm (0.012 to 0.018)
   Wear limit . . . .   1.0 mm (0.039 in)

Connecting rod
Axial play (wear limit) . . . .   0.37 mm (0.015 in)
Big-end bearing clearance (wear limit) . . . .   0.12 mm (0.005 in)

Camshaft
Axial play (wear limit) . . . .   0.15 mm (0.006 in)
Bearing clearance (wear limit) . . . .   0.15 mm (0.006 in)

Tappet clearances
Engine warm:
   Inlet . . . .   0.20 to 0.30 mm (0.008 to 0.012 in)
   Exhaust: . . . .   0.40 to 0.50 mm (0.016 to 0.020 in)
Engine cold:
   Inlet . . . .   0.15 to 0.25 mm (0.006 to 0.010 in)
   Exhaust . . . .   0.35 to 0.45 mm (0.014 to 0.018 in)
Adjusting shim thicknesses . . . .   3.00 to 4.25 mm (0.118 to 0.167 in) at 0.05 mm (0.002 in) intervals

Valve guides
Wear limit:
   Inlet . . . .   1.0 mm (0.039 in)
   Exhaust . . . .   1.3 mm (0.051 in)

Cylinder head
Minimum height (between faces) . . . .   132.55 mm (5.219 in)
Surface finish . . . .   15 microns

Oil pump
Gear backlash . . . .   0.05 to 0.20 mm (0.0020 to 0.0079 in)
Axial play (wear limit) . . . .   0.15 mm (0.006 in)

2.0 litre – Part B

General

	WA (High compression)	WF (Low compression)
Code letters	WA (High compression)	WF (Low compression)
Capacity	1984 cc (121 cu in)	1984 cc (121 cu in)
Output	85 kW (115 bhp) at 5500 rpm	77 kW (105 bhp) at 5500 rpm
Torque	168 Nm (124 lbf/ft) at 3500 rpm	155 Nm (115 lbf/ft) at 3500 rpm
Bore	86.5 mm (3.41 in)	86.5 mm (3.41 in)
Stroke	84.4 mm (3.32 in)	84.4 mm (3.32 in)
Compression ratio	9.3:1	7.0:1
Valve timing:		
Inlet opens	6° BTDC	6° BTDC
Inlet closes	42° ABDC	42° ABDC
Exhaust opens	46° BBDC	46° BBDC
Exhaust closes	2° ATDC	42° ATDC
Fuel octane rating	98 RON minimum	83 RON minimum
Oil pressure	2.0 kgf/cm² (28.5 lbf/in²)	2.0 kgf/cm² (28.5 lbf/in²)
Idle speed	950 ± 50 rpm	950 ± 50 rpm
Oil capacity:		
Including filter	5.0 litres, 8.8 Imp pt, 10.6 US pt	5.0 litres, 8.8 Imp pt, 10.6 US pt
Excluding filter	4.5 litres, 7.9 Imp pt, 9.5 US pt	4.5 litres, 7.9 Imp pt, 9.5 US pt
Compression pressure (engine at more than 30°C and throttle open):		
New	9-13 kgf/cm² (1280 to 1850 lbf/in²)	8 to 11 kgf/cm² (113.8 to 156.5 lbf/in²)
Wear limit	7.0 kgf/cm² (99.6 lbf/in²)	6.5 kgf/cm² (92.5 lbf/in²)
Max differential between cylinders	2.0 kgf/cm² (28.5 lbf/in²)	3.0 kgf/cm² (42.7 lbf/in²)

Crankshaft

Needle bearing depth	1.0 mm (0.040 in)	1.0 mm (0.040 in)
Endplay:		
New	0.10 to 0.19 mm (0.004 to 0.007 in)	0·10 to 0·19 mm (0.004 to 0.007 in)
Wear limit	0.25 mm (0.010 in)	0.25 mm (0.010 in)
Journal diameters:		
Main bearing:		
Original size	64.00 −0.022 to −0.042 mm (2.52 − 0.0009 to −0.0016 in)	
1st undersize	63.75 −0.022 to −0.042 mm (2.51 − 0.0009 to −0.0016 in)	
2nd undersize	63.50 −0.022 to −0.042 mm (2.50 − 0.0009 to −0.0016 in)	
3rd undersize	63.25 −0.022 to −0.042 mm (2.49 − 0.0009 to −0.0016 in)	
Big-end bearing:		
Original size	48.00 −0.022 to −0.042 mm (1.89 − 0.0009 to −0.0016 in)	
1st undersize	47.75 −0.022 to −0.042 mm (1.88 − 0.0009 to −0.0016 in)	
2nd undersize	47.50 −0.022 to −0.042 mm (1.87 − 0.0009 to −0.0016 in)	
3rd undersize	47.25 −0.022 to −0.042 mm (1.86 − 0.0009 to −0.0016 in)	

Pistons

Piston-to-bore clearance:		
New	0.03 mm (0.0012 in)	0.03 mm (0.0012 in)
Wear limit	0.08 mm (0.0013 in)	0.08 mm (0.0013 in)
Groove-to-ring clearance:		
New	0.04 to 0.07 mm (0.0016 to 0.0028 in)	0.04 to 0.07 mm (0.0016 to 0.0028 in)
Wear limit	0.10 mm (0.004 in)	0.10 mm (0.004 in)
Piston wear limit (difference between skirt diameter and nominal dimension of crown)	0.04 mm (0.0016 in)	0.04 mm (0.0016 in)
Piston oversizes:	**Piston diameter**	**Bore diameter**
Standard	86.48 mm (3.40473 in)	86.51 mm (3.40591 in)
	86.49 mm (3.40512 in)	86.52 mm (3.40631 in)
	86.50 mm (3.40552 in)	86.53 mm (3.40670 in)
1st oversize	86.73 mm (3.41457 in)	86.76 mm (3.41575 in)
	86.74 mm (3.41496 in)	86.77 mm (3.41615 in)
	86.75 mm (3.41536 in)	86.78 mm (3.41654 in)
2nd oversize	86.98 mm (3.42441 in)	87.01 mm (3.42558 in)
	86.99 mm (3.42479 in)	87.02 mm (3.42597 in)
	87.00 mm (3.42519 in)	87.03 mm (3.42637 in)
3rd oversize	87.48 mm (3.44408 in)	87.51 mm (3.44526 in)
	87.49 mm (3.44448 in)	87.52 mm (3.44566 in)
	87.50 mm (3.44487 in)	87.53 mm (3.44605 in)

Piston rings

Endgap clearance (ring 15 mm from bottom of bore):		
New	0.30 to 0.50 mm (0.0118 to 0.020 in)	0.30 to 0.50 mm (0.0118 to 0.020 in)
Wear limit	1.0 mm (0.040 in)	1.0 mm (0.040 in)

Connecting rod
Axial play (wear limit) . . . . 0.4 mm (0.016 in)   0.4 mm (0.016 in)
Big-end bearing clearance (wear limit) . . . . 0.10 mm (0.004in)   0.10 mm (0.004 in)

Tappet clearances
Engine warm:
  Inlet . . . . 0.20 to 0.25 mm (0.008 to 0.010 in)   0.20 to 0.25 mm (0.008 to 0.010 in)
  Exhaust . . . . 0.45 to 0.50 mm (0.018 to 0.020 in)   0.45 to 0.50 mm (0.018 to 0.020 in)

Engine cold:
  Inlet . . . . 0.10 to 0.15 mm (0.004 to 0.006 in)   0.10 to 0.15 mm (0.004 to 0.006 in)
  Exhaust . . . . 0.40 to 0.45 mm (0.016 to 0.018 in)   0.40 to 0.45 mm (0.016 to 0.018 in)
Tappet adjusters . . . . 1 complete turn alters clearance 0.05 mm (0.0020 in)   1 complete turn alters clearance 0.05 mm (0.0020 in)

Camshaft
Axial play (wear limit) . . . . 0.2 mm (0.008 in)   0.2 mm (0.008 in)

Valve guides
Wear limit:
  Inlet . . . . 0.9 mm (0.035 in)   0.9 mm (0.035 in)
  Exhaust . . . . 1.1 mm (0.043 in)   1.1 mm (0.043 in)

Cylinder head
Minimum height from lower edge of hole to face (see Fig. 1.74) . . . . . 139.5 mm (5.492 in)   139.5 mm (5.492 in)

2.2 litre – Part C

General
Capacity . . . . 2144 cc (130.8 cu in)

Code letters . . . .

	WB	WC	WD	WE (California)	WE (Sweden)	WG
Output						
kW/rpm	85/5500	100/5700	79/5300	79/5300	85/5300	100/5700
bhp/rpm	115/5500	136/5700	108/5300	108/5300	115/5300	136/5700
Torque						
Nm/rpm	166/3500	185/4200	155/4000	163/4000	168/4000	185/4200
lbf ft/rpm	122/3500	136/4200	114/4000	120/4000	124/4000	136/4200
Bore						
mm	79.5	79.5	79.5	79.5	79.5	79.5
in	3.1299	3.1299	3.1299	3.1299	3.1299	3.1299
Stroke						
mm	86.4	86.4	86.4	86.4	86.4	86.4
in	3.4016	3.4016	3.4016	3.4016	3.4016	3.4016
Compression ratio	8.3 : 1	9.3 : 1	8.0 : 1	8.0 : 1	8.0 : 1	9.3 : 1
Valve timing:						
Inlet open BTDC	6°	0°	6°	6°	6°	0°
Inlet closes ABDC	44°	51°	44°	44°	44°	51°
Exhaust opens BBDC	40°	40°	40°	40°	40°	40°
Exhaust closes ATDC	10°	10°	10°	10°	10°	10°
Fuel octane rating (RON minimum)	91	98	91	91	91	98

Oil pressure (minimum) . . . . 1.0 kgf/cm^2 (14.2 lbf/in^2)
Idle speed . . . . 900 ± 50 rpm
Oil capacity:
  Including filter . . . . 5.0 litres, 8.8 Imp pt, 10.6 US pts
  Excluding filter . . . . 4.5 litres, 7.9 Imp pt, 9.5 US pt
Compression pressure (engine at more than 30°C and throttle open:

	WC, WG	WB, WD, WE
New	13 to 19 kgf/cm^2 (128 to 185 lbf/in^2)	8.5 to 12 kgf/cm^2 (121 to170 lbf/in^2)
Wear limit	7.5 kgf/cm^2 (106.7 lbf/in^2)	7.0 kgf/cm^2 (99.6 lbf/in^2)
Main differential between cylinders	3.0 kgf/cm^2 (42.7 lbf/in^2)	3.0 kgf/cm^2 (42.7 lbf/in^2)

Crankshaft
Needle bearing depth . . . . 5.5 mm (0.217 in)
Endplay:
  New . . . . 0.07 to 0.18 mm (0.003 to 0.007 in)
  Wear limit . . . . 0.25 mm (0.010 in)
Journal diameters
  Main bearing:
    Original size . . . . 58.00 −0.022 to −0.042 mm (2.2835 −0.0009 to −0.0016 in)
    1st oversize . . . . 57.75 −0.022 to −0.042 mm (2.2736 −0.0009 to −0.0016 in)
    2nd oversize . . . . 57.50 −0.022 to −0.042 mm (2.2638 −0.0009 to −0.0016 in)
    3rd oversize . . . . 57.25 −0.022 to −0.042 mm (2.2539 −0.0009 to −0.0016 in)

Big-end bearing:
- Original size .... 46.00 −0.022 to −0.042 mm (1.8110 −0.0009 to −0.0016 in)
- 1st oversize .... 45.75 −0.022 to −0.042 mm (1.8012 −0.0009 to −0.0016 in)
- 2nd oversize .... 45.50 −0.022 to −0.042 mm (1.7913 −0.0009 to −0.0016 in)
- 3rd oversize .... 45.25 −0.022 to −0.042 mm (1.7726 −0.0009 to −0.0016 in)

Pistons
Piston-to-bore clearance:
- New .... 0.025 mm (0.001 in)
- Wear limit .... 0.07 mm (0.0028 in)

Groove-to-ring clearance:
- New .... 0.02 to 0.08 mm (0.0008 to 0.0032 in)
- Wear limit .... 0.1 mm (0.004 in)

Piston wear limit (difference between skirt diameter and nominal
dimension of crown) .... 0.04 mm (0.0016 in)

Piston oversizes:

	Piston diameter	Bore diameter
Standard	79.48 mm (3.129 in)	79.51 mm (3.130 in)
1st oversize	79.73 mm (3.139 in)	79.76 mm (3.140 in)
2nd oversize	79.98 mm (3.149 in)	80.01 mm (3.150 in)
3rd oversize	80.48 mm (3.169 in)	80.51 mm (3.170 in)

Piston rings
Endgap clearance (ring 15 mm from bottom of bore):
- New .... 0.25 to 0.5 mm (0.010 to 0.020 in)
- Wear limit .... 1.0 mm (0.40 in)

Connecting rod
Axial play (wear limit) .... 0.4 mm (0.016 in)
Bearing clearance (wear limit) .... 0.12 mm (0.005 in)

Tappet clearances
Engine warm:
- Inlet .... 0.20 to 0.30 mm (0.008 to 0.012 in)
- Exhaust .... 0.40 to 0.50 mm (0.016 to 0.020 in)

Engine cold:
- Inlet .... 0.15 to 0.25 mm (0.006 to 0.010 in)
- Exhaust .... 0.35 to 0.45 mm (0.014 to 0.018 in)

Adjusting shim thickness .... 3.00 to 4.25 mm (0.118 to 0.167 in) at 0.05 mm (0.002 in) intervals

Valve guides
Wear limit:
- Inlet .... 1.0 mm (0.039 in)
- Exhaust .... 1.3 mm (0.051 in)

Camshaft
Axial play (wear limit) .... 0.15 mm (0.006 in)

Cylinder head
Minimum height (face-to-face) .... 132.75 mm (5.226 in)
Surface finish .... 15 microns

Torque wrench settings

	Nm	lbf ft
Cylinder head		
Hexagon or polygon socket headed bolts (2.0 litre):		
Warm	120	89
Cold	100	74
Hexagon socket headed bolts (1.6 and 2.2 litre):		
Warm	85	63
Cold	75	55
Polygon socket headed bolts (cold, 1.6 and 2.2 litre)*	75 $+\frac{1}{4}$ additional turn	55 $+\frac{1}{4}$ additional turn

Do not retighten cylinder head bolts with polygon socket heads when engine is warm or after 620 miles (1000 km) of running

	Nm	lbf ft
Cylinder head cover:		
1.6 litre	6	4
2.0 litre	8	6
2.2 litre	10	7
Spark plugs	30	22
Temperature gauge sender	8	6
Camshaft sprocket	79	58
Timing belt tensioner:		
1.6 litre	44	32
2.0 litre	39	29
2.2 litre	20	15
Fuel injector lines	25	18
Sump bolts:		
1.6 litre	8	6
2.0 litre (M6 bolts)	8	6

	Nm	lbf ft
2.0 litre (M8 bolts)	15	11
2.2 litre	10	7
Sump drain plug:		
1.6 litre	30	22
2.0 and 2.2 litre	39	29
Oil pump-to-crankcase bolts:		
1.6 litre	20	14
2.0 litre	10	7
2.2 litre (M6 bolts)	10	7
2.2 litre (M8 bolt)	20	14
Oil pressure relief valve (2.0 and 2.2 litre)	40	29
Oil pump backplate setscrews:		
2.0 litre	8	6
2.2 litre	10	7
Oil pump cover and pick-up bolts (1.6 litre)	10	7
Oil pump pick-up-to-crankcase bolts (2.0 and 2.2 litre)	10	7
Oil pressure switch:		
1.6 litre and 2.0 litre	12	8
2.2 litre	15	11
Oil filler flange (1.6 litre)	25	18
Timing sprocket/vibration damper-to-crankshaft:		
1.6 litre	79	58
2.0 litre	245	180
2.2 litre	345	254
Intermediate shaft sprocket (1.6 litre)	79	58
Pulley/vibration damper-to-timing belt sprocket	20	15
Intermediate shaft sealing flange-to-cylinder block (1.6 litre)	25	18
Coolant pump:		
1.6 and 2.2 litre	20	15
2.0 litre (M6 bolts)	10	7
2.0 litre (M8 bolts)	20	15
Radiator thermostatic switch	49	36
Starter motor:		
1.6 litre	20	15
2.0 and 2.2 litre	58	43
Main bearings:		
1.6 and 2.2 litre	65	47
2.0 litre	80	58
No 5 main bearing outer bolts (2.0 litre)	65	47
Crankshaft rear seal flange:		
1.6 and 2.2 litre	10	7
2.0 litre	65	47
Crankshaft front seal flange (1.6 litre)	10	7
Connecting rod bearing caps:		
1.6 litre	45	33
2.0 litre	58	43
2.2 litre	49	36
Camshaft bearing caps	20	15

Part A – 1.6 litre engine

1　General description

The engine has four cylinders in-line and is liquid cooled. A belt driven pump circulates coolant around the combustion chambers and through a front mounted radiator; and cooling of the radiator is assisted by an electrically driven fan, which is thermostatically controlled.

The camshaft, driven from the crankshaft by a toothed belt, is mounted above the valves and operates them through bucket tappets. The valve clearance is adjusted by the use of shims.

The engine has a full-flow lubrication system from a gear type oil pump mounted in the sump, and driven by an extension of the distributor which is itself geared to the intermediate shaft. The oil filter is of the cartridge type, mounted on the left-hand side of the cylinder block.

2　Major operations possible with engine in place

1　The water pump, fuel pump, distributor and radiator can be removed with the engine installed in the car.

2　The cylinder head and camshaft can be removed for decarbonising and valve grinding; and new alternator and timing belts can be fitted with the engine in place.

3　The clutch, flywheel or driveplate (auto-transmission) are not accessible without removing either the engine or the gearbox; if the engine does not require major attention it is easier to remove the gearbox, leaving the engine in place.

4　It is possible to remove the sump and oil pump without removing the engine, but to do so the engine must be supported from above and the subframe front mounting bolts removed. Removal of the sump with the engine in position requires a hexagon socket with an extension to reach the bolts at the rear of the sump.

5　With the sump, oil pump, and cylinder head removed, the pistons and connecting rods can be removed through the top of the cylinder block although this job is best performed with the engine out of the car.

6　The intermediate shaft can be withdrawn if the fuel pump and distributor are first removed but as the engine will have to be raised or lowered to permit shaft removal, it is again a job to be done with the engine out of the car if at all possible.

3 Engine – removal and refitting

It is recommended that the engine is removed leaving the transmission in the car.

1   Disconnect the battery leads.

2   Remove the cap from the coolant reservoir to relieve the pressure in the system. Place a large bowl beneath the engine to catch the coolant, then loosen the clamps of the bottom hose and heater hose. Pull the hoses off and drain the coolant.

3   Remove the intake air hose from the air cleaner and remove the air cleaner, referring to Chapter 3 if necessary. After removing the air cleaner, cover the carburettor air intake with a clean rag, or plastic bag, to stop the entry of dirt.

4   With the help of an assistant, mark the position of the bonnet hinges, remove the bolts and lift the bonnet off.

5   Pull the engine bonnet lock cable towards the driver's side and detach the cable from the bracket on the radiator.

6   Unscrew the clutch cable adjusting nut to loosen the clutch cable and then detach the cable from the clutch operating lever on the bellhousing.

7   Loosen the clips on the two hoses attached to the coolant reservoir and detach the hoses. Loosen the clip at the engine end of the upper coolant hose and detach the hose.

8   Disconnect the plug connections of the radiator fan and the radiator thermostatic switch, then remove the two brackets from the bottom of the radiator and lift the radiator out.

9   Disconnect the throttle cable. On cars fitted with a manual gearbox this is done by removing the adjuster clip from the point where the outer cable is attached to the carburettor bracket and then disengaging the inner cable from the throttle quadrant. On cars with automatic transmission, remove the circlip from the end of the throttle cable at its attachment to the throttle lever and remove the take-up spring. Remove the nut from the ferrule of the cable adjuster and pull the throttle cable out of the bracket on the carburettor.

Fig. 1.1 Disconnect hoses to drain coolant (1.6 litre) (Sec 3)

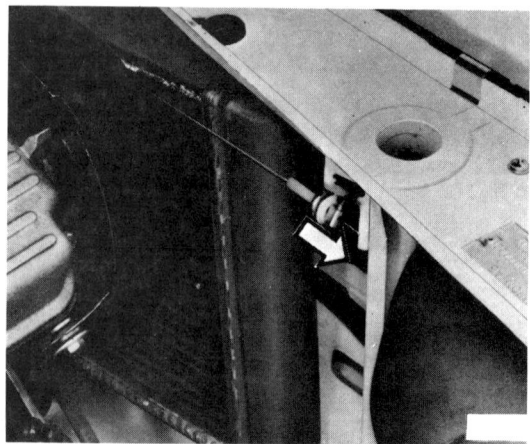

Fig. 1.2 Bonnet lock guide sleeve (Sec 3)

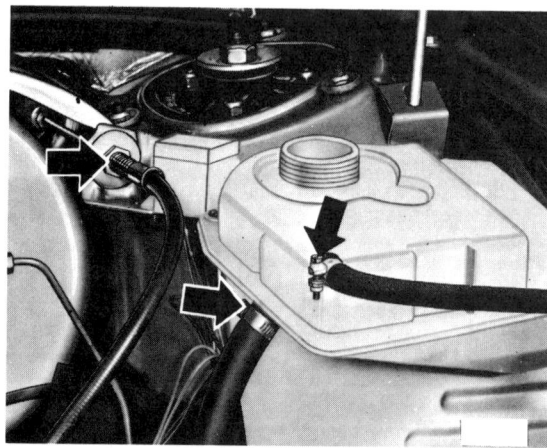

Fig. 1.3 Coolant reservoir hoses and clutch cable adjuster (Sec 3)

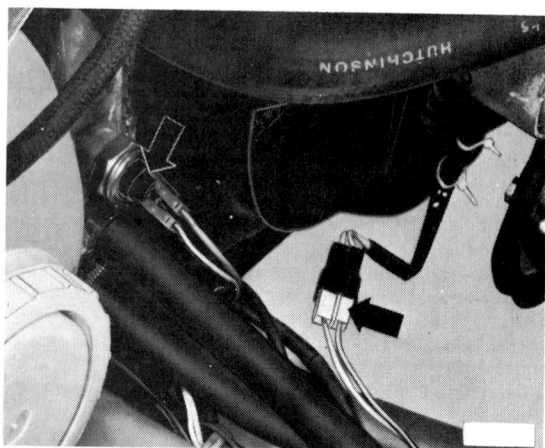

Fig. 1.4 Radiator fan and thermostatic switch connections (1.6 litre) (Sec 3)

Fig. 1.5 Radiator fixings (1.6 litre) (Sec 3)

Fig. 1.6 Throttle connection (1.6 litre manual) (Sec 3)

Fig. 1.7 Throttle connection (1.6 litre automatic) (Sec 3)

Fig. 1.8 Coolant, vacuum and electrical connections
(1·6 litre automatic) (Sec 3)

Fig. 1.9 Carburettor electrical connections (1.6 litre) (Sec 3)

Fig. 1.10 Oil pressure and temperature connections (1.6 litre)
(Sec 3)

Fig. 1.11 Fuel line disconnection points (1.6 litre) (Sec 3)

10 Disconnect the heater hoses from the inlet manifold and disconnect the wires from the inlet manifold thermostatic switch. Disconnect the two hoses to the oil cooler on vehicles with automatic transmission.

11 Disconnect the brake servo vacuum hose from the inlet manifold and pull the vacuum hose(s) off the distributor vacuum unit.

12 Disconnect the three electrical connections from the carburettor and disconnect the electrical connections to the oil pressure switch and the temperature sender.

13 Release the clamp and remove the hose to the heater from the

temperature sender housing.

14 Disconnect the high and low tension connections to the ignition coil and disconnect the wiring to the windscreen washer motor.

15 Disconnect the alternator plug connection.

16 Remove the cover from the right-hand engine mounting and remove the upper bolts from the bellhousing. A long socket extension will be required for this.

17 Disconnect the fuel pipe from the pump to the filter and disconnect the fuel return line from the Y-piece.

18 With a suitable container placed beneath the sump, remove the sump drain plug and drain out the oil. Refit the drain plug and tighten it.

19 Attach lifting slings to the alternator bracket and to the lifting lug at the rear of the engine. Ensure that the slings are in good condition, have a safe working load of at least 250 lb (110 kg), and are fitted so that there is no danger of their slipping. The front sling should be shorter than the rear one so that the engine, when free, will be at an angle of about 30°. Attach the slings to a hoist and raise the hoist until the weight of the engine is taken off the engine bearers.

20 Remove the mounting from the left-hand side of the engine, if necessary raising the hoist slightly to achieve this.

21 Remove the bolts attaching the right-hand engine mounting to the cylinder block and swivel the mounting on its connection to the chassis to push it away from the engine.

22 Remove the six nuts attaching the exhaust pipe to the exhaust manifold and pull off the exhaust pipe.

23 Note the position of the three electrical connections to the starter motor and then remove them. Remove the two starter motor fixing bolts and take the motor off.

24 On vehicles with automatic transmission, turn the starter ring so that each of the three torque converter mounting bolts is accessible in turn through the starter motor hole and remove the bolts attaching the converter to the driveplate.

25 Pack wooden blocks beneath the gearbox, so that it remains in the same position when the engine is removed.

26 On vehicles with manual transmission, remove the lower bolts connecting the engine to the gearbox. Remove the cover plate from the bottom of the bell housing.

27 Check that there is nothing attached to the engine which will prevent its removal and then separate the engine from the gearbox, which can be done by holding one of the support slings and pushing the car to the rear slightly.

28 As soon as the gearbox input shaft is free of its bearing in the crankshaft the engine can be lifted. Care must be taken to prevent damage to the input shaft, the clutch and the body. When the engine is clear of the gearbox, turn the engine sideways to make its removal easier. On vehicles with automatic transmission, secure the torque converter to prevent it from falling out.

29 Although refitting the engine is the reversal of the operations necessary for removing it, there are a few points which need particular care.

30 When fitting the engine to the gearbox, make sure that the mating faces of the engine and gearbox are aligned and parallel before attempting to push them together and if it is difficult to enter the input shaft into the clutch splines, turn the crankshaft pulley a small amount to line the splines up. If the clutch has been removed, make sure that it has been centred accurately (Chapter 5). Do not attempt to force the engine and gearbox together, because this will result in damage.

31 Connect the starter motor cable to the solenoid as shown in Fig. 1.15 and ensure that the cable is routed well clear of all parts of the engine and body. If this is not done, there is a risk of a short circuit and a fire.

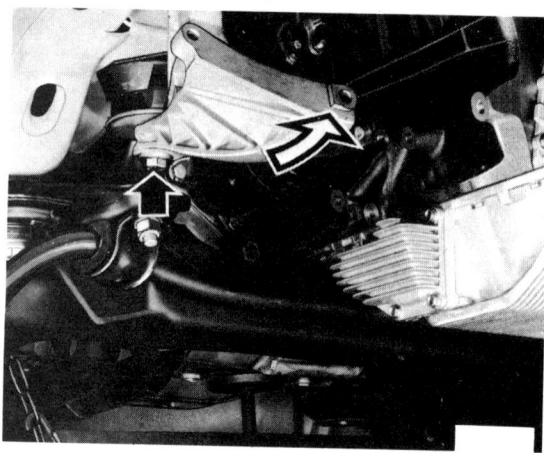

Fig. 1.12 Swing engine mounting aside (1.6 litre) (Sec 3)

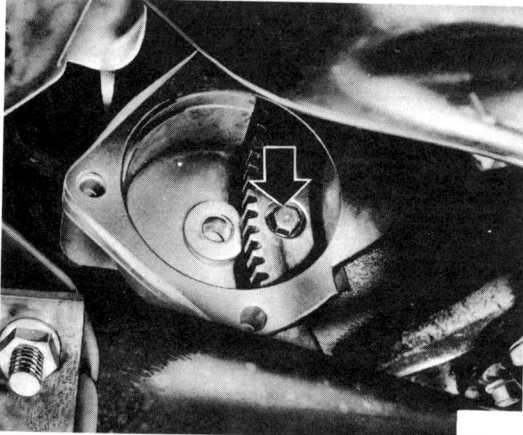

Fig. 1.13 Drive plate bolts (automatic transmission) (Sec 3)

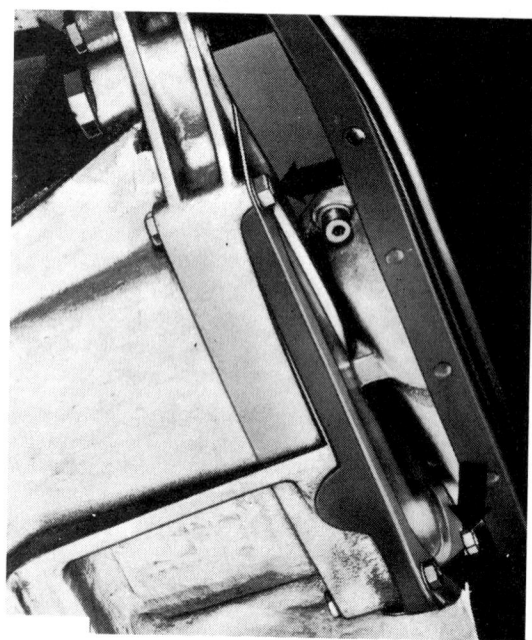

Fig. 1.14 Cover plate (1.6 litre manual transmission) (Sec 3)

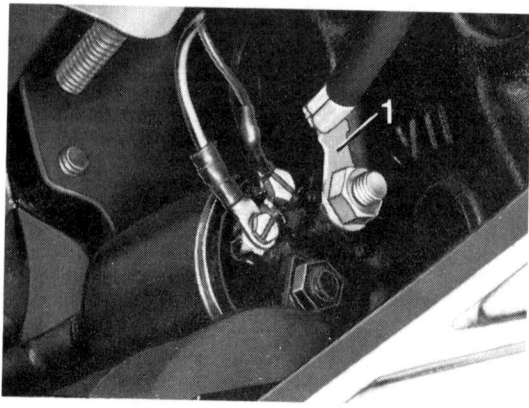

Fig. 1.15 Starter motor and solenoid connections (1.6 litre) (Sec 3)

1   *Starter motor cable*

32 Check that the engine has been filled with oil and that the cooling system is full before starting the engine.

33 Align the exhaust system so that it is free from strain.

34 Ensure that the rubber engine mountings are not strained, by leaving their final tightening until the engine is idling.

4 Cylinder head and camshaft – removal

1 If the cylinder head is to be removed without removing the engine, the following preliminary operations are necessary. Camshaft removal with the cylinder head in-situ or out of the vehicle, is covered in paragraphs 7 to 12.

(a) Disconnect the battery leads
(b) Drain the cooling system
(c) Remove the air cleaner
(d) Disconnect the throttle cable
(e) Disconnect the heater hoses
(f) Disconnect the carburettor electrical connections
(g) Disconnect the plug leads
(h) Disconnect the fuel pipe to the carburettor
(i) Disconnect the exhaust pipe from the manifold

These operations are described in detail in the previous Section. If the

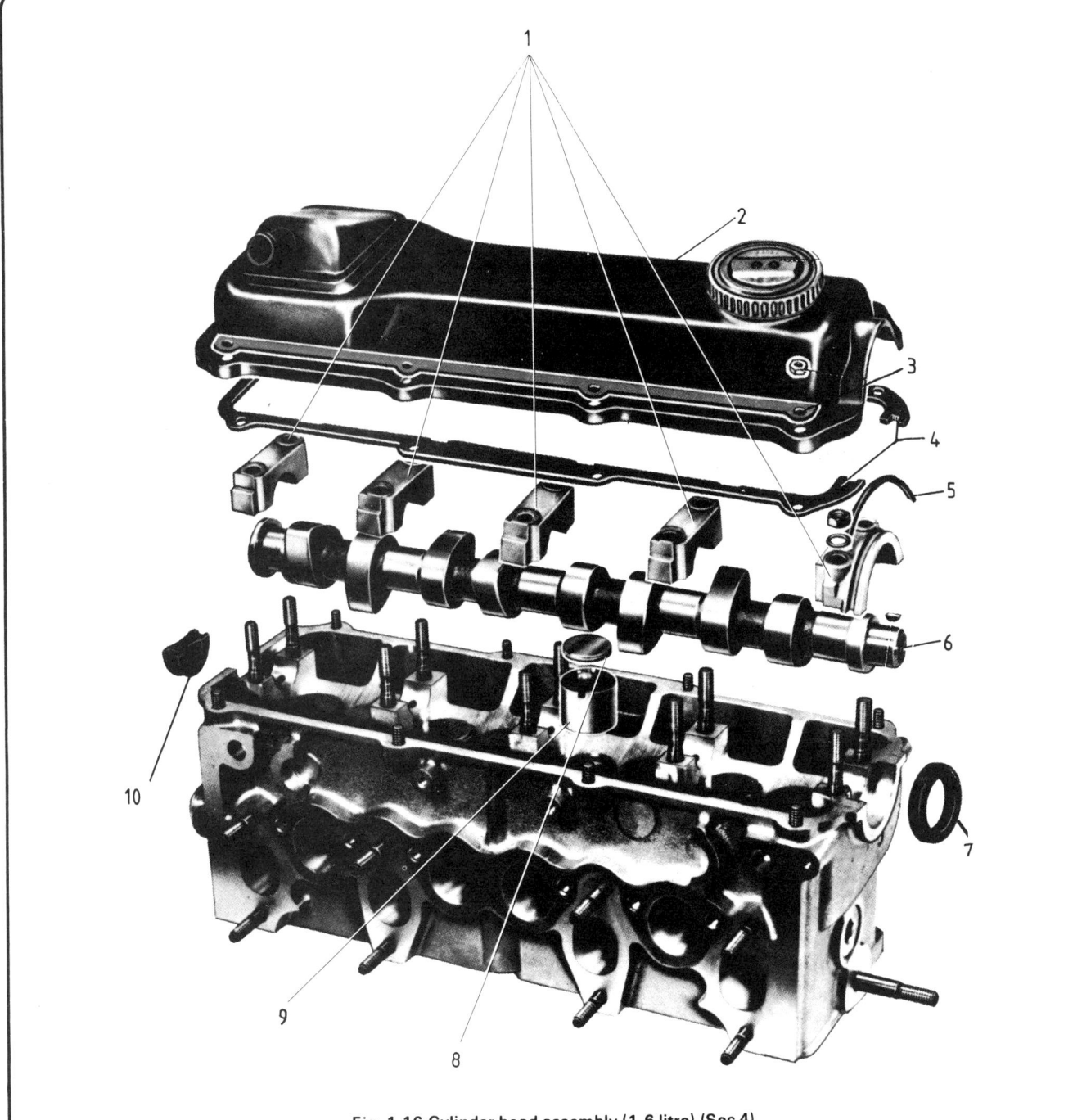

Fig. 1.16 Cylinder head assembly (1.6 litre) (Sec 4)

1	Camshaft bearing caps	4	Gasket	7	Camshaft oil seal	9	Bucket tappet
2	Cylinder head cover	5	Bearing gasket	8	Tappet shim	10	Sealing plug
3	Clamp plate	6	Camshaft				

Fig. 1.17 Crankshaft and intermediate shaft positions for No 1
cylinder at TDC (1.6 litre) (Sec 4)

Fig. 1.18 Camshaft sprocket position for No 1 cylinder at TDC
(1.6 litre) (Sec 4)

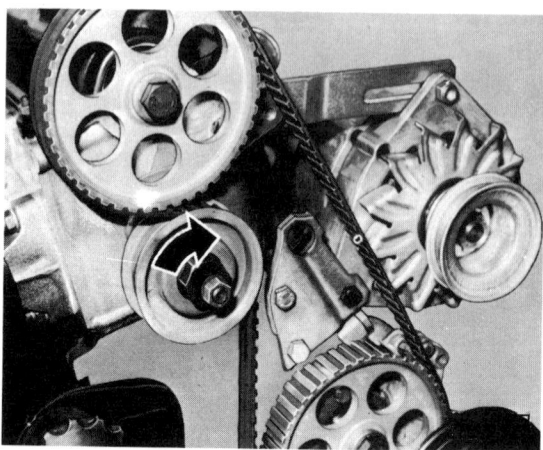

Fig. 1.19 Timing belt tension adjuster (1.6 litre) (Sec 4)

cylinder head is to be removed with the camshaft in position ignore
paragraphs 7 to 12 of this Section.

2   Slacken the alternator mountings and remove the V-belt. If a
power steering pump and/or compressor are fitted, slacken their
drivebelts and remove the belts.

3   Remove the bolts securing the toothed belt cover and take the
cover off.

4   Disconnect the breather pipe from the cylinder head cover.
Remove the eight nuts securing the cover and take off the cover and
the two clamping plates.

5   Fit a spanner to the crankshaft pulley nut and turn the crankshaft
until number one cylinder is at TDC. This is when the notch on the
crankshaft pulley and the mark on the intermediate shaft are as Fig.
1.17 and the mark on the back of the camshaft sprocket is in line with
the top of the casting (Fig. 1.18). Look at the cams operating the
valves of No 1 cylinder and check that the cam lobes are clear of the
tappets so that the valve springs are not compressed.

6   Loosen the nut in the centre of the toothed belt jockey pulley and
rotate the eccentric hub anti-clockwise to release belt tension.
Remove the toothed belt.

7   Unscrew and remove the bolt from the centre of the camshaft and
remove the camshaft sprocket and its key. Because the key is a tight
fit, it will need to be gripped with a hand vice or Mole wrench to pull it
out of the shaft.

8   Slacken the nuts on the camshaft bearing cap Nos 1, 3 and 5 (No
1 at timing bolt end of engine) and remove the nuts.

9   Loosen the nuts on bearing cap No 2 about two turns and then

Fig. 1.20 Camshaft bearing caps (1.6 litre) (Sec 4)

loosen the nuts on bearing cap No 4 two turns. Repeat the sequence until there is no tension on the studs and then screw the nuts right off. If the camshaft bearing nuts are not removed as described there is a danger of distorting the camshaft.

10 Check that each bearing cap has its number stamped on it and if not, make an identifying mark to ensure that each cap is put back where it was originally. Note that the caps are off-set and can only be fitted one way round.

11 Remove the camshaft bearing caps and lift the camshaft out. Discard the camshaft sprocket oil seal and the plug at the rear of the cylinder head.

12 Have ready a board with eight pegs on it or alternatively use a box with internal compartments, marked to identify cylinder number and whether inlet, or exhaust, or position in the head numbering from the front of the engine. As each tappet is removed, place it on the appropriate peg, or mark the actual tappet to indicate its position. Note that each tappet has a shim (disc) fitted into a recess in its top. This shim must be kept with its particular tappet.

13 To prevent damage to the cylinder head bolts and to ensure that they are tightened correctly requires a hexagon or polygon wrench depending upon which type of bolt is fitted. Although it is possible to remove and tighten the bolts without the proper tool, the practice is not recommended.

14 Loosen the cylinder head bolts a turn at a time in the reverse order to the tightening sequence shown in Fig. 1.22. When there is no longer any tension on the bolts, unscrew them and remove them.

15 If necessary tap the cylinder head with a soft-headed hammer, to release it. Lift off the cylinder head and remove the gasket.

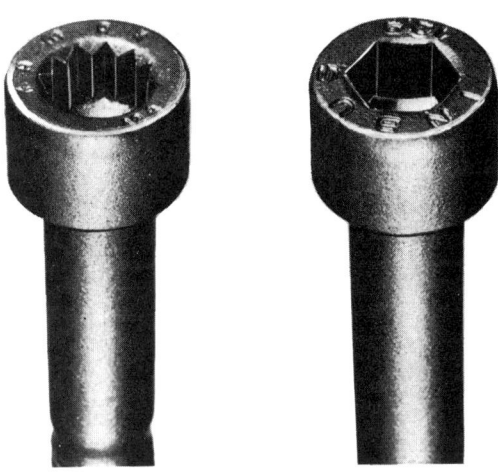

Fig. 1.21 Polygon and hexagon cylinder head bolts (Sec 4)

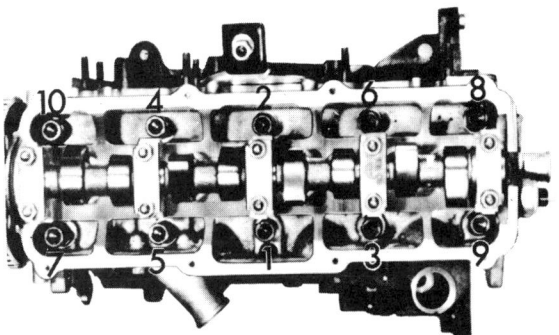

Fig. 1.22 Cylinder head bolt tightening sequence – reverse the sequence for loosening (1.6 litre) (Sec 4)

5 Valves – removal and renovation

1 With the cylinder head removed as previously described, the valve gear can be dismantled as follows. Because the valves are recessed deeply into the top of the cylinder head, their removal requires a valve spring compressor with long claws or the use of some ingenuity in adapting other types of compressor. One method which can be employed is to use a piece of tubing of roughly the same diameter as the valve spring cover and long enough to reach above the top of the cylinder head. To be able to remove the valve collets, either cut a window in the tube on each side, or cut a complete section away, so that the tube is about three quarters of a circle.

2 Have ready a board with holes in it, into which each valve can be fitted as it is removed, or have a set of labelled containers so that each valve and its associated parts can be identified and kept separate. Inlet valves are Nos 2-4-5-7, Exhaust valves are Nos 1-3-6-8, numbered from the timing belt end of the engine.

3 Compress each valve spring until the collets can be removed. Take out the collets, release the spring compressor and remove it.

4 Remove the valve spring cover, the outer and inner spring and the valve. Thread the springs over the valve stem to keep them with the valve and also put on the valve spring cover. It is good practice, but not essential, to keep the valve springs the same way up, so that parts are refitted exactly as they were before removal.

5 Prise off the valve stem seals, or pull them off with pliers and discard them, then lift off the valve spring seat and place it with its valve.

6 Examine the heads of the valves for pitting and burning, paying particular attention to the heads of the exhaust valves. The valve seats should be examined at the same time. If the pitting on the valve and seat is only slight, the marks can be removed by grinding the seats and valves together with coarse and then fine grinding paste. Where bad pitting has occurred, it will be necessary to have the valve seat re-cut and either use a new valve, or have the valve re-faced.

7 The refacing of valves and cutting of valve seats is not expensive and gives a far better result than grinding in valves which are badly pitted. Exhaust valves, if too worn for grinding in must be discarded. Re-machining of exhaust valves is not permissible.

8 Valve grinding is carried out as follows: Smear a small quantity of coarse carborundum paste around the contact surface of the valve, or seat and insert the valve into its guide. Apply a suction grinder tool to the valve head and grind in the valve by semi-rotary motion. This is produced by rolling the valve grinding tool between the palms of the hands. When grinding action is felt to be at an end, extract the valve, turn it and repeat the operation as many times as is necessary to produce a uniform matt grey surface over the whole seating area of the valve head and valve seat. Repeat the process using fine grinding paste.

9 Scrape away all carbon from the valve head and valve stem. Carefully clean away every trace of grinding paste, taking care to leave none in the ports, or in the valve guides. Wipe the valves and valve seats with a paraffin soaked rag and then with a clean dry rag.

6 Cylinder head – checking

1 Check the cylinder head for distortion, by placing a straight edge across it at a number of points, lengthwise, crosswise and diagonally, and measuring the gap beneath it with feeler gauges. If the gap exceeds the limit given in Specifications, the head must be re-faced by a workshop which is equipped for this work. Re-facing must not reduce the cylinder head depth below the minimum dimension given in Specifications.

2 Examine the cylinder head for cracks. If there are minor cracks of not more that 0.5 mm (0.020 in) width between the valve seats, or at the bottom of the spark plug holes (Fig. 1.25), the head can be re-used but a cylinder head cannot be repaired or new valve seat inserts fitted.

3 Check the valve guides for wear and rectify if necessary. Refer to Part B, Section 23, paragraphs 16, and 17 for details of this operation.

7 Camshaft and bearings – checking

1 Examine the camshaft for signs of damage, or excessive wear. If either the cam lobes, or any of the journals have wear grooves, a new

Fig. 1.23 Cylinder head and valves (1.6 litre) (Sec 5)

1	Valve cotters	7	Cylinder head bolt
2	Spring cover	8	Cylinder head
3	Valve springs	9	Inlet valve
4	Spring seat	10	Exhaust valve
5	Stem oil seal	11	Cylinder head gasket
6	Valve guide		

Fig. 1.24 Checking the cylinder head for distortion (1.6 litre) (Sec 6)

Fig. 1.25 Cracks in spark plug hole and between valve seats Width 'a' must not exceed 0.5 mm (0.020 in) (Sec 6)

camshaft must be fitted.

2   With the camshaft fitted in its bearings, but with the bucket tappets removed so that there is no pressure on the crankshaft, measure the axial play (endfloat) of the camshaft, which should not exceed the limit given in Specifications.

3   The camshaft bearings are part of the cylinder head and cannot be renewed. The bearing clearance is very small and the clearances can only be checked with a dial gauge. If there is excessive looseness in the camshaft bearings, do not attempt to decrease it by grinding or filing the bottoms of the bearing caps.

8   Valves – reassembly to cylinder head

1   When reassembling, fit the valve spring seats and then press a new seal on to the top of each valve guide. A plastic sleeve should be provided with the valve stem seals, so that the seals are not damaged when the valves are fitted.

2   Apply oil to the valve stem and the stem seal. Fit the plastic sleeve over the top of the valve stem and insert the valve carefully. Remove the sleeve after inserting the valve. If there is no plastic sleeve, wrap a piece of thin adhesive tape round the top of the valve stem, so that it covers the recess for the collets and prevents the sharp edges of the recess damaging the seal. Remove the tape after fitting the valve.

3   Fit the inner and outer valve springs, then the valve spring cover. If renewing springs, they must only be renewed as a pair on any valve.

4   Fit the spring compressor and compress the spring just enough to allow the collets to be fitted. If the spring is pressed right down there is a danger of damaging the stem seal.

5   Fit the collets, release the spring compressor slightly and check that the collets seat properly, then remove the compressor.

6   Tap the top of the valve stem with a soft-headed hammer to ensure that the collets are seated.

9   Cylinder head and camshaft – refitting

1   Before fitting the cylinder head, ensure that the top of the block is perfectly clean. Use a new gasket and fit the gasket to the block so that the word "OBEN" marked on it faces towards the cylinder head.

2   Check that the cylinder head face is perfectly clean. Fit a new plug to the rear end of the cylinder head. Place two long rods or pieces of dowel in two cylinder head bolt holes at opposite ends of the block, to position the gasket and give a location for fitting the cylinder head. Lower the head on to the block, remove the guides and insert the bolts and washers. Do not use jointing compound on the cylinder head joint.

3   Torque-tighten the cylinder head bolts in three stages to the 'cold' figure given in the Specifications, following the sequence shown in Fig. 1.22. Note the special method used for polygon headed bolts.

4   Fit the bucket tappets to their original positions, the adjustment shims on the top of the tappets must be fitted so that the lettering on them is downwards. Lubricate the tappets and the camshaft journals.

5   Lay the camshaft into the lower half of its bearings so that the lowest point of the cams of No 1 cylinder are towards the tappets and fit the bearing caps in their original positions, making sure that they are the right way round before fitting them over the studs.

6   Fit the camshaft nuts and washers and tighten each of the nuts on bearing cap Nos 1, 3 and 5 a few turns at a time in sequence until the specified torque is reached.

7   Tighten the nuts on bearing caps No 2 and 4 to the specified torque. Fit the camshaft Woodruff key.

8   If a new camshaft has been fitted, or if the valves have been ground, check and if necessary adjust the tappet clearances (Section 10).

9   Fit new gaskets to the camshaft front bearing and the cylinder head cover. Fit the cylinder head cover, the clamping plates and nuts and tighten the nuts a few turns at a time in a diagonal sequence similar to when tightening the cylinder head bolts. Do not tighten the cylinder head cover nuts beyond the specified torque because this tends to distort both the cover and the gasket and cause oil leaks.

10 Lightly oil the lip and the outer edge of a new camshaft sprocket oil seal. Enter the seal with its open face first and use a block of wood and a hammer to drive the seal in until its face is flush with the front of the cylinder head. Do not drive the seal in until it touches the bottom of its recess, because this will cover up an oil return hole.

11 Fit the camshaft pulley and tighten its bolt. Turn the camshaft pulley until the mark on its rear face is in line with the upper edge of the cylinder head cover gasket (Fig. 1.18).

Fig. 1.26 Cylinder head gasket correctly fitted (1.6 litre) (Sec 9)

Fig. 1.27 Checking camshaft drivebelt tension (1.6 litre) (Sec 9)

12 Ensure that the crankshaft pulley and intermediate shaft sprocket are in their No 1 cylinder at TDC positions (Fig. 1.17), then fit the toothed belt and tension it by rotating the hub of the jockey pulley clockwise.

13 When the belt is tensioned so that its longest span can just be twisted through 90° by thumb and finger pressure (Fig. 1.27), tighten the tensioner clamping bolt.

14 Fit the belt cover over the toothed belt, then fit the V-belt(s) and tension them.

15 The remainder of the operations are a reversal of those necessary for removal (Section 4).

16 Where the cylinder head is retained by conventional socket headed bolts, run the engine to attain the normal operating temperature then loosen each bolt in turn by 30° and re-tighten to the specified torque in the order shown in Fig. 1.22. Repeat this procedure after 620 miles (1000 km) of running.

10 Valve clearances – checking and adjusting

1   Valve clearances are adjusted by inserting the appropriate thickness shim to the top of the tappet. Shims are available in thicknesses from 3.00 to 4.25 mm (0.118 to 0.167 in) in increments

of 0.05 mm (0.0020 in).

2   Adjust the valve clearances for the initial setting-up after fitting a new camshaft, or grinding in the valves with the engine cold. The valve clearances should be re-checked when the engine is warm, with the coolant over 35°C (95°F), after 620 miles (1000 Km). Thereafter valve clearances should be checked when the engine is warm.

3   Pull the breather hose from the cylinder head cover and take the cover off.

4   Fit a spanner to the crankshaft pulley nut and turn the crankshaft until the highest points of the cams for one cylinder are pointing upwards and outwards at similar angles. Use feeler gauges to check the gap between the cam and the tappet (Fig. 1.28) and record the dimension.

5   Repeat the operation for all four cylinders and complete the list of clearances. Valves are numbered from the timing belt end of the engine. Inlet valves are Nos 2-4-5-7, exhaust valves are Nos 1-3-6-8.

6   Where any tolerances exceed those given in Specifications, remove the existing shim by placing the blade of a wide screwdriver against the top edge of the tappet, lever against the camshaft to depress the tappet and at the same time lift out the shim from the top of the tappet.

7   Note the thickness of the shim (engraved on its underside) and calculate the shim thickness required to correct the clearance. For example, if the measured clearance on an inlet valve is 0.35 mm (0.014 in) this is outside the tolerance specified for inlet valves which is 0.20 to 0.30 mm (0.008 to 0.012 in). The best adjustment is the mid-point of the range i.e. 0.25 mm (0.010 in) and the measured gap of 0.35 mm (0.014 in) is 0.1 mm (0.004 in) too great. If the shim which is taken out is 3.05 mm (0.120 in), it should be replaced by one of 3.15 mm (0.124 in).

8   Lever against the camshaft to depress the tappet and fit the new shim with its engraved side down.

9   Shims which have been removed can be re-used by interchanging if they are the right thickness for correcting the clearance of the other valve.

11 Flywheel, or driveplate – removing and refitting

1   If the gearbox is removed, the flywheel, or driveplate (automatic trans) can be removed with the engine still in place in the vehicle.

2   The engine timing mark is stamped on the rim of the flywheel, or driveplate, so it is important to put mating marks on the crankshaft and flywheel, or driveplate before starting to remove the bolts.

3   Insert a bolt into one of the holes in the engine-to-gearbox flange, choosing a hole which is near the rim of the flywheel. Use a piece of angle iron, or other suitably shaped piece of metal which will fit into the teeth of the starter ring and jam it against the bolt.

4   Remove the eight bolts securing the flywheel or driveplate to the crankshaft. The bolts are coated with locking compound on assembly and are difficult to remove.

5   If removing a driveplate, note that there is a spacer between the bolts and the driveplate and there may be another spacer behind the driveplate.

6   When refitting the flywheel to the crankshaft, line up the mating marks, which were made before removal. Coat the threads of the bolts with locking compound before inserting them and then tighten to the specified torque.

7   When refitting a driveplate, line up the mating marks which were made before removal and if a spacer was fitted behind the driveplate, do not forget to refit it. The spacer on the front of the driveplate is fitted with the chamfer towards the driveplate. Coat the threads of the bolts with locking compound before inserting them and then tighten to the specified torque.

Fig. 1.28 Measuring tappet clearance (1.6 litre) (Sec 10)

Fig. 1.29 Flywheel timing mark (1.6 litre) (Sec 11)

Fig. 1.30 Driveplate (automatic transmission) and spacers (Sec 11)

1   Front spacer   2   Rear spacer (if fitted)

Fig. 1.31 Measuring the projection of the driveplate (Sec 11)

8 If a replacement driveplate is to be fitted, its position must be checked and adjusted if necessary. The distance from the rear face of the block to the torque converter mounting face on the driveplate (Fig. 1.31) must be between 30.5 and 32.1 mm (1.20 and 1.26 in). If necessary, remove the driveplate and fit a spacer behind it to achieve the correct dimension.

12 Pistons and connecting rods – removing and dismantling

1 The pistons and connecting rods are removed from the top of the cylinders, so the cylinder head must be removed (refer to Section 4). If the engine is in the car, refer to Section 2, paragraph 4 to remove the sump.

2 If the engine is out of the car, set it on its side on the bench and remove the sump, having first ensured that the oil has been drained from it.

3 Remove the bolts securing the oil pump and take the oil pump off.

4 Mark each connecting rod with its cylinder number, so that the pistons and connecting rods can be refitted to the correct cylinder.

5 Turn the crankshaft so that the connecting rod big-end bearing cap nuts are accessible, remove the nuts and lift off the bearing cap.

Fig. 1.32 Piston and connecting rod assembly (1.6 litre) (Sec 12)

1	Piston rings	3	Piston pin	5	Connecting rod	7	Connecting rod bearing shell
2	Piston	4	Circlip	6	Piston pin bush	8	Bearing cap

6   Rotate the crankshaft until the piston has been pushed to the top of the bore, then disengage the connecting rod from the crankshaft and push the piston and connecting rod out of the top of the cylinder block. Put the bearing cap with its connecting rod and make sure that they both have the cylinder number marked on them. If any of the bearing shells become detached while removing the connecting rods and bearing caps, ensure that they are placed with their matching cap or rod.

7   Before removing the pistons from the connecting rods, mark the connecting rods to show which side of them is towards the front of the engine. The casting marks on the rod face towards the intermediate shaft.

8   Remove the circlips from the grooves in the piston pin holes and push the piston pin out enough for the connecting rod to be removed. Do not remove the pins completely unless new ones are to be fitted, to ensure that the pin is not turned end for end when the piston is refitted. If the piston pin is difficult to push out, heat the piston by immersing it in hot water.

9   New bushes can be fitted to the connecting rods, but as they need to be reamed to size after fitting, the job is best left to an VW/Audi agent.

10   Using old feeler gauges, or pieces of thin rigid plastic inserted behind the piston rings, carefully ease each ring in turn off the piston. Lay the rings out so that they are kept the right way up and so that the top ring can be identified. Carefully scrape the rings free of carbon and clean out the ring grooves on the pistons, using a piece of wood or a piece of broken piston ring.

13 Pistons and cylinder bores – checking

1   Examine the pistons and the bores for obvious signs of damage and excessive wear. If they appear to be satisfactory, make the following checks.

2   Measure the piston diameter at a position 10 mm (0.394 in) from the lower edge of the skirt and at 90° to the axis of the piston (Fig. 1.36) and compare this with the wear limit of the piston given in Specifications.

3   Push a piston ring into the cylinder bore and use a piston to push the ring down the bore so that it is square in the bore and about 15 mm (0.55 in) from the bottom of the cylinder. Measure the ring gap using a feeler gauge. If the gap is above the top limit, look for obvious signs of bore wear, or if a new piston ring is available, measure the gap when a new piston ring is fitted to the bore.

4   To measure the bore diameter directly a dial gauge with an internal measuring attachment is required. If one is available, measure each bore in six places and compare the readings with the wear limit given. Bore diameter should be measured 10 mm (0.394 in) from the top of the bore, 10 mm (0.394 in) from the bottom and at the mid-point. At each of the three stations measure in-line with the crankshaft and at right angles to it. If the bores are worn beyond the limit, they will need to be rebored and new pistons fitted.

5   If one bore is oversize, all four must be rebored and a new set of pistons fitted, otherwise the engine will not be balanced. Also, connecting rods must only be fitted as complete sets and not be replaced individually.

6   Fit the rings to the pistons and use a feeler gauge to measure the gap between the piston ring and the side of its groove. If the gap is beyond the wear limit, it is more likely that it is the piston groove, rather than the ring which has worn and either a new piston, or a proprietary oversize ring will be required. If new piston rings are fitted the wear ridge at the top of the cylinder bore must be removed, or a stepped top ring used.

14 Pistons and connecting rods – reassembly and refitting

1   Locate the piston onto the connecting rod so that with the rod in its correctly installed position, the mark on the piston crown will be

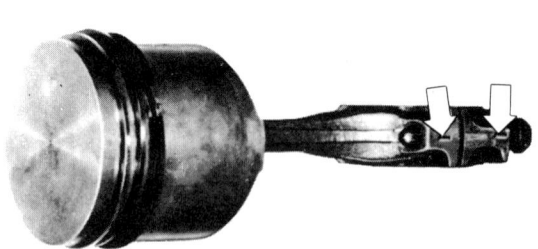

Fig. 1.33 Mark piston number on both parts of connecting rod (1.6 litre) (Sec 12)

Fig. 1.34 Cast marks on connecting rod face intermediate shaft (1.6 litre) (Sec 12)

Fig. 1.35 Piston marks showing nominal size and deviation – arrow points to front of engine (1.6 litre) (Sec 12)

Fig. 1.36 Measuring piston wear (Sec 13)

Fig. 1.37 Measuring piston ring gap (1.6 litre) (Sec 13)

Fig. 1.38 Measuring piston ring groove clearance (1.6 litre) (Sec 13)

Fig. 1.39 Piston ring markings (1.6 litre) (Sec 14)

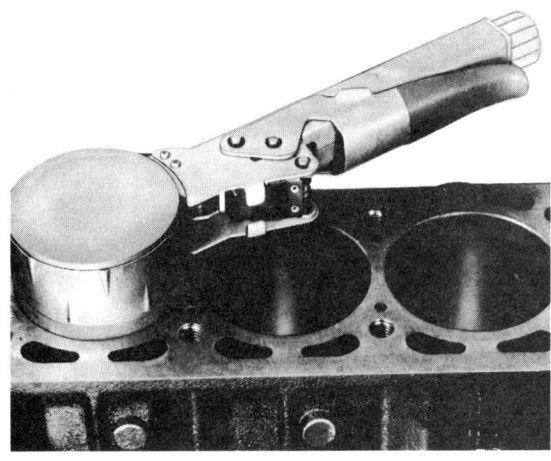

Fig. 1.40 Using a piston ring compressor (1.6 litre) (Sec 14)

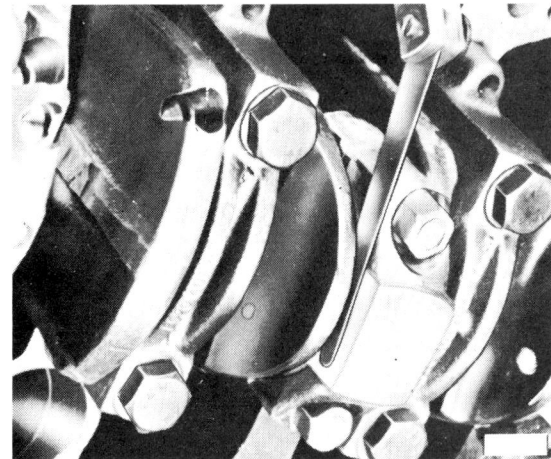

Fig. 1.41 Measuring connecting rod axial clearance (1.6 litre) (Sec 14)

towards the front of the engine and the casting marks on the connecting rod will be towards the intermediate shaft.

2   Before refitting the piston rings, or fitting new rings, check the gap of each ring in turn in its correct cylinder bore using a piston to push the ring down the bore, as described in the previous Section. Measure the gap between the ends of the piston ring, using feeler gauges. The gap must be within the limits given in Specifications.

3   If the piston ring gap is too small, carefully file the piston ring end until the gap is sufficient. Piston rings are very brittle, handle them carefully.

4   When fitting piston rings, look for the word TOP etched on one side of the ring and fit this side so that it is towards the piston crown.

5   Unless the big-end bearing shells are known to be almost new, it is worth fitting a new set when reassembling the engine. Clean the connecting rods and bearing caps thoroughly and fit the bearing shells so that the tang on the bearing engages in the recess in the connecting rod, or cap, and the ends of the bearing are flush with the joint face. Fit new bolts to the connecting rod.

6   To refit the pistons, first space the joints in the piston rings so that they are at 120° intervals. Oil the rings and grooves generously and fit a piston ring compressor over the piston. To fit the pistons without using a piston ring compressor is difficult and there is a high risk of breaking a piston ring.

7   Oil the cylinder bores and insert the pistons with the arrow on the piston crown (Fig. 1.35) pointing towards the front of the engine.

8   When the piston is pushed in flush with the top of the bore, oil the two bearing halves and the crankshaft journal and guide the connecting rod half-bearing on to the crankshaft journal.

9   Fit the big-end bearing cap complete with shell and tighten the nuts to the specified torque wrench setting.

10 Rotate the crankshaft to ensure that everything is free, before fitting the next piston and connecting rod.

11 Using feeler gauges between the machined face of each big-end bearing, and the machined face of the crankshaft web, check the axial

clearance (endfloat) which should be within the tolerance given in Specifications.

12 Refit the oil pump and the sump.

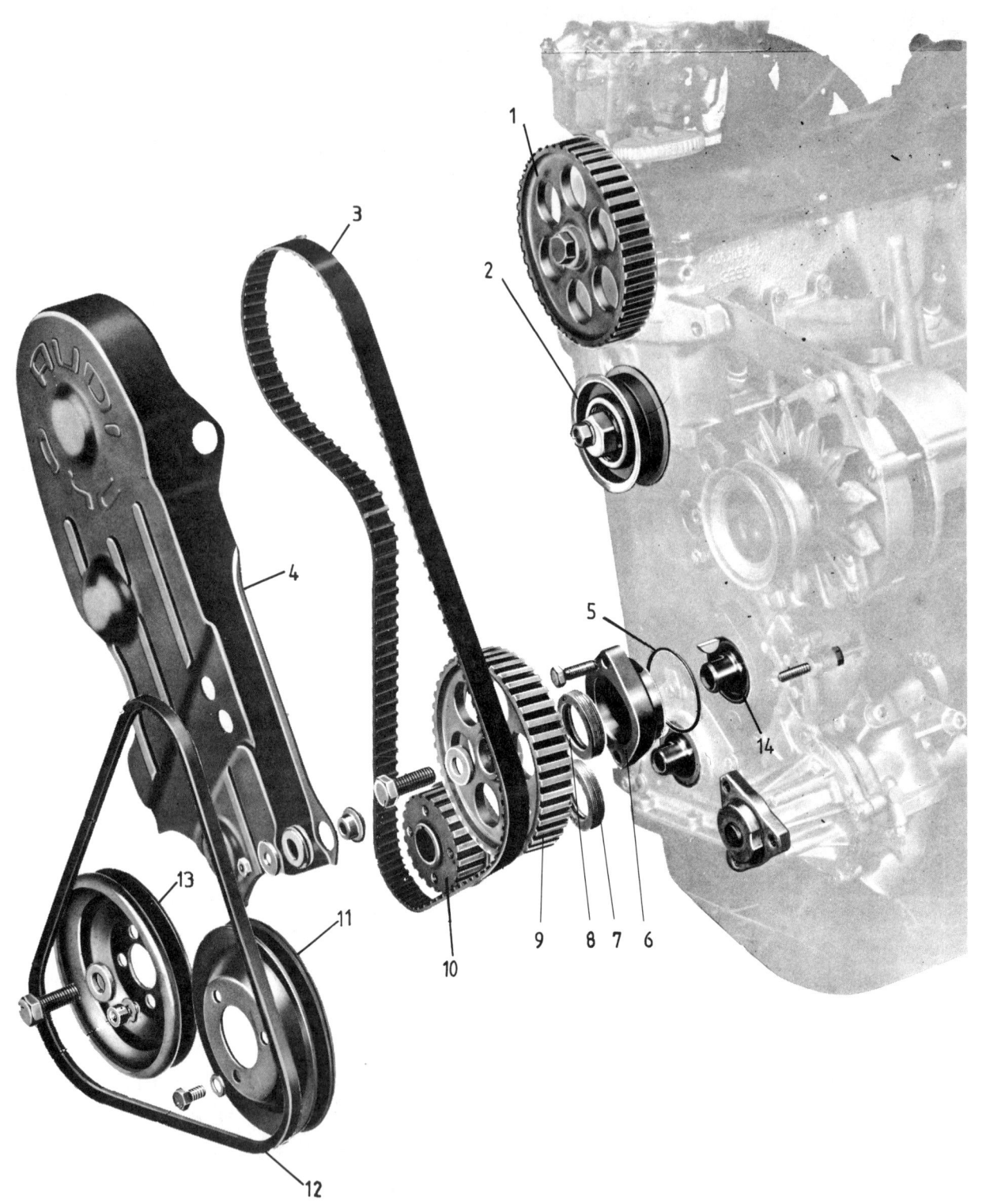

Fig. 1.42 Intermediate shaft and camshaft drive (1.6 litre) (Sec 15)

1 Camshaft sprocket	5 O-ring	9 Intermediate shaft sprocket	12 Vee belt
2 Tensioning pulley	6 Sealing flange	10 Crankshaft sprocket	13 Crankshaft pulley
3 Toothed belt	7 Crankshaft front oil seal	11 Water pump pulley	14 Intermediate shaft
4 Belt guard	8 Intermediate shaft oil seal		

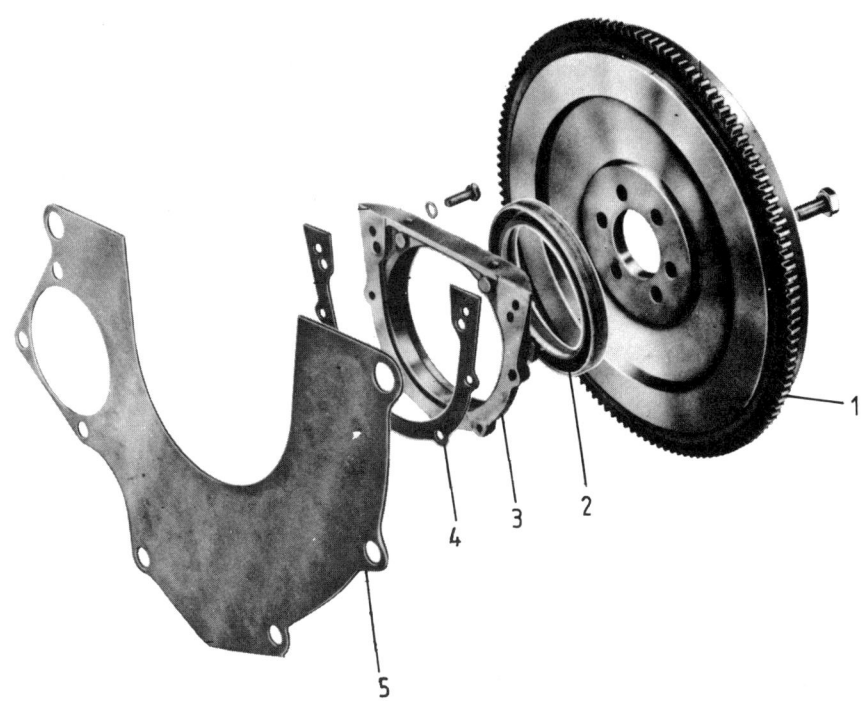

Fig. 1.43 Crankshaft rear oil seal (1.6 litre)
(Sec 16)

1   Flywheel
2   Oil seal
3   Sealing flange
4   Gasket
5   Intermediate shaft

15 Intermediate shaft – removal and refitting

1   Remove the timing belt cover and timing belt as described earlier in this Chapter (Section 4).
2   Check that the distributor and fuel pump have been removed.
3   Unscrew the bolt securing the sprocket to the intermediate shaft and remove the Woodruff key.
4   Remove the two bolts from the sealing flange, take off the sealing flange and the O-ring.
5   Withdraw the intermediate shaft from the block.
6   With the flange removed, the oil seal can be driven out. Fit a new seal with its open face towards the engine and use a block of wood to drive the seal in flush. Oil the lips of the seal before fitting the sealing flange.
7   Refitting the intermediate shaft is the reverse of removing it, but fit a new O-ring behind the sealing flange and fit the flange so that the oil drilling in it is towards the bottom of the engine.
8   Check that the shaft rotates freely and that its axial play (endfloat) is in accordance with Specifications.
9   Refit the timing belt and sprockets as described in Section 9.

16 Crankshaft oil seals – renewing

1   There are special tools which enable the seals to be extracted without removing the flanges carrying the seals, but without these the flanges have to be removed.
2   Remove the sump and the flywheel, or driveplate (automatic transmission).
3   The procedure is similar for both the front and the rear seal, it being necessary to drive out the old seal, taking care not to damage the seal housing. With the closed face of the seal outwards, drive the seal in using a block of wood across its face until the seal is flush with the outer face of its housing.
4   Fit the seal housing to the cylinder block, using a new gasket having first lubricated the lip of the seal with engine oil.

17 Crankshaft – removing and refitting

1   Having removed the sump, oil pump, connecting rods and the crankshaft oil seal flanges, place the crankcase upside down on the bench and check that the crankshaft bearing caps have their numbers stamped on them; if not, number them, starting at the front of the engine.

2   Remove the bolts from each bearing cap in turn, then remove the caps and lift out the crankshaft.
3   If the bearings are not being renewed, ensure that each half-bearing shell is identified so that it is put back in the same place from which it was removed.
4   If the engine has done a high mileage and it is suspected that the crankshaft requires attention, it is best to seek the opinion of a VW/Audi dealer, or crankshaft re-finishing specialist for advice on the need for regrinding.
5   Unless the bearing shells are known to be almost new, it is worth fitting a new set when the crankshaft is refitted. Clean the crankcase webs and bearing caps thoroughly and fit the bearing shells so that the tang on the bearing engages in the recess in the crankcase web, or bearing cap. Make sure that the shells fitted to the crankcase have oil holes, and that these line up with the drillings in the bearing housings. The shells fitted to the bearing caps do not have oil holes. Note that the bearing shell of the centre bearing (No 3) are different from the others, being flanged to act as a thrust bearing.
6   Fit the bearing shells so that the ends of the bearing are flush with the joint face.
7   Lubricate the crankcase web half-bearings, lubricate the crankshaft journals and lay the crankshaft in its bearings. Lubricate the bearing caps and lay them in their correct position and the correct way round (Fig. 1.44).

Fig. 1.44 Crankshaft main bearing caps correctly located (1.6 litre)
(Sec 17)

8   Fit the bolts to the bearing caps and tighten the bolts of the centre cap to the specified torque, then check that the crankshaft rotates freely. If it is difficult to rotate the crankshaft, check that the bearing shells are seated properly and that the bearing cap is the correct way round. Rotation will only be difficult if something is incorrect and the fault must be found. Dirt on the back of a bearing shell is sometimes the cause of a tight main bearing.

9   Working out from the centre, tighten the remaining bearing caps in turn, checking that the crankshaft rotates freely after each bearing has been tightened.

10 Check that the endplay of the crankshaft is within specification, by inserting feeler gauges between the crankshaft and the centre bearing thrust face (Fig. 1.46) while levering the crankshaft first in one direction and then in the other.

11 The remainder of the operations are the fitting of the seal housings, flywheel, crankshaft sprocket and pulley. These are the reverse of the removal operations.

12 The rear end of the crankshaft carries a needle roller bearing which supports the front end of the gearbox input shaft.

13 Inspect the bearing for obvious signs of wear and damage. If the gearbox has been removed and dismantled, fit the input shaft into the bearing to see if there is excessive clearance.

14 If the bearing requires renewing, insert a hook behind the bearing and pull it out of the end of the crankshaft.

Fig. 1.45 Crankcase assembly (1.6 litre) (Sec 17)

1 Main bearing caps	5 Intermediate shaft	8 O-ring	11 Gasket
2 Spigot bearing	6 Sealing flange	9 Crankshaft front oil seal	12 Bearing shell with thrust face
3 Crankshaft	7 Intermediate shaft oil seal	10 Front sealing flange	13 Plain bearing shells
4 Crankcase			

Fig. 1.46 Measuring crankshaft endfloat (1.6 litre) (Sec 17)

Fig. 1.47 Crankshaft needle bearing correctly installed (1.6 litre) (Sec 17)

'a' = 1.5 mm (0.059 in)

Fig. 1.48 Measuring oil pump gear backlash (1.6 litre) (Sec 18)

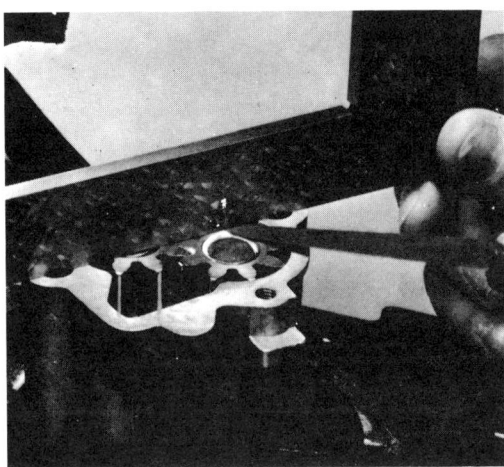

Fig. 1.49 Measuring oil pump gear axial play (1.6 litre)(Sec 18)

15 Install the new bearing with the lettering on the end of the bearing outwards. Press it in until the end of the bearing is 1.5 mm (0.059 in) below the face of the flywheel flange (Fig. 1.47).

18 Oil pump – removing, dismantling, checking and refitting

1 The sump must be removed to gain access to the oil pump (Fig. 1.50).
2 Remove the two socket head bolts from the pump and withdraw the pump and strainer assembly.
3 Remove the two hexagon headed bolts from the pump cover and lift off the cover.
4 Bend up the metal rim of the filter plate so that it can be removed and take the filter screen out. Clean the screen thoroughly with paraffin and a brush.
5 Clean the pump casing, cover and gears and reassemble the casing and gears.
6 Check the backlash of the gears with a feeler gauge (Fig. 1.48) and with a straight edge across the end face of the pump, measure the axial play of the gears (Fig. 1.49).
7 Examine the pump cover grooves worn by the ends of the gears, which will effectively increase the axial play of the gears.
8 If the wear on the pump is beyond the specified limits a new pump should be fitted.
9 After reassembling the pump, prime the pump by immersing the strainer in engine oil and turn the pump spindle until oil emerges from the outlet port, then refit the pump to the crankcase.

Part B – 2·0 litre engine

19 General description

In general the 2·0 litre engine is similar to the 1·6 litre engine (Section 1). but the following differences should be noted.

(a) An intermediate shaft is not used
(b) The distributor is gear driven from the rear end of the overhead camshaft
(c) The oil pump is mounted on the front end of the crankshaft
(d) The tappets (cam followers) incorporate a wedge type grub screw which has one flat face. The flat bears against the end face of the valve stem and as the screw is turned, it has the effect of expanding or contracting the tappet and so reducing or increasing the tappet to cam lobe clearance

20 Major operations possible with engine in place

1 The oil pump, water pump, fuel pump, distributor and radiator can be removed with the engine installed. The sump can also be removed, if the sub-frame front mounting bolts are removed.
2 The cylinder head can be removed for decarbonising and valve grinding; and new alternator and timing belts can be fitted with the

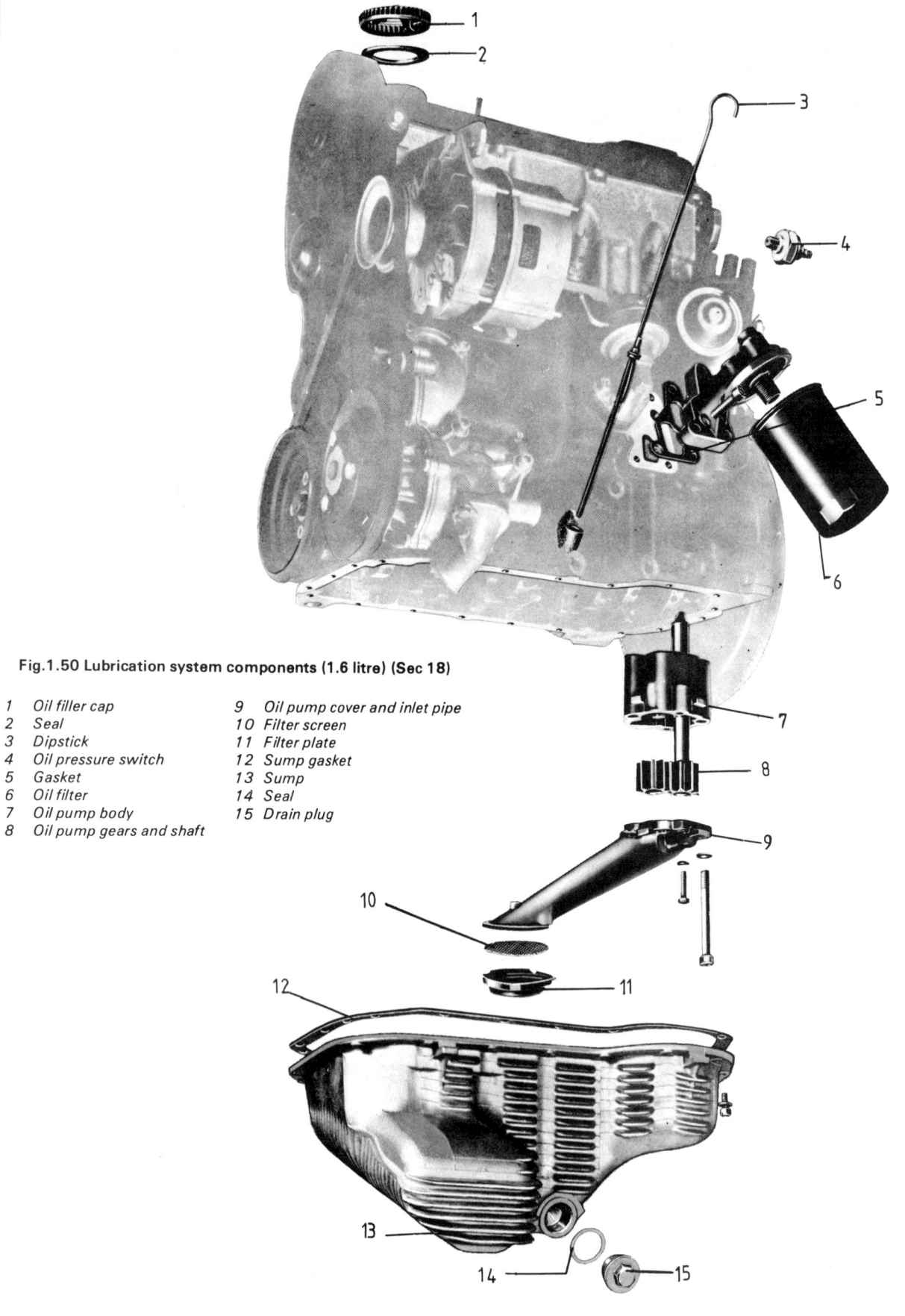

Fig.1.50 Lubrication system components (1.6 litre) (Sec 18)

1   Oil filler cap
2   Seal
3   Dipstick
4   Oil pressure switch
5   Gasket
6   Oil filter
7   Oil pump body
8   Oil pump gears and shaft

9   Oil pump cover and inlet pipe
10 Filter screen
11 Filter plate
12 Sump gasket
13 Sump
14 Seal
15 Drain plug

engine in place.

3   With the sump and cylinder head removed, it is possible to withdraw the piston/connecting rod assemblies although this work is best carried out with the engine out of the car.

4   The clutch and the flywheel are not accessible without removing either the engine or the transmission. If the engine does not require major attention, it is easier to withdraw the transmission leaving the engine in the car.

21 Engine – removal and refitting

1   Disconnect the battery leads.

2   On vehicles fitted with an air conditioner, set the heater control to *WARM*. Do not disturb any other air conditioning system connections except to unbolt the compressor and move it to one side of the engine compartment.

3   Remove the cap from the coolant reservoir to relieve the pressure in the system. Place a large bowl beneath the engine to catch the coolant, then loosen the clamp on the bottom hose. Pull the hose off and drain the coolant.

4   Remove the air intake hose from the air cleaner and remove the air

Fig. 1.51 Coolant draining point (2.0 litre) (Sec 21)

Fig. 1.53 Removing the radiator (2.0 litre) (Sec 21)

cleaner, referring to Chapter 3 if necessary. After removing the air cleaner, cover the carburettor air intake with a clean rag, or plastic bag, to stop the entry of dirt.

5   With the help of an assistant mark the position of the bonnet hinges, remove the bolts and lift the bonnet off.

6   Pull the engine bonnet lock cable towards the driver's side and detach the cable from the bracket on the radiator.

7   Unscrew the clutch cable adjusting nut to loosen the clutch cable and then detach the cable from the clutch operating lever on the bellhousing.

8   Loosen the clips on the two hoses attached to the coolant reservoir and detach the hoses. Loosen the clip at the thermostat end of the upper coolant hose and detach the hose.

9   Disconnect the plug connections of the radiator fan and the radiator thermostatic switch, then remove the two brackets from the bottom of the radiator and lift the radiator out.

10   Disconnect the throttle cable. On cars fitted with a manual gearbox, this is done by releasing the clamp screw where the inner cable is attached to the throttle lever on the carburettor and pulling the cable grommet out of the bracket. On cars with automatic transmission it is also necessary to remove the clip from the end of the pushrod attachment to the throttle lever and disengage the pushrod from the lever (Fig. 1.55).

11   Disconnect the two fuel pipes from the petrol pump and disconnect the fuel pipe from the fuel filter to the carburettor (Fig. 1.56).

12   Disconnect the electrical wiring from the carburettor. Disconnect the wires from the oil pressure switch and temperature sender unit (Fig. 1.57).

13   Disconnect the high and low tension wires from the ignition coil and disconnect the windscreen washer pump wires.

14   If the car is equipped with power steering, unbolt the pump and move it to one side of the engine compartment, alternatively, disconnect and plug the fluid hoses and remove the pump.

15   Disconnect the heater hoses at the points arrowed in Fig. 1.58. On

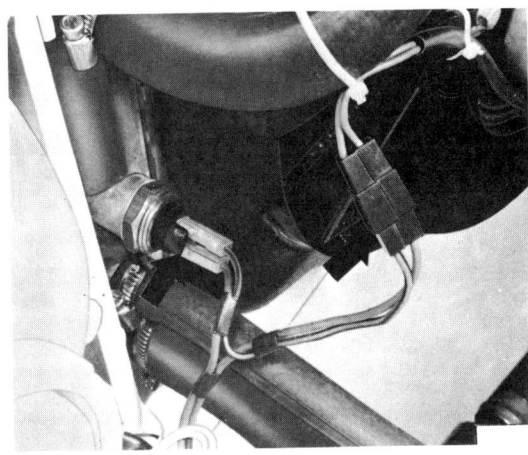

Fig. 1.52 Radiator fan and thermostatic switch connections
(2.0 litre) (Sec 21)

Fig. 1.54 Throttle cable disconnection (2.0 litre – manual) (Sec 21)

Fig. 1.55 Throttle cable and push rod disconnection (2.0 litre – automatic) (Sec 21)

Fig. 1.56 Fuel line disconnection points (2.0 litre) (Sec 21)

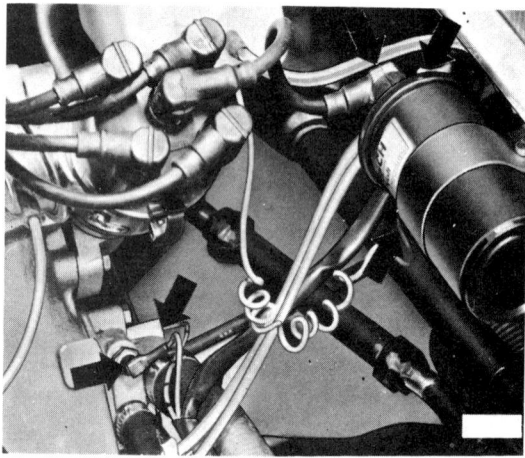

Fig. 1.57 Oil pressure switch, temperature gauge and ignition coil connections (2.0 litre) (Sec 21)

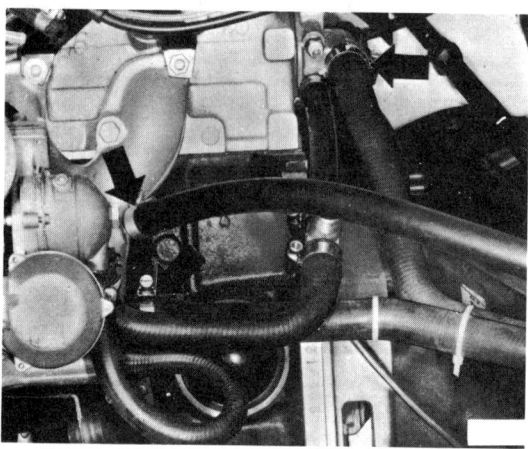

Fig. 1.58 Heater hose disconnection points (2.0 litre) (Sec 21)

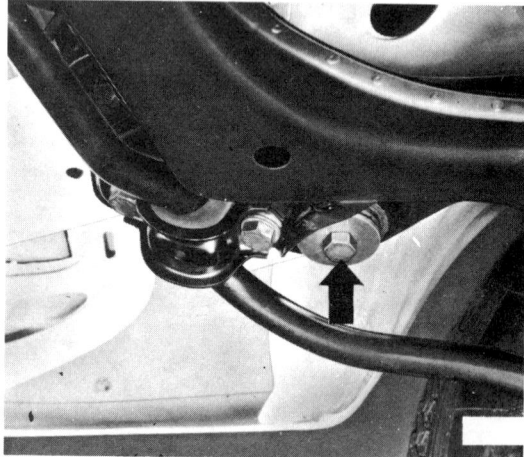

Fig. 1.59 Front sub-frame bolts (Sec 21)

vehicles with automatic transmission, also disconnect the two hoses to the oil cooler.

16 Disconnect the brake servo vacuum hose from the inlet manifold and pull the vacuum hose(s) off the distributor vacuum unit.

17 Disconnect the alternator plug connection.

18 Remove the upper bolts attaching the engine to the bellhousing.

19 With a suitable container placed beneath the sump, remove the sump drain plug and drain out the oil. Refit the drain plug and tighten it.

20 Attach lifting slings to the two lifting brackets on the left side of the engine. Ensure that the slings are in good condition, have a safe working load of at least 250 lb (110 kg), and are fitted so that there is no danger of their slipping. The front sling should be shorter than the rear one, so that the engine, when free, will be at an angle of about 30°. Attach the slings to a hoist and raise the hoist until the weight of the engine is taken off the engine mountings.

21 Remove the bolts from the subframe mountings on the left and right-hand sides.

22 Note the position of the four electrical connections to the starter motor and then remove them. Remove the two starter motor fixing bolts and take the motor off.

23 On vehicles with automatic transmission, turn the starter ring so that each of the three torque converter mounting bolts is accessible in turn through the starter motor hole and remove the bolts attaching the converter to the driveplate.

24 Pack wooden blocks beneath the gearbox, so that it remains in the same position when the engine is removed.

25 Remove the exhaust mountings from the gearbox and then remove the four nuts from the exhaust pipe-to-exhaust manifold joint. Separate the two parts, remove the gasket and discard it.

26 Remove the lower bolts attaching the engine to the bellhousing.

27 Remove the three socket headed bolts attaching the engine front support to the engine.

28 Remove the nut from the right-hand engine bearer and then lift the hoist until the left-hand engine bearer is just under tension. Remove the nut from the left-hand engine bearer.

29 Remove the three bolts from the engine support on the left-hand side.

30 Check that there is nothing attached to the engine which will

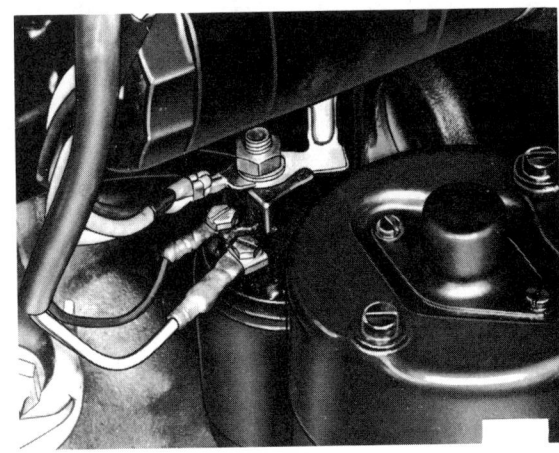

Fig. 1.60 Starter motor and solenoid cables (2.0 litre) (Sec 21)

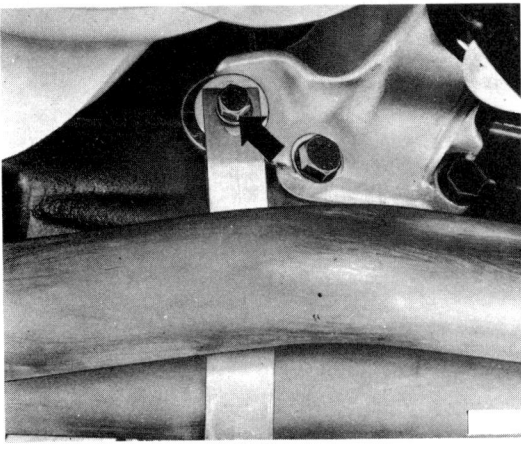

Fig. 1.61 Exhaust pipe to gearbox mounting (2.0 litre) (Sec 21)

Fig. 1.62 Front engine support (2.0 litre) (Sec 21)

Fig. 1.63 Left engine support and earth strap (2.0 litre) (Sec 21)

Fig. 1.64 Correct position of air cleaner housing (2.0 litre) (Sec 21)

prevent its removal and then separate the engine from the gearbox, which can be done by holding one of the support slings and pushing the car to the rear slightly.

31 As soon as the gearbox input shaft is free of its bearing in the crankshaft, the engine can be lifted taking care to prevent damage to the input shaft, the clutch and the body. When the engine is clear of the gearbox, turn the engine sideways to make its removal easier. On vehicles with automatic transmission, secure the torque converter to prevent it from falling out.

32 Although refitting the engine is the reversal of the operations necessary for removing it, there are a few points which require particular care.

33 When fitting the engine to the gearbox, make sure that the mating faces of the engine and gearbox are aligned and parallel before attempting to push them together and if it is difficult to enter the input shaft into the clutch splines, turn the crankshaft pulley a small amount to line the splines up. If the clutch has been removed, make sure that it has been centred accurately (Chapter 5). Do not attempt to force the engine and gearbox together, because this will result in damage.

34 Connect the starter motor cable to the solenoid as shown in Fig. 1.60 and ensure that the cable is well clear of all parts of the engine and body. If this is not done, there is a risk of a short circuit and a fire.

35 When fitting the air cleaner to the carburettor, ensure that it is fitted as shown in Fig. 1.64 and that the marks on the air intake and the cover are lined up (Fig. 1.65).

36 When fitting the left-hand engine support, refit the earth strap to the bottom bolt (Fig. 1.63).

37 When fitting the engine front support, ensure that it is not under strain by first loosening the bolts (Fig. 1.66) and leave the final tightening of all the engine mountings until the engine is idling.

38 Align the exhaust system so that it is free from strain.

39 Check that the engine has been filled with oil and that the cooling system is full before starting the engine. If the power steering pump was disconnected, bleed the system as described in Chapter 11.

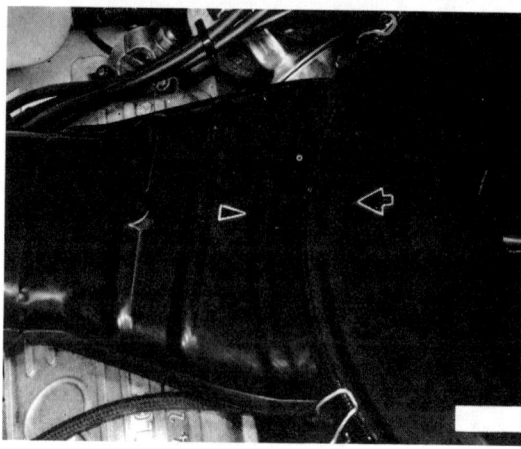

Fig. 1.65 Correct position of air cleaner cover (2.0 litre) (Sec 21)

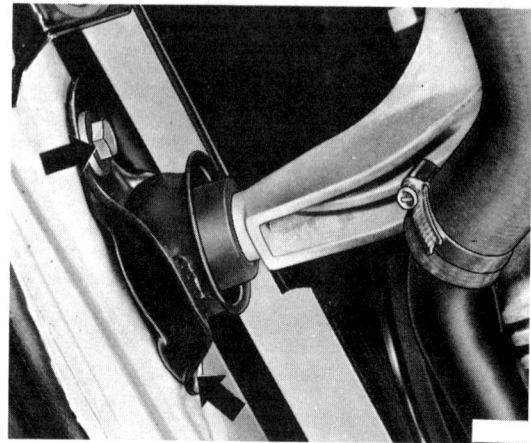

Fig. 1.66 Loosen front support bolts when installing engine
(2.0 litre) (Sec 21)

22 Camshaft – removal and refitting

1   The camshaft can be removed and refitted without disturbing the
cylinder head.
2   Set the crankshaft with No 1 piston at TDC, then:

   (a) Remove the air cleaner (Chapter 3)
   (b) Remove the cylinder head cover
   (c) Remove the fuel pump (Chapter 3)
   *(d) Remove the distributor, complete with the drive gear housing
      (Chapter 4)*
   (e) Remove the V-belt and the timing belt guard
   *(f) Engage 4th gear, apply the handbrake and loosen the
      camshaft sprocket bolt*
   (g) Remove the timing belt and camshaft sprocket

3   Check that each bearing cap has its number stamped on it and if
not, make an identifying mark to ensure that each cap is put back
where it was originally. Note that the caps are off-set and can only be
fitted one way round.
4   It is important that the camshaft is removed exactly as described,
so that there is no danger of it becoming distorted.
5   Remove the nuts securing the oil pipe to No 2 and No 4 camshaft
bearings. Pull off the oil pipe and screw the nuts back on finger tight.
6   Remove the nuts from bearing cap Nos 1, 3 and 5 and lift the
bearing caps off.

7   Loosen the nuts on bearing caps No 2 about two turns and then
loosen the nuts on bearing cap No 4 about two turns. Repeat the
sequence until there is no tension on the studs and then screw the
nuts right off.
8   Remove the two bearing caps and lift the camshaft out of its lower
half bearings. Check the camshaft and bearings as described in Part A
for the 1·6 litre engine (Section 7).
9   Refitting the camshaft is generally the reversal of the removal
operations, but the following points should be noted. Check that the
crankshaft is still set with No 1 piston at TDC.
10 Lay the camshaft into the lower half bearings with the cams of No
1 cylinder pointing upwards and outwards at equal angles.
11 Check that the off-set of each bearing cap is the right way round
before trying to fit it.
12 Tighten the nuts of bearing cap Nos 1, 3 and 5 about two turns at
a time in sequence until the specified torque is reached.
13 Fit bearing cap Nos 2 and 4, fit the oil pipe and then tighten the
bearing cap nuts. Do not exceed the specified torque when tightening
the bearing cap nuts, because this will distort the camshaft bearings.
14 When fitting the camshaft sprocket make sure that after the securing bolt is tightened that the sprocket is positioned so that the mark on
the back of the sprocket is vertically above the mid point of the
camshaft cover (Fig. 1.70). Fit the timing belt and tension it as
described in Section 23 (Fig. 1.71). Fit the belt cover.
15 When refitting the fuel pump, make sure that the pump plunger is
positioned properly on its operating cam on the camshaft. If a new
camshaft has been fitted check the valve clearances (see Section 24).

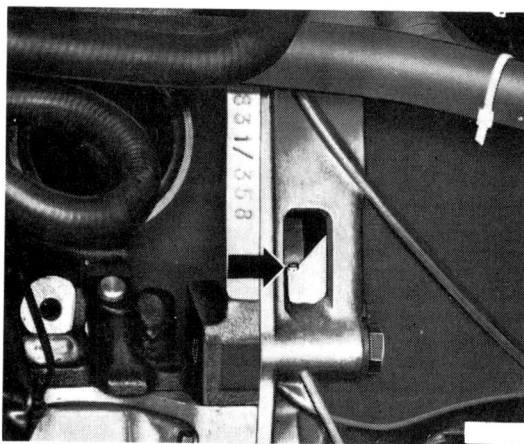

Fig. 1.67 TDC marks on bellhousing (2.0 litre) (Sec 22)

Fig. 1.68 TDC marks on crankshaft pulley (2.0 litre) (Sec 22)

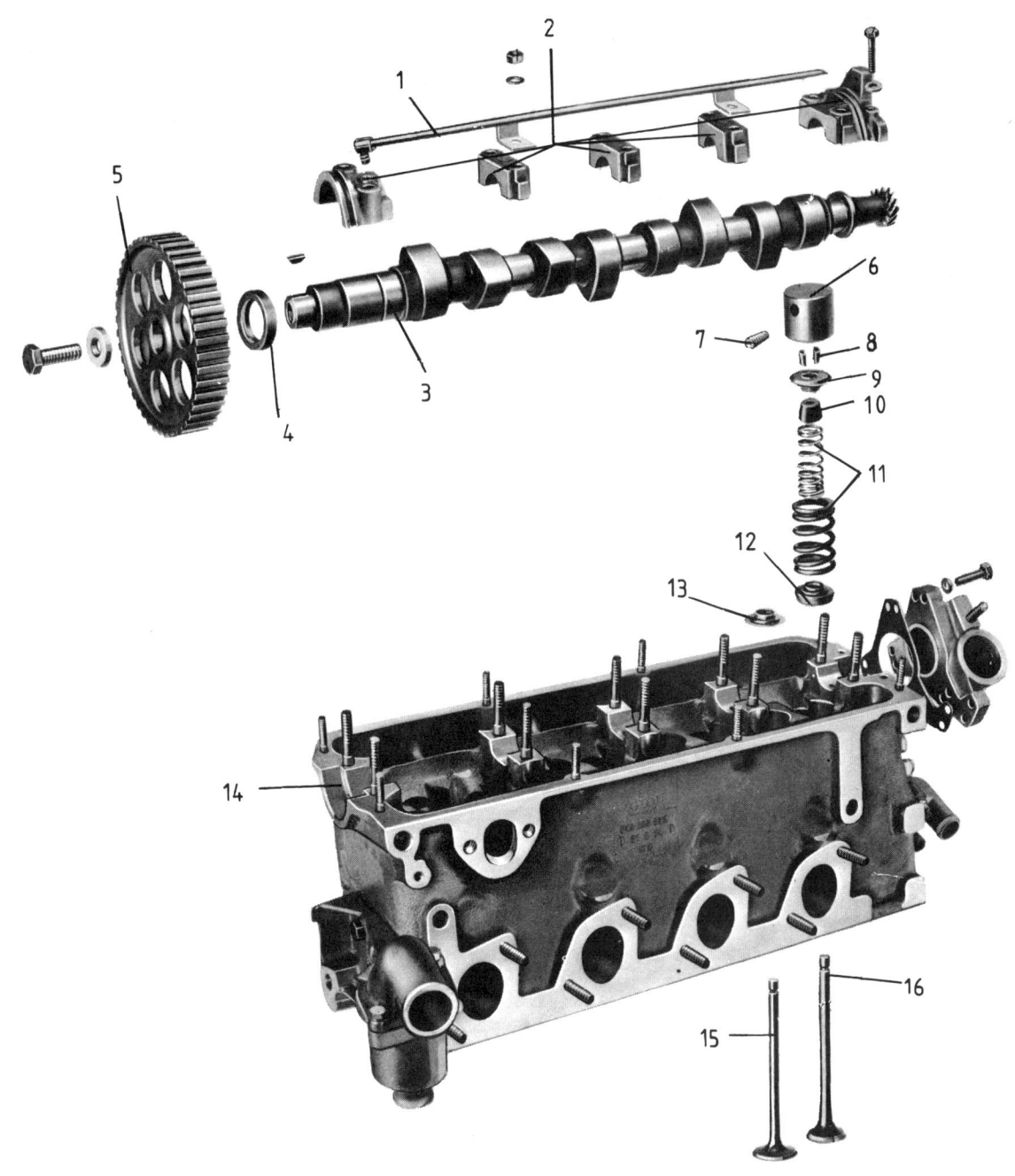

Fig. 1.69 Camshaft and valve gear (2.0 litre) (Sec 22)

1 Oil feed pipe
2 Camshaft bearing caps
3 Camshaft
4 Oil seal

5 Camshaft sprocket
6 Bucket tappet
7 Valve adjusting screw
8 Valve cotters

9   Valve spring cover
10 Stem oil seal
11 Valve springs
12 Rotocap (exhaust valves)

13 Spring seat (inlet valves)
14 Cylinder head
15 Inlet valve
16 Exhaust valve

Fig. 1.70 Camshaft timing mark and cylinder head cover pointer
(2.0 litre) (Sec 22)

Fig. 1.71 Camshaft belt tensioner (2.0 litre) (Sec 22)

23 Cylinder head – removal, servicing, checking and refitting

1   If the cylinder head is to be removed with the engine in the car, the
following preliminary operations are necessary.

    (a) Disconnect the battery leads
    (b) Drain the cooling system
    (c) Remove the air cleaner
    (d) Disconnect the throttle cable
    (e) Disconnect the heater hoses
    (f) Disconnect the carburettor electrical connections
    (g) Disconnect the plug leads
    (h) Disconnect the fuel pipe to the carburettor
    (i) Disconnect the exhaust pipe from the manifold

These operations are described in detail in the previous Section.
2   Slacken the alternator mountings and remove the V-belt. If a
power steering pump and/or compressor are fitted, slacken and
remove their drivebelts.
3   Remove the bolts securing the toothed timing belt cover and take
the cover off.
4   Remove the eight nuts securing the cylinder head cover and
remove the cover. Take off and discard the two piece cylinder head
cover gasket and the sealing strips of the two end camshaft bearing
caps.
5   Fit a spanner to the crankshaft pulley nut and turn the crankshaft
until No 1 cylinder is at TDC. If the engine is still in the vehicle, align
the TDC mark on the flywheel, or driveplate with the lug on the
bellhousing. If the engine has been removed, align the notch on the rim
of the crankshaft pulley with the mark on the oil pump housing. The
mark on the back of the camshaft sprocket should be vertically above
the mid-point of the cylinder head.
6   Loosen the nut in the centre of the toothed belt jockey pulley and
rotate the eccentric hub clockwise to release belt tension. Remove the

toothed belt.
7   The cylinder head may be removed with the camshaft in position
(See previous Section to remove camshaft). Slacken the cylinder head
bolts in the reverse sequence to Fig. 1.72 and then remove the bolts.
To prevent damage to the cylinder head bolts and to ensure that they
are tightened correctly requires the use of a hexagon or polygon
wrench, depending upon which type of bolt is fitted (see Fig. 1.21).
Although it is possible to remove and tighten the bolts without the
proper tool, the practice is not recommended.
8   Loosen the bolts a turn at a time in sequence and when there is no
longer any tension on them, unscrew them and remove them.
9   The cylinder head is fitted on two dowels and must be pulled, or
tapped up vertically to free it from the dowels. When it is free, lift it off
and discard the old gasket.
10   Dismantle the valve gear referring to Part A, Section 5 as
necessary.
11   If the camshaft is still in position it must now be removed from the
cylinder head (see Section 22).
12   Withdraw each tappet (cam follower) in turn and mark its position
(Numbered 1 to 8 from the timing belt end of the engine) using adhesive tape or a box with divisions. Adjusting shims are not used on the
2·0 litre engine, the tappets incorporate a screw adjustment device
(see Section 24).
13   When removing and refitting the valves note that the exhaust
valves have rotocaps beneath their valve springs and the inlet valves
have spring seats. The inner valve springs have the coils closer
together at one end, this end must be towards the cylinder head.
14   Check the cylinder head for distortion, by placing a straight edge
across it at a number of points, lengthwise, crosswise and diagonally
and measuring the gap beneath it with feeler gauges. If the gap
exceeds the limit given in Specifications, the head must be re-faced by
a workshop which is equipped for this work. Re-facing must not
reduce the cylinder head dimension in Fig. 1.74 below the limit given
in Specifications.
15   Examine the valve seats for damage and excessive wear. If pitting

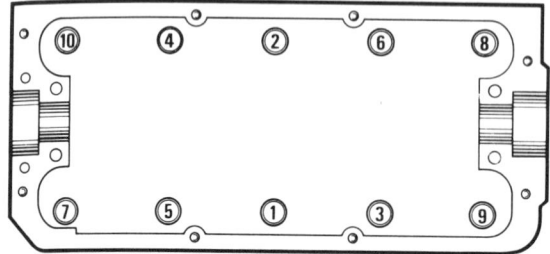

Fig.1.72 Cylinder head bolt tightening sequence – reverse order
for releasing (2.0 litre) (Sec 23)

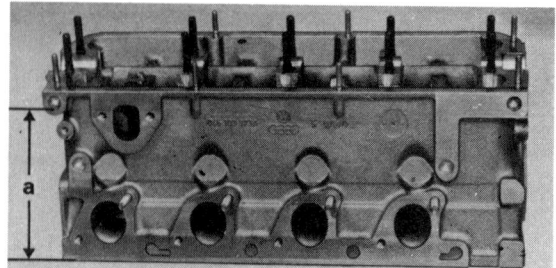

Fig. 1.73 Cylinder head re-finishing limit (2.0 litre) (Sec 23)

Dimension 'a' must not be reduced below 139.5 mm (5.5 in)

is significant, it is better to have the seats re-cut than try to remove all the marks by grinding in the valves.

16 Check the valve guides for wear. First clean out the guide with a cleaning reamer and then insert the stem of a new valve into the guide. Because the stem diameters are different, ensure that only an inlet valve is used to check the inlet valve guides, and an exhaust valve for the exhaust valve guides. With the end of the valve stem flush with the top of the valve guide, measure the total amount by which the rim of the valve head can be moved sideways. This can be done by pushing the valve head as far as possible in one direction and then placing a magnet on the cylinder head so that the magnet is just in contact with the valve head. Pull the valve in the opposite direction as far as possible and measure the gap between the valve head and the magnet with feeler gauges.

17 New valve guides can be fitted, but it is a job for a VW/Audi dealer, or specialist workshop. Replacement valve guides have an external

circlip which acts as a stop when the guide is pressed in and a new spring seat, having a recess to accommodate this circlip must also be fitted (Figs. 1.75 and 1.76).

18 Examine the cylinder head for cracks. If there are minor cracks of not more than 0·5 mm (0·020 in) width between the valve seats, or at the bottom of the spark plug holes, the head can be re-used.

19 Before fitting the cylinder head, ensure that the top of the block is perfectly clean. Use a new gasket and fit it over the cylinder block dowels (Fig. 1.77). Do not use jointing compound.

20 Check that the cylinder head face is perfectly clean.

21 If the cylinder head is being fitted with the engine still in the vehicle, positioning of the head is made easier if two long rods, or pieces of dowel are inserted in two of the bolt holes, to act as guides when lowering the head on to the block.

22 After fitting the head, remove the dowels and fit the cylinder head bolts and washers. Torque-tighten the bolts in three stages to the

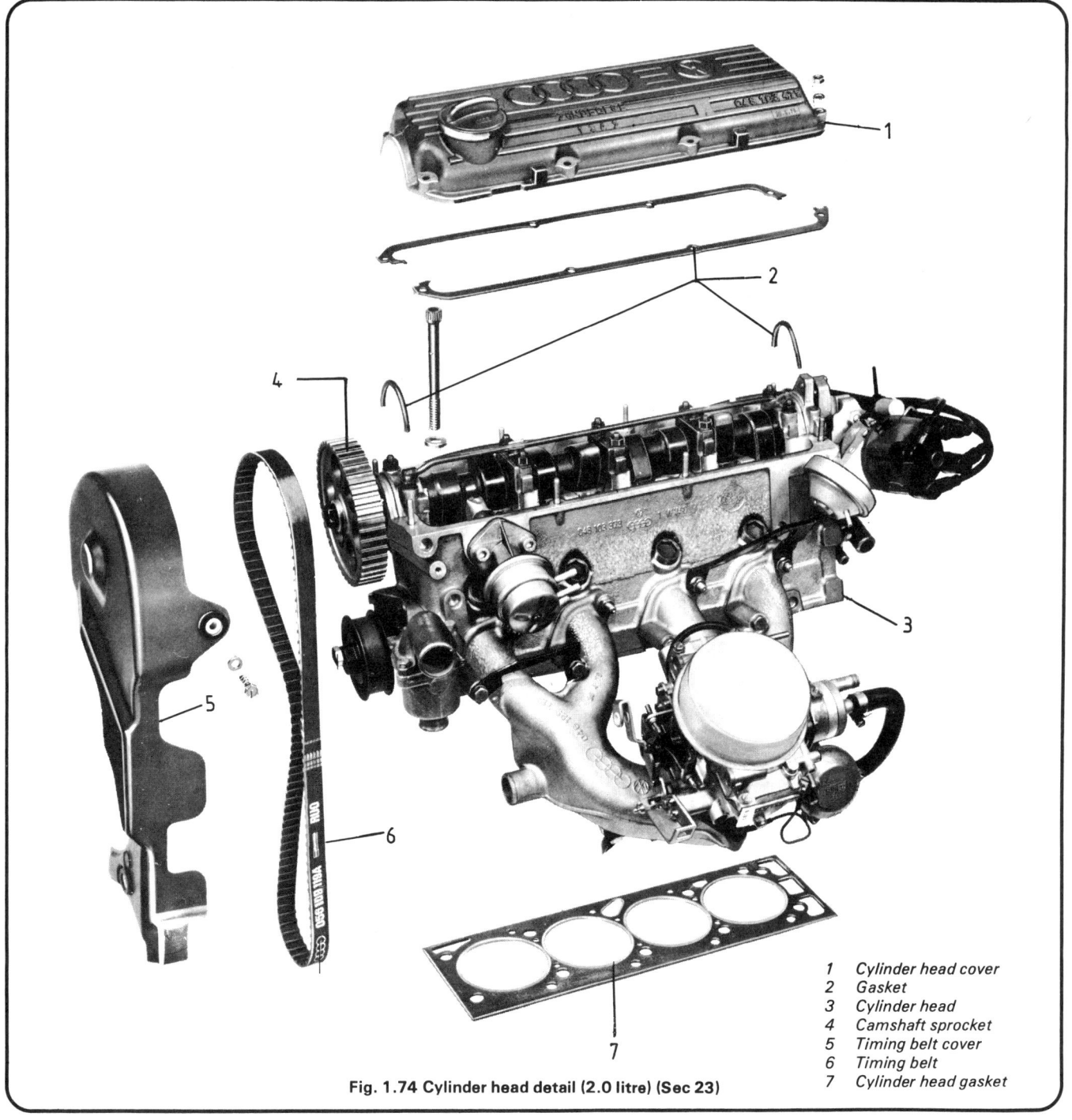

1 Cylinder head cover
2 Gasket
3 Cylinder head
4 Camshaft sprocket
5 Timing belt cover
6 Timing belt
7 Cylinder head gasket

Fig. 1.74 Cylinder head detail (2.0 litre) (Sec 23)

Fig. 1.75 Replacement valve guide (2.0 litre)(Sec 23)

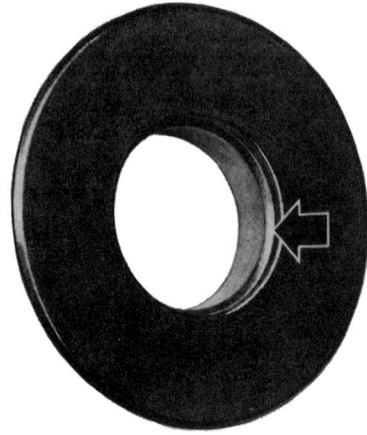

Fig. 1.76 Shouldered spring seat to fit replacement valve guide (2.0 litre) (Sec 23)

Fig. 1.77 Cylinder head gasket correctly located (2.0 litre) (Sec 23)

'cold' figure given in the Specifications, following the sequence shown in Fig. 1.72.

23 Fit new gaskets for the cylinder head cover and new seals to the end camshaft bearing. Fit the cylinder head cover on its studs, then fit the nuts and washers. Tighten the nuts to the specified torque, but do not over tighten them because this may distort the cover, or damage the gasket causing oil leaks.

24 Ensure that the mark on the back of the camshaft sprocket is in line with the pointer on the cylinder head cover. Check that the crankshaft is at TDC.

25 Fit the timing belt and tension it by turning the eccentric hub of the jockey pulley anti-clockwise with the pulley centre bolt just tight enough to hold the pulley in position. When the belt tension is such that gripping it between the thumb and forefinger, the belt can just be turned through 90° at the middle of its longest span, tighten the jockey pulley centre bolt.

26 Fit the belt cover over the toothed belt, then fit the V-belt(s) and tension them.

27 Check and adjust the valve clearances as described in the following Section.

28 Run the engine to attain the normal operating temperature then loosen each cylinder head bolt in turn by 30° and re-tighten to the specified torque in the order shown in Fig. 1.72. Repeat this procedure after 620 miles (1000 km) of running.

24 Valve clearances – checking and adjusting

1   The bucket tappets incorporate a socket-headed grub screw which has an inclined flat machined face on one side. This acts like a wedge which can be moved in and out to adjust the gap between the top of the valve stem and the cam.

2   Each complete turn on the screw alters the valve clearance by 0·05 mm (0·0020 in) and the screw must never be adjusted except by complete turns to ensure that the screw always has its flat side in contact with the valve stem.

3   For the initial setting-up after fitting a new camshaft, or grinding in the valves the valve clearances will be adjusted with a cold engine. The valve clearances should be re-checked when the engine is warm with the coolant at a temperature of at least 35°C (95°F), after 620 miles (1000 km). Thereafter valve clearances should be checked when the engine is warm.

4   Remove the cylinder head cover and fit a spanner to the crankshaft pulley nut. Turn the crankshaft until the highest points of the cams for one cylinder are pointing upwards and outwards at similar angles.

5   Use feeler gauges to check the gap between the cam and the tappet (Fig. 1.79) and calculate the number of turns required on the adjuster as follows.

6   If the measured clearance on an inlet valve is 0·35 mm (0·014 in) on a hot engine, this is outside the tolerance specified for inlet valves, which is 0·20 to 0·30 mm (0·008 to 0·012 in). The best adjustment is the mid-point of the range i.e. 0·25 mm (0·010 in) and the measured gap of 0·35 mm (0·014 in) is 0·1 mm (0·004 in) too great. To decrease the gap by this amount, screw the adjuster clockwise two complete turns.

7   When a clearance is too small, the adjusting screw must be turned anti-clockwise and each complete turn will increase the clearance by 0·05 mm (0·002 in).

8   To make the adjustment, insert a 3 mm Allen key into the socket on the end of the screw, or use a hexagon socket and a ratchet handle. If using a socket and ratchet handle, put a mark on the socket so that you can see when it has made a complete turn.

9   It is important that the adjuster screw is never moved in or out too

Fig. 1.78 Camshaft lobes positioned for valve clearance adjustment (2.0 litre) (Sec 24)

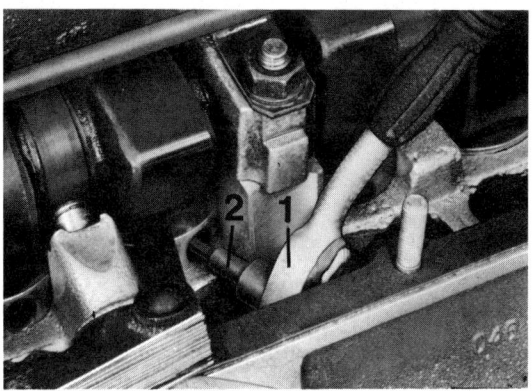

Fig. 1.79 Adjusting a valve clearance (2.0 litre) (Sec 24)

1   *Ratchet wrench*   2   *3mm socket*

Fig. 1.80 Marks on valve adjusting screw (2.0 litre) (Sec 24)

Left – Paint spot identification   Right – Grooves for identification

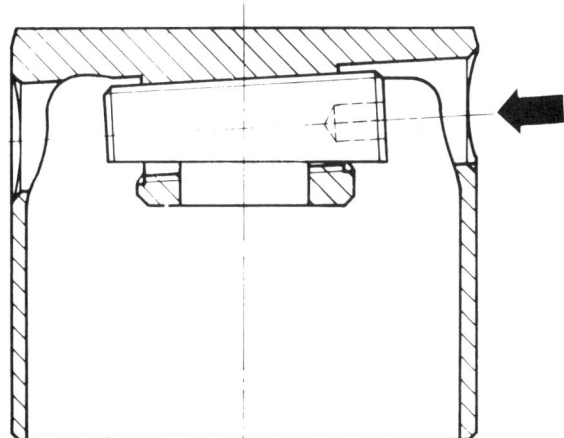

Fig. 1.81 Correct fitting of valve adjuster screw, pointing downward (2.0 litre) (Sec 24)

far so that it is not fully engaged in all the threads in the tappet; the head of the screw must never be more than 10 mm (0·394 in) in from the outer surface of the tappet. If correct valve clearance cannot be achieved without screwing the adjuster beyond the limit, a new screw must be fitted.

10 Four different screws are available and they are identified either by a coloured paint mark, or by a number of cuts on the end of the screw. Screws should normally be replaced by one with the same marking, but if a valve has been renewed, or a new camshaft fitted, a different screw may be necessary. In this case, measure the valve clearance with the adjuster screw at its mid-point and consult a VW/Audi dealer to find the right screw for giving the correct clearance.

11 When fitting a new screw, it must be inserted into the tappet from

the correct side. Mark the tappet before removing the screw to indicate which side of the tappet has the socket end of the screw. If a screw has been removed without marking the tappet, check that when entering the screw in the threads, the screw has to be pointed downwards slightly. If the screw is entered into the wrong side, it will have to be pointed slightly upwards to engage the threads (Fig. 1.81).

12 Valves are numbered from the timing belt end of the engine, inlet valves are Nos 1–3–5–7, exhaust valves are Nos 2–4–6–8.

25 Flywheel, or driveplate – removing and refitting

1   The procedure is identical with that described for the 1·6 litre engine in Part A (Section 11), except that the flywheel and crankshaft have mating marks scribed on them during production. Check that these marks are visible, or make new marks before removing the bolts.

2   The distance from the rear face of the block to the torque converter mounting face is different from that on the 1·6 litre engine. For the 2·0 litre engine the dimension should be between 18·0 and 18·8 mm (0·709 and 0·740 in).

26 Pistons and connecting rods – removal, dismantling, checking and reassembly

1   The pistons and connecting rods are removed from the top of the cylinders, so the cylinder head must be removed before they can be withdrawn.

2   If the engine is in the car, remove the sump (Section 19) and the cylinder head (Section 22). If the engine has been removed, place it on its side on the bench, remove the sump, having first ensured that the oil has been drained from it. Unbolt and remove the oil pick-up pipe and strainer.

3   Mark each connecting rod with its cylinder number on both parts of the connecting rod bearing (Fig. 1.82) so that the pistons and connecting rods can be refitted to the correct cylinder.

4   Turn the crankshaft so that the connecting rod big-end bearing cap nuts are accessible, remove the nuts and lift off the bearing cap.

5   Rotate the crankshaft until the piston has been pushed to the top of its bore, then disengage the connecting rod from the crankshaft and push the piston and connecting rod out of the top of the block. Put the bearing cap with its connecting rod and refit any half-bearing shell which may become detached.

6   Dismantling the piston/connecting rod is as described in Part A for the 1·6 litre engine (Section 12) except that it should not be necessary to mark the connecting rods to show which side is towards the front of the engine, because of the casting marks (Fig. 1.84).

7   To check the pistons and cylinder bores for wear, refer to Part A, Section 13, the procedure being identical.

8   Unless the bearing shells are known to be almost new, it is worth fitting a new set when the pistons have been removed. Clean the connecting rods and bearing caps thoroughly and fit the bearing shells so

Fig. 1.82 Connecting rods marked with cylinder number (2.0 litre) (Sec 26)

that the tang on the bearing engages in the recess in the connecting rod, or cap and the ends of the bearing are flush with the joint face.

9   To refit the pistons, first space the joints in the piston rings so that they are at 120° intervals. Oil the rings and grooves generously and fit a piston ring compressor over the piston (Fig. 1.85). To fit the pistons without using a piston ring compressor is difficult and there is a high risk of breaking a piston ring.

10   Oil the cylinder bores and insert the pistons with the arrow on the piston crown (Fig. 1.86) pointing towards the front of the engine.

11   When the piston is pushed in flush with the top of the bore, oil the two big-end bearing halves and the crankshaft journals and guide the connecting rod half-bearing on to the crankshaft journal.

12   If the pistons have been removed from the connecting rods check that they have been fitted the correct way round. When the arrow on the piston crown is pointing to the front of the engine, the cast marks on each part of the connecting rod bearing must also be towards the front of the engine.

13   Fit the big-end bearing cap and tighten the nuts.

14   Rotate the crankshaft to ensure that everything is free, before fitting the next piston and connecting rod.

15   Refit the oil pick-up, the sump and cylinder head.

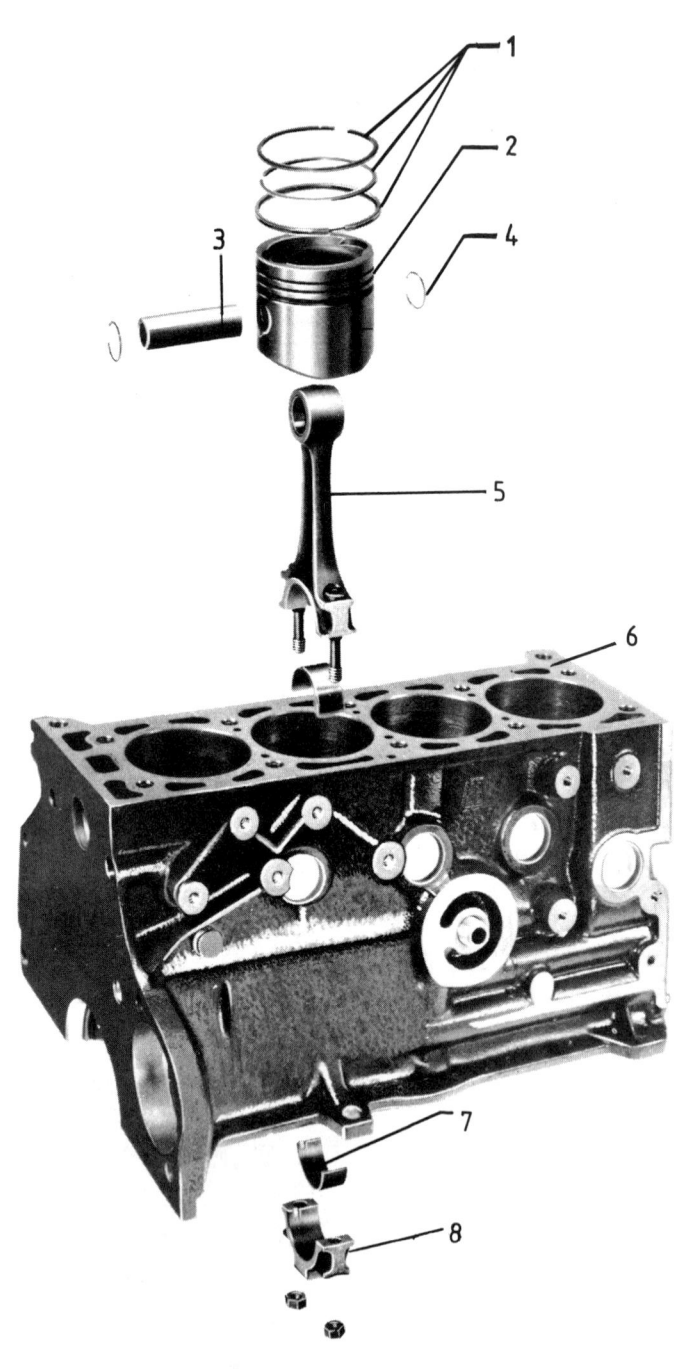

Fig. 1.83 Pistons and connecting rods (2.0 litre) (Sec 26)

1	Piston rings	3	Piston pin	5	Connecting rod	7	Bearing shell
2	Piston	4	Circlip	6	Cylinder block	8	Bearing cap

Fig. 1.84 Casting marks on front face of connecting rods (2.0 litre) (Sec 26)

Fig. 1.85 Using a piston ring compressor (Sec 26)

Fig. 1.86 Front facing arrows on piston crowns (2.0 litre) (Sec 26)

27 Crankshaft oil seals – renewing

1   The crankshaft front oil seal is incorporated in the oil pump and the rear oil seal is held between an extension to the crankshaft rear bearing and the crankshaft.

2   There are special tools which enable the seals to be renewed in-situ, but without these, it is necessary to remove the sump.

3   Renewing the front oil seal is included in the dismantling of the oil pump (Section 29).

4   To renew the rear oil seal, either remove the engine from the gearbox or the gearbox from the engine, the latter being easier. Remove the flywheel, or driveplate, from the crankshaft.

5   Drain the oil from the sump.

6   Remove the bolts from the sump and take off the sump. Remove the two parts of the sump gasket and the semi-circular seals from each end of the sump and discard them.

7   Loosen the two hexagon bolts and the two hexagon headed screws of No 5 crankshaft bearing and pull the oil seal off the crankshaft flange.

8   Oil the lip of a new seal and slide it over the crankshaft flange. The closed end of the seal should be towards the flywheel.

9   Push the seal as far forward as it will go, being careful to keep it square on the crankshaft and ensuring that the lip of the seal does not become twisted.

10   Tighten the bearing cap bolts to the specified torque.

11   Fit a new seal to the semi-circular surfaces at each end of the sump. Fit a new sump gasket and refit the sump.

12   Complete reassembly by reversing the order of operations for dismantling and fill the sump with oil to the correct level.

28 Crankshaft – removing and refitting

1   With the engine out of the car it is not necessary to remove the cylinder head and piston before removing the crankshaft, but if the crankshaft is being removed as part of a general engine overhaul, it is convenient to leave the crankshaft until last.

2   Remove the flywheel, the sump and the oil pump.

3   Position the engine upside down on the bench, if the cylinder head has been removed, or lying on its side if the cylinder head is still in place. Put marks on each bearing cap to indicate its position and also which side of it is towards the front of the engine.

4   Knock back the tabs of the lockplate on the oil intake pipe flange. Remove the two bolts from the flange and the bolt from the stay.

5   Remove the oil intake pipe and discard the lockplate and gasket.

6   Remove the bolts from each bearing cap in turn, then remove the caps and lift out the crankshaft.

7   If the bearings are not being renewed, ensure that each half-bearing is identified so that it is put back in the same position from which it was removed.

8   If the engine has done a high mileage and it is suspected that the crankshaft requires attention, it is best to seek the opinion of a VW/Audi dealer, or a crankshaft machining specialist.

9   Unless the main bearing shells are known to be almost new, it is worth fitting a new set when the crankshaft is removed. Clean the crankcase webs and bearing caps thoroughly and fit the bearing shells so that the tang on the bearing engages in the recess in the crankcase web, or bearing cap. Make sure that the shells fitted to the crankcase have oil holes, and that those line up with the drillings in the bearing housings. The shells fitted in the bearing caps do not have oil holes. Note that the bearing shells of the centre bearing (No 3) are different from the others, being flanged to act as a thrust bearing.

10   Fit the bearing shells so that the ends of the bearing are flush with the joint face.

11   Lubricate the crankcase web half-bearings, lubricate the crankshaft journals and lay the crankshaft on its bearings.

12   Lubricate the bearing caps and apply sealing compound to the joint face of No 5 bearing. Lay the bearings in their correct position and the right way round (Fig. 1.88).

13   Fit the bolts to the bearing caps and tighten the bolts of the centre cap to the specified torque, then check that the crankshaft rotates freely. If it is difficult to rotate the crankshaft, check that the bearing shells are seated properly and that the bearing cap is the correct way round. Rotation will only be difficult if something is incorrect and the fault must be found.

14   Working out from the centre, tighten the remaining bearing caps in turn, checking that the crankshaft rotates freely after each bearing has been tightened. Note that the rear (No 5) main bearing cap incorporates the rear oil seal housing and is retained by four bolts. The outer bolts are tightened to a lower torque than the inner ones (see Specifications).

15   Check that the endplay of the crankshaft is within specification by inserting feeler gauges between the crankshaft and the centre bearing thrust face at the same time levering the crankshaft first in one direction and then in the other.

16   Fit the oil intake pipe, using a new gasket and a new lockplate.

Fig. 1.87 Crankcase components (2.0 litre) (Sec 28)

1 Oil intake pipe	5 Plain bearing shell	9 Needle bearing	12 Gasket
2 Lock plate	6 Centre bearing shell	10 Crankshaft	13 Oil pump
3 Gasket	7 Flywheel	11 Crankcase	14 Oil seal
4 Main bearing caps	8 Crankshaft oil seal		

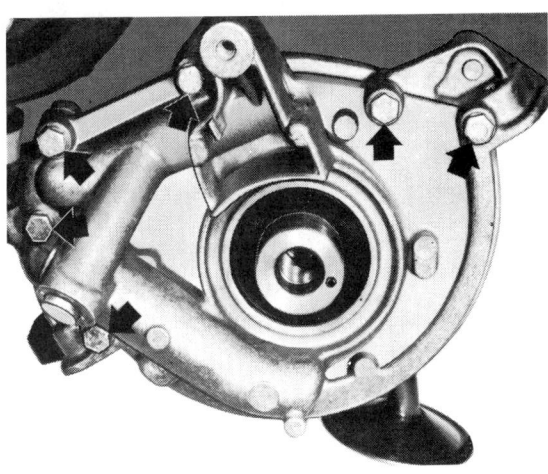

Fig. 1.89 Oil pump fixing bolts (2.0 litre) (Sec 29)

Bend up the corners of the lockplate to prevent the bolts from moving after they have been tightened.

17 The remainder of the operations are the fitting of the flywheel, oil pump (see Section 29) and sump. These are the reverse of the removal operations.

18 The rear end of the crankshaft carries a needle roller bearing which supports the front end of the gearbox input shaft.

19 Inspect the bearing for obvious signs of wear and damage. If the gearbox has been removed and dismantled, fit the input shaft into the bearing to see if there is excessive clearance.

20 If the bearing requires renewing, insert a hook in the bearing and pull it out of the end of the shaft.

21 Press in a new bearing, with the lettering on the end of the bearing outwards. Press the bearing in until the bearing is 1·0 mm (0·039 in) below the face of the flywheel flange in similar manner to the 1·6 litre engine (Fig. 1.47) except that the depth is different.

29 Oil pump – removing, dismantling, checking and refitting

1 The oil pump can be removed without removing the engine but the following preliminary work is necessary.

(a) Remove the radiator (Chapter 2)
(b) Remove the V-belt and timing belt
(c) Remove the crankshaft pulley and timing belt sprocket
(d) Drain the oil and remove the dipstick
(e) Remove the front subframe bolts and remove the sump

2 Remove the six bolts securing the oil pump to the front of the engine.

Fig. 1.88 Main bearing caps correctly fitted (2.0 litre) (Sec 28)

3 Remove the oil pump by pulling it over the end of the crankshaft. Remove and discard the gasket between the pump and the cylinder block and the semi-circular seal between the pump and the sump.

4 Remove the six countersunk screws securing the pump back plate and lift the back plate off, exposing the gears.

5 Put a mark on the gears to show which side of them is towards the engine and remove the gears.

6 Unscrew the pressure relief valve and remove the plug, sealing ring, spring and plunger (Fig. 1.90).

7 Clean all the parts thoroughly and examine the pump casing and backplate for signs of wear, or scoring. Examine the pressure relief valve plunger and its seating for damage and wear and check that the spring is not damaged, or distorted.

8 Check the gears for damage and wear. New gears may be fitted, but they must be fitted as a pair.

9 Prise out the oil seal from the front of the pump. Oil the lip of a new seal, enter the seal with its closed face outwards and use a block of wood to tap the seal in flush. If there is any scoring on the crankshaft in the area on which the lip of the seal bears, the seal may be pushed to the bottom of its recess so that the lip bears on an undamaged part of the crankshaft.

10 Reassemble the pump by fitting the gears and the backplate. The inner gear has its slotted end towards the crankshaft and although the outer gear can be fitted either way round, it should be fitted the same way round as it was before removal. Some gears have a triangle stamped on them and this mark should be towards the front plate.

11 When refitting the pump, use a new gasket and ensure that the inner gear is properly engaged with the drive keys on the crankshaft.

Part C – 2.2 litre engine

30 General description

The engine has five-cylinders in-line and is liquid cooled. A belt-driven pump circulates coolant around the combustion chambers and through a front mounted radiator; and cooling of the radiator is assisted by an electrically driven fan which is controlled thermostatically.

The camshaft, driven from the crankshaft by a toothed belt, is mounted above the valves and operates them through bucket tappets. The valve clearance is adjusted by the use of shims.

A gear on the end of the camshaft drives the distributor and on carburettor models the camshaft also drives the fuel pump.

The engine has a full-flow lubrication system. A gear and crescent type oil pump is mounted on the front of the crankshaft. The oil filter is of the cartridge type, mounted on the left-hand side of the cylinder block.

The engine is a hybrid of the 1.6 litre and 2.0 litre types and when appropriate, reference is made to these engines, to avoid repetition.

31 Major operations possible with engine in place

1 The water pump, fuel pump, distributor and radiator can be removed without removing the engine.

2 The cylinder head can be removed for decarbonizing and valve grinding; and new V-drivebelts and timing belts can be fitted with the engine in place.

3 The clutch is not accessible without removing either the engine, or the gearbox; if the engine does not require major attention, it is easier to remove the gearbox, leaving the engine in place.

4 It is possible to remove the sump and oil pump without removing the engine, but to do so, the engine must be supported from above and the subframe front mounting bolts removed. Before removing the oil pump, the vibration damper on the crankshaft end must be removed. This is kept in place by a bolt which has locking compound on its threads and is tightened to a very high torque. To remove this bolt with the engine is place requires special tools (Nos 2079 and 2084). Do not attempt this work without the special tools as there is no alternative way to secure the crankshaft against rotation while the bolt is released.

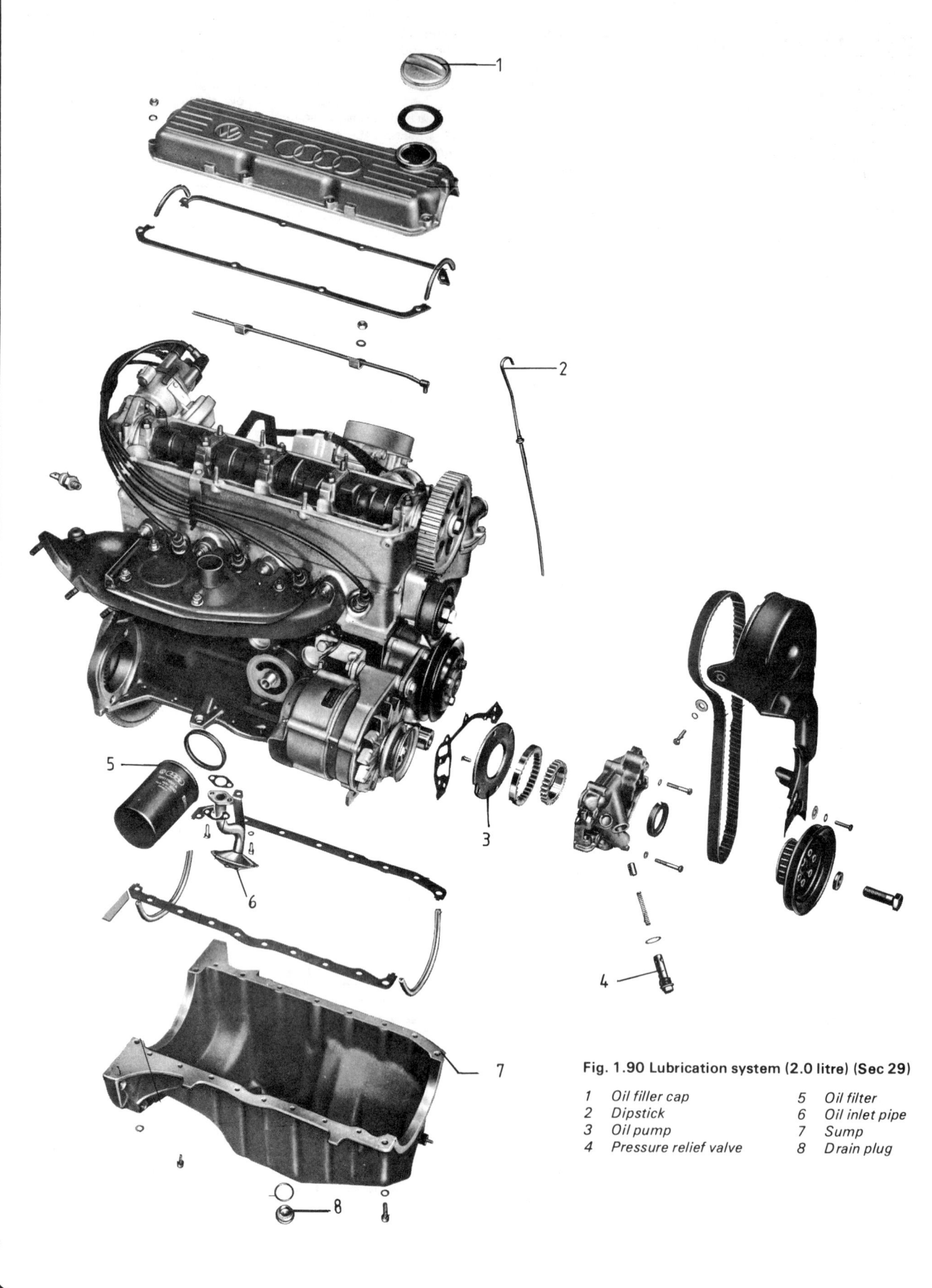

Fig. 1.90 Lubrication system (2.0 litre) (Sec 29)

1 Oil filler cap
2 Dipstick
3 Oil pump
4 Pressure relief valve
5 Oil filter
6 Oil inlet pipe
7 Sump
8 Drain plug

32 Engine – removal and refitting

1 Disconnect the battery leads.

2 Remove the cap from the coolant reservoir to relieve the pressure in the system. Place a large bowl beneath the engine to catch the coolant, then loosen the clamp and remove the hose at the bottom of the reservoir to drain the reservoir.

3 Disconnect the coolant hose at the connector (Fig. 1.92) and drain the coolant from the system. If an air conditioner is fitted, set the heating control to *cold*.

4 On fuel injection models, pull the ignition out of the inlet manifold, remove the two bolts and take the cold start valve from the manifold, remove the two bolts and take the warm-up valve off the cylinder block (photo). Secure the removed parts so that they are out of the way, but do not disconnect any of the fuel lines to them.

5 On carburettor models, remove the air cleaner. On injection models disconnect the air duct and vacuum hoses from the intake manifold and throttle housing, then release the clips on the air cleaner cover and take off the cover and the filter element. Cover the air inlet with a clean rag, or plastic bag to stop the entry of dirt.

6 With the help of an assistant, marking the position of the bonnet hinges, remove the bolts and lift the bonnet off.

7 Pull the engine bonnet lock cable towards the driver's side and detach the cable from the bracket on the radiator.

8 If an air conditioner is fitted, remove the radiator grille, dismount the condenser (but do not disconnect any pipes) and tilt it forwards.

9 Remove the bolts securing the power steering pump and tie the pump out of the way, but do not disconnect the pipes (photo).

10 On USA vehicles, remove the vacuum booster and detach the thermopneumatic valve from the cylinder head.

11 Loosen the clamp round the ignition coil, detach the electrical connections and remove the ignition coil from the front bulkhead.

12 Pull off the spark plug caps, remove the cap from the ignition coil after detaching the earth strap and take off the distributor cap and ignition leads. Remove the rotor arm from the distributor.

13 Disconnect the pipes and electrical connections from the windscreen washer container and take the container off the bulkhead.

14 On vehicles with a manual gearbox, disconnect the accelerator cable from the throttle housing of the carburettor, or the injection system and pull the cable out of its bracket (Chapter 3).

15 On vehicles with automatic transmission, disconnect the throttle control pushrod and the pull rod (Chapter 3, Section 32).

16 On carburettor engines, pull the fuel supply pipe off the fuel filter and pull the return pipe off the centre connection of the fuel return valve.

17 If an air conditioner is fitted, unbolt the compressor complete with its brackets, but do not disconnect the pipes. Tie the compressor clear of the engine.

18 Remove the power steering reservoir from its holder and secure it clear of the engine.

19 Disconnect the brake servo vacuum hose from the inlet manifold and pull the vacuum hose (3) off the distributor vacuum unit.

20 On carburettor models, disconnect the electrical connections to the carburettor.

21 Disconnect the wires to the oil pressure switch (photo), the oil temperature sender (on the sump) and the water temperature sender (photos).

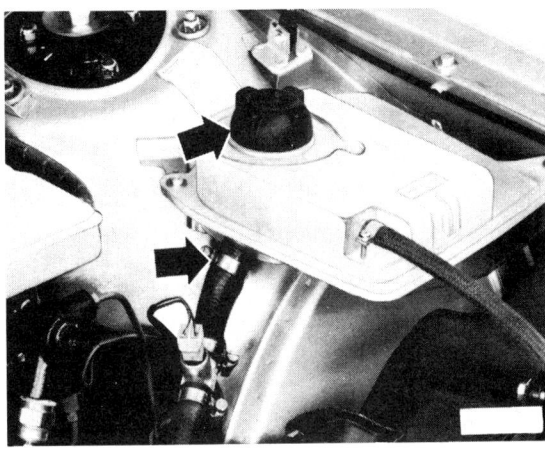

Fig. 1.91 Coolant reservoir drain point (2.2 litre) (Sec 32)

Fig. 1.92 Cooling system drain point (2.2 litre)(Sec 32)

32.4 Warm-up valve

32.9 Power steering pump tied to one side of engine compartment

Fig. 1.93 Securing the compressor (2.2 litre) (Sec 32)

22 Disconnect the alternator plug connections, remove the alternator fixing bolts and take off the alternator.

23 Note the position of the electrical connections to the starter motor and solenoid and then remove them. Remove the two starter motor fixing bolts and take the motor off.

24 On vehicles with automatic transmission, turn the starter ring until each of the three torque converter mounting bolts in turn is accessible through the starter motor hole and remove the bolts attaching the converter to the driveplate.

25 Remove the three nuts securing the exhaust pipe flange to the manifold and the bolt securing the exhaust pipe to the gearbox (photo).

26 Remove the front engine mounting.

27 With a suitable container placed beneath the sump, remove the sump drain plug and drain out the oil. Refit the drain plug and tighten it.

28 Pack wooden blocks beneath the gearbox so that it remains in the same position when the engine is removed and then remove the lower bolts connecting the engine to the gearbox.

29 Attach lifting slings to the eye attached to the front left-hand side of the cylinder head and to the eye on the left-hand side of the cylinder block (photo). Adjust the length of the slings so that when hoisted the engine will be inclined at an angle of about 15°, with the front higher than the rear. Attach the slings to a hoist and raise the hoist to take up the slack.

30 Remove the upper bolts connecting the engine to the gearbox. Remove the engine mounting bracket on the left-hand side of the engine and disconnect the right-hand engine mounting bracket from the engine mounting.

31 Check that there is nothing attached to the engine which will prevent its removal and then separate the engine from the gearbox by raising the hoist enough to lift the engine clear of the mounting and then holding the support sling and pushing the car to the rear slightly.

32 As soon as the gearbox input shaft is free of its bearing in the crankshaft, the engine can be lifted, guiding it to prevent damage to the input shaft, the clutch and the body. As soon as the engine is free, turn it to the right and hoist it clear of the engine compartment. On vehicles with automatic transmission, secure the torque converter to prevent it from falling out of the bellhousing.

33 Although refitting the engine is the reversal of the operations necessary for removing it, there are a few points which need particular care.

34 When fitting the engine to the gearbox, make sure that the mating faces of the engine and gearbox are aligned and parallel, before attempting to push them together. If it is difficult to enter the input shaft into the clutch splines on manual transmission models, turn the crankshaft pulley a small amount to line the splines up. If the clutch has been removed, make sure that the driveplate has been centralised accurately (Chapter 5). Do not attempt to force the engine and gearbox together, because this will result in damage.

35 Connect the starter motor cable to the solenoid as shown in Fig. 1.94 and ensure that the cable is well clear of all parts of the engine and body. If this is not done, there is a risk of a short circuit and fire.

36 When fitting the gasket to the joint between the exhaust manifold

32.21A Oil pressure switch

32.21B Oil temperature sender

32.21C Coolant temperature sender (arrowed)

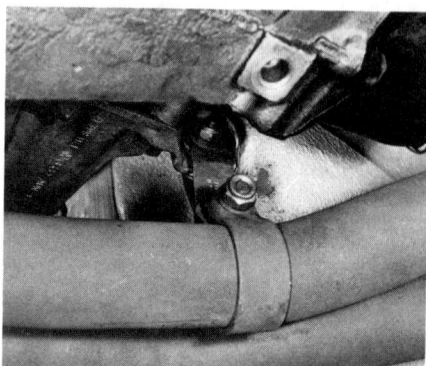

32.25 Exhaust pipe mounting to gearbox

32.29 Lifting slings in position

and the exhaust pipe, fit the gasket so that the lip on it is towards the exhaust pipe.

37 On engines fitted with exhaust gas recirculation attach the vacuum hoses as shown in Fig. 1.95.

38 Check that the engine has been filled with oil and that the cooling system is full before starting the engine.

39 Align the exhaust system so that it is free from strain.

40 Ensure that the rubber engine mountings are not strained, by leaving their final tightening until the engine is idling.

33 Camshaft – removal and refitting

1 The camshaft can be removed and refitted without disturbing the cylinder head.

2 Turn the crankshaft so that No 1 piston at TDC on its compression stroke (flywheel timing marks in alignment).

3 Carry out the following preliminary operations:

   (a) Remove the air cleaner (carburettor models) (Chapter 3)
   (b) Remove the cylinder head cover
   (c) Remove the fuel pump (carburettor models) (Chapter 3)
   (d) Remove the distributor (Chapter 4)
   (e) Remove the V-belts and the timing belt guard
   (f) Engage 4th gear, apply the handbrake and loosen the camshaft sprocket bolt
   (g) Remove the timing belt and camshaft sprocket

4 Check that each bearing cap has its number stamped on it and if not, make an identifying mark to ensure that each cap is put back where it was originally. Note that the caps are off-set and can only be fitted one way round.

5 It is important that the camshaft is removed exactly as described, so that there is no danger of it becoming distorted.

6 Loosen one of the nuts on bearing cap No 2 about two turns and then loosen the diagonally opposite nut on bearing cap No 4 about two turns. Repeat the operations on the other nut of bearing cap No 2 and bearing cap No 4. Continue the sequence until the nuts are free, then remove them.

7 Loosen and remove the nuts of bearing caps Nos 1 and 3 using a similar diagonal sequence.

8 Lift the bearing caps off and lift the camshaft out (photo). Check the camshaft and bearings for wear as described for the 1.6 litre engine in Part A of this Chapter.

9 With the camshaft removed, pull off the camshaft oil seal and discard it. The oil seal may be removed without removing the camshaft if bearing cap No 1 is removed and the seal is driven off the shaft.

10 Refitting the camshaft is generally the reversal of the removal operations, but the following points should be noted.

11 Check that the off-set of each bearing cap is the right way round, before trying to fit it (photo).

12 Tighten the nuts of bearing cap Nos 2 and 4 a turn at a time in diagonal sequence until the specified torque is achieved and then tighten the nuts of bearing cap Nos 1 and 3 in a similar manner. Do not exceed the specified torque when tightening the bearing cap nuts,

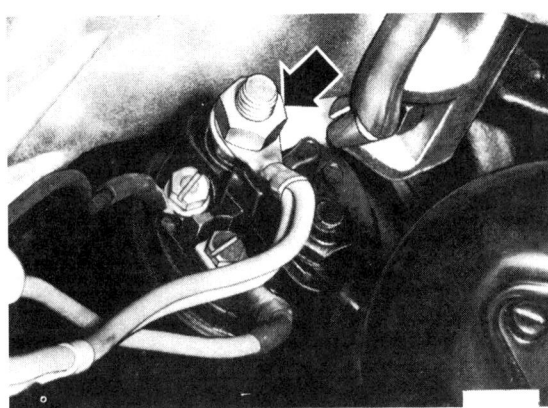

Fig. 1.94 Correct position of starter motor cable (2.2 litre) (Sec 32)

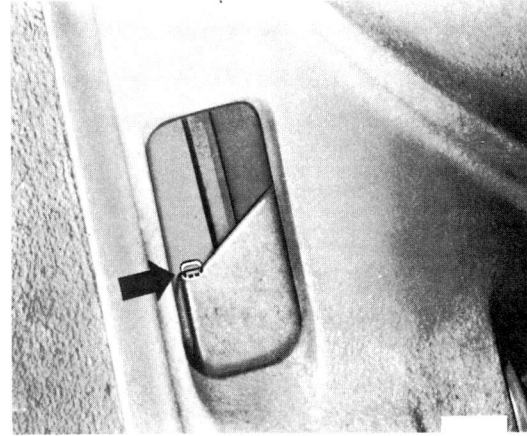

Fig. 1.96 Flywheel timing marks – No 1 piston at TDC (2.2 litre) (Sec 33)

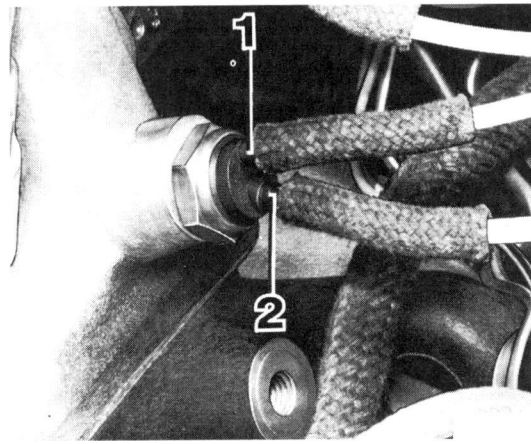

Fig. 1.95 Thermopneumatic valve connections (Sec 32)

   1   Straight adaptor to EGR valve
   2   Angled adaptor to vacuum booster

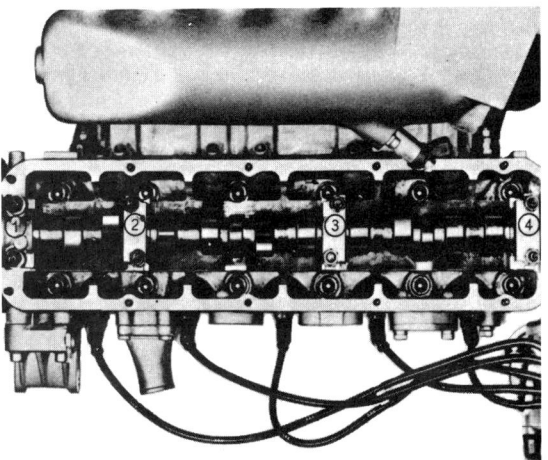

Fig. 1.97 Camshaft bearing markings (2.2 litre) (Sec 33)

33.8 Camshaft ready for removal

33.11 Fitting a camshaft bearing cap

because this will distort the camshaft bearings.

13 Lightly oil the lip and the outer edge of a new oil seal. Enter the seal with its open face first and use a block of wood and a hammer to drive the seal in until its face is flush with the front of bearing cap No 1. Do not drive the seal in until it touches the bottom of its recess, because this will cover up the oil return hole.

14 Fit the camshaft pulley and tighten its bolt. Turn the camshaft pulley until the mark on its rear face is in line with the upper edge of the cylinder head cover gasket.

15 Check that the crankshaft is still at its position for No 1 cylinder at TDC then fit and tension the timing belt.

34 Cylinder head – removal, servicing, checking, refitting

1 If the cylinder head is to be removed with the engine in the car, carry out the following preliminary operations.

   (a) Disconnect the battery leads
   (b) Drain the cooling system
   (c) Remove the air cleaner (carburettor models) or disconnect the air horn from the air flow meter (injection models)
   (d) Disconnect the throttle cable
   (e) Disconnect the HT lead from the ignition coil
   (f) Disconnect the electrical connections to the carburettor (carburettor models)
   (g) Unbolt the power steering pump and air compressor, if fitted and move them to one side of the engine compartment
   (h) Pull the injectors out of the manifold, remove the cold start valve and the warm-up valve (injection models)
   (i) Disconnect the fuel pipe to the carburettor (carburettor models)
   (j) Disconnect the exhaust pipe from the manifold
   (k) Pull the brake servo vacuum connection off the inlet manifold
   (l) Disconnect the low tension lead and the vacuum hoses from the distributor

2 Slacken the alternator mountings and remove the V-belt.

3 Remove the bolts securing the timing belt cover and take the cover off.

4 Remove the twelve nuts from the cylinder head cover and remove the cover. Remove and discard the main gasket, the gasket over the front camshaft bearing and the semicircular plug at the rear of the cylinder head.

5 Fit a spanner to the crankshaft pulley nut and turn the crankshaft until No 1 cylinder is at TDC. If the engine is still in the vehicle, align the TDC mark on the flywheel, or driveplate with the lug on the bellhousing (Fig. 1.96). If the engine has been removed, align the notch on the rim of the crankshaft pulley with the mark on the oil

Fig. 1.98 Camshaft sprocket alignment marks – No 1 piston at TDC (2.2 litre) (Sec 33)

Fig. 1.99 Crankshaft pulley alignment marks – No 1 piston at TDC (2.2 litre) (Sec 33)

pump housing (Fig. 1.99). The mark on the back of the camshaft sprocket should be in line with the upper edge of the rear part of the drive cover. If the cylinder head gasket is in place, the mark will be in line with the upper surface of the gasket (Fig. 1.98).

6 Loosen the three fixing bolts of the coolant pump and turn the pump clockwise to release the tension on the toothed belt. Remove the toothed belt.

7 The cylinder head may be removed with the camshaft in position. Slacken the cylinder head bolts in the reverse order to Fig. 1.100 and then remove the bolts. To prevent damage to the cylinder head bolts and to ensure that they are tightened correctly requires a hexagon or polygon wrench, depending upon which type of bolt is fitted (see Fig. 1.21). Although it is possible to remove and tighten the bolts without the proper tool, the practice is not recommended.

8 Loosen the bolts a turn at a time in sequence and when there is no longer any tension on them, unscrew them and remove them.

9 If necessary, tap the cylinder head with a soft-headed hammer to release it.

10 Remove and discard the old cylinder head gasket.

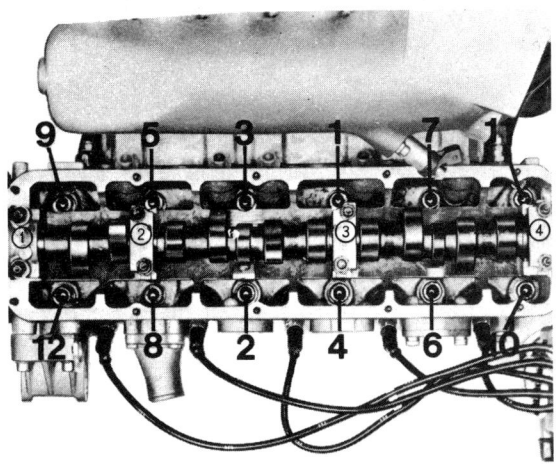

Fig. 1.100 Cylinder head bolt tightening sequence – reverse order for releasing (2.2 litre) (Sec 34)

Valves – dismantling, examination and renovation

11 These operations are as described for the 1.6 litre engine in Part A. Before work can start however, the camshaft must be removed if it is still fitted to the cylinder head.

12 Withdraw each tappet (cam follower) in turn and mark its position (1 to 8 numbering from the timing belt end of the engine) using adhesive tape or a box with divisions (photos). Take care to keep the adjustment shims with their respective tappets.

Valve removal and refitting

13 The removal and refitting of the valves is the same as that for the 1.6 litre engine described in Part A, Section 5 (photos).

Valves and valve seats

14 Examination and renovation is as described for the 1.6 litre engine in Part A, Section 5.

Cylinder head – checking

15 Check the cylinder head for distortion, by placing a straight edge across it at a number of points, lengthwise, crosswise and diagonally and measuring the gap beneath it with feeler gauges. If the gap exceeds the limit given in Specifications, the head must be re-faced by a workshop which is equipped for this work. Re-facing must not reduce the cylinder head dimension shown in Fig. 1.103 below the limit given in Specifications.

16 Examine the valve seats for damage and excessive wear. If pitting is significant, it is better to have the valve seats re-cut than to try to remove all the marks by grinding in the valves.

17 Check the valve guides for wear. First clean out the guide with a cleaning reamer and then insert the stem of a new valve into the guide. Because the stem diameters are different, ensure that only an inlet valve is used to check the inlet valve guides and an exhaust valve for the exhaust valve guides. With the end of the valve stem flush with the top of the valve guide, measure the total amount by which the rim of the valve head can be moved sideways. This can be done by pushing the valve head as far as possible in one direction and then placing a magnet on the cylinder head so that the magnet is just in contact with the valve head. Pull the valve in the opposite direction as far as

34.12A Removing a tappet (cam follower)

34.12B Method of keeping tappets in fitted sequence

34.13A Valve spring compressor

34.13B Removing valve spring cover and springs

34.13C Withdrawing a valve

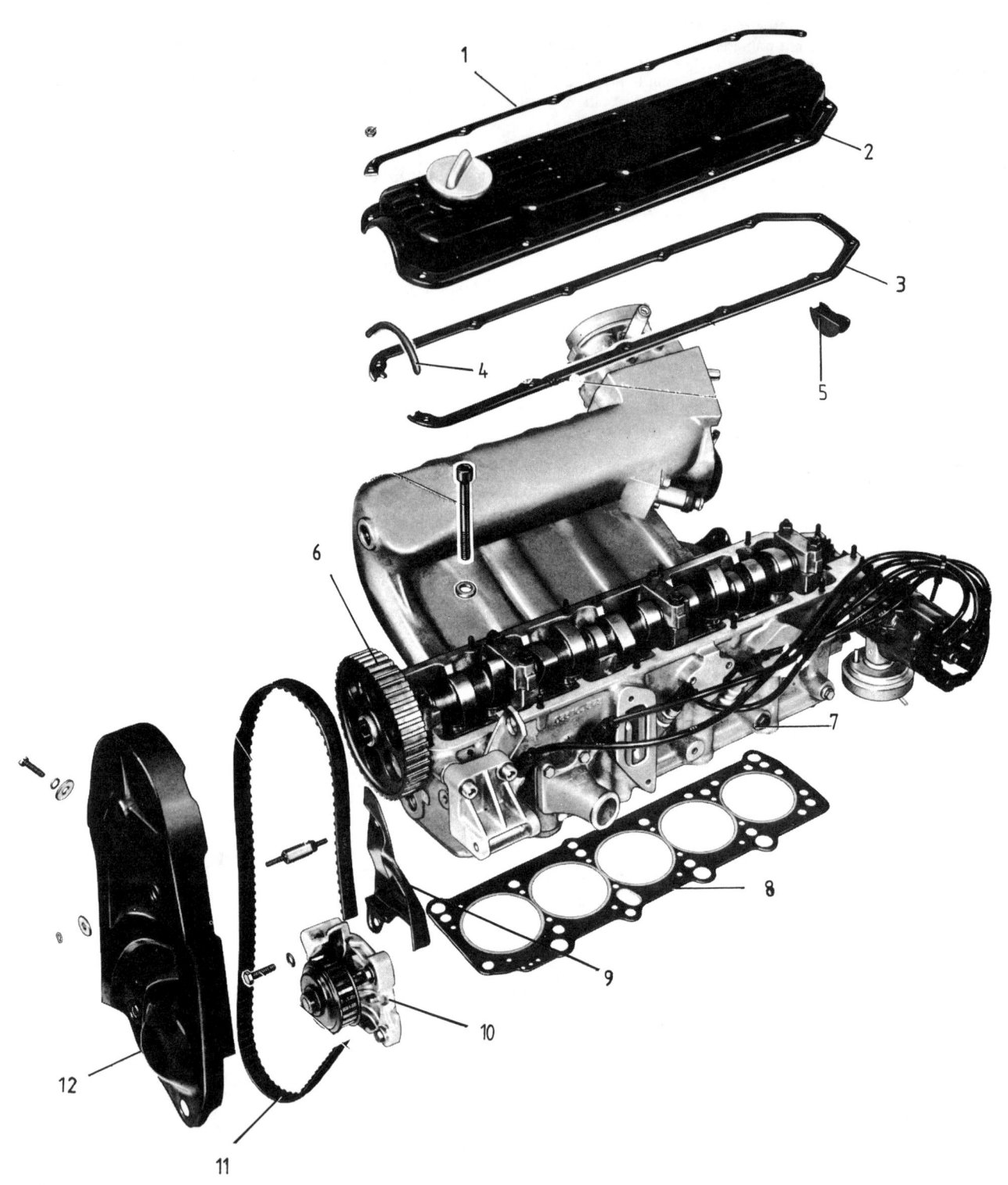

Fig. 1.101 Cylinder head assembly (2.2 litre) (Sec 34)

1	Clamping plate	4	Camshaft bearing gasket	7	Cylinder head	10	Coolant pump
2	Cylinder head cover	5	Semi-circular plug	8	Cylinder head gasket	11	Timing belt
3	Gasket	6	Camshaft sprocket	9	Timing belt rear cover	12	Timing belt front cover

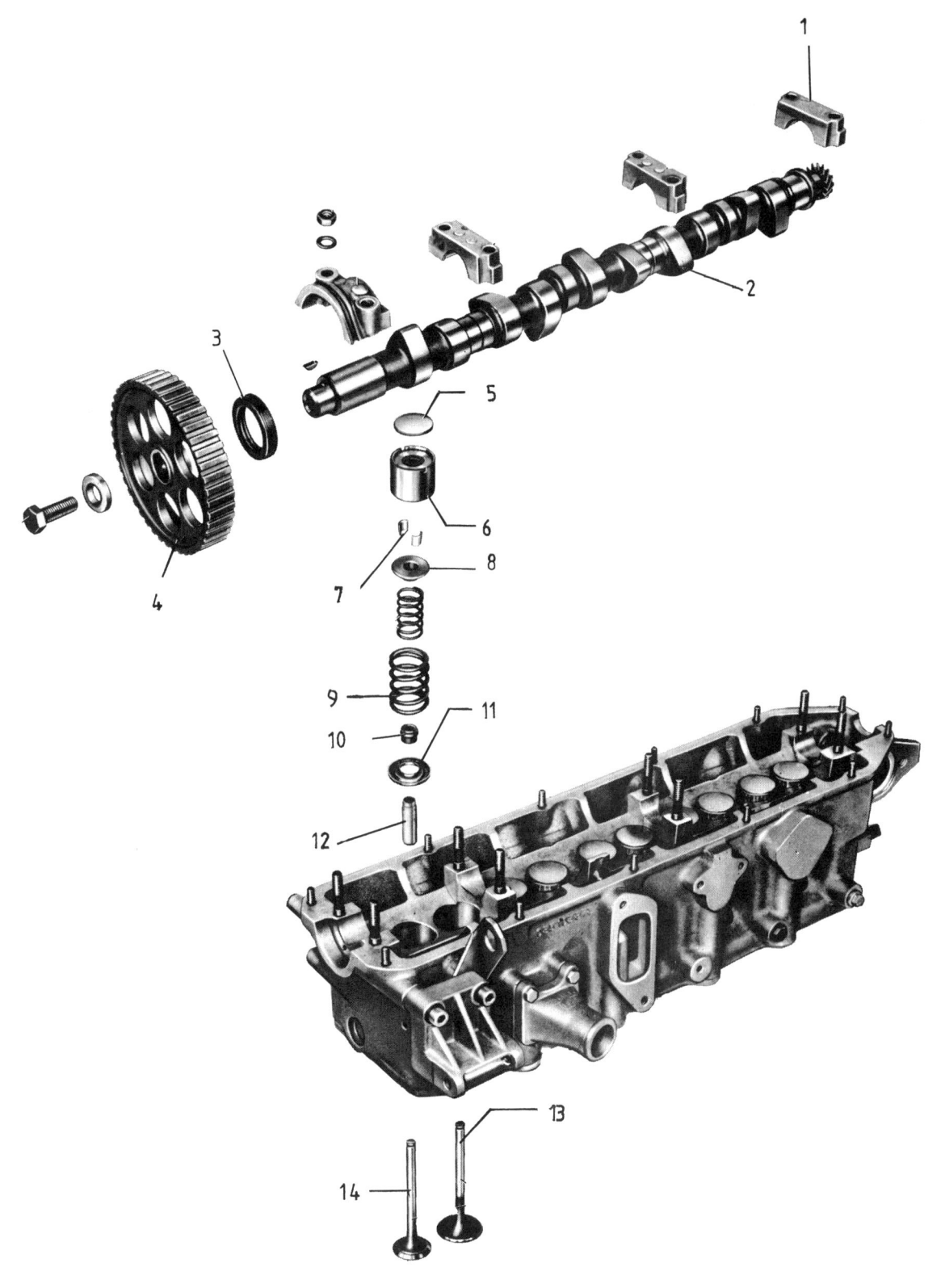

Fig.1.102 Camshaft and valves (2.2 litre) (Sec 34)

1 Camshaft bearing caps	5 Tappet shim	9 Valve springs	12 Valve guide
2 Camshaft	6 Tappet	10 Stem oil seal	13 Inlet valve
3 Oil seal	7 Valve cotters	11 Spring seat	14 Exhaust valve
4 Camshaft sprocket	8 Valve spring cap		

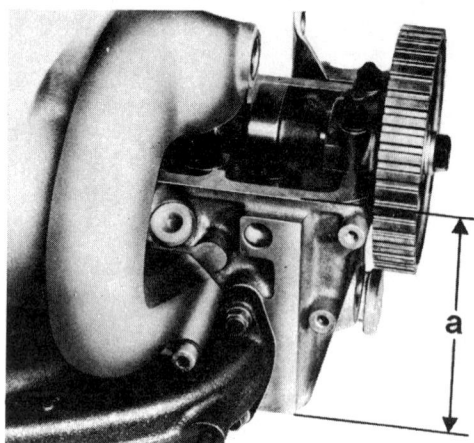

Fig.1.103 Cylinder head refinishing limit (2.2 litre) (Sec 34)

Dimension 'a' not to be reduced below 132.75 mm (5.23 in)

possible and measure the gap between the valve head and the magnet with feeler gauges.

18 New valve guides can be fitted, but it is a job for your VW/Audi dealer, or a specialist workshop.

19 Examine the cylinder head for cracks. A cracked cylinder head cannot be repaired and a new one must be fitted.

Cylinder head – refitting

20 Before fitting the cylinder head, ensure that the top of the block is perfectly clean. Use a new gasket and fit it so that the part number on it is uppermost. Do not use jointing compound on the cylinder head gasket.

21 Check that the cylinder head face is perfectly clean. Insert two

long rods, or pieces of dowel into cylinder head bolt holes at opposite ends of the block, to position the gasket and to give a location for fitting the cylinder head (photo). Lower the head on to the block, remove the guide dowels and insert the bolts and washers (photo).

22 Torque-tighten the cylinder head bolts in three stages to the 'cold' figures given in the Specifications, following the sequence shown in Fig. 1.100. Note the special method used for polygon headed bolts.

23 Fit a new gasket for the cylinder head cover, a new gasket to the front camshaft bearing and a new semi-circular plug to the rear of the cylinder head. Fit the cylinder head cover on its studs, fit the clamping plate to each side of the cylinder head cover (photo) and then fit the nuts. Tighten the nuts to the specified torque, but do not over tighten them, because this may distort the cover, or damage the gasket, causing oil leaks.

24 Ensure that the mark on the back of the camshaft sprocket is in line with the top of the rear part of the toothed belt cover. Check that the crankshaft is at TDC.

25 Fit the timing belt and tension it by turning the coolant pump anti-clockwise. When belt tension is such that gripping it between the thumb and forefinger, the belt can just be turned through 90° at the middle of its longest span, tighten the three water pump bolts.

26 Fit the belt cover over the toothed belt, then fit the V-belt(s) and tension them.

27 Check and adjust the valve clearances as described in the next Section.

28 Where the cylinder head is retained by conventional socket headed bolts, run the engine to attain the normal operating temperature then loosen each bolt in turn by 30° and re-tighten to the specified torque in the order shown in Fig. 1.100. Repeat this procedure after 620 miles (1000 km) of running.

35 Valve clearances – checking and adjusting

1 The procedure is as described for the 1.6 litre engine in Part A, Section 10 of this Chapter.

36 Flywheel, or driveplate – removing and refitting

1 If the gearbox is removed. the flywheel, or driveplate (automatic

34.21A Cylinder head gasket

34.21 B Installing the cylinder head

34.23 Camshaft cover clamp plate

Fig. 1.104 Tensioning camshaft belt (2.2 litre) (Sec 34)

transmission) can be removed with the engine still in place in the vehicle.

2 The engine timing mark is stamped on the rim of the flywheel, or driveplate, so it is important to put mating marks on the crankshaft and flywheel, or driveplate before starting to remove the bolts (photo).

3 Insert a bolt into one of the holes in the engine-to-gearbox flange, choosing a hole which is near to the rim of the flywheel. Use a piece of angle iron, or other suitably shaped piece of metal which will fit into the teeth of the starter ring and jam it against the bolt (photo).

4 Remove the eight bolts securing the flywheel or driveplate to the crankshaft. The bolts are coated with locking compound on assembly and are difficult to remove.

5 If removing a driveplate, note that there is a spacer between the bolts and the driveplate and there may be another spacer behind the driveplate.

6 When refitting the flywheel to the crankshaft line up the mating marks, which were made before removal. Coat the threads of the bolts with locking compound before inserting them and then tighten to the specified torque.

Fig.1.105 Checking camshaft belt tension (2.2 litre) (Sec 34)

7 When refitting a driveplate, line up the mating marks which were made before removal and if a spacer was fitted behind the driveplate, do not forget to refit it. The spacer on the front of the driveplate is fitted with the ridge on the washer (Fig. 1.106) towards the torque converter. Coat the threads of the bolts with locking compound before inserting them and then tighten to the specified torque.

8 If a replacement driveplate is to be fitted, its position must be checked and adjusted if necessary. The distance from the rear face of the block to the torque converter mounting face on the driveplate (Fig. 1.107) must be between 17.2 and 18.8 mm (0.667 and 0.740 in). If necessary, remove the driveplate and fit a spacer behind it to achieve the correct dimension.

9 If a new flywheel or driveplate is fitted the new part will have a TDC mark stamped on it, but not a timing mark. The position of the timing mark relative to the O-mark for TDC for the different engines is shown in Figs. 1.108, 1.109, 1.110 and 1.111.

37 Pistons and connecting rods – removal, dismantling, checking and reassembly

1 These operations are similar to those described for the small capacity engines in Parts A and B.

2 If the engine is removed from the car, the flywheel (or driveplate) can be removed and a length of flat steel bolted to the crankshaft rear flange to serve as a lever while the crankshaft damper bolt is unscrewed. Again a lever of good length will be required to release this bolt.

3 The connecting rods incorporate casting marks which should face the front of the engine when installed in the crankcase.

38 Crankshaft oil seals – renewal

1 The crankshaft front oil seal is incorporated in the oil pump and the rear oil seal is mounted in a carrying flange which is bolted to the rear face of the cylinder block.

2 There are special tools which enable the seals to be renewed in-situ, but without these, it is necessary to remove the sump.

36.2 Crankshaft and flywheel alignment marks

36.3 Jamming the flywheel starter ring gear

Fig. 1.106 Torque converter drive plate installation (2.2 litre) (Sec 36)

1   Washer with ridge arrowed   2   Spacer

Fig.1.107 Torque converter drive plate position (2.2 litre) (Sec 36)

Fig. 1.108 Timing marks WC, WG engines (2.2 litre) (Sec 36)

Ignition notch 12.1 mm (0.476 in) to left of TDC mark centre

Fig.1.109 Timing marks WD, WE engines (2.2 litre) (Sec 36)

Ignition notch 7.3 mm (0.287 in) to right of TDC mark centre

Fig. 1.110 Timing marks WB engines – manual (2.2 litre) (Sec 36)

Ignition notch 21.8 mm (0.858 in) to left of TDC mark centre

8   Drive out the old seal, taking care not to damage the seal housing.
9   Oil the lip and rim of a new seal and enter its open face into the housing, with the housing resting on its joint face. With a hammer and a block of wood, drive the seal in until its outer face is flush with the outer face of the housing.
10   Fit a new gasket to the cylinder block, carefully fit the seal over the crankshaft, line up the holes in the seal housing and cylinder block, then fit and tighten the bolts (photo).
11   Fit the sump, using a new gasket and on completion of assembly, fill the sump to the correct level.

39 Crankshaft – removing and refitting

1   With the crankcase upside down on the bench and having removed the pistons, the oil pump (Section 40) and the crankshaft rear oil seal flange, check that the crankshaft bearing caps have their numbers stamped on them (photo) and if not, number them, starting at the front of the engine.
2   Remove the bolts from each bearing cap in turn, then remove the caps and lift out the crankshaft (photo).
3   If the bearings are not being renewed, ensure that each half-bearing is identified, so that it is put back in the same place from which it was removed.
4   If the engine has done a high mileage and it is suspected that the crankshaft requires attention, it is best to seek the opinion of a VW/Audi dealer, or crankshaft refinishing specialist for advice on the need for regrinding.
5   Unless the bearing shells are known to be almost new, it is worth fitting a new set when the crankshaft is removed. Clean the crankcase

Fig. 1.111 Timing marks WB engines – automatic (2.2 litre) (Sec 36)

Ignition mark at centre of TDC mark

3   Renewing the front oil seal is included in the dismantling of the oil pump (Section 40).
4   To renew the rear oil seal, separate the engine from the gearbox and remove the flywheel, or driveplate, from the crankshaft.
5   Drain the oil from the sump.
6   Remove the twenty four bolts from the sump and take off the sump and the sump gasket.
7   Remove the six bolts securing the seal housing to the rear face of the cylinder block and take off the seal housing and gasket.

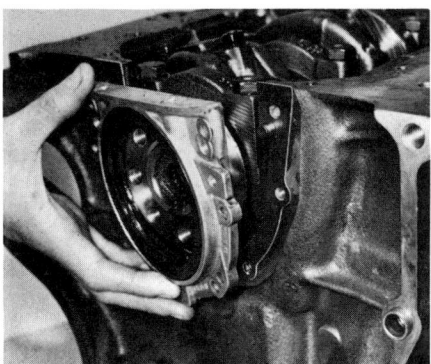

38.10 Fitting crankshaft rear oil seal

39.1 Main bearing cap number

39.2 Removing the crankshaft

39.5A Main bearing cap bearing shell (no oil hole)

39.5B No 4 main bearing cap

39.7 Lubricating crankcase main bearing shells (with oil hole)

webs and bearing caps thoroughly and fit the bearing shells so that the tang on the bearing engages in the recess in the crankcase web, or bearing cap. Note that the bearing shells for the crankcase webs are different from those for the bearing caps, in that the ones for the webs have an oil hole drilled in them, but the ones for the bearing caps do not (photo). Also note that the shells of No 4 bearing are different from all the others by being flanged to act as a thrust bearing (photo).

6 Fit the bearing shells so that the ends of the bearing are flush with the joint face. For the lower bearing shells, ensure that the oil hole in the bearing shell coincides with the drilling in the crankcase.

7 Lubricate the crankcase web half-bearings (photo), lubricate the crankshaft journals and lay the crankshaft in its bearings. Lubricate the bearing caps and lay them in their correct position and the correct way round (Fig. 1.112).

8 Fit the bolts to the bearing caps and tighten the bolts of No 4 cap to the specified torque, then check that the crankshaft rotates freely. If it is difficult to rotate the crankshaft, check that the bearing shells are seated properly and that the bearing cap is the correct way round. Rotation will only be difficult if something is incorrect and the fault must be found. Dirt on the back of a bearing shell can cause tightness in a bearing.

9 Working out from No 4, tighten the remaining bearing caps in turn, checking that the crankshaft rotates freely after each bearing has been tightened.

10 Check that the endplay of the crankshaft is within specification, by inserting feeler gauges between the crankshaft and the thrust face of No 4 bearing (See Fig. 1.46) and levering the crankshaft first in one direction and then the other.

11 The remainder of the operations are a reversal of the removal operations.

12 The rear end of the crankshaft carries a needle roller bearing which supports the front end of the gearbox input shaft.

13 Inspect the bearing for obvious signs of wear and damage. If the gearbox has been removed and dismantled, fit the input shaft into the bearing to see if there is excessive clearance.

14 If the bearing requires renewing, insert a hook in the bearing and pull it out of the end of the shaft.

Fig. 1.112 Correct fitting of main bearing caps (Sec 39)

15 Press in a new bearing, with the lettering on the end of the bearing outwards. Press the bearing in until the end of the bearing is 5.5 mm (0.217 in) below the face of the flywheel flange. Installation is similar to that for the 1.6 litre engine (Fig. 1.47).

40 Oil pump – removing, dismantling, checking and refitting

1 The oil pump can be removed without removing the engine, but because the vibration damper (photo) is bolted to the end of the crankshaft by a bolt which has locking compound on its threads (photo) and is tightened to a very high torque, removal of the damper is difficult with the engine in-situ, unless the special tools are available (see Section 31).

2 If the pump is removed with the engine in position, the following

Fig. 1.113 Crankcase assembly (2.2 litre) (Sec 39)

1	Oil intake pipe	5	Bearing shell	9	Oil seal carrier	12	Gasket
2	Lock plate	6	Crankshaft	10	Gasket	13	Oil pump
3	Gasket	7	Flywheel	11	Crankcase	14	Crankshaft front oil seal
4	Main bearing cap	8	Crankshaft rear oil seal				

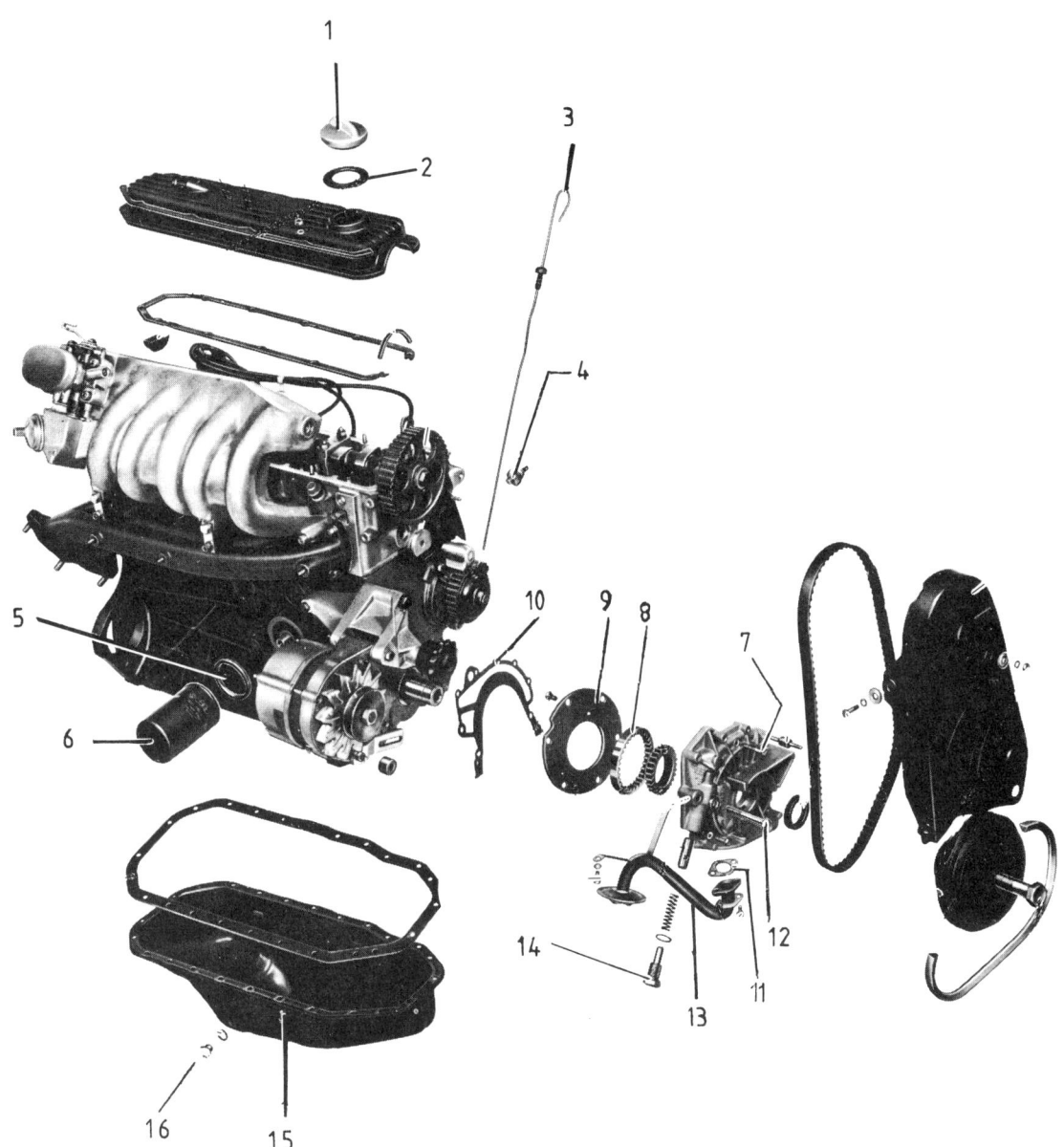

Fig. 1.114 Lubrication system components (2.2 litre) (Sec 40)

1	Oil filler cap	5	Gasket	9	Pump backplate	13	Oil intake pipe
2	Seal	6	Oil filter	10	Gasket	14	Pressure relief valve
3	Dipstick	7	Oil pump body	11	Locking plate	15	Sump
4	Oil pressure switch	8	Oil pump gears	12	Gasket	16	Oil drain plug

40.1A Crankshaft damper

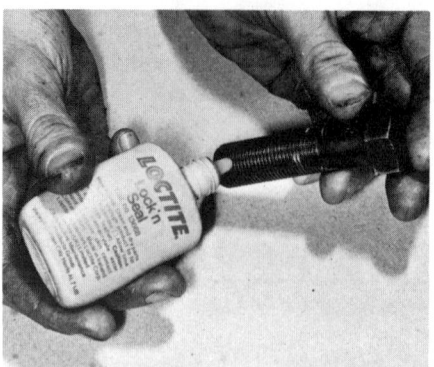

40.1B Crankshaft damper bolt with thread sealant

40.3A Oil pump pick up pipe and filter

40.3B Oil pump pick up pipe flange

40.4A Oil pump unit

40.4B Removing the oil pump

40.5 Oil pump with backplate removed

40.7 Oil pressure relief plug and valve assembly

preliminary work is necessary.

    (a) *Remove the V-belt(s) and timing belt*
    (b) *Remove the vibration damper (see Section 37, paragraph 3)*
    (c) *Drain the oil and remove the dipstick*
    (d) *Remove the front subframe bolts and remove the sump*

3   Remove the two bolts securing the oil intake pipe stay to the crankcase (photo). Knock back the tabs of the lockplate on the intake pipe flange (photo), remove the bolts and the intake pipe.
4   Remove the six bolts securing the oil pump (photo) and take off the oil pump and gasket (photo).
5   Remove the six countersunk screws securing the pump back plate and lift the back plate off, exposing the gears (photo).
6   Check that there is a mark on the exposed face of the gears and if not, make a mark to show which side of the gears is towards the engine before removing them.
7   Unscrew the pressure relief valve and remove the plug, sealing ring, spring and plunger (photo).

8   Clean all the parts thoroughly and examine the pump casing and backplate for signs of wear or scoring. Examine the pressure relief valve plunger and its seating for damage and wear and check that the spring is not damaged, or distorted.
9   Check the gears for damage and wear. New gears may be fitted, but they must be fitted as a pair.
10   Prise out the oil seal from the front of the pump. Oil the lip of a new seal, enter the seal with its closed face outwards and use a block of wood to tap the seal in flush. If there is any scoring on the crankshaft in the area on which the lip of the seal bears, the seal may be pushed to the bottom of its recess so that the lip bears on an undamaged part of the crankshaft.
11   Reassemble the pumps by fitting the gears and the backplate. The inner gear has its slotted end towards the crankshaft and although the outer gear can be fitted either way round, it should be fitted the same way round as it was before removal. Some gears have a triangle stamped on them and this mark should be towards the front plate.
12   When refitting the pump, use a new gasket and ensure that the inner gear is properly engaged with the drive keys on the crankshaft.

Part D

41 Fault diagnosis – engine

Symptom	Reason(s)
Engine fails to turn over when starter switch is operated	Discharged, or defective battery Dirty, or loose battery leads Defective solenoid, or starter switch Loose, or broken starter motor leads Defective starter motor Dirty, or defective engine to body earth strap
Engine spins, but does not start	Ignition components damp, or wet Disconnected low tension lead Dirty contact breaker, or defective ignitor Faulty condenser Faulty coil No petrol, or petrol not reaching engine Faulty petrol pump Water in fuel system Too much choke, leading to wet plugs
Engine stops and will not re-start	Ignition failure Fuel pump failure No petrol in tank Water in fuel system
Engine lacks power	Burnt exhaust valve Incorrect timing Blown cylinder head gasket Leaking carburettor, or inlet manifold gasket Incorrect mixture Blocked air intake, or dirty air filter Ignition automatic advance faulty
Excessive oil consumption	Oil leaks Defective valve stem oil seals Worn pistons and bores Blocked engine breather
Engine noisy	Incorrect valve clearances Worn distributor drive Worn bearings Worn pistons and bores

Chapter 2 Cooling system

Contents

Specifications

System type .... Pressurised thermo-syphon, pump and fan assisted

Thermostat
Starts to open .... 80°C ± 2° (176°F ± 4°)
Fully open .... 92°C ± 2° (197.6°F ± 4°)
Valve lift .... 7 mm minimum (0.28 in)

Thermostatic switch
Switch ON .... 90 to 95°C (194° to 203°F)
Switch OFF .... 84 to 89°C (183.2° to 192.2°F)

Reservoir cap
Relief pressure:
    Up to chassis No 4382 .... 0.9 to 1.15 bar (kg/cm²) (13 to 15 lbf/in²)
    From chassis No 4382 .... 1.2 to 1.35 bar (kg/cm²) (15 to 16 lbf/in²)

Antifreeze
Type .... Ethylene glycol, with corrosion inhibitor
Concentration ....

Protection down to	Percentage antifreeze by volume
- 25°C (- 14°F)	40
- 30°C (- 22°F)	45
- 35°C (- 31°F)	50

Cooling system capacity
1.6 litre engine .... 7 litres, 12.3 Imp pt, 14.8 US pt
2.0 litre engine:
    Front radiator .... 7.5 litres, 13.2 Imp pt, 15.8 US pt
    Side radiator .... 8 litres, 14.1 Imp pt, 16.9 US pt
2.2 litre engine .... 8 litres, 14.1 Imp pt, 16.9 US pt

Coolant level .... To point of arrow on coolant reservoir with engine cold

Torque wrench settings

	Nm	lbf ft
Radiator fixing bolts	15	11
Radiator shroud bolts	8	6
Thermostat cover bolts	10	7
Thermostat housing-to-engine	20	15
Water pump-to-body	20	15
Water pump pulley-to-spindle	20	15
Bleeder screw	20	15

1 General description

The engine is cooled by a pressurised, pump assisted thermo-syphon system and the excess heat is dissipated by a radiator mounted at the front of the vehicle. A thermostat mounted in the engine block prevents any circulation through the radiator until the engine has reached its normal operating temperature, but coolant is able to circulate through the heater core before the thermostat opens.

Dissipation of heat by the radiator is increased by a motor driven fan, operation of the fan being controlled by a thermostatic switch mounted in the radiator. It is a feature of the system that the fan operates at a pre-set temperature regardless of whether or not the engine is running, so that it is normal for the fan to continue to run for some time after the engine has been switched off. It should also be noted that great care is necessary if the engine is run with the bonnet lid open because the fan may initially be stationary, but will start rotating without any warning when the thermostatic switch operates.

There are differences in the types and positions of the water pumps, thermostats and radiators on the cooling systems of the different size engines, but the system is essentially the same.

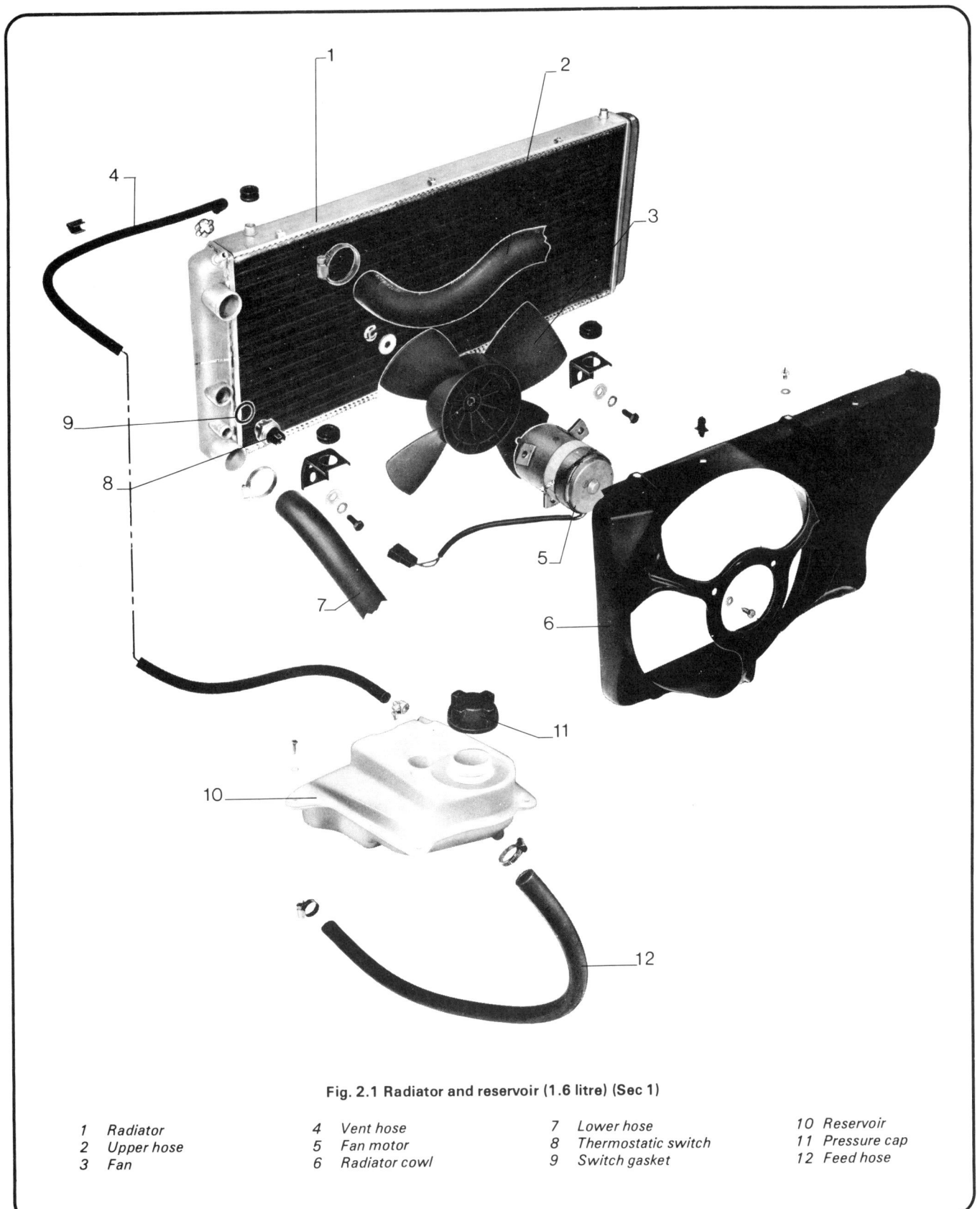

Fig. 2.1 Radiator and reservoir (1.6 litre) (Sec 1)

1	Radiator	4	Vent hose	7	Lower hose	10	Reservoir
2	Upper hose	5	Fan motor	8	Thermostatic switch	11	Pressure cap
3	Fan	6	Radiator cowl	9	Switch gasket	12	Feed hose

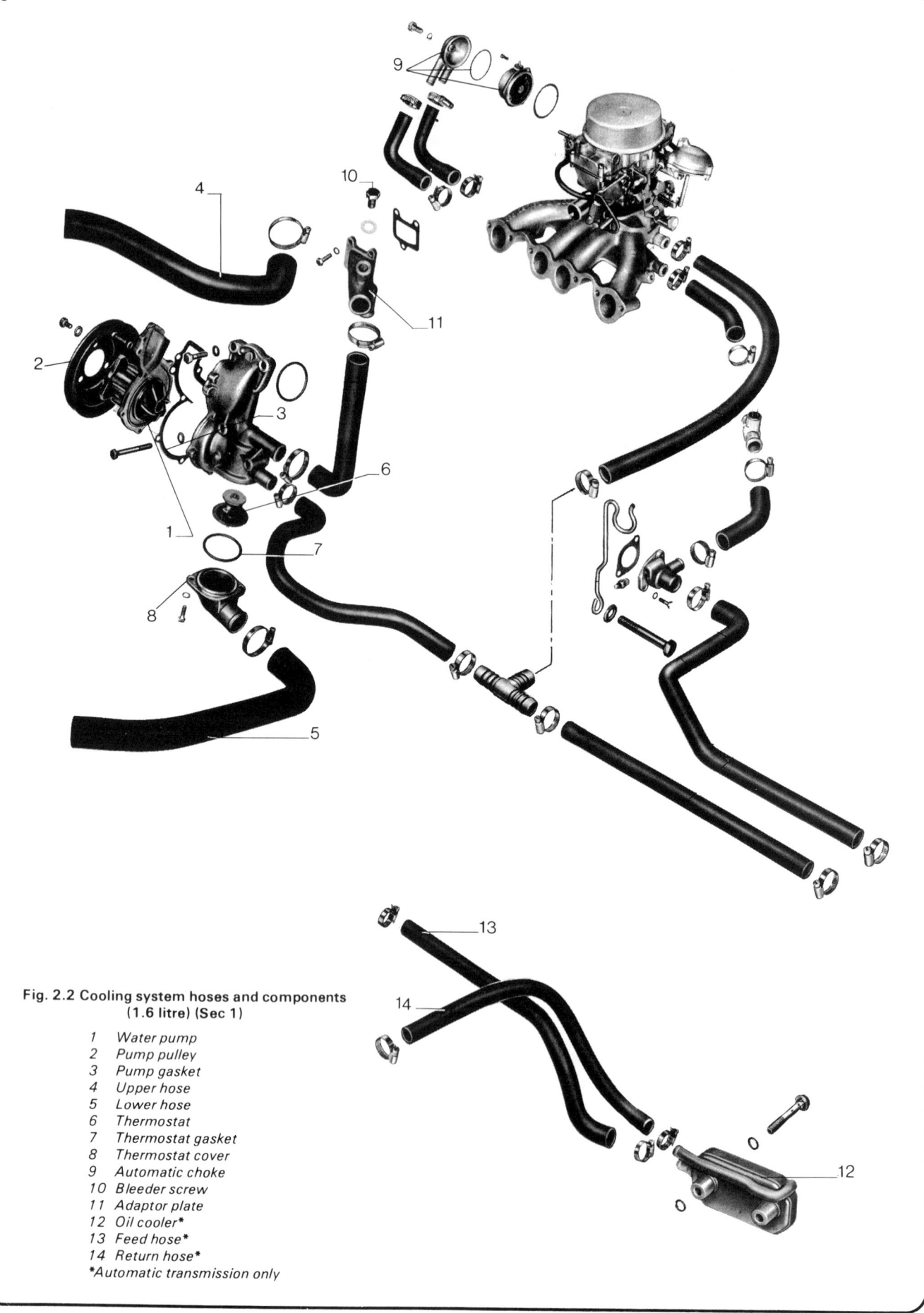

Fig. 2.2 Cooling system hoses and components
(1.6 litre) (Sec 1)

1   Water pump
2   Pump pulley
3   Pump gasket
4   Upper hose
5   Lower hose
6   Thermostat
7   Thermostat gasket
8   Thermostat cover
9   Automatic choke
10 Bleeder screw
11 Adaptor plate
12 Oil cooler*
13 Feed hose*
14 Return hose*
*Automatic transmission only

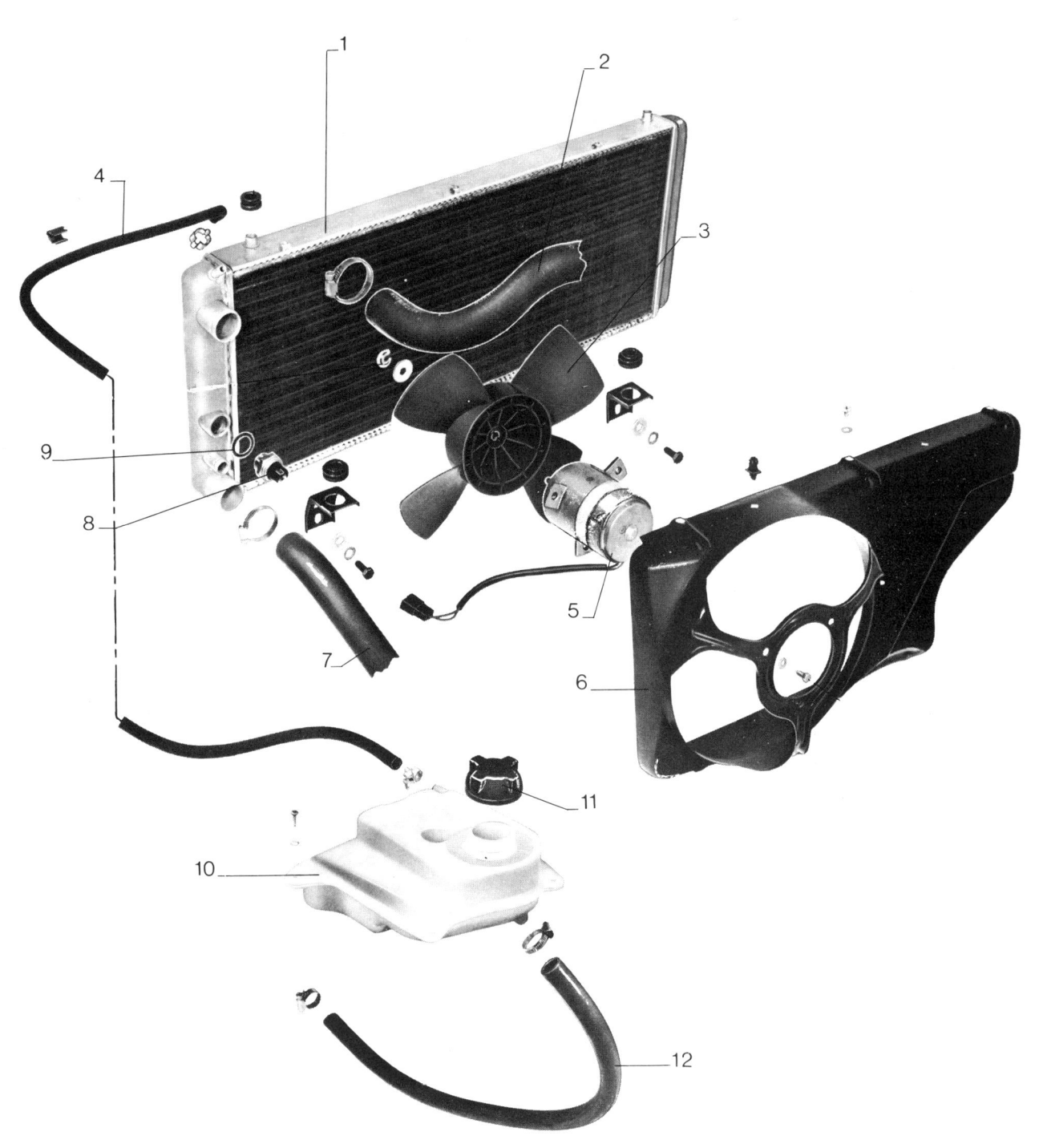

Fig. 2.3 Radiator and reservoir (2.0 litre) (Sec 1)

1 Radiator	4 Vent hose	7 Lower hose	10 Reservoir
2 Upper hose	5 Fan motor	8 Thermostatic switch	11 Pressure cap
3 Fan	6 Radiator cowl	9 Switch gasket	12 Feed hose

Fig. 2.4 Cooling system hoses and components
(2.0 litre) (Sec 1)

1 Water pump
2 Pump pulley
3 Pump gasket
4 Upper hose
5 Lower hose
6 Thermostat
7 Thermostat gasket
8 Thermostat cover
9 Automatic choke
10 Oil cooler*
11 Feed hose*
12 Return hose*
*Automatic transmission only

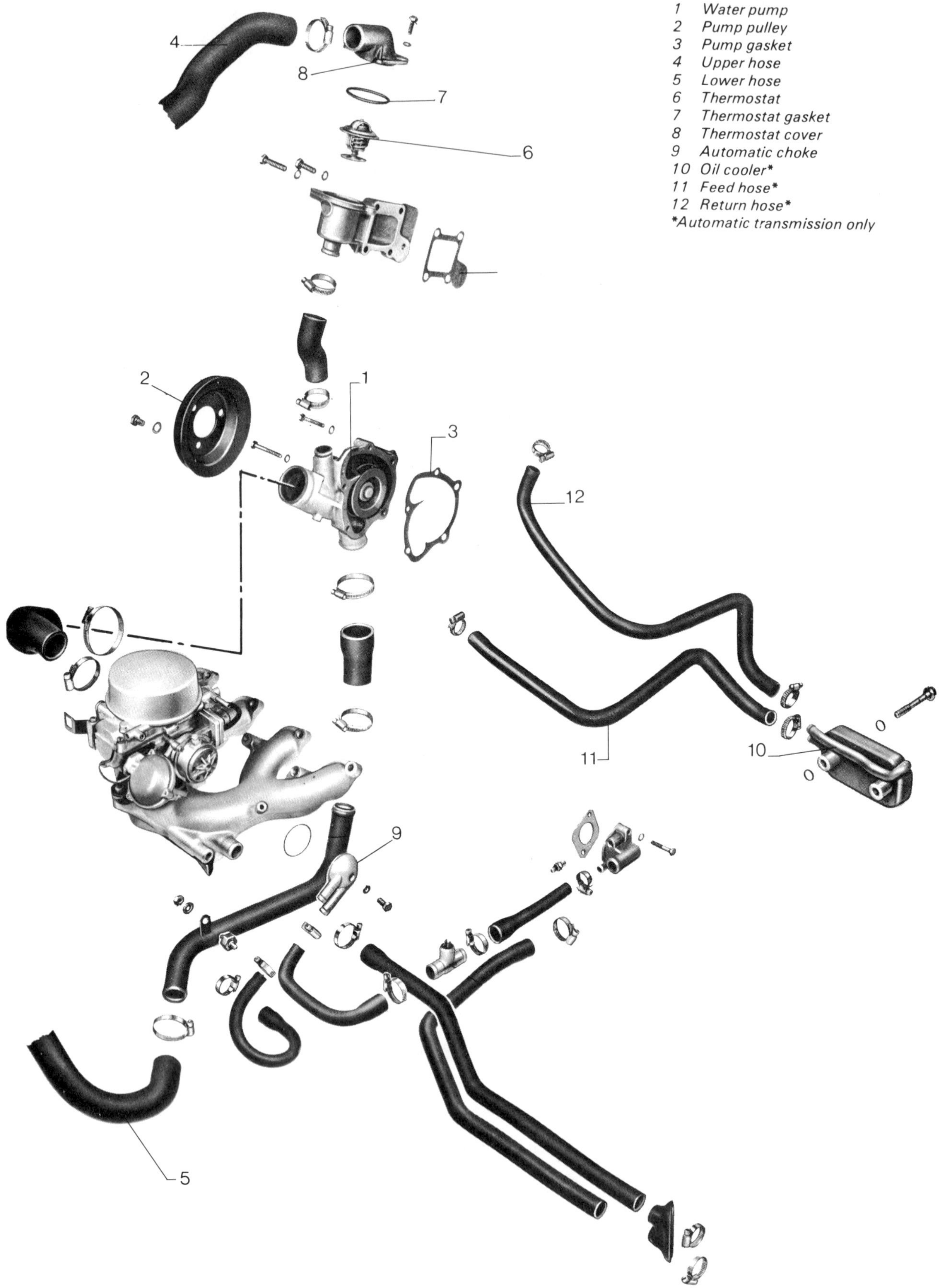

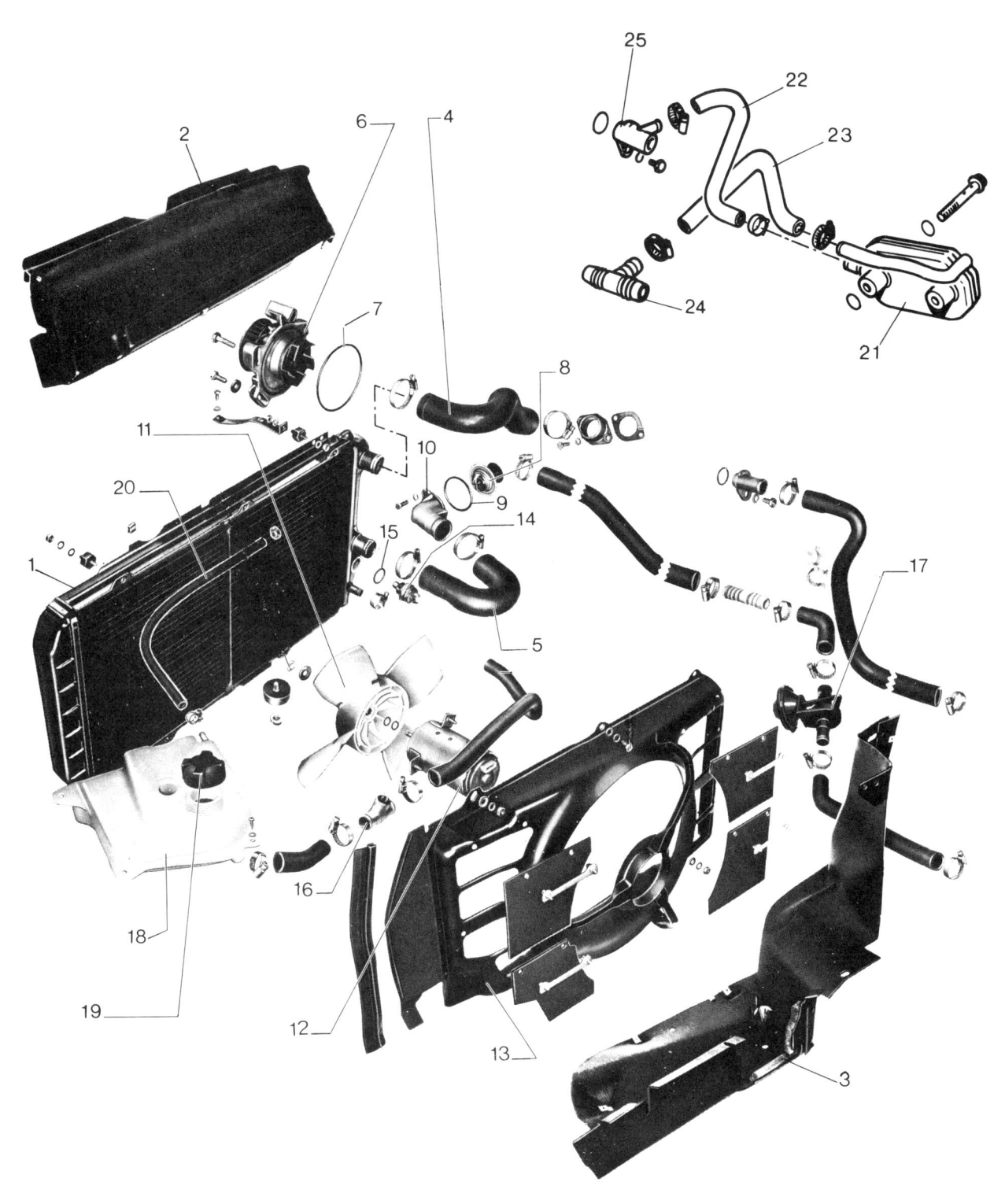

Fig. 2.5 Cooling system components (2.2 litre) (Sec 1)

1	Radiator	8	Thermostat	15	Switch gasket	22	Feed hose*
2	Upper cowl	9	Thermostat gasket	16	Thermostatic switch (a)	23	Return hose*
3	Lower cowl	10	Thermostat cover	17	Solenoid valve (a)	24	T-piece*
4	Upper hose	11	Fan	18	Reservoir	25	Cylinder block adaptor*
5	Lower hose	12	Fan motor	19	Pressure cap		*Automatic transmission only
6	Water pump	13	Radiator cowl	20	Vent hose		(a) Vehicles fitted with air
7	Pump sealing O-ring	14	Thermostatic switch	21	Oil cooler*		conditioner only

2 Cooling system – draining

1.6 litre engine

1   Remove the cap from the coolant reservoir to relieve any pressure in the system.

2   Unscrew the air bleeder screw on the adaptor (Fig. 2.6) until the hole drilled in the side of the screw is visible.

3   Place a container of about two gallons (9.0 litres) capacity beneath the water pump, then unscrew the hose clips from the water pump connections of the radiator bottom hose and the lower of the two heater hoses. Carefully lever the hoses off and allow the coolant to drain. Do not twist the hoses in an attempt to remove them because this tends to damage the hoses and may fracture the joints of the metal connections.

2.0 litre engine

4   Remove the coolant reservoir cap as in paragraph 1.

5   Place a clean two gallon (9.0 litres) container beneath the radiator bottom hose-to-cross pipe joint and on vehicles fitted with an air conditioner set the heater control to *Warm.*

6   Unscrew the hose clip and prise the hose off the cross pipe, allowing the coolant to drain. Do not twist the hose in an attempt to remove it, because this tends to damage the hoses and may fracture the joints of the metal connections.

2.2 litre engine

7   Remove the coolant reservoir cap as in paragraph 1 and on vehicles fitted with an air conditioner set the heater controls to *Warm.*

8   Place a suitable container under the coolant reservoir, loosen the hose clip on the supply hose, pull the hose off and drain the reservoir into the container.

9   Place a two gallon (9.0 litres) container on the ground beneath the hose connection arrowed in Fig. 2.7. Loosen the hose clip, prise off the hose and allow the coolant to drain into the container.

3 Cooling system – re-filling

1   Ensure that all hoses are in good condition, are fitted properly and that the hose clips have been tightened. If it is necessary to replace any hoses, it will be found that the new ones will be easier to fit if the inside of the hose at each end is smeared with soap, rubber grease, or hydraulic fluid.

2   If coolant drained from the system is to be re-used, make sure that the coolant is clean. If necessary filter the coolant through a paper towel.

1.6 litre engine

3   Ensure that the bleeder screw on the adaptor (Fig. 2.2) is unscrewed far enough to expose the hole drilled in its side.

4   Pour coolant into the coolant reservoir until it begins to flow out of the bleeder screw and then tighten the bleeder screw to the specified torque.

5   Continue adding coolant until the reservoir is full and then screw the reservoir cap on.

6   Start the engine and run it until the radiator is hot enough for the fan to switch on. Check that the level of coolant in the reservoir is a little above the arrow marked on the reservoir; the arrow indicates the correct level when the coolant is cold. Top-up if necessary.

2.0 litre engine

7   On vehicles fitted with an air conditioner, set the heater controls to *Warm.*

8   Pour coolant into the reservoir until the reservoir is full, then screw the reservoir cap on.

9   Run the engine and proceed as in paragraph 6.

2.2 litre engine

10   Proceed in exactly the same way as described for the 2.0 litre engine in paragraphs 7, 8 and 9.

4 Antifreeze mixture

1   The cooling system is filled at the factory with an antifreeze mixture which contains a corrosion inhibitor. The antifreeze mixture prevents freezing, raises the boiling point of the coolant and so delays the tendency of the coolant to boil, while the corrosion inhibitor reduces corrosion and the formation of scale. For these reasons the cooling system should be filled with antifreeze all the year round.

2   Any good quality antifreeze is suitable, if it is of the ethylene glycol type and also contains a corrosion inhibitor. Do not use an antifreeze preparation based on methanol, because these mixtures have a shorter life and methanol has the disadvantage of being inflammable and evaporates quickly.

3   The concentration of antifreeze should be adjusted to give the required level of protection selected from the table given in Specifications.

4   When topping-up the cooling system always use the same mixture of water and antifreeze which the system contains. Topping-up using water only will gradually reduce the antifreeze concentration and lower the level of protection against both freezing and boiling.

5   At the beginning of the winter season, check the coolant for antifreeze concentration and add pure antifreeze if necessary.

6   Antifreeze mixture should not be left in the system for longer than its manufacturers' recommendation which does not usually exceed three years. At the end of this time drain the system and refill with fresh mixture.

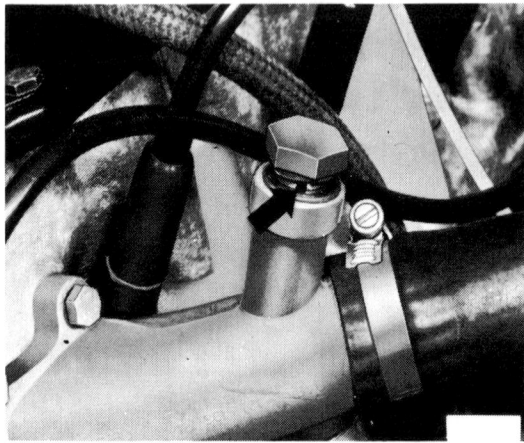

Fig.2.6 Coolant system bleeder screw (1.6 litre) (Sec 2)

Fig. 2.7 Coolant draining point (arrowed) (2.2 litre) (Sec 2)

5 Radiator – removing and refitting

1   Drain the cooling system, as described in the appropriate paragraphs of Section 2.
2   Disengage the cable control of the bonnet lock by pulling the guide sleeve in the direction of the arrow (Fig. 2.8) and then disengaging the cable from the clip on the radiator (front mounted radiator models only).

1·6 litre engine
3   Loosen the hose clips and detach the supply hose and vent hose from the coolant reservoir.
4   Loosen the hose clip of the upper coolant hose-to-engine joint and prise the hose off.
5   Disconnect the plug connections to the radiator fan and to the thermostatic switch.
6   Remove the two bolts securing the brackets at the bottom of the radiator to the car body and lift out the radiator assembly.

2·0 litre engine
7   The procedure is similar to that described for the 1·6 litre, except that the upper coolant hose is detached from its connection with the thermostat housing. When a side mounted radiator is fitted proceed as described for the 2·2 litre engine.

2·2 litre engine
8   Prise off the clips and remove the radiator top cowl.
9   Loosen the hose clip and disconnect the vent hose from the coolant reservoir.
10   Loosen the hose clips and disconnect the upper and lower coolant hoses from the radiator.
11   Disconnect the plug connections to the radiator fan and to the thermostatic switch (photos).
12   Remove the two bolts securing the brackets at the bottom of the radiator to the car body and the bolts securing the stay and bracket to the top of the radiator (photo) and lift out the radiator assembly (photo). On vehicles fitted with air conditioning, a slit has to be made in the lower cowl panel (Fig. 2.9), so that the panel can be threaded over the air conditioner hose.
13   Refitting the radiator is the reversal of the operations necessary for removal and the cooling system must then be re-filled as described in Section 3.

6 Thermostat – removing and refitting

1   Drain the cooling system, as described in the appropriate paragraphs of Section 2.

1·6 litre engine
2   Remove the two bolts securing the thermostat cover to the bottom of the water pump. Tap the cover with a soft-faced hammer to break the seal, pull off the cover and remove the thermostat and sealing ring.
3   Before refitting the thermostat, make sure that its seating in the water pump is clean and that both faces of the thermostat cover joint

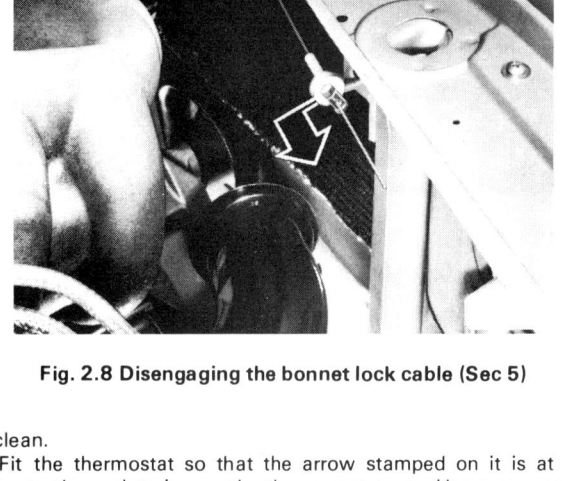

Fig. 2.8 Disengaging the bonnet lock cable (Sec 5)

are clean.
4   Fit the thermostat so that the arrow stamped on it is at right angles to the outlet pipe on the thermostat cover. Use a new sealing ring and tighten the bolts to the specified torque.
5   Re-connect the hose and then re-fill the cooling system.

2·0 litre engine
6   Except that the thermostat housing is not an integral part of the water pump, the procedure is the same as that for the 1·6 litre engine.
7   The correct position for the thermostat is shown in Fig. 2.10.

2·2 litre engine
8   The thermostat is mounted directly into the cylinder block (photos). The procedure for removing and refitting it is the same as for the 1·6 litre engine and its correct fitted position is shown in Fig. 2.11.

7 Thermostat – testing

1   Remove the thermostat from the engine and inspect it for obvious mechanical damage. Ensure that when the thermostat is at normal air temperature its plate valve is fully closed.
2   Place the thermostat in a pan of cold water with a thermometer and heat the water. Note the temperature at which it starts to open, continue heating and note the temperature at which it is fully open. The amount of opening should increase gradually with temperature and should not be jerky.
3   Measure the height of the valve plate when fully open and compare this with the value given in Specifications.
4   Cool the thermostat and check that it closes smoothly and is fully closed when cool.
5   If the operation of the thermostat is suspect, or if its operating temperature or lift are outside the specified values, discard it and fit a new one.

5.11a Radiator fan connection (2.2 litre)

5.11b Thermostatic switch connection (2.2 litre)

5.12a Radiator top fixings (2.2 litre)

5.12b Removing the radiator (2.2 litre)

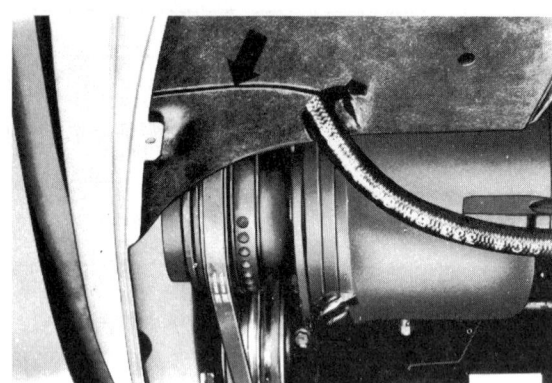

Fig. 2.9 Slit in lower cowl for air conditioned vehicles (2.2 litre) (Sec 5)

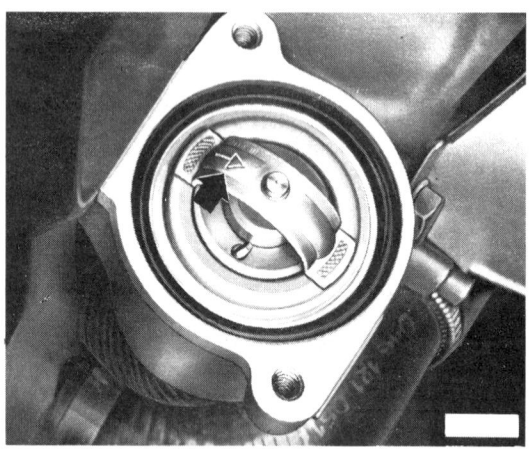

Fig. 2.10 Correct position of thermostat (2.0 litre) (Sec 6)

6.8a Fitting the thermostat ...

6.8b ... and cover (2.2 litre)

Fig. 2.11 Correct position of thermostat (2.2 litre) (Sec 6)

8 Water pump – removing and refitting

1   Drain the cooling system, as described in the appropriate paragraphs of Section 2.
2   Slacken the alternator mounting bolts and swing the alternator towards the engine to slacken the drivebelt. Disengage the drivebelt from the alternator pulley and then from the fan pulley.

1·6 litre engine

3   Remove the three bolts securing the water pump pulley to the pump spindle and take the pulley off.
4   Remove the bolts from the water pump flange, tap the pump with a soft-faced hammer to break the seal and pull the pump rotor assembly from its housing.
5   Before fitting the pump, remove all traces of dirt, old gasket and jointing compound from both faces of the pump joint. Fit the pump, using a new gasket and tighten the bolts to the specified torque.
6   Refit the pulley and drivebelt. Tension the drivebelt and re-fill the cooling system.

2·0 litre engine

7   The procedure is similar to that described for the 1·6 litre engine except that it is necessary to loosen the hose clips and remove the three water pump hoses before removing the flange bolts.
8   Refitting is similar also to the procedure for the 1·6 litre engine with the addition of re-connecting the hoses.

2·2 litre engine

9   It is not necessary to slacken the alternator mountings and remove the V-belt, because the water pump is driven from the timing belt for which it also acts as a belt tensioner.
10   Remove the fixings of the timing belt cover and take the cover off (photo).
11   Slacken the water pump fixing bolts, rotate the pump to slacken the belt, then remove the three pump fixing bolts (photo) and take off the pump (photo). It is important that the crankshaft and camshaft sprockets are not moved while the belt is slack, because this will alter the valve timing. In any event it is recommended that the timing is checked as described in Chapter 1, Part C.
12   When re-fitting the pump, ensure that the sealing O-ring fits properly in its groove (photo) and make sure that the belt is fitted into the teeth of the crankshaft and camshaft sprockets without any slack before engaging the water pump pulley in the belt.
13   Fit the water pump and insert its fixing bolts. Rotate the pump until the belt is taut and then tighten the pump bolts.
14   Complete the refitting by bolting on the belt cover and re-filling the cooling system.

8.10 Removing the timing belt cover (2.2 litre)

8.11a Water pump fixing bolts (2.2 litre)

8.11b Removing the water pump (2.2 litre)

8.12 Sealing ring and groove (2.2 litre)

9 Thermostatic switch – testing

1 Drain the cooling system, as described in the appropriate paragraphs of Section 2 and then unscrew the switch from the radiator, after disconnecting its plug.
2 Suspend the switch in a pan of water so that only the screwed end of the switch is immersed and the electrical contacts are clear of the water.
3 Either connect an ohmmeter between the switch terminals, or connect up a torch battery and bulb in series with the switch.
4 With a thermometer placed in the pan, heat the water and note the temperature at which the switch contacts close, so that the ohm meter reads zero, or the bulb lights. Allow the water to cool and note the temperature at which the switch contacts open. Discard the switch and fit a new one if the operating temperatures are not within the specified limits.
5 When refitting the switch, use a new joint washer. Refill the cooling system and re-connect the switch.

10 Fault diagnosis – cooling system

Symptom	Reason(s)
Loss of coolant	Loose hose clips or cracked hoses Radiator leaking or water pump leak Pump or thermostat gasket leaking Blown cylinder head gasket Reservoir pressure cap defective Cracked cylinder head, or block
Overheating	Coolant level low Water pump belt slipping Radiator core blocked Kinked hose Thermostat not opening fully Defective thermostatic switch Fan motor not running Ignition timing incorrect Carburettor adjustment too weak
Cool running	Excessively low ambient temperature Thermostat missing Thermostat opening too soon Thermostatic switch setting incorrect

Chapter 3 Fuel, exhaust and emission control systems

Contents

Specifications

Fuel tank capacity .... 60 litres, 15.9 US gall, 13.2 Imp gall

Fuel grade
1.6 litre .... Regular grade, not less than 91 RON
2.2 litre (115 bhp) engine code WD, WE .... Regular grade, not less than 91 RON
2.0 litre .... Premium grade, not less than 98 RON
2.2 litre (136 bhp) engine code WC, WG .... Premium grade, not less than 98 RON

Air cleaner .... Renewable paper element

Fuel pump
Type:
   Carburettor models .... Diaphragm type, mechanically operated from camshaft (2.0 and 2.2 litre) or intermediate shaft (1.6 litre)

   Injection models .... Electrically operated roller cell type
Operating pressure (mechanical type):
   1.6 litre .... 0.2 to 0.25 bar (2.84 to 3.56 lbf in^2)
   2.0 and 2.2 litre .... 0.35 to 0.40 bar (4.9 to 5.7 lbf in^2)
Operating data (electrical type):
   Pressure .... 4.2 to 5.2 bar (58 to 72 lbf in^2)
   Capacity .... 30 cc/sec (1.83 cu in/sec)
   Current loading .... 8.5 amps

Carburettor (1.6 litre – 2B2)
Type .... Zenith, twin-choke, downdraught

	Manual gearbox	Automatic transmission
Jets and settings:		
Venturi, Stages I/II	24/28	24/28
Main jet, Stage I/II	X117.5/X125	X117.5/X125
Air correction jet with emulsion tube, Stage I/II	135/92.5	135/92.5
Idle/idle air jet, Stage I	52.5/135	52.5/135
Idle/idle air jet, Stage II	40/125	40/125
By-pass fuel jet	42.5	42.5
By-pass air jet	130	130
Idle air jet for progression reserve	180	200
Idle fuel jet for progression reserve	130	100
Float needle valve, Stage I/II	2.0/2.0	2.0/2.0

	Manual gearbox	Automatic transmission
Injection pump tube	2X0.40	45
Enrichment valve	65	65
Throttle gap	0.65 + 0.05 mm	0.75 + 0.05 mm
	(0.026 + 0.002 in)	(0.030 + 0.002 in)
Float adjustment, Stage I/II	28 + 0.5/30 + 0.5 mm	28 + 0.5/30+ 0.5 mm
	(1.10 + 0.002/1.18 + 0.002 in)	1.10 + 0.002/1.18 + 0.002 in)
Injection capacity (slow) (cm³/stroke)	1.30 + 0.15	0.90 + 0.15
Choke gap	3.15 + 0.15 mm	4.50 + 0.15 mm
	(0.012 + 0.006 in)	(0.177 + 0.006 in)
Idle speed (rpm)	950 + 50	950 + 50
Idle CO (%)	1.5 + 0.3	1.5 + 0.3
Fast idle speed (rpm)	3400 + 50	3600 + 50

Carburettor (2.0 litre – 2B3)

Note:- The information given is for 1977 models onwards. There are some differences from these for 1976 models or those with engine code letters other than WF

Jets and settings:	Manual gearbox	Automatic transmission
Venturi, Stage I/II	24/28	24/28
Main jet, Stage I/II	125/142.5	125/142.5
Air correction jet, with emulsion tube, Stage I/II	140/92.5	140/92.5
Pilot jet, Stage I/II	52.5/145	52.5/140
Pilot air jet, Stage I/II	145/125	145/125
By-pass fuel jet	45	45
By-pass air jet	140	140
Idle air jet for progression reserve	130	130
Idle fuel jet for progression reserve	110	110
Float needle valve, Stage I/II	2.0/2.0	2.0/2.0
Enrichment valve	60	65
Throttle valve gap	1.45 + 0.05 mm	1.45 + 0.5 mm
	(0.057 + 0.002 in)	(0.057 + 0.002 in)
Float setting dimension, Stage I/II	28 + 0.5/30 + 0.5 mm	28 + 0.5/30 + 0.5 mm)
	1.10 + 0.020/1.18 + 0.020 in)	1.10 + 0.020/1.18 + 0.020 in)
Injection capacity (slow) (cm³/stroke)	1.3 + 0.2	1.3 + 0.2
Choke valve gap	4.7 + 0.15 mm	4.9 + 0.15 mm
	(0.185 + 0.006 in)	(0.193 + 0.006 in)
Idle speed (rpm)	950 + 50	950 + 50
Idle CO (%)	1.5 + 0.5	1.5 + 0.5
Fast idle speed (rpm)	4000 + 50	4300 + 50

Carburettor (2.2 litre – 2B2)

Jets and settings:	Manual gearbox	Automatic transmission
Venturi, Stage I/II	24/28	24/28
Main jet, Stage I/II	X120/X127.5	X120/X127.5
Air correction jet with emulsion tube, Stage I/II	135/115	135/115
Idling air jet, Stage I	45/120	42.5/120
Idling air jet, Stage II	40/125	40/125
By-pass fuel jet	42.5	42.5
By-pass air jet	127.5	127.5
Idling air jet for progression reserve, Stage II	205	205
Idling fuel jet for progression reserve, Stage II	95	95
Float needle valve, Stage I/II	2.0	2.0
Accelerator pump discharge tube	2X0.40	2X0.40
Enrichment valve	100	100
Throttle valve gap	1.1 + 0.05 mm	1.2 + 0.05 mm
	(0.043 + 0.002 in)	(0.047 + 0.002 in)
Float adjustment dimension, Stage I/II	28 + 1/30 + 1 mm	28 + 1/30 + 1 mm
	(1.10 + 0.04/1.18 + 0.04 in)	(1.10 + 0.04/1.18 + 0.04 in)
Injection capacity (slow) (cm³/stroke)	1.5 + 0.15	1.5 + 0.15
Choke valve gap (in)	3.9 + 0.15 mm	3.7 + 0.15 mm
	(0.154 + 0.006 in)	(0.146 + 0.006 in)
Idle speed (rpm)	900 + 50	900 + 50
Idle CO (%)	1.0 + 0.5	1.0 + 0.5
Fast idle speed (rpm)	3600 + 100	3700 + 100

Fuel injection system (2.2 litre)

Cold start valve injection time	See Fig. 3.52
Warm-up valve heater coil resistance	20 ohms
Injector opening pressure	3.2 – 3.8 bar
Idle speed (oil temperature above 60°C)	
Engine code:	
WC	900 + 50 rpm
WD	925 + 75 rpm
WE	925 + 75 rpm (except Sweden)
	900 + 50 rpm (Sweden only)
WG	900 + 50 rpm

Idle CO
    Engine code:
        WC .... 1.0 ± 0.2%
        WD .... 0.5 ± 0.4%
        WE .... 0.3% max (except Sweden)
                                                       2.0% max (Sweden only)
        WG .... 1.0 ± 0.2%

Torque wrench settings

	Nm	lbf ft
Fuel tank strap-to-body	25	18
Mechanical fuel pump-to-engine	20	14
Electric pump check valve	20	14
Electric pump fuel union	20	14
Check valve-to-filter (injection models)	40	29
Fuel pipe-to-filter (injection models)	10	7
Air filter-to-carburettor nuts	8	6
Warm air duct-to-engine nuts	20	14
Carburettor-to-engine bolts	10	7
Inlet manifold-to-engine bolts	25	18
Preheater-to-inlet manifold bolts	10	7
Carburettor upper part-to-body bolts	5	3
Automatic choke cover bolt	10	7
Carburettor lower part-to-body bolts	10	7
Fuel metering distributor-to-airflow meter bolts	4	3
Airflow meter-to-air cleaner bolts	4	3
Cold start valve-to-manifold bolts	10	7
Fuel pipe union bolts (injectors)	10	7
Fuel feed-to-metering distributor union bolt	25	18
Warm-up valve fixing bolts	20	14
Exhaust system-to-manifold nuts	30	22
Exhaust pipe-to-engine bracket bolt	25	18
Exhaust system flange and clamp bolts	25	18

1 General description

The fuel tank is mounted beneath the rear seat and fuel is drawn from it by a pump. On the 2.2 litre fuel injection model, the pump is electrically driven and is mounted beneath the rear right-hand wheel arch. On all carburettor models the pump is of the mechanical diaphragm type, driven from the camshaft (intermediate shaft on 1.6 litre engines).

Fuel is pumped via a filter to the carburettor, or on the 2.2 litre injection engine, to a fuel injection system. The twin-choke down-draught carburettors are fitted with automatic chokes, operated by the temperature of the engine coolant; the fuel injection is by the K-Jetronic system.

To reduce fuel consumption and achieve the best possible cold running performance the 2.2 litre carburettor engine has an electrical heating element inside the inlet manifold. This has several electrical resistors which heat up within a few seconds and their heat enables the fuel to mix with the air thoroughly, even at very low ambient temperatures.

The fuel injection system used on the 2.2 litre injection engine is of the continuous injection type which distributes fuel continuously to the injection valves while the engine is running, the amount of fuel injected being controlled by the intake airflow meter.

All models have an air cleaner of the renewable paper element type. On carburettor models it is circular and mounted on the top of the engine, with a vacuum operated flap valve which admits either cold air, or air warmed by the engine depending upon ambient temperature. The operation of the vacuum valve is controlled by a thermostatic control valve which is also mounted in the air cleaner. The air cleaner on the injection model does not have temperature control, except on models for Sweden and the USA. These latter models have a regulator box with an integral thermostat mounted between the air cleaner cover and the intake pipe.

Exhaust gas recirculation (EGR) is fitted on all vehicles exported to the USA and those for California are also fitted with catalytic converters in the exhaust system.

2 Air cleaner – element renewal

1 A dirty air cleaner element will cause a loss of performance and an increase in fuel consumption. A new element should be fitted every 30 000 miles (48 000 km) and the element should be cleaned every twelve months, or more frequently under dusty conditions.

Carburettor models

2 Release the spring clips securing the air cleaner lid and remove the lid.

3 Cover the carburettor entry port to prevent any dirt entering it when the element is lifted out, and remove the element. Wipe the inside of the air cleaner with a moist rag to remove all dust and dirt and then remove the covering from the entry port.

4 In a place well away from the vehicle, tap the air cleaner element to remove dust and dirt. If necessary use a soft brush to clean the outside, or blow air at very low pressure from the inside surface towards the outside.

5 Refit the element, clean the cover and put it in place, then clip the cover down, ensuring that the two arrows (Fig. 3.9) are aligned.

Injection models

6 Release the spring clips securing the air cleaner cover and lift the cover off.

7 Remove the element from the cover and clean it in a similar manner to that described in paragraph 4.

8 When refitting the element (photo), ensure that the fins of the element are horizontal.

9 Refit the air cleaner cover and clip it into place. On injection models with a regulator box, the rib and groove (Fig. 3.10) must be aligned.

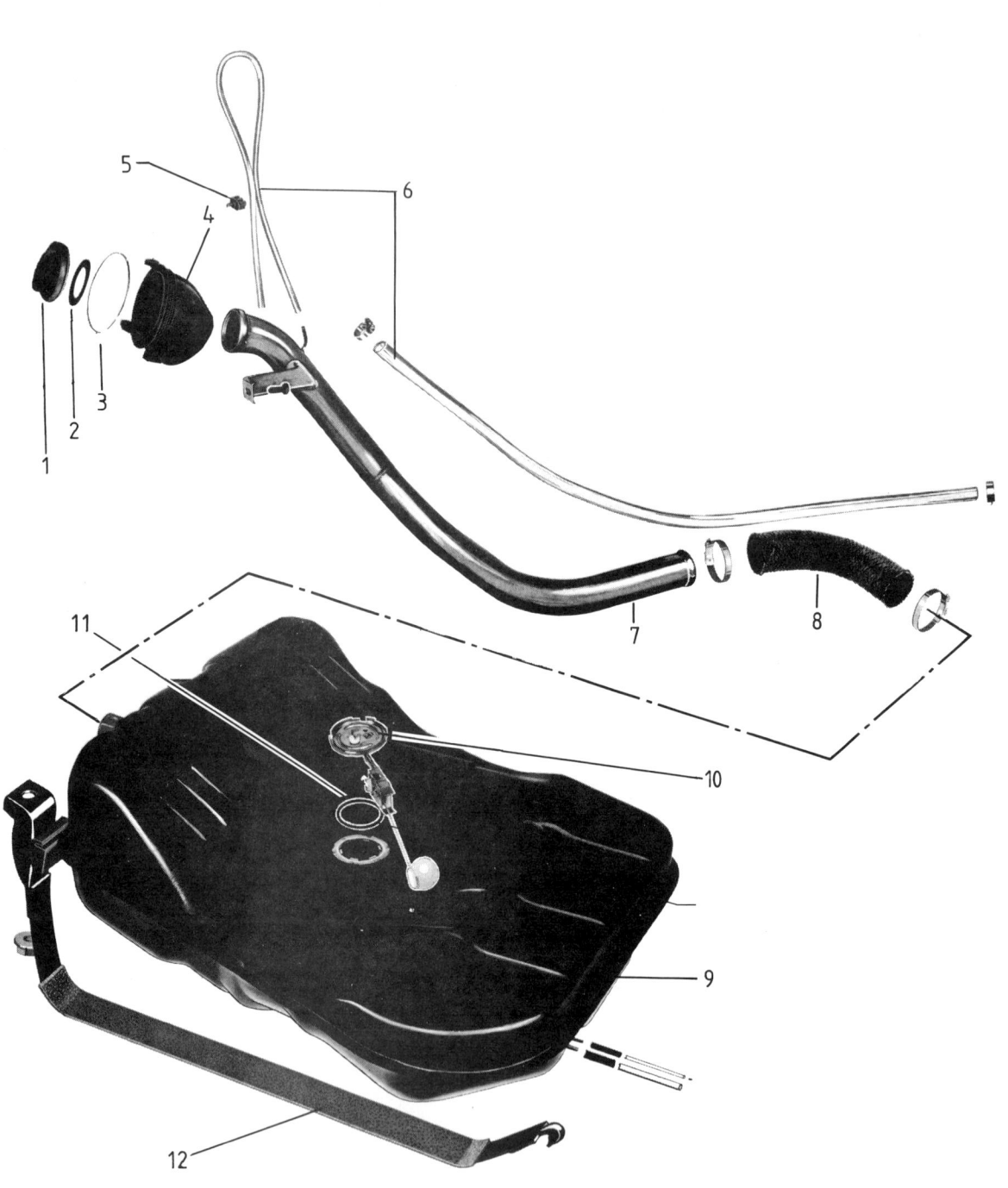

Fig. 3.1 Fuel tank and hoses (1.6 and 2.0 litre) (Sec 1)

1	Filler cap	4	Rubber adaptor	7	Filler pipe	10	Fuel gauge sender unit
2	Seal	5	Clip	8	Filler hose	11	Seal
3	Clamping ring	6	Vent pipes	9	Fuel tank	12	Strap

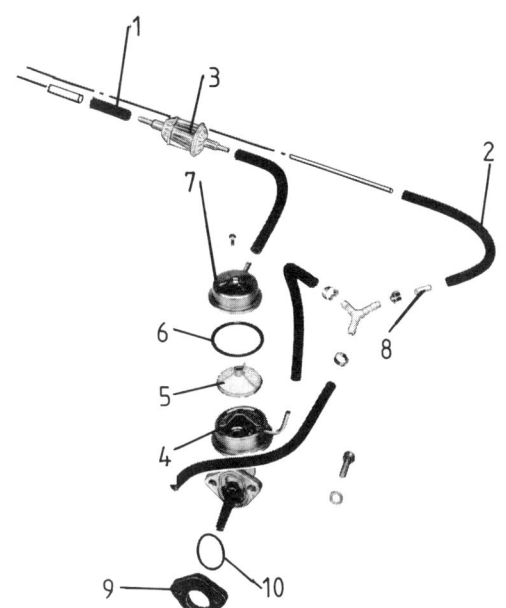

Fig. 3.2 Fuel pump and filter (1.6 litre) (Sec 1)

1	Suction line	6	Seal
2	Return line	7	Fuel pump cover
3	Fuel filter	8	Adaptor
4	Fuel pump	9	Sealing flange
5	Filter screen	10	Seal

Fig. 3.3 Fuel pump and filter (2.0 litre) (Sec 1)

1	Suction line	7	Fuel pump cover
2	Return line	8	Fuel reservoir
3	Fuel filter	9	Sealing flange
4	Fuel pump	10	Seal
5	Filter screen	11	Bracket
6	Seal		

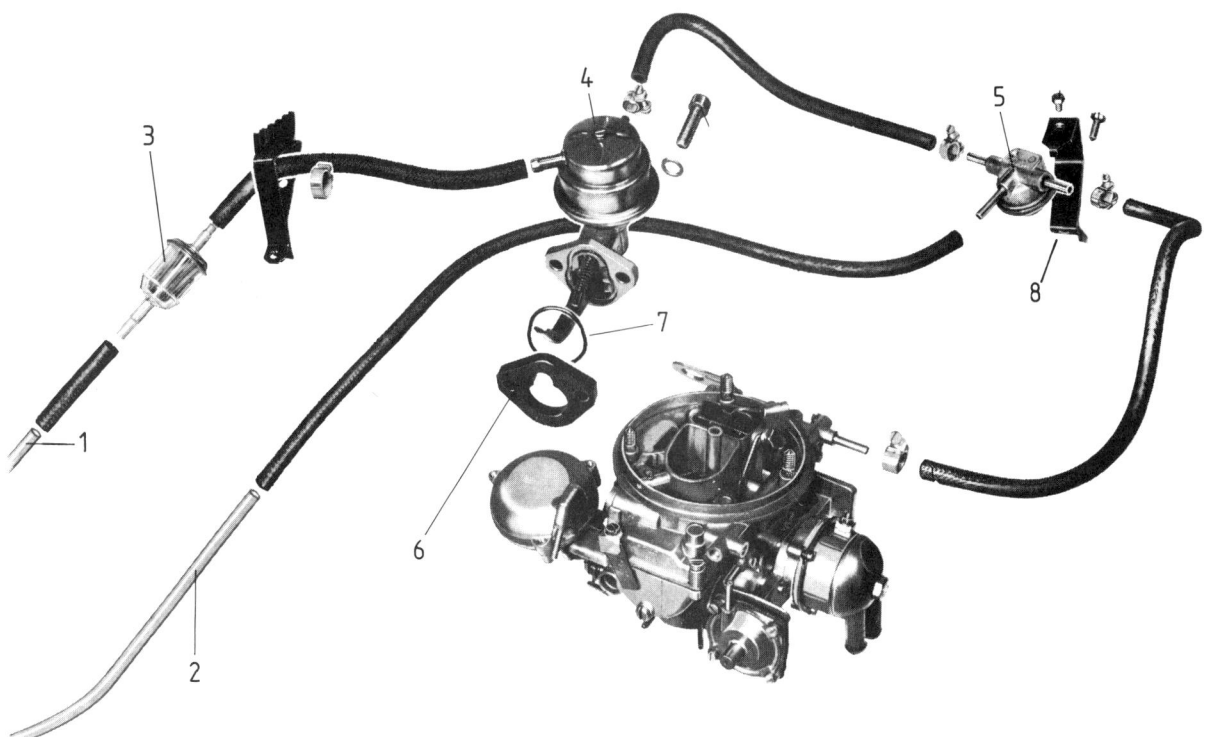

Fig. 3.4 Fuel pump and filter (2.2 litre – carburettor) (Sec 1)

1	Suction line	3	Fuel filter	5	Non-return valve	7	Seal
2	Return line	4	Fuel pump	6	Sealing flange	8	Bracket

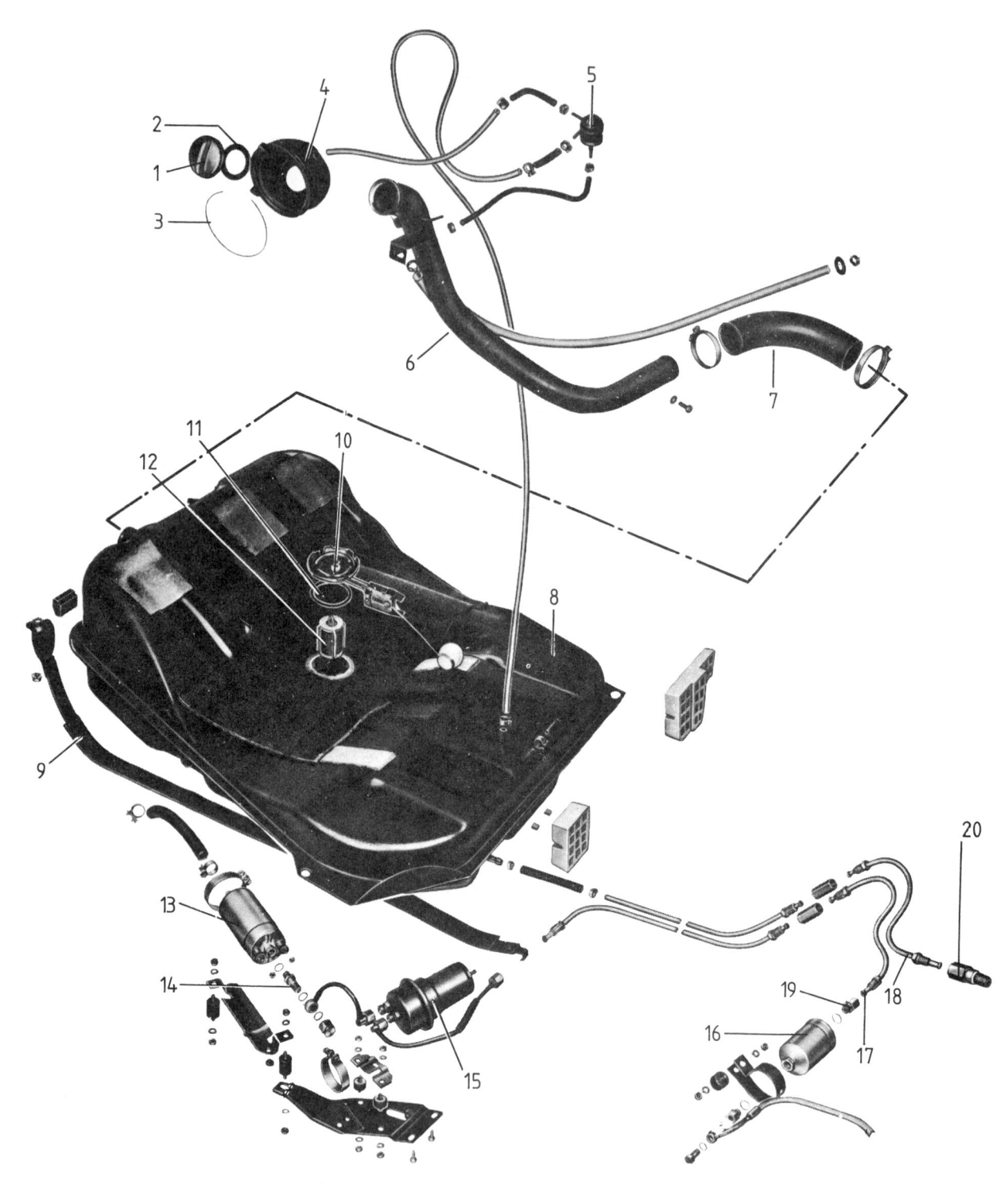

Fig. 3.5 Fuel system (2.2 litre injection) – except US (Sec 1)

1	Filler cap	6	Filler pipe
2	Seal	7	Filler hose
3	Clamping ring	8	Fuel tank
4	Rubber adaptor	9	Strap
5	Breather valve	10	Fuel gauge sender unit
11	Seal	16	Fuel filter
12	Filter	17	Feed line
13	Fuel pump	18	Return line
14	Fuel pump check valve	19	Check valve
15	Fuel accumulator	20	Check valve

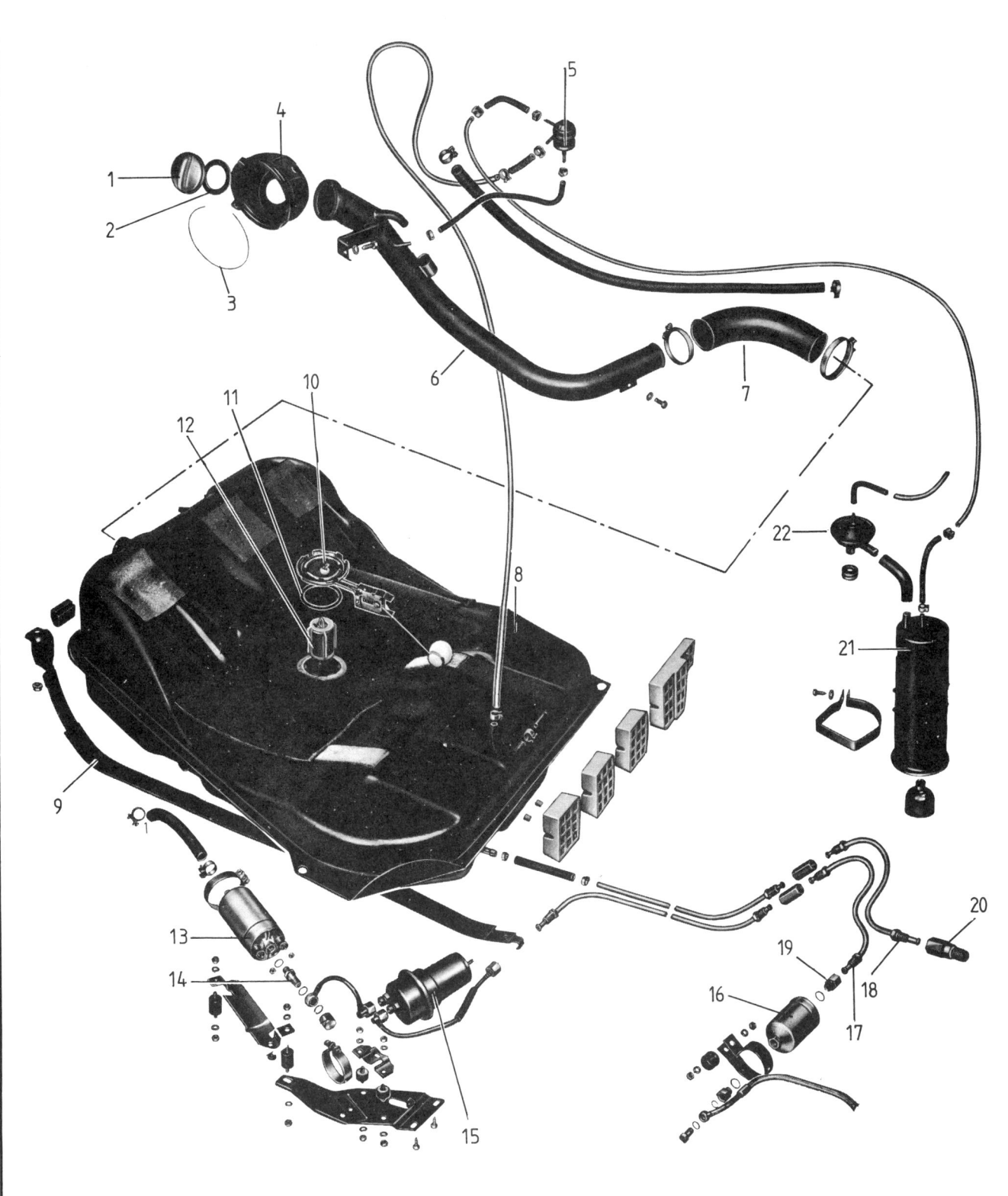

Fig. 3.6 Fuel system (2.2 litre injection) – US models (Sec 1)

1	Filler cap	7	Filler hose	13	Fuel pump	18	Return line
2	Seal	8	Fuel tank	14	Fuel pump check valve	19	Check valve
3	Clamping ring	9	Strap	15	Fuel accumulator	20	Check valve
4	Rubber adaptor	10	Fuel gauge sender unit	16	Fuel filter	21	Charcoal filter
5	Breather valve	11	Seal	17	Feed line	22	Charcoal filter valve
6	Filler pipe	12	Filter				

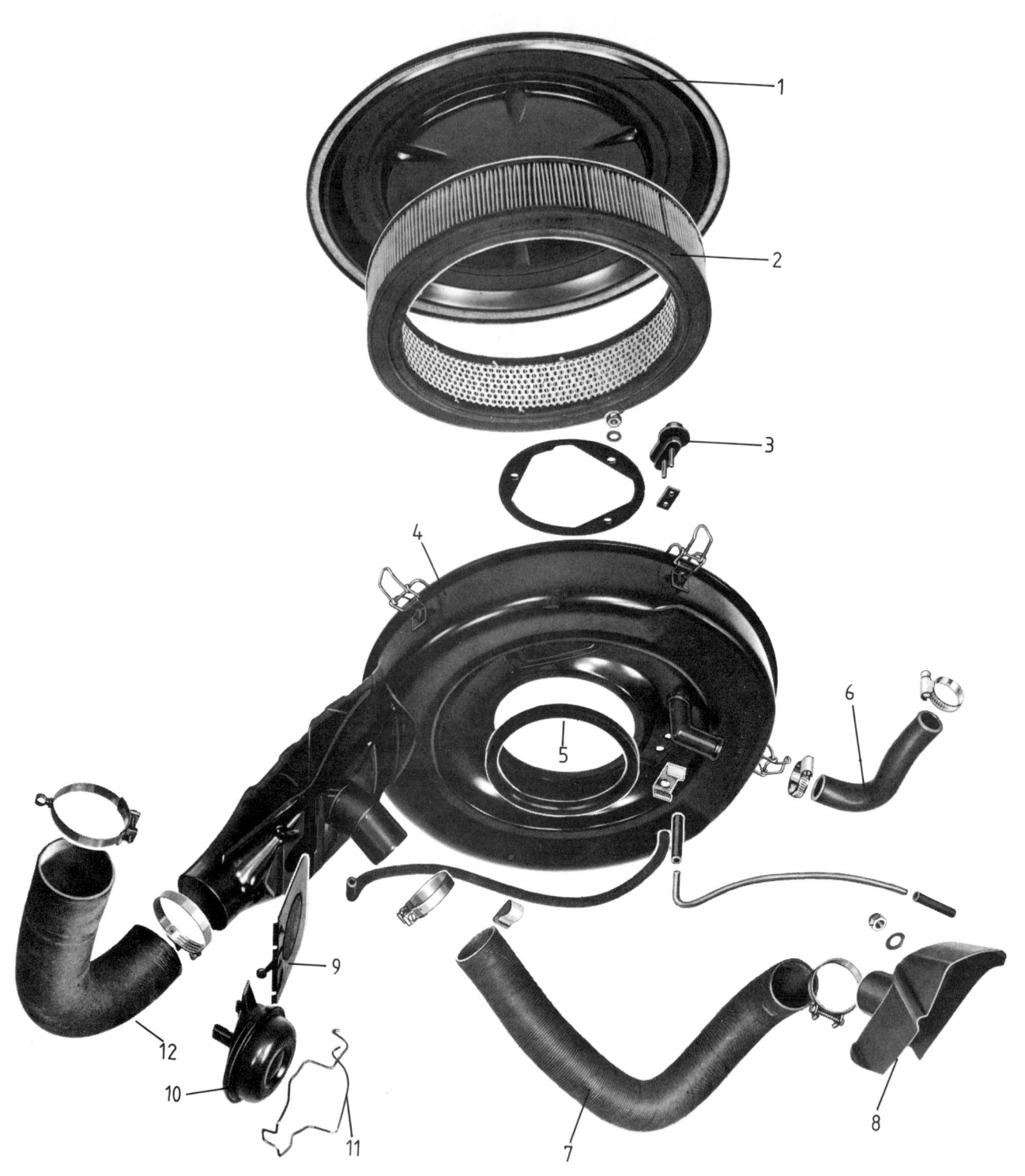

Fig. 3.7 Air cleaner assembly (1.6, 2.0 and 2.2 litre carburettor) (Sec 2)

1 Air cleaner cover	4 Air cleaner housing	7 Preheating hose	10 Vacuum unit
2 Filter element	5 Seal	8 Warm air duct	11 Spring clip
3 Thermostatic control valve	6 Crankcase breather hose	9 Regulator flap	12 Cold air duct

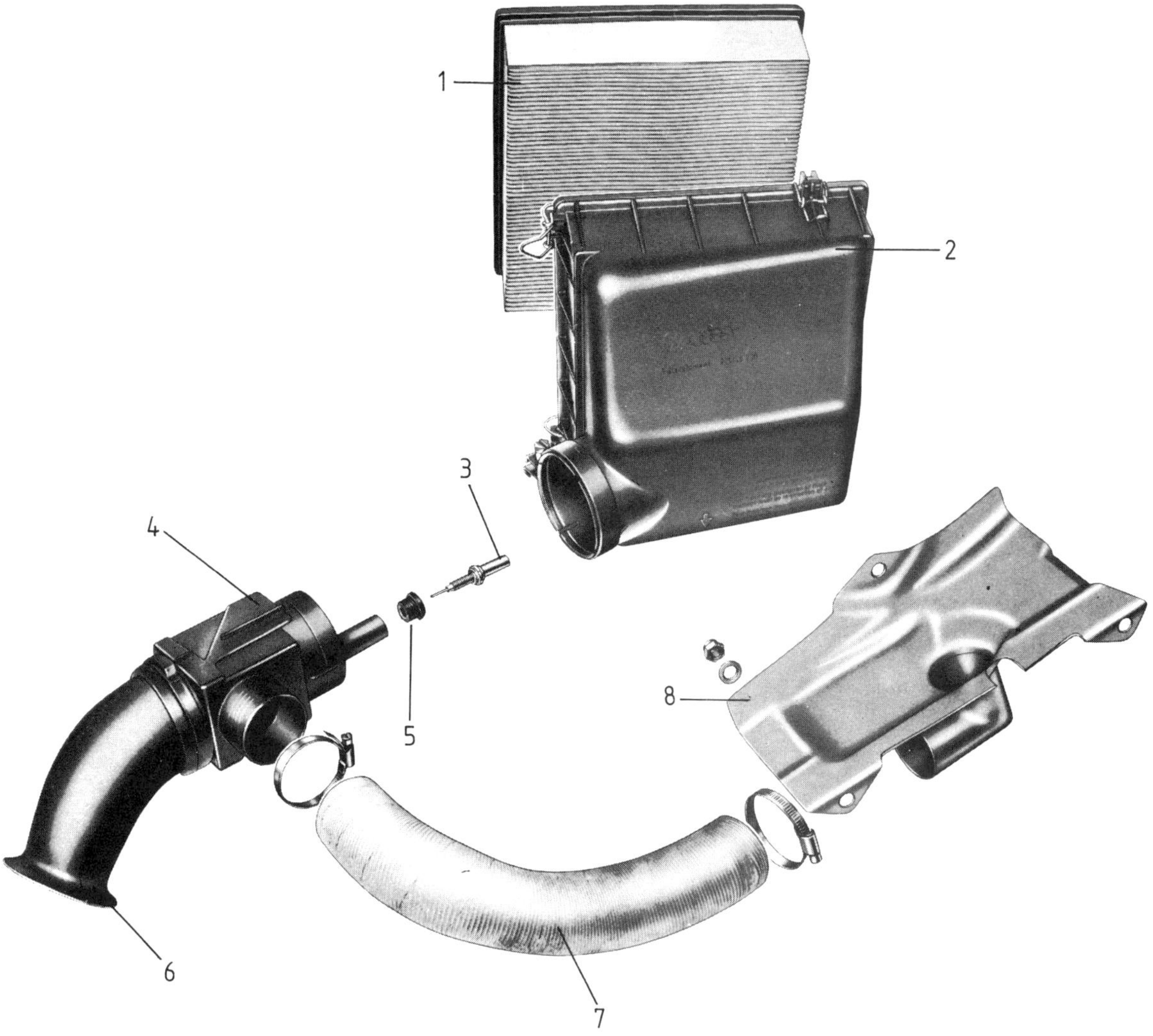

Fig. 3.8 Air cleaner assembly (2.2 litre injection) – US and Swedish models (Sec 2)

1 Filter element	3 Thermostat	5 Adaptor	7 Preheating hose
2 Air cleaner cover	4 Regulator box	6 Intake pipe	8 Warm air duct

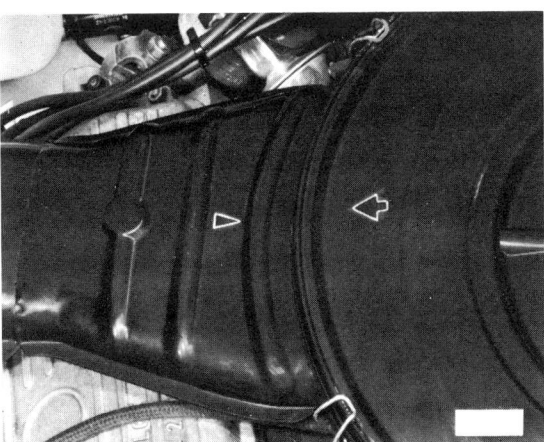

Fig. 3.9 Air cleaner cover alignment marks (Sec 2)

2.8 Fit air cleaner with fins horizontal (injection models)

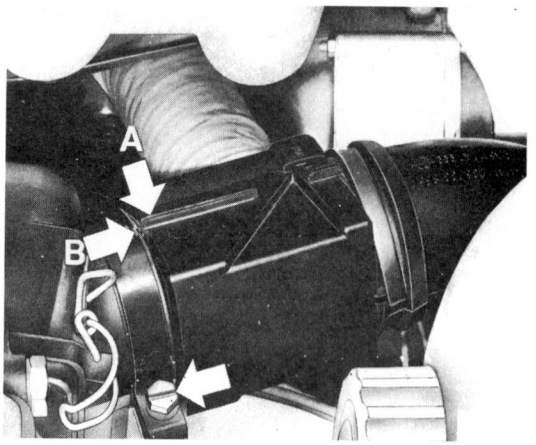

Fig. 3.10 Alignment rib and groove on regulator box (Sec 2)

3   Air cleaner – removing and refitting

1   On injection models the air cleaner is attached to the engine bay and its removal is unlikely to be necessary.
2   On carburettor models the air cleaner is attached to the carburettor by three nuts and washers.
3   Remove the air cleaner cover and element, taking the precaution of covering the carburettor air intake while removing the element.

Clean the inside of the air intake case before removing the port covering.
4   Depending on the model, there will be a variety of hoses attached to the air cleaner body. Release the clips retaining the air and breather hoses and remove them. Before pulling off any vacuum hoses, make a note of the pipes to which they are connected, or mark them in a way which ensures that they will be refitted correctly.
5   Refitting is a reversal of removal, but take care that all the hoses are fitted correctly, are not kinked or strained and that where hose clips are fitted, the clips are tightened. Ensure that the sealing ring is in good condition and use new self-locking nuts.

4   Vacuum unit – removing, checking and refitting

1   Remove the air cleaner as described in Section 3.
2   Press the spring clip in the direction of the arrow (Fig. 3.11) and remove the vacuum unit and flap.
3   Press the diaphragm plunger in (Fig. 3.12) and disengage the regulator flap from its two retaining lugs.
4   The vacuum unit may be tested without removing it from the air cleaner assembly, by proceeding as follows. With the engine cold, pull the preheating hose off the air cleaner and check that the regulator flap is closing the warm air inlet.
5   Connect vacuum hose 1 to pipe 2 (Fig. 3.13), or hose a to pipe b (Fig. 3.14) then start the engine and run it at idling speed. This should result in the regulator flap opening the warm air intake. After checking this, disconnect vacuum hose 3 and the regulator flap should then move to close the warm air intake.

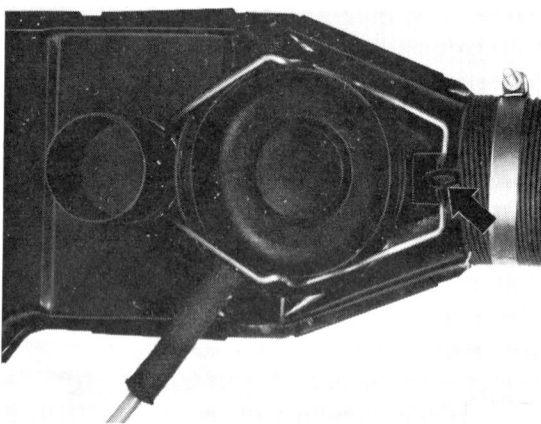

Fig. 3.11 Releasing the vacuum unit clip (Sec 4)

Fig. 3.12 Removing the regulator flap (Sec 4)

Fig. 3.13 Testing the vacuum unit (1.6 litre) – For key see text (Sec 4)

Fig. 3.14 Testing the vacuum unit (2.0 litre) – For key see text (Sec 4)

Fig. 3.15 Checking thermostatic valve (single valve) – for key see text (Sec 5)

6   Refit the vacuum pipes to their original positions and refit the pre-heating air hose.

5   Thermostatic control valve – testing

1   The thermostatic control valve is mounted inside the air cleaner body (carburettor models only) and may be either of the single, or double valve type, depending on vehicle chassis number. Vehicles up to Chassis No 76 063 038 have the single valve, Part No 113 129 828A. From Chassis No 72 063 039 a double valve is fitted and this valve may have one of three different identifications:

   (a) The valve may have the Part No 046 129 630 marked on its cover
   (b) The valve may have a yellow spot and Part No 113 129 828A marked on its cover
   (c) The cover may be yellow, with no part number marking

Single valve type
2   After ensuring that the vacuum unit is working properly, check the control flap is moving freely (see previous Section) and that the engine is cold; start the engine and run it at idling speed.
3   Disconnect the vacuum hose from the vacuum unit to the thermostatic valve, marked (a) in Fig. 3.15. Put a finger over the end of the hose to check that there is vacuum at the end of the hose, also check that the control flap closes the warm air intake when the hose is disconnected.

Double valve type
4   Pull the preheating hose off the air cleaner and check that the control valve flap is closing the warm air intake.
5   Start the engine, set it to idling speed and pull the vacuum hose off the carburettor (Fig. 3.16), the flap valve should open the warm air intake fully.
6   Attach the vacuum hose again and after leaving it for about two minutes, pull it off. The warm air supply should initially be open, but the flap should close it fairly quickly.
7   When the engine is warm, connect the vacuum hose and check that the flap valve keeps the warm air inlet closed.

6   Carburettor – dismantling, servicing and reassembling

1   Carburettor models use a single carburettor of the twin-choke downdraught type. Two different models of carburettor are used, the differences between them are minor (Figs. 3.18 and 3.19). Automatic transmission vehicles are fitted with a variant of the appropriate carburettor model. There are also differences of choke and jet size to cater for the different engine capacities.

2B2 carburettor
2   Remove the air cleaner as described in Section 3. All the jets

Fig. 3.16 Checking thermostatic valve (double valve) (Sec 5)

except the main jets are then accessible (Fig. 3.17). The jets, except the air correction jet of the main system, can then be unscrewed. Jets should be cleaned by blowing through them or, if this is not adequate, using a nylon bristle. Never attempt to clean out a jet with wire, because this will cause permanent damage. It is also important when removing carburettor parts to use a screwdriver or spanner which fits the part exactly, because brass components are easily damaged by ill fitting tools.
3   To remove the upper part of the carburettor, detach the choke crank lever by removing the cotter pin and washer (Fig. 3.20) and detach the accelerator pump operating rod by disconnecting the cranked end of the rod from the throttle linkage. Do not disturb the nut at the pump lever end of the rod, because this will alter the accelerator pump setting. Remove the six screws securing the upper and lower carburettor parts. Lift off the top and turn it over for access to the main jets (Fig. 3.21).
4   With the carburettor top removed, the enrichment valve and fuel jet for progression reserve are accessible (Fig. 3.22).
5   When dismantling a carburettor have handy several small clean containers so that components of each sub-assembly can be kept together. Wash parts in clean petrol and leave them to dry naturally. Make sure that any cleaning rag used is lint-free and observe the same

Fig. 3.17 Jet arrangement (2B2) upper part (Sec 6)

   1   Auxiliary air jet – Stage I
   2   By-pass fuel jet (beneath air jet)
   3   Main air correction jet
   4   Idling jet – Stage I
   5   Idling jet – Stage II
   6   Main air correction jet
   7   Progression reserve air jet

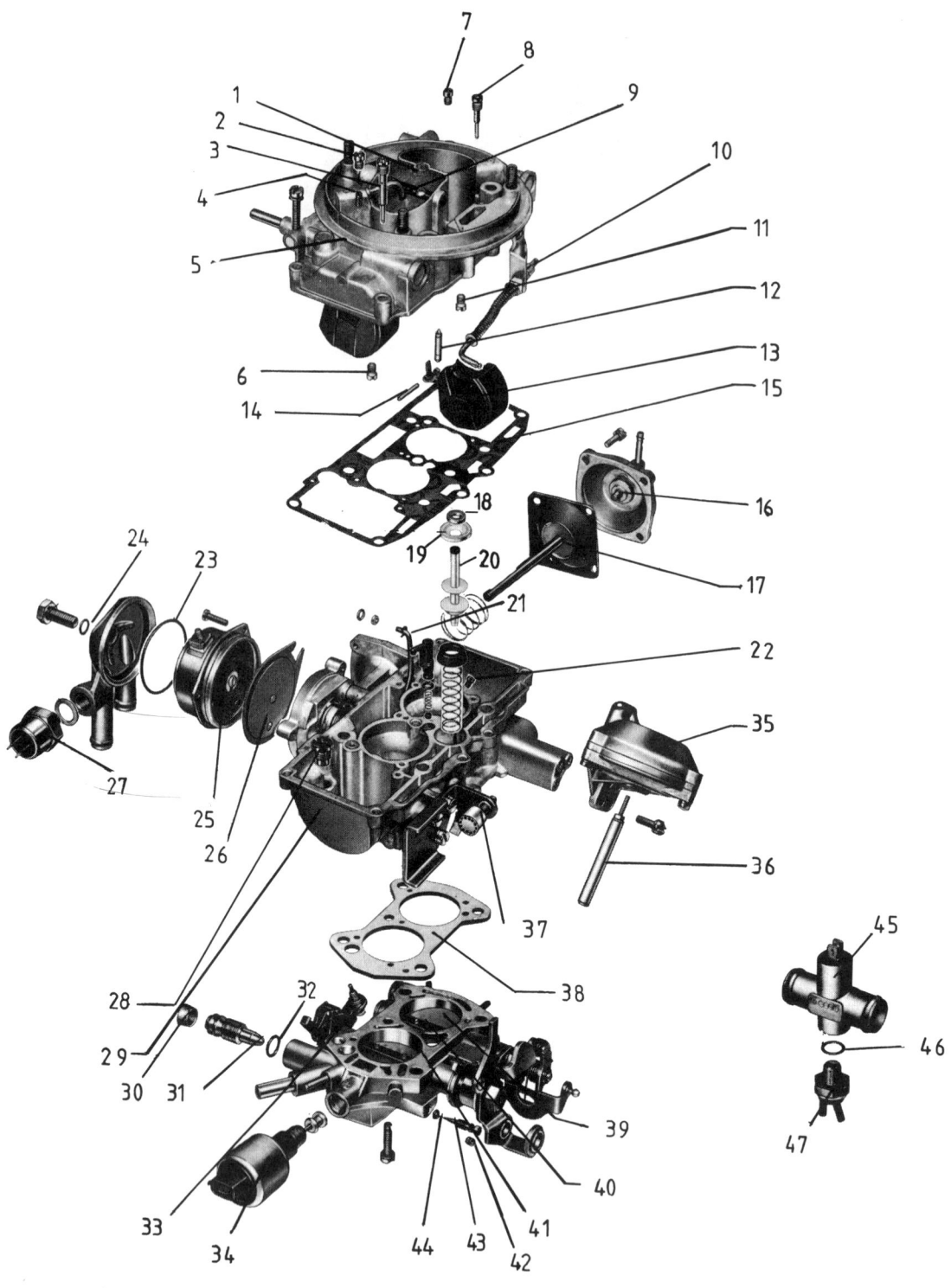

Fig. 3.18 2B2 carburettor components (Sec 6)

1 Choke valve	12 Float needle	24 O-ring	36 Pull rod
2 By-pass air jet	13 Float	25 Automatic choke	37 Throttle stop screw
3 Idling air jet (progression reserve)	14 Float pivot pin	26 Insulating disc	38 Gasket
4 By-pass fuel jet	15 Gasket	27 Thermo-switch	39 Stage II throttle adjuster
5 Carburettor, upper part	16 Choke adjusting screw	28 Enrichment valve	40 Throttle valve
6 Stage 1 main jet	17 Plunger and diaphragm	29 Carburettor body	41 Stage I throttle valve
7 Idling air jet	18 Felt ring	30 Idling adjuster cap	42 CO adjustment locking cap
8 Stage II idling air jet	19 Sealing ring	31 Idling adjuster	43 CO adjustment screw
9 Emulsion tube	20 Pump plunger	32 O-ring	44 O-ring
10 Accelerator pump adjuster	21 Injection tube	33 Fast idling speed adjuster	45 Thermo-switch
11 Stage II main jet	22 Progression reserve fuel jet	34 By-pass air valve	46 O-ring
	23 Automatic choke cover	35 Stage II vacuum unit	47 Thermo-pneumatic valve

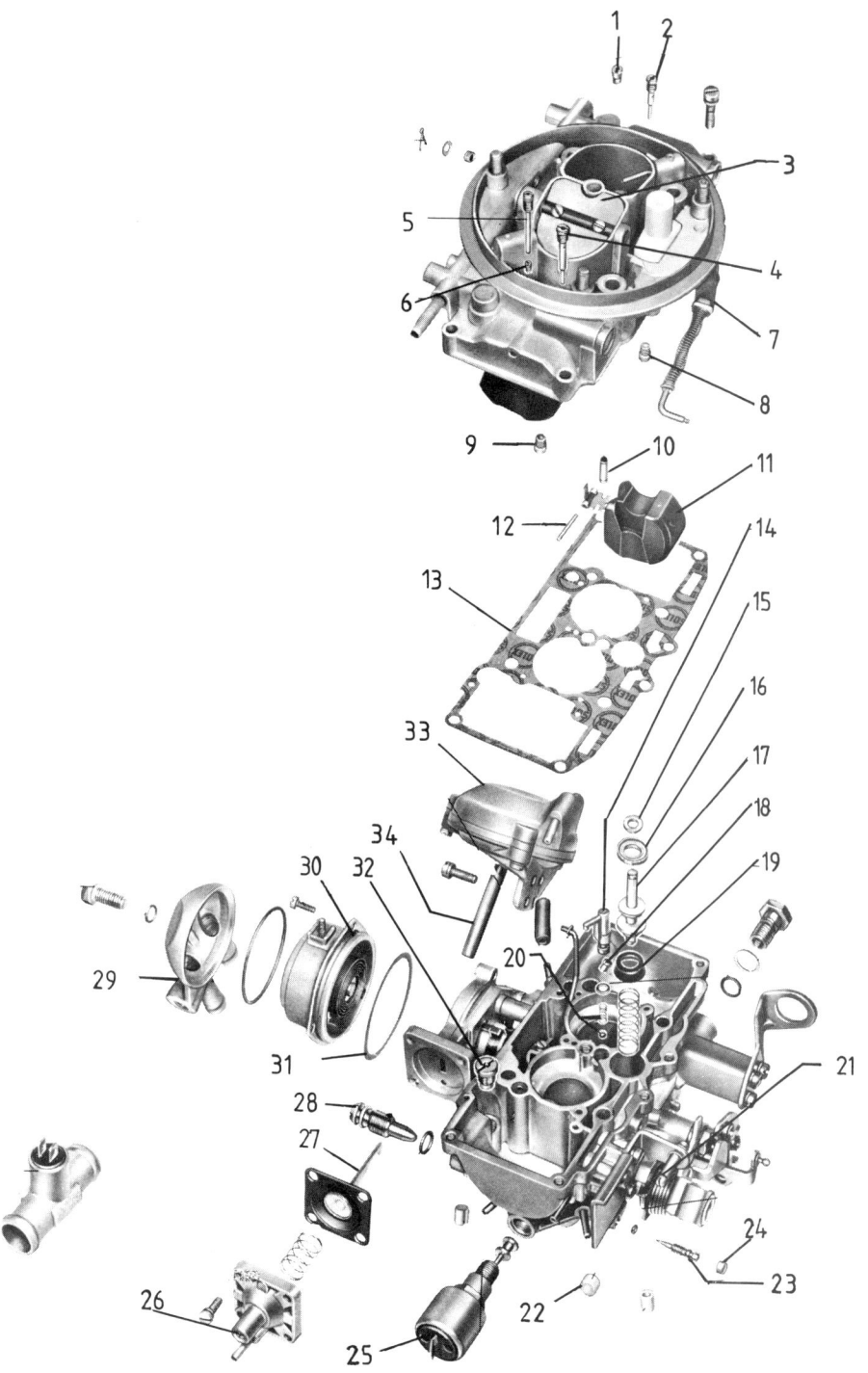

Fig. 3.19 2B3 carburettor components (Sec 6)

1 Idling air jet (progression reserve)
2 Stage II idle air jet
3 Choke plate
4 Stage I idle air jet
5 By-pass air jet
6 By-pass fuel jet
7 Accelerator pump adjuster
8 Stage II main jet
9 Stage I main jet
10 Float needle
11 Float
12 Float pivot
13 Gasket
14 Injection tube
15 Felt ring
16 Sealing ring
17 Pump plunger
18 Progression idle fuel jet
19 Pump seal
20 Check valve
21 Throttle limit screw
22 Throttle limit screw cap
23 CO adjusting screw
24 CO adjusting screw cap
25 By-pass air valve
26 Choke gap adjuster
27 Plunger and diaphragm
28 Idle speed adjuster
29 Automatic choke cover
30 Automatic choke
31 Gasket
32 Enrichment valve
33 Stage II vacuum unit
34 Pull rod

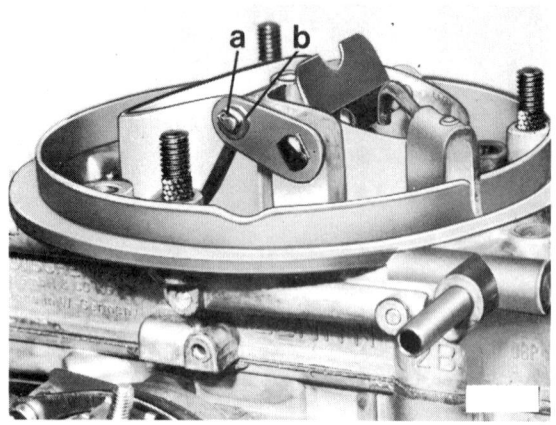

Fig. 3.20 Disconnecting the choke (Sec 6)

(a)   Cotter pin   *(b)   Washer*

precautions when cleaning out carburettor body passages as those for cleaning jets.

6   To remove the float and float needle, drive out the float pivot pin from the inside towards the outside of the carburettor. Remove the float and shake out the float needle.

7   To dismantle the automatic choke, unscrew the bolt in the centre of the choke cover and remove the bolt, O-ring, cover, O-ring, automatic choke and insulating disc in that order.

8   When reassembling the carburettor use new gaskets and sealing rings and when fitting gaskets be very careful to fit them so that the hole patterns of the gasket and its mating surfaces match.

9   The accelerator pump is mounted in the lower body and can be removed by pulling on the piston rod and removing the piston assembly and spring. When reassembling, first fit the spring, then the piston rod with the cup seal pointing downwards. Press the bearing ring in until it is flush with the rim of the pump bore and then fit the felt seal to the piston rod.

2B3 carburettor

10   There are minor constructional differences and the position of the jets is slightly different from the 2B2 carburettor, but the method of dismantling and reassembly is similar.

Fig. 3.21 Main jet arrangement (2B2) (Sec 6)

8   Main jet – Stage I   *9   Main jet – Stage II*

Fig. 3.23 Jet arrangement – upper part (2B3) (Sec 6)

1   By-pass air jet
2   By-pass fuel jet (beneath air jet)
3   Air correction jet – Stage I
4   Idle jet – Stage I
5   Idle jet – Stage 2
6   Air correction jet – Stage 2
7   Idle air jet (progression reserve)

Fig. 3.22 Jet arrangement – lower part (2B2) (Sec 6)

10   Progression reserve fuel jet   *11   Enrichment valve*

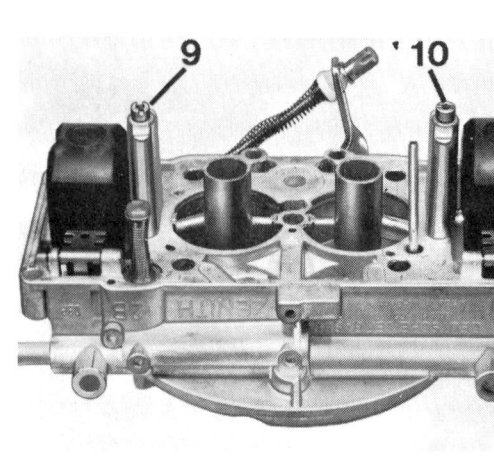

Fig. 3.24 Main jet arrangement (2B3) (Sec 6)

9   Main jet – Stage I   *10   Main jet – Stage II*

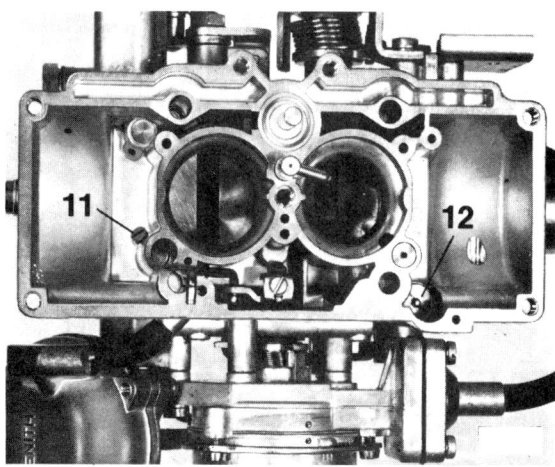

Fig. 3.25 Jet arrangement – lower part (2B3) (Sec 6)

11 Progression reserve fuel jet   *12 Enrichment valve*

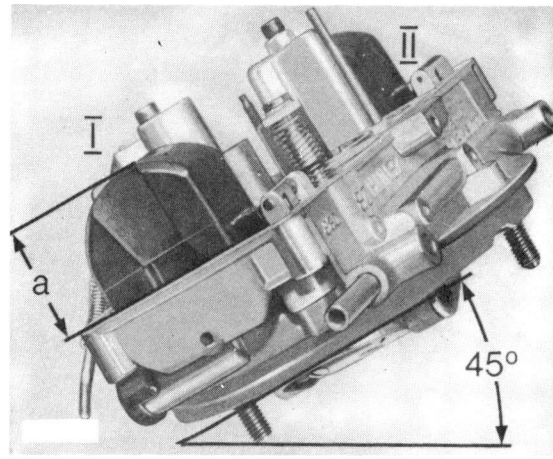

Fig. 3.26 Carburettor float adjustment

Stage I – a = 28mm ± 0.5 mm (1.1 ± 0.020 in)
Stage 2 – a = 30 mm ± 0.5 mm (1.18 ± 0.020 in)

Fig. 3.28 Choke valve adjusting screw (arrowed) (Sec 7)

7 Carburettor – adjustments

Float adjustment

1   With the upper part of the carburettor held at an angle of 45° (Fig. 3.26), measure the height of the bottom of the float from the joint face for both the Stage I and Stage II floats and compare the values with those given in Specifications. To alter the setting, remove the float as described in the previous Section and bend the float stop tab towards the float to decrease the height and away from the float to increase the height. Refit the float and check the measurement, repeating the operation if necessary.

Choke valve gap adjustment

2   If the upper part of the carburettor has been removed, or the choke dismantled, the choke valve should be adjusted.

3   With the choke mechanism removed, close the choke and press the pull rod of the choke adjuster diaphragm as far to the right as it will go (Fig. 3.27). Press the choke plate lightly in the direction of arrow (a). to take up the play in the bearings and link. With the plate in this position use a twist drill to check the gap between the lip of the choke plate and the bore of the venturi. The correct size of gap is given in Specifications.

4   If the choke plate requires adjustment, turn the adjusting screw (Fig. 3.28) and after completing the adjusting lock the screw in position by dropping a spot of thread locking liquid on the screw end.

5   When reassembling the automatic choke, the pipe connections should point downwards at about 20° and the marks on the choke assembly and the carburettor upper section should line up (Fig. 3.29).

Fig. 3.27 Choke gap adjustment (Sec 7)

Fig. 3.29 Automatic choke alignment marks (arrowed) (Sec 7)

Basic throttle setting (Stage 1)

6   The limiting screw (*a* in Fig. 3.30) is set at the factory and this setting should not be altered. If the screw is turned by mistake, or if the throttle has been dismantled, the correct setting can be re-established by the following method.

7   Break off the locking cap. It is not possible to remove the cap without breaking it and a new cap is required for fitting after the screw has been adjusted. Open and close the throttle quickly and then screw in screw *a* until it touches the stop, then turn it a further quarter turn.

8   After making the adjustment, fit a locking cap to the screw and then check the engine idle speed and CO level. Without an exhaust gas analyser, the latter job is of course one for your dealer.

Basic throttle setting (Stage II)

9   The limiting screw (*a* in Fig. 3.31) is set at the factory and this setting should not be altered. If the screw is turned by mistake, the correct setting can be re-established by the following method.

10   Ensure that the choke is open fully and that Stage I throttle is in its idling position. Remove the locking cap from screw *a* (Fig. 3.31) and unscrew the screw until there is a gap between the end of the screw and stop *b*.

11   Disconnect the vacuum unit pull rod from the throttle linkage (Fig. 3.32) and press the throttle linkage gently in the direction which closes the throttle.

12   Insert a piece of paper between the end of the screw *a* and stop *b*

and screw in the screw until its end just nips the piece of paper. Remove the paper and advance the screw a further quarter of a turn.

13   Fit the limiting screw locking cap and re-connect the vacuum unit pull rod.

14   After completing the adjustment, check the engine idle speed and CO level.

Adjusting throttle gap

15   With the carburettor removed from the engine, close the choke and turn the carburettor upside down to expose the throttle valves (Fig. 3.33).

16   Remove the locking cap from the adjusting screw *b* and turn the screw until a twist drill of the specified size can just be inserted between the lip of the throttle plate and the throttle bore.

17   After making the adjustment, fit the locking cap to the screw and then check the engine idle speed and CO level.

Vacuum unit pull rod adjustment

18   Disconnect the vacuum unit pull rod from the throttle linkage.

19   Loosen the locknut on the spindle (Fig. 3.34) and screw the pull rod up, or down as necessary until dimension *a* is between one and two millimetres (0.039 and 0.079 in).

20   Tighten the locknut without altering the setting of the pull rod and re-connect the rod to the throttle linkage.

Fig. 3.30 Basic throttle setting (Stage I) (Sec 7)

a = limit screw

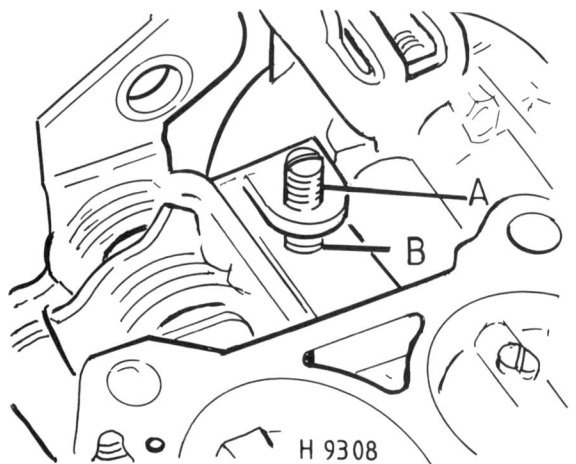

Fig. 3.31 Basic throttle setting (Stage II) (Sec 7)

a = limit screw, b = stop

Fig. 3.32 Disconnecting the vacuum unit (Sec 7)

Fig. 3.33 Adjusting throttle gap (Sec 7)

a = twist drill gauge   b = adjusting screw

Fig. 3.34 Vacuum unit pull rod adjustment (Sec 7)

a = 1 to 2 mm (0.039 to 0.079 in)

Fig. 3.36 Adjusting accelerator pump output (Sec 7)

1   Adjuster nut

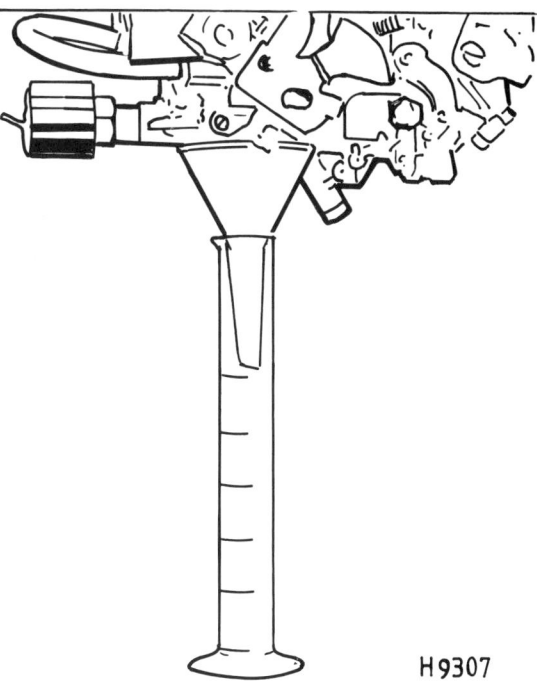

Fig. 3.35 Checking accelerator pump output (Sec 7)

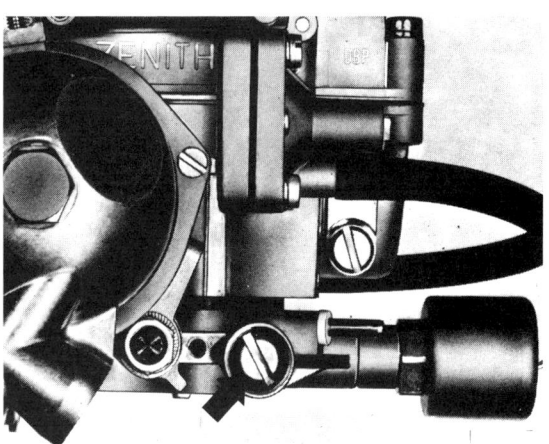

Fig. 3.37 Idle speed adjusting screw (arrowed) (Sec 7)

Accelerator pump adjustment

21 With the carburettor removed from the engine, hold the carburettor (with its float chamber full) above a funnel and measuring jar (Fig. 3.35).
22 Open the throttle valve fully and release it slowly, taking at least three seconds to complete the operation and then repeat the cycle until ten complete strokes have been completed. Read off the amount of fuel ejected and divide by ten to obtain the quantity delivered per stroke. Compare this with the value given in Specifications.
23 Adjust the pump output if necessary by turning the adjusting nut (Fig. 3.36) clockwise to increase capacity and anti-clockwise to decrease it. After completing the adjustment, lock the nut with a spot of thread locking liquid.
24 If the specified rate of ejection cannot be achieved by adjusting the nut, check the condition of the pump piston and cup washer and also ensure that the injection tube is not blocked or obstructed.

Idling speed adjustment

25 Ensure that the engine oil temperature is at least 60°C (140°F), that the choke is fully open and that all electrical accessories are switched OFF.
26 Disconnect the crankcase breather hose from the cylinder head and plug the hose.
27 Disconnect the radiator fan electrical connections so that the fan cannot run while the idling speed is being adjusted.
28 Break the locking cap on the adjusting screw (Fig. 3.37) and turn

the screw to give an idling speed of 950 ± 50 rpm. Lock the screw by fitting a new cap after making the adjustment and re-connect the breather hose and the radiator fan connections.

Fast idling speed adjustment

29 With the engine oil temperature at least 50°C (122°F) remove the cover of the air cleaner and remove the cap from the adjusting screw (Fig. 3.38).
30 Open the throttle, close the choke valve fully and then release the throttle so that the adjusting screw is left resting on the highest part of the fast idle cam.
31 Release the choke and check that it returns to its fully open position, then start the engine without touching the accelerator pedal.
32 Check the speed of the engine and if necessary turn the adjusting screw until the speed is in accordance with Specifications. The adjusting screw is not very accessible when it is resting on the highest part of the cam and it may be necessary to open the throttle in order to be able to turn the screw. If this is the case, turn the screw a small amount, release the throttle so that the screw again makes contact with the cam and repeat the process until the correct speed is achieved.
33 Fit a new limit cap to the fast idle screw.

Fig. 3.38 Fast idle speed adjusting screw (arrowed) (Sec 7)

Fig. 3.39 Idle mixture (CO) adjusting screw (arrowed) (Sec 8)

Fig. 3.40 Thermostatic switch (Sec 9)

Fig. 3.41 Thermo-pneumatic valve (automatic transmission) (Sec 10)

8 Idle mixture (CO) adjustment

1   The following adjustment can be made if an exhaust gas analyser is available. The CO content of the exhaust gas is limited by statutory regulations in some countries and where this is the case it is necessary to have a check of CO level carried out after making any adjustments to the carburettor.

2   Ensure that the engine oil temperature is at least 60°C (140°F) that the choke is fully open and that all electrical accessories are switched *OFF*.

3   Disconnect the crankcase breather hose from the cylinder head and plug the hose.

4   Disconnect the radiator fan electrical connections so that the fan cannot run while the CO level is being adjusted.

5   Connect the exhaust gas analyser to the tail pipe as directed by the equipment manufacturer. Break the limit cap on the adjusting screw (Fig. 3.39) and turn the screw to achieve the specified CO level.

6   After adjusting the CO level, check the idling speed, adjust it if necessary (see paragraph 25) and then re-check the CO level.

7   Lock the adjuster screw with a new cap and re-connect the crankcase breather hose. It may be noted that the CO level rises when the breather hose is re-connected. This effect is due to an increase in the dilution of oil in the crankcase by fuel as a result of the stopping and starting necessary to do the CO check. This increase is temporary and will disappear after about thirty minutes of fast driving, or may be overcome by changing the crankcase oil if an oil change is due.

9 Thermostatic switch – checking

1   The automatic choke mechanism is heated by engine coolant and

the flow of coolant is controlled by an electrically operated thermostatic valve (Fig. 3.40). Some models also have a similar valve controlling the flow of coolant through the inlet manifold.

2   To test the switch, connect a continuity meter, or battery and bulb between the terminals. With the switch cold (below about 30°C) (86°F) the switch should be *ON* and give continuity. If the valve body is heated, by immersing it in hot water, the switch should change to *OFF* at above about 40°C (104°F).

3   The temperatures given in the preceding paragraph are approximate because there are differences between the valve settings used on different models and those used for choke heating have a different setting from those used for manifold heating. The latter may be *ON* in the temperature range below 45°C (113°F) to below 26°C (78°F) and may be *OFF* from above 55°C (131°F) to above 28°C (84°F).

10 Thermo-pneumatic valve – checking

1   Some automatic transmission models have a thermo-pneumatic valve (Fig. 3.41) screwed into the thermostatic switch and this valve is in the vacuum line to the vacuum unit of the Stage II throttle positioner.

2   To check the valve without removing it from the vehicle remove the two hoses from the valve and attach a length of tubing to one of the connections on the valve. Blow down the pipe when the engine is cold and the valve should not pass any air.

3   Run the engine until it is at normal operating temperature and again blow down the pipe. With the engine hot the valve should be open and allow free passage of air.

4   Remove the piece of tubing from the valve and re-connect the vacuum pipes to it.

5   If the valve is removed from the car for checking it will first be necessary to drain the cooling system before unscrewing the thermo-pneumatic valve from the thermostatic switch. Use a piece of tubing on one port to blow into the valve when it is cold and then immerse the valve in water to heat it. It should not be possible to blow through the valve if the valve temperature is below 58°C (136°F) and it should give free passage at a temperature above 62°C (144°F).

6   When refitting the thermo-pneumatic valve to the thermostatic switch, use a new sealing ring.

---

11   Carburettor – removing and refitting

1   An insulator is fitted between the carburettor and the inlet manifold and it is easier to leave the insulator in position when removing the carburettor.

2   Remove the air cleaner as described in Section 3, and drain the cooling system as described in Chapter 2.

3   Disconnect the leads from the battery.

4   Remove the throttle cable connection. The connecting link must also be removed on automatic transmission models (See Section 32).

5   Unclamp and remove the fuel and coolant hoses from the carburettor, marking the hoses before they are removed if there is likely to be any doubt in refitting them to the correct pipe.

6   Label all the vacuum hoses to indicate the pipes to which they were connected and then remove them (Figs. 3.43 and 3.44).

7   Remove the four through-bolts and washers from the upper part of the carburettor and lift the carburettor off its insulator. To free the carburettor completely, it is necessary to disconnect one end of the earth bonding wire between the carburettor and the inlet manifold.

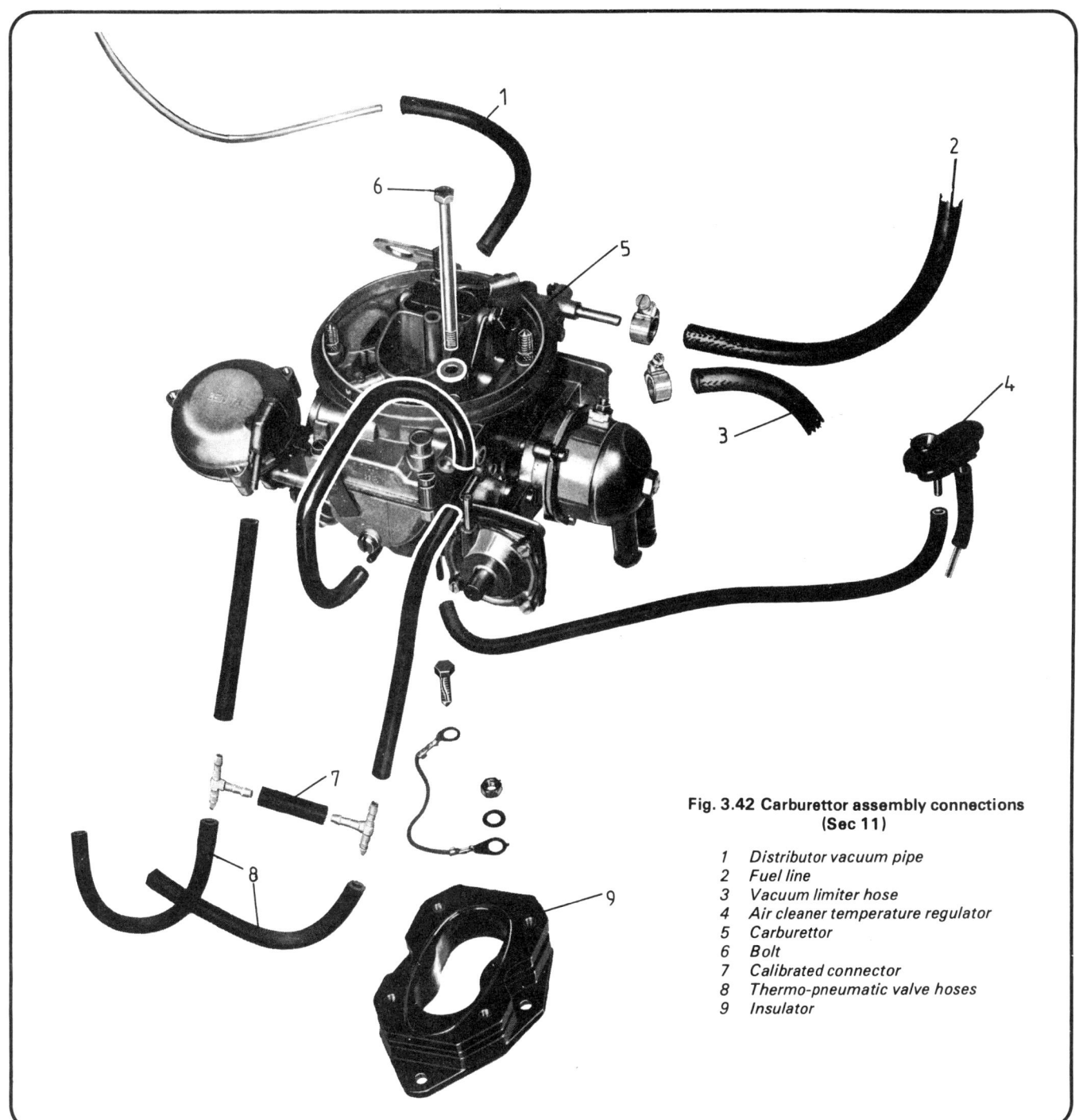

Fig. 3.42 Carburettor assembly connections (Sec 11)

1   *Distributor vacuum pipe*
2   *Fuel line*
3   *Vacuum limiter hose*
4   *Air cleaner temperature regulator*
5   *Carburettor*
6   *Bolt*
7   *Calibrated connector*
8   *Thermo-pneumatic valve hoses*
9   *Insulator*

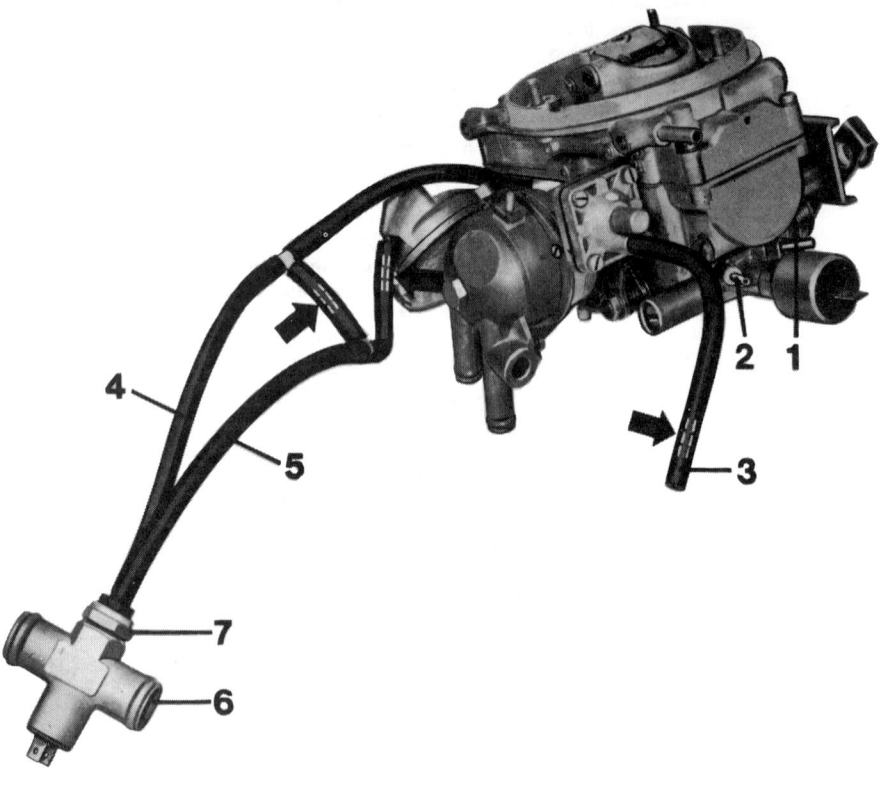

Fig. 3.43 Vacuum connections
(manual transmission) (Sec 11)

1   Air cleaner temperature control unit
2   Distributor vacuum unit
3   Brake servo
4   Thermo-pneumatic valve – angled
     pipe
5   Thermo-pneumatic valve – straight
     pipe
6   Choke thermo-switch
7   Carburettor 2nd Stage thermo-
     pneumatic valve

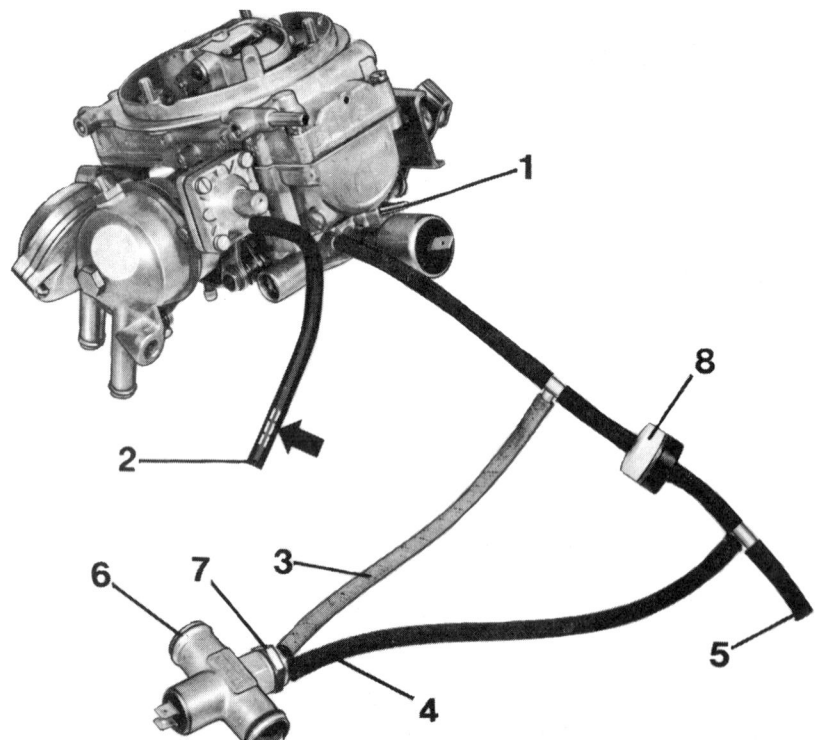

Fig. 3.44 Vacuum connections
(automatic transmission) (Sec 11)

1   Air cleaner temperature control unit
2   Brake servo
3   Thermo-pneumatic valve angled pipe
4   Thermo-pneumatic valve – straight
     pipe
5   Distributor vacuum unit
6   Choke thermo-switch
7   Thermo-pneumatic valve for vacuum
     advance of ignition
8   Check valve for vacuum advance of
     ignition

12 Inlet manifold – removing and refitting

1   Remove the carburettor as described in the previous Section.
2   Unclamp and remove the four coolant hoses connected to the inlet manifold, the vacuum hose to the brake servo and any other vacuum hoses which may be connected.
3   On vehicles fitted with an electrical preheater in the manifold,

disconnect its plug from the wiring harness.
4   Remove the bolts securing the inlet manifold to the cylinder head (photo) and remove the manifold and gasket.
5   When refitting the manifold, ensure that the mating faces are clean and use a new joint gasket. Tighten the securing bolts to the torque given in Specifications. Refit the hoses, tightening the clamps where appropriate and re-connect the preheater cable.

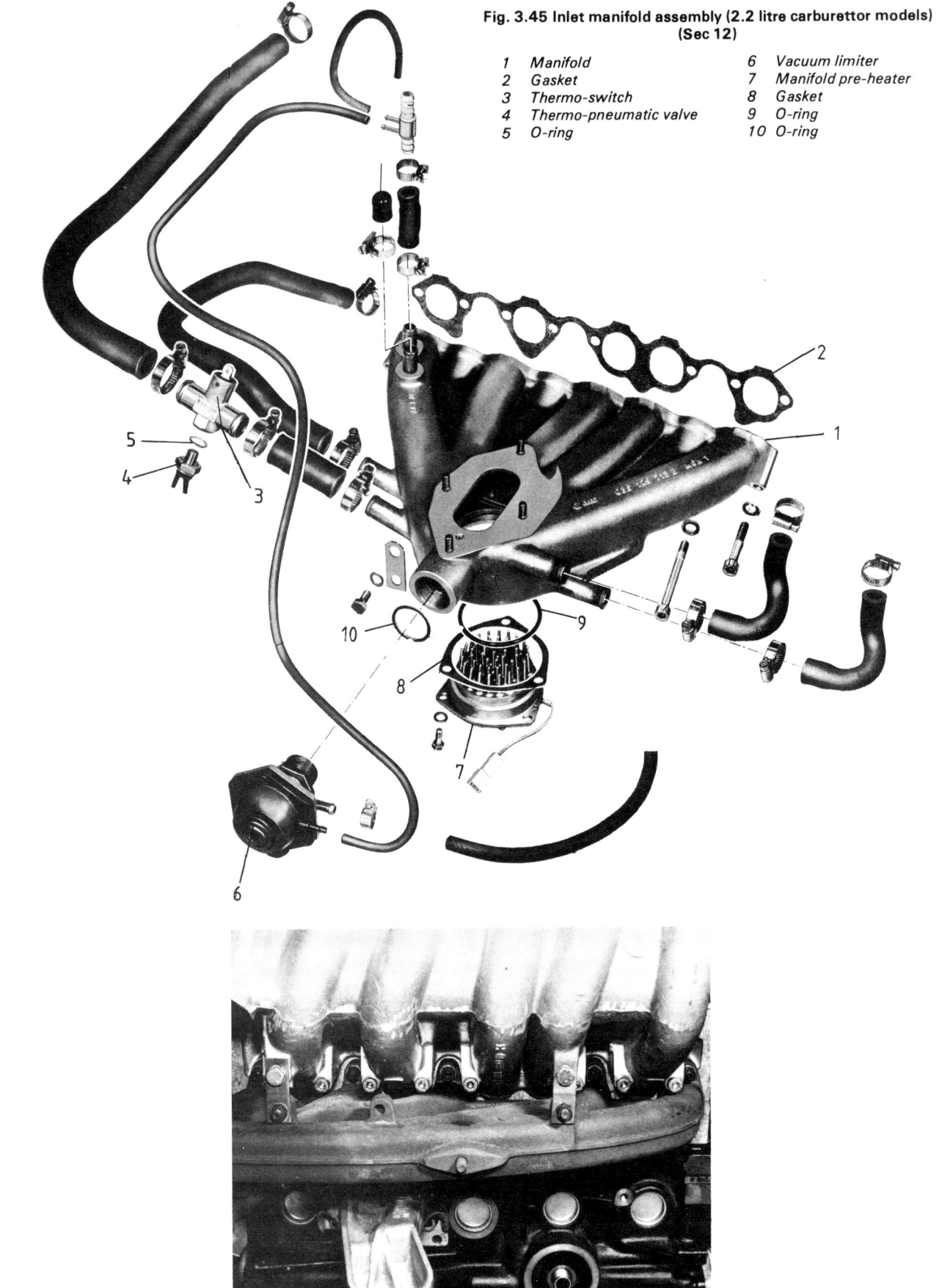

Fig. 3.45 Inlet manifold assembly (2.2 litre carburettor models) (Sec 12)

1 Manifold
2 Gasket
3 Thermo-switch
4 Thermo-pneumatic valve
5 O-ring
6 Vacuum limiter
7 Manifold pre-heater
8 Gasket
9 O-ring
10 O-ring

12.4 Inlet manifold bolts (2.2 litre)

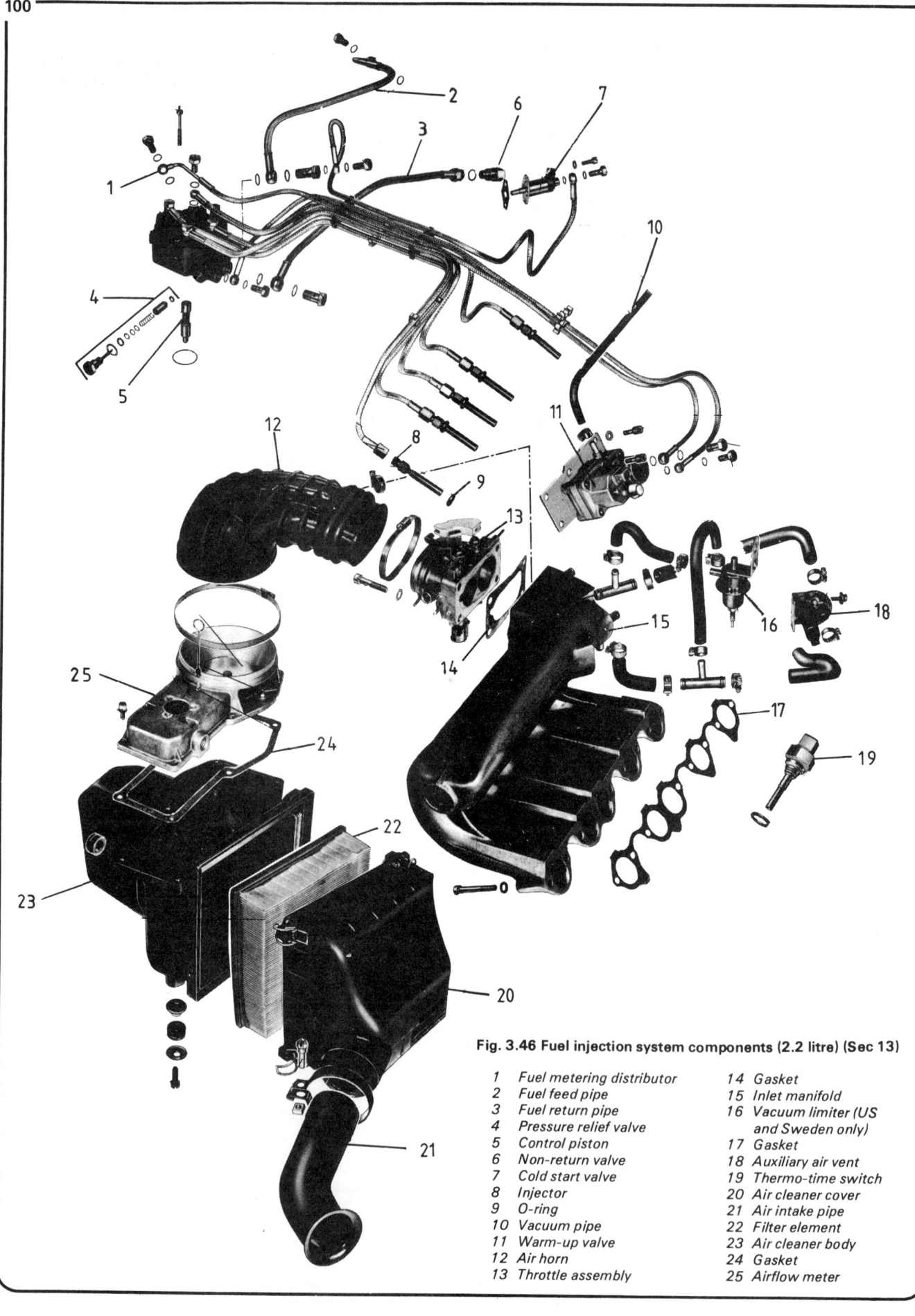

Fig. 3.46 Fuel injection system components (2.2 litre) (Sec 13)

1 Fuel metering distributor	14 Gasket
2 Fuel feed pipe	15 Inlet manifold
3 Fuel return pipe	16 Vacuum limiter (US
4 Pressure relief valve	and Sweden only)
5 Control piston	17 Gasket
6 Non-return valve	18 Auxiliary air vent
7 Cold start valve	19 Thermo-time switch
8 Injector	20 Air cleaner cover
9 O-ring	21 Air intake pipe
10 Vacuum pipe	22 Filter element
11 Warm-up valve	23 Air cleaner body
12 Air horn	24 Gasket
13 Throttle assembly	25 Airflow meter

13 Fuel injection system – general description

Although the fuel injection system is known as the "K-jetronic", it is not an electronically controlled system. The principle of the system is very simple and there are no specialised electronic components. There is an electrically driven fuel pump and there are electrical sensors and switches, but these are no different from those in general use on cars.

The following paragraphs describe the system and its various elements. Later Sections describe the tests which can be carried out to ensure whether a particular unit is functioning correctly, but dismantling and repair procedures of units are not generally given because repairs are not possible.

The system measures the amount of air entering the engine and determines the amount of fuel which needs to be mixed with the air to give the correct combustion mixture for the particular conditions of engine operation. The fuel is sprayed continuously by an injection nozzle to the inlet channel of each cylinder (photo). This fuel and air is drawn into the cylinders when the inlet valves open.

Air flow meter

1   This measures the volume of air entering the engine and relies on the principle that a circular disc, when placed in a funnel through which a current of air is passing, will rise until the weight of the disc is equal to the force on its lower surface which the air creates. If the volume of air flowing is increased and the plate were to remain in the same place, the rate of flow of air through the gap between the cone and the plate would increase and the force on the plate would increase.

2   If the plate is free to move, then as the force on the plate increases, the plate rises in the cone and the area between the edge of the plate and the edge of the cone increases, until the rate of air-flow and hence the force on the plate, becomes the same as it was at the former lower flow rate and smaller area. Thus the height of the plate is a measure of the volume of air entering the engine.

3   The airflow meter consists of an air funnel with a sensor plate mounted on a lever which is supported at its fulcrum. The weight of the airflow sensor plate and its lever are balanced by a counterweight and the upward force on the sensor plate is opposed by a plunger. The plunger, which moves up and down as a result of the variations in airflow, is surrounded by a sleeve having vertical slots in it. The vertical movement of the plunger uncovers a greater or lesser length of the slots, which meters the fuel to the injection valves.

4   The sides of the air funnel are not a pure cone because optimum operation of the engine requires a different air/fuel ratio under different conditions such as idling, part load and full load. By making parts of the funnel steeper than the basic shape, a richer mixture can be provided for at idling and full load. By making the funnel flatter than the basic shape, a leaner mixture can be provided.

Fuel supply

5   Fuel is pumped continuously while the engine is running by a roller cell pump running at constant speed; excess fuel is returned to the tank. The fuel pump is operated when the ignition switch is in the *START* position, but once the starter is released a switch connected to the air plate prevents the pump from operating unless the engine is running.

6   The fuel line to the fuel supply valve incorporates a filter and also a fuel accumulator. The function of the accumulator is to maintain pressure in the fuel system after the engine has been switched off and so give good hot re-starting.

7   Associated with the fuel accumulator is a pressure regulator which is an integral part of the fuel metering device. When the engine is switched off, the pressure regulator lets the pressure to the injection valves fall rapidly to cut off the fuel flow through them and so prevent the engine from "dieseling" or "running on". The valve closes at just below the opening pressure of the injector valves and this pressure is then maintained by the pressure accumulator.

Fuel distributor

8   The fuel distributor is mounted on the air metering device and is controlled by the vertical movement of the airflow sensor plate. It consists of a spool valve which moves vertically in a sleeve, the sleeve having as many vertical slots around its circumference as there are cylinders on the engine.

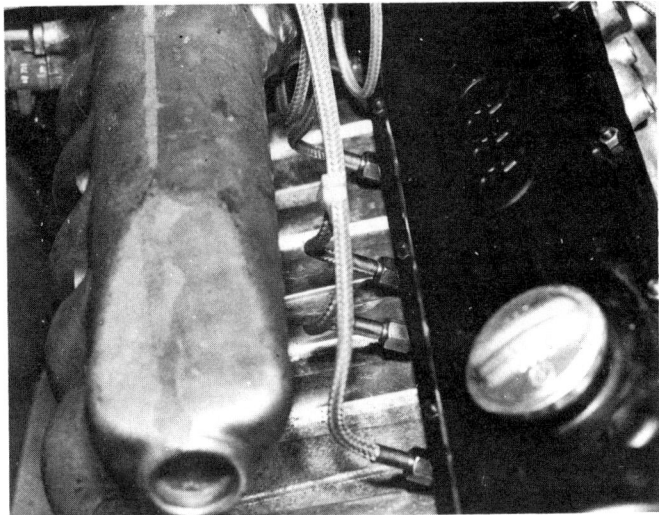

13.3 Inlet manifold and injectors (2.2 litre)

9   The spool valve is subjected to hydraulic pressure on the upper end and this balances the pressure on the air plate which is applied to the bottom of the valve by a plunger. As the spool valve rises and falls it uncovers a greater or lesser length of metering slot and so controls the volume of fuel fed to each injector.

10   Each metering slot has a differential pressure valve, which ensures that the difference in pressure between the two sides of the slot is always the same. Because the drop in pressure across the metering slot is unaffected by the length of slot exposed, the amount of fuel flowing depends only on the exposed area of the slots.

Compensation units

11   For cold starting and during warming up, additional devices are required to adjust the fuel supply to the different fuel requirements of the engine under these conditions.

Cold start valve

12   The cold start valve is mounted in the intake manifold and sprays additional fuel into the manifold during cold starting. The valve is solenoid operated and is controlled by a thermo-time switch in the engine cooling system. The thermo-time switch is actuated for a period which depends upon coolant temperature, the period decreasing with rise in coolant temperature. If the coolant temperature is high enough for the engine not to need additional fuel for starting, the switch does not operate.

Warm-up regulator

13   While warming up the engine needs a richer mixture to compensate for fuel which condenses on the cold walls of the inlet manifold and cylinder walls. It also needs more fuel to compensate for power lost because of increased friction losses and increased oil drag in a cold engine. The mixture is made richer during warming up by the warm-up regulator. This is a pressure regulator which lowers the pressure applied to the control plunger of the fuel regulator during warm-up. This reduced pressure causes the air flow plate to rise higher than it would do otherwise, thus uncovering a greater length of metering slot and making the mixture richer.

14   The valve is operated by a bi-metallic strip which is heated by an electric heater. When the engine is cold the bi-metallic strip presses against the delivery valve spring to reduce the pressure on the diaphragm and enlarge the discharge cross-section. This increase in cross-section results in a lowering of the pressure fed to the control plunger.

15   When the engine is started, the electrical heater of the bi-metallic strip is switched *ON*. As the strip warms it rises gradually until it ultimately rises free of the control spring plate and the valve spring becomes fully effective to give normal control pressure.

Auxiliary air device

16   Compensation for power lost by greater friction is compensated for by feeding a larger volume of fuel/air mixture to the engine than is

supplied by the normal opening of the throttle. The auxiliary air device by passes the throttle with a channel having a variable aperture valve in it. The aperture is varied by a pivoted plate controlled by a spring and a bi-metallic strip.

17   During cold starting the channel is open and increases the volume of fuel/air mixture passing to the engine, but as the bi-metallic strip bends it allows a control spring to pull the plate over the aperture until at normal operating temperature the aperture is closed. The heating of the bi-metallic strip is similar to that of the warm-up regulator described in paragraphs 14 and 15.

14 Fuel metering distributor – removing and refitting

1   Disconnect the battery terminals.
2   Ensure that the vehicle is in a well ventilated space and that there are no naked flames or other possible sources of ignition.
3   While holding a rag over the joint to prevent fuel from being sprayed out, loosen the control pressure line from the warm-up valve. The control pressure line is the one connected to the large union of the valve.
4   Mark each fuel line, and it's port on the fuel distributor. Carefully clean all dirt from around the fuel unions and distributor ports and then disconnect the fuel lines.
5   Unscrew and remove the connection of the pressure control line to the fuel metering distributor.
6   Remove the locking plug from the CO adjusting screw, then remove the three screws securing the fuel metering distributor (Fig. 3.47).
7   Lift off the fuel metering distributor, taking care that the metering plunger does not fall out (Fig. 3.48). If the plunger does fall out accidentally, clean it in petrol and then re-insert it with its chamfered end downwards.
8   Before refitting the metering distributor, ensure that the plunger moves up and down freely. If the plunger sticks, the distributor must be renewed, because the plunger cannot be repaired or replaced separately.
9   Refit the distributor, using a new sealing ring, and after tightening the screws, lock them with paint.
10 Refit the fuel lines and the cap of the CO adjusting screw and tighten the union on the warm-up valve.

15 Airflow meter – removing and refitting

1   Remove the fuel lines from the distributor, as described in paragraphs 1 to 5 of the previous Section.
2   Loosen the clamps at the air cleaner and throttle assembly ends of the air scoop and take off the air scoop.
3   Remove the six socket head bolts securing the airflow meter to the air cleaner and lift off the airflow meter and fuel metering distributor.
4   The fuel metering plunger should be prevented from falling out when the fuel metering distributor is removed from the airflow meter (see previous Section).
5   Refitting is the reverse of removing, but it is necessary to use a new gasket between the airflow meter and the air cleaner.

16 Pressure relief valve – removing, servicing and refitting

1   Release the pressure on the fuel system, as described in paragraphs 1 to 3 of Section 14.
2   Unscrew the non-return valve plug and remove the plug and its sealing washer.
3   Take out the O-ring, shims, spring, plunger and O-ring in that order.
4   When refitting the assembly, use new O-rings and ensure that all the shims which were removed are refitted.

17 Deceleration valve – checking

1   The deceleration valve is only fitted to models for Sweden and US (except California), having manual transmissions.
2   Unclamp and remove the hose from the side pipe of the deceleration valve and plug the hose.

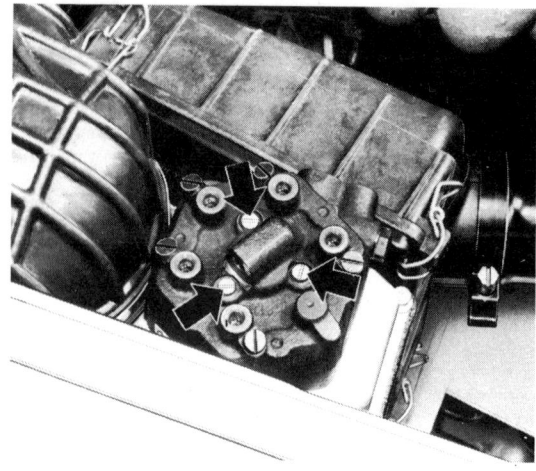

Fig. 3.47 Fuel metering distributor fixing screws (arrowed) (Sec 14)

Fig. 3.48 Restraining the metering plunger (Sec 14)

Fig. 3.49 Airflow meter fixing bolts (arrowed) (Sec 15)

3   Start the engine and run it at 3000 rpm for a few seconds.
4   Let the throttle valve snap shut and at the same time put a finger over the side pipe of the deceleration valve to check for suction.
5   Disconnect the vacuum hose to the bottom of the deceleration valve at the T-connector (Fig. 3.51).
6   Repeat the procedure of starting the engine and testing for suction as described in paragraphs 3 and 4, but this time there should not be

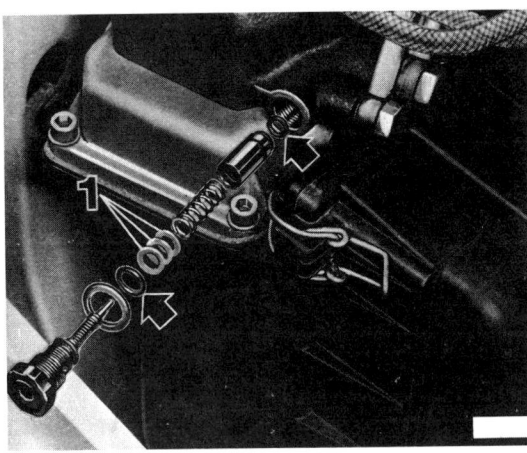

Fig. 3.50 Pressure relief valve components (Sec 16)

1   Shims

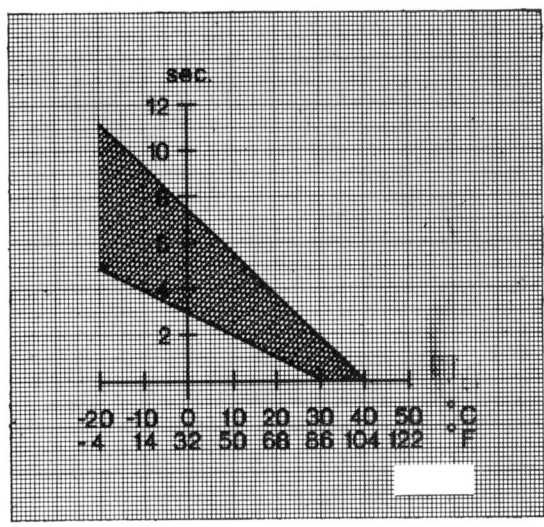

Fig. 3.52 Thermoswitch time/temperature characteristic (Sec 18)

(Shaded area shows switch ON period)

Fig. 3.51 Deceleration valve (side pipe and T-connection arrowed)
(Sec 17)

Fig. 3.53 Checking the cold start valve (Sec 19)

suction. If suction is felt when the vacuum pipe is disconnected, the deceleration valve is defective and a new one must be fitted.

18 Thermo-time switch – checking

1   The thermo-time switch energises the cold start valve for a short time on starting and the time for which the valve is switched on depends upon engine temperature (as shown in Fig. 3.52).
2   Pull the connector off the cold start valve and connect a test lamp across the contacts of the connector.
3   Pull the high tension lead off the centre of the distributor and connect the lead to earth.
4   Operate the starter for 10 seconds and note the interval before the test lamp lights and the period for which it remains alight. Reference to the graph will show that at a coolant temperature of 30°C (86°F) the lamp should light immediately and stay on for two seconds.
5   The check should not be carried out if the coolant temperature is above 30°C (86°F).
6   Refit the high tension lead onto the distributor, and reconnect the lead to the cold start valve.

19 Cold start valve – checking

1   Ensure that the coolant temperature is below 30°C (86°F) and

that the car battery is fully charged.
2   Pull the high tension lead off the centre of the distributor and connect the lead to earth.
3   Pull the connectors off the warm-up valve and the auxiliary air unit.
4   Remove the two bolts securing the cold start valve to the inlet manifold and remove the valve, taking care not to damage the gasket.
5   With fuel line and electrical connections connected to the valve, hold the valve over a glass jar and operate the starter for 10 seconds. The cold start valve should produce an even cone of spray during the time the thermo-time switch is ON.
6   After completing the checks refit the valve and reconnect the leads that were disturbed.

20 Warm-up valve – checking

1   With the engine cold, pull the connectors off the warm-up valve and the auxiliary air unit.
2   Connect a voltmeter across the terminals of the warm-up valve connector (photo) and switch the ignition ON. The voltage across the terminals should be a minimum of 11.5 volts.
3   Switch the ignition OFF and connect an ohmmeter across the terminals of the warm-up valve. If the meter does not indicate a resistance of about 20 ohms, the heater coil is defective and a new valve must be fitted.

20.2 Warm-up valve electrical connector

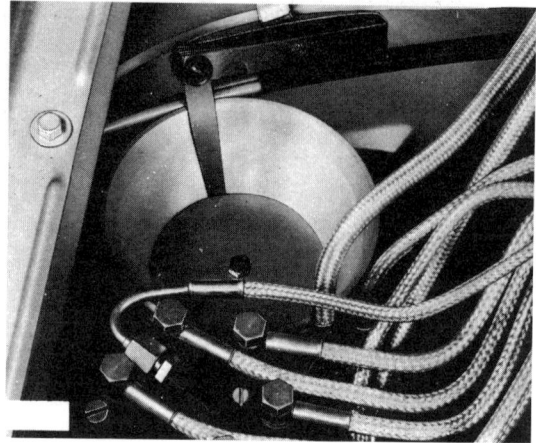

Fig. 3.54 Centring the airflow plate (Sec 21)

21 Air lever and control plunger – checking

1   For the correct mixture to be supplied to the engine it is essential that the sensor plate is central in the venturi and that its height is correct.

2   Loosen the hose clips at each end of the air scoop and remove the scoop. If the sensor plate appears to be off centre, loosen its centre screw and carefully run a 0.10 mm (0.004 in) feeler gauge round the edge of the plate to centralise it, then re-tighten the bolt.

3   Raise the airflow sensor plate and then quickly move it to its rest position. No resistance should be felt to this movement and if there is resistance the airflow meter is defective and a new one must be fitted.

4   If the sensor plate can be moved downwards easily, but has a strong resistance to upward movement, the control plunger is sticking. Remove the fuel distributor (Section 14) and clean the control plunger in petrol. If this does not cure the problem, a new fuel distributor must be fitted.

5   Release the pressure on the fuel distributor, as described in Section 14 and then check the rest position of the airflow sensor plate. The upper edge of the plate should be flush with the bottom edge of the air cone (Fig. 3.56). It is permissible for the plate to be lower than the edge by not more than 0.5 mm (0.020 in), but if higher, or lower than the permissible limit, the plate must be adjusted.

6   Adjust the height of the plate by lifting it and bending the wire clips attaching the plate to the balance arm (Fig. 3.57), but take care not to scratch or damage the surface of the air cone.

7   After making the adjustment, tighten the warm-up valve union and check the idle speed and CO concentration.

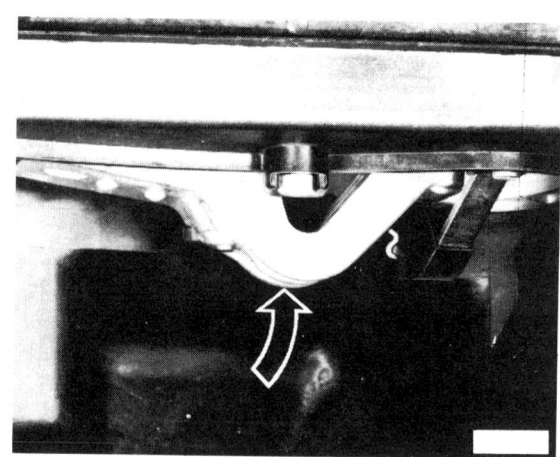

Fig. 3.55 Lifting the airflow plate (Sec 21)

22 Idle speed adjustment (injection models)

1   Run the engine until the oil temperature is at least 60°C (140°F).

2   Check the ignition timing (Chapter 4, Section 7), adjusting it if necessary.

3   If the car is fitted with an air conditioner, this must be turned OFF, but the main headlights should be turned ON.

4   Remove the locking cap from the adjustment screw on the throttle assembly (Fig. 3.58) and turn the screw to achieve the slow running speed given in the Specifications.

5   After making the adjustment, refit the locking cap over the adjustment screw.

23 Idle mixture (CO) adjustment (injection models)

1   The idle CO adjustment screw alters the height of the fuel metering distributor plunger relative to the air control plate of the airflow meter.

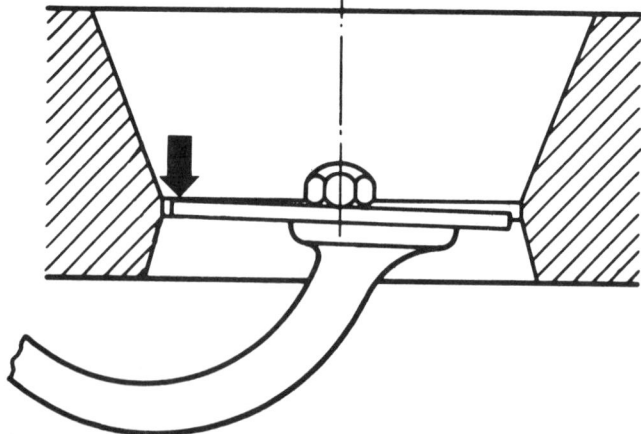

Fig. 3.56 Rest position of airflow plate (Sec 21)

2   The screw is accessible by removing the locking plug from between the air duct scoop and the fuel metering distributor on the airflow meter casing.

3   Although a special tool is recommended for this adjustment, it can be made using a long, thin screwdriver.

4   Ensure that the engine is running under the same conditions as those necessary for adjusting the idling speed (see previous Section) and that the idling speed is correct.

5   Connect the exhaust gas analyser to the tail pipe as directed by

Fig. 3.57 Airflow plate height adjuster (arrowed) (Sec 21)

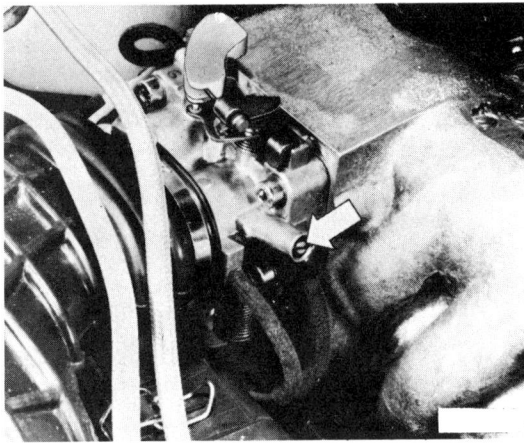

Fig. 3.58 Idle speed adjusting screw (arrowed) (Sec 22)

25.1 Fuel pump (B) and fuel accumulator (A) (2.2 litre)

the equipment manufacture and read the CO level.
6   Turn the adjusting screw clockwise to raise the percentage of CO and anti-clockwise to lower it. It is important that the adjustment is made without pressing down on the adjusting screw, because this will move the airflow sensor plate and affect the adjustment.
7   Remove the tool, accelerate the engine briefly and re-check. If the

tool is not removed before the engine is accelerated there is a danger of the tool becoming jammed and getting bent.

24 Mechanical fuel pump – removing, servicing and refitting

1   When a mechanical fuel pump is fitted, it is attached to the left-hand side of the engine. On the 1.6 litre engine it is mounted on the crankcase and the sump operating lever is in contact with a cam on the intermediate shaft. On the 2.0 litre and 2.2 litre engine the fuel pump is attached to the cylinder head and the pump operating plunger is in contact with the camshaft.
2   Disconnect the battery leads.
3   Ensure that the car is in a well ventilated place and that there is no danger of ignition from sparks, or naked flames. Never work on any part of a fuel system when the car is over an inspection pit.
4   Unclamp and disconnect the fuel lines from the pump. Remove the two securing bolts and lift the pump off.
5   The pump is not repairable and the only servicing operation possible is cleaning the filter. To do this, remove the screw from the centre of the pump and take off the cover, sealing ring and filter.
6   Clean the pump cover with a lint-free cloth and wash the filter in petrol.
7   Refit the filter, then a new sealing ring and finally the cover. When fitting the cover, the notch on its rim must engage in the corresponding recess in the pump body. Tighten the centre screw firmly, but do not distort the pump cover.
8   When fitting the pump to the engine, note that the sealing flange is fitted in contact with the engine, then follows the sealing ring and then the pump.
9   When offering up the pump to the engine, ensure that its lever, or plunger fits correctly against the cam, not under it.
10 Bolt the pump in place and attach the suction (fuel inlet) pipe, which is the pipe from the fuel filter, to the pipe on the cover of the pump.
11 Place a container against the pump delivery pipe, re-connect the battery leads and disconnect and earth the high tension cable from the ignition coil to the centre of the distributor to prevent the engine firing.
12 With an assistant operating the starter for a few seconds check that the pump is delivering regular spurts of fuel.
13 If satisfactory, fit the pump delivery hose and tighten the clamps.

25 Electric fuel pump – removing, testing and refitting

1   The electric fuel pump is mounted beneath the vehicle and alongside the fuel tank (photo). It is a sealed unit and the brushes and commutator are not accessible for servicing. The only replacement part available is the check valve on the fuel outlet.
2   To remove the pump, first ensure that the car is in a well ventilated place and that there is no danger of ignition from sparks, or naked flames. Never work on any part of a fuel system when the car is over an inspection pit.
3   Disconnect the battery leads and then disconnect the wires from the pump, noting which wire is connected to which terminal (Fig. 3.59).
4   Thoroughly clean all dirt away from the fuel pipe unions on the pump. Disconnect the fuel pipe from the fuel tank to the pump and seal the end of the pipe to prevent fuel leakage. Disconnect the fuel pipe from the outlet check valve on the pump and cover the pipe end to keep out dirt.
5   Remove the two bolts securing the fuel pump clamp and remove the clamp.
6   The outlet check valve may be unscrewed if necessary, but the pump body must not be held in a vice. Either grip the hexagon of the valve in the vice and turn the pump by hand, or use a spanner on the valve and a strap wrench on the pump body (Fig. 3.60).
7   The pump is designed to work with all its moving parts immersed in petrol and it will be damaged irreparably if it is run without being connected to the fuel system.
8   The capacity of the pump is much greater than the fuel requirement of the engine and it is unlikely that pump output will fall to a point where it is inadequate. If the pump is suspect, test it while on the vehicle as follows.
9   Measure the voltage across the pump terminals when the pump is running. If the voltage is less than 11.5 volts, check the condition of the battery and the cleanliness and tightness of the pump connections.

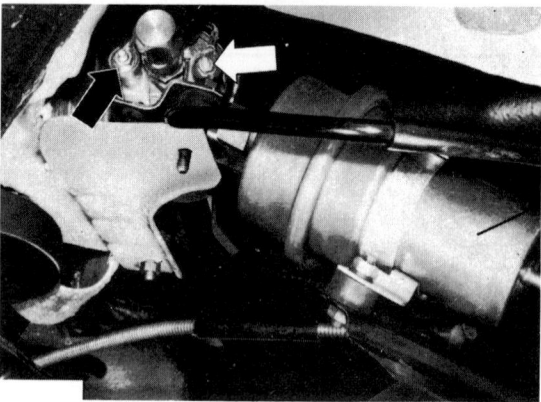

Fig. 3.59 Fuel pump electrical connections (arrowed) (Sec 25)

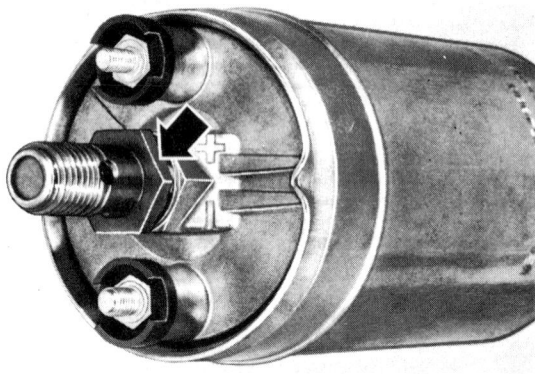

Fig. 3.60 Removing the pump outlet valve (Sec 25)

B   *Fuel accumulator*

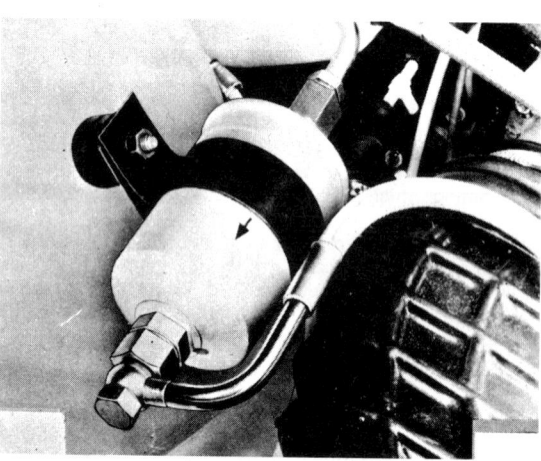

Fig. 3.61 Fuel filter (arrow denotes direction of flow) (Sec 26)

10   Connect an ammeter into the pump circuit, again run the pump and check that it is taking a current of about 8.5 amps. If the current exceeds this figure a new pump must be fitted.

11   If the pump gives satisfactory voltage and current readings but its output is still suspect, check that the fuel filter is connected so that the arrow on it points in the direction of flow and that a new filter was fitted at the correct maintenance interval.

26 Fuel filter – fitting

1   A disposable fuel filter is fitted in the fuel line. On carburettor engines it is fitted in the suction line to the pump and hangs in the fuel line near the pump. On injection models it is held by a clip to the front bulkhead.

2   On carburettor models, pull the hoses off the filter. Because the filter is on the suction side of the pump the hoses do not normally have hose clips. Fit a new filter, taking care to ensure that the arrow on it points in the direction of fuel flow.

3   On injection models, unscrew the pipe unions from each end of the filter. Unscrew the nut securing the filter mounting bracket to the bulkhead and take off the filter and bracket.

4   Open the filter bracket until it can be slipped off the filter.

5   Fit the bracket to the new filter so that when the fixing hole in the bracket is uppermost, the curved end of the filter is to the left.

6   Fit the bracket to the bulkhead and reconnect the fuel pipes. If the bracket has been fitted as above, the pipe connections should be correct, but check that the arrow on the filter points in the direction of fuel flow.

27 Fuel tank breather valve – removing, checking and refitting

1   Pull the three hoses off the valve (photo) and then unclip the valve from its bracket.

2   To test the valve, plug the centre connection of the valve and attach a piece of tubing to the top connection. Put the open end of the tubing in a glass of water and while holding the valve vertically blow into the bottom connection of the valve.

3   When the valve is vertical there should be some resistance to blowing and air bubbles should emerge from the immersed end of the tube.

4   While still blowing into the bottom connection, tilt the valve to an angle of 45°. Bubbles should continue to be seen, but the flow of air should be reduced.

5   If the valve is satisfactory refit it to its bracket and attach the hoses. The correct connections for the three hoses are shown in Fig. 3.62.

28 Fuel tank – removing and refitting

1   Empty the fuel tank as far as possible by normal usage.

2   With the car in a well ventilated place, free of any naked flames, or sources of ignition, disconnect the battery leads and jack the rear of the car as high as possible. Support the rear of the car on axle-stands and chock the front wheels. Removing the fuel tank should not be done with the car over a pit because of the danger of the pit becoming

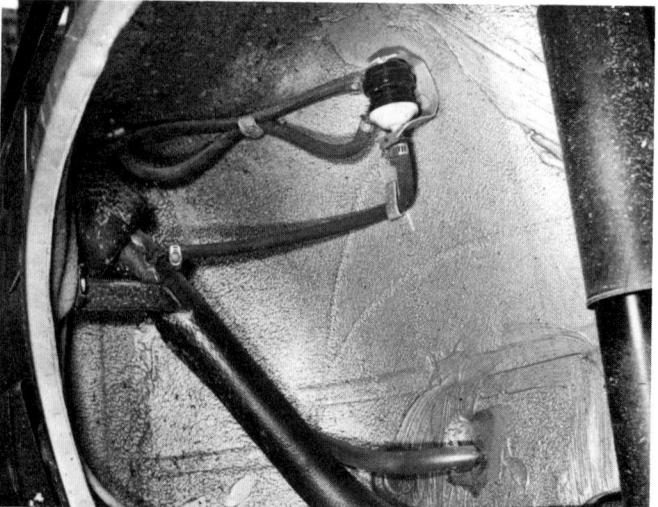

27.1 Fuel tank breather valve location

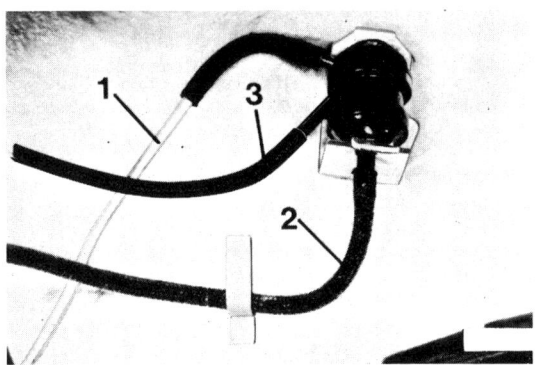

Fig. 3.62 Fuel tank breather valve connections (Sec 27)

1   Hose to charcoal filter   3   Hose to fuel tank
2   Hose to fuel filler neck

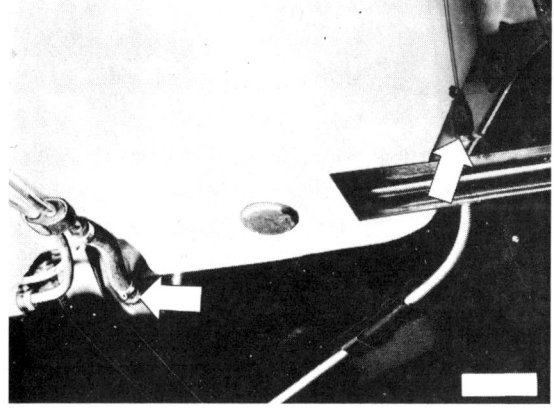

Fig. 3.63 Handbrake and fuel pipe connections to tank (arrowed)
(Sec 28)

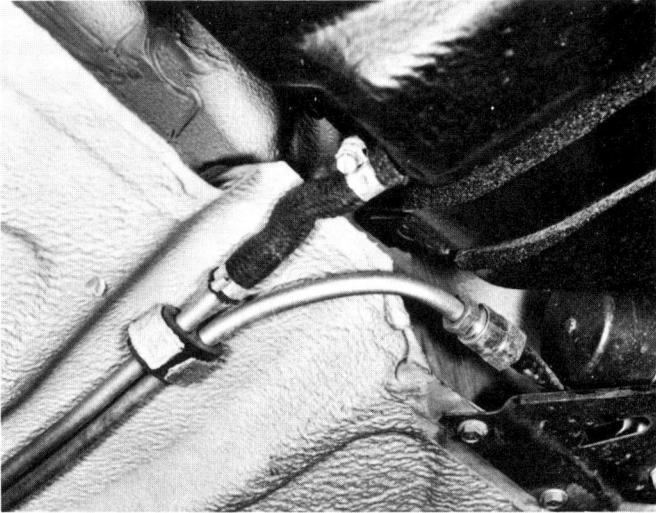

28.4 Fuel tank pipe connections

28.5 Fuel tank straps and hose connections

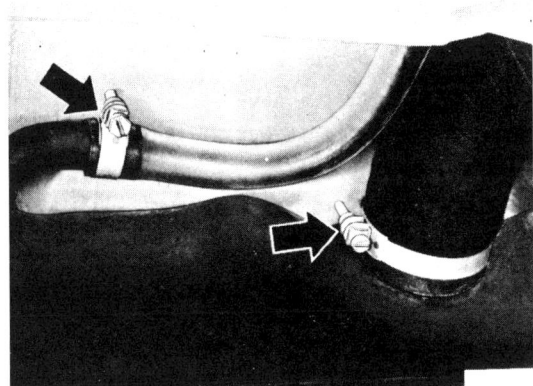

Fig. 3.64 Vent hose and filler pipe connections (Sec 28)

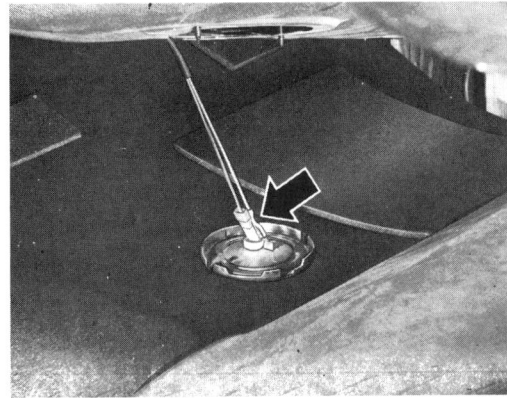

Fig. 3.65 Fuel tank sender unit connections (Sec 28)

filled with inflammable vapour.

3   Disconnect the handbrake cable from its mounting (Fig. 3.63).
4   Have ready a suitable metal container and a funnel to collect the fuel which runs out and then loosen the clips and pull the fuel lines off the tank (photo). Plug both the tank pipes and the hoses when the fuel has finished draining and store the drained fuel in a safe place.
5   Loosen the clamps on the vent hose and filler pipe (photo) and detach the hose and pipe from the tank.

6   Prop the tank and then remove the nut and washer from each of the two support straps. Swing the straps downwards clear of the tank.
7   Lower the tank until the cable connector on the fuel gauge sender unit is accessible and then disconnect the cable from the sender unit.
8   Remove the tank to a well ventilated place. Do not attempt to do any repair work on a tank unless it has been steamed out and made completely safe.

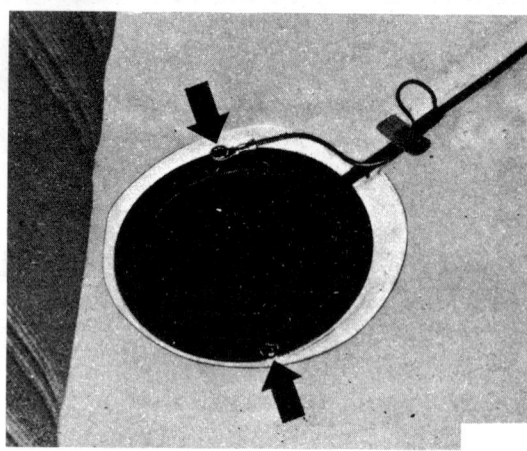

Fig. 3.66 Fuel tank sender unit cover (Sec 29)

29 Fuel gauge sender unit – removing and refitting

1   The fuel gauge sender unit may be withdrawn without removing the fuel tank.

2   Ensure that the tank is less than half full of fuel before removing the unit.

3   Remove the rear seat to reveal the cover plate (Fig. 3.66), then remove the two screws securing the cover and the earth wire.

4   Lift the cover to gain access to the sender unit and disconnect the cable from the unit.

5   Turn the clamp ring on the top of the tank unit. If no tool is available to fit the ring it may be tapped round with a hammer and soft drift.

6   Lift out the tank unit and its sealing washer.

7   Before refitting the unit, ensure that the joint faces are clean and use a new sealing washer.

8   Fit the tank unit so that the float arm is towards the front of the car and tighten the clamp ring so that the sealing ring is compressed slightly.

9   After refitting the unit, fill the fuel tank to well above the half way mark and check that the sealing ring is not leaking before refitting the cover plate and the rear seat cushion.

30 Emission control systems – general

1   Although careful attention to the correct ignition and mixture settings minimises the amount of harmful gases released by the exhaust system, the increasingly stringent legislation in some countries has made the introduction of additional systems necessary.

Crankcase ventilation system

2   Some of the products of combustion blow past the piston rings and enter the crankcase, from whence they would escape to the atmosphere if special precautions were not taken.

3   To prevent these gases from escaping to the atmosphere the crankcase breather is connected by a hose to the air cleaner so that the crankcase gases mix with the air/fuel mixture in the manifold and are consumed by the engine.

Exhaust gas recirculation

4   The principle of the system is that some of the hot exhaust gas is ducted from the exhaust manifold to the inlet manifold where it mixes with the fuel/air mixture and again enters the cylinders. This dilution of the inlet manifold mixture lowers the temperature of combustion in the cylinders and reduces the oxides of nitrogen content of the exhaust.

5   The system is controlled by a thermostatic valve and by a vacuum valve, controlled by inlet manifold pressure and system operation must be checked annually as a maintenance item.

6   Check the physical condition of the hoses of the system, looking for cracks and splits.

7   Run the engine and check that there are no leaks in the line from the EGR valve to the exhaust manifold.

8   Disconnect the yellow coloured vacuum hose from the straight connection of the temperature control valve and connect it to the T-piece on the hose to the inlet manifold. If the idling speed of the engine falls, or the engine stalls, the EGR valve is working properly. If the idle speed does not change, check that none of the hoses is blocked and if the hoses are clear the EGR valve is faulty and must be renewed.

Catalytic converter

9   This is only fitted to cars intended for California and it consists of an additional component in the exhaust pipe and silencer system.

10   The converter contains a catalyst which induces a chemical reaction to turn the carbon monoxide and hydrocarbons in the exhaust gas into carbon dioxide and water.

11   The converter does not require any maintenance, but should be examined periodically for signs of physical damage.

12   The catalyst in the converter can be poisoned and rendered ineffective by lead and other fuel additives and it is important that only unleaded petrol is used and that the fuel contains no harmful additives.

13   The catalytic converter contains a ceramic insert which is fragile and is liable to fracture if the converter is hit, or dropped.

Evaporative fuel control

14   To prevent petrol vapour escaping to the atmosphere the fuel tank is vented to a carbon canister. The fuel tank has an expansion chamber and vent lines which are arranged so that no fuel, or vapour can escape even though the car may be at a very high temperature, or may be driven or parked on a very steep incline.

15   The vent lines are connected to a canister containing carbon which absorbs the hydrocarbon vapours. When the engine is not running, fuel vapour collects in the carbon canister. When the engine is running, fresh air is sucked through the canister and the vapours are drawn from the canister through the air cleaner and into the engine, where they are burnt.

31 Emission control systems – operating precautions

1   The efficiency and reliability of the emission control system is dependent upon a number of operating factors and the following precautions must be observed.

2   Ensure that the fuel and ignition systems are serviced regularly and that only unleaded fuel, free from harmful additives is used.

3   Do not alter or remove any parts of the emission control system, or any controls which have been fitted to the vehicle to protect the environment.

4   Do not continue to use the car if it is misfiring, or showing any other symptoms of faulty operation of the engine.

5   Do not leave the car unattended when the engine is running, because any indications of improper operation will not be noticed and prolonged idling can cause the engine to overheat and be damaged.

6   If a catalytic converter is fitted, take care not to park the car on areas of dry grass or leaves, because the external temperature of the converter may be sufficient to ignite them.

7   Do not apply any additional undersealing, or rustproofing material to the exhaust system, or anywhere very near to it, because this may lead to a fire.

8   If a catalytic converter is fitted, the car must never be pushed or towed to start it and the engine must not be turned off if the car is moving. To do so would allow unburnt fuel to enter the converter and damage it.

32 Throttle cable – removing and refitting

1.6 litre engine (manual transmission)

1   Remove the interior trim (Chapter 12) to gain access to the accelerator pedal.

2   Unhook the throttle cable eye from the accelerator pedal, remove the circlip from each end of the accelerator pedal rod and remove the pedal.

3   Press in the sides of the throttle cable bearing (Fig. 3.67) and push the bearing through into the engine compartment.

4   Remove the air cleaner. Disengage the cable nipple from the throttle quadrant and pull the outer cable from the mounting bracket (Fig. 3.68).

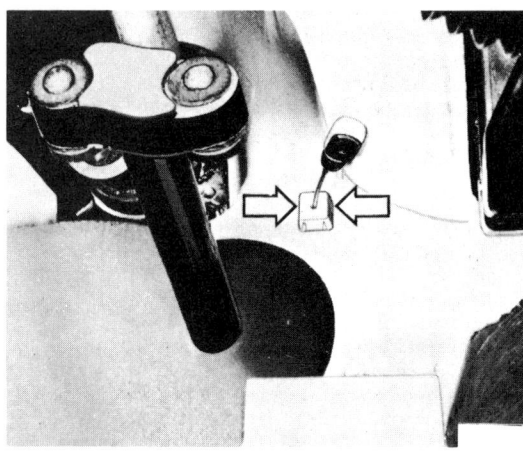

Fig. 3.67 Throttle cable bearing (1.6 litre) (Sec 32)

Fig. 3.68 Removing the throttle cable from the carburettor (1.6 litre) (Sec 32)

Fig. 3.69 Spring clip (arrowed) cable adjustment (1.6 litre) (Sec 32)

Fig. 3.70 Throttle cable routing (1.6 litre – automatic) (Sec 32)

Fig. 3.71 Cable attachment to throttle lever (1.6 litre – automatic) (Sec 32)

5 When fitting a throttle cable, first ensure that the cable is not kinked. Do not fit a cable which has been kinked as it is liable to break.

6 Remove the circlip from the outer cable adjuster, thread the outer cable through the bracket and attach the cable end to the throttle valve lever.

7 Route the cable through the engine compartment so that the cable is free of obstructions and is not bent sharply. Fit the cable bearing into

its cut out in the toe board.

8 Fit the accelerator pedal and set it to its idle position, with the pedal plate a distance of 60 mm (2.36 in) from the stop, then engage the cable eye on to the end of the pedal rod.

9 Check that the choke is fully open and the throttle is in its idle position, then insert the circlip into a slot in the throttle cable so that all the slack is taken up (Fig. 3.69).

10 Check that the accelerator pedal moves freely over the whole range of its travel and that when the accelerator pedal is at its full throttle position, the clearance between the throttle lever and its stop does not exceed 1 mm (0.039 in).

1.6 litre (automatic transmission)

11 The general procedure is similar to that for the manual transmission, but the cable first has to be guided between the engine subframe (Fig. 3.70) and the oil filter and the ball socket pressed on to the ball of the operating lever on the gearbox.

12 Guide the other end of the cable from the gearbox lever through the bracket on the carburettor and attach it to the throttle lever (Fig. 3.71).

13 Cable adjustment is made under the same choke and throttle conditions as the manual model, but adjustment is made on the screwed ferrule (Fig. 3.72).

14 When the cable has been adjusted check the movement of the pedal over its whole range, making sure that when the accelerator pedal is at the full throttle position (not pressed past the kickdown point), the take-up spring (Fig. 3.73) is not compressed.

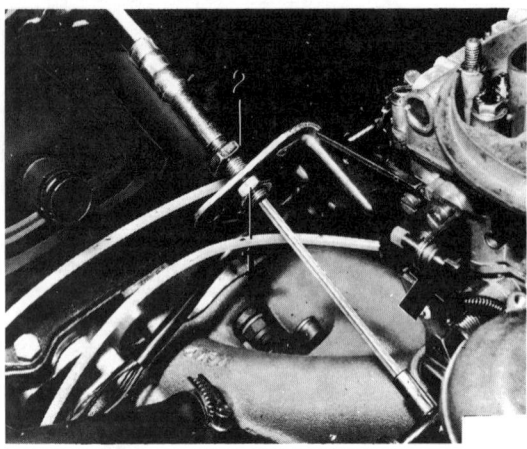

Fig. 3.72 Cable adjuster (1.6 litre – automatic) (Sec 32)

Fig. 3.73 Spring (arrowed) must not be compressed (1.6 litre – automatic) (Sec 32)

Fig. 3.74 Cable adjustment (2.0 litre – manual) (Sec 32)

2.0 litre (manual transmission)

15 The procedure is similar to that for the 1.6 litre, except that adjustment is made on the inner cable by means of the clamp screw on the throttle lever (Fig. 3.74).

2.0 litre (automatic transmission)

16 The procedure for fitting the cable to the pedal is the same as for the 1.6 litre model described previously.

17 Disconnect the connecting rod from the crank lever and after ensuring that the choke is fully open and the throttle at its idle position, it should be possible to insert the connecting rod pin without strain into its hole in the crank lever. If necessary loosen the adjusting plate clamp-bolt and move the rod until it can be inserted easily. Tighten the clamp-bolt and fit the clip to retain the end of the rod in the crank lever.

18 The link (Fig. 3.75) should not have been detached, but if it has been, hold the throttle lever against the idle adjustment stop screw, push the connecting link as far as it will go in the direction of the arrow, and then tighten the clamp screw.

19 Connect the accelerator pedal cable to the rocker lever (Fig. 3.76) and adjust it so that all slack is taken up.

20 Check the movement of the pedal over its entire range, making sure that when the accelerator pedal is at full throttle position (not pressed past the kickdown point), the take up spring (Fig. 3.78) is not compressed.

2.2 litre (manual transmission)

21 The arrangements are similar on both carburettor and injection models and the procedure is as described for the 1.6 litre engine.

2.2 litre (automatic transmission)

22 The throttle cable is connected to the gearbox lever and the throttle valve is controlled by rods and linkages between the gearbox lever and the throttle lever (Fig. 3.79).

23 Adjustment of the pedal and linkage is carried out as follows. On

Fig. 3.75 Connecting link adjustment (2.0 litre – automatic) (Sec 32)

Fig. 3.76 Throttle cable connections (2.0 litre – automatic) (Sec 32)

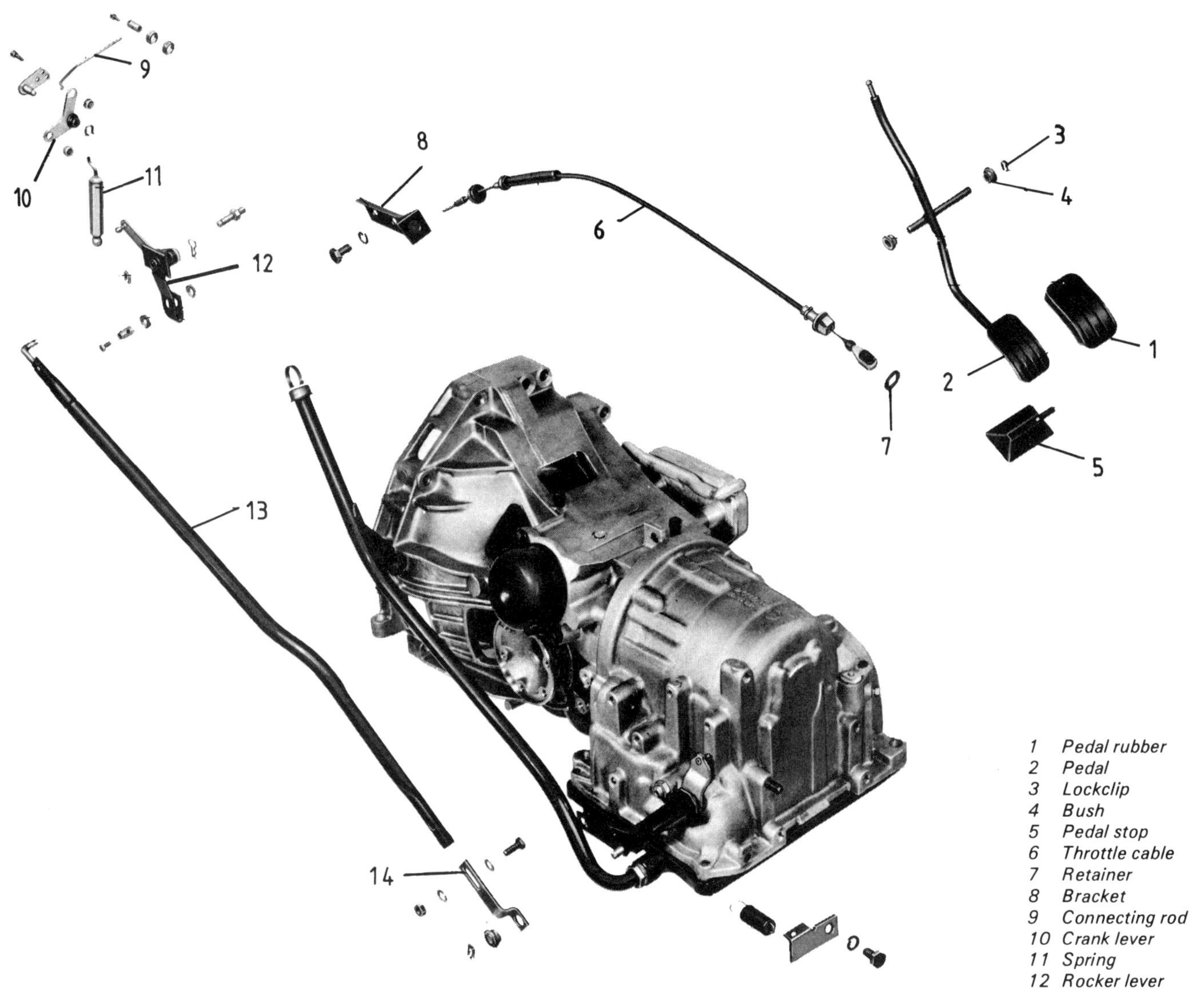

Fig. 3.77 Throttle cable arrangement (2.0 litre – automatic)
(Sec 32)

1   Pedal rubber
2   Pedal
3   Lockclip
4   Bush
5   Pedal stop
6   Throttle cable
7   Retainer
8   Bracket
9   Connecting rod
10 Crank lever
11 Spring
12 Rocker lever
13 Connecting rod
14 Adjusting plate

Fig. 3.78 Spring (arrowed) must not be compressed (2.0 litre –
automatic) (Sec 32)

carburettor engines it is first necessary to ensure that the choke is fully open.

24 Disconnect the throttle pull rod from the pull rod lever and set the throttle valve to its idling position.

25 Move the pull rod lever to its stop, by turning it anti-clockwise as far as possible (Fig. 3.80).

26 With both the throttle valve and the pull rod lever held in these positions, see if it is possible to fit the pull rod without any strain. If necessary move the balljoint adjuster until this can be achieved (Fig. 1.81).

27 With the clamp-bolt on the connecting rod slackened and with the throttle still in its idling position, move the gearbox lever to its idle speed position and then tighten the clamp-bolt.

28 Move the accelerator pedal to its idling position. On carburettor engines this is when the distance between the kickdown stop and the point of the pedal which contacts it is 60 mm (2.36 in). On fuel injection engines the distance between pedal and kickdown stop should be 75 to 80 mm (2.95 to 3.15 in).

29 Thread the throttle cable through the hole in the gearbox bracket and clip the square adaptor into its hole. Thread the inner cable through the hole in the clamping bush in the gearbox lever (Fig. 1.83).

30 With the accelerator pedal held in its idling position, apply tension to the throttle cable inner wire to take up all slack and secure it in this

Fig. 3.79 Throttle cable arrangement (2.2 litre – automatic)
(Sec 32)

1   Throttle assembly (injection
    models) or carburettor
2   Throttle cable
3   Retainer
4   Square adapter
5   Pedal rubber
6   Pedal
7   Pedal stop
8   Circlip
9   Bush
10 Engine bracket
11 Pull rod lever
12 Connecting rod lever
13 Pull rod
14 Connecting rod
15 Adjuster arm
16 Gearbox bracket
17 Clamping screw and bush
18 Return spring (not on US
    vehicles)

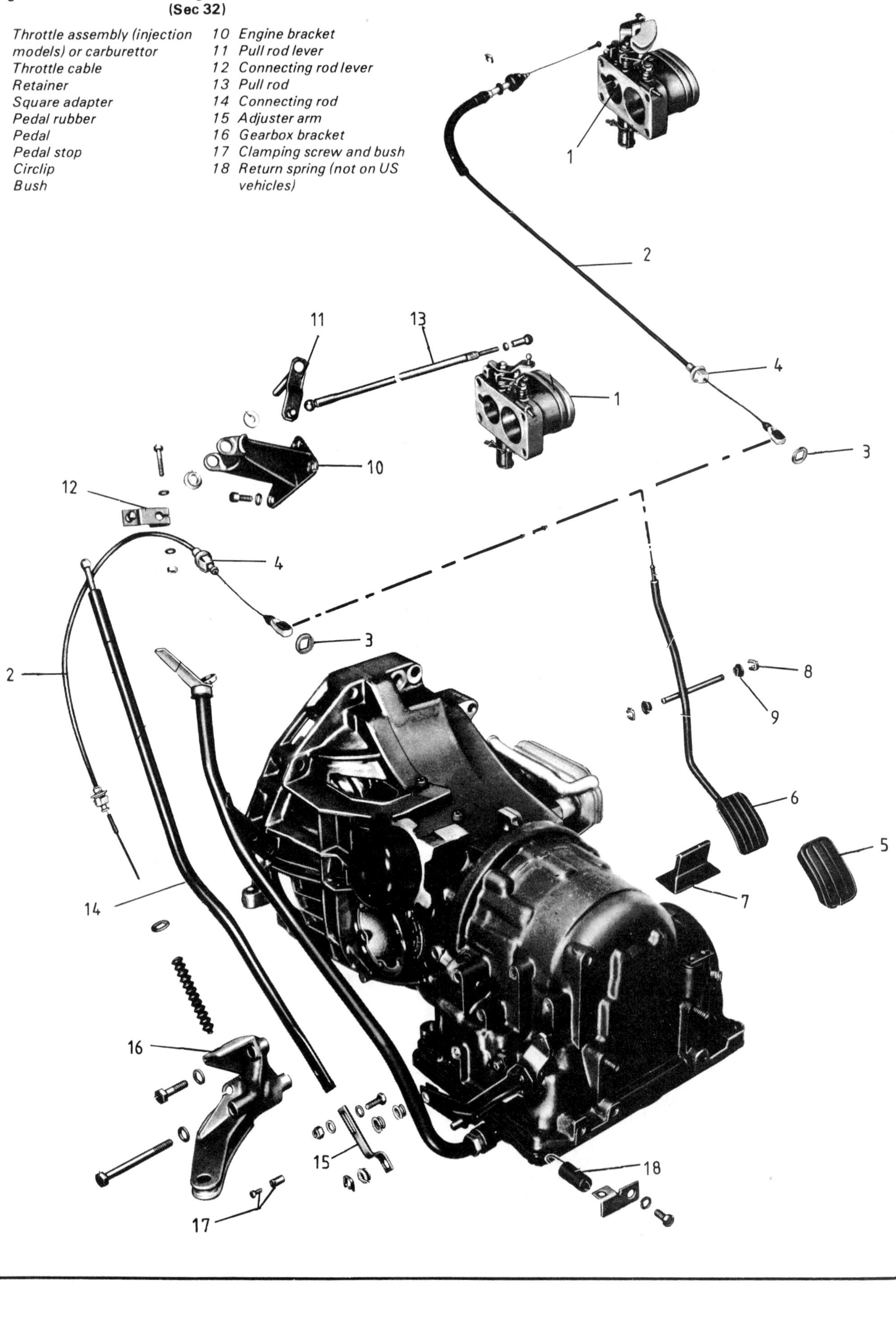

Fig. 3.80 Move pull rod lever to stop (2.2 litre – automatic) (Sec 32)

Fig. 3.81 Pull rod adjustment (2.2 litre – automatic) (Sec 32)

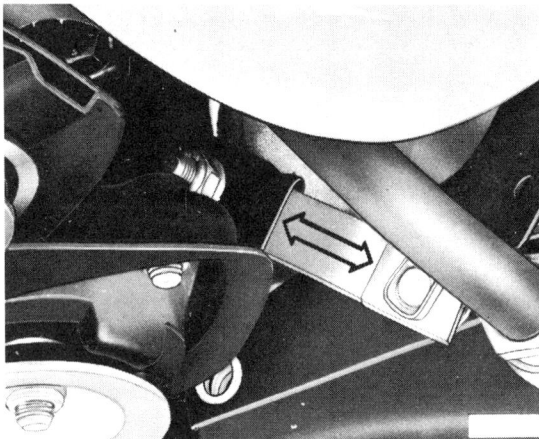

Fig. 3.82 Connecting rod adjustment (2.2 litre – automatic) (Sec 32)

Fig. 3.83 Throttle cable clamp (2.2 litre – automatic) (Sec 32)

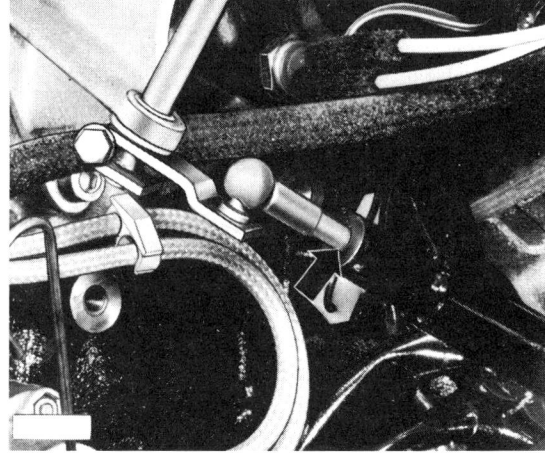

Fig. 3.84 Spring (arrowed) must not be compressed at full throttle setting (2.2 litre – automatic) (Sec 32)

position by tightening the clamping screw.
31 Check that the pedal moves freely and smoothly over its entire range and that when it is in the full throttle position (not pressed past the kickdown point), the throttle valve is fully open and that the kickdown spring is not compressed.

33 Exhaust system – general

1 The exhaust system varies considerably between different models, but the main silencer and rear silencer are similar on all models.
2 The front pipes on models fitted with automatic transmission are different from those for manual models with the 2.0 and 2.2 litre engines.
3 Models for California have a catalytic converter and an intermediate pipe in place of the front silencer. The catalytic converter must be handled with care and must never be banged, or dropped, because this may fracture its ceramic insert.

34 Exhaust system – removing and refitting

1 Before doing any dismantling work on the exhaust system, wait until the system has cooled down and then saturate the fixing bolts and joints with a proprietary anti-corrosion fluid.
2 When refitting the system new nuts and bolts should be used and it may be found easier to cut through the old bolts with a hack saw, rather than unscrew them.
3 When renewing any part of the exhaust system, it is usually easier to undo the manifold to front pipe joint and remove the complete system from the car, then separate the various pieces of the system, or cut out the defective part, using a hacksaw, to make removal easier.
4 Refit the system a piece at a time, starting with the front pipe. Use a new joint gasket and note that if it has a flanged side, the flanged side should face towards the exhaust pipe.
5 Smear all the joints with a proprietary exhaust sealing compound

Fig. 3.85 Exhaust system (1.6 litre) (Sec 34)

1 Exhaust manifold
2 Front pipe
3 Gearbox bracket
4 Clamp and bracket (automatic models)
5 Sealing ring
6 Main silencer
7 Rubber mounting
8 Rear silencer

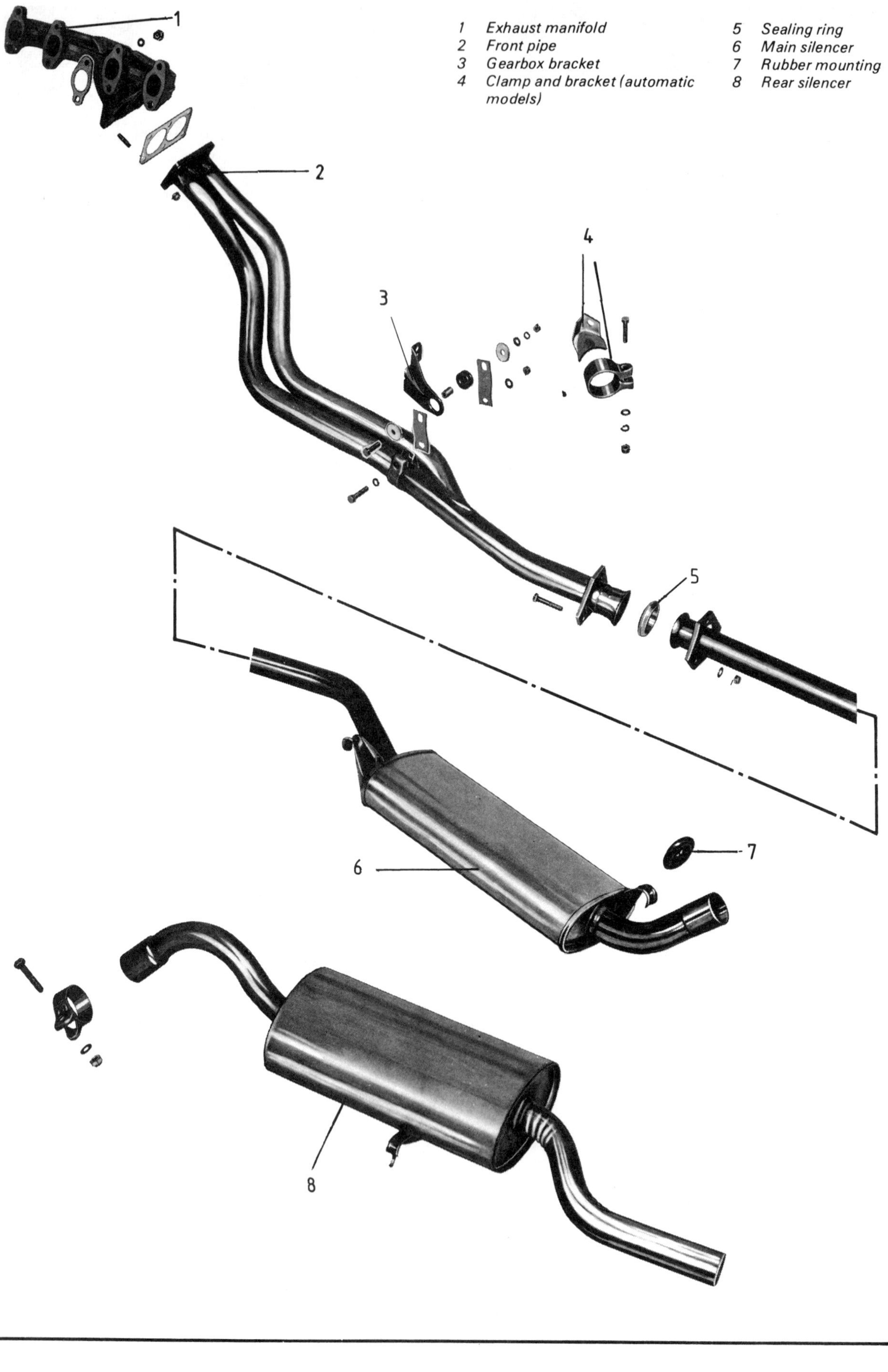

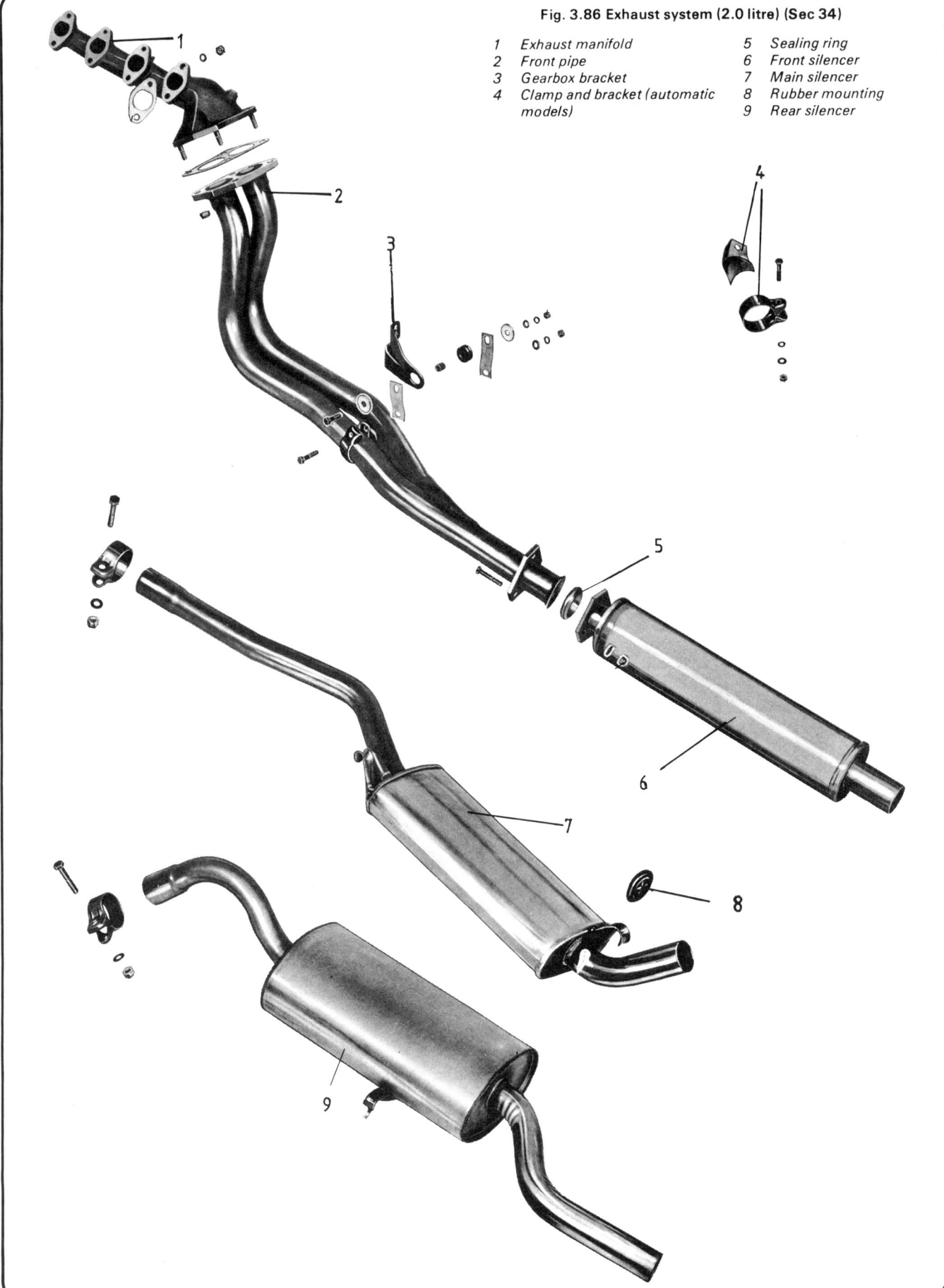

Fig. 3.86 Exhaust system (2.0 litre) (Sec 34)

1 Exhaust manifold
2 Front pipe
3 Gearbox bracket
4 Clamp and bracket (automatic models)
5 Sealing ring
6 Front silencer
7 Main silencer
8 Rubber mounting
9 Rear silencer

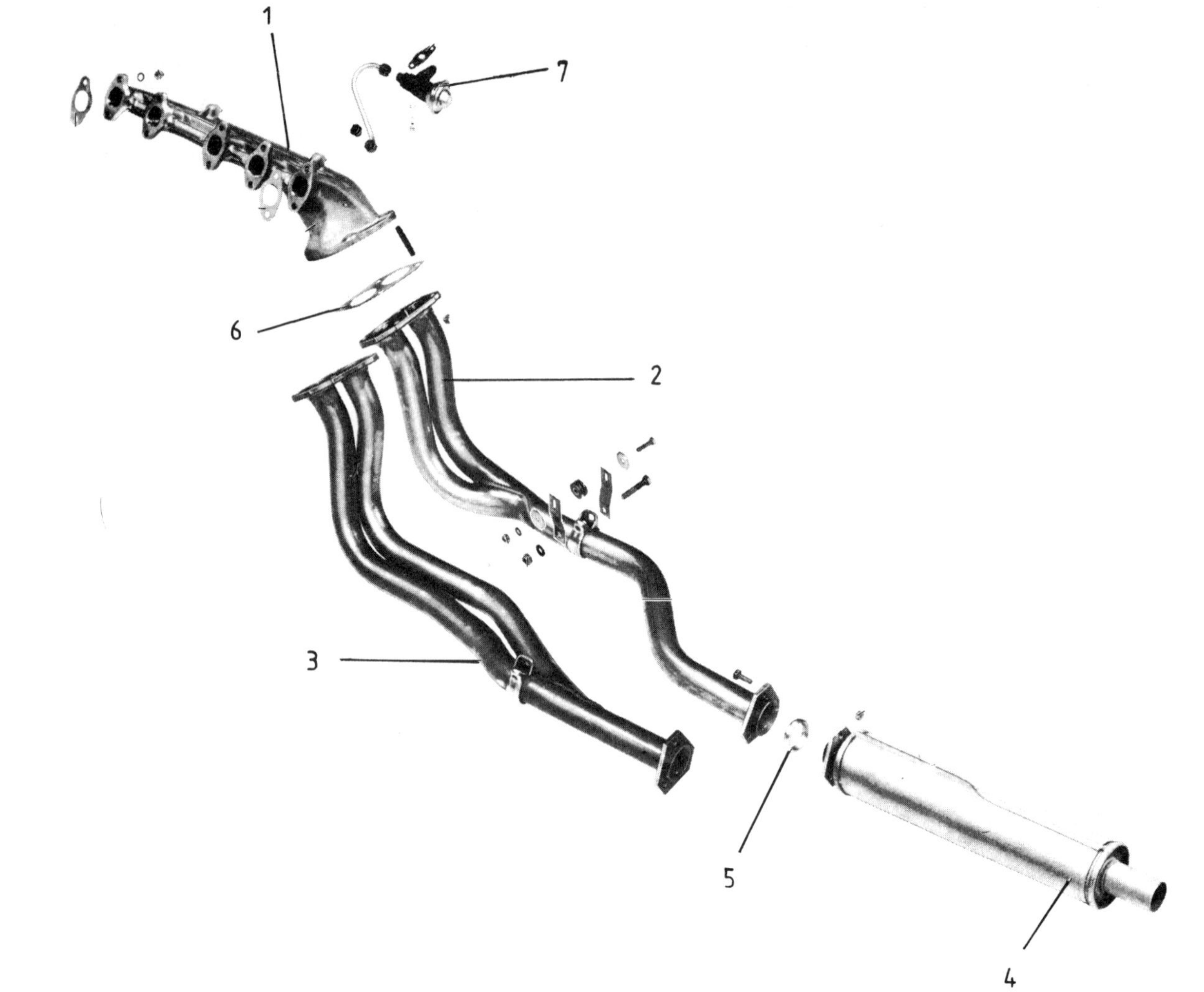

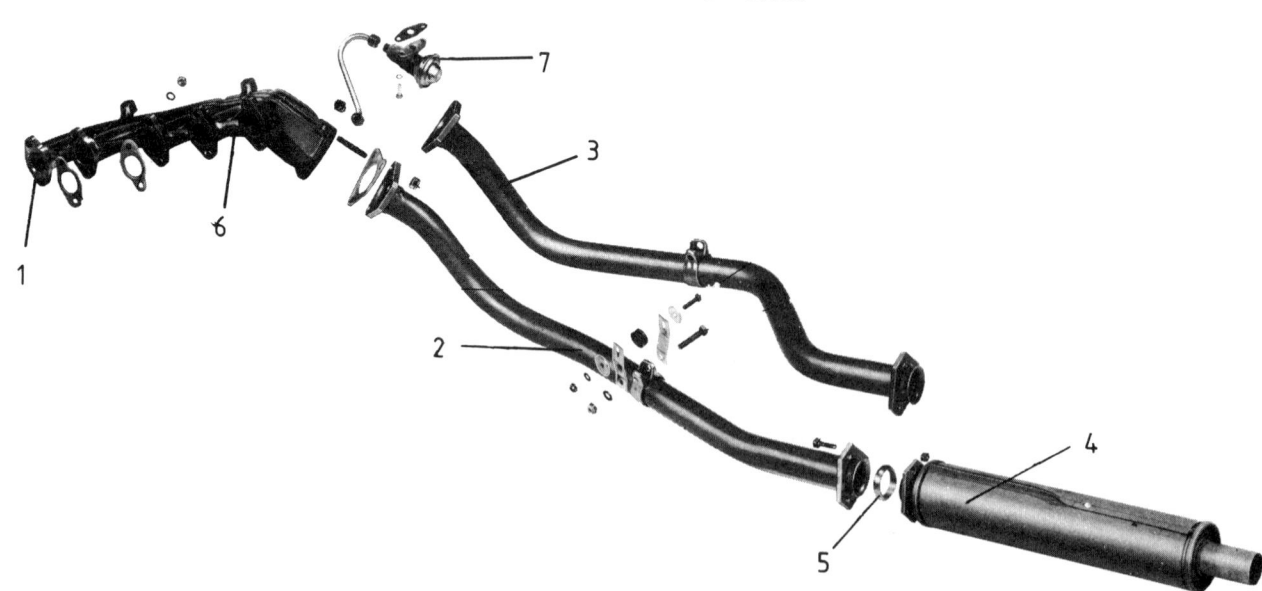

Fig. 3.87 Front pipe assembly (2.2 litre – WB, WC, WG, and Swedish WE engines) (Sec 34)

1 Exhaust manifold	3 Front pipe (manual models)	5 Sealing ring	7 EGR valve (if fitted)
2 Front pipe (automatic models)	4 Front silencer	6 Gasket	

Fig. 3.88 Front pipe assembly (2.2 litre – WD engines) (Sec 34)

1 Exhaust manifold	3 Front pipe (manual models)	5 Sealing ring	7 EGR valve (if fitted)
2 Front pipe (automatic models)	4 Front silencer	6 Gasket	

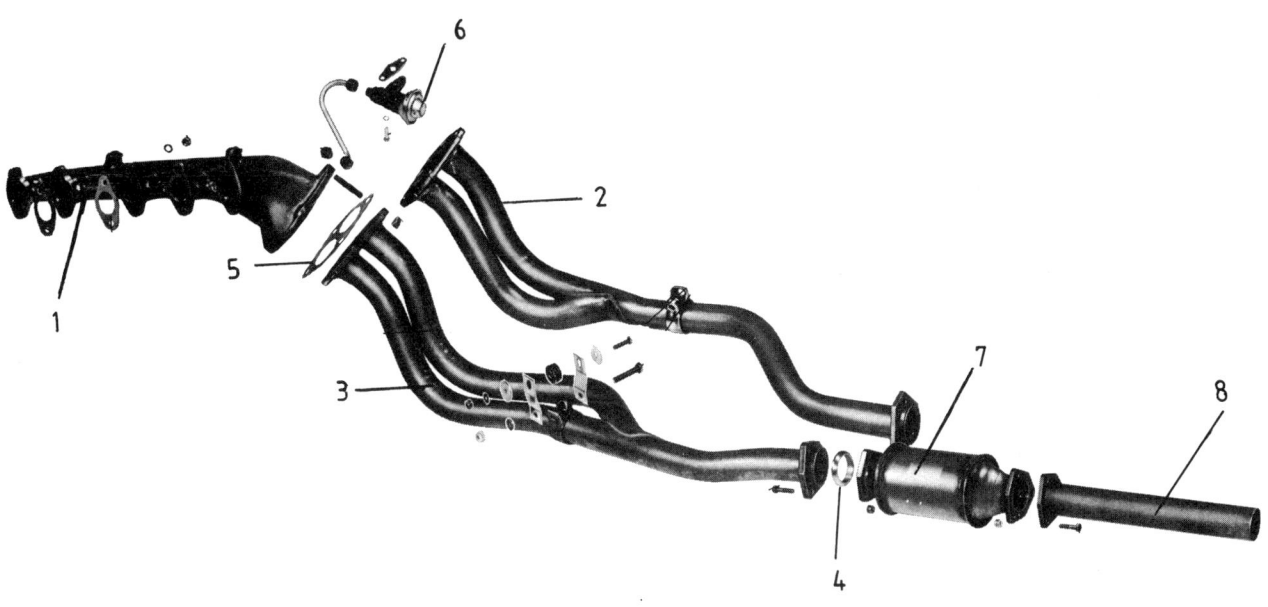

Fig. 3.89 Front pipe assembly (2.2 litre – WE) (Sec 34)

1	Exhaust manifold	3 Front pipe (manual models)	5 Gasket	7 Catalytic converter (California
2	Front pipe (automatic models)	4 Sealing ring	6 EGR valve (if fitted)	only)
				8 Intermediate pipe

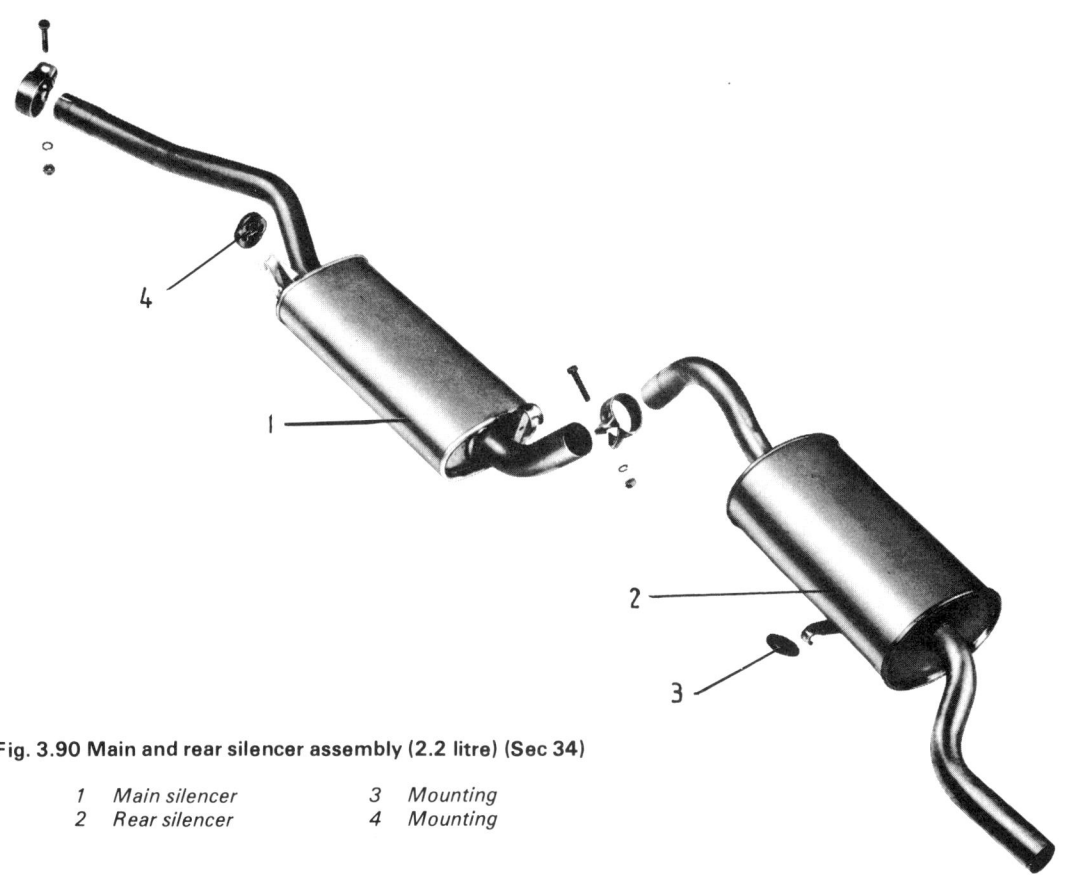

Fig. 3.90 Main and rear silencer assembly (2.2 litre) (Sec 34)

1	Main silencer	3	Mounting
2	Rear silencer	4	Mounting

before assembly. This makes it easier to slide the pieces to align them and ensures that the joints will be gas tight. Leave all bolts loose.

6   Run the engine until the exhaust system is at normal temperature and then, with the engine running at idling speed, tighten all the mounting bolts and clips, starting at the manifold and working towards the rear silencer. Take care to avoid touching any part of the system with bare hands because of the danger of painful burns. The catalytic converter, if fitted, requires particular care because of its very high temperature.

7   When the bolts and clips are tightened, it is important to ensure that there is no strain on any part of the system.

35 Fault diagnosis – fuel system (carburettor models)

Symptom	Reason(s)
Smell of petrol with engine stopped	Leaking fuel tank Leaking fuel pipe, or joints
Smell of petrol with engine running	Leaking fuel pipe Float chamber level too high
Excessive fuel consumption without obvious petrol leakage	Worn jets Dirty air cleaner
Engine will not start	Fuel not reaching carburettor Automatic choke not working Carburettor flooding
Engine hunts, or stalls at idling	Leak in vacuum hose Leak on inlet manifold Leak in EGR hose Blocked jets
Engine will not accelerate smoothly from idle	Accelerator pump not working properly Partial or full load enrichment system blocked Fuel pump output low
Engine lacks power	Dirty air filter Blocked jet

36 Fault diagnosis – fuel system (injection models)

Symptom	Reason(s)
Engine difficult to start	Air leaks at injectors, mixture control unit, or auxiliary air regulator Fuel pump defective Air sensor plate stuck or fuel control plunger sticking Cold start valve defective Thermo-time switch defective
Engine starts, then stops	Auxiliary air regulator closed EGR valve defective Throttle valve stuck
Lack of power	Faulty EGR valve Fuel pressure low Pump output low Air sensor plate, or fuel control plunger not moving freely
Fuel consumption high	Fuel leaks Idle CO incorrect Control pressure regulator defective Cold start valve leaking

Chapter 4 Ignition system

Contents

Specifications

Ignition coil

Primary resistance:	
Contact breaker ignition	1.7 to 2.1 ohms
Transistorised ignition	0.95 to 1.4 ohms
Secondary resistance:	
Contact breaker ignition	7 to 12 k ohms
Transistorised ignition	5.5 to 8 k ohms

Distributor

Dwell angle setting:	
1.6 litre	47 ± 3°
2.0 litre	47 ± 3°
2.2 litre	43 to 65° (not adjustable)
Dwell angle limits:	
1.6 litre	42 to 58°
2.0 litre	42 to 58°
Contact breaker points gap (1.6 and 2.0 litre).............	0.40 mm (0.016 in)
Induction coil resistance (electronic ignition distributor)	890 to 1285 ohms
Rotor arm resistance:	
1.6 litre	5 k ohms
2.0 litre	4 to 6 k ohms
2.2 litre	5 k ohms

Ignition timing

	1.6 litre YV	2.0 litre WA	WB Manual	WB Automatic	2.2 litre WC	WD/WE	WG
					Engine identification		
Firing point	TDC	10°BTDC	9°BTDC	TDC	5°BTDC	3°ATDC	5°BTDC
Engine speed (rpm)	950±50	950±50	900±50	900±50	900±50	925±75	900±50
Vacuum hoses	on	off	off	on	on	on	on
Centrifugal advance:							
Begins (rpm)	1050–1400	1000–1250	950	950	900	1000	1000
Ends:							
rpm	3000	3800	6000	6000	6000	4500	4500
degrees	18–22	23–28	31–35	31–35	12–17	21–25	21–25
Vacuum advance max (degrees)	11–15	12–16	15–19	15–19	8–12	4–8	0–2
Vacuum retard max (degrees)	7–9		–	8–10	12–14	8–10	12–14

Spark plugs

Type:							
Bosch	W175 T30	W225 T30	W175 T30	W175 T30	W200 T30	W175 T30	W200 T30
Beru	175/14/ 3A	225/14/ 3A	175/14/ 3A	175/14/ 3A	200/14/ 3A	175/14/ 3A	200/14/ 3A
Champion	N8Y	N7Y	N7Y	N7Y	N7Y	N8Y	N7Y

	1.6 litre YV	2.0 litre WA	WB Manual	WB Automatic	2.2 litre WC	WD/WE	WG
Electrode gap:							
mm	0.6–0.7	0.6–0.7	0.7	0.7	0.7	0.9	0.7
in	0.024–0.028	0.024–0.028	0.028	0.028	0.028	0.035	0.028

Firing order

1.6 litre	1–3–4–2
2.0 litre	1–3–4–2
2.2 litre	1–2–4–5–3

Plug lead resistance

Vehicles with radio (k ohms)	1 ± 0.2
Vehicles without radio (k ohms)	zero

Spark plug connectors

Suppressed (k ohms)	5 ± 1
Not suppressed (k ohms)	1 ± 0.2

Torque wrench settings

	Nm	lbf ft
Spark plugs	30	22
Ignition coil clamp screw	8	6
Ignition coil-to-bulkhead nuts	10	7
Distributor clamp screw (1.6 litre)	14	10
Distributor clamp nut (2.0 litre)	20	15
Distributor drive housing bolts (2.0 litre)	10	7
Ignition coil terminal nuts	3	2
Plug lead cable clips	8	6

1 General description

For an engine to run at maximum efficiency, the spark must ignite the fuel/air charge in the combustion chamber at exactly the right moment for the particular engine speed and load conditions.

The ignition system comprises the ignition coil, which consists of two windings coupled electromagnetically; and the distributor which is a mechanically-driven rotary switch. The distributor applies battery voltage to the low tension winding of the ignition coil and at the instant when the low tension, or primary winding is switched off, a very high voltage is induced in the high tension secondary winding. This very high voltage is routed to the appropriate cylinder by the distributor rotor and jumps to earth across the electrodes of the spark plug.

On all models except the 2·2 litre, the distributor is of the conventional type, with a contact breaker, operated by a cam. On the 2·2 litre model the switching is electronic (contactless) and is controlled by electro-magnetic induction from a toothed rotor and a pick-up coil.

On 1·6 litre engines, the distributor driveshaft is geared to the intermediate shaft. A lower extension of the distributor driveshaft drives the oil pump which is mounted within the crankcase. On 2·0 and 2·2 litre engines, the distributor is driven from a gear on the rear end of the overhead camshaft.

A vacuum diaphragm, connected to the inlet manifold, causes the ignition timing to be varied according to inlet manifold suction and therefore engine load, while a centrifugally operated cam varies the timing dependent upon engine speed. Some models have a vacuum connection to each side of the diaphragm so that the basic ignition timing can be either advanced, or retarded. This additional provision is to reduce exhaust pollution.

2 Distributor – removing and refitting

1   Pull the high tension connection from the centre of the ignition coil and remove the caps from the spark plugs.
2   Release the two spring clips securing the distributor cover, then remove the distributor cover with the ignition harness attached. On the 2·2 litre model, which has a metal screening round the top of the distributor, it is necessary to remove the screw from the bonding strap before the cover can be taken off (photo).
3   Remove the connection from the low tension lead to the contact breaker.
4   Note the exact position of the rotor arm, so that the distributor can be fitted with the rotor arm in the same position and also put mating

2.2 Distributor cap bonding lead (2.2 litre)

2.7 Fitting the distributor (2.2 litre)

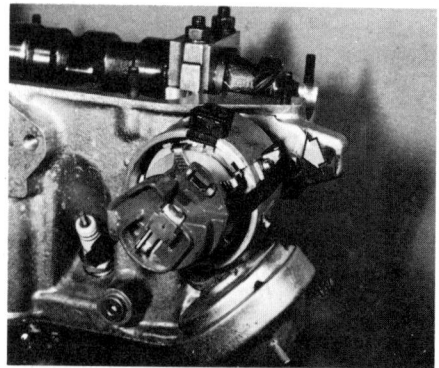

2.8 Distributor with clamp plate (2.2 litre)

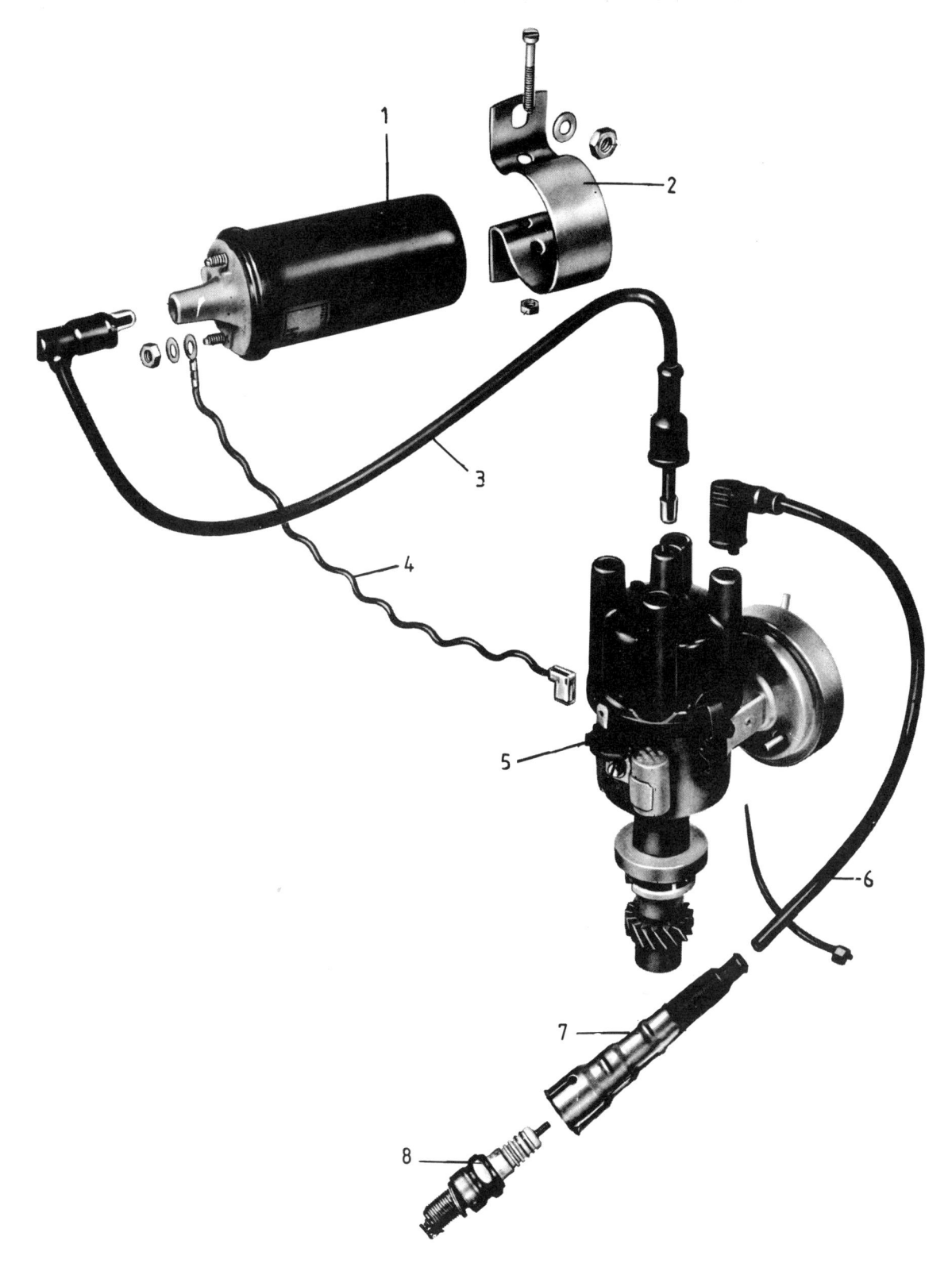

Fig. 4.1 Ignition system components (1.6 litre) (Sec 1)

| 1 | Ignition coil | 3 | Distributor-to-coil HT lead | 5 | Distributor | 7 | Plug connector |
| 2 | Coil clamp | 4 | Distributor-to-coil LT lead | 6 | Plug lead | 8 | Spark plug |

marks on the distributor mounting flange and the cylinder head. By marking these positions and also ensuring that the crankshaft is not moved while the distributor is off, the distributor can be refitted without upsetting the ignition timing.

5   Pull the vacuum pipe(s) from the vacuum control unit, marking the position of the pipes if there is more than one.

6   Remove the nut and washer, or bolt and washer from the distributor clamp plate and take the clamp plate off.

7   When refitting the distributor, provided the crankshaft has not been moved, turn the rotor arm to such a position that when the distributor is fully installed and the gears mesh, the rotor will turn and take up the position which it held before removal (photo). On the 1·6 litre engine if the distributor will not seat fully, withdraw the unit and use pliers to turn the oil pump driveshaft slightly, then try again.

8   Fit the clamp plate and washer, then fit the nut or bolt and tighten it (photo).

9   Fit the distributor cap and clip it in place, then re-connect the high and low tension wires.

10 If the engine has been the subject of overhaul, the crankshaft has been rotated or a new distributor is being fitted, then the procedure for installing the distributor will differ according to engine capacity, refer to Section 6 of this Chapter.

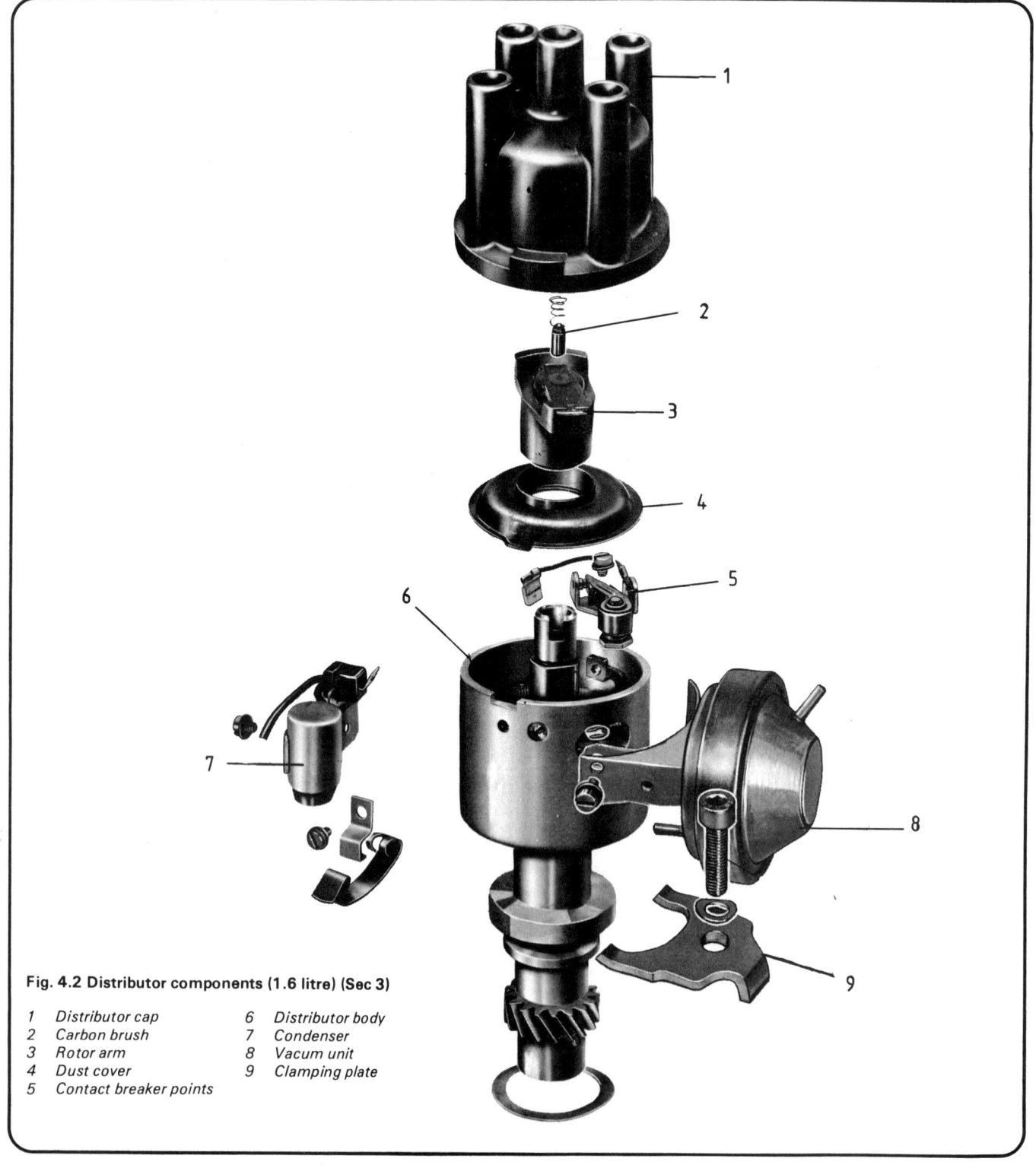

Fig. 4.2 Distributor components (1.6 litre) (Sec 3)

1	Distributor cap	6	Distributor body
2	Carbon brush	7	Condenser
3	Rotor arm	8	Vacum unit
4	Dust cover	9	Clamping plate
5	Contact breaker points		

Fig. 4.3 Distributor components (2.0 litre) (Sec 3)

1 Distributor cap
2 Carbon brush
3 Rotor arm
4 Dust cover
5 Contact breaker points
6 Distributor body
7 Condenser
8 Vacuum unit
9 Clamping plate
10 Distributor drive housing

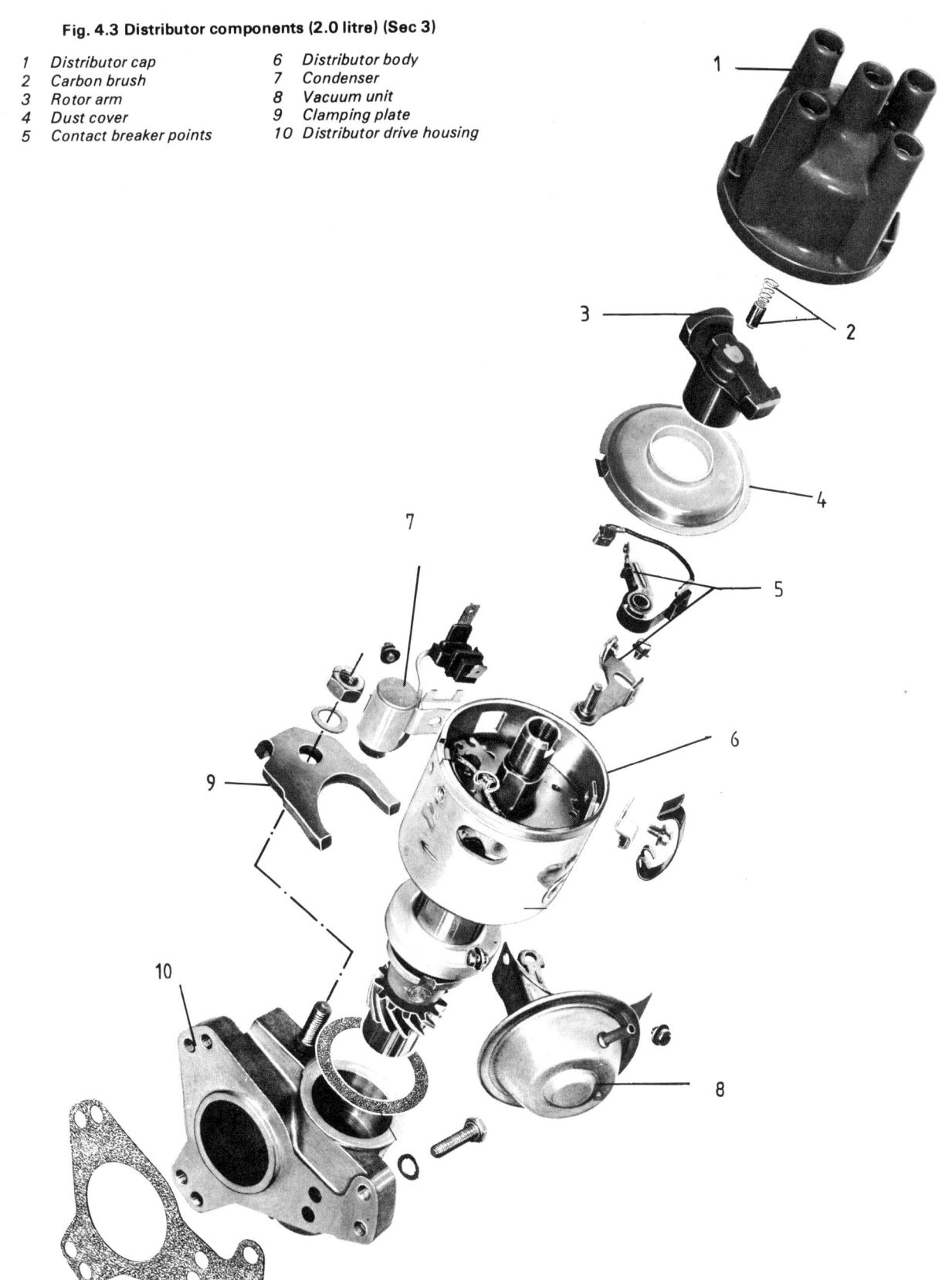

3 Distributor – dismantling, inspection and reassembling

1.6 and 2.0 litre engine

1 Release the two spring clips retaining the cap and lift the cap off.

2 Pull the rotor arm off the cam spindle and then lift off the dust cover beneath it.

3 Disconnect the contact breaker lead from the terminal on the side of the distributor. Remove the clamp screw and washer from the contact breaker and lift the breaker assembly off the base plate.

4 Disconnect the condenser lead from the terminal on the side of the distributor. Remove the condenser fixing screw and take off the condenser.

5 Remove the small spring clip which secures the operating rod of the vacuum unit to the pin on the contact breaker base plate. Remove the screw securing the vacuum unit to the distributor case and take off the vacuum unit. This is the limit of dismantling which should be attempted, because none of the parts beneath the contact breaker plate, nor the drivegear can be renewed individually.

6 Inspect the inside of the distributor cap for signs of burning, or tracking. Make sure that the small carbon brush in the centre of the distributor cap is in good condition and can move up and down freely under the influence of its spring.

7 Check that the rotor arm is not damaged. Use an ohm-meter to measure the resistance between the brass contact in the centre of the rotor arm and the brass contact at the edge of the arm. The measured value of resistance should be between 4000 and 6000 ohms.

8 Suck on the pipe connection to the vacuum diaphragm and check that the operating rod of the diaphragm unit moves. Retain the diaphragm under vacuum to check that the diaphragm is not perforated.

9 The contact breaker and condenser are relatively inexpensive items and it is recommended that the old ones are discarded and new ones fitted on reassembly.

10 Before reassembling, make sure that all the parts are clean and take great care not to get any oil, grease or dirt on the contacts. Smear the cam with grease and after fitting the vacuum unit, apply a single spot of oil to the junction of the operating rod and the pin on the contact breaker plate.

11 Fit and adjust the contact breaker as described in Section 5.

2.2 litre engine

12 The engine has a transistorised coil ignition (TCI) system which is liable to be damaged unless special precautions are taken (see Section 4) and it should not be dismantled unnecessarily.

13 Release the two spring clips and fit pads to them so that it is impossible for them to fall into the distributor (Fig. 4.4).

14 Pull the rotor arm off the cam spindle and then lift off the dust cover beneath it.

15 Remove the circlip and wave washer, then pull off the rotor, taking care to recover its drive key.

16 Remove the screw from the low tension plug retainer, remove the retainer and pull out the plug.

17 Remove the screw securing the socket of the low tension connections to the side of the distributor. Remove the circlip from the distributor spindle and lift out the induction coil and the insulating disc beneath it.

18 Remove the screw securing the vacuum unit to the distributor body, unhook the vacuum unit operating rod from its connection to the stator plate and remove the vacuum unit.

19 Further dismantling by removing the centrifugal advance mechanism is not recommended.

20 Before reassembling, check that all parts are clean.

21 Measure the resistance between the two terminals of the induction coil. This should be between 890 ohms and 1285 ohms. If outside these limits the coil must be discarded and a new one fitted.

22 Measure the resistance between the centre and the outer contact of the rotor arm. The nominal value for this is 5000 ohms and a new rotor arm should be fitted if the resistance of the existing arm varies by more than 10% from the nominal value.

23 After fitting the stator and rotor, measure the radial clearance (air gap) between the stator and rotor teeth (Fig. 4.4). The correct clearance is 0.25 mm (0.010 in) and is adjusted by bending the rotor, or stator teeth.

24 Before fitting the rotor arm, apply two or three spots of thin oil to the felt pad at the top of the rotor spindle.

Fig. 4.4 Measuring rotor-to-stator gap (2.2 litre) (Sec 3)

Note pads to prevent clips from getting into distributor

25 Before fitting the distributor cap, ensure that there are no cracks, signs of burning or tracking on the plastic. Also ensure that the carbon brush in the centre of the distributor moves freely under the influence of its spring.

26 After fitting the distributor cap and the high tension and low tension connections, ensure that the braid bonding wire from the distributor cap is clamped to the distributor body.

4 Transistorised coil ignition system (2.2 litre) – safety measures

1 To prevent personal injury and damage to the ignition system, the following precautions must be observed when working on the ignition system.

2 Do not attempt to disconnect any plug lead or touch any of the high tension cables when the engine is running, or being turned by the starter motor.

3 Ensure that the ignition is turned *OFF* before disconnecting any of the ignition wiring.

4 Ensure that the ignition is switched *OFF* before connecting or disconnecting any ignition testing equipment such as a timing light.

5 Do not connect a suppression condenser or test lamp to the coil negative terminal (1).

6 Do not connect any test appliance or stroboscopic lamp requiring a 12 volt supply to the coil positive terminal (15).

7 If the HT cable is disconnected from the distributor (terminal 4), the cable must immediately be connected to earth and remain earthed if the engine is to be rotated by the starter motor, for example if a compression test is to be done.

8 If a high current boost charger is used, the charger output voltage must not exceed 20 volts and the time must not exceed one minute.

9 The ignition coil of a transistorised system must never be replaced by the ignition coil from a contact breaker type ignition system.

10 If an electric arc welder is to be used on any part of the vehicle, the car battery must be disconnected while welding is being done.

11 If a stationary engine is heated to above 80°C (176°F) such as may happen after paint drying, or steam cleaning, the engine must not be started until it has cooled.

12 Ensure that the ignition is switched *OFF* when the car is washed.

5 Contact breaker points (1.6 and 2.0 litre) – removing, refitting and adjusting

1 Release the two clips securing the distributor cap and remove the cap.

2 Pull the rotor arm off the cam spindle and remove the dust cover beneath the rotor arm.

3 Disconnect the contact breaker wire from the terminal inside the distributor. Remove the clamp screw and washer from the contact breaker assembly and remove the assembly.

4 Before fitting the new points, smear the distributor cam with grease and grease the pivot pin of the moving contact breaker contact.

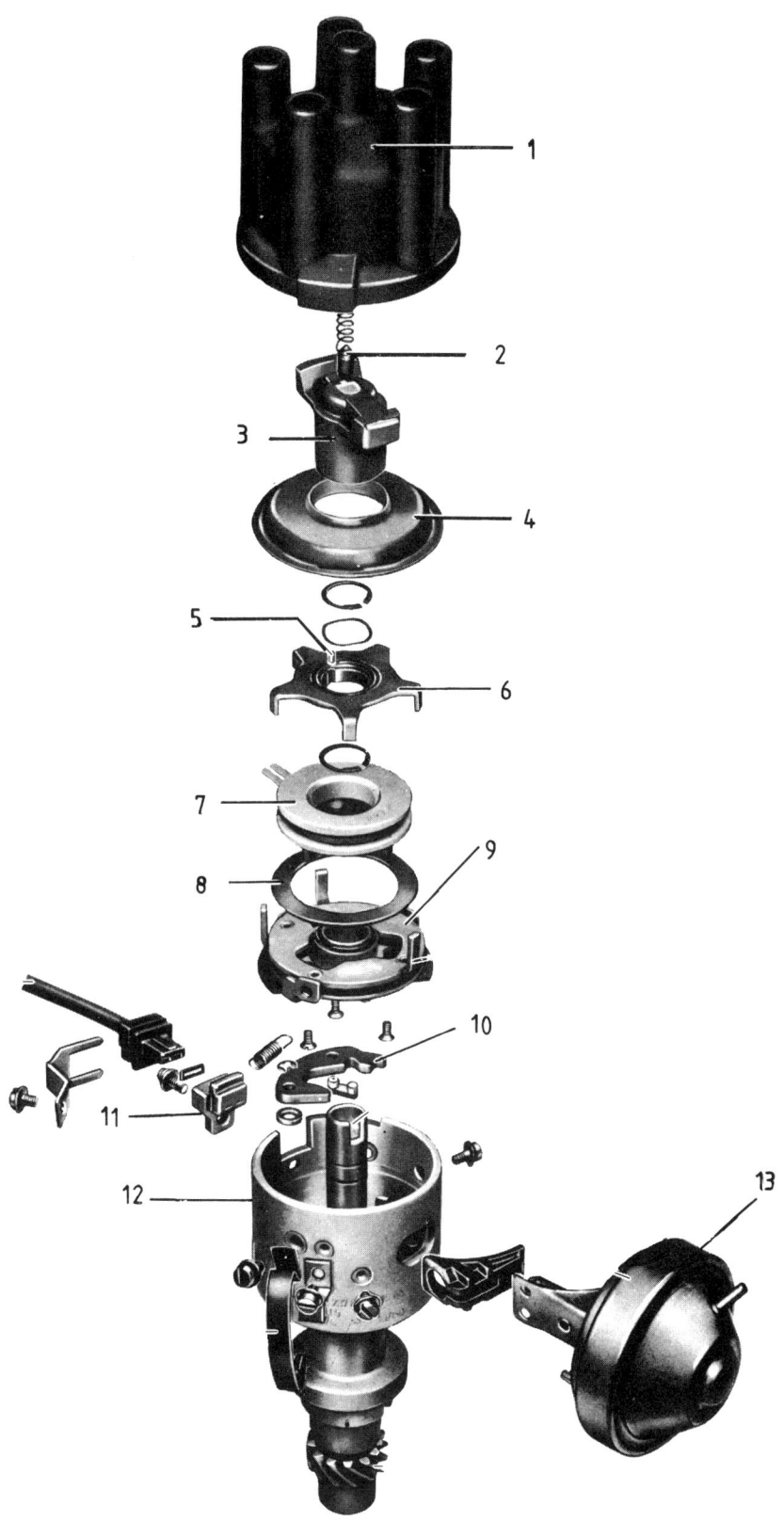

Fig. 4.5 Distributor components (2.2 litre) (Sec 3)

1 Distributor cap	5 Drive key	8 Insulating disc	11 Coil connector
2 Carbon brush	6 Rotor	9 Stator	12 Distributor body
3 Rotor arm	7 Induction coil	10 Centrifugal weight	13 Vacuum unit
4 Dust cover			

5   Fit the contact breaker assembly and tighten the clamp screw so that the fixed contact is just clamped to the base plate. Either rotate the crankshaft until the plastic cam follower is on the highest point of the cam, or release the distributor clamp plate and turn the distributor body until the contacts are at their maximum separation. If the latter method is used, mark the position of the distributor before moving it, so that it can be re-clamped in its original position.

6   With the cam follower on the highest point of the cam, lever the fixed contact plate until the contacts are at the specified gap and then tighten the clamp screw. This should only be regarded as a nominal setting. For optimum engine performance the setting of the contact breaker points should be checked with a dwell meter.

7   Ensure that the contact breaker lead is securely attached to the contact on the side of the distributor and then refit the distributor cover.

---

6   Ignition timing – basic

1   If the distributor has been removed and the basic timing of the engine has been disturbed, this setting must be restored before the engine timing can be set properly. The way this is done for the various engines is as follows.

1.6 litre engine

2   Turn the engine until the TDC mark (O) appears opposite the pointer seen through the aperture in the flywheel cover (Fig. 4.6).

3   Ensure that the timing mark on the rear face of the camshaft sprocket is in line with the upper edge of the rocker cover gasket (Fig. 4.7). If the flywheel is at TDC and the camshaft mark is not in its correct position, turn the crankshaft one complete revolution.

4   Turn the oil pump shaft until its lug is parallel with the crankshaft (Fig. 4.8).

5   Hold the distributor over its recess in the cylinder block with the vacuum unit at 90° to the engine centre line and the contact end of the rotor arm pointing in the direction of the mark on the rim of the distributor body. Insert the distributor fully and as the drive gears mesh, the rotor arm should turn to align with the No 1 HT lead segment in the distributor cap (when installed in its fitted position). A certain amount of trial and error may be required for this, also if the distributor cannot be fully inserted into its mounting hole, slightly reposition the oil pump driveshaft lug. Turn the distributor body until the original body-to-cylinder head marks are in alignment or if a new distributor is being fitted, until the contact points are just about to open, then clamp the distributor in position.

2.0 litre engine

6   Turn the crankshaft until the mark on the rear face of the camshaft sprocket is vertically above the pointer at the front of the rocker box cover (Fig. 4.10).

7   If the distributor is being installed with its drive housing attached, turn the rotor until it is in line with the distributor low tension connection (Fig. 4.11).

8   Fit the distributor and its mounting and tighten the mounting bolts (Fig. 4.12). The rotor arm should now be pointing to the mark on the rim of the distributor housing, having rotated by the meshing of the drivegears. If this is not the case, release the distributor clamp and turn the distributor body until the rotor does line up with the mark. Re-clamp the distributor.

9   If the distributor has been withdrawn by removing its clamp plate

Fig. 4.6 Flywheel timing mark (1.6 litre) (Sec 6)

Fig. 4.7 Camshaft timing mark (1.6 litre) (Sec 6)

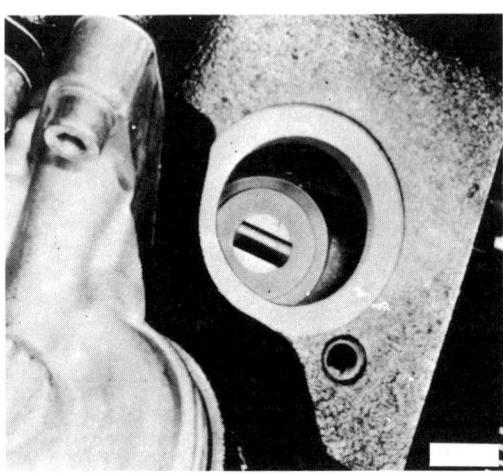

Fig. 4.8 Oil pump lug parallel with crankshaft (1.6 litre) (Sec 6)

Fig. 4.9 Rotor set to No 1 cylinder mark (1.6 litre) (Sec 6)

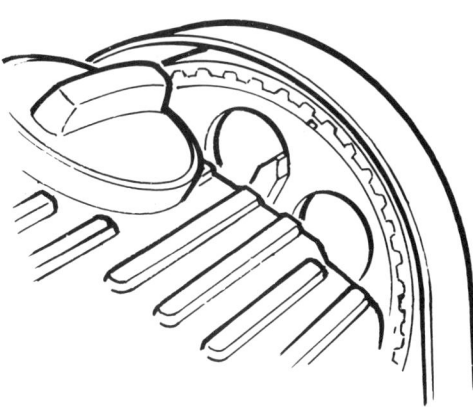

Fig. 4.10 Camshaft timing mark (2.0 litre) (Sec 6)

Fig. 4.12 Distributor drive housing fixing bolts (2.0 litre) (Sec 6)

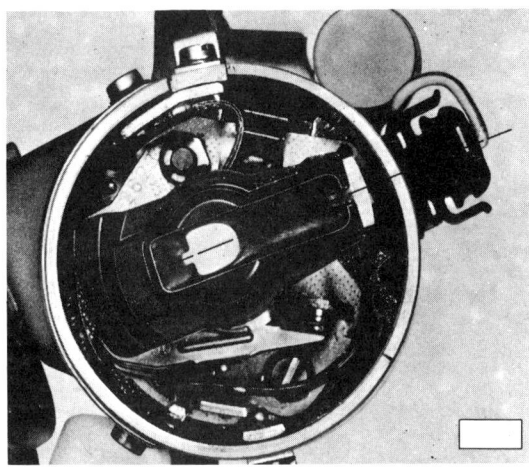

Fig. 4.11 Rotor arm position (2.0 litre) – fitting distributor and drive housing (Sec 6)

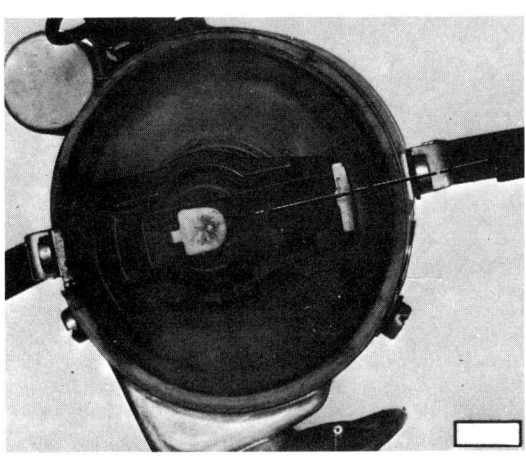

Fig. 4.13 Rotor arm position (2.0 litre) – fitting distributor with drive housing installed (Sec 6)

and leaving the distributor housing attached to the engine, hold the distributor over its recess so that the vacuum unit is pointing towards the front of the engine and downwards at about 30° to the top surface of the camshaft cover. Turn the rotor so that its contact end points towards the distributor cap securing clip which is furthest from the condenser (capacitor).

10 Install the distrubutor and the rotor will turn to align with the mark on the distrubutor body rim, this rotation being caused by the meshing of the drivegears. Turn the distributor body to align the original mark with the one on the drive housing or if a new distributor is being fitted, until the contact points are just about to open, then clamp the distributor in position.

2.2 litre engine

11 Turn the engine until the TDC mark (O) appears opposite the reference mark in the window of the flywheel or drive plate cover (Fig. 4.14.).

12 Ensure that the timing mark on the rear face of the camshaft sprocket is in line with the upper edge of the rocker cover gasket (Fig. 4.7). If the flywheel is at TDC and the camshaft mark is not in its correct position, turn the crankshaft one complete revolution.

13 On all engines except those of 7:1 compression ratio i.e. all engines which do not have the code letters WD or WE, turn the rotor until it is in the position shown in Fig. 4.15.

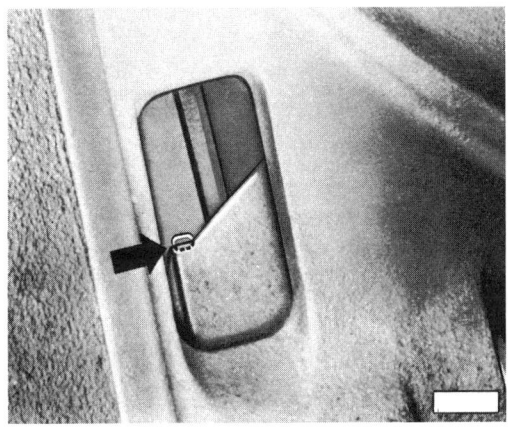

Fig. 4.14 Flywheel timing mark (2.2 litre) (Sec 6)

Fig. 4.15 Rotor arm position when inserting distributor (2.2 litre) – except WD and WE (Sec 6)

Fig. 4.16 Rear arm position when inserting distributor (2.2 litre) – WD and WE (Sec 6)

14 On engines with the code letters WD and WE, turn the rotor until it is in the position shown in Fig. 4.16.

15 Hold the distributor over its mounting recess with the vacuum unit pointing downward and push the distributor fully home. As the drivegears mesh, the rotor will turn and align with the mark (No 1) on the rim of the distributor body.

16 Align the distributor body and cylinder head marks made before removal or if a new unit is being installed, turn the body until the ends of the impulse sender are square to the stator contact lugs. Clamp the distributor.

17 With all types of engine and distributor, check the ignition timing after installation.

7 Dwell angle and ignition timing – dynamic

Dwell angle

1 To check the dwell angle on 1.6 and 2.0 litre engines which have a conventional (mechanical contact breaker) type ignition system, connect a dwell meter in accordance with the maker's instructions.

2 The dwell angle is the number of degrees through which the distributor cam turns during the period between the instants of closure and opening of the contact breaker points.

3 The correct dwell angle is a given in Specifications. If the angle is too large, increase the points gap, if too small, reduce the gap.

4 The dwell angle not only provides a more accurate setting of the contact breaker points gap but the method also evens out any variations in gap caused by wear in the distributor shaft or bushes or differences in the heights of the cam peaks.

5 Always check and adjust the dwell angle before checking or adjusting the ignition timing.

Timing (dynamic)

6 Connect a timing light in accordance with its manufacturer's instructions, noting that on the 2.2 litre engine any light requiring a 12 volt battery supply must not take that supply directly from the distributor (see Section 4).

7 Start the engine and then proceed as follows according to the engine fitted to the vehicle.

8 1.6 litre engine.

   (a)   *Leave the hose(s) connected to the vacuum unit*

   (b)   *Run the engine at idling speed, adjusting the idling speed to the correct value if necessary*

   (c)   *Ensure that engine oil temperature is at least 30°C (86°F) and that the choke valve is fully open*

   (d)   *Shine the timing light through the timing mark aperture in the flywheel or drive plate cover. If the correct timing mark (given in Specifications) does not appear in line with the pointer, release the distributor clamp and turn the distributor body until the correct position is achieved. Clamp the distributor firmly after correcting the timing*

9 2.0 litre engine.

   The procedure is identical with that for the 1.6 litre engine, except that the vacuum hose must be disconnected from the distributor

10 2.2 litre engine.

   (a)   *On distributors with a single vacuum hose connection, pull the hose off. On distributors with two vacuum hoses, leave the hoses connected*

   (b)   *Run the engine at idling speed, adjusting the idling speed to the correct value if necessary*

   (c)   *Ensure that engine oil temperature is at least 30°C (86°F) and that the choke valve is fully open. On vehicles with air conditioning, switch this OFF, (ECON button pressed)*

   (d)   *Shine the timing light through the timing mark aperture in the flywheel, or drive plate cover. If the correct timing mark given in Specifications is not in line with the reference edge of the aperture, note whether the ignition needs to be advanced, or retarded and unclamp and turn the distributor as necessary until alignment is achieved. Do not connect or disconnect the timing light while the engine is running or the ignition is switched on (Figs. 4.17, 4.18 and 4.19)*

8 Automatic advance – checking

1 It is difficult to check whether the amount of advance is within the manufacturer's specification unless special equipment is available, but the following tests are adequate for determining whether or not the automatic advance is working.

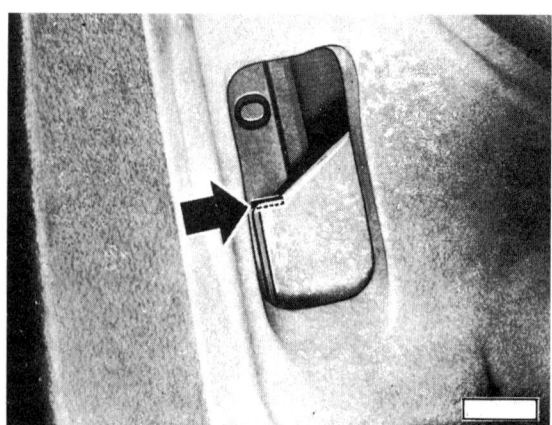

Fig. 4.17 Timing mark (2.2 litre) – engines timed BTDC (Sec 7)

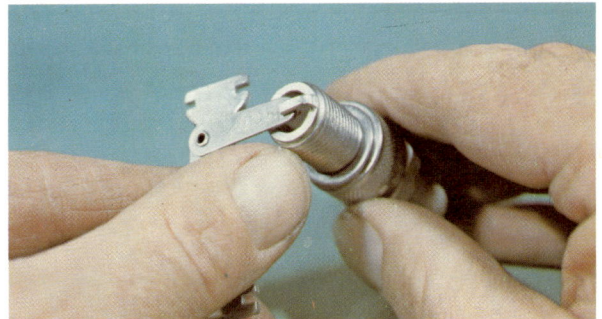

Measuring plug gap. A feeler gauge of the correct size (see ignition system specifications) should have a slight 'drag' when slid between the electrodes. Adjust gap if necessary

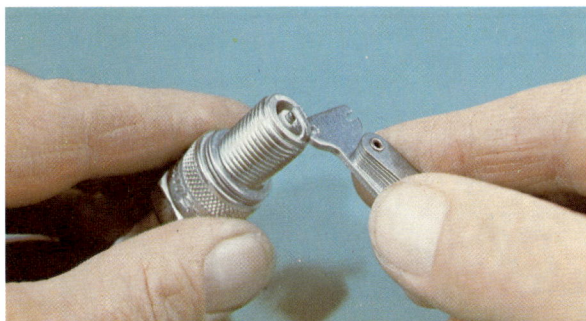

Adjusting plug gap. The plug gap is adjusted by bending the earth electrode inwards, or outwards, as necessary until the correct clearance is obtained. Note the use of the correct tool

Normal. Grey-brown deposits, lightly coated core nose. Gap increasing by around 0.001 in (0.025 mm) per 1000 miles (1600 km). Plugs ideally suited to engine, and engine in good condition

Carbon fouling. Dry, black, sooty deposits. Will cause weak spark and eventually misfire. Fault: over-rich fuel mixture. Check: carburettor mixture settings, float level and jet sizes; choke operation and cleanliness of air filter. Plugs can be re-used after cleaning

Oil fouling. Wet, oily deposits. Will cause weak spark and eventually misfire. Fault: worn bores/piston rings or valve guides; sometimes occurs (temporarily) during running-in period. Plugs can be re-used after thorough cleaning

Overheating. Electrodes have glazed appearance, core nose very white – few deposits. Fault: plug overheating. Check: plug value, ignition timing, fuel octane rating (too low) and fuel mixture (too weak). Discard plugs and cure fault immediately

Electrode damage. Electrodes burned away; core nose has burned, glazed appearance. Fault: pre-ignition. Check: as for 'Overheating' but may be more severe. Discard plugs and remedy fault before piston or valve damage occurs

Split core nose (may appear initially as a crack). Damage is self-evident, but cracks will only show after cleaning. Fault: pre-ignition or wrong gap-setting technique. Check: ignition timing, cooling system, fuel octane rating (too low) and fuel mixture (too weak). Discard plugs, rectify fault immediately

Fig. 4.18 Timing mark (2.2 litre) —engines timed at TDC (Sec 7)

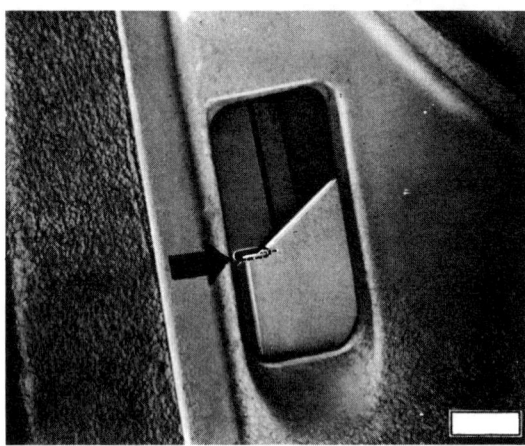

Fig. 4.19 Timing mark (2.2 litre) – engines timed ATDC (Sec 7)

10.1 Ignition coil (2.2 litre)

positive terminal. Open the contact breaker points, either by removing the distributor cap and prising the points apart with a screwdriver, or turn the engine so that the distributor cam opens the points. When the points are separated, the test lamp should not be alight. If the test lamp is alight when the contact breaker points are open, the condenser is short-circuited.

4   An open-circuited condenser will cause burning of the points and the engine will be difficult to start. If either of these troubles is experienced a new condenser should be fitted.

10 Ignition coil – testing

1   It is rare for an ignition coil (photo) to fail, but if there is reason to suspect it, use an ohmmeter to measure the resistance of the primary and secondary circuits.
2   Measure the primary resistance between the terminals 1 and 15 and the secondary resistance between the centre HT terminal and terminal 15. The correct resistance values are given in Specifications.

11 Spark plugs

1   It is important that only spark plugs of the recommended type are used and that these are set to the correct gap.
2   Unless the bores of the cylinders are very worn and the engine is burning oil, the spark plugs should not need any attention between recommended intervals for fitting new plugs.
3   The external surface of the plug's porcelain insulator should be kept clean, because dirty insulators are the most frequent cause of difficult starting in damp weather.
4   When fitting spark plugs, start by screwing them in by hand to ensure that they are not cross-threaded. When tightening the plugs, do not exceed the torque setting given in Specifications.

12 HT leads and suppressor caps

1   The spark plug leads and spark plug connectors have resistors incorporated in them for radio interference suppression and it is important that the plug leads are not replaced with wire leads.
2   The correct resistance values for the leads and the plug connectors are given in Specifications.

13 Transistorised coil ignition system (2.2 litre) – testing

Distributor
1   Check that the distributor is connected correctly as shown in Fig. 4.20.

Centrifugal advance
2   Disconnect the vacuum hoses. When two vacuum hoses are connected, the retard hose, which is the one connected to the flatter side of the vacuum unit, must be sealed off with a plug.
3   With a timing light connected, proceed as for dynamic ignition timing described in the previous Section.
4   After checking that the timing is correct at idling speed, gradually increase the speed of the engine. At about 1000 to 1250 rpm the ignition should begin to advance and continue to advance as engine speed is increased to its maximum. The overall advance should be about 25° at maximum speed.

Vacuum advance
5   With the engine idling, connect the vacuum pipe on the advance (domed) side of the vacuum diaphram. When the pipe is connected the ignition should advance by about 10° and fall again when the pipe is pulled off.

9 Condenser – testing

1   A high voltage insulation tester is required to test a condenser satisfactorily and it is usually simpler to try substituting another condenser if the original is suspect.
2   Condensers used in mechanical contact breaker type distributors are more liable to fail by short-circuiting than by going open circuit. A short-circuited condenser will result in there being no spark and the engine will not fire.
3   Remove the low tension wire from the distributor and connect a 12 volt test lamp between the distributor terminal and the battery

Fig. 4.20 Distributor connections (2.2 litre) (Sec 13)

A – green cable   *B – brown cable*

2   Check and if necessary adjust the gap between the stator and rotor teeth (see Section 3, paragraph 22).

3   Measure the resistance between the two terminals on the induction coil with the plug connector pulled off. If the value is outside the limits 890 to 1285 ohms, a new distributor must be fitted.

Control unit

4   Ensure that the battery is fully charged, all cables are connected and that the ignition is switched *ON*.

5   Measure the voltage between chassis earth and the coil negative terminal (1). The indicated voltage should be less than 2 volts.

6   Measure the voltage between chassis earth and the coil positive terminal (15). The indicated voltage should exceed 5 volts.

7   Check that there is electrical continuity between the cable attached to terminal 1 on the coil and terminal 6 on the control unit plug.

8   Check that there is electrical continuity between chassis earth and terminal 5 of the control unit plug.

9   If the foregoing checks are satisfactory, connect all the low tension cables. Pull the high tension wire from the centre of the distributor (terminal 4) and earth the end of the HT cable.

10   Connect a voltmeter between chassis earth and terminal 1 on the coil. Operate the starter and check that the indicated voltage oscillates between 1 and 12 volts. If it does not, the control unit is defective and a new one must be fitted.

14 Fault diagnosis – ignition system

1   There are two distinct symptoms of ignition faults. Either the engine will not start or fire, or it starts with difficulty and does not run normally.

2   If the starter motor spins the engine satisfactorily, there is adequate fuel and yet the engine will not start, the fault is likely to be on the LT side.

3   If the engine starts, but does not run satisfactorily, it is more likely to be an HT fault.

Engine fails to start

4   If the starter motor spins the engine satisfactorily, but the engine does not start, first remove the petrol pipe to the carburettor, spin the engine and check that fuel is being fed to the carburettor. Also check that the choke valve is in its correct position for the temperature of the engine i.e. closed for cold engine and open for hot engine.

5   Check for broken or disconnected wires to the coil and distributor.

6   For vehicles with electronic ignition follow the procedure detailed in Section 13.

7   For vehicles with contact breaker distributors, remove the LT lead from the distributor and connect a 12 volt test lamp between the end of the lead and the terminal on the side of the distributor. Spin the engine and check that the lamp flashes on and off as the engine turns. If it does, there is no fault in the LT wiring. If it does not flash, but either remains alight, or fails to light, check the contact breaker, condenser and LT wiring.

Engine starts, but misfires

8   Bad starting and intermittent misfiring can be an LT fault, such as an intermittent connection of either the distributor, coil LT leads, or a loose condenser clamping screw.

9   If these are satisfactory look for signs of tracking and burning inside the distributor cap, then check the plug leads, plug caps and plug insulators for signs of damage.

10   If the engine misfires regularly, it indicates that the fault is on one particular cylinder. On vehicles with contact breaker type distributors, the following test may be done, but it should not be done if transistorised ignition is fitted (see Section 4). While the engine is running, grip each plug cap in turn with a piece of clean dry rag, to avoid getting an electric shock and pull the cap off the plug. If there is no difference in engine running when a particular plug lead is removed, it indicates a defective plug, or lead. Stop the engine, remove the suspect plug and insert is in a different cylinder. Repeat the test, to see whether the plug performs satisfactorily in the new position and whether a different plug is satisfactory in the position from which the suspect one was removed.

Chapter 5 Clutch

Contents

Specifications

Type . . . . Single dry plate, diaphragm spring, manual operation on 1.6 and 2.0 litre models, hydraulic operation on 2.2 litre models

Driven plate
Diameter . . . . 8.46 or 8.98 in (215 or 228 mm)
Maximum run-out:
    215 mm (8.46 in) diameter . . . . 0.4 mm (0.016 in)
    228 mm (8.98 in) diameter . . . . 0.5 mm (0.020 in)

Pressure plate distortion . . . . 0.3 mm max (0.012 in)

Diaphragm spring finger wear . . . . 0.3 mm max (0.012 in)

Clutch free-play (cable operation) . . . . 15 mm (0.591 in)

Clutch adjustment (hydraulic operation) . . . . Clutch pedal approximately 10 mm (0.394 in) higher than brake pedal

Torque wrench settings

	lbf ft	Nm
Clutch housing-to-flywheel	18	25
Clutch release lever retainer (hydraulic control)	10	15
Pedal bracket-to-body nuts	18	25
Master cylinder-to-bracket bolts (hydraulic control)	14	20
Clutch lever-to-release shaft clamp-bolt (mechanical control)	18	25

1 General description

All manual transmission models have a single dry plate type clutch with a diaphragm spring. Except on the 2.2 litre model, the clutch is operated by a cable attached to the clutch pedal and clutch free-play adjustment is provided by a screwed adjuster, which is easily accessible inside the engine compartment. It is important that the amount of free-play on the clutch pedal is kept to the figure given in Specifications.

2.2 litre models have a hydraulically operated clutch with a slave cylinder fitted into a pocket in the clutch bellhousing. The clutch master cylinder is mounted behind the clutch pedal and fluid is fed from the combined brake/clutch reservoir mounted remotely in the engine compartment. The only adjustment which needs to be made on the hydraulic clutch is the height of the clutch pedal which should be maintained at the specified figure by adjusting the screwed clevis on the clutch master cylinder operating rod.

2 Clutch adjustment

Cable operated clutch

1 Open the bonnet lid to gain access to the clutch adjuster which is fitted to a bracket adjacent to the shock absorber top mounting (Fig. 5.2).

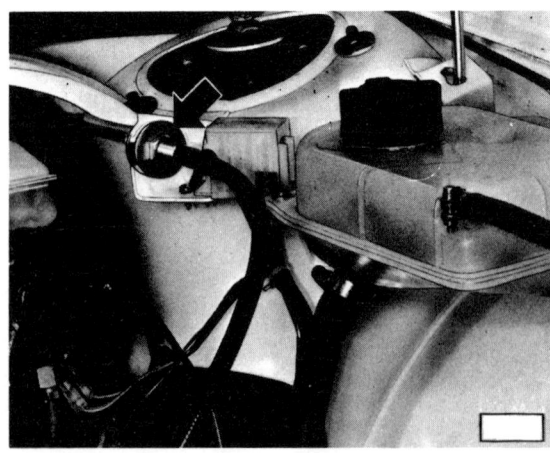

Fig. 5.1 Clutch cable adjuster (arrowed) (Sec 2)

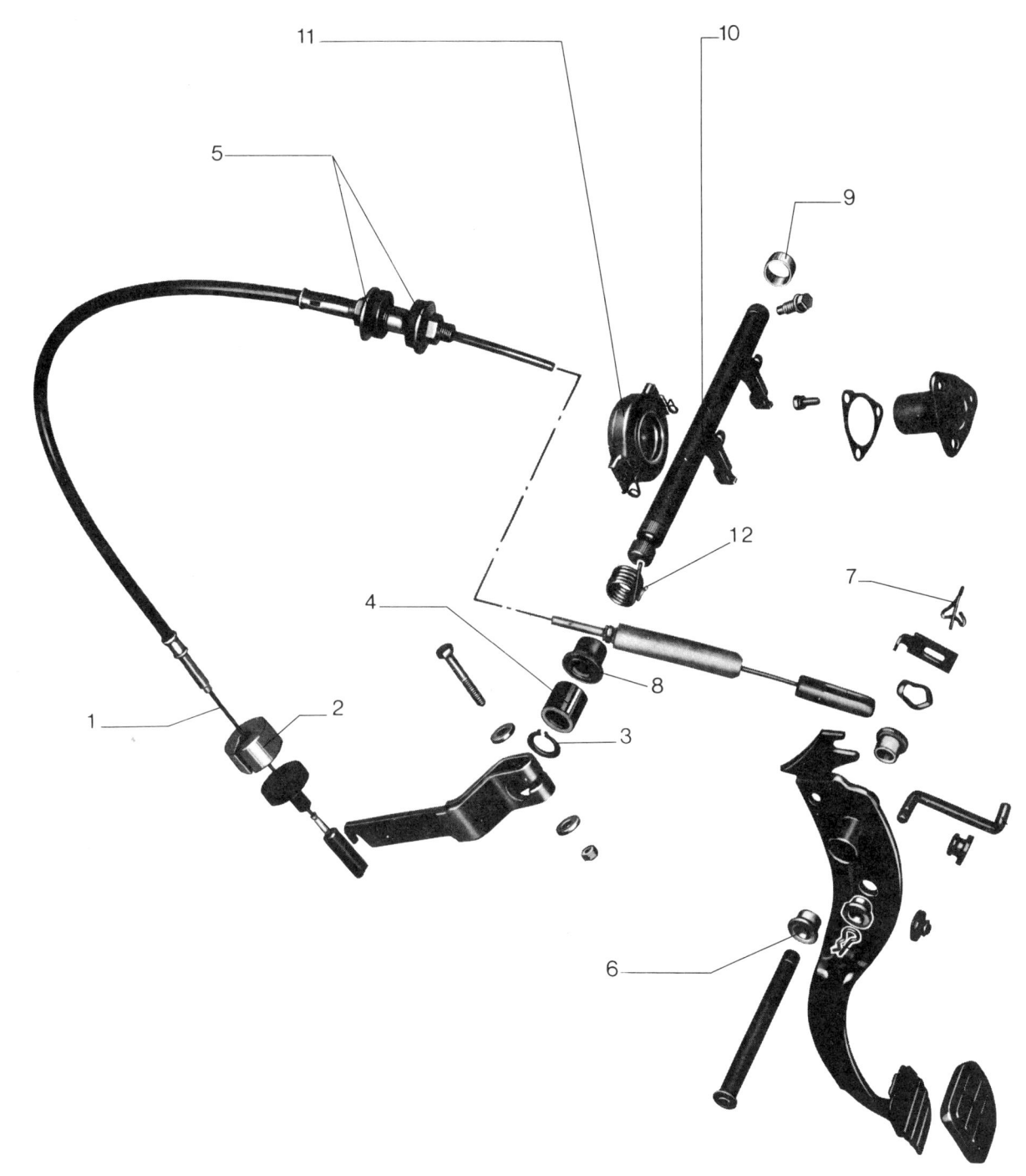

Fig. 5.2 Mechanical clutch control (1.6 and 2.0 litre) (Sec 2)

1 Clutch cable	4 Rubber spring	7 Locking clip	10 Release shaft
2 Balance weight	5 Clutch cable adjuster	8 Release shaft outer bush	11 Release bearing
3 Circlip	6 Pivot bush	9 Release shaft inner bush	12 Release shaft spring

2   Slacken the locknuts so that the screwed cable ferrule is free to turn. If the cable is to be tightened hold the front locknut with a spanner and screw the threaded ferrule further out of the nut until the specified amount of pedal free-play is achieved. While still holding the locknut with a spanner, tighten the other locknut.

Hydraulically operated clutch

3   Remove the parcel shelf (see Chapter 12) to gain access to the clutch master cylinder.

4   Release the locknut behind the clevis on the clutch master cylinder operating rod and turn the rod until the correct pedal height is achieved.

5   Depress the clutch pedal and then release it to ensure that the over-centre spring returns the pedal properly. After the pedal has returned, check that the pedal is clear of the pedal stop. If the pedal is against the pedal stop in the rest position, premature wear of the clutch facing will result.

6   When the operation of the pedal is satisfactory, tighten the clevis locknut and refit the parcel shelf.

3   Clutch cable – removal and refitting

1   Remove the parcel shelf (see Chapter 12) to gain access to the

upper end of the clutch pedal.

2   Release the two locknuts on the clutch cable adjuster in the engine compartment and slide the cable assembly out of its anchorage.

3   Unhook the clutch cable connection from the hook on the upper end of the clutch pedal and from the hook on the end of the clutch operating lever.

4   Pull the clutch cable through the front bulkhead into the engine compartment and remove the assembly.

5   When fitting a new cable, fit the pedal end first and when installation has been completed, check and if necessary adjust the pedal free-play.

4   Clutch – removal and refitting

1   Access to the clutch is obtained either by removing the engine (Chapter 1, Sections 3, 21 or 32) or by removing the transmission (Chapter 6, Sections 2 or 13). If the clutch requires attention and the engine is not in need of a major overhaul, it is preferable to gain access to the clutch by removing the gearbox, provided that either a pit is available, or the car can be put on ramps to give a good ground clearance.

2   Put a mark on the rim of the clutch pressure plate cover and a

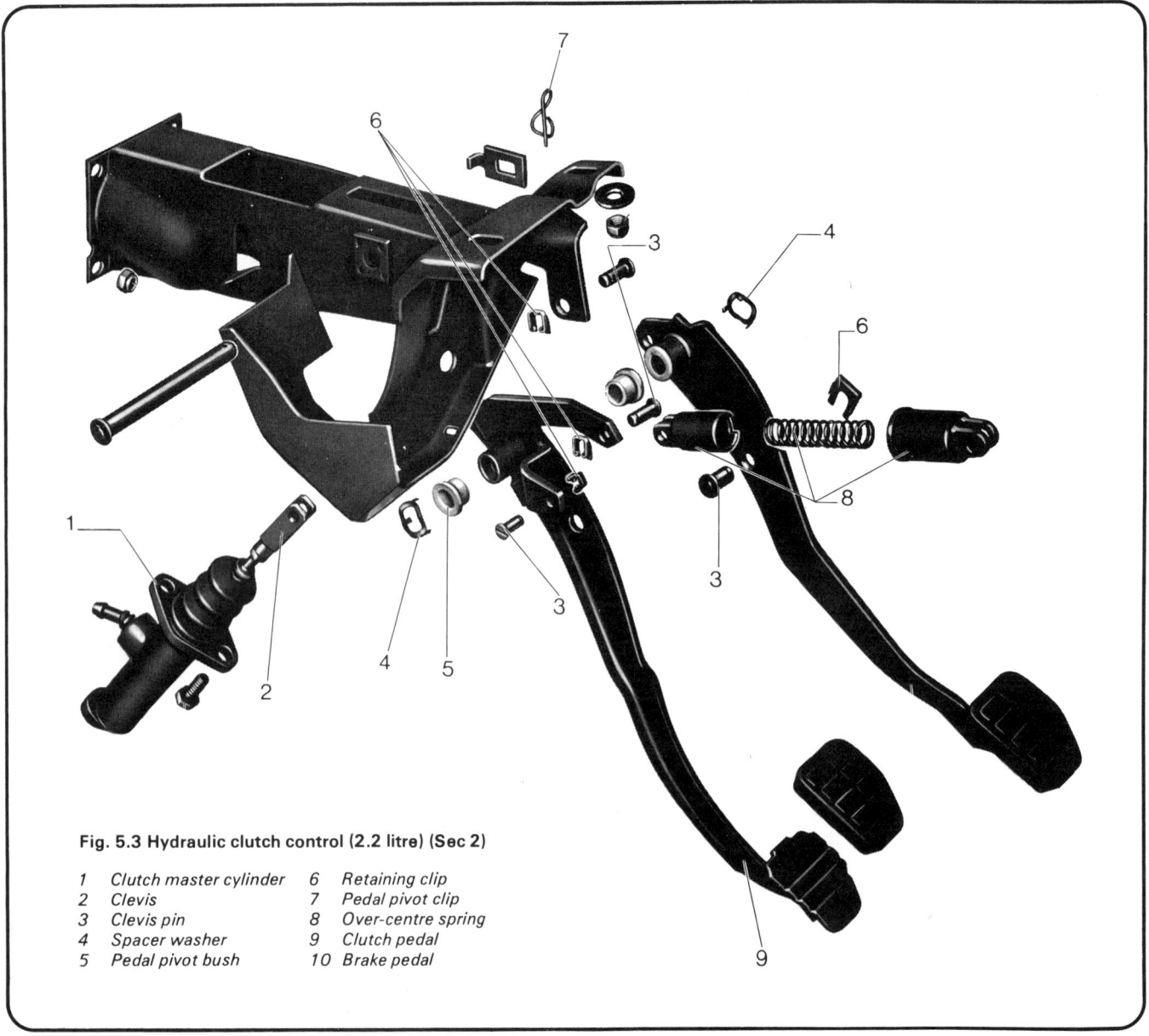

Fig. 5.3 Hydraulic clutch control (2.2 litre) (Sec 2)

1 Clutch master cylinder	6 Retaining clip
2 Clevis	7 Pedal pivot clip
3 Clevis pin	8 Over-centre spring
4 Spacer washer	9 Clutch pedal
5 Pedal pivot bush	10 Brake pedal

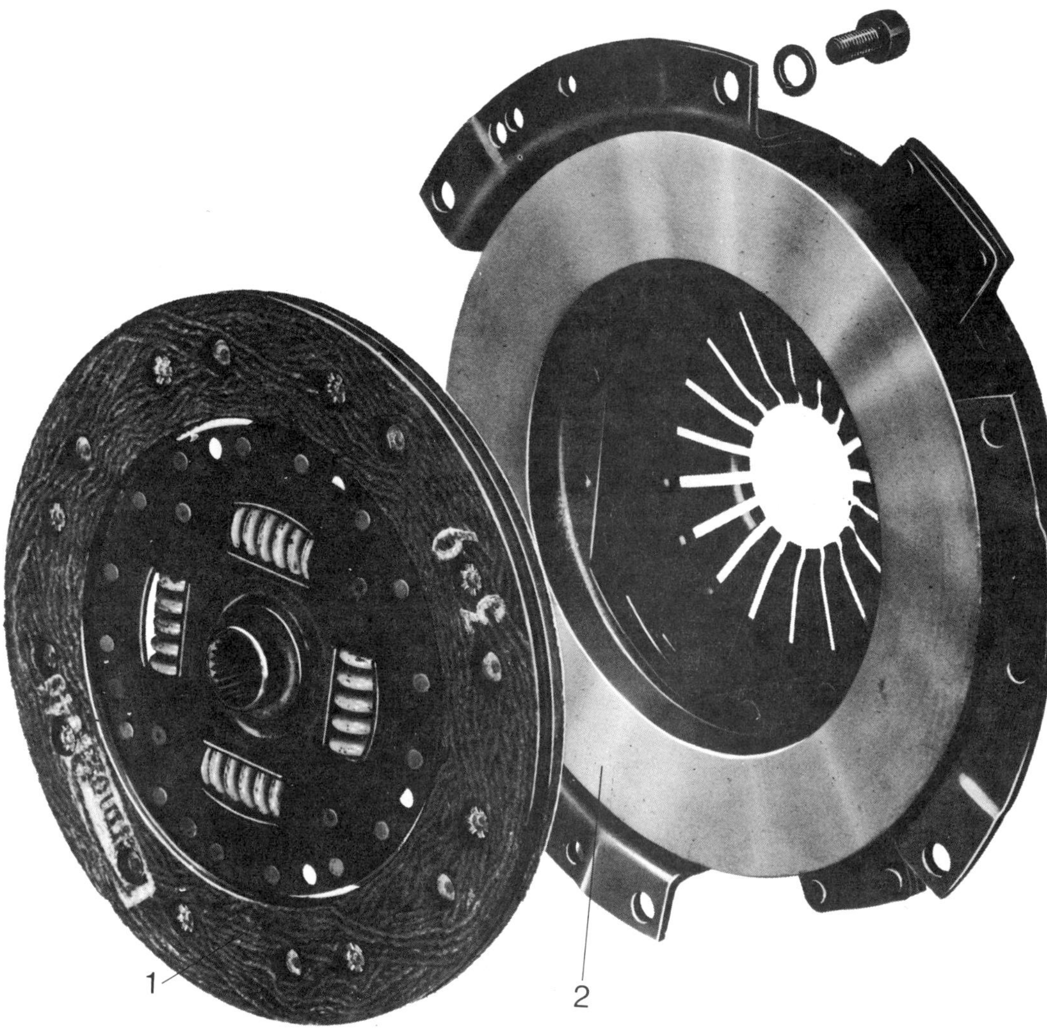

Fig. 5.4 Clutch components (Sec 4)

1   Friction plate (driven plate)   *2   Pressure plate assembly*

corresponding mark on the flywheel so that the clutch can be refitted in exactly the same position.

3   Slacken the clutch cover retaining bolts a turn at a time, working in diagonal pairs round the casing. When all the bolts have been loosened enough to release the tension on the diaphragm spring, remove the bolts and lift off the clutch cover and the friction plate.

4   Clean the parts with a damp cloth, ensuring that the dust is not inhaled. Because the dust produced by the wearing of the clutch facing may contain asbestos, which is dangerous to health, parts should not be blown clean or brushed to remove dust.

5   Examine the fingers of the diaphragm spring for signs of wear, or scoring. If the depth of any scoring exceeds 0.3 mm (0.012 in), a new cover assembly must be fitted.

6   Lay the clutch cover on its diaphragm spring end, place a steel straight edge diagonally across the pressure plate and test for distortion of the plate (Fig. 5.5). If a 0.3 mm (0.012 in) feeler gauge can be inserted in any gap beneath the straight edge, the clutch cover must be discarded and a new one fitted. The check for distortion should be made at several points round the plate.

7   Check that the plate is not badly distorted or scored, and shows no signs of cracking, or burning. The maximum run-out figure is given in Specifications.

8   Inspect the friction plate and fit a new plate if the surface of the

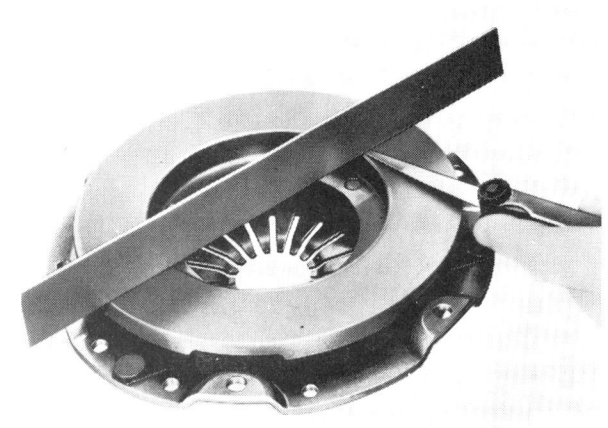

Fig. 5.5 Checking pressure plate distortion (Sec 4)

friction material left is approaching the level of the rivets. Discard the plate if the friction material has become impregnated with oil, or shows signs of breaking into shreds.

9   Examine the friction plate splined hub for signs of damage, or wear. Check that when the hub is on the gearbox input shaft, the hub slides smoothly along the shaft and that the radial clearance between the gearbox shaft and clutch hub is small.

10   If there is reason to suspect that the clutch hub is not running true, it should be checked by mounting the hub between centres and checking it with a dial gauge. Unless you have the proper equipment, get your local dealer to make this check.

11   Do not re-use any part which is suspect. Having gone to the trouble of dismantling the clutch, it is well worth ensuring that when reassembled it will operate satisfactorily for a long time. Check the flywheel for scoring and tiny cracks caused by overheating; refinish or renew as necessary (see Chapter 1).

12   Ensure that all the parts are clean, free of oil and grease and are in a satisfactory condition before reassembling.

13   Fit the friction plate so that the torsion spring cages are towards the pressure plate (photo).

14   Fit the clutch cover to the flywheel ensuring that the marks made before dismantling are lined up and insert all bolts finger tight to hold the cover in position.

15   Centralise the friction plate (photo), either by using a proprietary tool (photo), or by making up a similar tool to hold the friction plate concentric with the hole in the end of the crankshaft. If the clutch cover is tightened without the friction plate being centralised, it will be impossible to refit the gearbox as the input shaft will not pass through the drive plate hub and engage the spigot bearing.

16   With the centraliser holding the clutch friction plate in position, tighten all the clutch cover bolts a turn at a time in diagonal sequence until the specified torque is achieved.

17   Remove the centering tool and smear the hub splines with molybdenum disulphide lubricant.

5   Clutch release mechanism – removal and refitting

Cable operated clutch

1   Release the two spring clips, being careful to note how they are fitted and then slide the bearing over the release bearing guide sleeve.

2   Put a mark on the clutch operating lever and a mating mark on the end of the release shaft, to ensure that the lever and shaft splines are not moved relative to each other when the lever is refitted. Release the clamp bolt on the lever and pull the lever off the end of the shaft.

3   Prise the end of the clutch lever spring out of its recess inside the bellhousing and then rotate the shaft so that the shaft is no longer restrained by the guide sleeve.

4   Remove the circlip from the splined end of the release shaft and prise out the flanged bush. Pull the shaft to free it from the bush at its inner end and then remove the shaft from inside the bellhousing.

5   Clean the release bearing with a dry cloth. Do not wash the bearing in solvent, because this will cause its lubricant to be washed out. If the bearing is noisy, or has excessive wear, discard it and obtain a new one.

6   Inspect the release shaft and its bushes for wear. Do not remove the inner bush unless a new one has to be fitted. If a new inner bush is required, the old one will need a special extractor to remove it.

7   Before refitting the release shaft, coat it with molybdenum disulphide grease and ensure that the return spring is fitted to the shaft.

8   Reassemble the clutch operating mechanism by reversing the dismantling procedure.

Hydraulically operated clutch

9   Remove the release bearing as described in paragraph 1.

10   Unscrew and remove the bolt securing the clutch release lever retainer and leaf spring (photo). Remove the retainer and spring, then take out the clutch release lever (photo).

4.13 Assembling clutch with drive plate torsion springs away from flywheel

4.15a Centralising the clutch

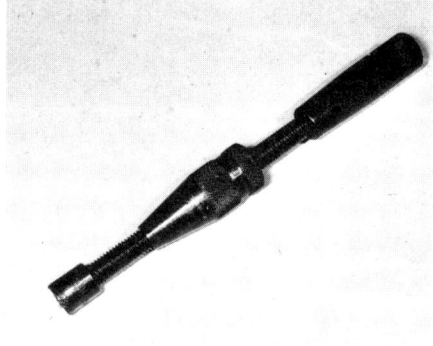
4.15b Clutch centralising tool

5.10a Clutch lever retainer leaf spring (arrowed)

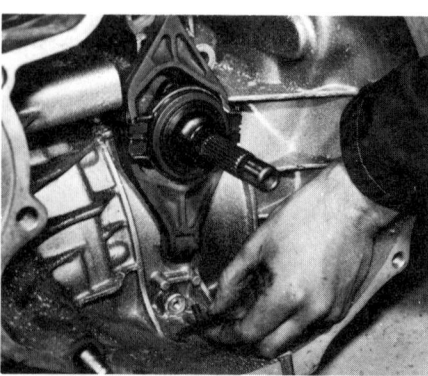
5.10b Removing the retainer and spring leaf

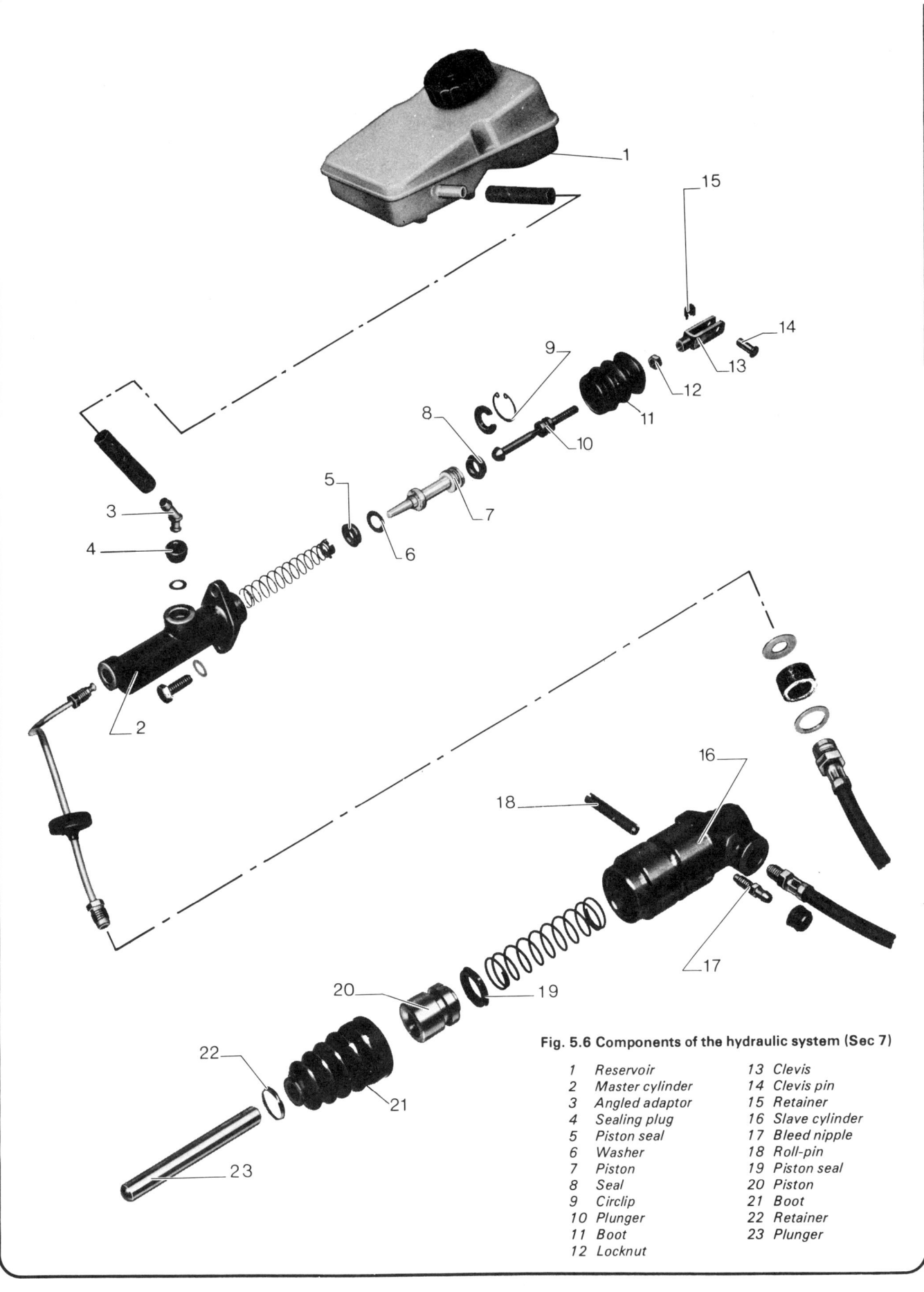

Fig. 5.6 Components of the hydraulic system (Sec 7)

1	Reservoir	13	Clevis
2	Master cylinder	14	Clevis pin
3	Angled adaptor	15	Retainer
4	Sealing plug	16	Slave cylinder
5	Piston seal	17	Bleed nipple
6	Washer	18	Roll-pin
7	Piston	19	Piston seal
8	Seal	20	Piston
9	Circlip	21	Boot
10	Plunger	22	Retainer
11	Boot	23	Plunger
12	Locknut		

11 Clean the release bearing as described in paragraph 5. Coat the top of the ball cap inside the bellhousing and also all the working surfaces of the clutch operating lever with molybdenum disulphide grease and refit the arm and release bearing by reversing the removal procedure.

6 Bleeding the clutch hydraulic system

1 If any part of the hydraulic system is dismantled, or if air has accidentally entered the system, the system will need to be bled. The presence of air is characterised by the pedal having a "spongy" feel (which lessens if the pedal is pumped a few times) and it results in difficulty in changing gear.

2 Bleeding the system requires the help of an assistant, unless you have some form of one man (pressure bleeding) equipment which is obtainable at low cost from accessory shops.

3 Attach a piece of tight fitting tubing to the bleed nipple of the clutch slave cylinder, which is at the top of the gearbox housing. Pour about an inch (25.4 mm) of clutch fluid of approved specification into a small clean jar and immerse the other end of the tube in the jar. Fix the end of the tube so that it cannot come above the fluid and secure the jar so that it cannot be knocked over.

4 Top-up the fluid reservoir to its fullest extent and then unscrew the bleed nipple one full turn.

5 Instruct an assistant to depress the clutch pedal fully and keep it depressed until told to release it. As the assistant depresses the pedal, watch for bubbles coming from the end of the immersed tube, then while the pedal is still depressed, screw in the bleed nipple until it is closed.

6 Repeat the sequence of opening the nipple, depressing the pedal, closing the nipple and releasing the pedal as many times as is necessary to ensure that the ejected fluid is free from air bubbles, but top-up the fluid reservoir after every four or five sequences to prevent more air being drawn in due to the feed pipe from the reservoir becoming uncovered.

7 When bleeding has been completed, close the bleed nipple securely and remove the tubing and jar.

8 Discard any fluid which is bled from the system, even if it looks clean. Brake fluid absorbs water and its re-use can cause internal corrosion of the master and slave cylinders, leading to excessive wear and failure of the seals.

7 Servicing the hydraulic system

Master cylinder

1 Remove the parcel shelf (see Chapter 12) to gain access to the master cylinder. Remove the retainer from the master cylinder clevis and withdraw the clevis pin.

2 Remove the two bolts securing the master cylinder to the pedal bracket (photo) and free the cylinder from the bracket.

3 Place a large tray beneath the cylinder to prevent any hydraulic fluid spilling on to the carpet. Pull the fluid feed hose off the angled adaptor on the master cylinder and plug the hose to stop the escape of fluid.

4 Unscrew the union from the end of the cylinder, withdraw the pipe and either plug the pipe, or put a cap over its end to seal it.

5 Dismantle the master cylinder in the following sequence. First slacken the clevis locknut, screw the clevis and the locknut off the master cylinder operating rod. Pull off the rubber boot, remove the circlip from the mouth of the cylinder bore and pull out the piston assembly and spring. Note which way round the two piston seals are fitted. The lip of each of the seals should be towards the closed end of the cylinder.

6 Dismantle the piston assembly as shown in Fig. 5.6 Reassemble it using all the parts supplied in the repair kit and coat the seals and pistons lightly with brake cylinder grease before installation. When inserting the piston assembly into the cylinder, take care not to fold back the lips of the seals and if necessary use a pointed matchstick to ease the lips of the seals into the bore.

7 After refitting the cylinder by reversing the removal operations, bleed the hydraulic system and adjust the pedal height as described in Sections 6 and 2 respectively.

Slave cylinder

8 Drive out the roll-pin assembly securing the slave cylinder to the clutch bellhousing and withdraw the cylinder.

9 Hold the flexible pipe union with a spanner and screw the slave cylinder off the pipe, taking care not to lose any sealing washer fitted between the union and the cylinder. Seal the end of the pipe to prevent dirt from entering and fluid from escaping.

10 Dismantle the cylinder by pulling out the operating rod, removing the boot, removing the retaining ring from the mouth of the bore and pulling out the piston and spring. Note that the lip of the piston seal points towards the spring.

11 Reassemble the cylinder using all the parts supplied in the repair kit and coat the seal and piston lightly with brake grease before installation. When inserting the piston into the cylinder, take care not to fold back the lip of the seal and if necessary use a pointed matchstick to ease the lip of the seal into the bore.

12 After refitting the cylinder, by reversing the removal operations, bleed the hydraulic system and check the pedal height, as described in Sections 6 and 2 respectively.

13 Do not use any solvent to clean any components of the hydraulic system. Methylated spirit may be used, but rubber parts should be dropped in the spirit and then removed and must not be left soaking in methylated spirit.

14 If the bores of cylinders are scored, or are rusty, new seals are only likely to be effective for a short time and it is preferable to fit a new cylinder assembly.

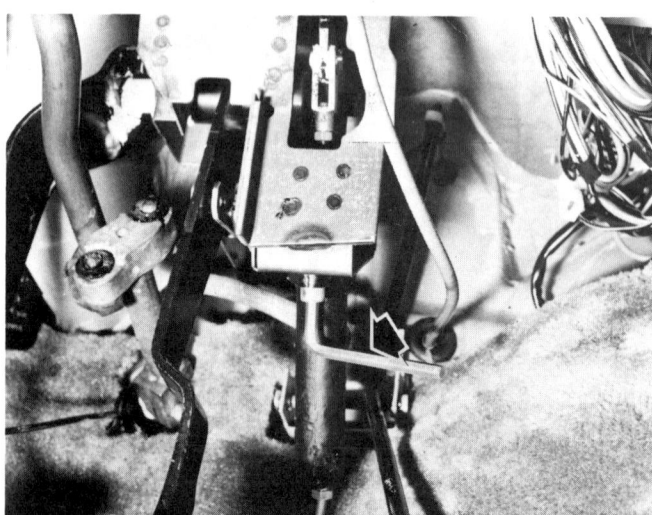

7.2 Removing a clutch master cylinder bolt (Allen key arrowed)

8.4 Over-centre spring assembly (arrowed) – 2.2 litre clutch pedal

8 Clutch pedal – removal and refitting

1   The clutch and brake pedals share a common bracket assembly and there are slight differences in the bracket for the 2.2 litre with hydraulic clutch, compared with the other models.

2   Remove the parcel shelf, then remove the clips from the clevis pins connecting the clutch and brake controls to their respective pedals and withdraw the pins.

3   Remove four self-locking nuts securing the pedal assembly to the front bulkhead, and the two self-locking nuts securing the front mount-ing, and withdraw the assembly.

4   Withdraw the spring clip from the end of the pedal pivot pin and withdraw the pin. In the 2.2 litre model also remove the pin securing the over-centre spring assembly (photo).

5   To renew the pedal bushes, drive out the old ones with a punch and press in the new ones between the jaws of a vice. If necessary ream the bushes to give a satisfactory fit for the pivot pin.

6   Before reassembly, smear all contact surfaces with molybdenum disulphide grease. Renew all self-locking nuts, spring clips and spacers and reassemble as the reverse of dismantling. On completion check that the pedal settings are correct.

9 Fault diagnosis – clutch

Sympton	Reason(s)
Judder when taking up drive	Loose engine mountings Oil contaminated clutch facing Worn splines on driven plate or gearbox input shaft
Clutch slip	Oil contaminated clutch facing Lack of lubrication of clutch splines Worn driven plate Incorrect cable adjustment
Clutch spin	Oil on clutch facing Incorrect cable adjustment
Noise on depressing clutch pedal	Dry, or worn clutch release bearing
Difficulty in disengaging clutch	Fault in master or slave cylinder Incorrect cable adjustment Air in hydraulic system Lack of lubrication on clutch splines

Chapter 6 Manual gearbox and final drive

Contents

Specifications

1.6 litre engine
Gearbox type . . . . 014/11, four forward speeds and reverse, in unit with final drive, synchromesh on all forward speeds

Code letters . . . . YS

Gear ratios:

Final drive	40 : 9	4.44 : 1
1st gear	38 : 11	3.45 : 1
2nd gear	35 : 18	1.94 : 1
3rd gear	36 : 28	1.29 : 1
4th gear	30 : 33	0.909 : 1
Reverse	38 : 12	3.17 : 1

Oil capacity . . . . 1.7 litre, 3 Imp pt, 3.6 US pt

Oil specification . . . . Hypoid gear oil, SAE 80 or 80W 90

2.0 litre engine
Gearbox type . . . . 088, four forward speeds and reverse, in unit with final drive, synchromesh on all forward speeds

Code letters . . . . XY or XU

Gear ratios:

Final drive	35 : 9	3.89 : 1
1st gear	36 : 10	3.60 : 1
2nd gear	34 : 16	2.125 : 1
3rd gear	34 : 25	1.36 : 1
4th gear	29 : 30	0.996 : 1
Reverse	42 : 12	3.50 : 1

Oil capacity . . . . 2.6 litre, 4.69 Imp pt, 5.5 US pt

Oil specification . . . . Hypoid gear oil SAE 80 or 80W 90

2.2 litre engine (115 HP carburettor and 136 HP injection)
Code letters XV
All other details as 2.0 litre

2.2 litre engine (108 HP injection and 115 HP injection)
Code letters . . . . XW

Final drive . . . .   37 : 9   4.11 : 1
All other details as 2.0 litre

Torque wrench settings

1.6 litre

	Nm	lbf ft
Driveshaft flange	45	32
Gearbox-to-engine	55	40
Starter-to-gearbox	20	15
Driveflange-to-gearbox	20	15
Oil drain plug	25	18
Bearing carrier-to-gearbox housing	25	18
Pinion nut	100	72
Gearshift housing-to-gear casing	25	18
Clutch release shaft bolt	15	11
Oil filler plug	25	18
Relay lever bolt	35	25
Reversing light switch	30	22
Gearshift linkage side plates	30	22
Gearshift adaptor-to-selector lever	15	11
Gearshift lever-to-shift rod	10	7
Lever housing-to-floor	10	7
Lever bearing-to-lever housing	10	7
Final drive cover	25	18
Gearbox support-to-subframe	45	32
Gearbox support-to-gearbox	25	18

2.0 and 2.2 litre

	Nm	lbf ft
Driveshaft flange	45	33
Gearbox-to-engine	55	40
Starter-to-gearbox	60	43
Bearing carrier-to-gearbox housing	25	18
Drive flange-to-gearbox	25	18
Selector shaft cover	10	7
Mainshaft securing bolt	25	18
Oil drain plug	25	18
Oil filler plug	25	18
Reverse gear shaft bolt	25	18
Rocker lever bolt	35	25
Detent plugs	30	22
Reversing light switch	30	22
Gearlever base-to-floor	10	7
Gearlever-to-gearshift rod	10	7
Gearshift rod clamp-bolt	15	11
Selector lever clamp-bolt	15	11
Stop and cover plate-to-gear lever base	10	7
Final drive cover	25	18
Gearbox support-to-gearbox	40	28
Gearbox support-to-subframe	40	28
Subframe-to-body	110	79

Part A – 1.6 litre models (Type 014/11 gearbox)

1   General description

1.6 litres models are fitted with the Type 014/11 gearbox. The 2.0 and 2.2 litre models are fitted with the Type 088 gearbox. These gearboxes differ in several respects, although they both have four forward gears and reverse and incorporate the final reduction gear and differential assembly within the gearbox casing, using a common lubrication system. Both gearboxes have an input shaft and a pinion output shaft and have similar gear arrangements. The clutch bellhousing which incorporates the clutch release mechanism is an integral part of the gearbox housing.

All models have a floor mounted gear change lever with a linkage connecting the lever to the gearbox, but the shift mechanism and selector layout on the Type 014/11 gearbox (1.6 litre model) is completely different from the Type 088 gearbox used on the 2.0 and 2.2 litre models.

2   Gearbox – removal and refitting (engine in vehicle)

1   This can be done much more easily if the vehicle is over a pit. If this is not possible, the front wheels may be put on ramps, but it is unsafe to attempt to remove the gearbox with the car supported on jacks.
2   Disconnect the battery leads.
3   Remove the nuts securing the exhaust pipe to the manifold and then undo the clip securing the exhaust pipe to the gearbox.
4   Remove the upper bolts attaching the gearbox to the engine.
5   Disengage the clutch cable from the clutch lever.
6   Unscrew the speedometer drive from the final drive casing, then tie the cable out of the way.
7   Using a socket wrench, remove the bolts from the driveshaft flange couplings. Separate the coupling parts and rest the driveshafts on the subframe.

8   Remove the cover plate and then remove the lower bolts attaching the gearbox to the engine.

9   Remove the bolts securing the starter motor and pull the starter motor back towards the engine support as far as it will go.

10 Mark the gear shift rod so that it can be re-inserted in the shift finger in exactly the same way. It is important to mark both the distance to which it is inserted and also to ensure that the splines are mated in exactly the same way, otherwise there will be difficulty in engaging all the gears.

11 Detach the gear shift rod and also press the support strut off its balljoint.

12 Disconnect the cables from the reversing light switch.

13 Raise the gearbox slightly by using a jack beneath it, but place a block of wood between the jack and the gearbox casing.

14 Remove the bolts securing the gearbox support to the subframe and then prise the gearbox away from the engine until the mainshaft is clear of the clutch plate.

15 Lower the gearbox and remove it from beneath the car.

16 The gearbox is refitted by reversing the above operations, but noting the following points:

(a) *The splines on the mainshaft should be coated with molybdenum disulphide powder, or smeared with graphite grease before it is inserted into the clutch and care is necessary to ensure that the shaft is not strained while being inserted*

(b) *Take care not to damage the shaft of the starter motor when refitting the gearbox and the starter motor*

(c) *Fit the gearbox on to the dowel sleeves and when fitting the gearbox mounting make sure that neither it nor the engine mounts are under strain*

3   Gearbox – removal and refitting (engine out of vehicle)

1   If the engine and radiator have already been removed, the removal of the gearbox is simplified. The gearbox mounting will already have been disconnected and the gearbox supported on a jack.

2   Disconnect the driveshaft coupling flanges and support the driveshafts on the subframe.

3   Disconnect the gear change rod, taking the precautions detailed in paragraph 10 of Section 2.

4   Disconnect the speedometer drive. Disconnect the clutch cable and tie both the speedometer drive and the clutch cable out of the way.

5   Disconnect the cables from the reversing light switch.

6   Check that the gearbox is free and then move it forward and lift it out of the engine compartment.

4   Gearbox – dismantling

1   Remove the gearbox drain plug, drain out the oil and refit the plug. Clean away external dirt from the gearbox casing.

2   Remove the bolts from the selector housing. If necessary give the selector housing a light tap to separate it from the gear housing and then manoeuvre the selector housing off the gear housing. Remove the shim and gasket.

3   Carefully pull the 3rd/4th gear selector rod out of the casing until the small interlock plunger (Fig. 6.4) can be removed. Be careful not to pull the shaft out further than is absolutely necessary because the locking keys of the synchro-hub may fall out.

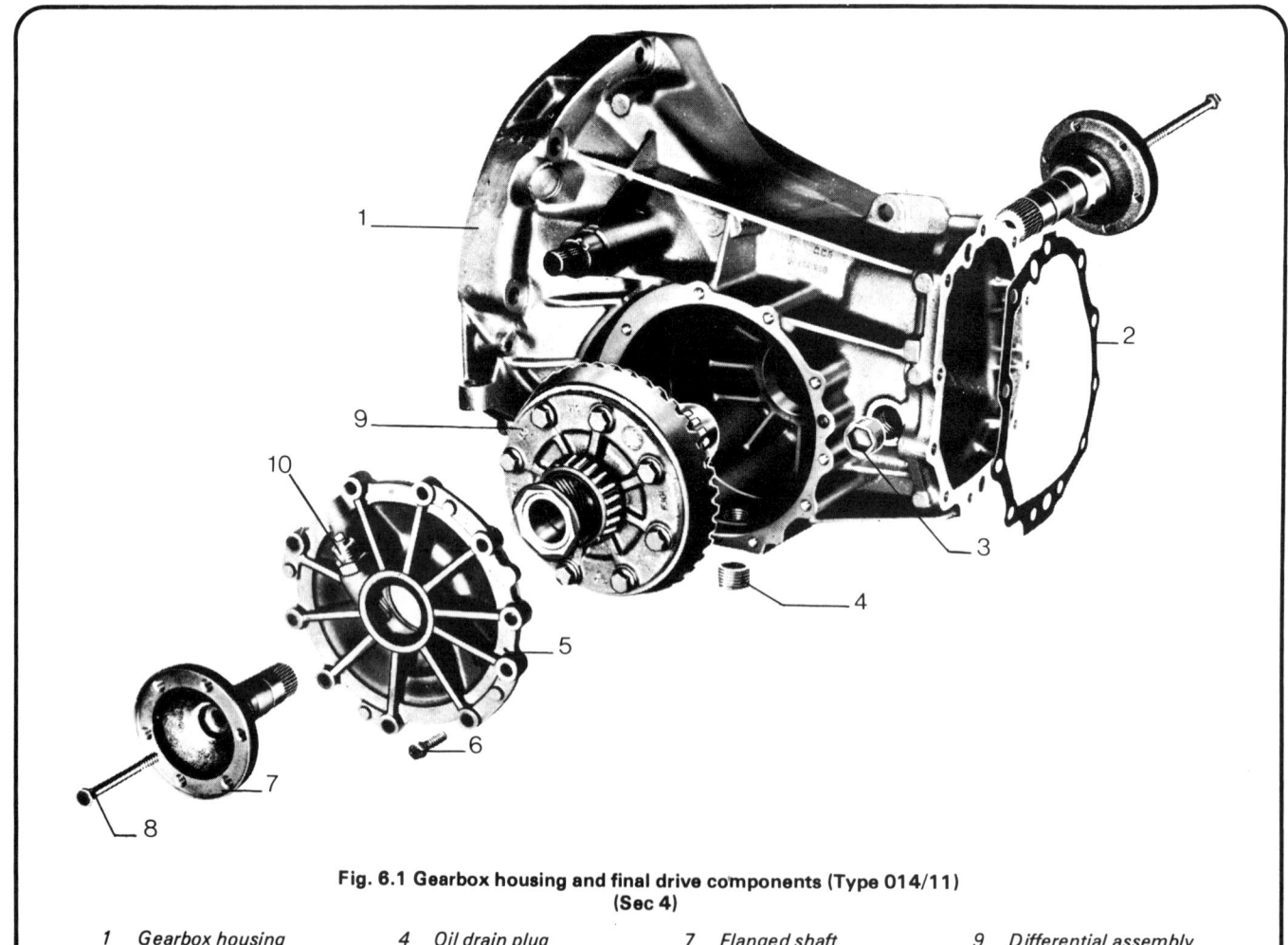

Fig. 6.1 Gearbox housing and final drive components (Type 014/11)
(Sec 4)

1	Gearbox housing	4	Oil drain plug	7	Flanged shaft	9	Differential assembly
2	Gasket	5	Final drive cover	8	Shaft retaining bolt	10	Speedometer drive
3	Oil filler plug	6	Cover bolt				

Fig. 6.2 Selector housing bolts (Type 014/11) (Sec 4)

1   M8 x 75 with washer (3)
2   M8 x 45 with washer (12)
3   M8 x 80 with spring washer (5)
4   M8 x 44/15 special bolt (1)

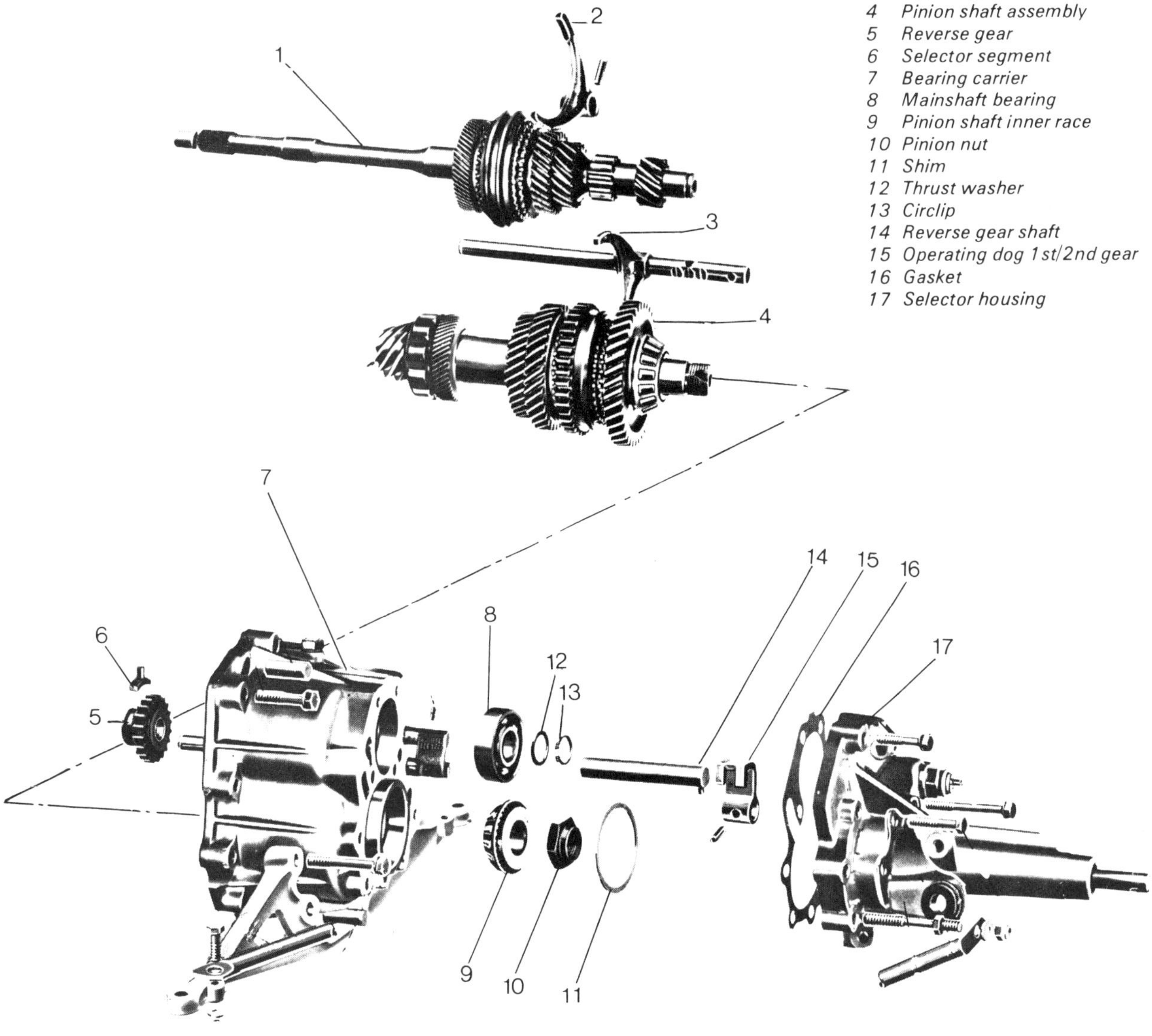

Fig.6.3 Bearing carrier and selector housing components (Type 014/11) (Sec 4)

1   Mainshaft assembly
2   3rd/4th gear selector fork
3   1st/2nd gear selector fork
4   Pinion shaft assembly
5   Reverse gear
6   Selector segment
7   Bearing carrier
8   Mainshaft bearing
9   Pinion shaft inner race
10 Pinion nut
11 Shim
12 Thrust washer
13 Circlip
14 Reverse gear shaft
15 Operating dog 1st/2nd gear
16 Gasket
17 Selector housing

Fig. 6.4 Removing the interlock plunger (Type 014/11 gearbox) (Sec 4)

Fig. 6.5 Engaging 1st and reverse gears (Type 014/11 gearbox) (Sec 4)

Fig. 6.6 Driving out 3rd/4th gear selector pin (Type 014/11 gearbox) (Sec 4)

Fig. 6.7 Removing reverse gear shaft (Type 014/11 gearbox) (Sec 4)

4 Having removed the plunger, push the shaft back in to its neutral position. If the locking keys of the synchro-hub have fallen out it will not be possible to push the rod back in and the alternative method of removing the pinion nut given in the next paragraph will have to be used.

5 Pull the upper selector rod out to engage reverse gear and the lower one out to engage first gear (Fig. 6.5). By engaging the two gears at once the shafts will be locked and the pinion nut can be undone. If two gears cannot be engaged, it will be necessary to hold the pinion shaft by gripping fourth gear in a soft-jawed vice so that the pinion nut can be undone.

6 Remove the circlip and thrust washer from the end of the input shaft.

7 The next step is to remove the ball bearing from the input shaft and this operation requires the use of a special bearing extractor.

8 Remove the bolts securing the bearing carrier and gearbox housing and detach the bearing carrier with the input shaft and pinion shaft.

9 Drive the dowel pins back until they are flush with the joint face.

10 Clamp the gearbox in a soft-jawed vice. Support the free end of the 3rd/4th gear selector shaft by jamming a block of hardwood under it and drive the roll-pin out of the selector shaft. If the free end of the shaft is not supported while the pin is driven out, the bore for the shaft in the gear carrier may be damaged.

11 Pull out the 3rd/4th gear selector shaft until the 3rd/4th gear selector fork can be removed and then push the shaft back to its neutral position.

12 Remove the input shaft assembly.

13 Drive out the reverse gear shaft and remove reverse gear and its selector segment.

14 Drive out the roll-pin from the 1st/2nd gear operating dog and remove the dog from the selector shaft.

15 Using a soft-faced hammer, or a hammer and drift, drive the pinion shaft out of its bearing. While doing this check that the 1st/2nd gear selector shaft does not become jammed and if necessary tap the shaft lightly to free it. Recover the taper-roller bearing race when the shaft is removed.

16 Dismantle the gearbox housing as follows. First insert a suitable rod through one of the bolt holes of a coupling flange so that the rod is against one of the cover ribs and so prevents the flange from rotating, then remove the bolt from the centre of the flange (photo). Repeat the operation on the other coupling flange and then use two levers to prise out the flanged shafts. Mark each shaft as it is removed to ensure that it is fitted to its correct side of the gearbox housing.

17 Remove the ten bolts from the differential cover, remove the cover, and take out the differential (photos).

5 Mainshaft – dismantling and reassembly

1 Remove the circlip from the end of the shaft (photo) and then remove the thrust washer.

2 Lift off the 4th gearwheel with its needle roller bearing (photo). If the bearing is removed from the gear, put a paint mark on the bearing and the gear so that the bearing is not turned end-for-end on reassembling.

3 Remove the 4th gear synchro-ring.

4 Remove the circlip retaining the synchro-hub (photo) and take the hub off the shaft. It may be possible to hold the 3rd gearwheel and tap the shaft out of the synchro-hub, or it may be necessary to have the hub pressed off.

5 Remove the 3rd gear synchro-ring, the 3rd gearwheel and its needle roller bearing.

6 Mark the gear and bearing so that the bearing is not turned end-for-end on reassembly.

7 Before starting reassembly, ensure that all parts are clean and inspect them for signs of damage or excessive wear. Gearbox components are very expensive and if any gears or shafts are required it may be economic to fit an exchange gearbox.

8 Lubricate the 3rd gear needle roller bearing with gear oil and fit

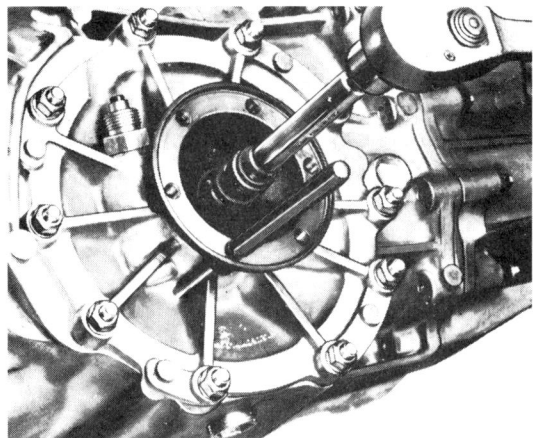

Fig. 6.8 Removing the driveflange bolt (Type 014/11 gearbox) (Sec 4)

the bearing onto the shaft, ensuring that the bearing is the same way up as it was before removal.

9 Fit the 3rd gearwheel.

10 If the synchroniser has been dismantled, look for mating marks etched on the outer edge (Fig. 6.10). If so, the hub must be assembled with these marks in line. Later models do not having mating marks and do not need to be reassembled in a particular position.

11 Fit the three locking keys into the hub before fitting the sleeve and then retain the keys with the circlips, positioning the circlips as shown in Fig 6.10, with the angled end of the spring fitted into the hollow of the locking key.

12 Fit the 3rd gear synchro-ring onto the cone of the gear and measure the gap "a" in Fig. 6.11, using a feeler gauge. This gap must not exceed 0.5 mm (0.020 in) otherwise a new synchro-ring must be fitted.

13 Note that the splines on the bore of the synchro-hub are chamfered at one end. The chamfered end of the hub goes onto the shaft first, facing 3rd gear. The hub also has an additional groove at one end (Fig. 6.12) and this groove faces 4th gear.

14 Press the synchroniser on to the mainshaft, first turning the 3rd gear synchro-ring so that the grooves on it are aligned with the synchroniser locking keys.

15 Insert the circlip on top of the synchro-hub and then press the synchroniser back against the circlip. This increases the gap between the synchroniser and 3rd gear which ensures better lubrication of the 3rd gear bearing.

16 Fit the 4th gear synchro-ring, aligning the grooves in it with the synchroniser locking keys, then check its clearance, as in paragraph 12.

17 Fit 4th gear and its bearing, first lubricating the bearing with gear oil, fit the thrust washer and finally the circlip.

18 Measure the axial clearance between 4th gear and the thrust washer (Fig. 6.13). This clearance should be at least 0.10 mm (0.004 in), but less than 0.40 mm (0.016 in). If it exceeds the upper limit, a thicker thrust washer must be fitted and these are available in three thicknesses, 3.47 mm (0.136 in), 3.57 mm (0.141 in) and 3.67 mm (0.144 in).

4.16 Removing the drive flange retaining bolt (Type 088 gearbox shown)

4.17a Removing the differential cover plate (Type 088 gearbox shown)

4.17b Removing the differential assembly (Type 088 gearbox shown)

5.1 Removing the mainshaft circlip (Type 088 gearbox shown)

5.2 Removing 4th gearwheel and synchro-ring (Type 088 gearbox shown)

5.4 Removing the synchroniser circlip (Type 088 gearbox shown)

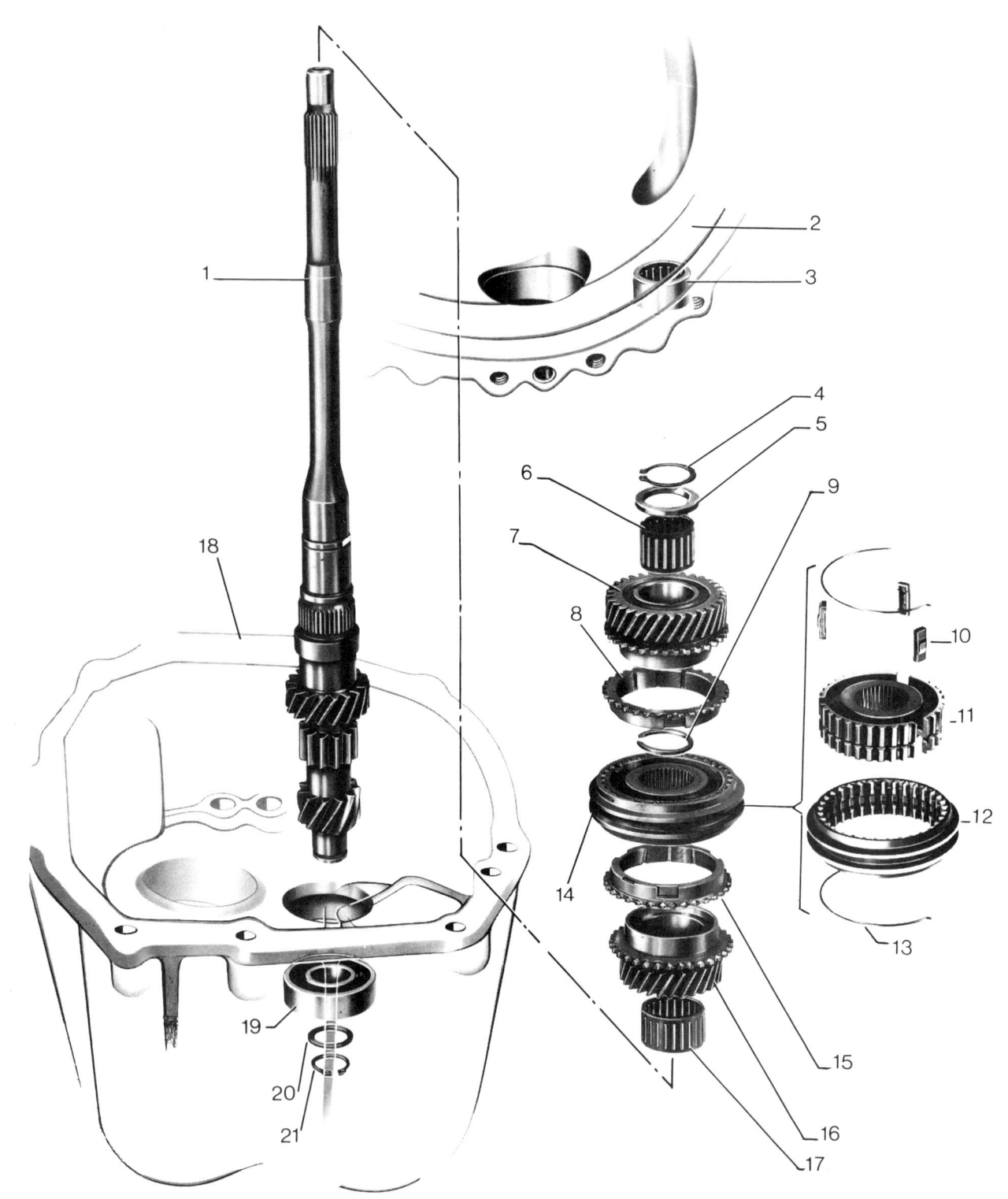

Fig. 6.9 Mainshaft components (Type 014/11 gearbox) (Sec 5)

1	Mainshaft	7	4th gearwheel	12	Synchro-sleeve
2	Gearbox housing	8	4th gear synchro-ring	13	Wire circlip
3	Mainshaft needle bearing	9	Circlip	14	Synchroniser assembly
4	Circlip	10	Locking keys	15	3rd gear synchro-ring
5	Thrust washer	11	Synchro-hub	16	3rd gearwheel
6	4th gear bearing				

17   3rd gear bearing
18   Bearing carrier
19   Mainshaft bearing
20   Thrust washer
21   Circlip

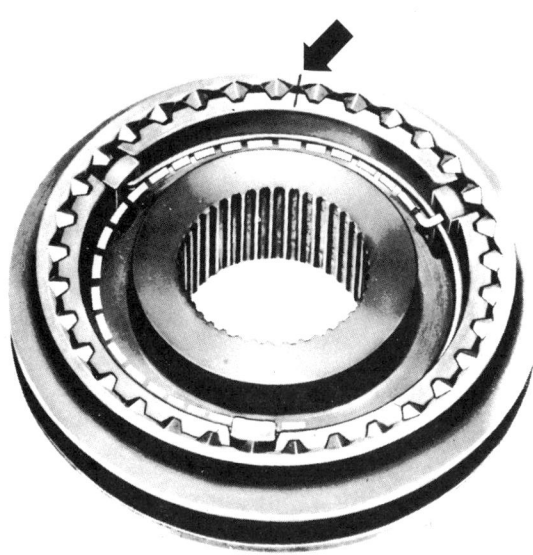

Fig. 6.10 Synchroniser mating marks (arrowed) (Type 014/11 gearbox) (Sec 5)

Fig. 6.11 Checking the synchroniser rings (Type 014/11 gearbox) (Sec 5)

Dimension "a" must not exceed 0.5 mm (0.02 in)

Fig. 6.12 3rd/4th gear synchroniser assembly (Type 014/11 gearbox) (Sec 5)

*Chamfer on splines (black arrow) towards 3rd gear
Groove in end (white arrow) towards 4th gear*

Fig. 6.13 Checking 4th gear axial clearance (Type 014/11 gearbox) (Sec 5)

6 Pinion shaft – dismantling and reassembly

1 The depth of the pinion's engagement with the crownwheel is adjusted during manufacture to the optimum position for quiet running and long life. When components affecting the pinion engagement are changed, adjustments must be made to regain this optimum position. Before the pinion shaft is dismantled or replacement items fitted, the position of the pinion must be established by measurement. Because this requires the use of specialist measuring equipment the work should be entrusted to your Audi dealer. The components which affect the pinion engagement are the gearbox casing, the bearing carrier, the double taper-roller bearing, and the 1st gear needle roller bearing. The crownwheel and pinion must be replaced as a matched pair and the pinion engagement adjusted to the figure etched onto the crownwheel – a job for your Audi dealer.

2 Using a suitable puller, remove the 2nd inner bearing race from the end of the shaft and then remove the 1st speed gear, its needle roller bearing and sleeve. Ensure that the needle roller assembly and the sleeve are marked so that they are not turned end-for-end when refitted.

3 Lift off the 1st gear synchro-ring.

4 Using a puller with its legs placed beneath the 2nd gearwheel, draw off the gear and the 1st/2nd gear synchroniser assembly.

5 Lift off the 2nd gear needle roller bearing and mark it to ensure correct refitting.

6 The 3rd speed and 4th speed gears are pressed and shrunk on to the shaft and if they need to be removed, the work should be entrusted to an Audi dealer.

7 Reassembly will commence with the pinion end bearing, 4th gear, 3rd gear and the circlip already on the pinion shaft; complete reassembly of the shaft as follows.

8 Lubricate the 2nd gear needle roller bearing with gear oil and fit it to the shaft.

9 Fit the 2nd gearwheel onto its bearing, then place the synchro-ring on the gear. Measure the gap as in Fig. 6.11. If the gap exceeds 0·5 mm (0·020 in), a new synchro-ring must be fitted.

10 If the synchroniser assembly has been dismantled, it must be reassembled in the following way. The sleeve and the hub may have matching marks, if so they must be assembled with these marks (Fig. 6.15) lined up. Fit the three locking keys into their slots and secure the keys with the circlips. The circlips should be spaced 120° apart and the angled end of the circlip should be engaged in the hollow of a locking key. If there are no matching marks on the hub and sleeve the two parts need not be assembled in any particular position, except that the groove on either the hub spline, or the end of the hub (Fig. 6.16)

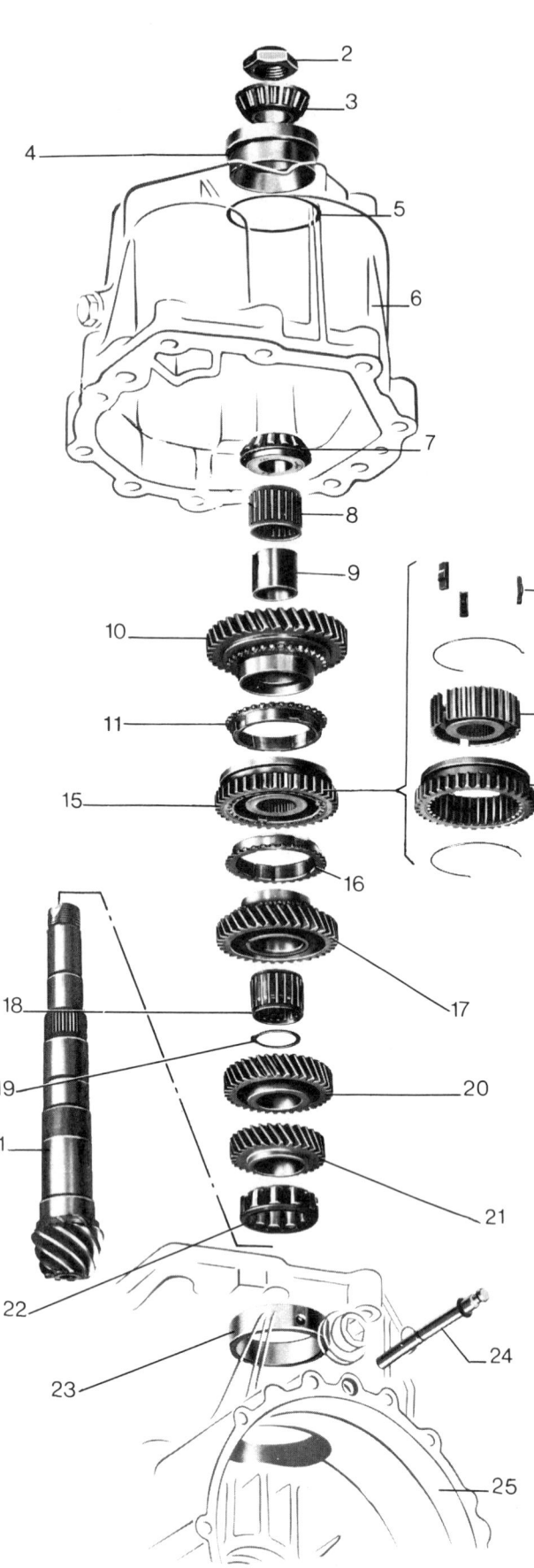

Fig. 6.14 Pinion shaft components (Type 014/11 gearbox)
(Sec 6)

1	Pinion shaft	14	Synchro-sleeve
2	Pinion nut	15	Synchroniser assembly
3	1st inner race	16	2nd gear synchro-ring
4	Outer track	17	2nd gearwheel
5	Shim	18	2nd gear bearing
6	Bearing carrier	19	Circlip
7	2nd inner race	20	3rd gearwheel
8	1st gear bearing	21	4th gearwheel
9	1st gear sleeve	22	Roller bearing
10	1st gearwheel	23	Bearing outer track
11	1st gear synchro-ring	24	Bearing track retaining pin
12	Locking keys	25	Gearbox housing
13	Synchro-hub		

Fig. 6.15 Synchroniser mating marks (arrowed) (Type 014/11
gearbox) (Sec 6)

must face towards 1st gear.

11 Fit the synchroniser assembly to the shaft, with the end of the
sleeve having external teeth towards the pinion. Before pressing the
hub down fully, turn the 2nd gear synchro-ring so that the slots in it
are aligned with the locking keys in the synchroniser assembly.

12 Fit the 1st gear synchro-ring, lining up its slots with the locking
keys in the synchroniser assembly. Later models have a modified
synchro-ring with a tooth missing at three points (Fig. 6.17). The tooth
angle on these synchro-rings was altered from 120° to 110° to
improve the engagement of 1st gear. This type of ring must only be
used on 1st gear and if the 1st gear ring is being renewed, the 120°
type, having the full number of teeth, should be fitted.

13 Fit the 1st gear bearing sleeve, then lubricate the needle roller
bearing with gear oil and fit it over the sleeve.

14 Fit the 1st gearwheel and then press on the 2nd inner race of the
tapered roller bearing.

7 Gearbox housing – servicing

1   The removal and re-fitting of the clutch release mechanism fitted
in the gearbox housing is described in Chapter 5, Section 5.

Input shaft needle bearing (Fig. 6.18)

2   Using a drift, or piece of hardwood dowel of suitable size, drive the
bearing out from the clutch bellhousing end of the casing. Fit the new
bearing so that the lettering on the bearing faces the drift used for
installation. Enter the bearing into the bore squarely from the gearbox
side of the casing and using a drift, or a piece of hardwood, knock it in
until it is flush with the face of the casting.

Fig. 6.16 1st/2nd gear synchroniser assembly (Type 014/11 gearbox) (Sec 6)

Groove on hub splines (white arrow) or end of hub (black arrow) must be towards 1st gear

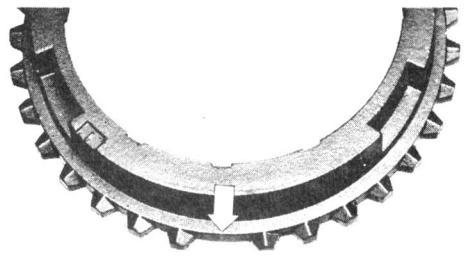

Fig. 6.17 Identification of 110° synchro-ring for 1st gear (Type 014/11 gearbox) (Sec 6)

7.8 Removing the guide sleeve (Type 088 gearbox shown)

Pinion bearing

3   The outer track of the pinion bearing is secured by a pin which engages a depression in the outer circumference of the bearing. Grip the grooved end of the pin and pull it out at least $\frac{1}{8}$ in (3·2 mm) so that the other end is clear of the bearing. Using a suitable drift, tap the outer race out of the end of the casing. When fitting a new outer track, line up the depression in the outer track with the pin and then drive the track in flush with the face of the casting before tapping home the pin (the grooves marking on the end face of the bearing track should face towards the gearbox). Renewing the roller assembly of the bearing is a job for an Audi agent, the 3rd and 4th gearwheels are shrunk onto the shaft and will require a substantial press tool to remove. On refitting the gears must be heated to 120°C (230°F) before being pressed into position (wide shoulder on each gear faces the pinion).

Driveshaft oil seals

4   The driveshaft oil seals in the gearbox housing and in the final drive cover may be prised out with a large screwdriver.
5   Fit new seals with the lips of the seal inwards. Take care to enter the seal squarely into the housing and drive it in fully using a hammer and a block of wood.
6   After fitting the seal, smear its lip with gear oil and fill the space between the lips with multipurpose grease.

Input shaft oil seal

7   Remove the clutch release bearing as described in Chapter 5.
8   Remove the three bolts attaching the guide sleeve to the housing and remove the guide sleeve (photo).
9   Use a hooked lever to remove the oil seal, or prise it out with a short lever. If the bush is also to be removed, this must be driven out towards the bellhousing using a piece of tubing of suitable diameter, which is long enough to extend into the gearbox housing. To renew the oil seal only, it is not necessary to dismantle the gearbox housing.
10   Drive the bush into the housing until the flat end of the bush seats against the bottom of the recess.
11   If the oil seal is being fitted with the input shaft in position, slide a piece of plastic sleeving over the splines of the input shaft, or wrap plastic tape round them before sliding the seal over the shaft. This will prevent the splines from damaging the seal. Fit the seal with its flat face outwards and oil the lips with gear oil before fitting it. Drive the seal in flush, using a hammer and a block of wood.
12   Fit the guide sleeve and re-insert and tighten its fixing bolts. If the guide sleeve is plastic, it should be kept free from grease.

8   Bearing carrier – servicing

1   If the bearing carrier is being renewed, the meshing of the crown-wheel and pinion is affected (see Section 6, paragraph 1). To ensure correct meshing, the pinion projection will need to be measured by an Audi agent before and after the new carrier is fitted. They can then advise on the appropriate thickness of shim and gasket to be fitted between the new gear carrier and the gearbox housing to regain the original pinion projection.

Pinion bearing renewal (Fig. 6.19)

2   The outer track of the bearing can be driven out of the case using a suitable drift, but the fitting of a new bearing and determining the correct thickness of shim needs to be done by an Audi agent (See Section 6, paragraph 1).

Gear detents – removing and refitting

3   Remove the pin from the reverse selector rod (Fig. 6.20) and pull the rod from the bearing carrier.
4   Pull the 3rd/4th gear selector rod out of the bearing carrier, taking care to recover the small interlock plunger within the rod.
5   To remove the detent plug at the top of the bearing carrier (Fig. 6.19), cut a 6 mm thread in the plug, screw a bolt into the plug and pull the bolt to extract the plug. With the plug removed, the spring and the detent can be removed.
6   The two detents in the side of the box arc removed by driving in their plugs until the plugs can be removed from the gear selector rod bore (Fig. 6.21). The detent, spring and sleeves can then be shaken out.
7   Refitting is the reverse of removal. The correct position of the detents and interlock plungers is shown in Fig. 6.24.

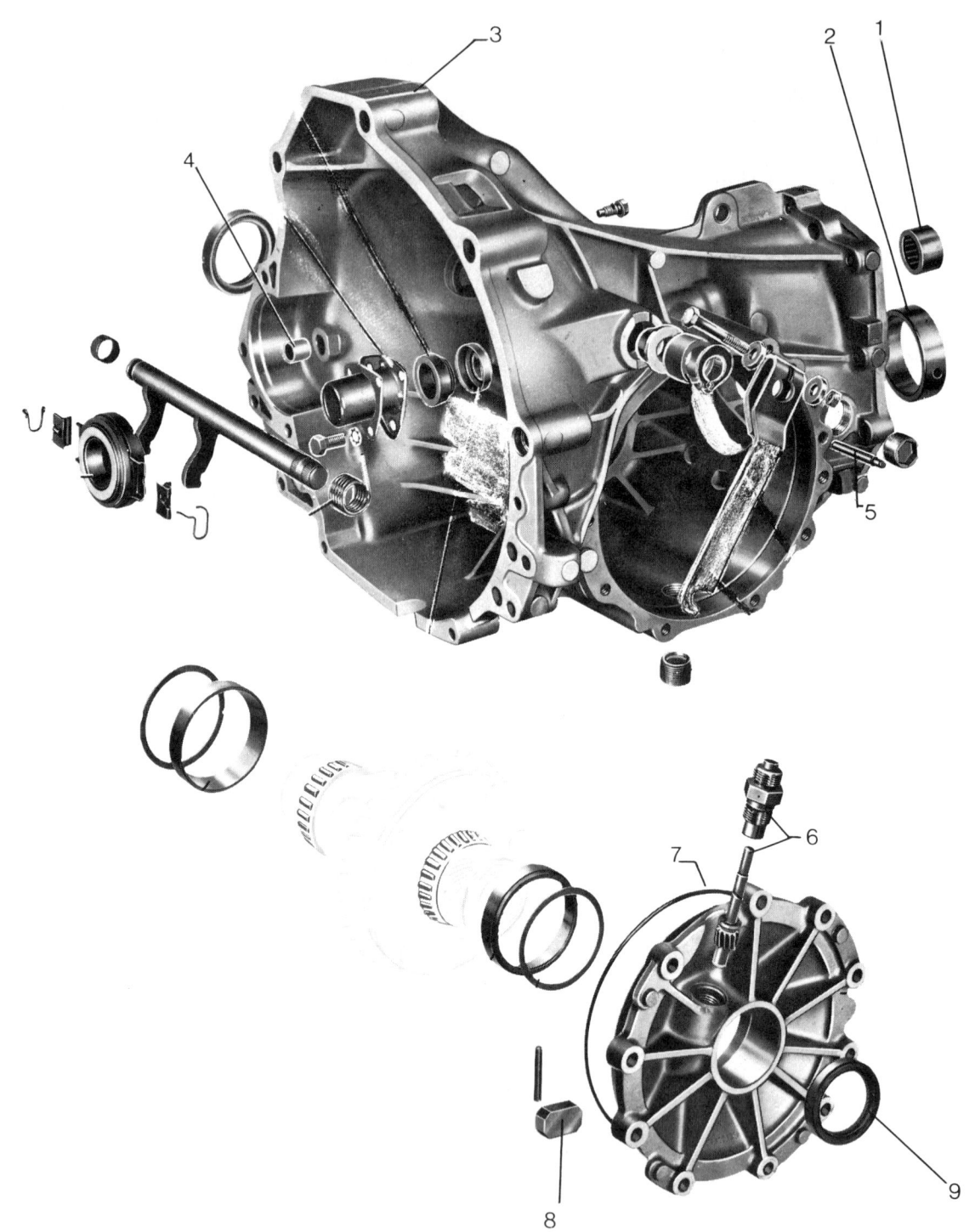

Fig. 6.18 Gearbox housing components (Type 014/11 gearbox) (Sec 7)

1	Input shaft needle bearing	4	Starter bush	6	Speedometer drivegear	8	Magnet
2	Pinion bearing outer track	5	Bearing outer track retaining	7	O-ring	9	Driveshaft oil seal
3	Gearbox housing		pin				

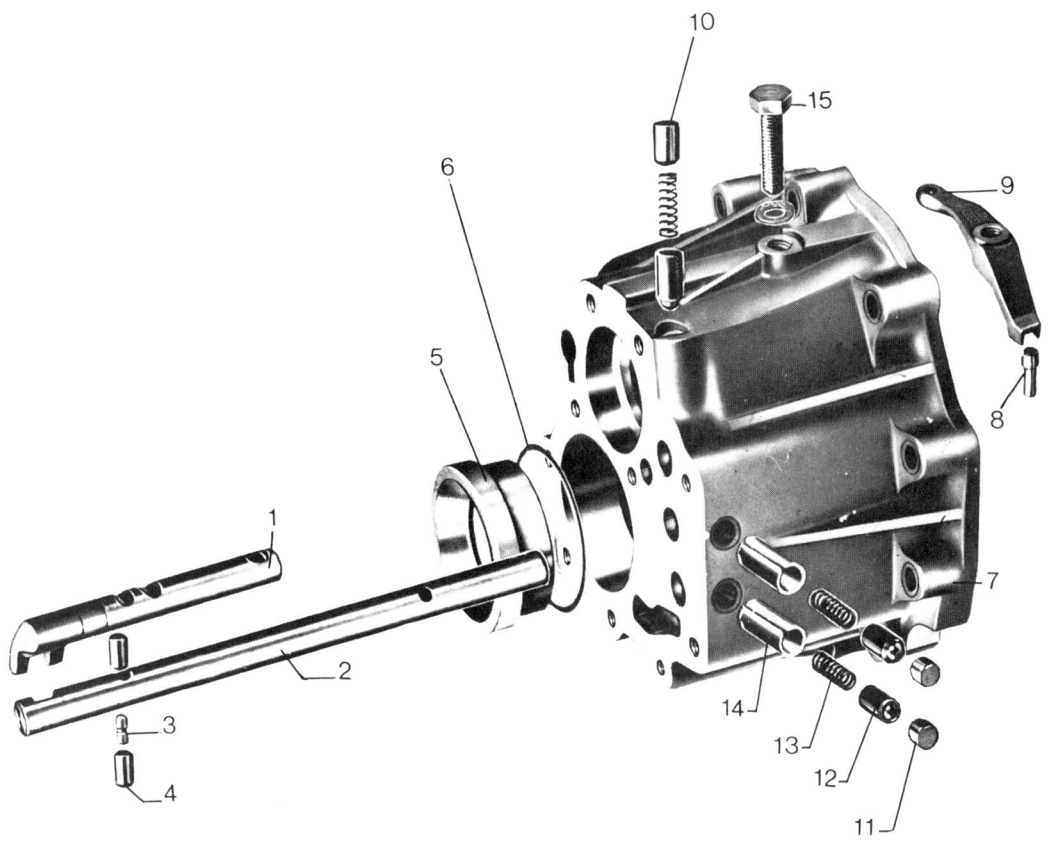

Fig. 6.19 Bearing carrier components (Type 014/11 gearbox) (Sec 8)

1	Reverse gear selector rod	5	Pinion bearing outer track	9	Relay lever	13	Detent spring
2	3rd/4th gear selector rod	6	Shim	10	Long plug	14	Sleeve
3	Small interlock plunger	7	Bearing carrier	11	Short plug	15	Relay lever bolt
4	Interlock plunger	8	Reverse gear selector rod pin	12	Detent		

Fig. 6.20 Removing the reverse gear selector rod pin (Type 014/11 gearbox) (Sec 8)

Fig. 6.21 Removing the short plugs (Type 014/11 gearbox) (Sec 8)

Relay lever adjustment

8   It is not necessary to remove the selector rods in order to adjust the relay lever.

9   Fit reverse gear and its shaft and then insert the relay lever and selector link.

10   Fit the relay lever bolt and washer. Screw the bolt in until it touches the relay lever, while the relay lever is being pressed in the direction of the arrow (Fig. 6.22).

11   Press the relay lever against the end of the bolt and then screw in the bolt until it just starts to engage the threads in the relay lever.

12   While still holding the relay lever in the same position, screw the bolt in and tighten it to the torque given in Specifications. The relay lever should now be set at the correct distance from the gearcase.

13   Move the reverse gear selector rod to the reverse gear position several times and check that the relay mechanism moves freely in all positions.

14   If the relay lever has been adjusted with the selector rods removed, reverse gear must be removed again before the selector rods can be fitted.

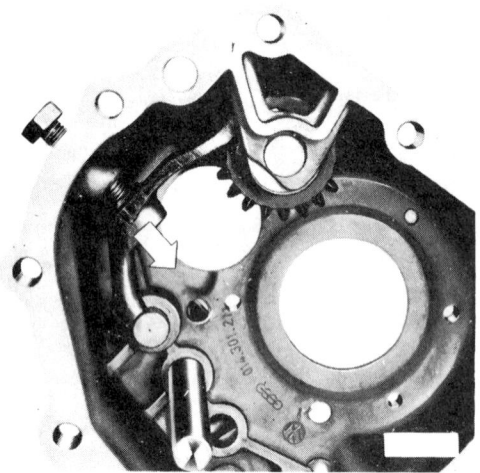

Fig. 6.22 Adjusting the relay lever (Type 014/11 gearbox) (Sec 8)

9 Gearshift housing – servicing

Front and rear bushes

1   Pull out the selector rod and spring.
2   Before removing the rear bush, lever out the rear oil seal and then use a long drift to tap out the bush from the front end of the housing.
3   Enter the new bush squarely into the rear of the housing and tap it home flush with the end of the casting, using a block of wood. In order to drive the new bush in fully, rub the outside diameter of the old bush with a piece of emery cloth to reduce its diameter enough to make it an easy fit in the casting, then use this bush as a drift.
4   Fit a new oil seal, with the open end of the seal inwards, and using a block of hardwood against the seal, drive it in until its face is flush with the end of the casting.
5   The procedure for removing and fitting the front bush is similar except that there is no oil seal and it is necessary to note which way round the bush is fitted.
6   Lubricate the bushes and smear the lip of the oil seal with gear oil before refitting the selector rod.

10 Gearbox – reassembly

1   If the selector rods have been removed from the bearing carrier, check that they have been inserted correctly and that the interlock plungers are in their proper places (Fig. 6.24).
2   Fit the pinion assembly and the 1st/2nd gear selector fork into the bearing carrier.
3   Using a suitable piece of tubing as a drift, tap the outer part of the taper-roller bearing on to the end of the shaft, but while doing this make frequent checks to ensure that the 1st/2nd gear selector shaft has not jammed. If it has jammed, tap it lightly to free it.
4   Fit the 1st/2nd gear operating dog on the shift rod, line up its hole with the hole in the shift rod, then drive in the roll-pin.
5   Fit reverse gear and its selector link into the bearing carrier and then drive in the reverse gear shaft.
6   Fit the input shaft assembly loosely into the box without its bearing.
7   Pull back the 3rd/4th gear selector rod until the 3rd/4th gear selector fork can be fitted into the groove in the synchro-hub sleeve. Push the selector rod back to its neutral position and line up the hole in the selector rod with the hole in the fork. Support the free end of the shaft in the same way as when removing the selector fork and drive in the roll-pin.
8   Fit a new gasket to the gearbox housing and fit the bearing carrier, with the input and pinion shaft assemblies, to the gearbox housing. Line up the holes and drive the dowel pins in. Insert and tighten the bolts.
9   Fit the input shaft ball bearing squarely on to the end of its shaft, ensuring that the closed side of the bearing cage is towards the bearing carrier. Using a suitable tube, or a block of hardwood, drive the bearing in, taking care to see that it stays square to the shaft.
10   Fit the thrust washer and circlip on top of the input shaft bearing.
11   Pull back the two selector rods until 1st and reverse gears are both engaged and the shafts are locked together. Fit the pinion shaft nut, tighten it to the specified torque and lock the nut to the shaft. Move the selector shafts back to their neutral position and check that both shafts are able to rotate freely.
12   The next operation requires great care if unnecessary work is to be avoided. Very carefully pull out the 3rd/4th gear selector rod just enough for the small interlock plunger to be inserted. Smear grease on to the plunger, insert it into the hole and push the selector rod back in. If the rod is pulled out too far, the locking keys of the synchro-hub can come out and the gear assembly will have to be separated from the gearbox housing so that the locking keys can be re-inserted into the synchro-hub.

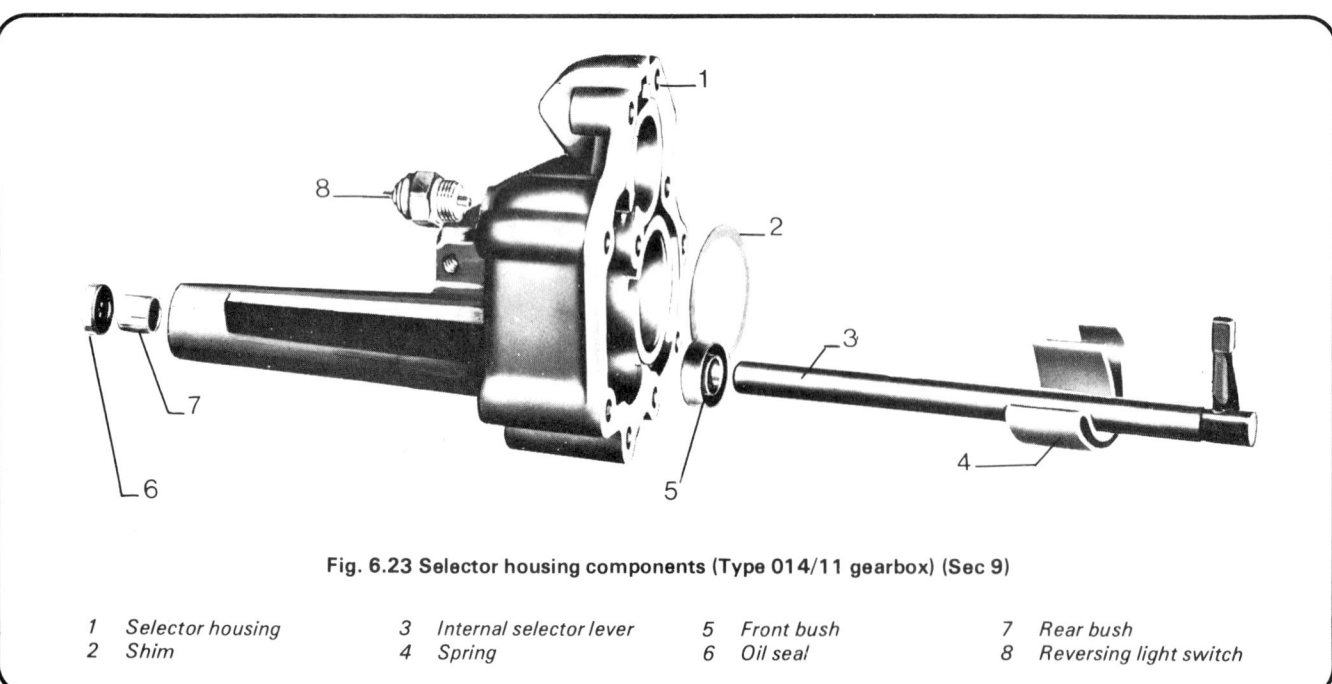

Fig. 6.23 Selector housing components (Type 014/11 gearbox) (Sec 9)

1 Selector housing	3 Internal selector lever	5 Front bush	7 Rear bush
2 Shim	4 Spring	6 Oil seal	8 Reversing light switch

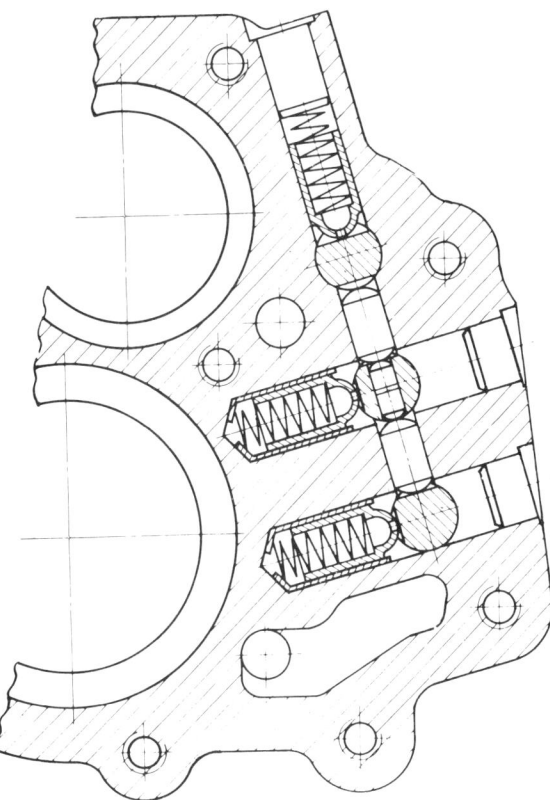

Fig. 6.24 Arrangement of interlock plungers (Type 014/11 gearbox) (Sec 10)

Fig. 6.25 Fitting 1st/2nd gear operating dog (Type 014/11 gearbox) (Sec 10)

Fig. 6.26 Measuring mainshaft bearing projection (Type 014/11 gearbox) (Sec 10)

Fig. 6.27 Fitting the spring clip to the selector lever (Type 014/11 gearbox) (Sec 10)

Fig. 6.28 Compressing the spring clip (Type 014/11 gearbox) (Sec 10)

13 When refitting the gearshift housing to the bearing carrier, use a new gasket, but because the thickness of gasket influences the position of the pinion, the correct thickness must be fitted. If no parts of the bearing carrier have been renewed, measure the thickness of the old gasket, which will be either 0·30 or 0·40 mm (0·012 or 0·016 in) and use a new gasket of the same thickness.

14 If a new input shaft bearing has been fitted, measure the amount by which the outer race projects from the end face of the gear assembly (Fig. 6.26). If this is between 0·20 and 0·26 mm (0·008 and 0·010 in) use a 0·30 mm (0·012 in) thick gasket. If the projection is between 0·27 and 0·32 mm, (0·011 and 0·013 in), use a 0·40 mm (0·016 in) thick gasket.

15 When refitting the gearshift housing, first ensure that the shim is in place in the housing recess, with the recess in the shim towards the spring clip.

16 Fit the spring clip by first putting it over the internal selector lever (Fig. 6.27). Compress the clip and slide the clip and the internal selector lever into the housing so that the end of the clip rests against the end of the housing and the shim (Fig. 6.28). Move the spring and the selector lever into the housing as far as they will go and turn the selector lever so that the spring and selector lever are as shown in Fig. 6.29.

17 Insert the finger of the selector lever into the slots in the selector rods and push the gearshift housing into place. Insert the bolts and tighten them to the specified torque.

Fig. 6.29 Final position of spring clip (Type 014/11 gearbox)
(Sec 10)

11   Gearshift lever – removing, refitting and adjusting

1   The adjustment of the gearshift linkage requires a special tool, so if
the linkage is undone, it is very important to mark the position of the
shift rod in the shift finger before separating them.

2   Put a mark to show how far the shift rod is inserted into the clamp
and also mark a horizontal line on both the shift finger and the shift rod
so that they can be reconnected without any rotational change.

3   Release the bolt on the clamp and separate the shift rod from the
shift finger.

4   From inside the car, remove the four nuts and washers securing
the lever housing to the car floor and remove the gear lever assembly
and shift rod.

5   To separate the shift rod from the gear lever, undo and remove the
shift rod clevis bolt.

6   After refitting the gear lever, by reversing the removal operations,
the basic setting of the linkage should be tested by engaging 1st gear
and then moving the gear lever as far to the left as it will go. Release
the lever and measure the distance which it springs back on its own.
This should be between 5 and 10 mm (0·20 and 0·39 in). If this basic

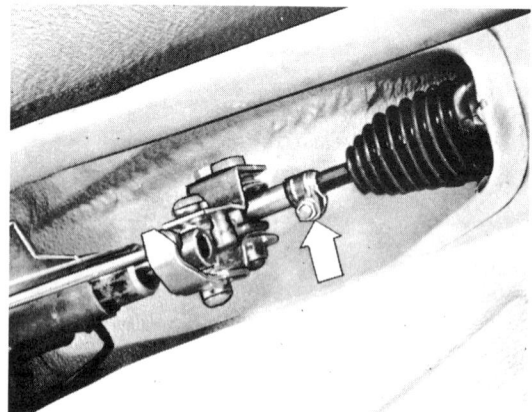

Fig. 6.30 Gear rod clamp (Type 014/11 gearbox) (Sec 11)

Fig. 6.31 Gearshift components (Type 014/11 gearbox) (Sec 11)

1	Gear knob	9	Spring
2	Circlip	10	Shell
3	Washer	11	Lower ball
4	Spring	12	Gear lever
5	Gearlever bearing assembly	13	Gearlever housing
6	Gearlever plate	14	Stop pad
7	Rubber guide	15	Reverse stop
8	Upper ball		

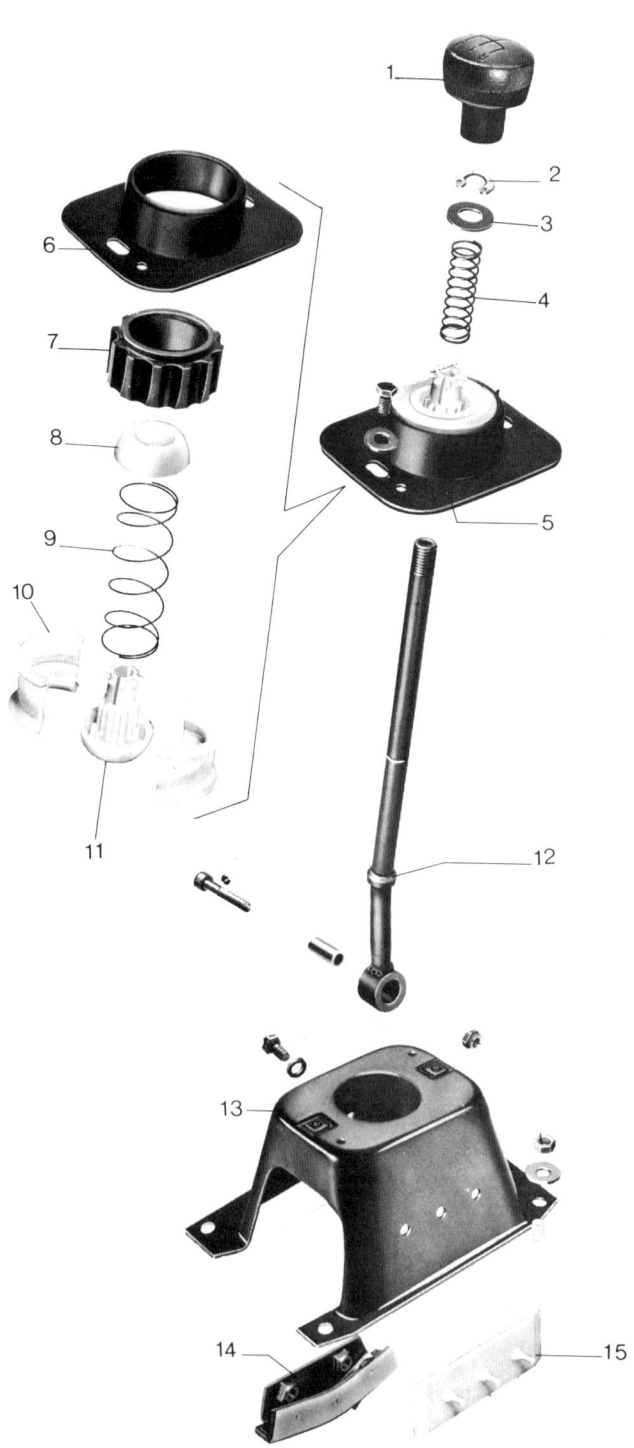

adjustment is incorrect, it is unlikely that all the gears can be engaged. The gear lever will either have to be set up using a special VW gauge, or the adjustment can be made by a lengthy process of trial and error.

12 Gearshift linkage – dismantling and reassembly

1   The gearshift linkage consists of two principal parts, the shift rod coupling assembly and the lever assembly.

Gearlever assembly

2   Remove the gear lever as described in the previous Section.

3   Dismantle the assembly by unscrewing the gear knob, removing the circlip from the gear lever and lifting off the washer and spring. The gear lever can then be pulled out of the lever bearing assembly.

4   Before separating the lever bearing assembly from the lever housing, mark round the lever bearing plate with a scriber so that it can be returned to exactly the same position, then remove the two screws and washers from the plate.

5   Do not dismantle the bearing unless it is necessary to grease it. Dismantling is done by pushing the rubber guide downwards out of the plate and then pushing the balls, shells and spring out of the plate.

6   When reassembling have the rubber guide with its shouldered end uppermost and press the two shells into it. Press the lower ball half into the shells, then the spring and finally press in the upper ball half,

pushing the shells slightly apart if necessary.

7   After assembling the parts into the rubber guide, push the assembly up into the lever bearing plate.

8   When inserting the lever into the bearing, note that the lever is cranked to the left and when refitting the lever bearing plate to the housing, take care to line up the plate with the scribed mark made before dismantling.

Shift rod coupling

9   To dismantle the shift rod coupling, remove the bolt from the end of the support rod. Mark the position of the adaptor on the gearbox selector lever then remove the wire from the bolt, loosen the bolt and remove the shift rod coupling assembly.

10 Prise the ball coupling of the support off its mounting on the side plate. Remove the bolt which clamps the two side plates together and extract the shift finger and its bushes.

11 When reassembling the shift rod coupling, note that the adaptor should be fitted so that the hole for the clamp-bolt is towards the front and the groove for the clamp-bolt on the shift finger is on the left-hand side. Make sure that the holes in the two side plates are exactly in line, so that the coupling is assembled without any strain.

12 All the joints and friction surfaces of the shift rod coupling should be lubricated with special lubricant AOS 126 000 06 and after refitting the assembly to the gear box, the clamp-bolt should be tightened and then locked with soft iron wire.

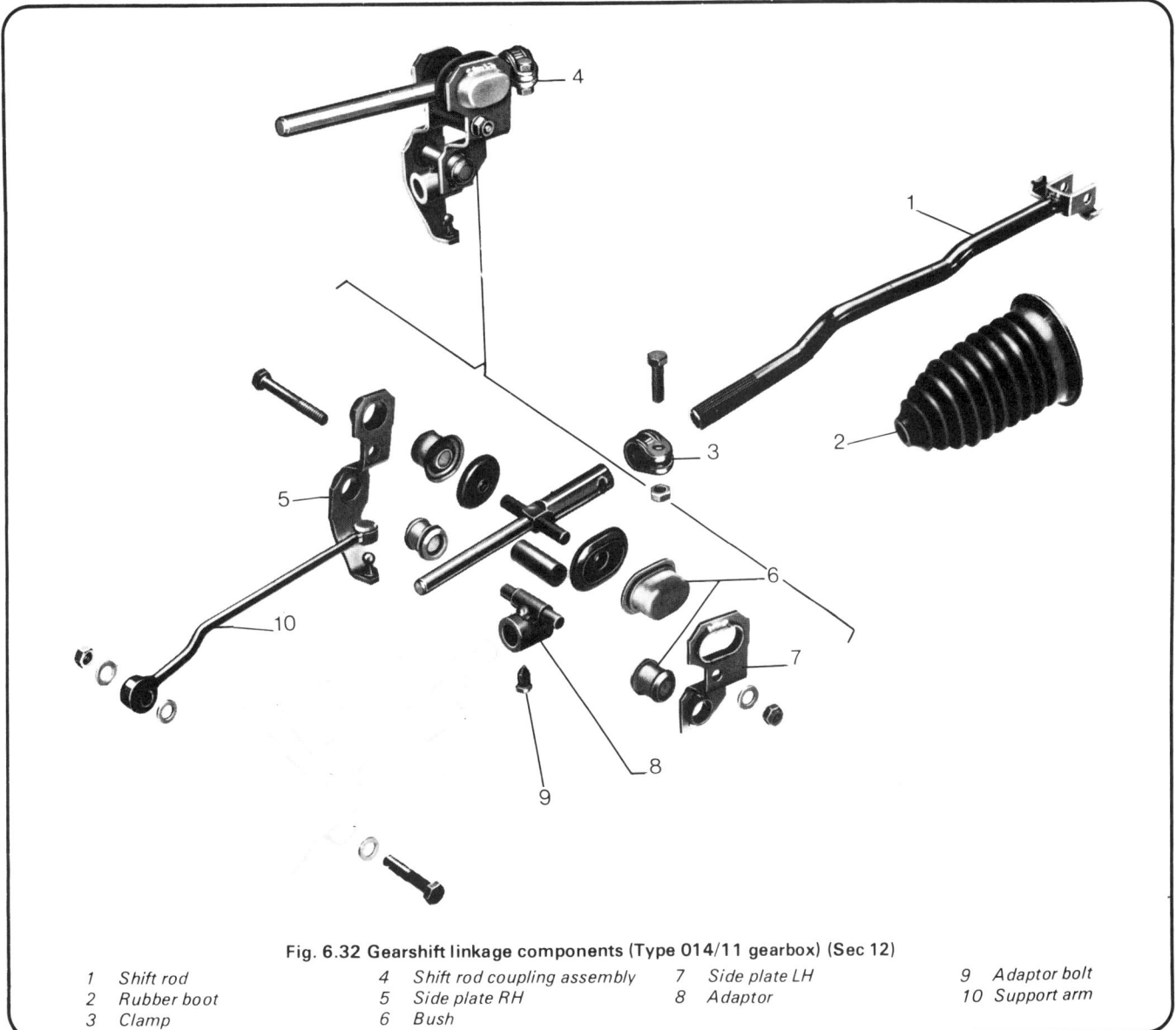

Fig. 6.32 Gearshift linkage components (Type 014/11 gearbox) (Sec 12)

1	Shift rod	4	Shift rod coupling assembly	7	Side plate LH	9	Adaptor bolt
2	Rubber boot	5	Side plate RH	8	Adaptor	10	Support arm
3	Clamp	6	Bush				

Part B – 2·0 and 2·2 litre models (Type 088 gearbox)

13 Gearbox – removal and refitting (engine in vehicle)

1   This can be done much more easily if the vehicle is over a pit. If this is not possible, the front wheels may be put on ramps, but it is unsafe to attempt to remove the gearbox with the car supported on jacks.

2   Disconnect the battery leads.

3   To improve access to the top of the engine, lift out the windscreen washer container and place it in the heater compartment.

4   Undo and remove the bolts from the top of the gearbox.

5   Disconnect the speedometer cable from the left-hand side of the gearbox housing (photo).

6   On 2·2 litre models, drive out the roll-pin securing the clutch slave cylinder and detach the slave cylinder. It is not necessary to detach the hydraulic pipe from the cylinder and the clutch cylinder can then be refitted without the need for bleeding the system. Tie the clutch slave cylinder out of the way.

7   On 2·0 litre engines with a cable operated clutch, detach the clutch cable from the clutch operating lever.

8   Remove the nuts securing the exhaust pipe to the manifold and then undo the clip securing the exhaust pipe to the gearbox.

9   Support the front of the engine by a sling from the engine lifting lug to an overhead support. It is not advisable to support the engine by jacking the sump.

10   Remove the deflector plate from above the right-hand driveshaft coupling, then using a socket wrench remove the bolts from the driveshaft couplings. Separate the coupling parts and rest the driveshafts on the sub-frame (photos).

11   Disconnect the cables from the reversing light switch (photo).

12   Disconnect the gearbox from the gearshift linkage by pressing the shift rod and the adjusting rod off their ball studs (photo).

13   Remove the lower bolts connecting the engine to the gearbox.

14   Remove the bolts securing the starter motor and pull the starter clear (photo).

13.5 Disconnecting the speedometer drive

13.10a Separating the driveshaft coupling

13.10b Driveshaft resting on subframe

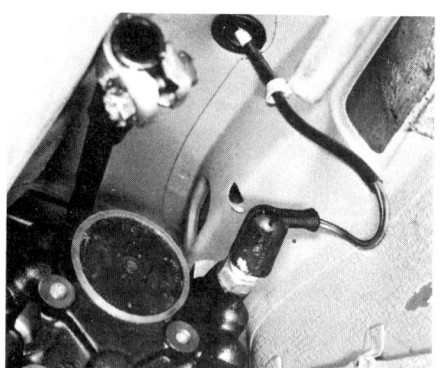
13.11 Reversing light switch cables

13.12 Shift rod and adjusting rod balljoints (arrowed)

13.14 Removing the starter motor

13.16 Supporting the gearbox

13.18 Removing the gearbox bracket

15 Detach the deflector plate from the subframe.

16 Raise the gearbox slightly by using a jack beneath it, but place a block of wood between the jack and the gearbox casing (photo).

17 Remove the two rear bolts securing the subframe to the body and detach both gearbox supports from the subframe.

18 Remove the three bolts and take off the right-hand gearbox support bracket (photo).

19 Prise the gearbox away from the engine until the input shaft is clear of the clutch plate and then lower the gearbox and remove it from beneath the car.

20 The gearbox is refitted by reversing the above operations, but noting the following points.

> *(a) The splines on the mainshaft should be coated with molybdenum disulphide powder, or smeared with graphite grease before it is inserted into the clutch and care is necessary to ensure that the shaft is not strained while being inserted*
>
> *(b) Take care not to damage the shaft of the starter motor when refitting the gearbox and the starter motor*
>
> *(c) Fit the gearbox onto the dowel sleeves before inserting any of the fixing bolts, then fit the lower bolts*
>
> *(d) Keep the driveshafts out of the way by laying them on the top of the subframe until the gearbox has been fitted*
>
> *(e) Ensure that neither the engine or the gearbox mountings are under any strain and then tighten the mounting bolts to the specified torque*

14 Gearbox – removal and refitting (engine out of vehicle)

1 If the engine and radiator have already been removed, the removal of the gearbox is simplified. The gearbox mountings will have been disconnected and the gearbox supported on a jack.

2 Disconnect the driveshaft coupling flanges and support the driveshafts on the subframe. It is also necessary to remove the deflector plate from above the right-hand coupling.

3 If not already removed, remove the two rear bolts securing the subframe to the body and detach the gearbox supports from the subframe.

4 Disconnect the gearbox from the gearshift linkage by pressing the shift rod and adjusting rod off their ball studs.

5 Disconnect the speedometer cable from the left-hand side of the gearbox housing.

6 On 2·2 litre models, drive out the roll-pin securing the clutch slave cylinder and detach the slave cylinder. It is not necessary to detach the hydraulic pipe from the cylinder and the clutch cylinder can be refitted without the need for bleeding the system. Tie the clutch slave cylinder out of the way.

7 Disconnect the cables from the reversing light switch.

8 Check that the gearbox is free and then either move it forward and lift it out from the engine compartment, or remove it from beneath the car.

15 Gearbox – dismantling

1 The clutch operating mechanism is different on the gearboxes fitted to the 2·0 and 2·2 litre engines; the removal of this mechanism is described in Chapter 5. Otherwise the gearbox dismantling operations are the same for both models.

2 Remove the gearbox drain plug, drain out the oil and refit the plug.

3 Mark the position of the shift lever on its splines (photo) and then release the clamp-bolt and pull the shift lever off.

4 Remove the two bolts from the selector shaft cover, take off the cover and remove the small spring (photo).

5 Remove the circlip from the shaft (photo) and take off the washer and large spring (photo).

6 Remove the bolts securing the bearing carrier to the gearbox housing and drive out the two dowel pins.

7 Push the selector shaft in as far as possible, so that it is disengaged from the dogs on the shift rods and then separate the bearing carrier with the gear assembly from the gearbox housing.

8 Remove the cover from the end of the bearing carrier (photo). If a

15.3 Punch mark (arrowed) to show position of selector lever on shaft

15.4 Selector cover and small spring

15.5a Removing the selector shaft circlip ...

15.5b ... washer and large spring

15.8 Bearing carrier cover (rubber)

metal cover is fitted, tap the cover out with a drift and remove the O-ring. If a rubber plug is fitted, pierce the centre of the plug with a large screwdriver and lever the plug out. If the gearbox has a metal cover, a rubber plug must not be fitted, because it would block an oil hole.

9   Clamp the input shaft in a soft-jawed vice and unscrew and remove the hexagon bolt from the end of the shaft.

10 Support the free end of the 3rd/4th gear selector shaft by jamming a block of hardwood under it and drive the roll-pin out of the selector shaft.If the free end of the shaft is not supported while the pin is driven out, the bore for the shaft in the bearing carrier may be damaged.

11 Pull out 3rd/4th gear selector rod (photo), leaving the selector fork engaged in the sleeve of the synchroniser and taking care not to lose the interlock plunger which is in the rod (photo).

12 Use a soft metal drift and a hammer to drive the end of the mainshaft out of its bearing and then manoeuvre the mainshaft assembly out.

13 Remove the pinion shaft with the 1st/2nd gear selector rod and fork. It will be necessary to move it to one side slightly to get it past reverse gear.

14 Remove 3rd/4th gear selector fork.

15 Dismantle the gearbox housing as described in paragraphs 16 and 17 of Section 4, Part A.

16 Mainshaft – dismantling and reassembly

1   Dismantling and reassembly of the mainshaft is identical to that of the Type 014/11 gearbox described in Part A (Fig. 6.38).

2   When assembling the 3rd/4th gear synchro-hub and sleeve there are no mating marks and no special position is necessary, but when fitting the assembly to the shaft, the grooved end of the hub is towards 4th gear as on the Type 014/11 gearbox.

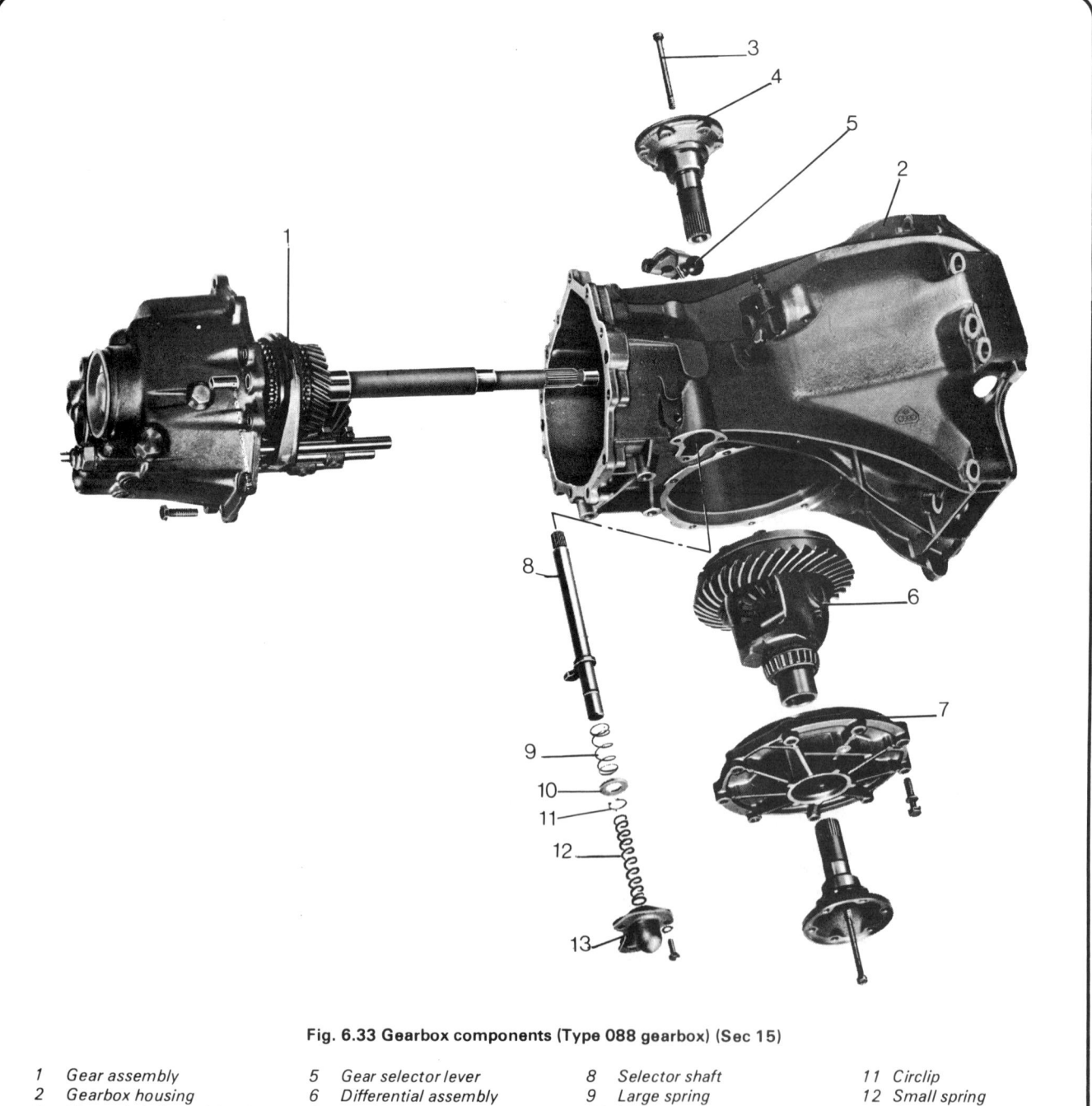

Fig. 6.33 Gearbox components (Type 088 gearbox) (Sec 15)

1	Gear assembly	5	Gear selector lever	8	Selector shaft	11	Circlip
2	Gearbox housing	6	Differential assembly	9	Large spring	12	Small spring
3	Flanged shaft retaining bolt	7	Final drive cover	10	Washer	13	Selector shaft cover
4	Flanged shaft						

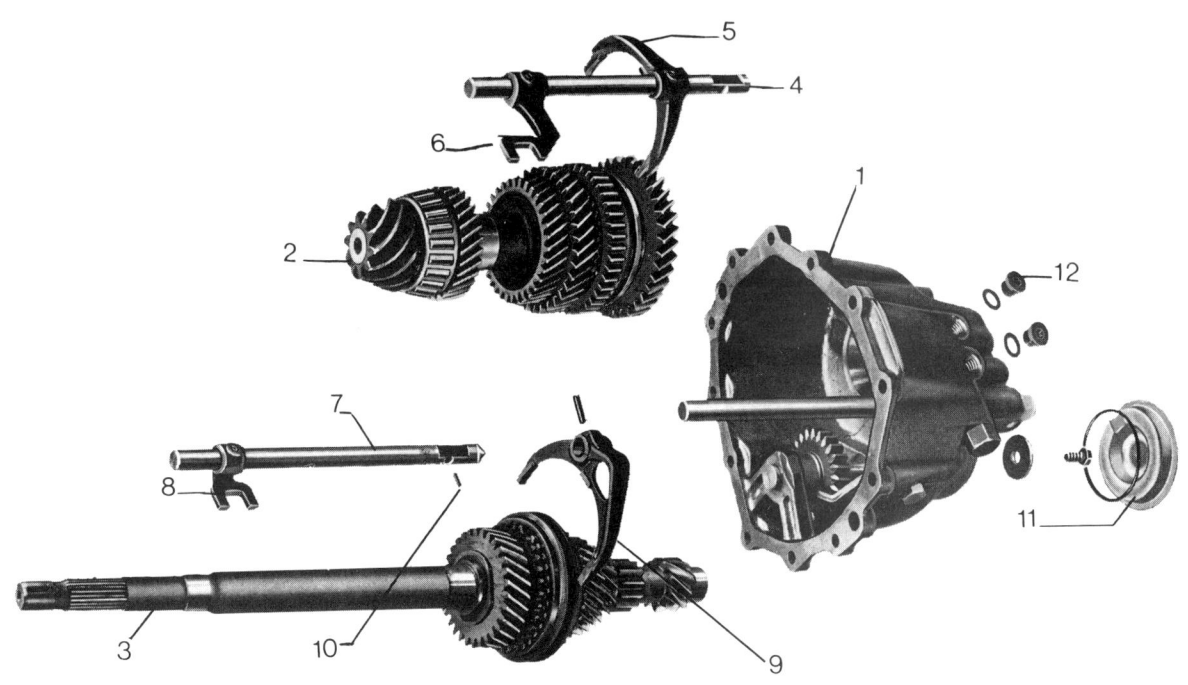

Fig. 6.34 Bearing carrier and gearshaft components (Type 088 gearbox) (Sec 15)

1	Bearing carrier	7	3rd/4th gear selector rod
2	Pinion assembly	8	3rd/4th gear selector dog
3	Mainshaft assembly	9	3rd/4th gear selector fork
4	1st/2nd gear selector rod	10	Small interlock plunger
5	1st/2nd gear selector fork	11	Bearing cover
6	1st/2nd gear selector dog	12	Detent plug

Fig. 6.35 Unscrewing the mainshaft bolt (Sec 15)

Fig. 6.36 Driving the pin from 3rd/4th gear selector fork (Sec 15)

15.11 Pulling out 3rd/4th gear selector rod

15.11b Small interlock plunger in 3rd/4th gear selector rod

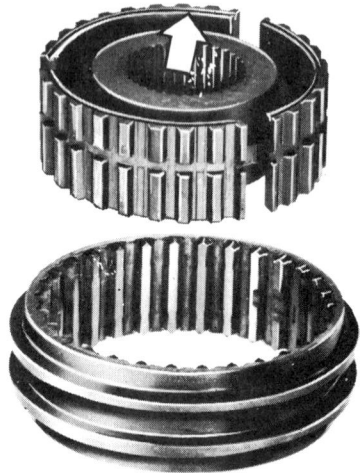

Fig. 6.37 3rd/4th gear synchro-hub (Type 088 gearbox) (Sec 17)

Groove on hub (arrowed) faces 4th gear

17 Pinion shaft – dismantling and reassembly

1   The depth of the pinion's engagement with the crownwheel is adjusted during manufacture to the optimum position for quiet running and long life. When components affecting the pinion engagement are changed, adjustments must be made to regain this optimum position. Before components are dismantled or replacement items fitted, the position of the pinion must be established by measurement. Because this requires the use of specialist equipment its work should be entrusted to your Audi dealer. The components which affect the pinion engagement are the gearbox casing, the bearing carrier, and the pinion shaft bearings (Fig. 6.39).

2   Using a soft-jawed vice, grip the pinion shaft assembly on the plain part between 3rd and 4th gear and loosen the bolt in the end of the shaft (Fig. 6.40).

3   Remove the bolt and washer, then use a puller to remove the bearing inner race.

4   Lift off the 1st gearwheel and its needle bearing (photo). Fit the bearing back into the gear the same way round as when fitted to the shaft.

5   Remove the 1st gear synchro-ring and fit it to the gear.

6   Remove the circlip located against the synchro-hub (photo).

7   Using a puller with its legs placed beneath the 2nd gearwheel,

draw off the 2nd gearwheel and the 1st/2nd gear synchroniser assembly.

8   Lift off 2nd gear needle roller assembly and fit it inside the gear the same way round as when fitted to the shaft.

9   The 3rd and 4th speed gears are pressed and shrunk on to the shaft and if they need to be removed, or the pinion end bearing renewed, the work should be entrusted to an Audi dealer.

10   Reassembly will commence with the large bearing inner race, 4th gear, its circlip, 3rd gear and its circlip already on the shaft; complete reassembly of the shaft as follows.

11   Lubricate the 2nd gear needle roller bearing with gear oil and fit it to the shaft.

12   Fit the 2nd gearwheel onto its bearing (photo), then place the synchro-ring on the gear (photo). Measure the gap as in Fig. 6.11. If the gap exceeds 0·5 mm (0·02 in), a new synchro-ring must be fitted.

13   If the synchroniser assembly has been dismantled, it must be reassembled in the following way. Fit the three locking keys into their slots in the hub and secure the keys with circlips. The circlips should be spaced 120° apart and the angled end of the circlip should be engaged in the hollow of a locking key. Slide the operating sleeve over the synchro-hub, no special position of the sleeve relative to the hub is necessary.

14   Fit the synchroniser assembly to the shaft, the end of the sleeve having external teeth facing towards the pinion (photo). Before pressing the hub down fully, turn the 2nd gear synchro-ring so that the slots in it are aligned with the locking keys in the synchroniser assembly.

15   Fit the circlip against the synchro-hub and with the hub pressed down as far as possible, measure the clearance between the hub and the circlip (Fig. 6.41). The clearance should be between zero and 0·04 mm (0·002 in) and preferably nearer to the lower value. If the clearance exceeds the upper limit fit a new circlip of suitable thickness. The thicknesses available are 1·50, 1·55 and 1·60 mm (0·059, 0·061, 0·063 in).

16   Fit the 1st gear synchro-ring, lining up its slots with the locking keys in the synchroniser assembly. It may be found that the synchro-ring has a tooth missing at three points (Fig. 6.17). This denotes a later modification when the tooth angle on the synchro-ring was altered from 115° to 110° to improve the engagement of 1st gear. This type of ring must only be used on 1st gear and if the 1st gear ring is being renewed, the 115° type, having the full number of teeth, should be fitted.

17   Lubricate the 1st gear needle roller bearing with gear oil and fit it to the shaft, then fit 1st gear.

18   Measure the distance between the teeth on the synchro-ring and the synchronising teeth on the gear as in paragraph 11 and fit a new synchro-ring if the gap exceeds 0·5 mm (0·020 in).

19   Tap the bearing inner race on to the end of the shaft, using a tubular drift, or a block of hardwood. Grip the shaft in a soft-jawed vice as during dismantling and fit the bolt and washer.

20   Tighten the bolt to the torque value specified.

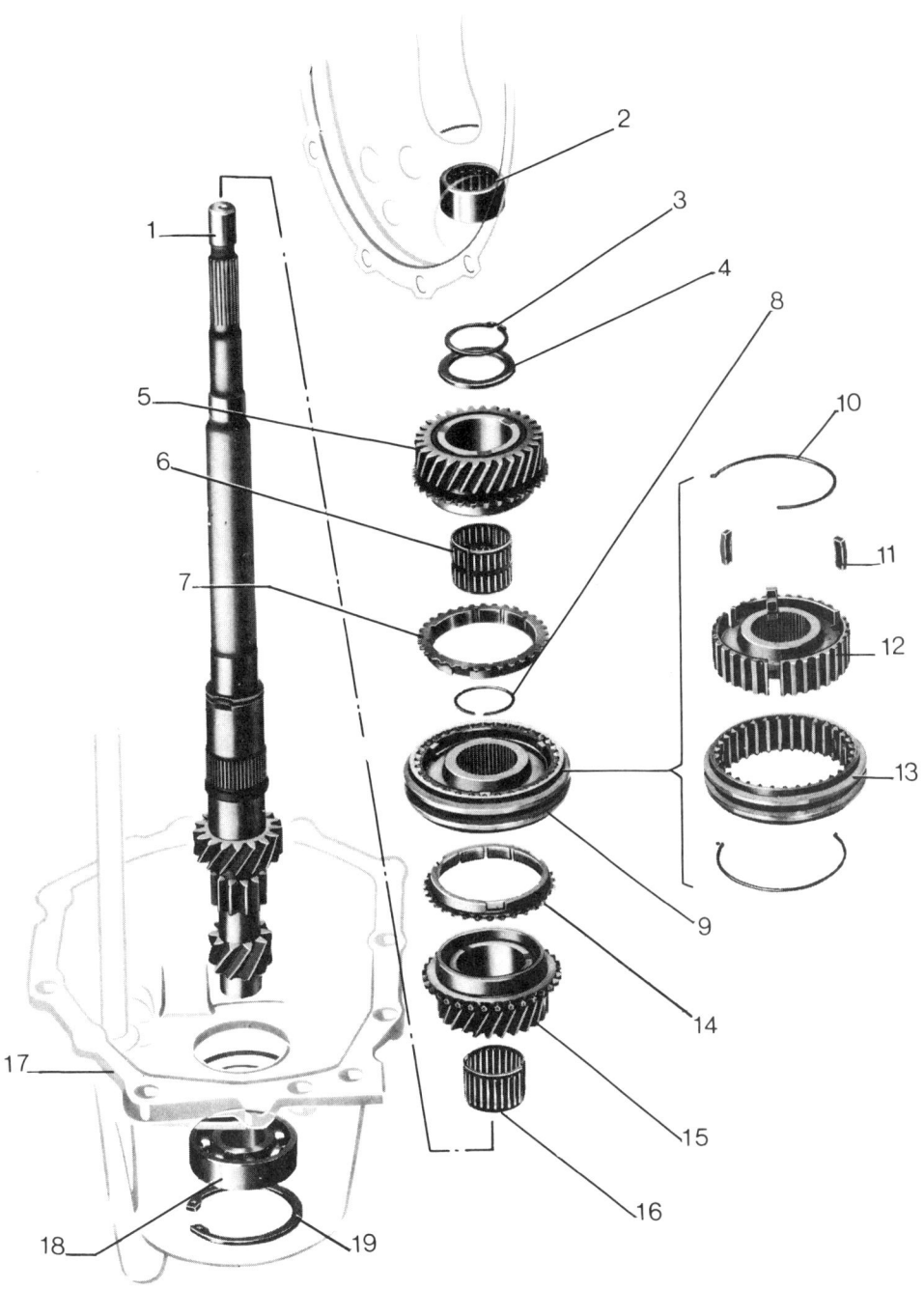

Fig. 6.38 Mainshaft assembly (Type 088 gearbox) (Sec 16)

1	Mainshaft	6	4th gear needle bearing	11	Locking keys	16	3rd gear needle bearing
2	Needle bearing	7	4th gear synchro-ring	12	Synchro-hub	17	Bearing carrier
3	Circlip	8	Circlip	13	Synchro-sleeve	18	Mainshaft bearing
4	Thrust washer	9	Synchroniser assembly	14	3rd gear synchro-ring	19	Circlip
5	4th gearwheel	10	Wire circlip	15	3rd gearwheel		

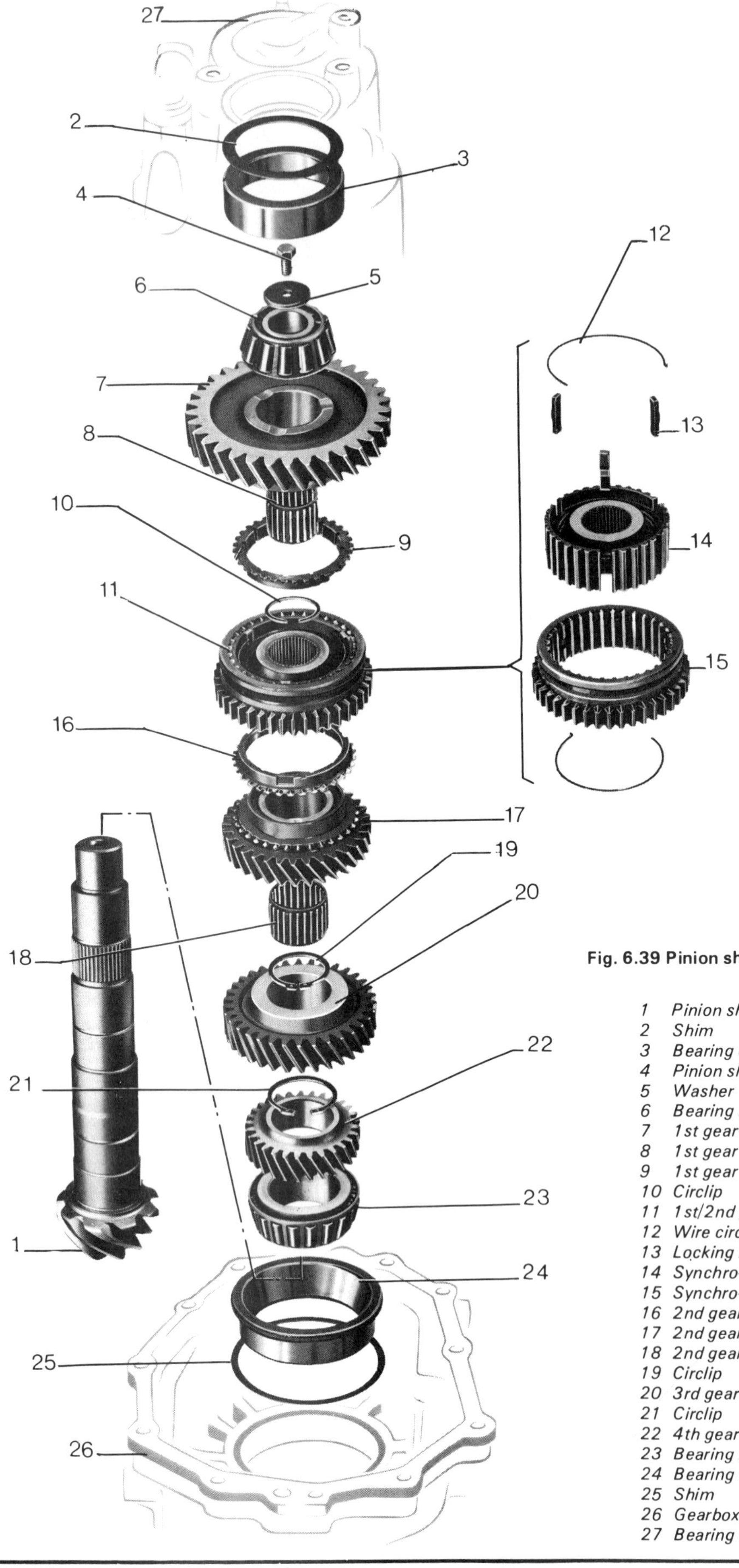

**Fig. 6.39 Pinion shaft assembly (Type 088 gearbox)
(Sec 17)**

1 Pinion shaft
2 Shim
3 Bearing outer track
4 Pinion shaft bolt
5 Washer
6 Bearing race
7 1st gearwheel
8 1st gear needle bearing
9 1st gear synchro-ring
10 Circlip
11 1st/2nd gear synchroniser assembly
12 Wire circlip
13 Locking keys
14 Synchro-hub
15 Synchro-sleeve
16 2nd gear synchro-ring
17 2nd gearwheel
18 2nd gear needle bearing
19 Circlip
20 3rd gearwheel
21 Circlip
22 4th gearwheel
23 Bearing race
24 Bearing outer track
25 Shim
26 Gearbox housing
27 Bearing carrier

Fig. 6.41 1st/2nd gear synchroniser axial clearance (Sec 17)

Fig. 6.40 Loosening the pinion bolt (Sec 17)

A – soft vice jaws

17.4 Removing 1st gear and its bearing from pinion shaft

17.6 Removing the synchro-hub circlip from pinion shaft

17.12a Fitting the 2nd gearwheel to pinion shaft ...

17.12b ... followed by its synchro-ring

17.14 Fitting the synchroniser assembly to pinion shaft

18 Gearbox housing – servicing

1   The operations for servicing the gearbox housing are the same as those for the Type 014/11 gearbox described in Part A with the exception of the pinion bearing.

2   The outer track of the pinion bearing is flanged (photo) and is a shrink fit. It requires a special mandrel and a slide hammer to remove it and when fitting a new track either the complete gearbox housing, or the area round the bearing must be heated to 150°C (302°F). Shims are fitted between the bearing track and the gearbox housing to adjust the pinion engagement in the crownwheel and if the track is to be replaced it is a job for your Audi dealer (see Sect 19, paragraph 1).

19 Bearing carrier – servicing

1   If the bearing carrier is being renewed, the meshing of the crownwheel and pinion is affected. To ensure correct meshing, the pinion projection will need to be measured by an Audi agent, who can then advise the appropriate thickness of shim for the pinion bearing.

Pinion bearing renewal

2   Renewing the pinion bearings affects the meshing of the crownwheel and pinion and removing and refitting either of the bearings requires special equipment so it is inadvisable for the owner to attempt this.

18.2 Mainshaft needle roller bearing and pinion bearing outer track

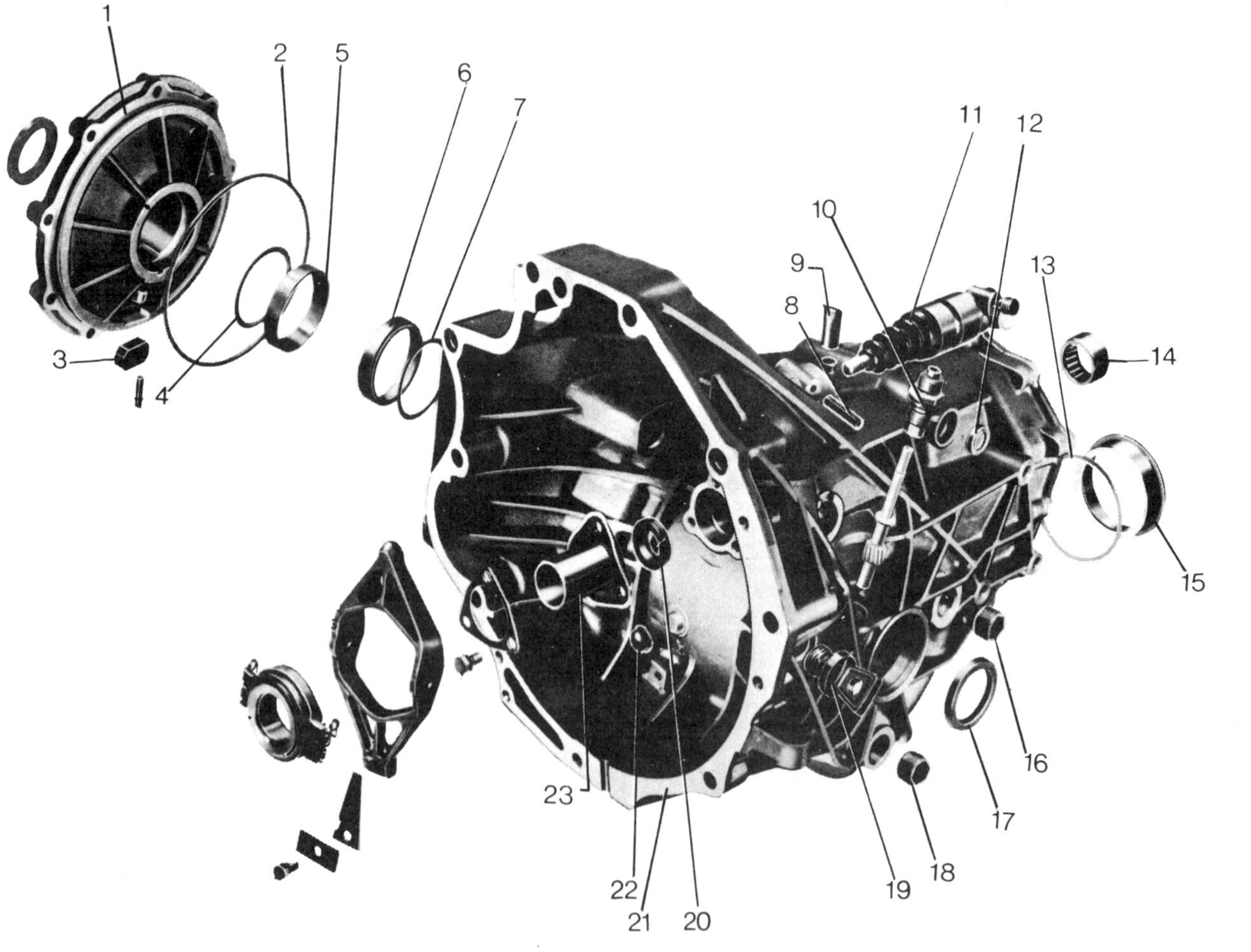

Fig. 6.42 Gearbox housing components (Type 088 gearbox) – 2.2 litre (2.0 litre is the same except for clutch mechanism) (Sec 18)

1 Final drive cover	7 Shim	13 Shim	19 Bellhousing plug
2 O-ring	8 Clutch cylinder pin	14 Mainshaft needle roller bearing	20 Mainshaft oil seal
3 Magnet	9 Vent	15 Pinion bearing outer track	21 Gearbox housing
4 Shim	10 Speedometer drive	16 Oil filler plug	22 Clutch lever ball cap
5 Differential small bearing outer track	11 Clutch cylinder	17 Drive flange oil seal	23 Guide sleeve
6 Differential large bearing outer track	12 Selector shaft seal	18 Oil drain plug	

Gear detents – removing and refitting

3   The gear detents are removed by taking out the two socket-headed plugs on the side of the gearbox and tapping out the plungers and springs.

4   Refit the spring and then the plunger, but leave out the plug until the appropriate shift rod has been fitted, then screw in the plug with a paper gasket beneath it.

5   The detent operating the interlock plungers is beneath the hexagon-headed plug at the top rear of the casing. Remove the plug and tip out the spring and detent. It is likely that the interlock plungers will also fall out.

6   Refit the interlock plungers by holding them on a magnet and inserting them through the selector rod holes (Fig. 6.45). Fit the selector rods and then insert the detent plunger and spring. Screw in the plug and tighten it.

7   If the plug is made of steel, it should have a sealing washer beneath it. If the plug is of aluminium it should be installed without any washer.

Mainshaft bearing renewal

8   If a special ball bearing extractor is available, a new bearing can be fitted without removing the mainshaft, but the procedure is similar when the shaft is removed and does not need a special extractor.

9   Remove the cover from the end of the gearbox as described in paragraph 8 of Section 15.

10   Remove the circlip which retains the bearing and if the gearbox has not been dismantled, unscrew and remove the bolt from the end of the shaft. To do this, put the car into gear and apply the handbrake to lock the transmission. Use an impact wrench to release the bolt, or in the absence of one, use a spanner and give it a sharp blow with a soft-headed hammer.

11   Draw out the bearing, or drift it out from inside the bearing carrier (photo).

12   Fit the new bearing, taking care to enter the bearing outer track

19.11 Mainshaft ball bearing

squarely. If the gearbox mainshaft is in position screw a bolt into the end of the shaft to assist in entering the shaft into the bearing. Drive the bearing in to the bottom of its recess and fit the bolt and washer to the mainshaft.

13   Fit the cover plug (see Section 20, paragraph 11).

Reverse gear – removing and refitting

14   Unscrew and remove the bolt on the left-hand side of the gearbox

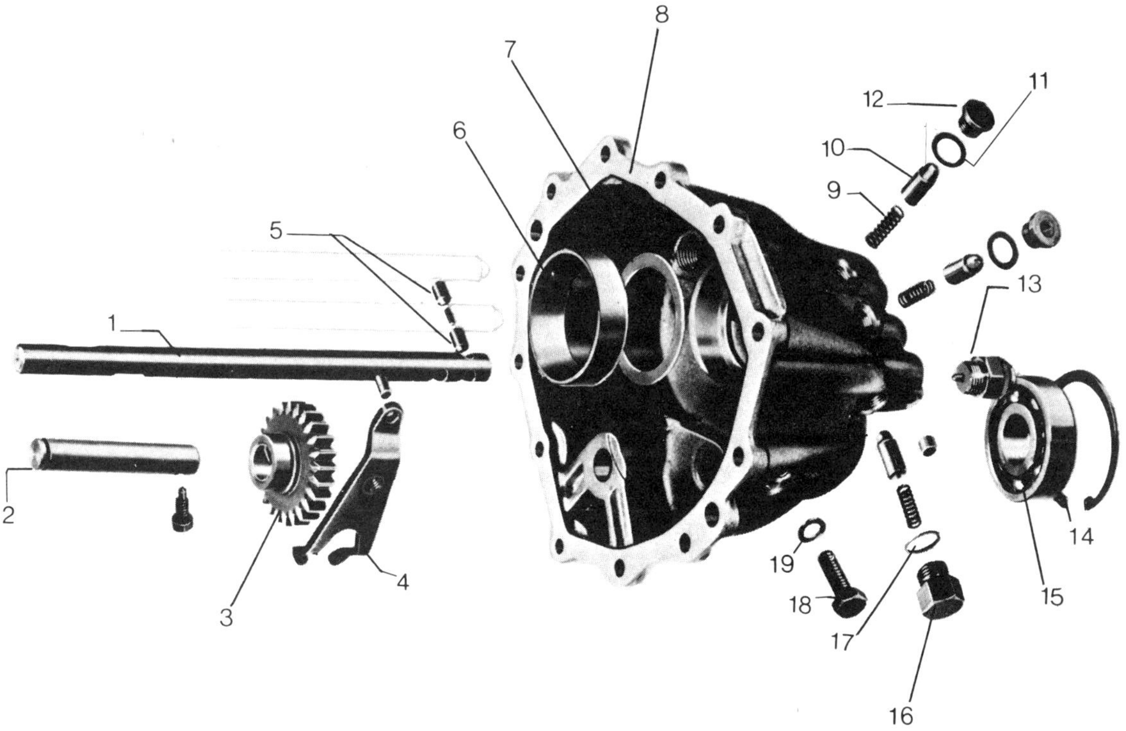

Fig. 6.43 Bearing carrier components (Type 088 gearbox) (Sec 19)

1	Reverse gear selector rod	6	Pinion bearing outer track	11	Paper gasket	16	Threaded plug
2	Reverse gear spindle	7	Shim	12	Detent plug	17	Washer (see text)
3	Reverse gearwheel	8	Bearing carrier	13	Reversing light switch	18	Relay lever bolt
4	Relay lever	9	Detent spring	14	Circlip	19	Relay lever washer
5	Interlock plungers	10	Detent plunger	15	Mainshaft bearing		

which secures the spindle of the reverse gear. Pull the spindle out from inside the box and extract the gear.

15 Unscrew and remove the relay lever adjusting bolt which is on the top of the gearbox. Unhook the relay lever from the reverse gear selector rod and remove the relay lever and the selector rod.

16 Refit the parts by reversing the dismantling operations, noting that the reverse gear is inserted with the boss on the gear towards the inside of the gearbox.

17 After inserting the reverse gear spindle, check that the drilling in the spindle to locate the shaft securing bolt is opposite the bolt hole in the casting and then insert and tighten the bolt (photo).

18 Adjust the relay lever as follows.

Relay lever adjustment

19 Put the washer on the relay lever bolt and screw the bolt into the casing until the end of the bolt touches the relay lever when the lever is pressed as far as possible in the direction of the arrow (Fig. 6.44).

20 Press the relay lever against the end of the bolt and then screw in the bolt until it just starts to engage the threads in the relay lever.

21 While still holding the relay lever in the same position, screw the bolt in and tighten it to the torque given in Specifications. The relay lever should now be set at the correct distance from the gearcase.

22 Move the reverse gear selector rod to reverse gear position several times and check that the relay mechanism moves freely in all positions.

20 Gearbox – reassembly

1 Remove the plugs from the bores of the detent plungers (photos) and ensure that the interlock plungers and the detents (photo) are as shown in Fig. 6.45.

2 Insert the 3rd/4th gear selector fork in the gear casing, with the hole in the web of the selector fork fitted over the reverse selector rod.

3 Fit the 1st/2nd gear selector fork into the groove in its synchro-sleeve and fit the pinion shaft and selector rod into the housing as an assembly. When the parts are in place, slide the selector fork forward to engage 2nd gear.

4 Fit the mainshaft assembly into the housing, guiding the 3rd/4th gear selector fork into its operating sleeve groove.

5 Using an 8 mm bolt, nut and large washer as shown in Fig. 6.46, pull the mainshaft into its bearing.

6 Set the reverse and the 1st/2nd gear selector rods to their neutral positions.

7 Ensure that the small interlock plunger is in its bore in the 3rd/4th gear selector rod and then insert the selector rod through the bore of its selector fork and into its bore in the housing.

8 Align the holes in 3rd/4th gear selector fork and rod, support the free end of the rod in similar manner to when dismantling and hammer in the roll-pin to secure the fork to the shaft.

9 Fit new paper gaskets to the screw plugs of the detent bores and screw the plugs in.

10 Grip the input shaft in a soft-jawed vice, remove the bolt used for drawing the shaft into the bearing and fit and tighten the mainshaft bolt and washer.

11 If a metal cover is fitted over the mainshaft bearing, fit a new O-ring, align the cover so that the recess in the cover is opposite the oil drilling in the gear carrier and tap the plug in. If a rubber plug was fitted, drive in a new one, but do not replace a metal plug with a rubber one.

12 The reassembly of the gearbox housing is the reverse of the dismantling procedure described in paragraphs 16 and 17 of Section 4, Part A.

13 After reassembling the gearbox housing, push in the selector shaft

19.17 Reverse gear spindle bolt

Fig. 6.44 Adjusting the relay lever (Sec 19)

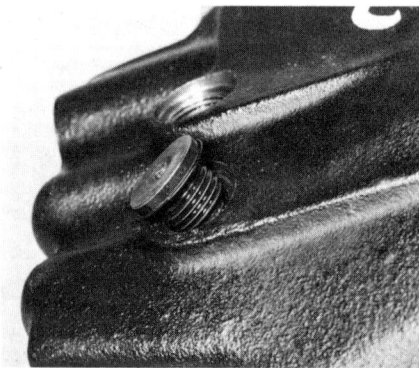

20.1a Detent plunger plug

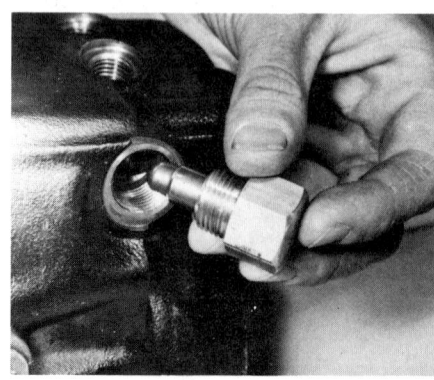

20.1b Interlock plunger plug and detent

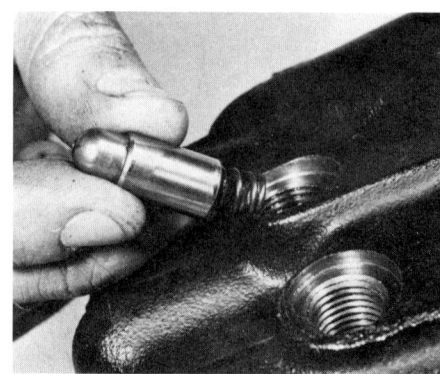

20.1c Selector shaft detent and spring

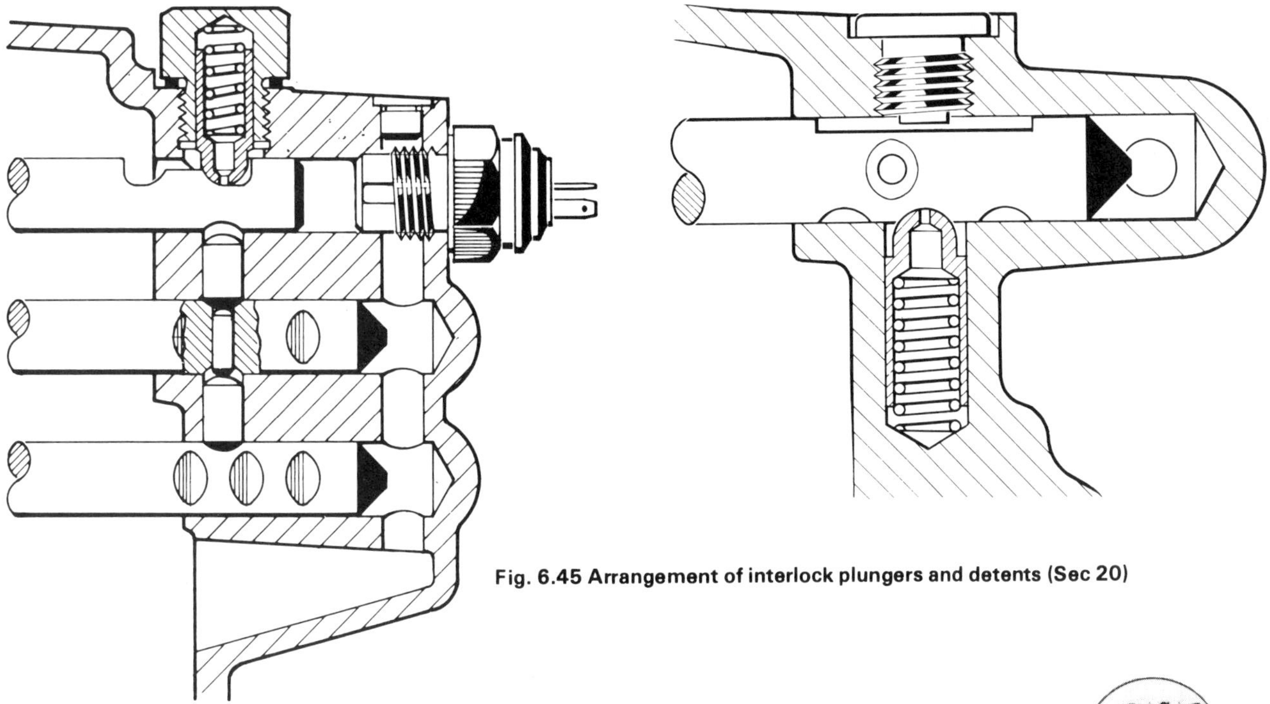

Fig. 6.45 Arrangement of interlock plungers and detents (Sec 20)

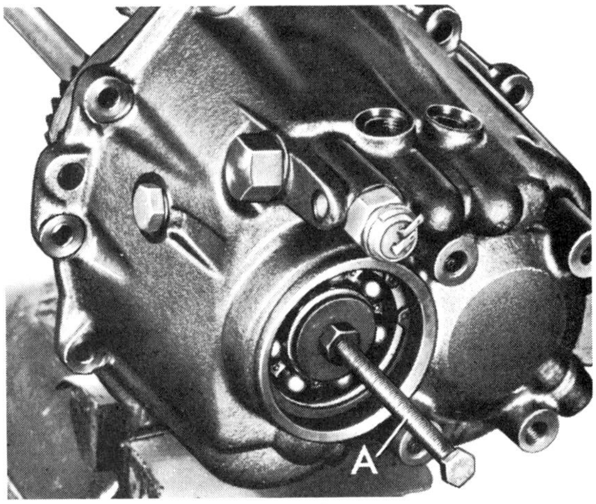

Fig. 6.46 Drawing the mainshaft into its bearing (Sec 20)

A – Bolt M8

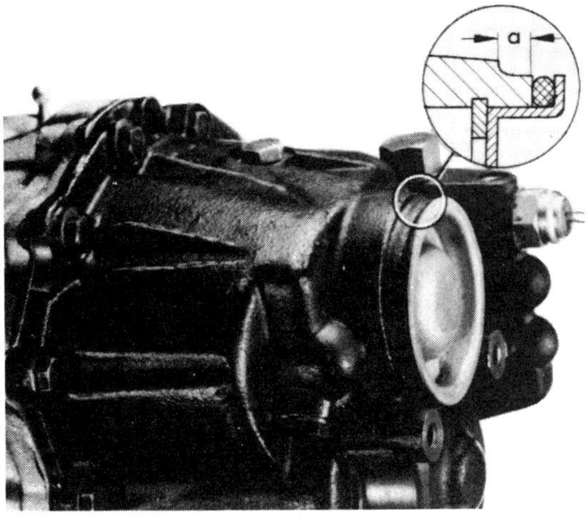

Fig. 6.47 Metal end cover and O-ring (Sec 20)

Used if shoulder "a" is 7mm (0.28 in)

Fig. 6.48 Rubber plug (Sec 20)

Used if shoulder "a" is 12 mm (0.47 in)

as far as possible, coat the joint faces with a thin coat of genuine VW D3 sealant and fit the gear assembly to the gearbox housing (photos). There is no gasket between the bearing carrier and the gearbox casing.

14 Line up the holes and drive the dowel sleeves in fully, then insert and tighten the bolts.

15 Complete the assembly by fitting the large spring and then the washer to the selector shaft, then fit the circlip. Fit the small spring, the selector cover and its two bolts and washers, then tighten the bolts to the specified torque.

16 Fit the shift lever to the end of the selector shaft so that the outer face of the lever is flush with the end of the splines. If the position of the lever on the splines was not marked on dismantling, set the lever so that the rear of the ball is 104 mm (4·1 in) from the joint face (Fig. 6.50).

21 Gearshift lever – removing, refitting and checking

1 Screw off the gear lever knob and remove the console (Chapter 12) to give access to the gear lever assembly.

2 Remove the bolt securing the gearshift rod to the gear lever.

3 Remove the four bolts and washers securing the gear lever base to the floor and remove the gear lever assembly.

4 Check the basic setting of the gearshift linkage by engaging 1st

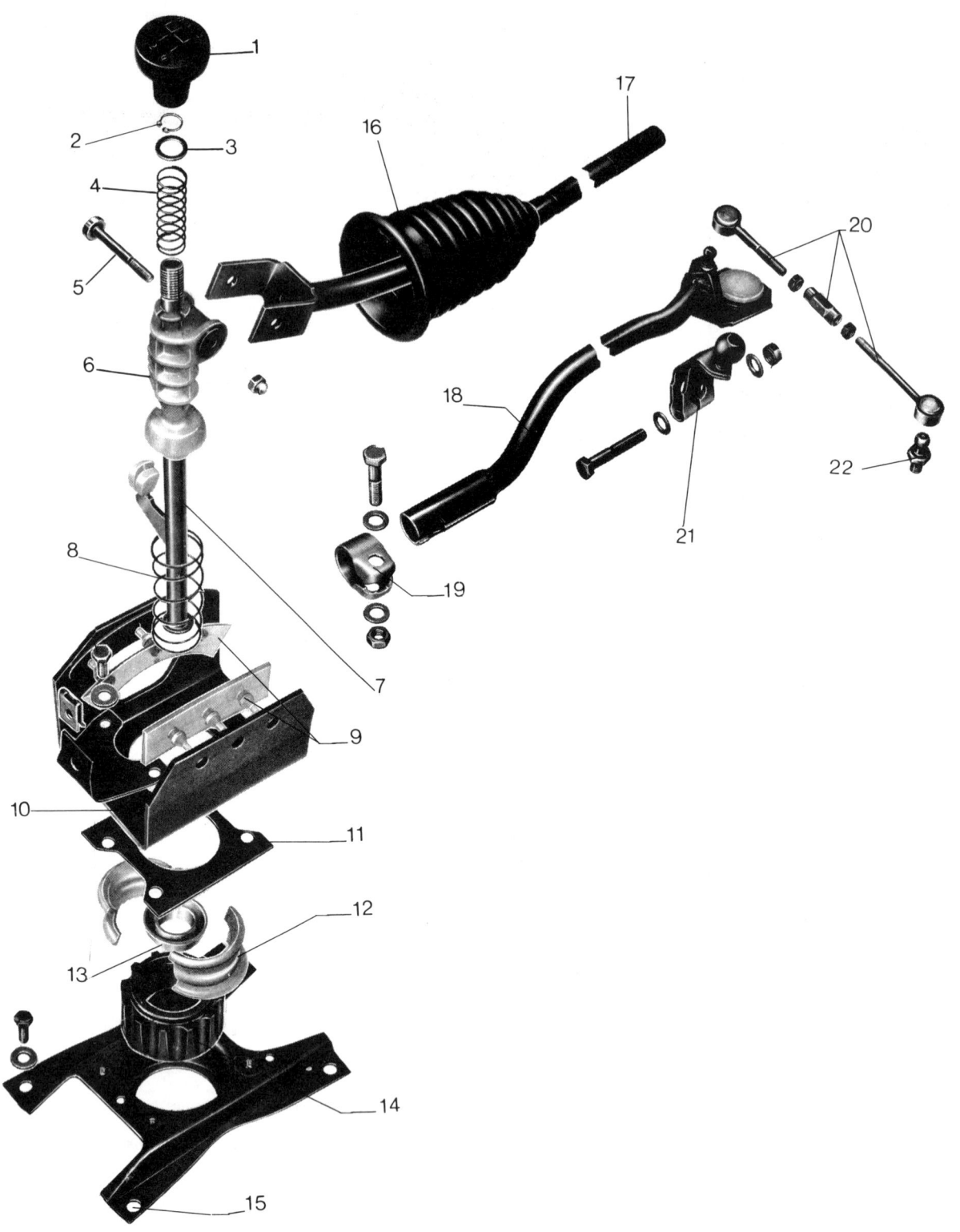

Fig. 6.49 Gearshift components (Type 088 gearbox) (Sec 21)

1	Gear knob	7	Gear lever	13	Lower ball section	18	Front gearshift rod
2	Circlip	8	Spring	14	Rubber guide	19	Clamp
3	Washer	9	Stop pads	15	Gear lever base	20	Adjusting rod
4	Spring	10	Stop	16	Rubber boot	21	Gearbox selector lever
5	Bolt	11	Cover plate	17	Rear gearshift rod	22	Ball stud
6	Upper ball section	12	Shells				

20.13a Fitting the gear assembly to the gearbox housing   20.13b Position of selector shafts and dogs   20.13c Selector shaft engaged with shift rods

Fig. 6.50 Position of selector lever (Sec 20)

Distance "a" is 104 mm (4.1 in)

gear and then pressing the gear lever to the left as far as it will go.
5   Release the gear lever and measure the amount by which it springs to the right. If the movement is not between 5 and 10 mm (0·20 and 0·34 in) the position must be adjusted as described in the following Section.

22 Gearshift linkage – dismantling, reassembly and adjusting

1   Remove the gearshift lever as described in the previous Section and then remove the gearshift rods as follows.
2   Press the front gearshift rod off its ball coupling on the selector lever and press the adjusting rod off its ball stud on the gearbox.
3   Remove the rod assembly from beneath the car.
4   The gear lever assembly should only be dismantled if it needs greasing.
5   Remove the four bolts which clamp the stop, the cover plate and the gear lever base together. Lift off the stop and the cover plate.
6   Pull the rubber guide out of the gear lever base and from it remove the upper ball section, spring, shells and lower ball section.
7   Grease all joints and moving surfaces with special grease AOS 126 000 06.
8   Commence reassembly with the shoulder of the rubber guide uppermost, and press in the lower ball section. Fit the spring and the gear lever, then press the upper ball section into place, spreading the shells slightly if necessary.
9   Fit the assembled rubber guide into the base plate and fit the cover plate and stop, screwing the three parts together.
10   Before tightening the screws, ensure that the centering holes in the stop and gear lever base are aligned (Fig. 6.51), then fit the spring, washer and circlip.

Adjusting the gearshift linkage

11   If the basic setting described in the previous Section is not correct,

Fig. 6.51 Align centering holes (arrowed) (Sec 22)

adjust the gear linkage as follows.
12   With the gearbox in neutral, ensure that the rear of the ball of the gearbox selector lever is 104 mm (4·1 in) from the joint face (Fig. 6.49). When the selector lever is positioned correctly, push the lever on to the shaft until it is flush with the end of the splines and tighten the clamp-bolt.
13   Set the adjusting rod so that the distance between the centres of the balljoints is 134 mm (5·28 in) (Fig. 6.52) then press the gearshift rod onto the ball of the gearbox selector lever and fit the adjusting rod.
14   Set the gear lever so that the joint on its plastic stop is in line with the centre hole of the left-hand stop pad when the gear lever is in neutral in the plane of 1st/2nd gear (Fig. 6.53) and fix the lever in this position.
15   Check that the centering holes in the stop and the gear lever base are aligned.
16   Loosen the clamp between the front and rear selector rods so that the rods can move freely.
17   Check that the front gearshift rod and the gear selector are still in the neutral position. Adjust it if necessary by moving the front gearshift rod without moving the rear one, then tighten the clamp between the rods and free the gearchange lever.
18   Check that all gears, including reverse can be engaged freely without sticking.
19   Fit the console and the gear lever boot and screw on the gear knob until it touches the boot.

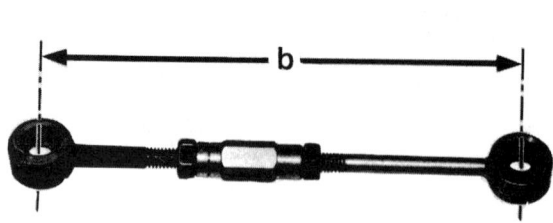

Fig. 6.52 Adjusting rod setting (Sec 22)

Dimension b = 134 mm (5.3 in)

Fig. 6.53 Position of lever when adjusting gearshift (Sec 22)

23 Fault diagnosis – manual gearbox

Symptom	Reason(s)
Synchromesh not giving smooth gear change	Worn synchro-rings Worn synchroniser
Jumps out of gear	Weak detent springs Worn selector forks Worn synchro-hubs
Vibration and/or whining noise	Worn bearings Damaged gears
Gears difficult to engage	Worn synchroniser Worn synchro-rings Clutch fault Gearshift out of adjustment

Chapter 7 Automatic transmission

Contents

Specifications

1.6 litre engine

Gearbox type 089

Code letters . . . . KE

Gear ratios:
Final drive . . . . 11 : 45   4.1 : 1
1st gear . . . .   2.55 : 1
2nd gear . . . .   1.45 : 1
3rd gear . . . .   1.00 : 1
Reverse . . . .   2.46 : 1

Oil capacity

	Gearbox (ATF)	Final drive
Total	6.0 litres, 10.6 Imp pts, 12.7 US pts	1.0 litres, 1.76 Imp pts, 2.1 US pts
At fluid change	3.0 litres, 5.3 Imp pts, 6.4 US pts	Filled for life. No change required

Oil specification . . . . ATF Dexron   Hypoid gear oil, SAE 90

Shift speeds . . . .

Gear shift	Full throttle		Kickdown	
	mph	kph	mph	kph
1–2	20–23	32–37	36–39	58–63
2–3	51–54	82–87	68–69	109–111
3–2	31–36	50–58	64–65	103–105
2–1	15–17	24–27	32–35	52–56

Torque converter
Max diameter of bush . . . . 34.25 mm (1.35 in)
Max out of round . . . . 0.03 mm (0.001 in)

Accelerator pedal
Height of underside of pedal-to-stop . . . . 80 mm (3.15 mm)

2.0 and 2.2 litre

Gearbox type 087

Code letters
2.0 litre . . . . RJ
2.2 litre (carburettor) . . . . RA
2.2 litre (injection) . . . . RB

Gear ratios

Final drive	11 : 41	3·73 : 1
1st gear		2·55 : 1
2nd gear		1·45 : 1
3rd gear		1·00 : 1
Reverse		2·46 : 1

Oil capacity

	Gearbox (ATF)	Final drive
Total	10·6 Imp pts, 6·0 litres, 12·6 US pts	1·8 Imp pts, 1·0 litre, 2·16 US pts
At fluid change	5·3 Imp pts, 3·0 litres, 6·4 US pts	Filled for life No change required

Oil specification

Oil specification	ATF Dexron	Hypoid gear oil, SAE 90

Shift speeds

Gear shift	Full throttle		Kickdown	
	mph	kph	mph	kph

2·2 litre, 115 BHP ....

1–2	21–27	34–44	39–43	63–69
2–3	55–58	88–94	72–73	116–117
3–2	34–41	55–66	68–70	110–112
2–1	16–17	26–28	36–39	58–62

2·0 litre, 115 BHP ....

1–2	20–25	33–41	38–41	61–66
2–3	53–57	85–91	70–71	112–114
3–2	32–38	52–61	66–67	106–108
2–1	16–17	25–28	34–37	54–59

2·2 litre, 136 BHP ....

1–2	24–30	39–48	43–46	69–74
2–3	58–62	94–99	76–77	122–124
3–2	37–42	59–68	72–73	116–118
2–1	17–18	27–29	39–42	63–68

Torque converter

Max diameter of bush	34·12 mm (1·34 in)
Max out of round	0·03 mm (0·001 in)

Accelerator pedal

Height of underside of pedal-to-stop	80 mm (3·15 in)

Torque wrench settings

	Nm	lbf ft
Driveshaft-to-flange	45	32
Oil pan-to-gearbox	20	15
Gearbox-to-engine	55	40
Torque converter-to-driveplate	30	22
Selector cable-to-operating lever	8	6
Starter-to-gearbox (1·6 litre)	20	15
(2·0 and 2·2 litre)	60	44
Selector lever-to-floor	15	11
Gearbox-to-bellhousing	30	22

1 General description

The automatic transmission consists of three main assemblies which have a common casing, these being the torque converter, which is directly coupled to the engine; the final drive unit which incorporates the differential assembly; and the planetary gearbox with its hydraulically operated multi-disc clutches and brake bands. The gearbox also houses an oil pump, which is coupled to the torque converter housing and this pump supplies automatic transmission fluid to the planetary gears, hydraulic controls and torque converter. The fluid performs a triple function by lubricating the moving parts, cooling the automatic transmission system and providing a torque transfer medium. The final drive lubrication is separate from the transmission lubrication system, unlike the manual gearbox where the final drive shares a common lubrication system. Lubricant for the differential assembly and final drive is SAE 90 hypoid gear oil.

The torque converter is a sealed unit which cannot be dismantled. It is bolted to the crankshaft drive plate and replaces the clutch found on an engine with manual transmission. Inside the torque converter are two turbine discs which can rotate independently of each other and the fluid transfers engine torque to the input shaft of the gearbox.

The gearbox is of the planetary type with epicyclic gear trains operated by brakes and clutches through a hydraulic control system. The correct gear is selected by a combination of three control signals, a manual valve operated by the gearshift cable, a vacuum valve operated by vacuum from the inlet manifold and a governor which controls the fluid pressure. The manual valve allows the driver to select a specific gear and over-ride the automatic control if desired. The vacuum valve provides a control which reflects engine load and the governor control reflects engine speed.

Because of the need for special test equipment, the complexity of some of the parts and the need for scrupulous cleanliness when servicing automatic transmissions the amount which the owner can do is limited, but those operations which can reasonably be carried out are detailed in the following Sections.

2 Automatic transmission – operation

1 The automatic transmission has three forward speeds and one reverse, controlled by a six position lever with the following positions:

P	Park
R	Reverse
N	Neutral
D	Drive
2	Low
1	Low

The selector lever has a push button which must be depressed when selecting the following positions:

From P to R
  R to P
  N to R
  2 to 1

The selector lever can be moved freely between all other positions. If the lever is set to positions D, or 2, the automatic transmission changes gears automatically.

Position D

2 This position is for normal driving and once selected the three forward gears engage automatically throughout the speed range from zero to top speed.

Position 2

3 With the lever in this position, the two lower gears will engage automatically but the highest gear will not engage. For this reason position 2 should only be selected when the speed of the car is below 75 mph (121 kph). Selecting Position 2 will make use of the engine's braking effect and the actual change can be made without letting up the accelerator pedal.

Position 1

4 The position is needed rarely such as on steep inclines or declines. The transmission remains in the lowest gear and Position 1 should only be selected when the car speed is below 40 mph (64 kph).

Reverse

5 Reverse must only be selected when the car is absolutely stationary and with the engine running at idling speed.

Park

6 In the park position the transmission is locked mechanically by the engagement of a pawl. This position must only be selected when the car is absolutely stationary, otherwise the transmission will be damaged.

3 Automatic transmission – precautions

Starting the engine

1 A safety switch prevents the engine from being started unless the selector lever is in the *Neutral* or *Park* positions.

Emergency starting

2 A car fitted with automatic transmission cannot be started by pushing or towing. If the battery is discharged, the car can be started using jumper cables and the correct procedure for doing this is given in Introduction and Maintenance.

Towing

3 If the car is being towed, the ignition key must be inserted so that the steering wheel is not locked and the gear selector must be in *Neutral*. Because the lubrication of the transmission is limited when the engine is not running, the car must not be towed for more than 30 miles (48 km), or at a speed greater than 30 mph (48 kph) unless the front wheels of the car are lifted clear of the road.

4 Automatic transmission – maintenance

1 The only routine maintenance necessary is to check the level of the fluid and if necessary top it up every 12 months or 10 000 miles (16 000 km) and to change the fluid every 30 000 miles (48 000 km).
2 Checking the fluid level should be done when the engine is warm and running at idling speed with the selector lever in *Neutral* and the handbrake applied. Withdraw the dipstick and wipe it with a piece of clean, lint-free rag. It is important that the rag is both clean and lint-free, because even a tiny speck of dirt can damage or cause a malfunction of the transmission. The level of fluid is satisfactory anywhere between the two marks on the dipstick, but either too high, or too low a level must be avoided.

5 Automatic transmission – draining and refilling

1 This job should not be attempted unless clean, dust free conditions can be achieved.
2 With the car standing on level ground, place a container of at least six pints capacity beneath the oil pan of the transmission. Remove the drain plug and allow the fluid to drain out. Refit and tighten the plug.
3 Remove the bolts securing the oil pan, pull off the oil pan and

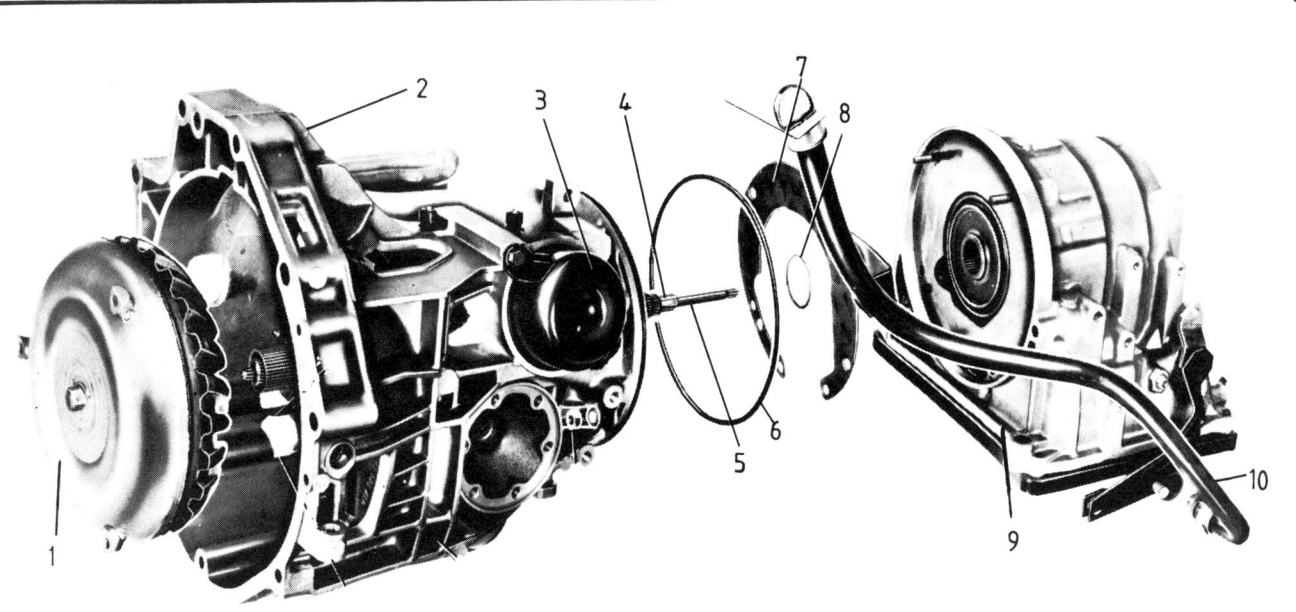

Fig. 7.1 Automatic transmission assembly (Sec 1)

1	Torque converter	3	Governor
2	Bellhousing and final drive casing	4	Turbine shaft
		5	Pump shaft

6	Sealing ring	9	Gearbox asssembly
7	Gasket	10	Filler pipe
8	Shim		

remove the gasket.

4   Remove the bolt from the centre of the oil filter screen cover plate and remove the cover plate and screen.

5   While the oil pan is off, tie a piece of plastic sheeting, or clean paper over the base of the gearbox to prevent the entry of dust and dirt. Do not run the engine, or move the vehicle while the oil pan is off, or while there is no fluid in the gearbox.

6   Clean the oil pan, the filter and the cover plate and wipe them with a clean lint-free cloth. Absolute cleanliness of all parts of the automatic transmission is essential.

7   Fit the oil screen with its rim against the gasket on the valve assembly. Refit the screen cover and tighten its fixing bolt.

8   Ensure that the joint faces of the gearbox and oil pan are perfectly clean, then refit the oil pan using a new gasket. Fit the oil pan bolts and tighten them to the specified torque.

9   If the fluid drained from the oil pan shows severe contamination, such as results from the transmission overheating, the torque converter hub must be drained of fluid before the system is refilled. Draining the hub is described in Section 6.

10   To fill the system, first wipe round the top of the filler tube and

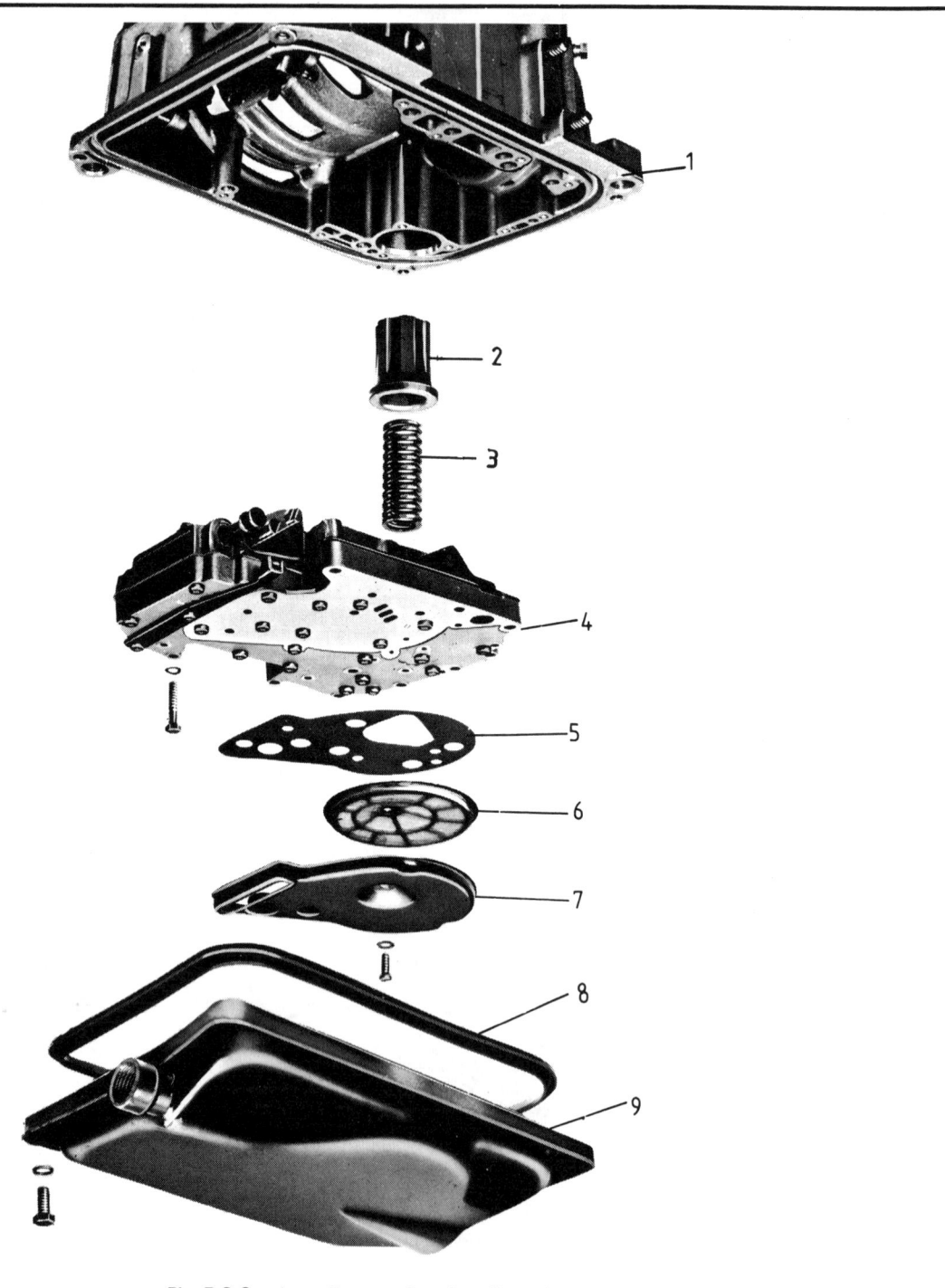

Fig. 7.2 Gearbox oil pan and strainer (Sec 2)

1	Gearbox casing	4	Valve assembly	6	Oil screen	8	Oil pan gasket
2	Accumulator piston	5	Gasket	7	Oil screen cover	9	Oil pan
3	Accumulator spring						

dipstick, then remove the dipstick.

11 If a funnel is to be used, make sure that it is absolutely clean and then pour in about 4 pints (2.5 litres) of fluid. The fluid must be of the "Dexron" type, without any lubricant additives.

12 Start the engine and with the handbrake applied, select every gear position once. With the engine idling and the transmission in *Neutral*, check the level of the fluid on the dipstick and if necessary top-up to the lower mark.

13 Road test the vehicle until the engine is at normal temperature then again check the fluid level and top-up if necessary.

14 The amount of fluid which must be added to raise the level from the lower mark to the upper mark on the dipstick is about half a pint (0.4 litre).

15 Do not overfill the transmission because an excess of fluid will upset its operation and any excess fluid will have to be drained.

6 Automatic transmission – removing and refitting

1.6 litre engine

1 This can be done much more easily if the vehicle is over a pit. If this is not possible, the front wheels may be put on ramps, but it is unsafe to attempt to remove the transmission with the car supported on jacks.

2 Disconnect the battery leads.

3 Remove the air cleaner.

4 Either clamp off the two hoses to the fluid cooler, or drain the cooling system. Place a pan beneath the fluid cooler to catch any spillage of engine coolant and remove the two hoses.

5 Attach lifting slings to the engine and take the weight of the engine on a hoist. Do not take the weight of the engine by placing a jack under the sump. Having taken the weight of the engine, remove the upper bolts attaching the engine to the transmission bellhousing.

6 Disconnect the speedometer cable from the final drive housing. This will require the use of a special split tubular spanner as shown in Fig. 7.4.

7 Disconnect the accelerator pedal cable and the throttle cable from the gearbox operating lever.

8 Remove the nuts securing the exhaust pipe to the manifold and then undo the clip securing the exhaust pipe to the gearbox.

9 Using a socket wrench, remove the bolts from the driveshaft couplings. Separate the coupling parts and rest the driveshafts on the subframe.

10 Remove the bolts securing the starter motor and pull the starter motor as clear as possible from its hole in the engine backplate.

11 Remove the selector cable bracket and disengage the selector cable from the operating lever on the gearbox (Fig. 7.7).

12 Remove the guard plate from the right-hand side of the subframe and then remove the bolts attaching the gearbox supports to the subframe (Fig. 7.8).

13 Turn the engine driveplate until each of the three torque converter mounting bolts in turn is accessible through the starter motor hole and remove the bolts (Fig. 7.9).

14 Jack the gearbox slightly, placing a hardwood block between the

Fig. 7.3 Disconnect the fluid cooler hoses (Sec. 6)

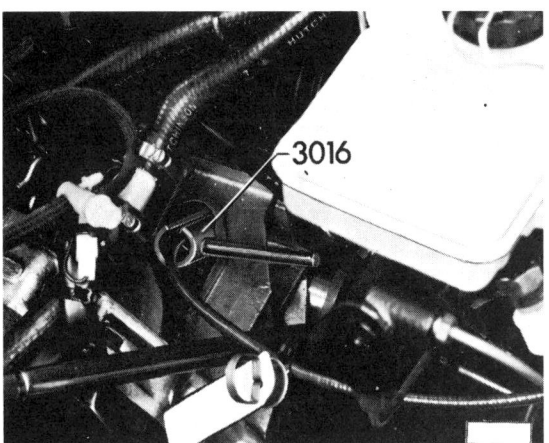

Fig. 7.4 Disconnect the speedometer cable using the special tool (Sec. 6)

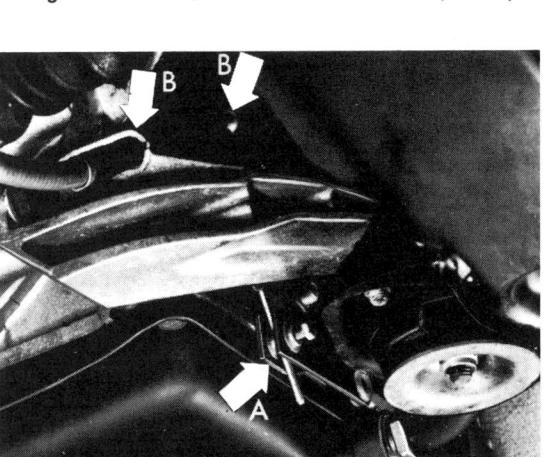

Fig. 7.5 Disconnect gearbox controls (1.6 litre) (Sec. 6)

A *Accelerator pedal cable*   B *Carburettor cable*

Fig. 7.6 Disconnect driveshafts (Sec. 6)

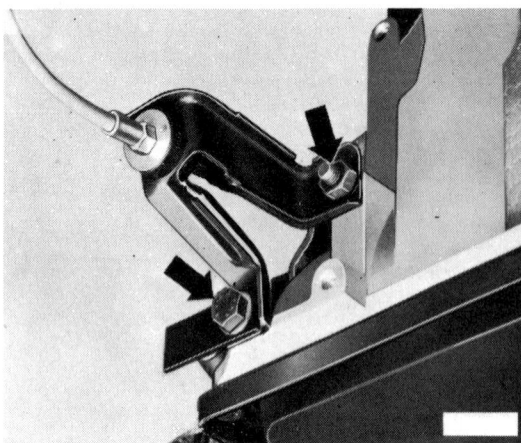

Fig. 7.7 Remove selector cable bracket (Sec. 6)

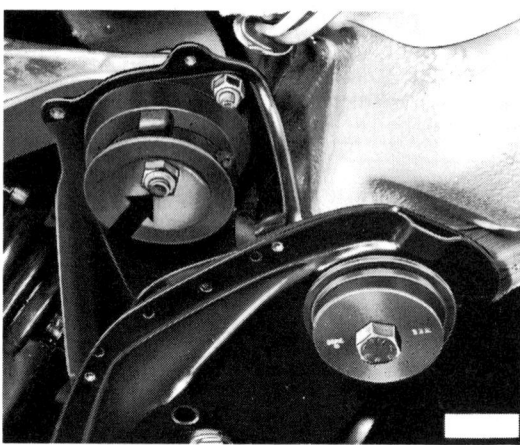

Fig. 7.8 Bolts attaching gearbox to subframe (Sec. 6)

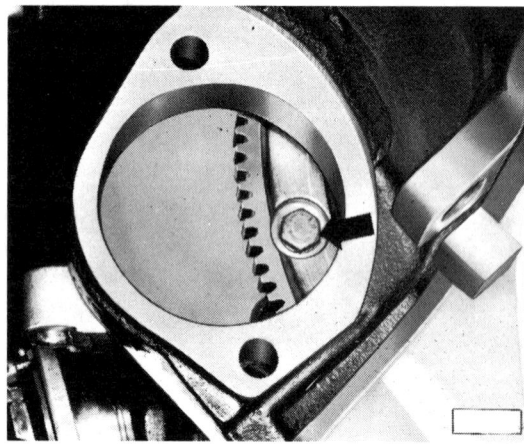

Fig. 7.9 Torque converter mounting bolts (Sec. 6)

jack and the gearbox. The positioning of the jack and the placing of the wood requires great care to ensure that no load is placed on the oil pan.

15 Remove the lower bolts attaching the engine to the bellhousing and remove the bolts from the rear subframe.

16 Prise the gearbox away from the engine carefully until the dowels are disengaged.

17 Lower the gearbox carefully, taking care to prevent the torque converter from falling out of the bell housing and then remove the gearbox from beneath the car.

2.0 and 2.2 litre engines

18 The majority of the operations are the same as those required on the transmission of the 1.6 litre engine, but there are a few differences as follows.

19 The accelerator linkage rod is disengaged at the carburettor end (Fig. 7.10) and only the accelerator linkage is disengaged from the gearbox operating lever (Fig. 7.11).

20 Before refitting the automatic transmission to the engine, the torque converter must be fitted inside the bellhousing.

21 Make sure that the pump shaft is engaged in its splines and then fit the torque converter. If the pump shaft is correctly engaged, the boss of the torque converter will be about 10 mm (0.39 in) from the open end of the bellhousing (Fig. 7.12). If the boss of the torque converter is found to be flush with the open end of the bellhousing (Fig. 7.13) it is likely that the pump shaft has pulled out of the pump driveplate splines. The pump driveplate will be destroyed if the gearbox is bolted to the engine with the pump shaft in this position.

22 Fit the gearbox, making sure that the torque converter does not slip forward and install the lower bolts attaching the gearbox to the engine.

23 Attach the subframe to the gearbox and then bolt the subframe to the body.

Fig. 7.10 Disconnect the carburettor linkage (2.0 and 2.2 litre) (Sec 6)

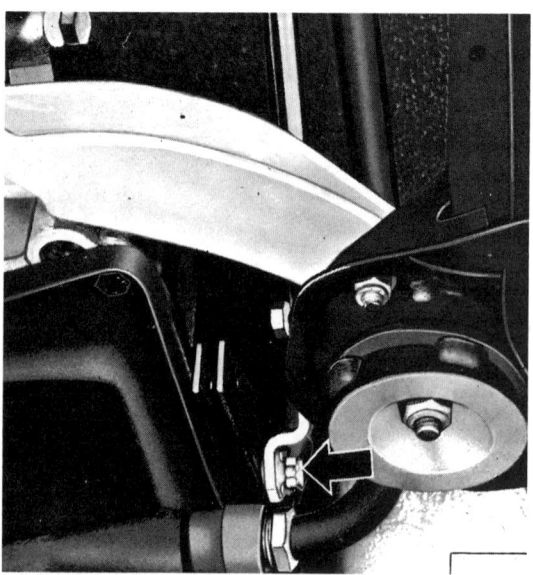

Fig. 7.11 Disconnect the accelerator linkage (2.0 and 2.2 litre) (Sec. 6)

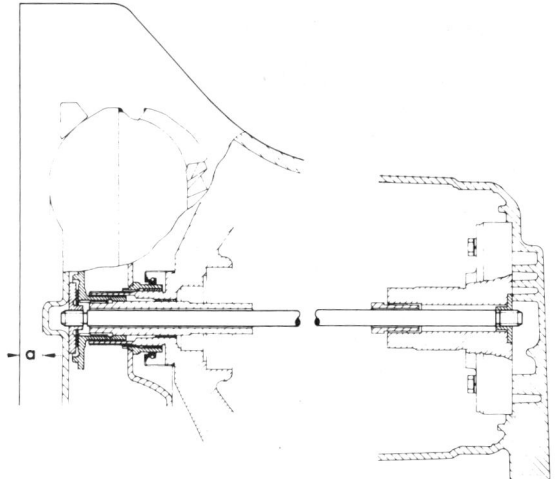

Fig. 7.12 Correct fitting of torque converter (Sec. 6)

*Dimension a is about 10 mm
(0.39 in)*

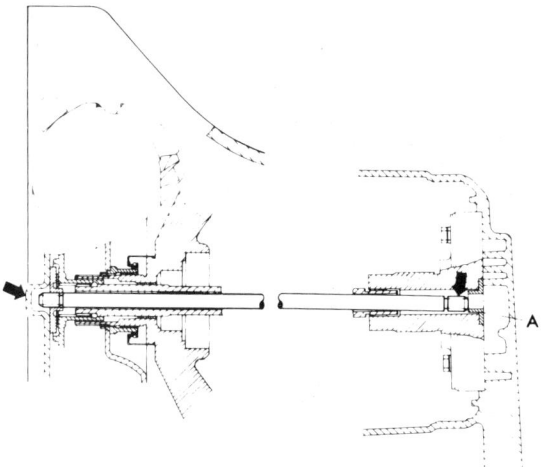

Fig. 7.13 Incorrect fitting of torque converter (Sec. 6)

*Boss is flush and pump shaft has
slipped out of engagement at
point A*

24 Attach the driveshafts to the engine and tighten the coupling bolts.
25 Fit the torque converter bolts and tighten them, then refit the starter motor.
26 Connect the linkages and cables as a reversal of the removal operations, then check the adjustment of the accelerator linkage and selector cable.
27 Reconnect the coolant hoses to the cooler and top-up the cooling system.

7 Torque converter – checking and draining

1 The torque converter is a welded unit and if it is faulty the complete unit must be replaced. Only the bush can be renewed.
2 Examine the bush for signs of scoring and wear. To check for wear requires an internal micrometer or dial gauge and if one is available measure the bore diameter to see if it exceeds the wear limit given in Specifications.
3 To remove the bush requires a commercial extractor and a slide hammer. After fitting a new bush its diameter must be between the limits given and if not the bush must be removed and another one fitted. For this reason the job is really one for an Audi agent.
4 Check that the cooling vanes on the converter are secure.
5 Fit the turbine shaft into the converter and check that the turbine turns freely.
6 If the fluid was dirty when drained from the oil pan, drain the fluid from the torque converter before the automatic transmission is refitted.
7 Have ready a container of about half a gallon (2 litres) capacity, a washing-up liquid bottle and a piece of plastic tubing of not more than 8 mm (0.32 in) outside diameter.
8 Put the torque converter on the bench and support it so that it is tipped up slightly.
9 Cut one end of the plastic tube on an angle so that the end of the tube will not be blocked if it comes against a flat surface and push this end into the torque converter hub until it touches the bottom.
10 Connect the spout of the washing up liquid bottle to the other end of the tube, hold the bottle below the level of the torque converter and squeeze the bottle. As the bottle expands again, fluid will be sucked into it and as soon as the fluid begins to syphon, pull the tube end off the bottle and rest the tube end in the larger container. Syphon as much fluid as possible from the torque converter. On reassembly and installation, the converter will fill with fluid as soon as the engine is started.

8 Gearbox assembly – dismantling and reassembly

1 The gearbox may be separated from the final drive assembly and the governor may be removed, but dismantling of the gearbox is not recommended.

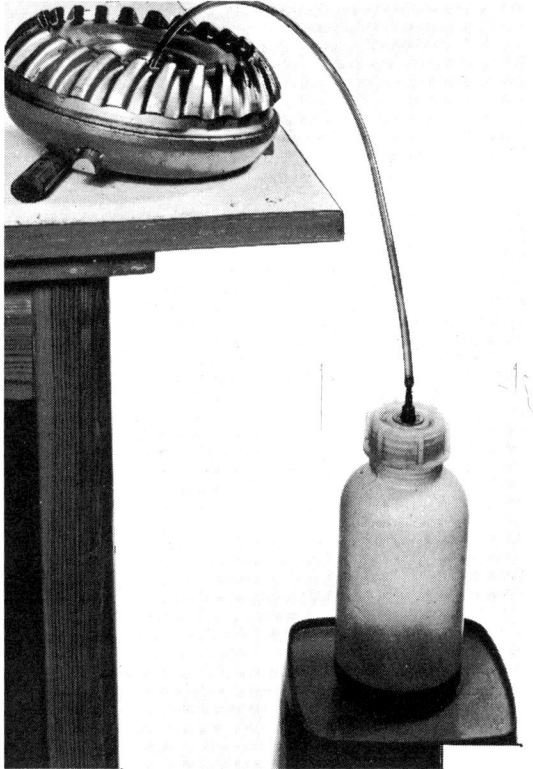

Fig. 7.14 Draining the torque converter (Sec. 7)

2 With the gearbox on the bench, pull out the torque converter if not already removed.
3 Unscrew and remove the fluid filler pipe if the fluid has been drained.
4 Remove the four nuts and washers which secure the gearbox to the bellhousing and prise away the gearbox. Remove the sealing ring, gasket and the shim.
5 With the gearbox removed the turbine shaft and pump shaft can be pulled out and examined. When examining the turbine shaft, check that the sealing rings (Fig. 7.15) are seated properly.
6 Both the pump shaft and the turbine shaft are available in various lengths so it is important to take the old shaft when obtaining a new one.
7 When reassembling be sure to refit the shim to the front of the gearbox and use a new gasket and sealing ring.

Fig. 7.15 Turbine shaft sealing rings (arrowed) (Sec. 8)

8   Make sure that the pump shaft is inserted properly (Section 6, paragraph 21) before fitting the torque converter.

9 Bellhousing – servicing

1   The removal and dismantling of the differential and final drive assembly is not recommended.
2   Removal of the driveshafts and renewal of the oil seals is similar to the procedure for the manual gearbox described in Chapter 6, Section 8.

Torque converter oil seal

3   Using the access holes in the side of the bellhousing, drive off the old seal with a hammer and chisel (Fig. 7.16). Fit a new seal over the boss, taking care to keep the seal square and then carefully drive it on fully with a hammer and wood block.

10 Governor – removing, dismantling, reassembling and refitting

1   The governor assembly is attached to the bellhousing by two bolts with spring and plain washers. Remove the bolts and washers and withdraw the governor assembly.
2   Remove the two bolts which pass through the assembly and remove the governor shaft, the balance weight, transfer plate and filter.
3   If the thrust plate is scored, fit a new one.
4   If the governor shaft is worn, a new shaft can be fitted, but the

Fig. 7.16 Removing the torque converter oil seal (Sec. 9)

balance weight must not be changed.
5   Remove the circlip from the end of the pin and remove the centrifugal weight, the valve, the spring and the spring cup.
6   Clean all the parts thoroughly and lubricate them with transmission fluid before reassembly.
7   When fitting the transfer plate and filter make sure that they are fitted in the position shown in Fig. 7.17.
8   When refitting the governor, ensure that the ring seal inside the cover is in place and in good condition.

11 Accelerator pedal and linkage – adjusting

1   The accelerator linkage must be adjusted so that the operating lever on the gearbox is at its idle position when the throttle is closed. If the adjustment is incorrect the shift speeds will be too high when the throttle is partially open and the main pressure will be too high when the engine is idling.
2   The adjustment of the linkage depends upon the engine and the model of automatic transmission which is fitted, but the adjustment of the accelerator pedal cable is the same for all models.

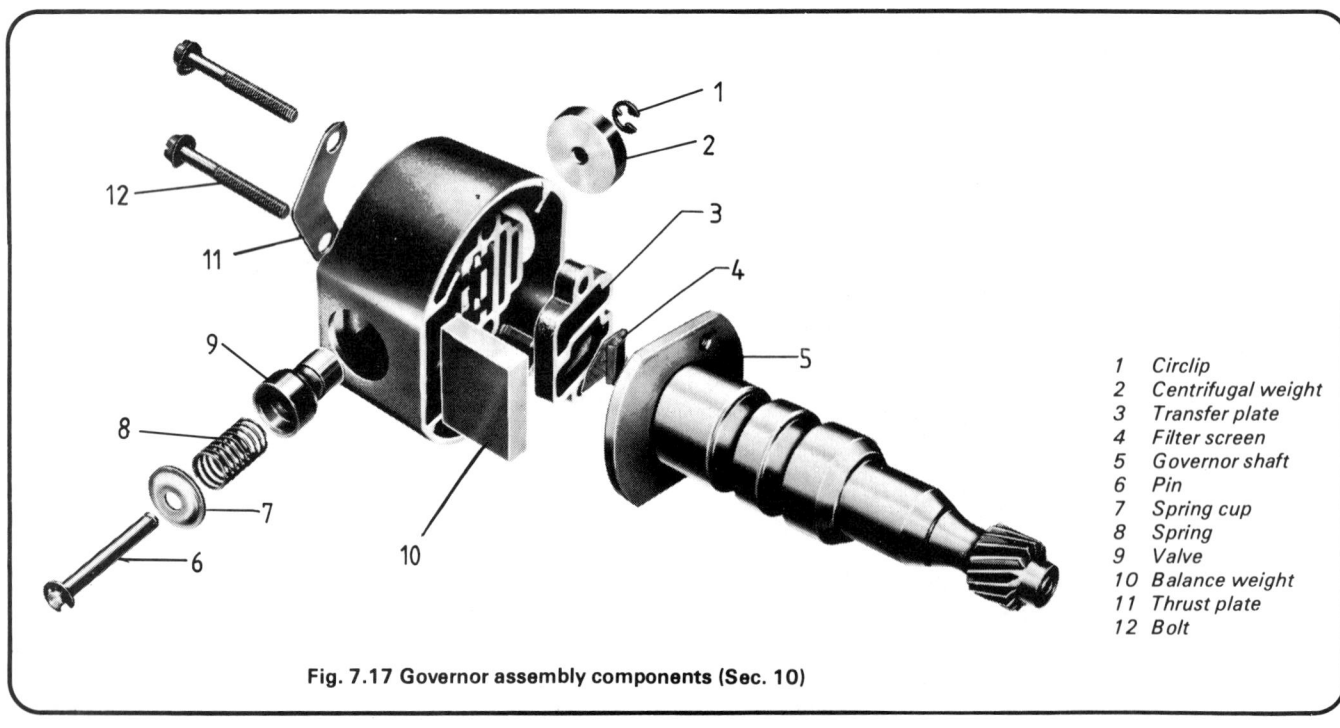

1   Circlip
2   Centrifugal weight
3   Transfer plate
4   Filter screen
5   Governor shaft
6   Pin
7   Spring cup
8   Spring
9   Valve
10 Balance weight
11 Thrust plate
12 Bolt

Fig. 7.17 Governor assembly components (Sec. 10)

1.6 litre

3   Remove the air cleaner to provide better access to the carburettor.

4   Ensure that the engine is at normal operating temperature so that the choke is fully open (off) and that the engine idling speed is adjusted to the correct figure.

5   With the engine switched off, loosen the locknut (Fig. 7.18) at the carburettor bracket and turn the adjusting nut until there is no slack in the carburettor cable, but at the same time ensure that the gearbox lever does not move from its neutral position.

6   Depress the accelerator pedal until resistance is felt and check that this corresponds to the full throttle position with the throttle lever against its stop.

7   Continue pressing the pedal until it reaches the floor stop and check that the operating lever on the gearbox has moved from its neutral position and is contacting its stop.

8   Disconnect the ball socket of the carburettor cable from its ball on the gearbox operating lever. With the throttle in its idling position and the gearbox operating lever against its stop, check that the ball socket is aligned with the ball so that the balljoint can be connected without strain.

2.0 litre

9   Carry out the procedures detailed in paragraphs 3 and 4.

10   Loosen the clamping screw on the carburettor and push the connecting rod (Fig. 7.19) as far as it will go in the direction of the arrow. Tighten the clamping screw.

11   Loosen the clamping screw on the pushrod. Push the rod so that the throttle is held in its idling position and at the same time hold the gearbox lever in its idling position. With both parts held in these positions, tighten the clamping screw.

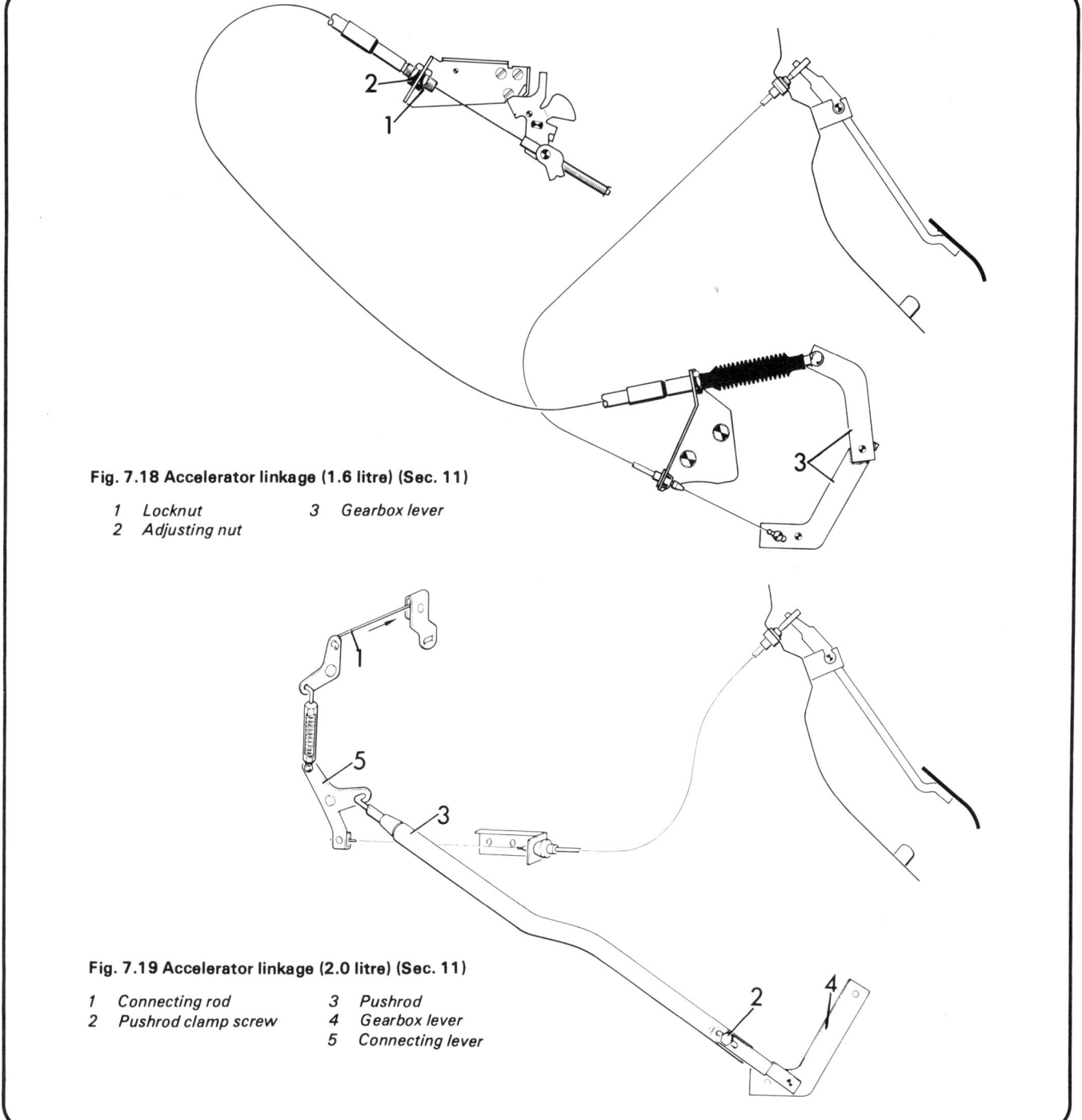

Fig. 7.18 Accelerator linkage (1.6 litre) (Sec. 11)

1	Locknut	3	Gearbox lever
2	Adjusting nut		

Fig. 7.19 Accelerator linkage (2.0 litre) (Sec. 11)

1	Connecting rod	3	Pushrod
2	Pushrod clamp screw	4	Gearbox lever
		5	Connecting lever

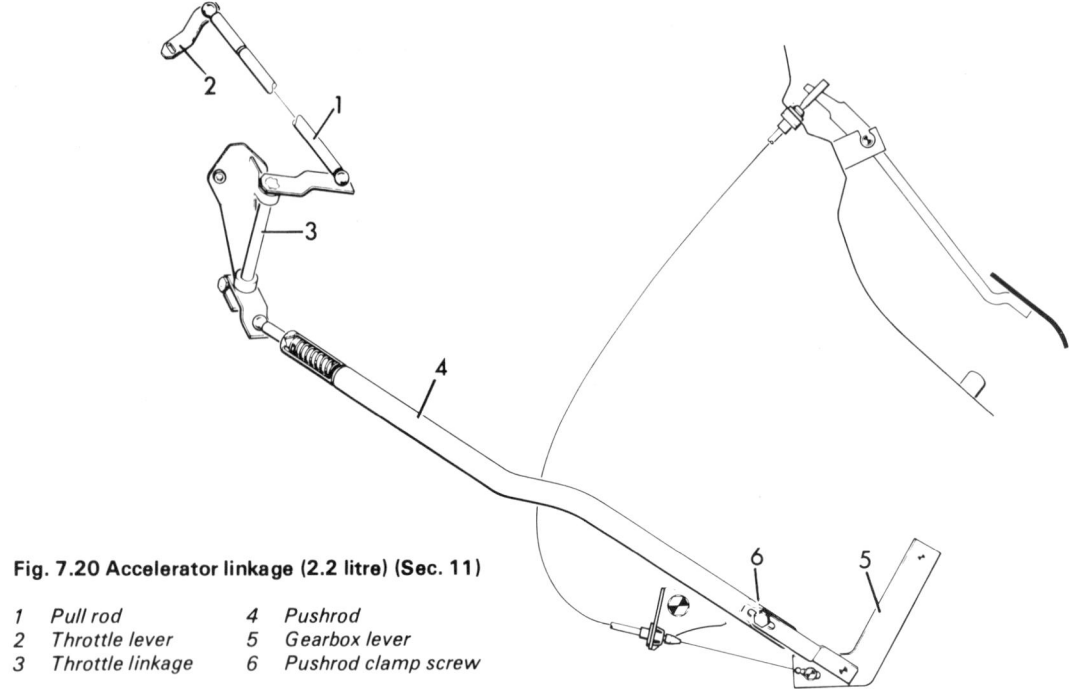

Fig. 7.20 Accelerator linkage (2.2 litre) (Sec. 11)

1 *Pull rod*	4 *Pushrod*
2 *Throttle lever*	5 *Gearbox lever*
3 *Throttle linkage*	6 *Pushrod clamp screw*

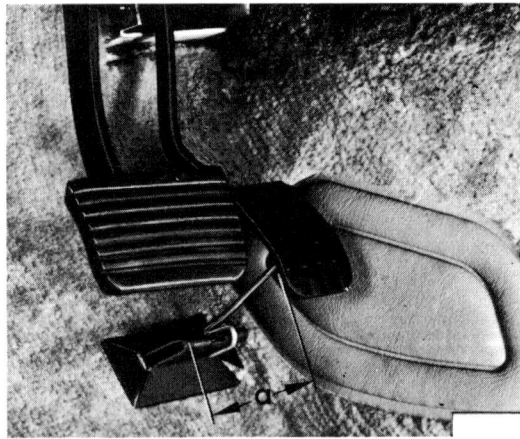

Fig. 7.21 Accelerator pedal adjustment (Sec. 11)

Dimension "a" is 80 mm (3.15 in)

12   Carry out the checks described in paragraphs 6 and 7.
13   Detach the pushrod at its clevis connection with the gearbox operating lever. Push the rod so that the throttle is in its idling position and hold the gearbox lever against its stop. With both parts in these positions ensure that the clevis can be reconnected without strain.

2.2 litre
14   Although the linkage is slightly different (Fig. 7.20), the basic procedure for the 2.2 litre is the same as for the 2.0 litre. Before loosening the clamp screw however, check the pull rod for freedom of movement of the balljoints of the throttle lever and linkage.

Accelerator pedal adjustment
15   Make up a gauge by bending a piece of rod and fit it over the accelerator stop (Fig. 7.21). The gauge should be adjusted so that the curved part of the underside of the pedal is 80 mm (3.15 in) from the highest point of the pedal stop.

16   With the pedal held in this position, connect the accelerator pedal to the operating lever on the gearbox. The method of adjusting the accelerator cable is described in Chapter 3, Section 32.

12   Gear selector mechanism – removing and refitting

1   Disconnect the battery terminal.
2   Release the grub screw in the selector knob and pull the knob off, then lift out the gear selector cover.
3   Remove the two screws securing the console and remove the console.
4   Disconnect the gear selector illumination bulb and also the starter inhibitor switch from the cable harness.
5   Unscrew the cable clamp-nut and pull the cable clear.
6   Remove the four bolts securing the bracket to the floor and lift out the lever assembly.
7   Refit the assembly by reversing the above operations and then adjust the selector cable and check the correct operation of the inhibitor switch before fitting the console and knob.

13   Selector cable – adjustment

1   Ensure that the cable is not bent sharply, kinked, or frayed and that the cable is lightly greased.
2   Remove the console, set the selector lever to P and loosen the nut on the cable clamp.
3   Set the gearbox lever to its P position, which is rearwards until it engages the stop and then tighten the nut on the cable clamp.

14   Inhibitor switch – adjustment

1   The switch consists of a contact bridge which is fixed to the selector lever and a contact plate attached to the lever bracket.
2   With the selector lever in R, D, 2 and 1, operate the starter switch. The starter motor should not operate with the lever in any of these positions. If it does operate, loosen the two clamp screws and slide the contact plate backwards, or forwards until the starter no longer operates. Clamp the plate in this position and recheck.
3   Select each of the positions P and N and check that the starter will operate with the lever in these positions.

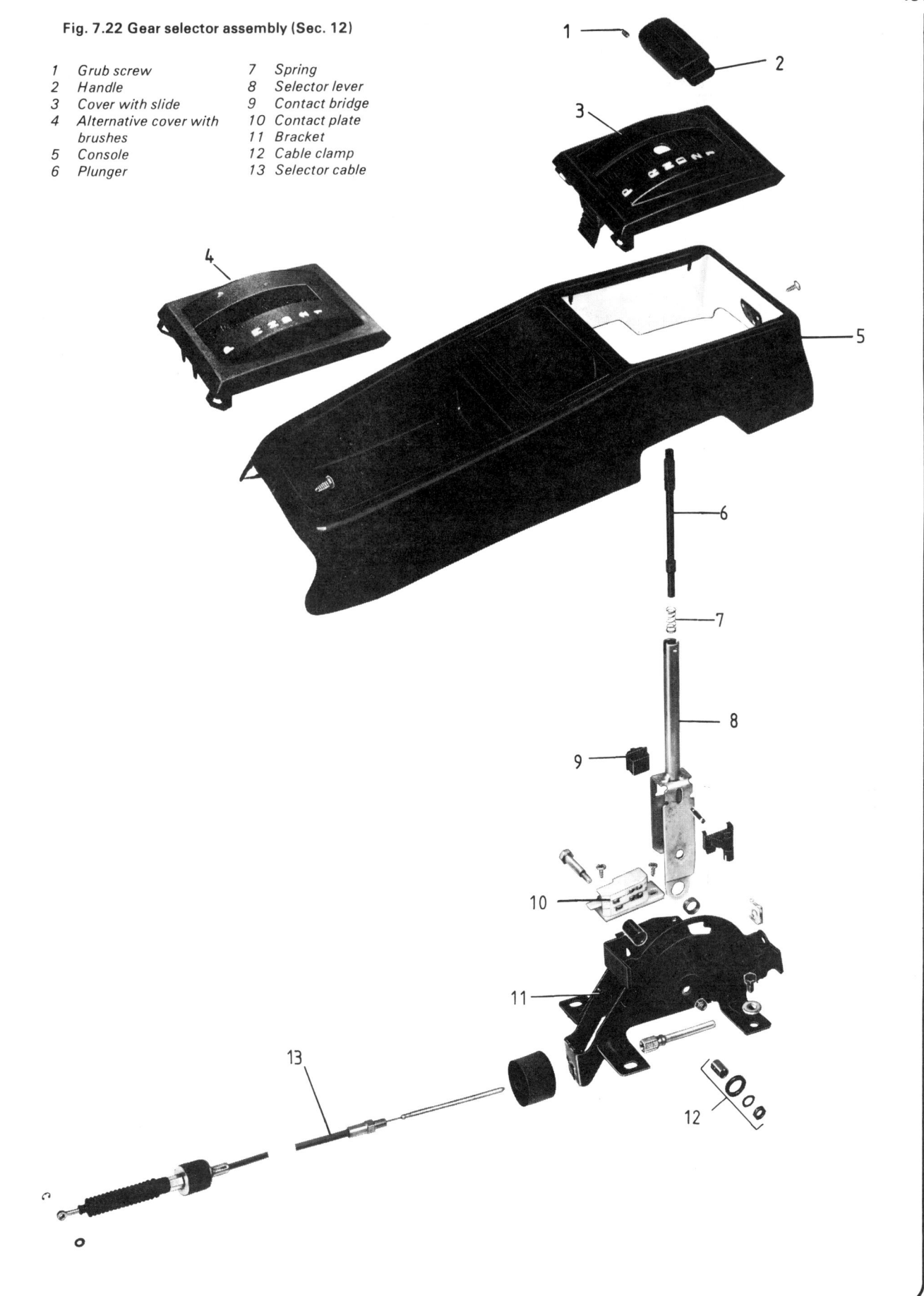

Fig. 7.22 Gear selector assembly (Sec. 12)

1   Grub screw
2   Handle
3   Cover with slide
4   Alternative cover with brushes
5   Console
6   Plunger
7   Spring
8   Selector lever
9   Contact bridge
10   Contact plate
11   Bracket
12   Cable clamp
13   Selector cable

15 Fault diagnosis – automatic transmission

Symptom	Reason(s)
No drive in any gear	Fluid level too low
Erratic drive in forward gears	Fluid level too low Dirty filter
Gear changes at above normal speed	Accelerator linkage adjustment incorrect Dirt in governor
Gear changes at below normal speeds	Dirt in governor
Gear engagement jerky	Idle speed too high
Gear engagement delayed on upshift	Fluid level too low Accelerator linkage adjustment incorrect
Kickdown does not operate	Accelerator linkage adjustment incorrect
Fluid dirty or discoloured	Brake bands and clutches wearing
Parking lock not effective	Selector lever out of adjustment Parking lock defective

Chapter 8 Rear axle and suspension

Contents

Specifications

Suspension type . . . . Trailing arms and diagonal Panhard rod

Shock absorbers . . . . Hydraulic, telescopic double-acting, or pressurised hydraulic spring cylinders

Springs . . . . Coil

Self-levelling suspension system
Fluid type . . . . ARAL 1010
Fluid capacity . . . . 2·8 litres, 4·9 Imp pt, 5·9 US pt
Oil pump delivery rate (Minimum with engine idling) . . . . 0·6 litres, 1·1 Imp pt, 1·3 US pt/min
Suspension reservoir gas pressure:
  New . . . . $24-25$ kg/cm^2 ($340-355$ lbf/in^2 at 20°C (68°F)
  Minimum . . . . 15 kg/cm^2 (213 lbf/in^2) at 20°C (68°F)

Rear wheel alignment
(For checking purposes only – angles set in production)
Camber . . . . 1° negative to 0°
Max difference between left and right-hand side . . . . 0° 30'
Toe-in . . . . 0° 10' to 0° 35'

Torque wrench settings

	Nm	lbf ft
Panhard rod-to-rear axle and body	90	65
Rear axle control arm-to-body	70	51
Shock absorber-to-rear axle	55	40
Shock absorber-to-body	20	15
Brake backplate-to-rear axle	30	22
Wheel bolts	110	80

Self-levelling suspension

	Nm	lbf ft
Pump pulley-to-spindle	60	44
Inlet pipe banjo	40	29
Pressure line banjo	20	15
Pump mounting bolts	20	15
Suspension reservoir mountings	20	15
Regulator arm adjusting bolts	10	7
Regulator arm linkage nuts	6	4
Regulator valve fixing bolts	10	7

1 General description

The rear axle is a torsion beam which is carried on two trailing arms, with lateral location provided by a transverse stabiliser (Panhard rod) (photo). The axle is of fabricated steel construction and attached to each end of it is a stub axle, carrying the hub and brake assemblies. If the rear axle is damaged, or distorted, it must not be straightened, or welded and it is important that the car is never raised by means of a jack placed under the rear axle.

The trailing arms are pivoted at their forward ends on bolts carried in bonded rubber bushes. The rear ends of the trailing arms are rigidly attached to the axle beam. The shock absorbers are of the double-acting piston type, but some models have self-levelling hydraulic suspension.

The self-levelling suspension system consists of an engine-driven hydraulic pump supplying hydraulic pressure. The pressure is regulated by a valve which responds to the position of the rear axle and this pressure is fed via a suspension reservoir to a hydraulic cylinder which is fitted in place of the conventional shock absorber. The hydraulic

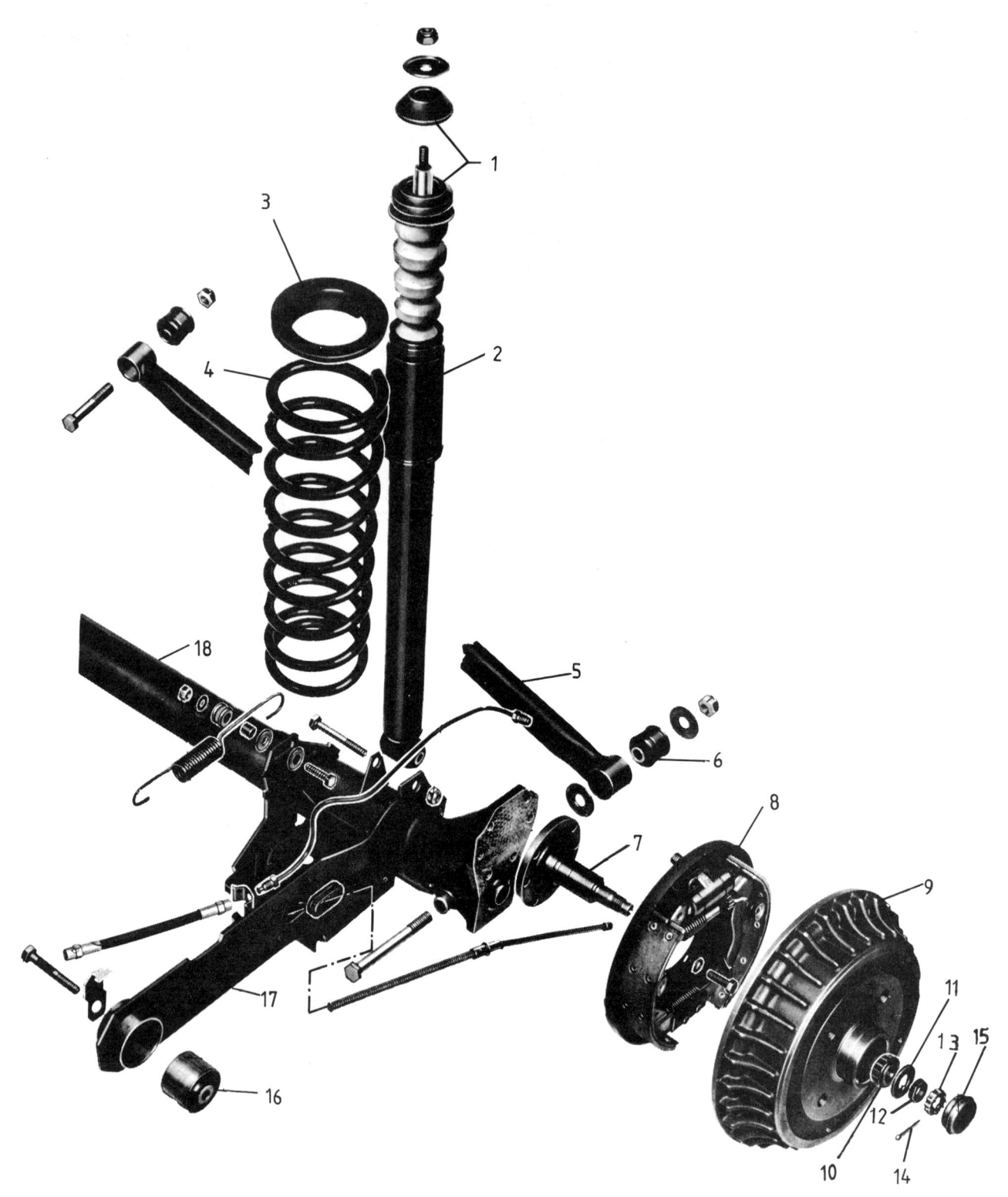

Fig. 8.1 Rear suspension components (Sec. 2)

1	Rubber bearing	6	Bonded rubber bush	11	Thrust washer	15	Hub cap
2	Shock absorber strut	7	Stub axle	12	Hub nut	16	Bonded rubber bush
3	Damper ring	8	Brake backplate assembly	13	Nut locking device	17	Trailing arm
4	Coil spring	9	Brake drum	14	Split-pin	18	Axle assembly
5	Panhard rod	10	Wheel bearing				

1.1 Panhard rod transverse stabiliser

2.2 Panhard rod-to-axle attachment

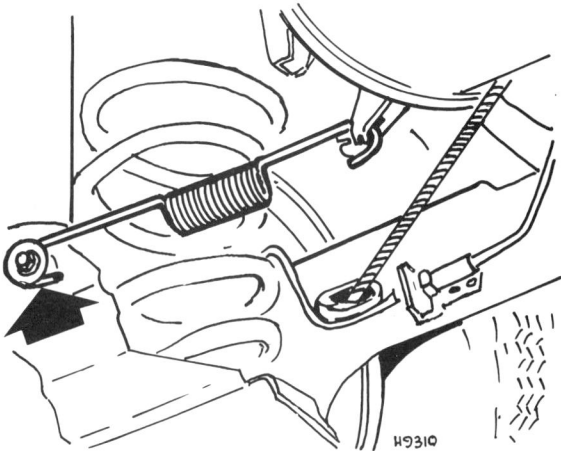

Fig. 8.2 Detach brake pressure regulator spring (arrowed) (Sec. 2)

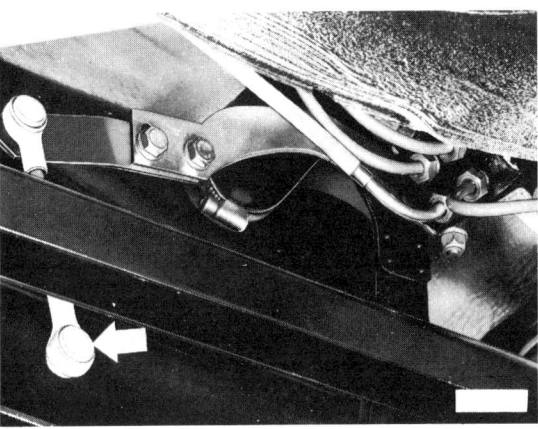

Fig. 8.3 Regulator valve linkage attachment (arrowed)– self levelling suspension (Sec. 2)

2 Rear axle – removing and refitting

1   Slacken the wheel nuts of both the rear wheels, but do not remove the wheels at this stage.

2   Remove the bolt attaching the Panhard rod to the rear axle (photo).

3   Unscrew the union of the right-hand brake pipe to the brake hose and seal the pipe ends to prevent the entry of dirt and loss of fluid.

4   Unhook the end of the brake pressure regulator spring from the bolt on the shock absorber bracket.

5   Detach and seal the left-hand brake hose.

6   On vehicles with self-levelling suspension, remove the nut and washer from the regulator valve linkage to the rear axle. While the linkage is detached, the engine must not be started, so as a precaution, remove the battery leads.

7   Remove the nut and washer from the fuel tank retaining strap on the right-hand side of the car.

8   Disconnect the handbrake cable from the fuel tank.

9   Detach the handbrake cable mounting clip on the left-hand side, then remove the nut from the handbrake compensator and disengage the handbrake cable (Fig. 8.5).

10   Remove the lining from the spare wheel cover and remove the cover to expose the shock absorber mountings. Remove the top covers from the mountings.

11   Hold the top of the piston rod stationary by fitting a spanner to its flats and unscrew and remove the nut from the top of each shock absorber (Fig. 8.6).

12   Using a jack under each side of the car, raise the body until the

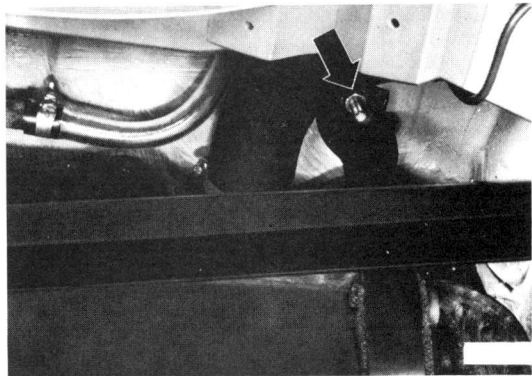

Fig. 8.4 Fuel tank strap attachment (arrowed) (Sec. 2)

system for the self-levelling suspension does not have to be bled in the same way as clutch and brake hydraulic systems. The hydraulic fluid circulates when the rear axle rebounds with the engine running and the system bleeds itself when the car is driven.

Fig. 8.5 Handbrake compensator nut (arrowed) (Sec. 2)

Fig. 8.6 Piston rod nut (arrowed) (Sec. 2)

2.12 Rear spring-to-axle mounting

2.14 Rear silencer rubber mountings

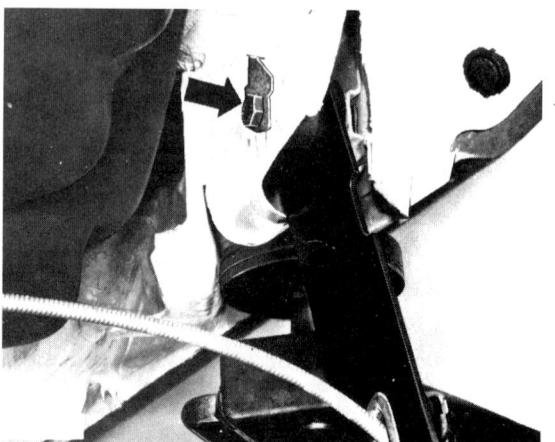

Fig. 8.7 Trailing arm pivot bolt (arrowed) (Sec. 2)

rear springs (photo) are free and remove the springs and damper rings. Keep the springs separate so that the right and left-hand ones are not interchanged.

13 Support the body on stands, and then remove the rear wheels.

14 Unhook the rubber mountings of the rear silencer (photo).

15 Support the ends of the axle so that the control arms are not resting against their stops and then unscrew and remove the control arm pivot bolts.

16 Guide the handbrake cable over the rear silencer and exhaust tail pipe until the cable is clear and then lift the axle clear from beneath the car.

17 The rubber bushes in the ends of the control arms and Panhard rod are pressed in and their removal and the fitting of new ones is a job for an Audi agent.

18 Refitting the rear axle requires three people for one of its stages and is carried out as follows.

19 Place the rear axle in position beneath the car, thread the hand-brake cable over the rear silencer and re-connect the silencer rubber mountings.

20 Fit the two control arm mounting bolts, but do not tighten them.

21 Fit the two rear wheels and lower the vehicle so that the tyres are just in contact with the ground.

22 Fit the damper ring to the top of each spring and with one person holding each of the springs in position, gradually lower the vehicle on to them.

23 Apply talcum powder (French chalk) to the rubber top bearing of the shock absorber and fit the shock absorbers. When tightening the nuts, hold the piston rod stationary with a spanner as when dismantling.

24 Raise the vehicle body again and ensure that the rear springs are positioned properly by turning them backwards and forwards.

25 Lower the vehicle until the full weight is on the suspension and with the car standing level tighten the control arm pivot bolts.

26 Re-connect the Panhard rod, the brake hoses, the brake regulator spring and the fuel tank strap.

27 Tighten the wheel bolts.

28 Bleed the brake system (Chapter 9, Section 15).

29 Attach the handbrake cable and adjust the handbrake (Chapter 9, Section 18).

3 Shock absorbers – removing and refitting

Models except Avant

1 With the vehicle standing on its rear wheels, but preferably on a ramp, or over a pit, remove the spare wheel cover to expose the shock absorber mountings. Remove the top covers from the mountings.

2 Hold the top of the piston rod stationary by fitting a spanner to its flats and unscrew and remove the nut from the top of each shock absorber, the washer and the rubber cone.

3 Remove the bolt from the lower end of the shock absorber and take the shock absorber out.

Avant models

4 With the vehicle standing on its rear wheels, but preferably on a ramp, or over a pit, tip forward the rear seat cushion and bend open the metal tab retaining the seatback padding (Fig. 8.8).

5 Remove the seatback padding, tip the seatback forward and remove the shelf.

6 Peel back the self-adhesive lining at the sides of the luggage space to reveal the covers giving access to the shock absorbers (Fig. 8.10). Prise the covers off with a screwdriver.

7 Remove the damper as described in paragraphs 2 and 3 except that the operation requires tubular spanners because the piston rod and nut are recessed (Fig. 8.11).

8 Refitting is the reverse of removal, but apply talcum powder (French chalk) to the rubber bearings at the top of the piston rod before refitting them.

4 Shock absorbers – testing

1 Defective shock absorbers tend to make noises when the car is driven; to make the car unstable when cornering and are illegal.

2 A quick check to test whether they are effective is to press down on the corner of the car as far as it will go and then release it. If the

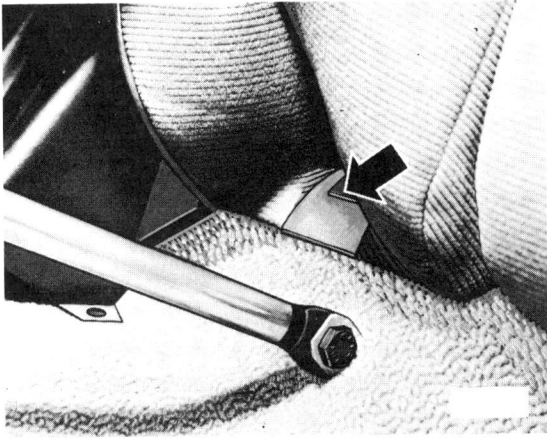

Fig. 8.8 Metal tab for seatback padding – Avant (Sec. 3)

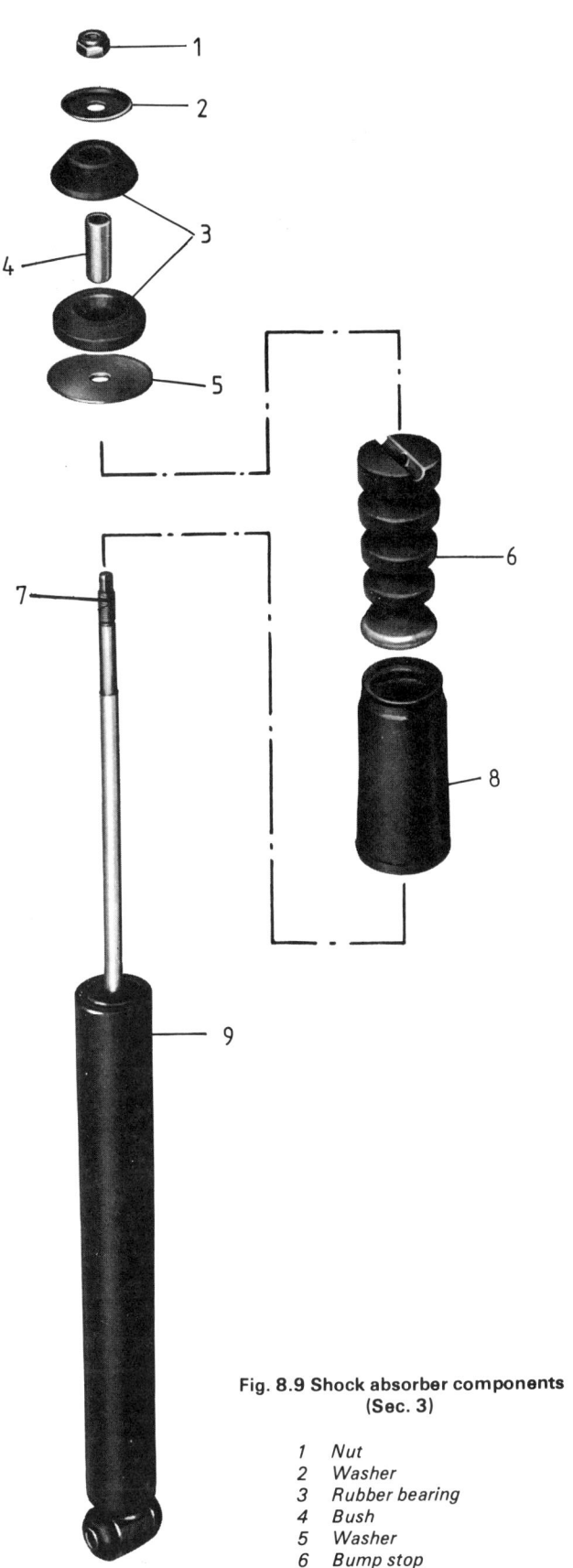

**Fig. 8.9 Shock absorber components
(Sec. 3)**

1   *Nut*
2   *Washer*
3   *Rubber bearing*
4   *Bush*
5   *Washer*
6   *Bump stop*
7   *Piston rod*
8   *Protective sleeve*
9   *Shock absorber strut*

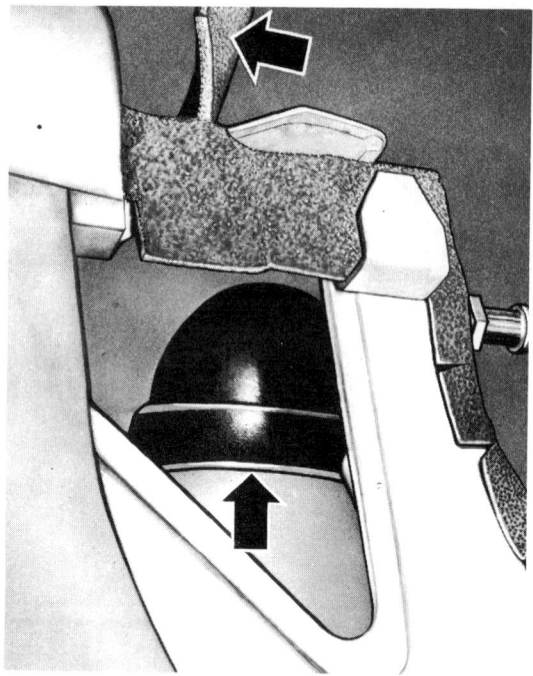

Fig. 8.10 Self-adhesive lining and shock absorber access cover (Avant) (Sec. 3)

Fig. 8.11 Unscrewing the rear shock absorber top mounting (Avant) (Sec. 3)

shock absorber is effective, the car will rebound and then settle immediately whereas with a defective shock absorber there will be several bounces before coming to rest.

3   With the shock absorbers removed, examine them for oil leaks and obvious signs of damage. Hold the shock absorber vertically and check its operation by pulling the piston rod out fully and then pushing it in fully by hand several times. Resistance should be even and the movement smooth over the entire stroke. If a shock absorber has been stored horizontally for a long time, it may require pumping up and down several times before it becomes effective.

4   If there has been excessive leakage of oil from the shock absorber, it may be ineffective on the rebound stroke, but if there is only a slight oil seepage from a shock absorber which operates correctly, it may be refitted.

5   Self-levelling suspension – general description

The self-levelling system is hydraulically operated and keeps the rear of the car at the same height, irrespective of load.

An engine-driven pump delivers hydraulic fluid to a regulator valve

Fig. 8.12 Oil pressurising pump belt tensioning (Sec. 6)

  1   *Clamping nuts*   2   *Adjusting nut*

which controls the pressure applied to the two spring cylinders attached to the rear axle in place of the standard shock absorbers. These spring cylinders perform as shock absorbers and also augment the coil springs. The regulator valve is connected to the rear axle by an adjustable linkage, and a gas charged suspension reservoir is provided between the regulator valve and each spring cylinder (Fig. 8.14).

As the load on the axle varies, the hydraulic pressure in the spring cylinders is increased, or decreased, thus raising or lowering the rear of the vehicle.

6   Self-levelling suspension – maintenance

1   The system is self-bleeding but two items require regular checking, these being the pump drivebelt tension and the fluid level.

2   With the vehicle unladen and the engine switched off, check the level of fluid in the reservoir. If the level is below the *MAX* mark, remove the reservoir cap and pour in the specified fluid until the level reaches the mark, but do not fill above the mark.

3   Unscrew the top of the reservoir and pull out the retaining bar and filter. If the filter is dirty, remove it from the retaining bar and wash it in petrol before refitting it.

4   If the pump drivebelt is tensioned correctly, it should be possible to deflect the mid-point of the longest span of the belt about 10 mm (0·39 in) with thumb pressure.

5   To adjust the belt tension, loosen the nuts on the pump mountings (Fig. 8.12) and turn the tensioner nut until the tension is satisfactory. Finally, tighten the nuts of the mountings.

7   Regulator valve – testing

1   With the vehicle standing on its wheels and with the engine running at idling speed, measure the height above the ground of the sill at the rear jacking point.

2   Load the vehicle by having two people sit on the rear seat and after waiting about a minute so that the system has time to operate, check the height from the ground at the same point.

3   Unload the vehicle, and after allowing the same time interval, check the height again to see that the levelling system has lowered the suspension system to counteract the rise caused by unloading.

8   Regulator valve – linkage adjustment

1   Cut two blocks, $7\frac{1}{2}$ in (196·5 mm) long from a piece of 2 in by 2 in (50 mm by 50 mm) timber.

2   If possible have the vehicle over a pit, or on ramps to make access to the regulator valve easier and place the blocks at the measuring points shown in Fig. 8.15.

3   Load the luggage compartment so that the measuring points only

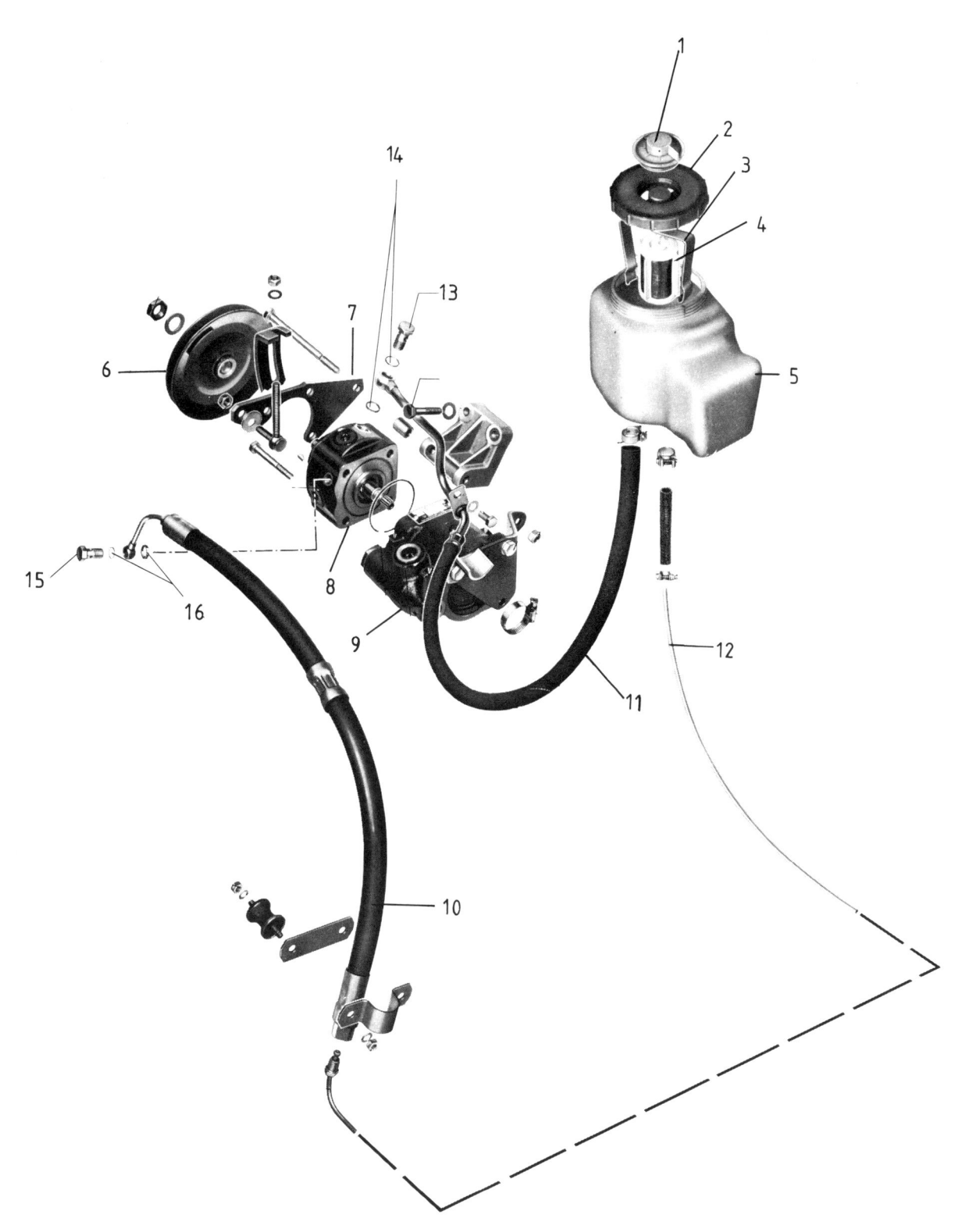

Fig. 8.13 Self-levelling suspension pump and fluid reservoir (Sec. 5)

1	Cap	5	Reservoir	9	High pressure impeller pump	13 Banjo bolt
2	Cover	6	Pump pulley	10	Expansion hose	14 Seals
3	Retaining bar	7	Adjuster plate	11	Inlet hose	15 Banjo bolt
4	Filter	8	Oil pressuring pump	12	Return line	16 Seals

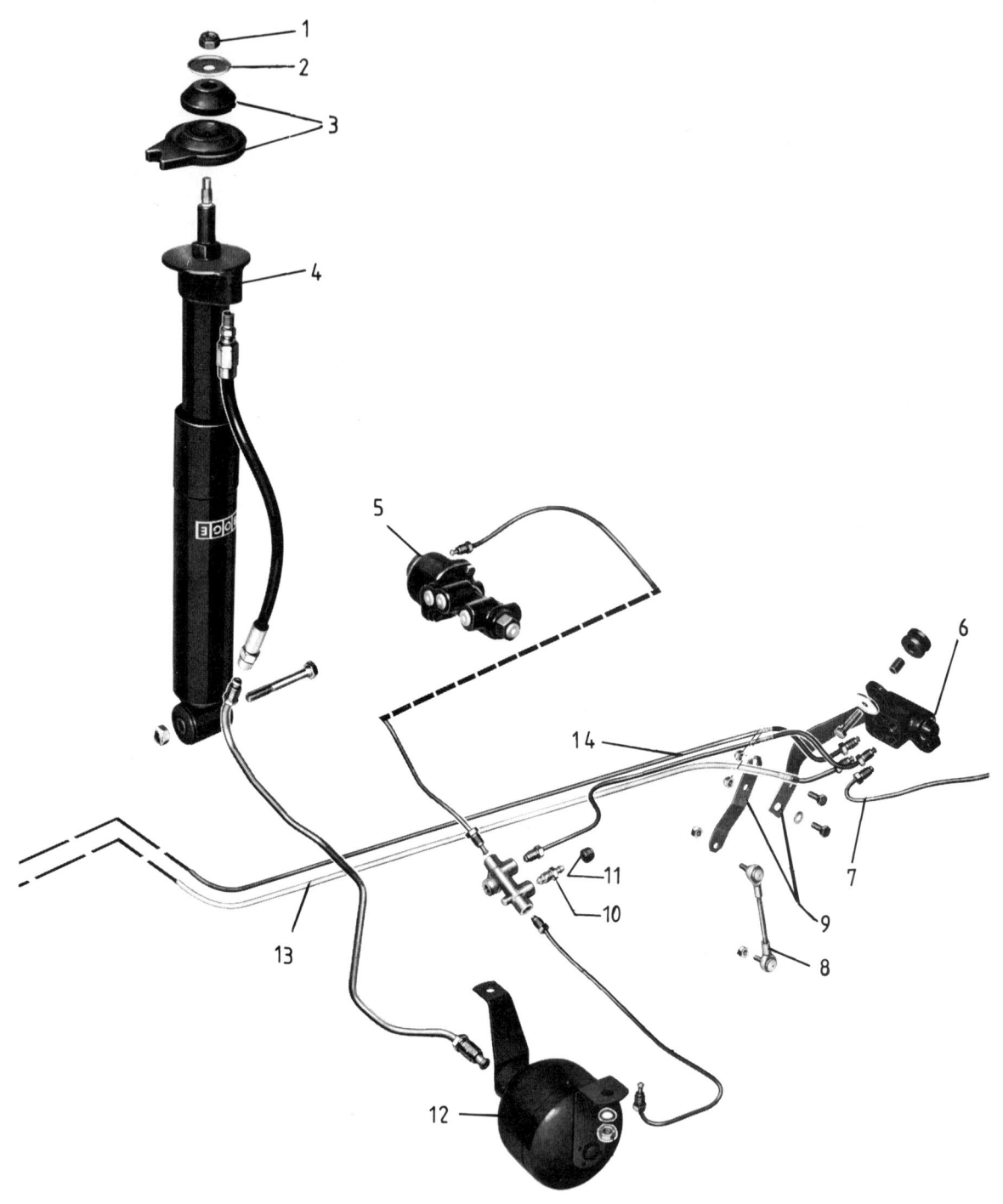

Fig. 8.14 Self-levelling suspension cylinder and regulator (Sec. 5)

1	Nut	5	Brake pressure regulator	8	Regulator valve rod	12	Suspension reservoir
2	Washer	6	Regulator valve	9	Regulator valve linkage	13	Return line
3	Rubber bearing	7	Pressure line to RH	10	Bleed screw	14	Pressure line
4	Spring cylinder		suspension reservoir	11	Dust cap		

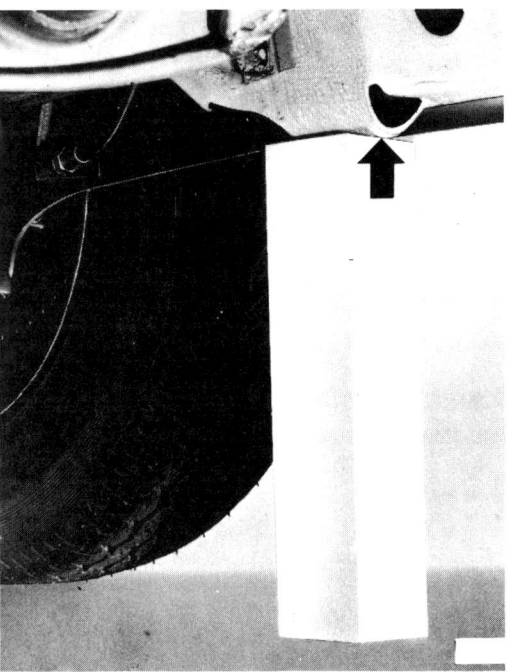

Fig. 8.15 Position of wooden blocks (Sec. 8)

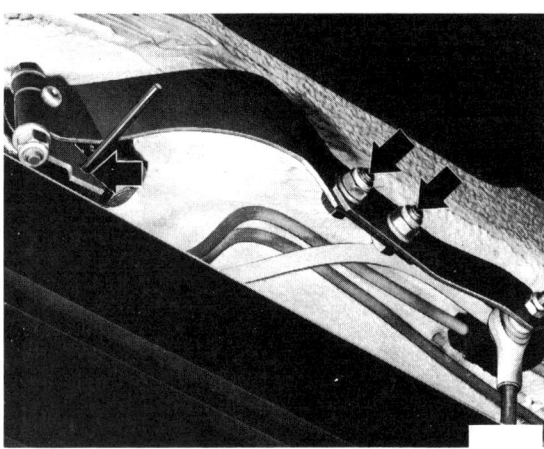

Fig. 8.17 Rod locating regulator valve (Sec. 8)

Fig. 8.16 Regulator valve linkage adjuster (Sec. 8)

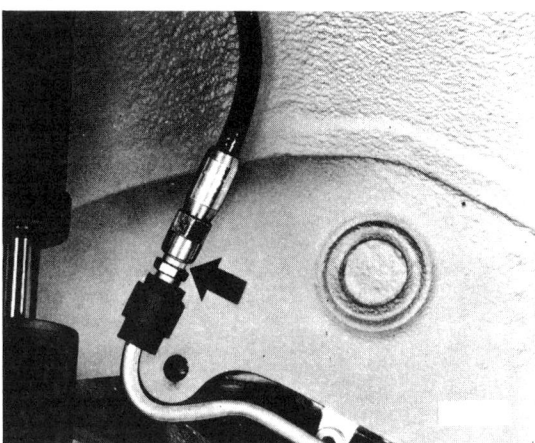

Fig. 8.18 Spring cylinder hose connection (Sec. 9)

just touch the ends of the blocks. This will require a load of about 75 kg (165 lb).

4   Loosen the two clamp bolts on the regulator linkage (Fig. 8.16) and then set the regulator valve by pushing a short piece of welding rod, or thick wire through the hole in the arm and into the locating hole on the valve body.

5   With the valve set, tighten the clamp bolts and then remove the wire from the locating hole.

9   Spring cylinders – removing and refitting

1   The procedure is similar to that for the removal of the shock absorbers described in Section 3, except that before the bolt at the lower end of the spring cylinder is removed, the hydraulic pipe must be disconnected.

2   To do this, first remove the dust cap from the bleed screw and attach to the screw a piece of tubing as used for bleeding the braking system. Put the free end of the tube into a clean jar and open the bleed screw. The residual pressure in the system will expel some fluid into the jar.

3   When pressure has been released, close the bleed screw, remove the tubing and fit the dust cap.

4   Disconnect the flexible hose from the feed pipe (Fig. 8.18) and then remove the lower mounting bolt.

10   Suspension reservoirs

1   The suspension reservoirs are gas pressurised and a loss of gas pressure will result in heavy knocks from the rear axle when the vehicle is driven.

2   Testing of the reservoirs is carried out with them in position on the car, but it is not a job which can be done by the home mechanic. If the gas pressure is low the reservoir must be renewed.

3   To replace a reservoir which is known to be defective, remove the dust cap from the bleed screw on the pipe connector and fit a piece of plastic tube over the nipple.

4   With the open end of the tube in a jar to catch the expelled fluid, open the bleed screw until the residual pressure has been released and fluid flow ceases. Close the screw, remove the pipe and fit the dust cap.

5   Disconnect the two hydraulic pipes from the reservoir and cover their open ends to prevent the entry of dirt and loss of fluid.

6   Remove the two mounting nuts and washers and lift the reservoir clear.

7   Fitting a new reservoir is the reversal of removal.

8   Refill the system with fluid and the system will self-bleed during normal operation.

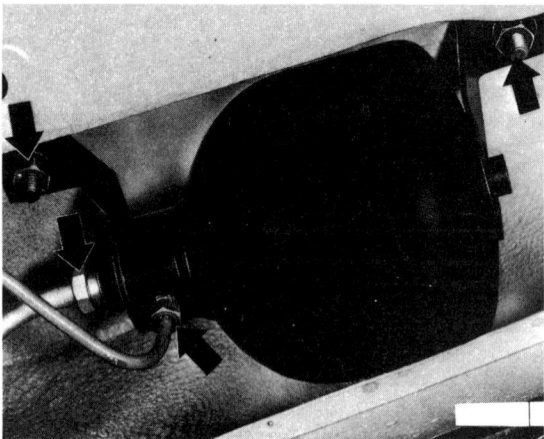

Fig. 8.19 Suspension reservoir fixing nuts and pipe connections (Sec. 10)

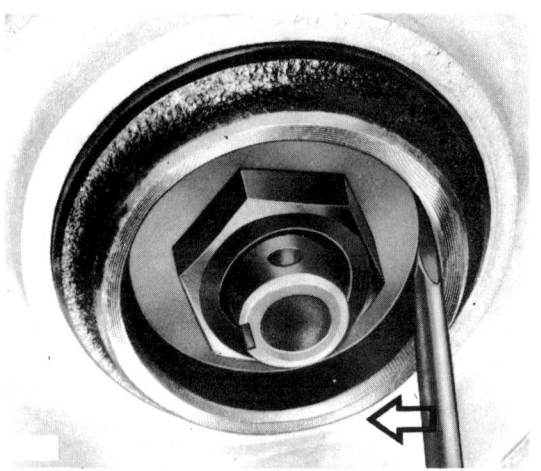

Fig. 8.20 Checking wheel bearing adjustment (Sec. 12)

brake back plate. Insert a screwdriver and use its tip to unscrew the brake adjusting ratchet until the shoes are well clear of the drum. On models with lever operated self-adjusting brakes, it is necessary to insert a piece of stiff wire through a wheel bolt hole to press the operating lever away from the ratchet before the ratchet can be backed off (refer to Chapter 9).

6   Pull off the brake drum, taking care that the wheel bearing does not fall out.

7   Disconnect the handbrake cable from the brake operating lever on the backplate.

8   Unscrew the brake pipe from the brake cylinder, cap the end of the pipe and plug the hole in the cylinder to prevent loss of fluid and the entry of dirt.

9   Unscrew and remove the four bolts which secure the brake backplate assembly and the stub axle to the end of the axle tube.

10 After refitting the components in the reverse order, adjust the handbrake (Chapter 9, Section 18), bleed the brake hydraulic system (Chapter 9, Section 15) and adjust the wheel bearing play as described in the following Section.

11.4 Rear hub bearing thrust washer

12 Wheel bearing – adjustment

1   Remove the rear wheel, brake drum, split-pin and nut locking device as described in the previous Section.

2   Tighten the nut so that when a screwdriver is placed against the edge of the thrust washer, the washer can be moved axially by finger pressure on the screwdriver (Fig. 8.20). Do not test the movement of the washer by rotating the screwdriver, or levering.

3   When adjusting, turn the hexagon nut, at the same time turning the wheel so that the bearing does not jam.

4   When bearing adjustment is correct, fit the nut lock and secure it with a new split-pin. Bend the ends of the split-pin back round the spindle to ensure that the pin cannot fall out.

5   Fill the hub with general purpose lithium based grease and fit the hub cap.

6   Refit the roadwheel and lower the jack.

11 Stub axles – removing and refitting

1   Chock the front wheels securely, loosen the bolts of the rear wheel, jack the car and remove the wheel.

2   Use a screwdriver to prise off the hub cap.

3   Remove the split-pin from the end of the stub axle and take off the nut locking device.

4   Unscrew and remove the nut and lever off the thrust washer beneath it (photo).

5   Remove the rubber plug which is adjacent to the brake pipe on the

13 Fault diagnosis – rear axle and suspension

Symptom	Reason(s)
Wheel wobble and vibration	Wheel nuts loose
Excessive tyre wear	Tyre pressure incorrect Rear axle distorted
Bumping of rear axle	Defective shock absorbers
Rear of car low, or tilted	Rear springs broken or strained

14 Fault diagnosis – self-levelling suspension

Symptom	Reason(s)
Noise of pump audible in vehicle	Pressure line, or expansion hose touching body, or other components
Rear of vehicle not raised	Fluid level too low so that pump is taking in air Regulator valve linkage incorrect Pump defective
Heavy knocks from rear axle when driving	Defective suspension reservoir
Rear of car drops noticeably about 15 minutes after switching off engine	Regulator valve leaking
Rear suspension too high, or too low	Regulator valve linkage damaged, or adjusted incorrectly

Chapter 9 Braking system

Contents

Specifications

System type ....

Hydraulically operated, disc front, drum rear, with vacuum servo assistance. Tandem master cylinder with independent twin diagonal brake circuits. Handbrake mechanical on rear wheels only

Front brakes

	1·6 and 2·0 litre	2·2 litre carburettor	2·2 litre injection
Disc diameter	257 mm (10·1 in)	257 mm (10·1 in)	258 mm (10·2 in)
Disc thickness	13 mm (0·51 in)	13 mm (0·51 in)	22 mm (0·87 in)
Wear limit	11 mm (0·433 in)	11 mm (0·433 in)	20 mm (0·787 in)
Thickness variation (max.)	0·02 mm (0·0008 in)	0·02 mm (0·0008 in)	0·02 mm (0·0008 in)
Runout limit	0·1 mm (0·0039 in)	0·1 mm (0·0039 in)	0·1 mm (0·0039 in)
Pad thickness	14 mm (0·551 in)	14 mm (0·551 in)	14 mm (0·551 in)
Pad wear limit (including backplate)	6 mm (0·236 in)	6 mm (0·236 in)	6 mm (0·236 in)
Pad wear limit (pad only)	2 mm (0·079 in)	2 mm (0·079 in)	2 mm (0·079 in)

Rear brakes

	1·6 and 2·0 litre	2·2 litre carburettor	2·2 litre injection
Drum diameter	200 mm (7·87 in)	230 mm (9·06 in)	230 mm (9·06 in)
Wear limit	201 mm (7·91 in)	231 mm (9·10 in)	231 mm (9·10 in)
Lateral runout at wheel contact surface	0·2 mm (0·0079 in)	0·2 mm (0·0079 in)	0·2 mm (0·0079 in)
Radial runout at brake contact surface	0·1 mm (0·0039 in)	0·1 mm (0·0039 in)	0·1 mm (0·0039 in)
	1·6 litre	**2·0 litre**	**2·2 litre**
Wheel cylinder diameter	15·87 mm (0·625 in)	17·46 mm (0·687 in)	17·46 mm (0·687 in)
Lining thickness (new)	5·25 mm (0·207 in)	5·25 mm (0·207 in)	5·25 mm (0·207 in)
Wear limit	2·50 mm (0·098 in)	2·50 mm (0·098 in)	2·50 mm (0·098 in)

Brake fluid specification .... SAE J 1703

Torque wrench settings

	Nm	lbf ft
Wheel bolts	110	80
Caliper-to-suspension strut	115	83
Brake backplate-to-rear axle	30	22
Brake backplate-to-suspension strut	10	7
Brake servo-to-bulkhead	25	18
Master cylinder-to-brake servo	25	18

1 General description

The braking system is hydraulic with servo-assistance and there are disc brakes on the front wheels and drum brakes on the rear. The system has a tandem master cylinder which operates two completely independent braking circuits, each circuit operating a front wheel and the diagonally opposite rear wheel. This ensures that if one circuit fails, the car can still be brought to rest in a straight line, even though the braking distance will be greater.

Most models incorporate a brake pressure regulator, which limits the pressure applied to the rear brake cylinders to a proportion of that applied to the front and so prevents the rear wheels from locking.

There are three different types of front brake caliper, the type used on a particular vehicle being dependent upon engine size and power. These are also variations to the rear brakes according to the engine fitted to the vehicle. There are three possible types, two of which are self-adjusting and a manually adjustable type. The handbrake lever applies to the rear brakes only.

2   Front brake pads – inspection, removing and refitting

1   Pad thickness can be checked without removing the road wheel. Turn the wheel until the brake pad is visible through one of the openings in the wheel rim.

2   With the aid of a torch to increase visibility, measure the thickness of each brake pad including its metal backplate and compare this with the minimum value given in Specifications. A rough guide to the amount of life remaining in brake pads which are nearing their minimum is that the rate of wear is about 1 mm (0·039 in) for every 1000 km (620 miles) driving.

3   If the brake pads are to be re-used, they must be refitted to the position from which they were taken. To ensure this, mark the pads to show which is the inner and which the outer before removing them.

4   Jack the car and remove the roadwheel, then proceed as follows.

1·6 and 2·0 litre engines

5   Use a punch to drive out the retaining springs and take out the spring retainer.

6   Use a hook to pull out the inner pad.

7   Press the floating caliper frame outwards (Fig. 9.2) to disengage the pad from the projection on the caliper frame and then pull out the outer pad.

2·2 litre carburettor engine

8   Push the cylinder housing in the direction indicated by the arrow in Fig. 9.3. This will press back the piston and in so doing will displace

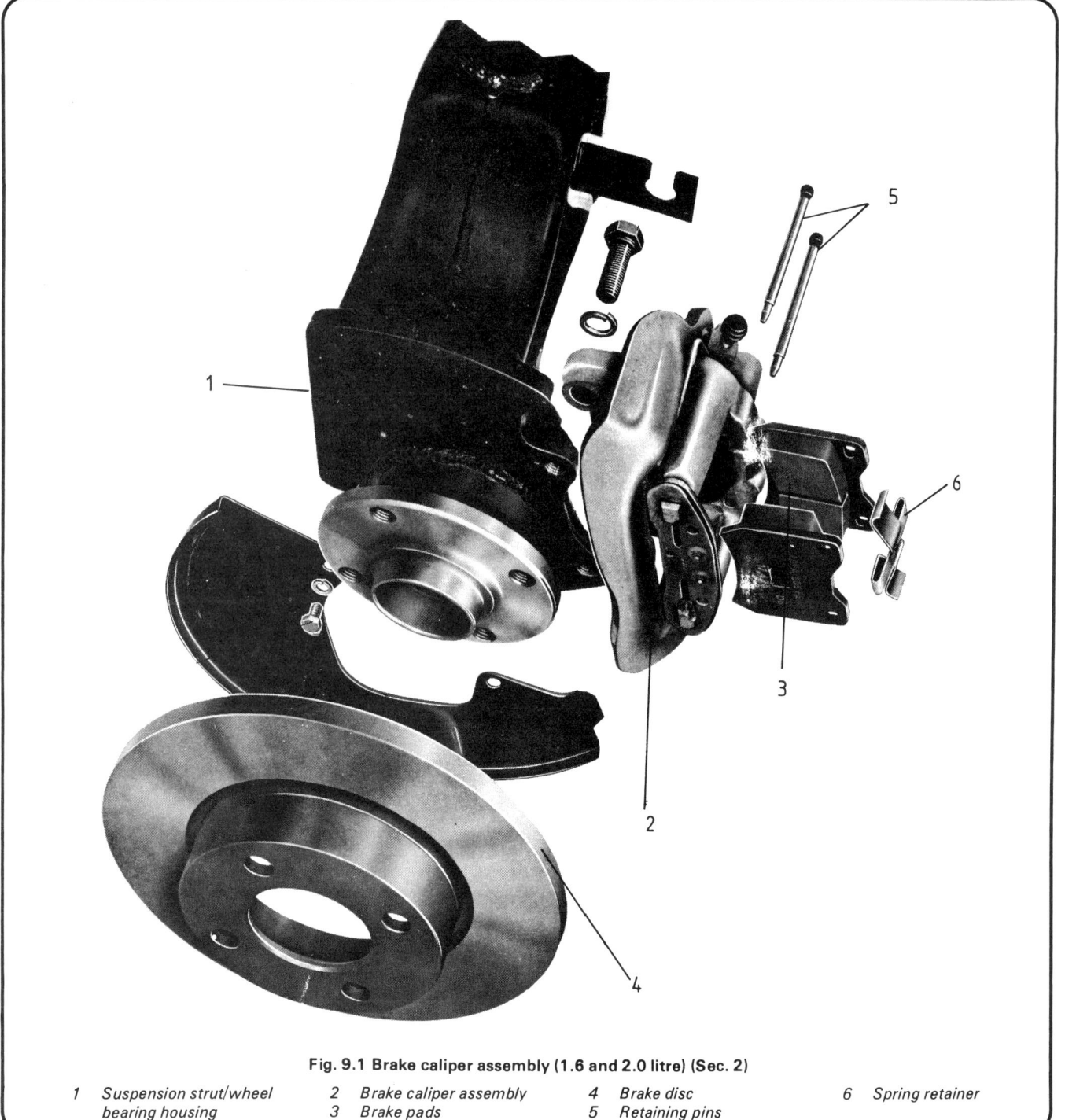

Fig. 9.1 Brake caliper assembly (1.6 and 2.0 litre) (Sec. 2)

1 Suspension strut/wheel bearing housing	2 Brake caliper assembly 3 Brake pads	4 Brake disc 5 Retaining pins	6 Spring retainer

Fig. 9.2 Disengaging the outer pad from the caliper frame
(1.6 and 2.0 litre) (Sec. 2)

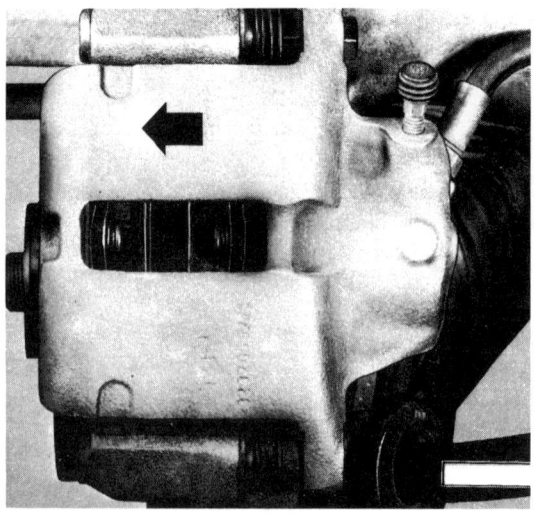

Fig. 9.3 Push housing in direction of arrow (2.2 litre carburettor)
(Sec. 2)

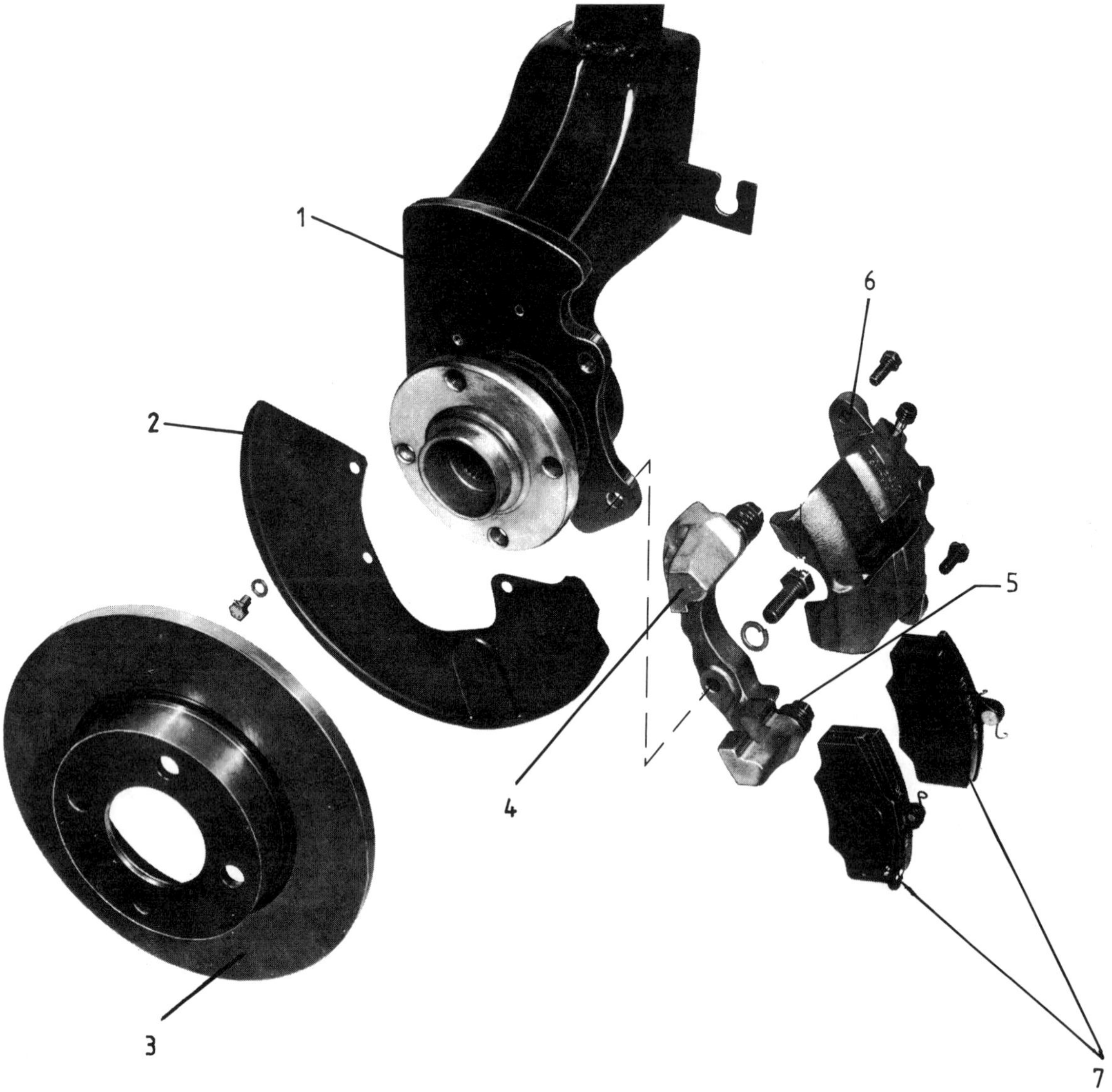

Fig. 9.4 Brake caliper assembly (2.2 litre carburettor) (Sec. 2)

1	Suspension strut/wheel bearing housing	2	Brake backplate	4	Brake carrier	6	Cylinder housing
		3	Brake disc	5	Guide pins	7	Brake pads

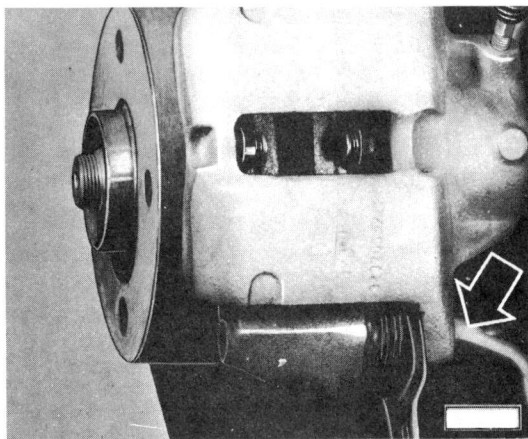

Fig. 9.5 Holding guide pin to undo bolt (2.2 litre carburettor) (Sec. 2)

Fig. 9.6 Pivoting the cylinder to remove the pads (2.2 litre carburettor) (Sec. 2)

2.13a Disc pad retaining spring (2.2 litre)

2.13b Removing the disc pad retaining pins (2.2 litre)

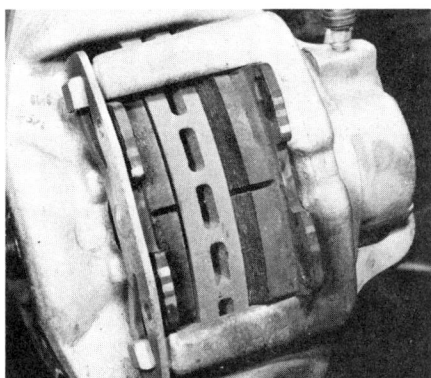

2.13c Withdrawing a disc pad (2.2 litre)

some hydraulic fluid back into the reservoir. Unless the level of fluid in the reservoir is low, some fluid will first have to be taken from the reservoir and this can be done by squeezing a plastic bottle to suck out some fluid. Brake fluid is poisonous and it must not be sucked out using a pipe.

9 While holding the guide pin with an open ended spanner, unscrew and remove the lower mounting bolt of the cylinder housing (Fig. 9.5).

10 Pivot the housing upwards and then pull out the pads.

11 The repair kit includes two new housing mounting bolts and both bolts should be used in place of the existing ones.

2·2 litre injection engine

12 The procedure is identical with that for the 1·6 and 2·0 litre engined models described in paragraphs 5 to 7, except that the retaining spring (photo) must be removed from the retaining pins (photos) before they are punched out and must be refitted after the pins have been inserted (Fig. 9.7).

13 Fitting brake pads is the reversal of removing them. On completion of the operation the brake pedal should be pressed firmly several times with the vehicle stationary, so that the brake pads take up their normal running position. On the 2·2 litre carburettor model, if fluid was removed from the reservoir, the reservoir must be topped-up to its correct level.

---

3 Front brake caliper – removing and refitting

1 Remove the roadwheel and brake pads as described in Section 2.

1·6 and 2·0 litre engine

2 Unscrew the brake pipe about a quarter of a turn at its connection

with the caliper cylinder.

3 Unscrew and remove the two bolts securing the caliper assembly to the front hub, holding the caliper assembly to prevent it from hanging from the brake pipe.

4 Have ready a plug, or cap for the end of the brake pipe and place a drip tray under the caliper assembly.

5 Holding the end of the brake pipe stationary with a spanner fitted to the hose union, unscrew the caliper assembly off the end of the brake hose.

2·2 litre carburettor engine

6 Unscrew the brake pipe about a quarter of a turn at its connection with the caliper cylinder.

7 Remove the upper bolt securing the caliper assembly while holding the guide pin stationary with an open ended spanner, in a similar manner to that used for the lower bolt when removing the brake pads.

8 Remove the caliper assembly as described in paragraphs 4 and 5.

2·2 litre injection engine

9 Proceed as described for the 1·6 and 2·0 litre engine in paragraphs 2 to 5.

10 After refitting the brake caliper, bleed the hydraulic system as described in Section 15.

---

4 Front brake caliper – dismantling, repairing and reassembling

1·6 and 2·0 litre engine

1 Press the mounting frame off the floating frame (Fig. 9.8).

Fig. 9.7 Brake caliper assembly (2.2 litre injection) (Sec. 2)

1	Brake disc	3	Suspension strut/wheel	4	Brake caliper	6	Retaining spring
2	Brake backplate		bearing housing	5	Retaining pins	7	Brake pads
						8	Spring retainer

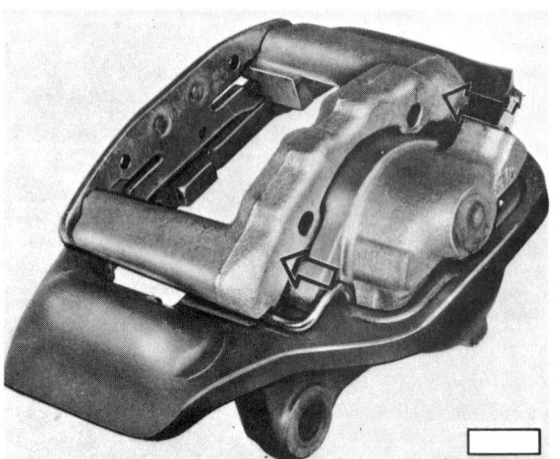

Fig. 9.8 Pressing mounting frame off sliding frame (1.6 and 2.0 litre) (Sec. 4)

Fig. 9.9 Removing the brake cylinder (1.6 and 2.0 litre) (Sec. 4)

**Fig. 9.10 Brake caliper components
(1.6 and 2.0 litre) (Sec. 4)**

1 Bleed valve
2 Brake cylinder
3 Seal
4 Piston
5 Dust cap
6 Circlip
7 Mounting frame
8 Slide
9 Floating frame
10 Locating spring

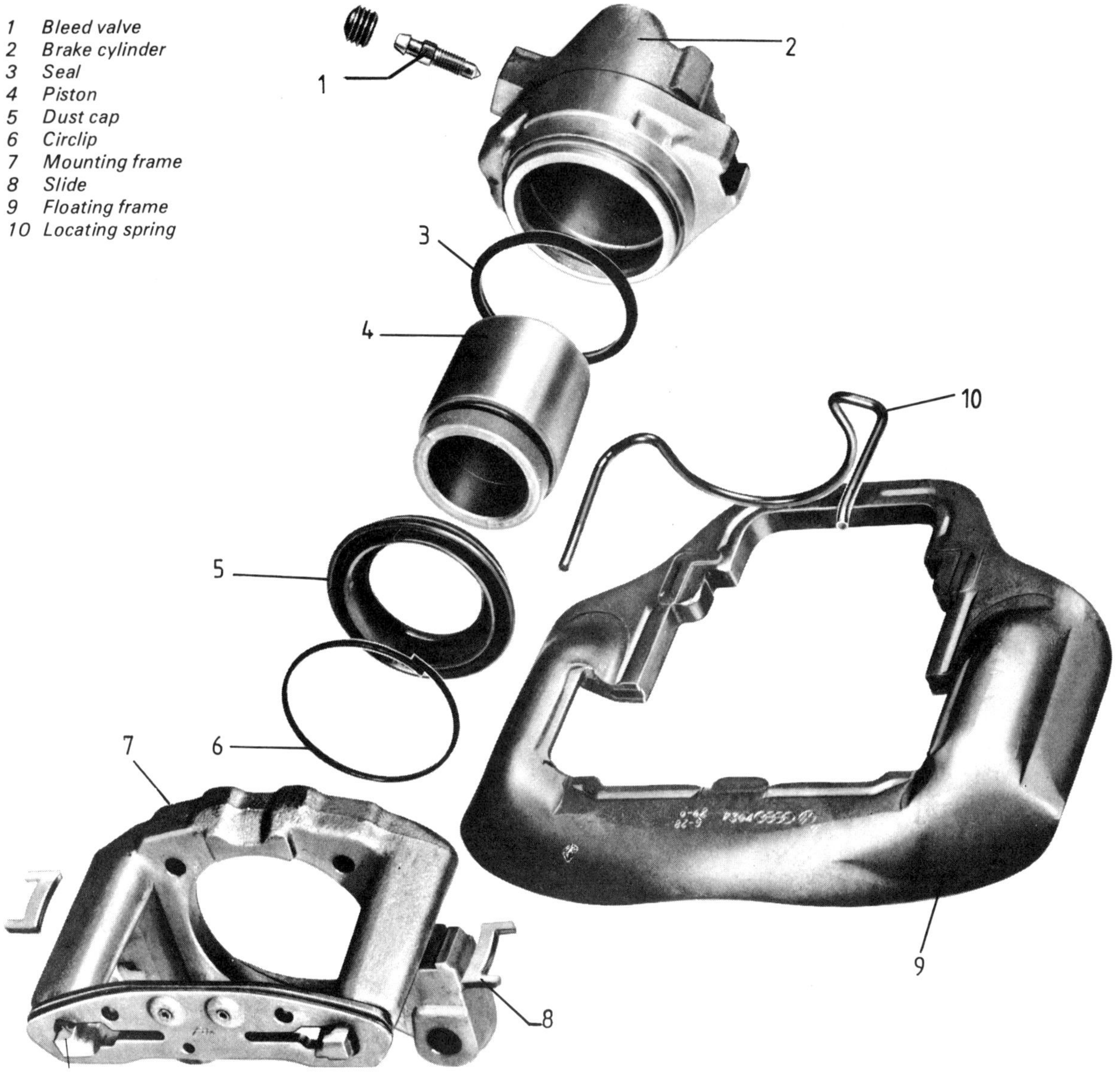

2 Place a block of wood in the floating frame and drive out the cylinder assembly, using a soft metal drift (Fig. 9.9).
3 Use a foot pump or a compressed air supply to blow the piston out of the cylinder, but support the cylinder with the piston facing downwards to avoid the risk of injury when the piston is ejected (Fig. 9.11).
4 Use a blunt screwdriver to prise the seal out of the piston bore, taking great care not to scratch the bore of the cylinder.
5 Fit a new seal into the groove in the cylinder bore. Apply a thin coat of brake rubber grease to the seal and to the cylinder. Then squeeze the piston into the cylinder using a vice fitted with soft jaws (Fig. 9.12).
6 Fit the locating spring into the groove on the brake cylinder. One end of the spring will be seen to be bent much more sharply than the other and this sharply bent end should be at the leading end of the cylinder for the normal direction of rotation of the disc (Fig. 9.13).
7 Fit the two slides into the mounting frame, as shown in Fig. 9.14 and fit the mounting frame to the floating frame.
8 Before refitting the caliper assembly, turn the piston so that the line of the step on its end is at an angle of 20° to the upper guide surface (Fig. 9.15). Check the angle by making a simple gauge.

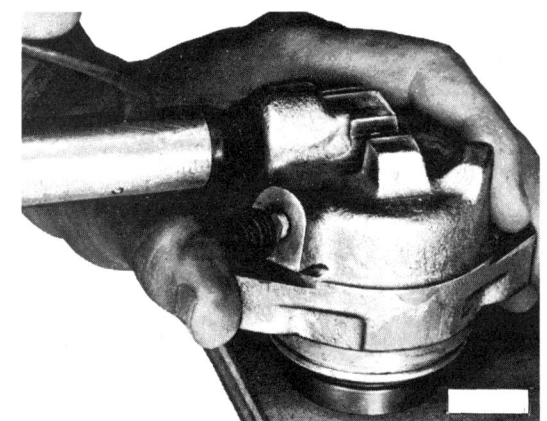

Fig. 9.11 Removing the piston from the cylinder using an air line
(1.6 and 2.0 litre) (Sec. 4)

Fig. 9.12 Pressing the piston into the cylinder (1.6 and 2.0 litre)
(Sec. 4)

Fig. 9.13 Installing the brake cylinder (1.6 and 2.0 litre) (Sec. 4)

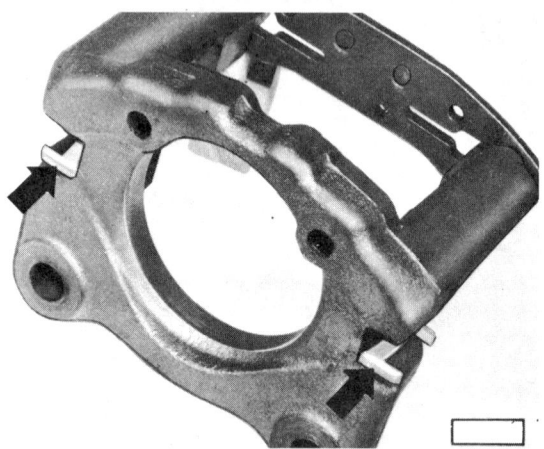

Fig. 9.14 Fitting the slides to the mounting frame (1.6 and 2.0 litre)
(Sec. 4)

Fig. 9.15 Setting the piston stop to 20° to top guide surface
(1.6 and 2.0 litre) (Sec. 4)

2·2 litre carburettor engine

9   Use a foot pump, or a compressed air supply to blow the piston
out of the cylinder, but place a block of wood inside the frame to
prevent damage to the piston (Fig. 9.16).

10   Use a blunt screwdriver to prise the seal out of the piston bore,
taking great care not to scratch the bore of the cylinder.

11   Fit a new seal into the groove in the cylinder bore. Apply a thin
coat of brake rubber grease to the seal and to the cylinder.

12   Fit the dust cap on to the piston as shown in Fig. 9.18 and then
offer the piston up to the cylinder and fit the sealing lip of the dust cap
into the groove of the cylinder bore, using a screwdriver (Fig. 9.19).

13   Smear brake rubber grease over the piston and then press the
piston into the cylinder until the outer lip of the dust cap springs into
place in the piston groove.

14   Examine the brake carrier, guide pins and protective caps. If any
component is damaged, the complete assembly must be replaced by a
new one.

2·2 litre injection engine

15   Dismantling is similar to that of the 1·6 and 2·0 litre engine,
described in paragraphs 1 to 4, but there are no slides as loose parts of
the mounting frame assembly (Fig. 9.20).

16   Reassembly is similar to paragraphs 5 to 8, except for the absence
of the slides in the mounting frame and the fact that the cylinder locating spring is symmetrical.

Fig. 9.16 Removing the piston from the cylinder using an air line
(2.2 litre carburettor) (Sec. 4)

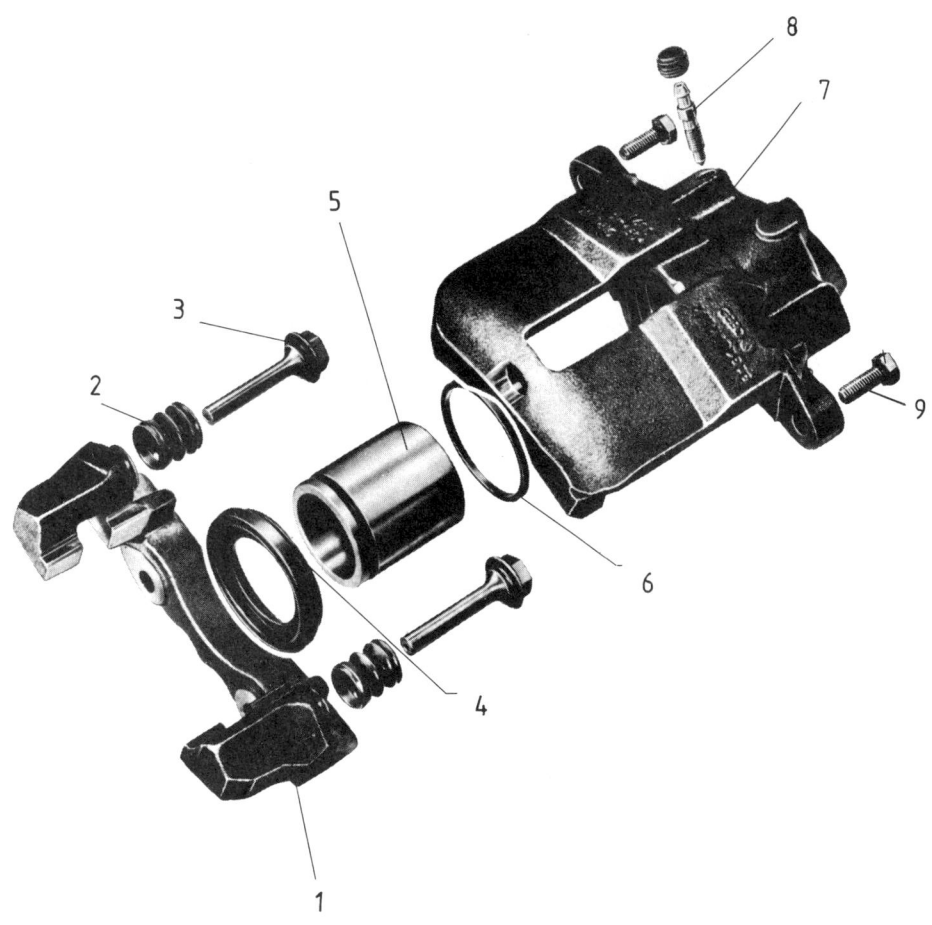

Fig. 9.17 Brake caliper components (2.2 litre carburettor) (Sec. 4)

1	Brake carrier	4	Dust cap	6	Piston seal	8	Bleed valve
2	Protective cap	5	Piston	7	Cylinder housing	9	Self-locking bolts
3	Guide pin						

Fig. 9.18 Fitting the piston dust cap (2.2 litre carburettor) (Sec. 4)

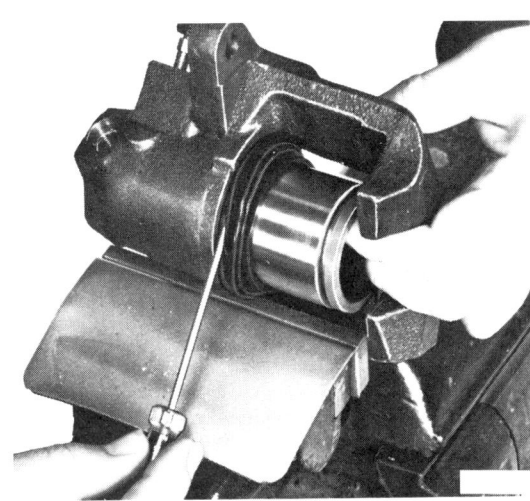

Fig. 9.19 Fitting lip of dust cap to cylinder (2.2 litre carburettor) (Sec. 4)

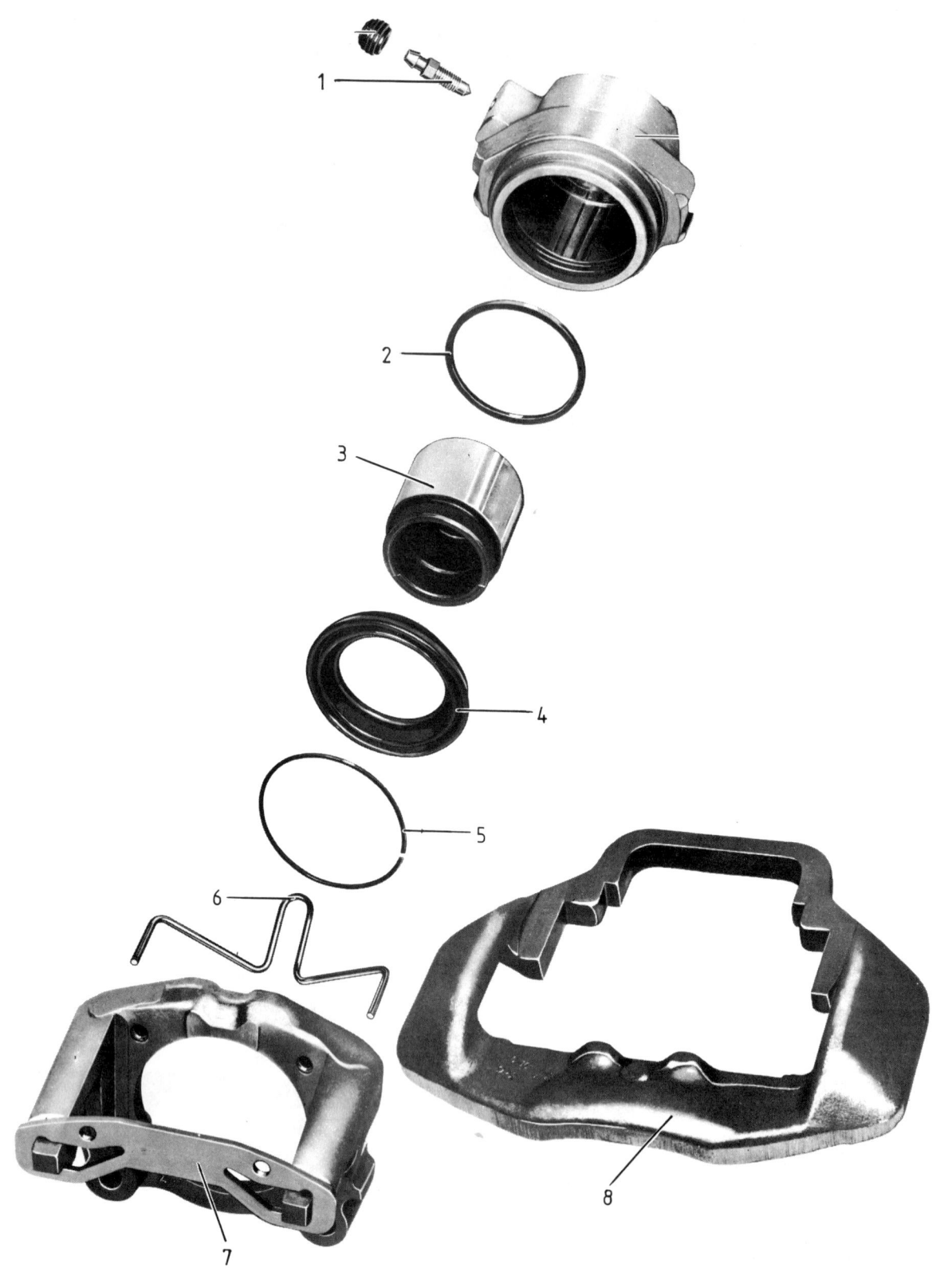

Fig. 9.20 Brake caliper components (2.2 litre carburettor) (Sec. 4)

1	Bleed valve	3	Piston	5	Circlip	7	Mounting frame
2	Piston seal	4	Piston dust cap	6	Locating spring	8	Floating frame

5 Brake discs – removing, inspecting and refitting

1   Remove the caliper assembly as described in the relevant paragraphs of Section 3.

2   The brake disc is secured to the hub by the wheel bolts, so the disc can be lifted off after the caliper has been removed, but before taking the disc off, mark its position on the hub so that it can be fitted in the same position as it was before removal.

3   Examine the disc for signs of scoring, burning, or uneven wear and check that its thickness is within the limits given in Specifications. If the disc is scored, it may be skimmed, but the same amount must be taken from both sides and the final thickness must not be less than the minimum specified.

4   If a new disc is fitted, it may be found that the brake catches at one point if the wheel is turned after it has been refitted. If this is the case, remove the wheel and turn the disc 90° on the hub, then refit the wheel again. If a satisfactory position cannot be found, remove the disc and check that there is no dirt on the mating surfaces of the disc and hub.

5   Brake discs must be replaced or refinished as pairs, it is not permitted to skim or replace one disc only.

6 Rear brake linings – inspection for wear and adjustment

1   The thickness of the rear brake linings can be checked without removing the brake drums.

2   Remove the rubber plug which is adjacent to the handbrake cable entry on the brake backplate (Fig. 9.21). Use a torch to increase visibility and check the thickness of friction material remaining on the brake shoes. If the amount remaining is close to the minimum given in Specifications, remove the brake drums, as described in Section 7 and make a close examination of the linings.

3   Adjustment is automatic on most models but manually adjustable types can be identified by the star wheel adjuster and larger diameter shoe upper return spring (see Fig. 9.23). To adjust these brakes press the lever on the pressure regulator several times (see Fig. 9.27), then turn the adjuster until the shoes lock the drum and back it off until the drum is just free to turn. Repeat the operation on the opposite brake and refit the rubber plugs.

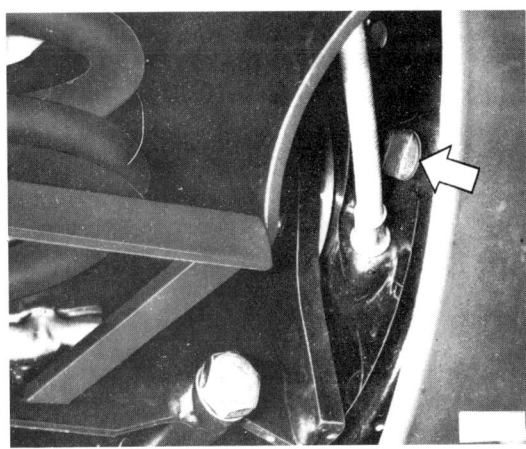

Fig. 9.21 Brake lining inspection hole (Sec. 6)

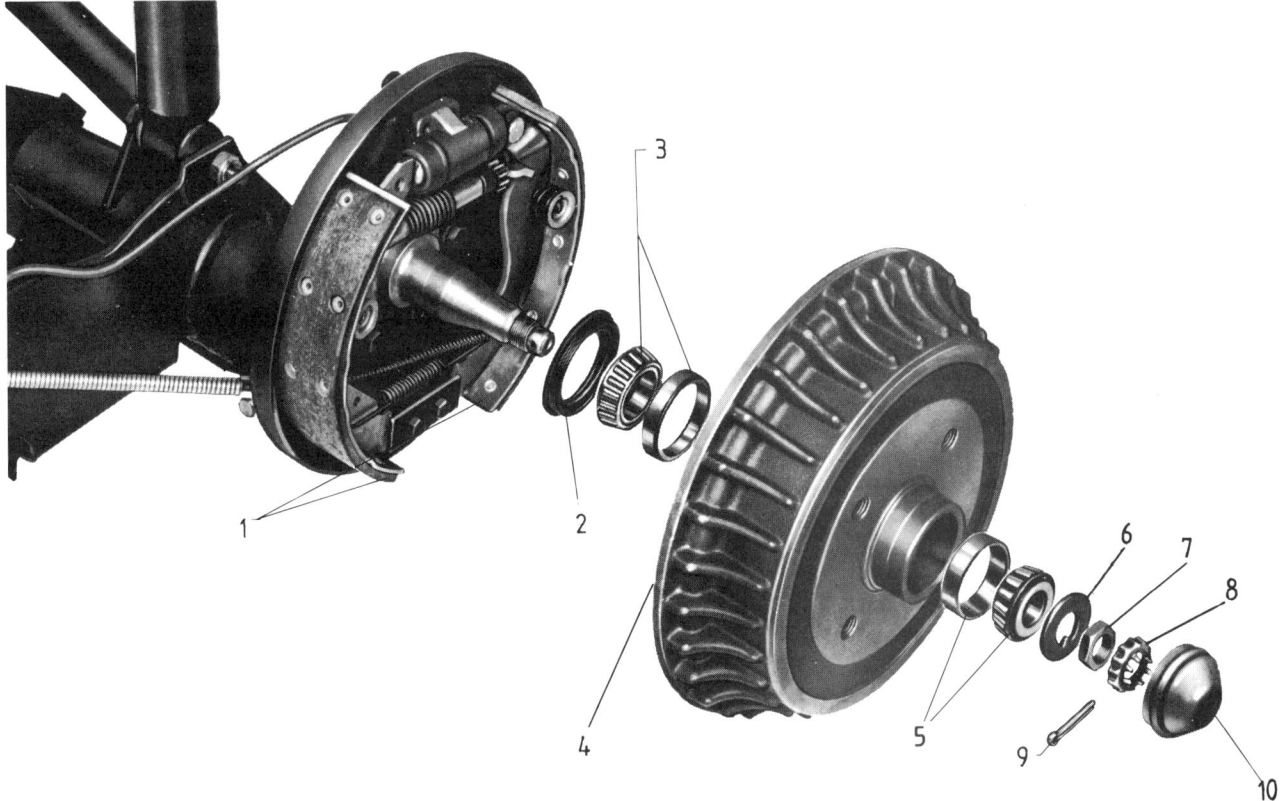

Fig. 9.22 Rear brake components (manual adjusters) (Sec. 7)

1 Brake shoes	4 Brake drum	7 Hexagon nut	9 Cotter pin
2 Seal	5 Outer wheel bearing	8 Nut locking device	10 Hub cap
3 Inner wheel bearing	6 Thrust washer		

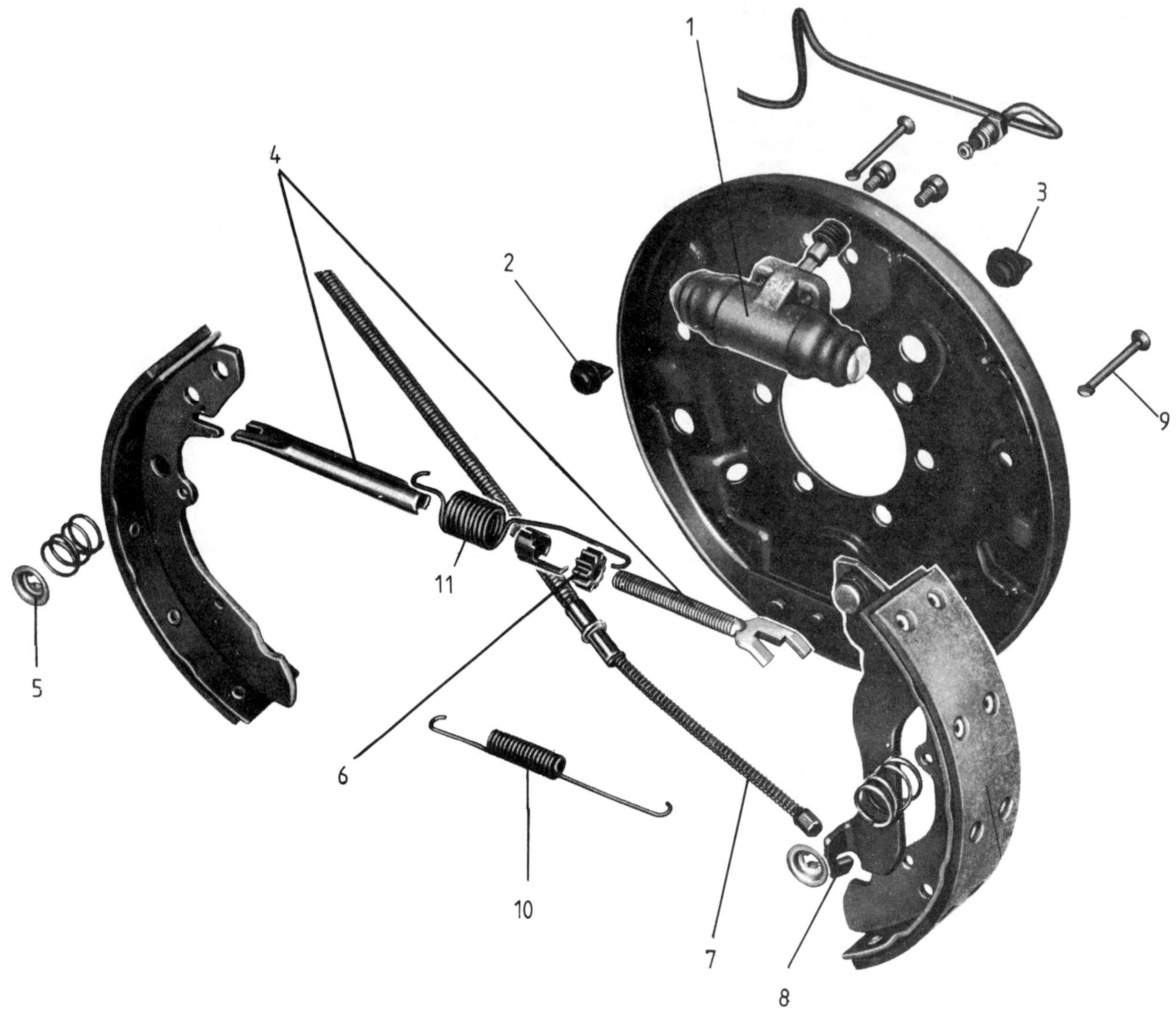

Fig. 9.23 Brake shoe arrangement (manual adjusters) (Sec. 7)

1	Wheel cylinder	4	Adjuster pushrod	7	Handbrake cable
2	Inspection hole plug	5	Spring retainer	8	Brake lever
3	Adjuster hole plug	6	Adjuster pinion	9	Retaining pin

10	Lower return spring
11	Upper return spring

7 Rear brake shoes – removing and refitting

1 Chock the front wheels securely, loosen the bolts of the rear wheel, jack the car and remove the wheel.

2 Use a screwdriver to prise the hub caps off.

3 Remove the cotter pin from the end of the stub axle and take off the nut locking device.

4 Unscrew and remove the nut and pull off the thrust washer beneath it.

5 Remove the rubber plug which is adjacent to the brake pipe on the brake back plate (Fig. 9.24). Insert a screwdriver and use its tip to unscrew the brake adjusting ratchet until the shoes are well clear of the drum. On models with lever operated self-adjusting brakes, it is necessary to insert a piece of stiff wire through a wheel bolt hole to press the operating lever away from the ratchet before the ratchet can be backed off.

6 Pull off the brake drum, taking care that the outer wheel bearing does not fall out.

7 Before starting to remove the brake shoes, make a drawing showing the position of the brake springs and of the self-adjusting mechanism if fitted (photo).

8 Disengage the handbrake cable from the brake shoe lever.

Fig. 9.24 Brake adjuster plug (Sec. 7)

7.7 Brake springs and adjuster (2.2 litre)

9 Use pliers to press in and turn the brake shoe steadying spring retainers. Remove the retainers, springs and pins.

10 Pull the brake shoes sideways and disengage them from the brake cylinder pistons and then pull their lower ends clear of the brake backplate.

11 Clean the dust from the brake shoes, brake drums and backplates by wiping them with a damp cloth. Brake lining material contains asbestos and can be dangerous if inhaled, so brakes should never be cleaned by brushing, or by the use of compressed air.

12 Inspect the brakes for signs of hydraulic leaks. If the friction linings have been contaminated with hydraulic fluid, they should not be re-used. Check that the brake lining thickness is at least equal to the minimum figure given in Specifications and if not fit new linings, or replacement shoes. If fitting new linings or shoes, a complete set must be fitted, otherwise uneven braking may result.

13 Check that the brake drums have not worn unevenly, are not scored excessively, or worn beyond the limit given in Specifications.

14 Apply a small amount of brake grease to the threads of the brake adjusters and to all the points of the brake shoes which make metal-to-metal contact,

15 Fit the springs to the brake shoes and fit the shoe and spring assemblies to the backplate. It is usually easier to fit the lower ends of the brake shoes before fitting the upper ends.

16 Screw the brake adjuster in to its fullest extent (fully retracted) noting that the left-hand rear brake adjuster has a right-hand thread and that the right-hand rear brake adjuster has a left-hand thread.

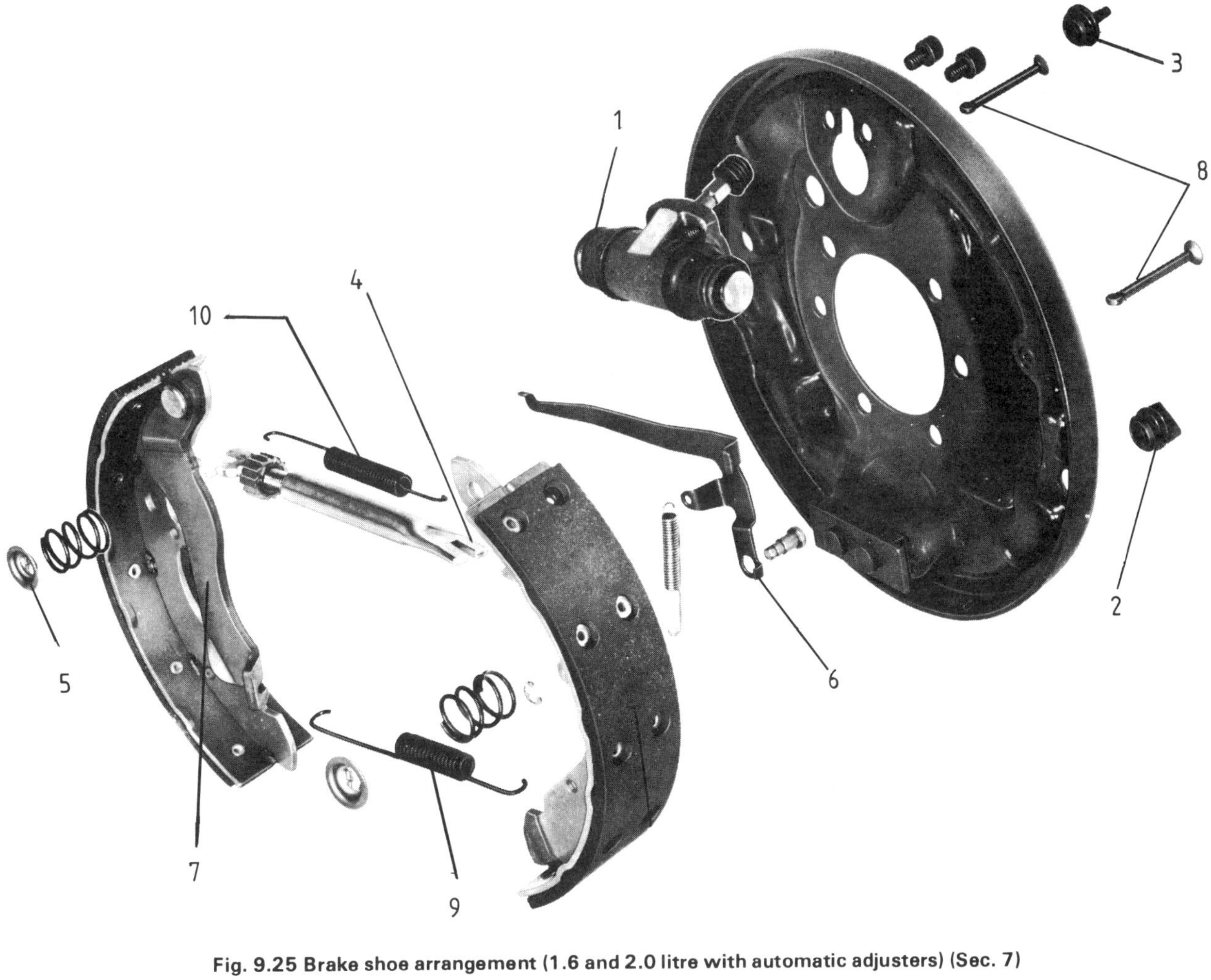

Fig. 9.25 Brake shoe arrangement (1.6 and 2.0 litre with automatic adjusters) (Sec. 7)

1 Wheel cylinder	4 Adjuster pushrod	7 Brake lever	9 Lower return spring
2 Inspection hole plug	5 Spring retainer	8 Retaining pin	10 Upper return spring
3 Adjuster hole plug	6 Adjuster operating lever		

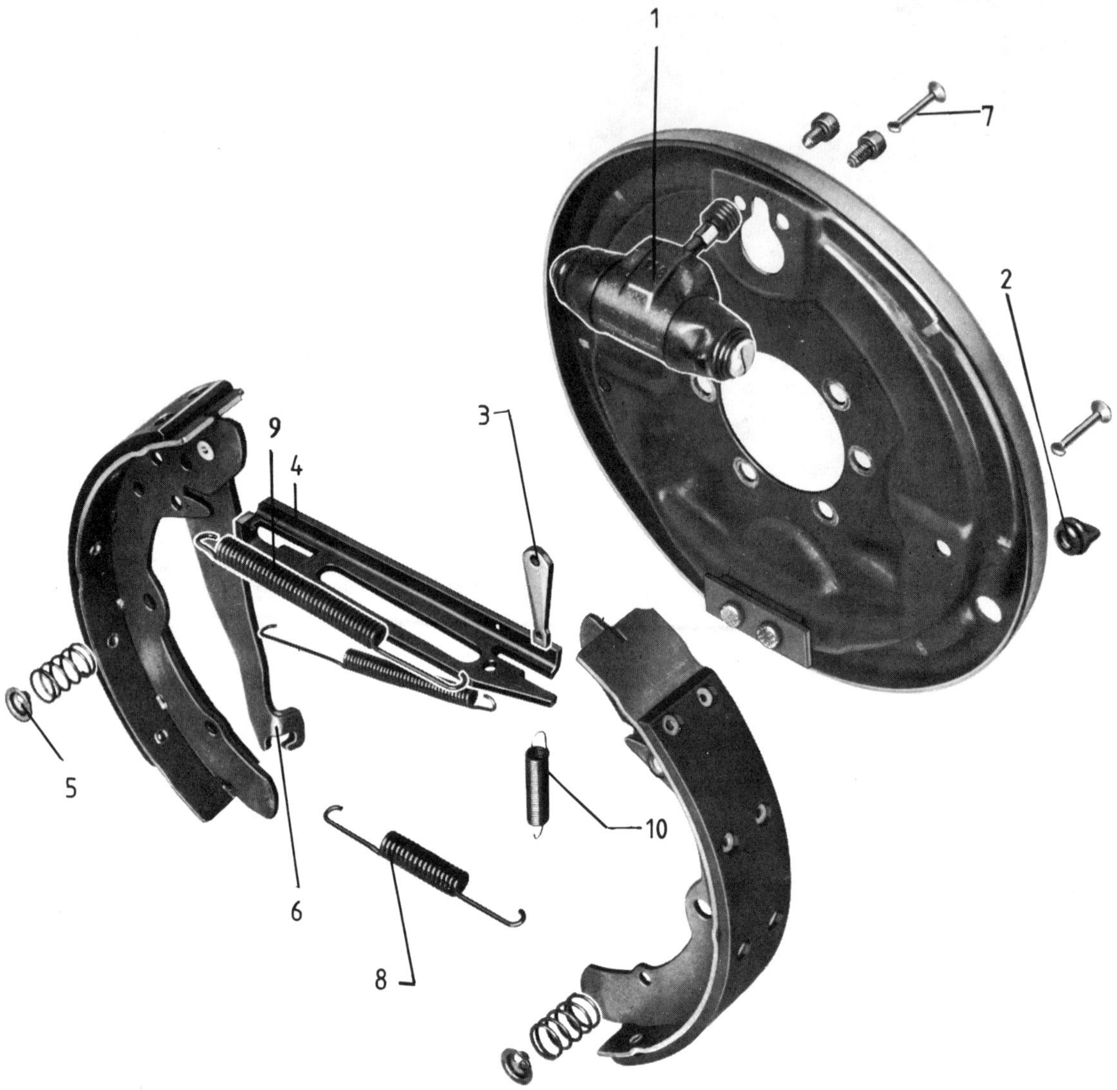

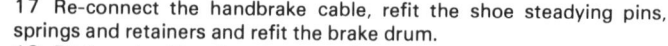

Fig. 9.26 Brake shoe arrangement (1979 on models with automatic adjusters) (Sec. 7)

1	Wheel cylinder	4	Adjuster pushrod
2	Inspection hole plug	5	Spring retainer
3	Draw key	6	Brake lever

7	Retaining pin	9	Upper return spring
8	Lower return spring	10	Draw key spring

17 Re-connect the handbrake cable, refit the shoe steadying pins, springs and retainers and refit the brake drum.

18 Fit the wheel bearing thrust washer and nut and tighten the nut so that the thrust washer can just be moved by prising sideways lightly with a screwdriver. Turn the wheel while adjusting the bearing nut, to prevent the bearing from jamming.

19 When the bearing adjustment is correct, fit the nut locking device and secure it with a new split-pin. Bend the ends of the split-pin back round the stub axle to ensure that the pin cannot fall out.

20 Fill the hub with general purpose lithium based grease and fit the hub cap.

21 Relieve the residual pressure, by pressing the brake regulator lever (Fig. 9.27) several times in the direction of the arrow. Insert a screwdriver through the brake backplate and rotate the ratchet until the brake shoes are in contact with the drums, then back off the adjuster until the wheel can be turned by hand freely.

22 Ensure that both rubber plugs are in place in the backplate and then refit the wheel.

8   Rear brake cylinder – removing, servicing and refitting

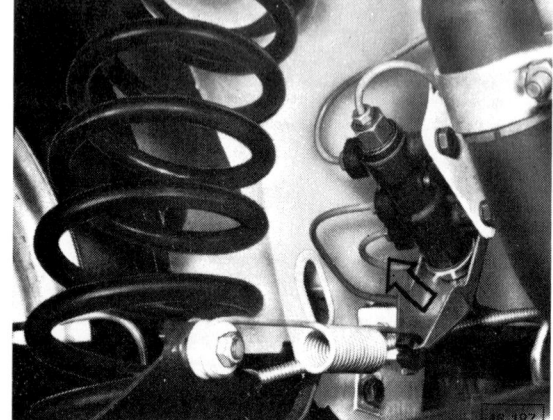

Fig. 9.27 Relieving brake residual pressure (load sensitive pressure regulator) (Sec. 7)

1   Remove the brake shoes as described in the previous Section.

2   Place a drip tray beneath the brake backplate and have ready a plug, or cap for the end of the brake pipe.

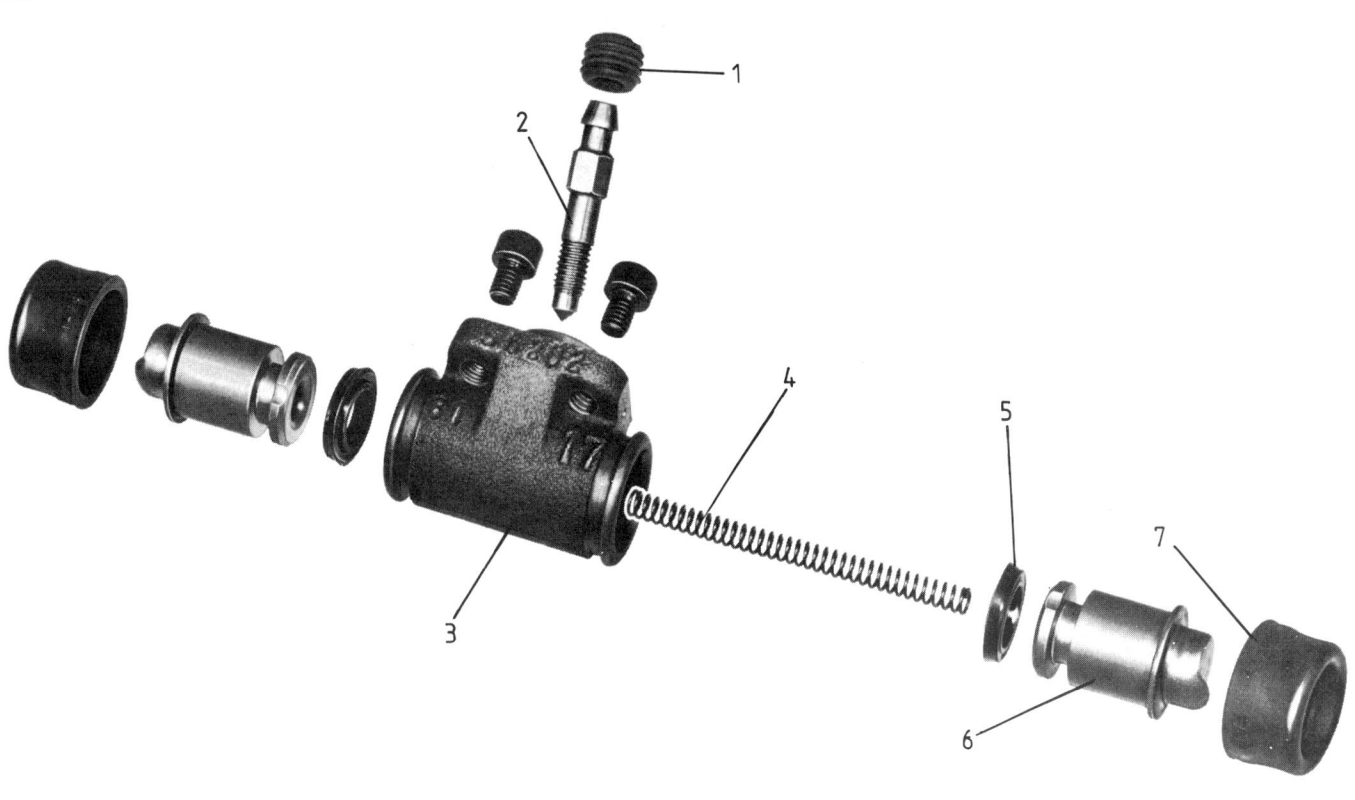

Fig. 9.28 Rear wheel brake cylinder components (Sec. 8)

1	Dust cap	4	Spring	6	Piston
2	Bleed valve	5	Cup	7	Boot
3	Cylinder housing				

3   Unscrew and remove the brake pipe from the brake cylinder and seal its end to prevent loss of fluid and the entry of dirt.

4   Remove the two screws securing the brake cylinder to the back-plate and remove the cylinder.

5   Remove the rubber boots from the ends of the cylinder and extract the two pistons and the spring between them.

6   Inspect the cylinder bore for signs of scoring and corrosion, inspect the pistons and seals for wear. If the cylinder is satisfactory a repair kit can be used; otherwise the cylinder should be discarded and a new complete assembly fitted.

7   If servicing a cylinder, use all the parts in the repair kit. Clean all the metal parts, using methylated spirit if necessary, but never petrol or similar solvents, then leave the parts to dry in the air, or dry them with a lint-free cloth.

8   Apply brake rubber grease to the seals and fit them so that their larger diameter end is nearest to the end of the piston.

9   Smear brake rubber grease on to the pistons and into the bore of the cylinder. Fit a piston into one end of the cylinder and then the spring and other piston into the other end. Take care not to force the pistons into the cylinders because this can twist the seals. If it is difficult to get the seals to enter the cylinder, use a pointed matchstick to help the seal flange enter the bore, but do not use anything metallic. When the pistons have been inserted, fit the boots to the cylinder ends.

10 Refit the cylinder as a reversal of removal. and after refitting the brake shoes and brake drum, bleed the hydraulic system as described in Section 15.

9   Brake master cylinder – removing and refitting

1   Remove the cap from the brake fluid reservoir, place a sheet of thin polythene over the reservoir neck and screw the cap back on. This will minimise the loss of fluid when the cylinder pipe connections are undone.

2   Place a drip tray undrneath the master cylinder and have ready suitable plugs for the pipe connections of the master cylinder and for the brake pipes. Brake fluid will cause damage to the car paintwork.

3   Disconnect the two brake pipes from the cylinder and plug the pipes and cylinder.

4   On models fitted with a brake warning light, disconnect the two connectors from the contacts on the brake fluid reservoir cap. Disconnect the brake light switch connections from the master cylinder.

5   Remove the two nuts and spring washers securing the brake master cylinder to the brake servo and remove the brake master cylinder and seal.

6   When refitting the master cylinder to the servo, use a new seal. Fill the reservoir with fresh hydraulic fluid after fitting and bleed the hydraulic system, as described in Section 15.

10   Brake master cylinder – dismantling, servicing and reassembling

1   Empty the master cylinder and reservoir and discard the fluid.

2   Pull the reservoir off the master cylinder.

3   Remove the stop screw from the cylinder and then remove the circlip from the mouth of the bore.

4   Pull out the piston pushrod assembly, the secondary piston assembly and finally the loose spring.

5   Inspect the bore of the cylinder for signs of wear, damage and corrosion. If the cylinder is in good condition it may be re-used with a service kit, otherwise obtain a new cylinder assembly.

6   Clean all the metal parts, using methylated spirit if necessary, but never petrol or similar solvents, then leave the parts to dry in the air, or dry them with a clean lint-free cloth.

7   Use all the parts supplied in the repair kit and moisten all components with brake fluid before fitting them.

8   Reassemble the secondary piston assembly in the following order. Fit the two piston seals at the larger diameter end of the piston. The

Fig. 9.29 Master cylinder components (Sec. 10)

1 Cap
2 Sealing washer
3 Strainer
4 Reservoir
5 Plugs
6 Master cylinder housing
7 Pressure valves
8 Brake light switch
9 Sealing ring
10 Stop screw
11 Short spring
12 Support ring
13 Primary cup
14 Cup washer
15 Secondary piston
16 Piston seals
17 Stroke limiting screw
18 Stop sleeve
19 Long spring
20 Support ring
21 Primary cup
22 Cup washer
23 Pushrod piston
24 Metal washers
25 Secondary cups
26 Plastic washer
27 Circlip

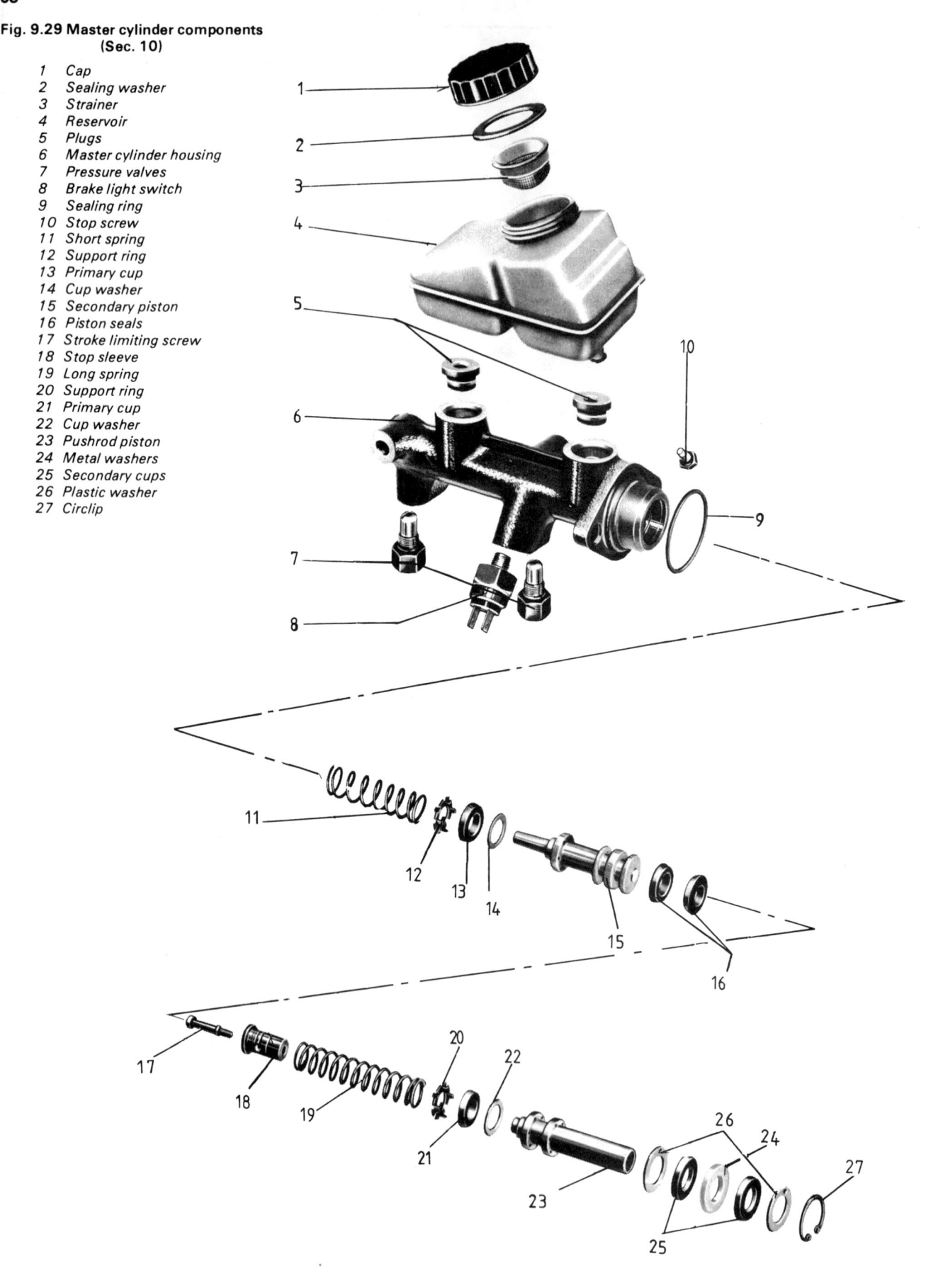

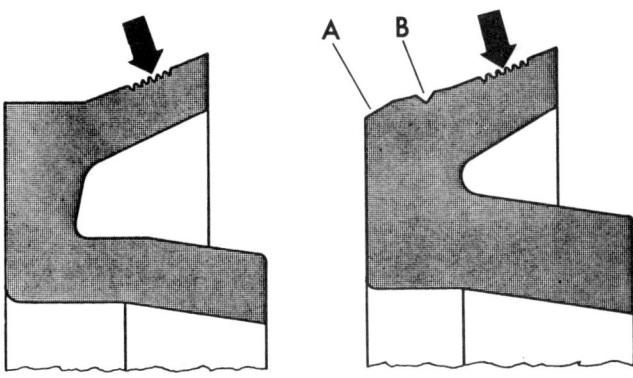

Fig. 9.30 Identification of cups and piston seals (Sec. 10)

Left – primary cup
Right – piston seal with chamfer A and groove B

Fig. 9.31 Inserting the secondary piston into master cylinder (Sec. 10)

piston seals are identified by their chamfer and groove (Fig. 9.30), the sealing lips of the two seals should face away from each other. Fit the cup washer, the primary cup with its lip towards the closed end of the cylinder, the support ring and finally the shorter of the two springs.

9   While holding the master cylinder body vertically with its open end pointing downwards, feed the secondary piston assembly into the cylinder. Guide the lip of the piston seal into the bore carefully, if necessary pressing it in with a very blunt tool, but do not force it in, because this may cause the seal to twist.

10   Fit the cup washer, primary cup, support ring, the longer of the two springs, the stop sleeve and the stroke limiting screw to the short end of the pushrod and tighten the screw firmly. To the longer end of the pushrod piston fit the metal washer, the secondary cup with its lip towards the washer, the plastic washer, the other secondary cup, with its lip facing the same way as the first one and finally the second metal washer.

11   Insert the pushrod piston assembly into the cylinder bore with the spring end first. Insert the stop screw and if necessary move the piston so that the stop screw can be screwed in fully. After screwing in the stop screw, fit the circlip to the mouth of the cylinder bore.

12   Fit a new seal over the end of the master cylinder.

11   Brake servo – removing and refitting

1   Remove the two nuts and spring washers securing the brake master cylinder to the servo (Fig. 9.32).

2   Unscrew the hose clip on the vacuum hose and pull the hose from the non-return valve.

3   Remove the parcel shelf (Chapter 12).

4   Disconnect the brake operating rod clevis from the brake pedal, as described in Chapter 5, Section 8.

5   Remove the four self-locking nuts securing the brake servo to the front bulkhead and the servo can then be removed from the engine compartment.

6   When refitting the servo, use new self-locking nuts and fit a new seal to the end of the brake master cylinder. Ensure that the vacuum hose seats properly on to the non-return valve and that the hose clip is tight.

12   Brake servo – servicing

The brake servo is a sealed unit. If from the fault diagnosis in Section 19 it appears that the servo is defective, a new one must be fitted.

13   Brake servo – testing

1   With the engine off, depress and release the brake pedal several times to release all the vacuum in the system.

2   Apply moderate pressure to the brake pedal and while holding the pedal in this position, start the engine. If the servo is working properly, the pedal will be felt to give slightly as servo-assistance becomes effective.

14   Brake pressure regulator

1   The brake pressure regulator is mounted on the vehicle body and is controlled by a spring attached to the rear axle (photo).

2   The regulator should be inspected for leaks, if topping-up of the hydraulic fluid reservoir is required at frequent intervals.

3   Operation of the regulator can be checked by connecting a pressure gauge to the left-hand front wheel caliper and the right-hand rear wheel brake cylinder and bleeding both gauges.

4   Depress the brake pedal and check that the front and rear pressures are in accordance with Specifications.

5   To adjust the regulator when the rear wheel cylinder pressure is too high, slacken the regulator spring. Tighten the regulator spring if the rear wheel cylinder pressure is too low.

15   Brake system – bleeding

1   The brake system should be bled in the following sequence:

Right-hand rear wheel cylinder
Left-hand rear wheel cylinder
Right-hand front caliper
Left-hand front caliper

2   Inspect the system for leaks and if any are evident find and rectify them before proceeding with the bleeding.

3   Top-up the brake fluid reservoir.

4   Unless you have a single handed bleeding device available, you will need the assistance of another person.

5   Connect one end of a length of flexible tubing to the bleed nipple and place the other end of the tube in a small jar containing about an inch (25·4 mm) depth of clean brake fluid. Ensure that the end of the tube is below the surface of the fluid.

6   Open the bleed screw one full turn and when it is open, instruct the assistant to depress the brake pedal fully and hold it depressed. While the pedal is still depressed, close the bleed screw and then instruct the assistant to release the brake pedal fully.

7   Continue the sequence of opening the screw, depressing the pedal, closing the screw and releasing the pedal until no bubbles are expelled when the pedal is depressed. Every four or five times that the

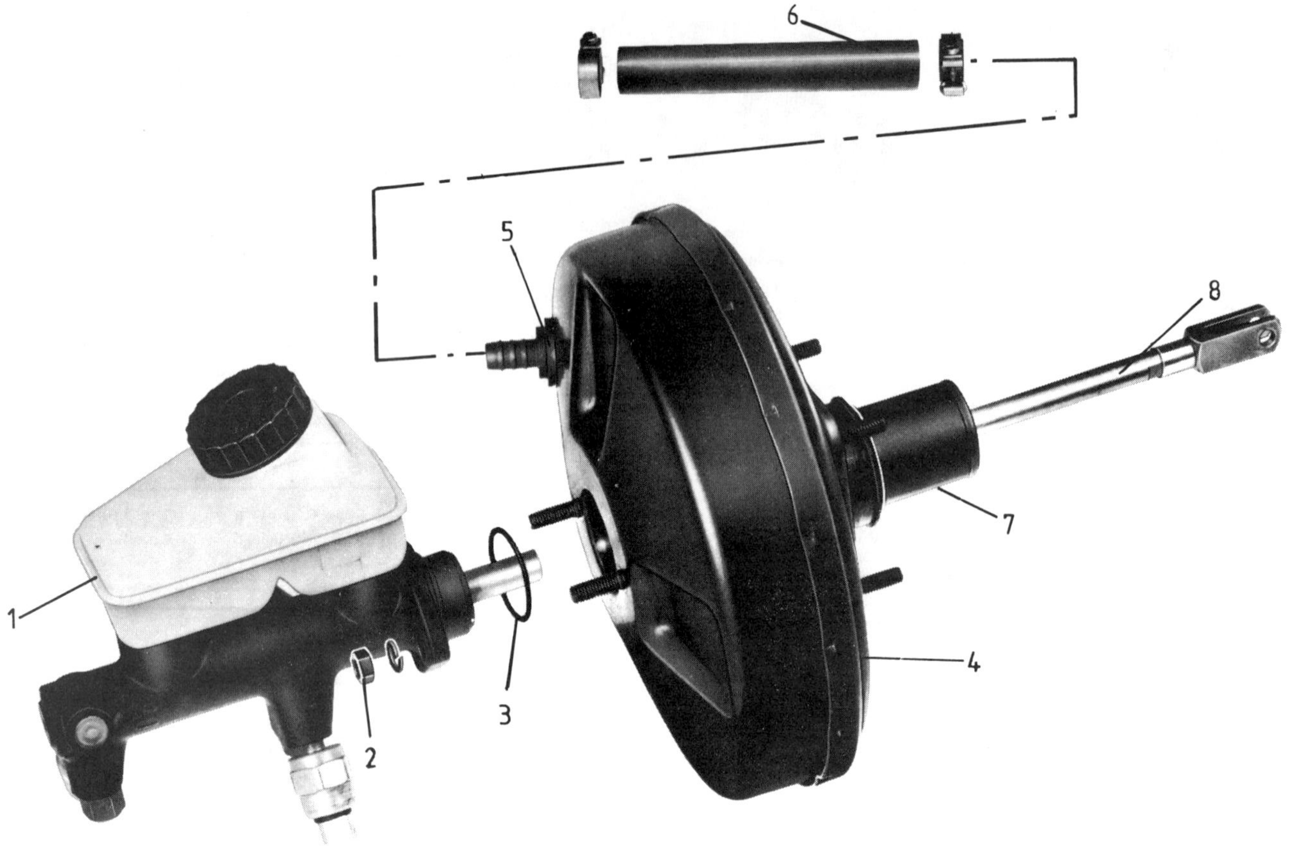

Fig. 9.32 Brake servo assembly (Sec. 11)

1 *Master cylinder*	3 *Seal*	5 *Non-return valve*	7 *Self-locking nut*
2 *Nut*	4 *Servo*	6 *Vacuum hose*	8 *Operating rod*

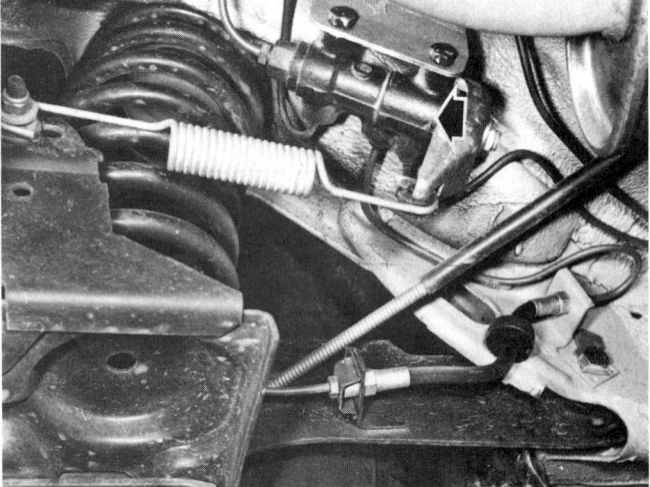

14.1 Brake pressure regulator

sequence has been completed, top-up the fluid reservoir with clean fluid. If the reservoir level is allowed to fall too low, air will enter the system through the reservoir and the entire process will have to be started again.

8　After bleeding each brake completely, proceed to the next one.

9　After bleeding all four brakes, top-up the fluid reservoir to its normal level.

16 Brake pedal – removing and refitting

The brake pedal and clutch pedal share a common bracket assembly and the removal and refitting of the pedals and bracket assembly is described in Chapter 5, Section 8.

17 Handbrake – removing and refitting

1　Unscrew and remove the nut from the compensator bar beneath the vehicle and take off the compensator bar.

2　Remove a circlip from the end of the handbrake pivot pin on the handbrake bracket. Push the pivot pin out to separate the handbrake lever from the bracket.

3　Pull the handbrake lever until the operating rod attached to the lever comes through the rubber boot and into the vehicle.

4　To separate the ratchet and the operating rod from the handbrake lever, it is necessary to grind away one end of their pivots and to reassemble using a new pivot.

5　Refitting is the reverse of removing, but grease all the pivots before refitting and on completion, adjust the handbrake as described in the following Section and grease the surface of the compensator bar.

18 Handbrake – adjustment

1　Raise each of the rear wheels in turn and then support the vehicle body on stands, or blocks, so that both the rear wheels are clear of the ground.

2　For vehicles manufactured in 1977, pull the handbrake control

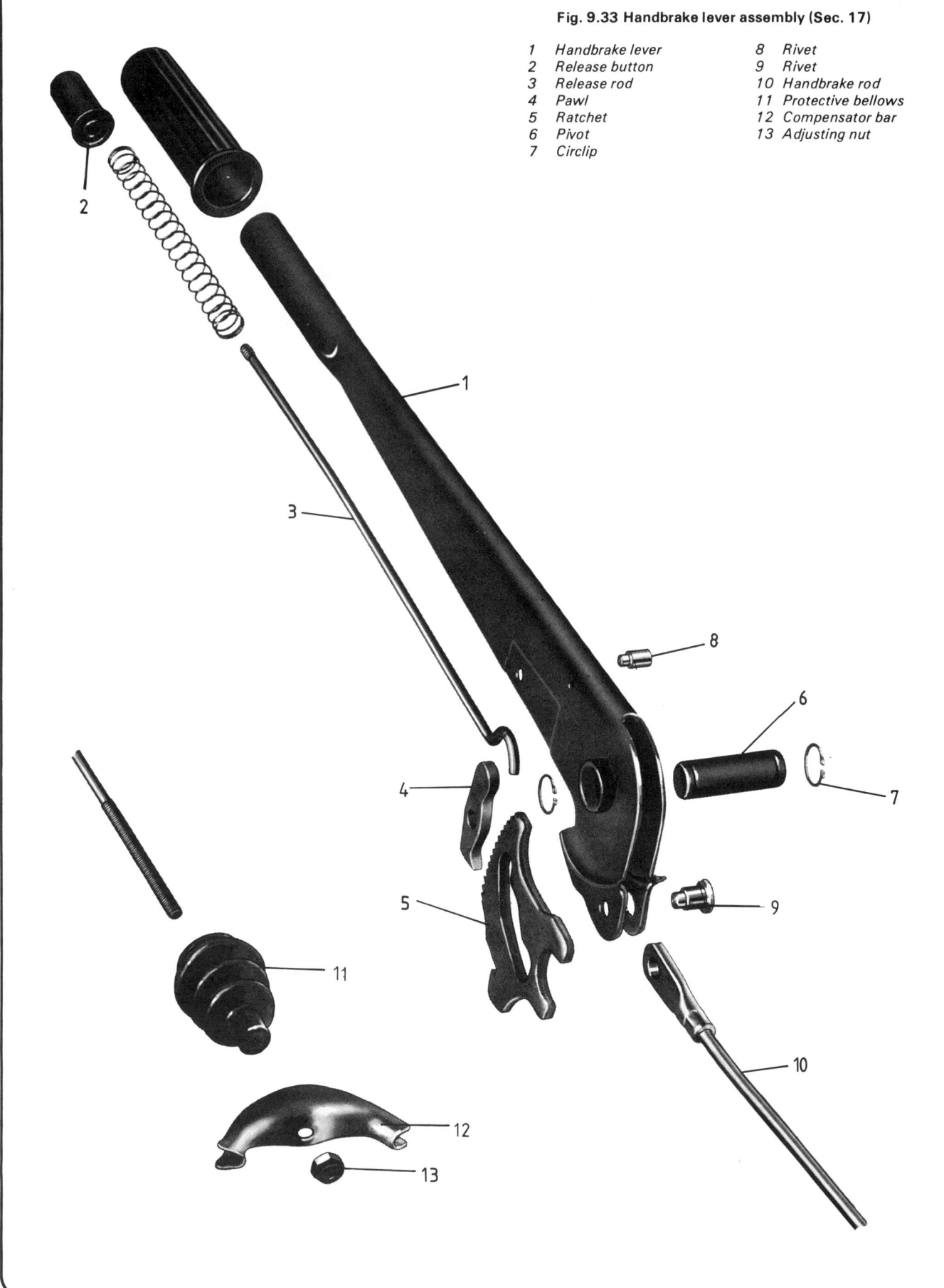

Fig. 9.33 Handbrake lever assembly (Sec. 17)

1 Handbrake lever
2 Release button
3 Release rod
4 Pawl
5 Ratchet
6 Pivot
7 Circlip
8 Rivet
9 Rivet
10 Handbrake rod
11 Protective bellows
12 Compensator bar
13 Adjusting nut

18.3 Handbrake adjuster and cable equaliser

lever to the fourth tooth of the ratchet. For 1978 vehicles, put the handbrake lever on the first tooth. For 1979 and later vehicles with self-adjusting rear brakes, put the handbrake on the third tooth of the ratchet.

3   After setting the handbrake lever, turn the nut on the equalizer (photo) until both the rear wheels can only just be turned by hand.
4   Release the handbrake and check that both rear wheels turn freely and if satisfactory, lower the vehicle on to its wheels.

19 Fault diagnosis – braking system

Symptom	Reason(s)
Pedal travels a long way before brakes operate	Brake shoes set too far from drums (automatic adjusters not operating)
Stopping ability poor, even though pedal pressure is firm	Linings, discs, or drums badly worn, or scored Failure of one of the braking systems One or more wheel cylinder siezed so that its shoe or pad is not effective Brake linings contaminated with oil, or hydraulic fluid Not all the pads, or shoes have the same friction material
Car veers to one side when brakes are applied	Brake pads or linings on one side are contaminated Different friction materials on some discs and shoes One disc distorted causing uneven braking on one side
Pedal feels spongy when brakes are applied	Air in hydraulic system
Pedal feels springy when brakes are applied	Brake linings not bedded down after fitting new ones Master cylinder of wheel cylinder mountings loose Discs out of true
Pedal travels right down to floor with little or no resistance and brakes are virtually non-operative	Fluid reservoir empty due to leak in the system Failure of both halves of master cylinder
Excessive pedal pressure required, no servo assistance	Vacuum line leaking Defective seal between master cylinder and servo Defective servo diaphragm Non-return valve on servo unit remains closed
Force on pedal becomes excessive from a certain position onwards	Pushrod piston scored allowing air to pass the seal at some positions

Chapter 10 Electrical system

Contents

Specifications

Battery

Type	12 volts
Capacity:	
Audi 100	54 Amp hours
Audi 5000	63 Amp hours
Minimum voltage under load	9·6 volts at 110 Amps
Acid level	5 mm (0·20 in) above separator plates, or at acid level mark
Battery acid specific gravity:	
Discharged	1·12 kg/dm^3
Half-charged	1·20 kg/dm^3
Charged	1·28 kg/dm^3

Alternator

Type	Integral regulator
Polarity	Negative earth
Regulator voltage	12·5 – 14·5 volts
Rating (depending on vehicle model):	
Motorola	35A, 55A or 65A
Bosch	35A, 55A, 65A, 75A or 90A
Brush length	
Motorola:	
New	9 mm (0·36 in)
Wear limit	5 mm (0·20 in)
Bosch:	
New	10 mm (0·40 in)
Wear limit	5 mm (0·20 in)
Rotor resistance	
Bosch	3 to 4 Ohms
Motorola	3·4 to 3·75 Ohms

Starter motor

Type	Pre-engaged
Minimum voltage at solenoid terminal	8 volts
Commutator diameter (minimum)	33·5 mm (1·32 in)
Axial play	0·1 to 0·3 mm (0·004 to 0·012 in)
Run-out (maximum)	0·03 mm (0·001 in)
Undercutting depth	0·5 to 0·8 mm (0·020 to 0·032 in)
Brushes (minimum length)	13 mm (0·512 in)

Fuses

No	Function	Rating (Amps)	Colour
1	Air conditioner, large blower	25	Blue
2	Foglights	8	White
3	High beam headlight, left	8	White
4	High beam headlight, right	8	White
5	Fuel pump (K-jetronic fuel injection)	16	Red
6	Right side light, right tail light	8	White
7	Left side light, left tail light, engine compartment light	8	White
8	Glove compartment light, number plate light, instrument panel illumination	8	White
9	Horn, combination instrument, heater blower motor (N models)	16	Red
10	Radiator fan motor	25	Blue
11	Brake lights, left and right	16	Red
12	Cigar lighter, radio, clock, interior light	16	Red
13	Low beam headlight, right	8	White
14	Low beam headlight, left	8	White
15	Reversing lights, wiper motor	16	Red
16	Heated rear window	25	Blue
17	Flasher unit	8	White

Bulbs

Headlamps:	
Audi 100 L/GL (H4)	55/55W
Audi 100 (Twin filament)	40/45W
Side light	5W
Front turn indicator	21W
Rear turn signal	21W
Brake light	21W
Rear foglight	21W
Tail light	10W

1   General description

The electrical system operates at 12 volts and is negative earth. Power is supplied by an alternator which has integral rectifiers and voltage control system and the rating of the alternator fitted to a particular model is able to cater for all the vehicle's requirements, even at low engine speeds.

Power from the battery and alternator is fed to a relay plate and fuse panel mounted in the engine compartment and from this it is distributed to the various electrically operated items by individually fused circuits.

2   Battery – removing and refitting

1   With the bonnet lid propped up, remove the cover from the plenum chamber at the rear of the engine compartment to expose the battery.

2   Unscrew the nuts on the battery terminals and pull the terminals off.

3   Release the bolt from the clamp which secures the bottom of the battery and remove the bolt and clamp (photo).

4   Lift the battery out, taking care to keep it level to avoid spilling any electrolyte.

5   When refitting the battery, ensure that the battery and battery tray are dry and free of corrosion.

6   Ensure that the terminals on the battery and on the battery leads are clean and free from corrosion. Smear them with petroleum jelly or a proprietary product for inhibiting battery terminal corrosion.

7   Fit the battery so that its negative terminal is nearest to the non-insulated battery lead. Fit the battery terminals and tighten the bolts to clamp the terminals tightly. Do not tighten the bolts so much that the terminals are distorted.

8   Refit the clamp and tighten the bolt until the battery is held sufficiently firmly to prevent it from moving.

3   Battery – maintenance

1   The essentials of battery maintenance are to ensure that the level of electrolyte is maintained, the terminals and leads are free from corrosion and that the battery is maintained fully charged.

2.3 Battery retaining clamp

2   At least once a month, remove the plug from each cell and check that the level of electrolyte just reaches the bottom of the filler spouts. Add distilled water as required, but do not fill the cells higher than the bottom of the spouts. Take care not to spill any water on the top of the battery and in the event of doing so, wipe it off immediately.

3   If the battery terminals are corroded, clean them down to bare metal and smear them with a proprietary acid resisting grease or petroleum jelly.

4   Battery – charging

1   When a battery remains in a low state of charge, its plates deteriorate as a result of an irreversible chemical reaction and its capacity is lessened. If the car is not used for several days at any time of the year, the battery's life will be prolonged if it is put on charge.

2   During the winter, when much of the car's electrical equipment is

Fig. 10.1 Alternator installation (1.6 litre) (Sec. 5)

1 Earth strap
2 Bracket
3 Rubber bearing with bush
4 Cup washer
5 Alternator support
6 Rubber bearing
7 Cup washer with guide collar
8 Alternator
9 Rubber bearing with bush
10 Bracket

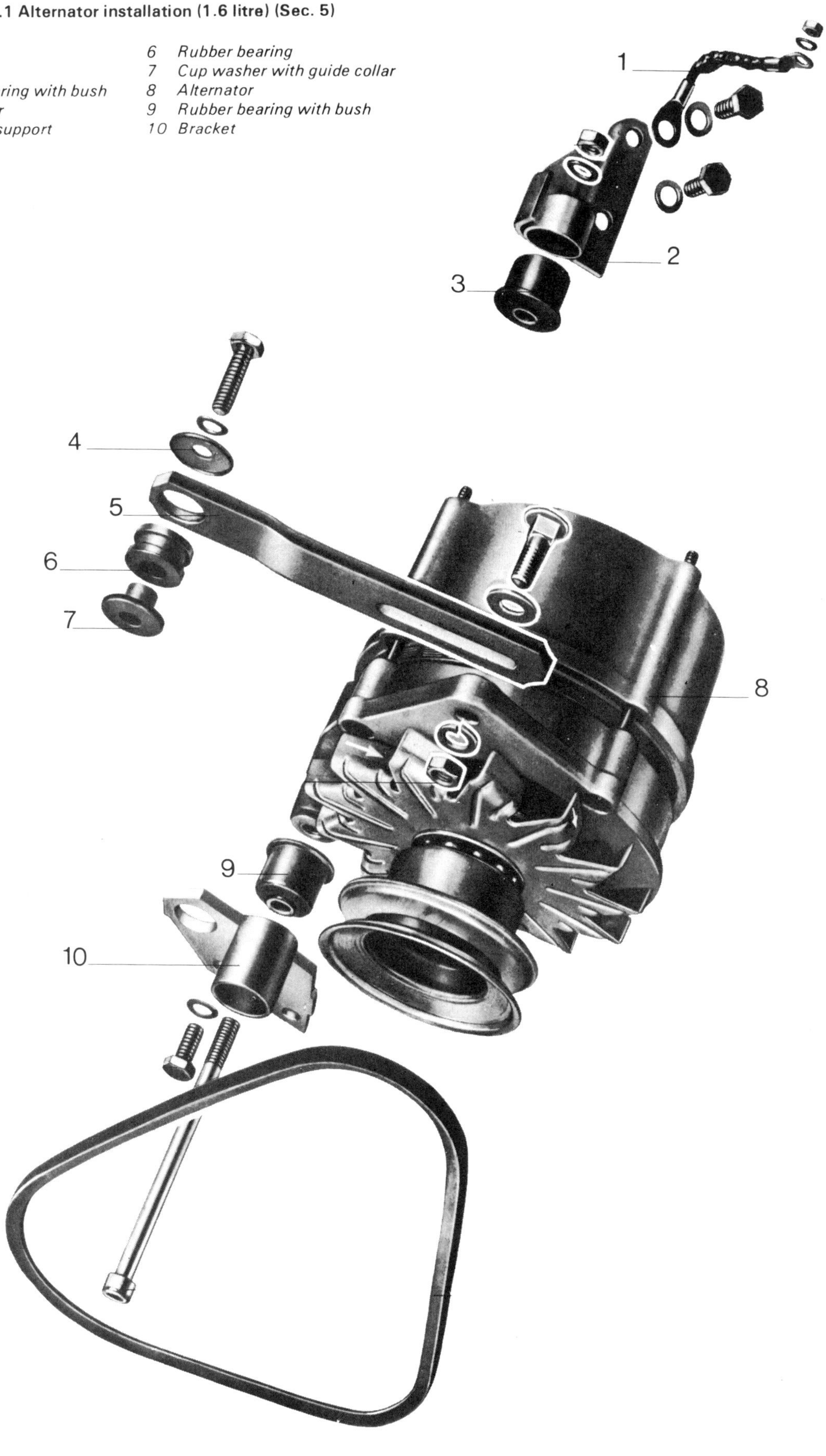

in use and there is little spare capacity for the alternator to charge the battery, the use of an external charger every week is worth while.

3   Disconnect the battery from the electrical system of the car before charging. In addition it is preferable to remove the battery from the car to avoid damage by acid spray during charging.

4   Remove all the cell plugs and connect the positive terminal of the battery charger to the positive battery terminal and the negative terminal of the battery charger to the negative battery terminal.

5   Avoid high rates of charge if possible. The normal rate of charge is the 10 hour rate, which means that if the battery capacity is 45 ampere hours (Ah), it should be charged at 4·5 amps. Continue charging until all cells are gassing vigorously, then disconnect the battery from the charger, check the electrolyte level and top-up if necessary and leave the battery for about 20 minutes to finish gassing before screwing in the cell plugs.

6   If during severe weather the battery electrolyte freezes, the battery must not be charged until the electrolyte has thawed.

7   During charging, electrolyte temperature must not exceed 40°C (104°F). If the battery reaches this temperature, reduce the charging rate.

5   Alternator – removing and refitting

1   There are four different methods of mounting the alternator and a range of different capacity alternators by different manufacturers is used.

2   There are three basic steps in removing the alternator and these are to release the tension on the V-belt so that it can be removed, to disconnect the electrical connections and to remove the fixing bolts (photo).

3   The way in which these operations can be carried out can be seen from Figs. 10.1, 10.2, 10.3 and 10.4.

4   Refitting the alternator is the reverse of removal, but on 2·0 litre and some 2·2 litre models the positioning of the wiring harness requires care. It is essential on these models that the cables are positioned as shown in Fig. 10.5.

5   After refitting the alternator, tension the drivebelt as described in the following Section.

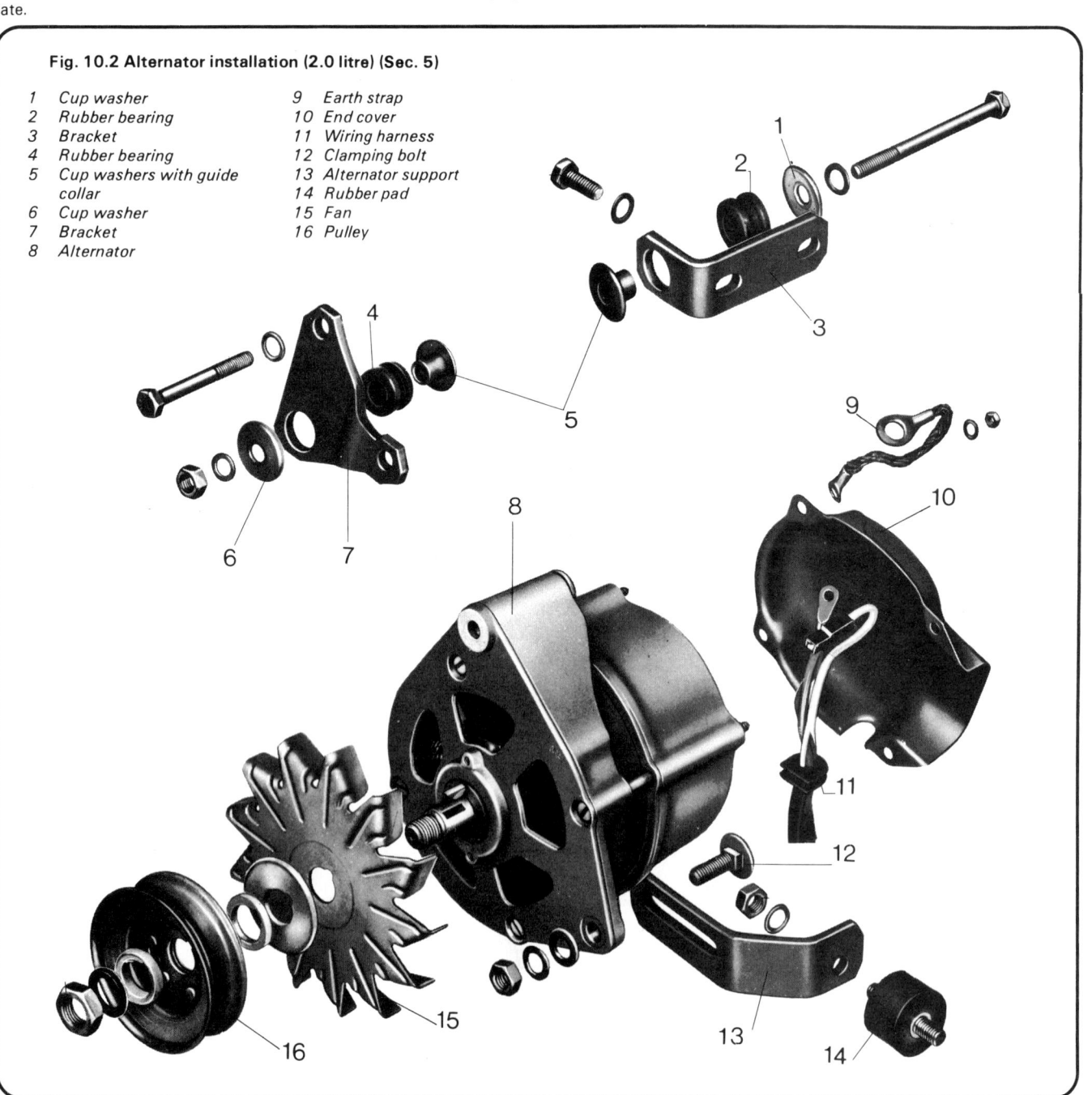

Fig. 10.2 Alternator installation (2.0 litre) (Sec. 5)

1	Cup washer	9	Earth strap
2	Rubber bearing	10	End cover
3	Bracket	11	Wiring harness
4	Rubber bearing	12	Clamping bolt
5	Cup washers with guide collar	13	Alternator support
6	Cup washer	14	Rubber pad
7	Bracket	15	Fan
8	Alternator	16	Pulley

5.2 Bosch alternator (2.2 litre)

6 Alternator – drivebelt tensioning

1·6 litre

1 Loosen the clamping bolt, arrowed in Fig. 10.6 and swivel the alternator outwards by pulling on the top or levering it with a piece of wood placed between the alternator and the engine.

2 Tighten the clamping bolt just enough to prevent the alternator from moving and check the belt tension by pressing with the thumb the mid-point of the span between the alternator and crankshaft pulleys.

3 If the deflection is between 10 and 15 mm (0·39 and 0·59 in) tighten the clamping bolt firmly, otherwise make the necessary adjustment to the alternator.

2·0 litre

4 The method of adjustment is the same as for the 1·6 litre engine, but before making the adjustment it is necessary to loosen both the mounting bolt and the clamping bolt (Fig. 10.7).

2·2 litre

5 The adjustment of alternator belt tension on the 2·2 litre engine is the same regardless of the type of alternator which may be fitted.

6 The clamping bolt is shown in Fig. 10.8 and the method of adjustment is the same as for the 1·6 litre engine.

Fig. 10.3 Alternator installation – 65A alternator (2.2 litre) (Sec. 5)

1 End cover	5 Alternator support
2 Wiring harness	6 Fan
3 Mounting bracket	7 Pulley
4 Alternator	

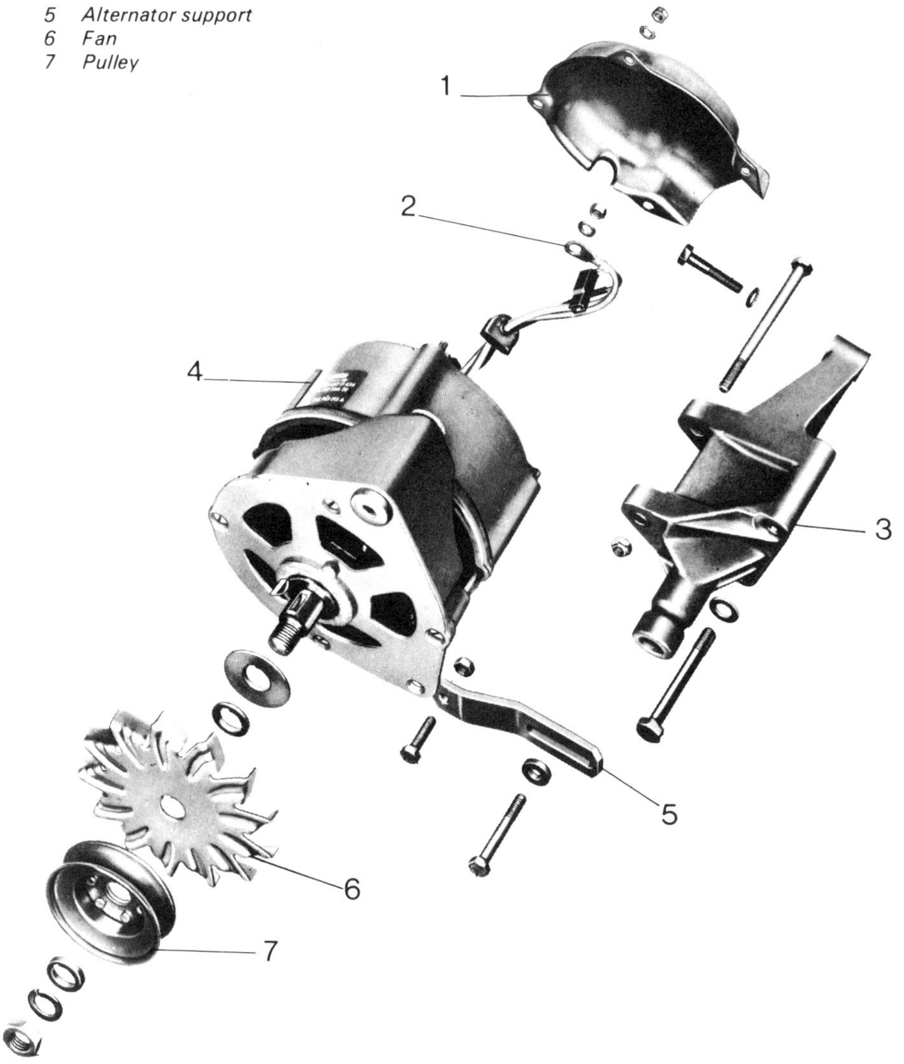

Fig. 10.4 Alternator installation – 75/90A alternator (2.2 litre)
(Sec. 5)

1 End cover
2 Alternator
3 Mounting bracket

4 Alternator supports
5 Fan
6 Pulley

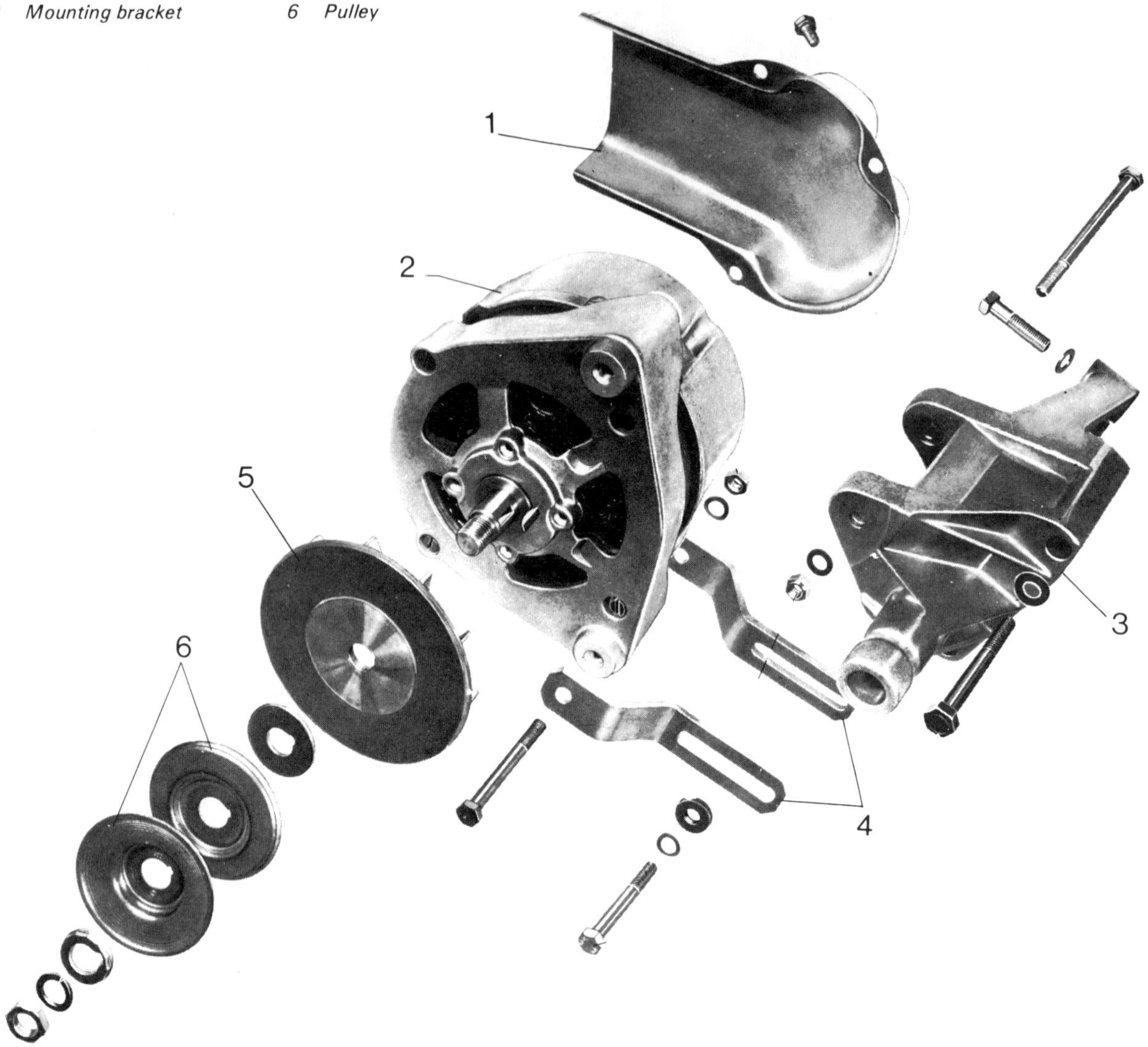

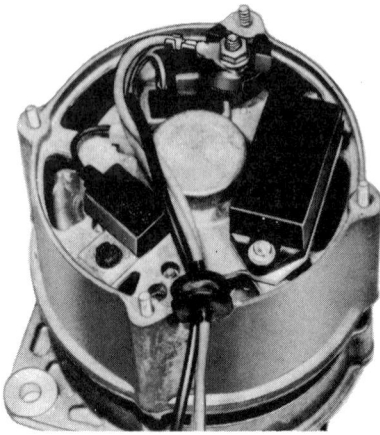

Fig. 10.5 Positioning the alternator wiring harness (Sec. 5)

Fig. 10.6 Alternator belt tensioning (1.6 litre) (Sec. 6) (Clamping bolt arrowed)

Fig. 10.7 Alternator belt tensioning (2.0 litre) (Sec. 6)

A   *Upper mounting bolt*   B   *Clamping bolt*

7   Alternator – servicing

1   Complete dismantling of an alternator should not be undertaken by anyone who is not experienced in soldering semiconductor devices, but the brushes may be renewed and the voltage regulator can be replaced.
2   Before removing the alternator from the engine, grip the drivebelt to prevent the alternator from rotating and loosen the alternator pulley nut.
3   After removing the alternator, remove the pulley nut and washer, draw off the pulley, withdraw the key and remove the fan and any spacers and collars which may be fitted.

Motorola alternators, 35A, 55A and 65A versions
4   Remove the two screws from the voltage regulator, lift the regulator and pull off the two wiring connectors to free the regulator. On some alternators it may first be necessary to remove the suppressor condenser (Fig. 10.10).
5   Remove the two screws from the brush box and lift the brush box out. Measure the exposed length of brush and fit new brushes if they are worn to the limit given in Specifications.
6   To fit new brushes, unsolder the ends of the braids (Fig. 10.11),

Fig. 10.8 Alternator belt tensioning (2.2 litre) (Sec. 6)
(Clamping bolt arrowed)

withdraw the brushes and insert the new ones. Use radio quality solder for soldering the braids.
7   Mark the bearing housing to show its position relative to the alternator housing, then remove the two bolts and washers clamping the

Fig. 10.9 Voltage regulator connections (Motorola) (Sec. 7)

1   *DF (green lead)*   2   *D + (red lead)*

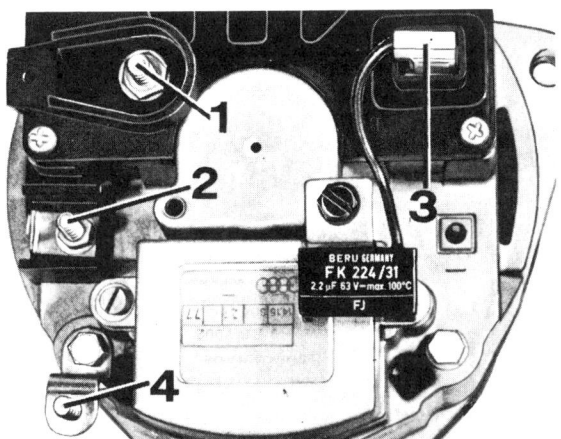

Fig. 10.10 Alternator external connections (Motorola) (Sec. 7)

1   B+
2   D+ (lead to charge indicator light)
3   B+ (connection to suppressor condenser)
4   Earth cable to engine

Fig. 10.11 Brush holder (Motorola) (Sec. 7)

(Soldered connections arrowed)

Fig. 10.12 Motorola alternator components (Sec. 7)

1	Pulley	4	Bearing	7	Alternator housing	10 Diode plate
2	Fan	5	Rotor	8	Brush holder	11 Cover
3	Bearing housing	6	Stator	9	Voltage regulator	

Fig. 10.13 Diode plate testing (Motorola) (Sec. 7)

1	Positive heat sink	3	Negative heat sink
2	Stator connections	4	Contact strip (D+)

Fig. 10.14 Diode plate soldered connections (arrowed) (Sec. 7)

alternator halves and separate them. The stator will stay in the alternator housing and the rotor and bearing will stay in the bearing housing.

8 Using a commercial bearing puller on the inner race of the slip ring end bearing, pull the bearing off, being careful to avoid damage to the slip rings.

9 Remove the screws securing the cover plate inside the front end bearing and press the rotor and bearing out of the bearing housing. Draw the bearing off the shaft with a commercial puller.

10 Clean the rotor and slip rings and check the resistance between the slip rings and the resistance between the slip rings and the rotor body. The correct value of the resistance between slip rings is given in Specifications and the resistance between the slip rings and the rotor body should be infinity.

11 Clean the stator and diode plate and look for signs of damage or overheating. If there is any reason to suspect that either of these parts is defective, it is better to take them to an auto electrician for testing, unless you have the necessary skill and equipment to do the testing yourself.

12 Using an ohm meter with a range of 200 ohms, the diodes can be tested as follows. With the red lead of the meter on point 1 in Fig. 10.13, take a reading with the black lead connected in turn to each of the three points marked 2. Repeat the test with the black lead connected to point 3 and the red lead connected in turn to each of the three points 2. Finally, connect the red lead on contact strip 4 and the black lead in turn to each of the three points marked 2. For every

measurement the reading should be in the range 50 to 80 ohms and a new diode plate must be fitted if this reading is not obtained.

13 To disconnect the diode plate from the stator windings, first label the four leads to indicate the points to which they are connected (Fig. 10.14). Grip the diode connection with a pair of long nosed pliers to dissipate the heat and use an instrument soldering iron of not more than 30 watts rating to unsolder the stator wires.

14 The resistance of the stator windings is very low and requires a special instrument to check it, but the resistance between the windings and frame can be checked, and should be infinite.

Bosch alternators, 35A, 55A and 65A versions

15 There are constructional differences between the Motorola and the Bosch alternators, but the method of dismantling is similar.

16 The voltage regulator is integral with the brushes and can be removed and refitted without removing the alternator, by undoing the fixing screw and taking off the unit. New brushes can be fitted in a similar manner to those of the Motorola alternator.

17 To test the diodes, connect the red lead of an ohm meter to point 1 on Fig. 10.16 and the black lead to each point 2 in turn. Repeat the test with the black lead connected to point 3 and test each point 2 in turn. Finally, connect the red lead to point 4 and connect the black lead to each of the points 2 in turn. For every measurement the reading should be in the range 50 to 80 ohms and a new diode plate must be fitted if this reading is not obtained.

18 The disconnection of the stator winding from the diode plate

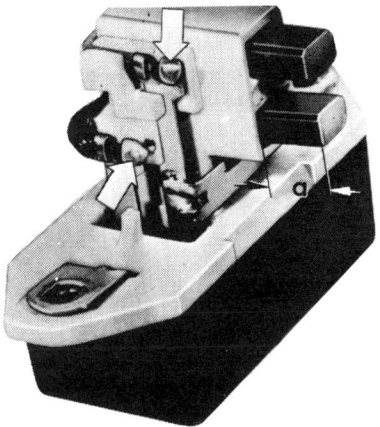

Fig. 10.15 Brush holder (Bosch) (Sec. 7)

(soldered connections arrowed)

Fig. 10.16 Diode plate testing (Bosch) (Sec. 7)

1	Positive heat sink	3	Negative heat sink
2	Stator connections	4	Contact strip (D+)

Fig. 10.17 Bosch alternator (35A, 55A, 65A versions) (Sec. 7)

1 Bearing housing
2 Drive end bearing
3 Rotor
4 Slip ring end bearing
5 Alternator housing
6 Brushes
7 Stator
8 Diode plate
9 Voltage regulator
10 Suppressor condenser

requires the unsoldering of the three wires, as shown in Fig. 10.18, taking the precautions explained in paragraphs 13.

Bosch alternators, 75A and 90A versions

19 Apart from minor differences in construction this version is essentially the same as the lower power alternator and the procedures for renewing the brushes and testing the diodes are identical.

8 Alternator – safety precautions

1 The alternator is wired for a negative earth supply. Be careful not to connect the battery the wrong way round, or the alternator will be damaged.

2 Do not run the alternator without its output wires connected.

3 To prevent surges reaching and damaging the diodes in the alternator, the battery should be disconnected and the alternator leads disconnected if any arc welding is being done on the car.

4 If the battery is being charged without removing it from the car,

Fig. 10.18 Disconnecting the diode plate (Sec. 7)

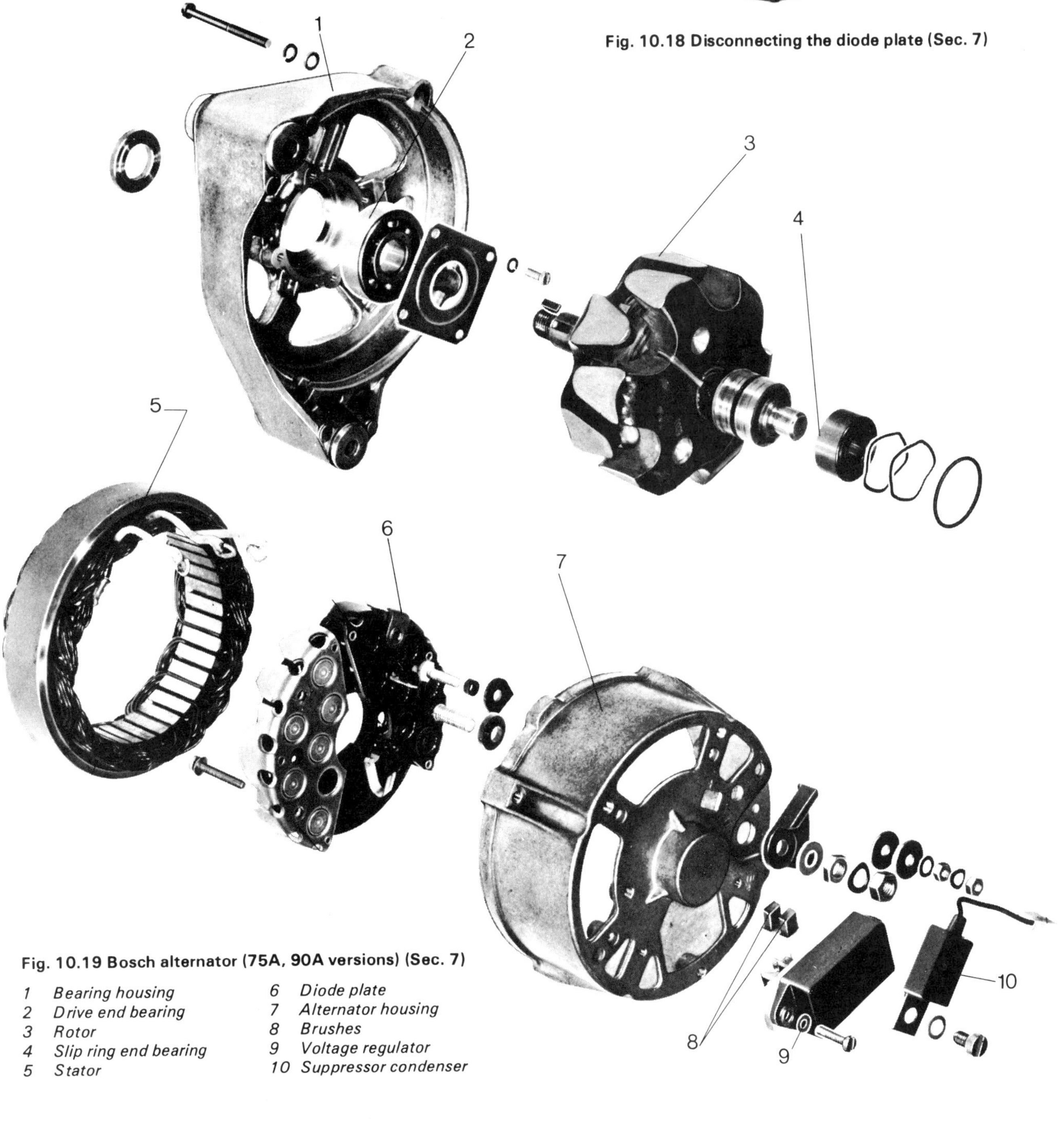

Fig. 10.19 Bosch alternator (75A, 90A versions) (Sec. 7)

1 Bearing housing	6 Diode plate
2 Drive end bearing	7 Alternator housing
3 Rotor	8 Brushes
4 Slip ring end bearing	9 Voltage regulator
5 Stator	10 Suppressor condenser

disconnect the battery leads before connecting the charger to the battery.

5   If the car is being started by using a booster battery, follow the procedure given under the heading **Jacking, towing and emergency starting on page 12.**

9   Starter motor – testing in car

1   If the starter motor fails to respond when the starter switch is operated, first check that the fault is not external to the starter motor.

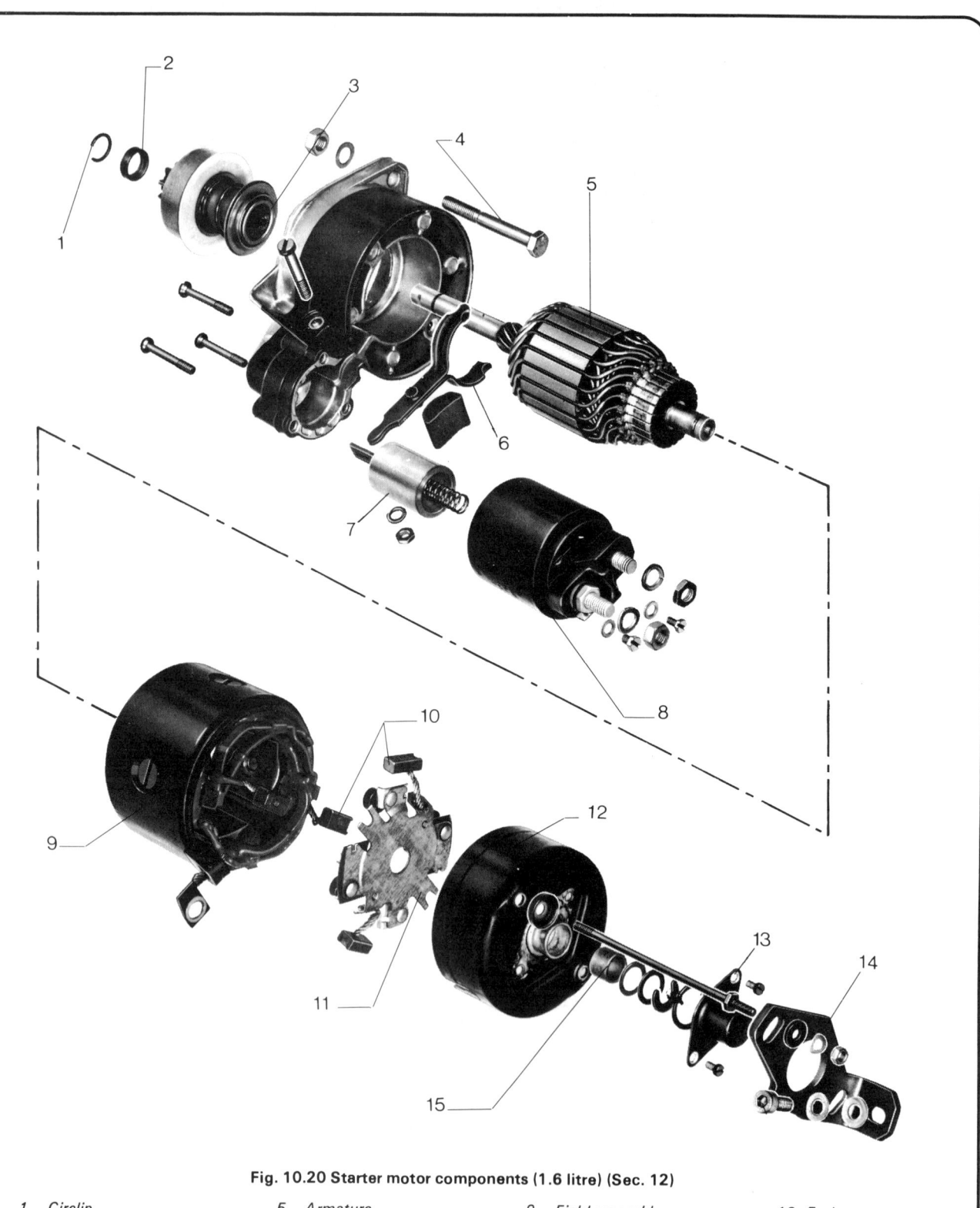

Fig. 10.20 Starter motor components (1.6 litre) (Sec. 12)

1 Circlip	5 Armature	9 Field assembly	13 End cap
2 Stop ring	6 Operating lever	10 Brushes	14 Support plate
3 Pinion drive	7 Solenoid plunger	11 Brush plate	15 Bush
4 Bearing housing	8 Solenoid body	12 End cover	

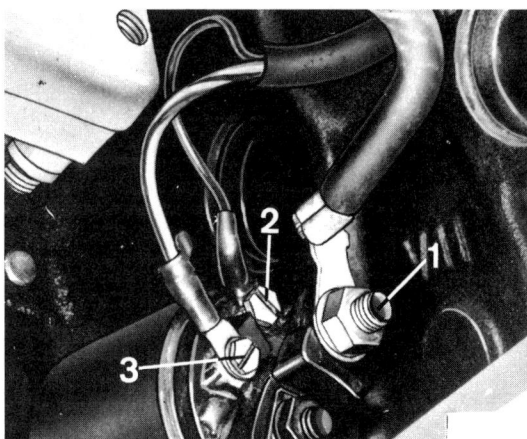

Fig. 10.21 Starter motor connections (1.6 litre) (Sec. 9)

1 *Terminal 30 (to battery and*   3 *Terminal 50 (to ignition/*
   alternator)   *starter switch)*
2 *Terminal 16 (to ignition coil)*

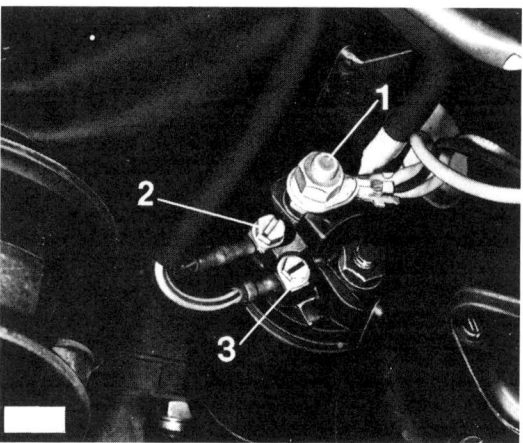

Fig. 10.22 Starter motor connections (2.0 and 2.2 litre) (Sec. 9)

1 *Terminal 30 (to battery and*   3 *Terminal 50 (to ignition/*
   alternator)   *starter switch)*
2 *Terminal 16 (to ignition coil)*

2   Connect a test lamp between chassis earth and the large terminal on the starter solenoid, terminal 30. This terminal is connected directly to the battery and the test lamp should light whether or not the ignition switch is operated.

3   Remove the test lamp connection from the large terminal (30) and transfer it to the smaller terminal (50) on the solenoid. The lamp should light only when the starter switch is in its *Start* position.

4   If both these tests are satisfactory the fault is in the starter motor.

5   If the starter motor is heard to operate, but the engine fails to start, check the battery terminals, the starter motor leads and the engine-to-body earth strap for cleanliness and tightness.

10 Starter motor – general description

1   The starter motor on the 1·6 litre is different from that on other models, but both are of the pre-engaged type.

2   Operation of the starter switch energises a solenoid and this causes the starter pinion to move into mesh with the starter ring on the flywheel, or driveplate.

3   When the teeth are in mesh and the solenoid reaches the limit of its travel, it operates contacts which switch current to the starter motor.

4   Incorporated in the starter motor drive is a one way clutch. This prevents the engine from driving the starter motor and damaging it after the engine has fired.

11 Starter motor – removing and refitting

1   Disconnect the battery leads.

2   Note the position of each of the wires connected to the starter motor and then remove them.

3   Unscrew and remove the two bolts securing the starter motor to the bellhousing and withdraw the starter motor.

4   When refitting the motor, make sure that both the starter flange and its mating surface on the bellhousing are clean. Insert and tighten the bolts and ensure that the two mating faces are flush.

5   The routing of the starter motor cables is critical and they must lie well clear of all parts of the engine and body. Refer to Chapter 1 and route the cable connections as shown in Figs. 1.15, 1.60 or 1.94 as appropriate. If this is not done, there is a great risk of a short circuit and a fire.

12 Starter motor – dismantling, servicing and reassembly

1·6 litre

1   Remove the support plate from the end cover.

2   Remove the screws from the shaft end cover. Take off the cover and remove the circlip and shims.

3   Remove the two through-bolts and lift off the end cover to expose the armature, brush assembly and commutator.

4   Lift the brush springs and withdraw the two brushes attached to the field windings.

5   To remove the mounting bracket from the drive end of the shaft, push back the stop ring to expose the circlip beneath it. Remove the circlip and the stop ring and withdraw the armature.

6   Disengage the drive pinion and clutch assembly from the operating lever and withdraw the assembly, after removing the pivot bolt from the operating lever.

7   Clean all the parts and examine them for damage. Examine the drive pinion for damaged teeth and check that it will only rotate in one direction.

8   Clean the commutator with a rag moistened with petrol. Minor scoring can be removed with fine glass paper, but deep scoring will necessitate the commutator being skimmed in a lathe and then being undercut. Commutator refinishing is a job which is best left to a specialist.

9   Measure the length of the brushes. If less than the minimum given in Specifications, fit new brushes. Crush the old brushes to free the copper braid and file the excess solder off the braid. Fit new brushes to the braid and hold the braid with a pair of flat nosed pliers below the carbon brush, to prevent solder from flowing down the braid. Solder the brushes on using radio quality solder and a heavy duty soldering iron of at least 250 watt rating. Check that the brushes move freely in their holders and if necessary dress the brushes with a fine file.

10   Reassemble by reversing the operations required for dismantling. To fit the brush assembly over the commutator, either hook the brush springs on to the edge of the brush holder, or bend pieces of wire to hold the springs off the brushes until the brush assembly has been fitted. As soon as this has been done, release the brush springs and position them so that they bear on the centres of the brushes.

11   When assembling the starter motor, apply sealing compound to the points indicated in Fig. 10.24 and smear the splines of the commutator with molybdenum disulphide grease.

12   Fit a new circlip to the pinion end of the shaft and ensure that the circlip groove is not damaged. Any burrs on the edges of the groove should be removed with a fine file.

13   New bushes can be fitted to the end housing. The old bush should be pressed out and a new bush should be soaked for five minutes in hot oil before being pressed in.

2·0 and 2·2 litre

14   There are minor constructional differences (Fig. 10.23) compared with the 1·6 litre engine starter motor, but the procedure for dismantling and assembly is the same.

15   The sealing points for this starter motor are shown in Fig. 10.25.

Fig. 10.23 Starter motor components (2.0 and 2.2 litre) (Sec 12)

1 Bush
2 Bearing housing
3 Circlip
4 Stop ring
5 Pinion drive
6 Armature
7 Yoke
8 Operating lever
9 Solenoid plunger
10 Solenoid body
11 Field coils
12 Brushes
13 Brush plate
14 End cover
15 Bush
16 End cap

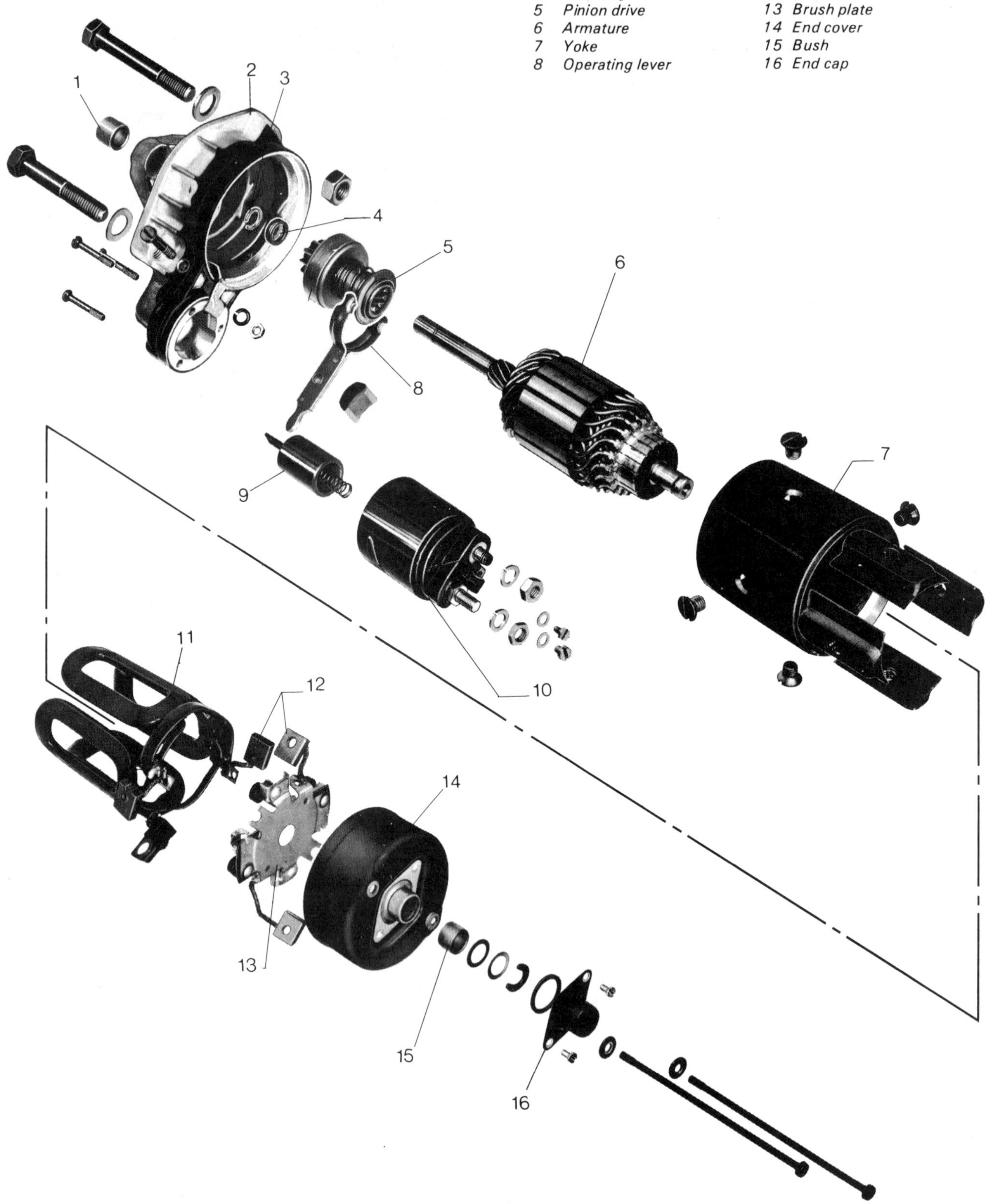

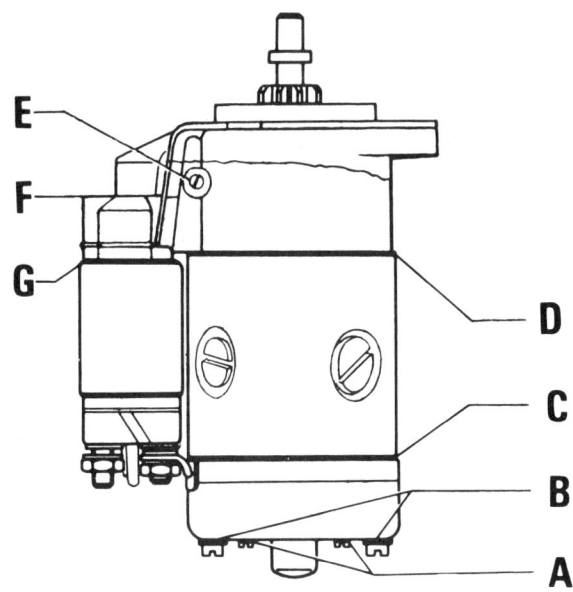

Fig. 10.24 Sealing points (1.6 litre) (Sec 12)

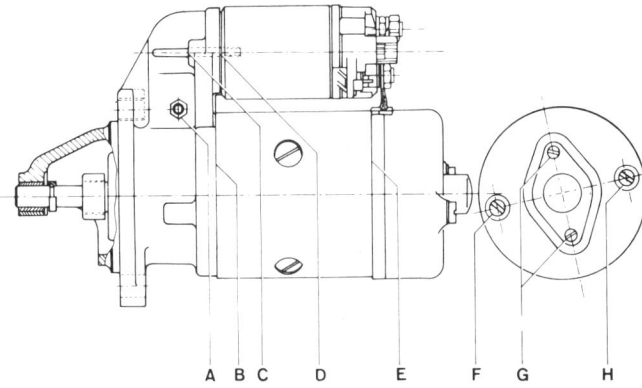

Fig. 10.25 Sealing points (2.0 and 2.2 litre) (Sec 12)

Fig. 10.26 Headlamp rim removal (single headlamps) (Sec. 13)

Fig. 10.27 Headlight mounting screws (single headlamps) (Sec. 13)

13 Headlamps – removing and refitting

1   Remove the radiator grille, by pulling the grille out of its retaining clips.

2   For vehicles with single headlamps (photo), prise off the three clips and remove the screw from the headlight rim and remove the rim.

3   Unscrew the knob from the beam height compensation control on headlights with H4 bulbs (photo). Remove the two screws from the top and the two screws from the front of the headlamp and pull the headlamp forward (photo).

4   Slide back the rubber sleeve from the turn indicator bulb, press in the clips at the top and bottom of the lampholder and remove the lampholder. Remove the cap and the 3-pin plug from the headlamp, to free the headlamp from the vehicle.

5   For vehicles with twin headlamps, remove the headlamp trim by removing the screw which is accessible between the two headlights when the bonnet is raised and then swinging the trim forward.

6   Remove the three screws which retain the lamp bezel. These three screws are equally spaced round the bezel and should not be confused with the beam adjustment screws which have springs on them.

13.2 Single headlamp installation

13.3(a) Beam height compensator

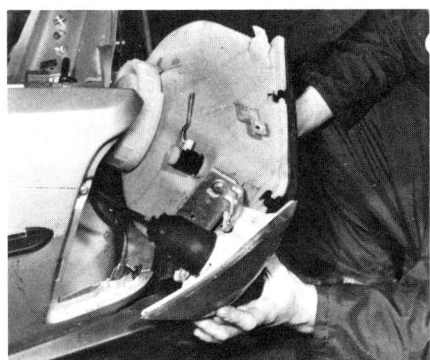

13.3(b) Removing a single headlamp assembly

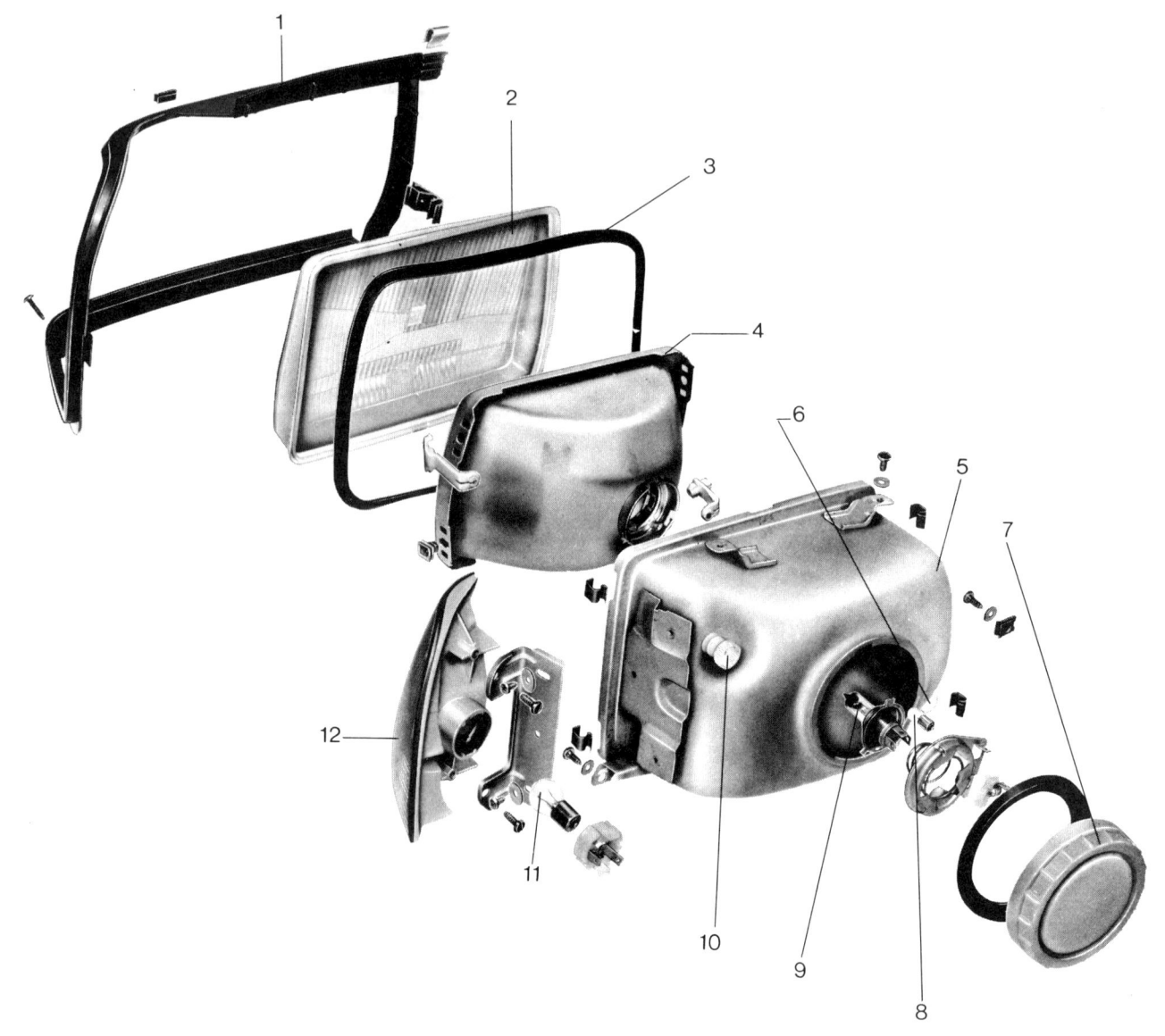

Fig. 10.28 Single headlamp assembly (Sec. 13)

1 Headlamp rim	4 Reflector	7 Cap	10 Vertical beam adjuster
2 Lens	5 Casing	8 Sidelight bulb	11 Turn indicator bulb
3 Seal	6 Lateral beam adjuster	9 Headlight bulb	12 Turn indicator lens

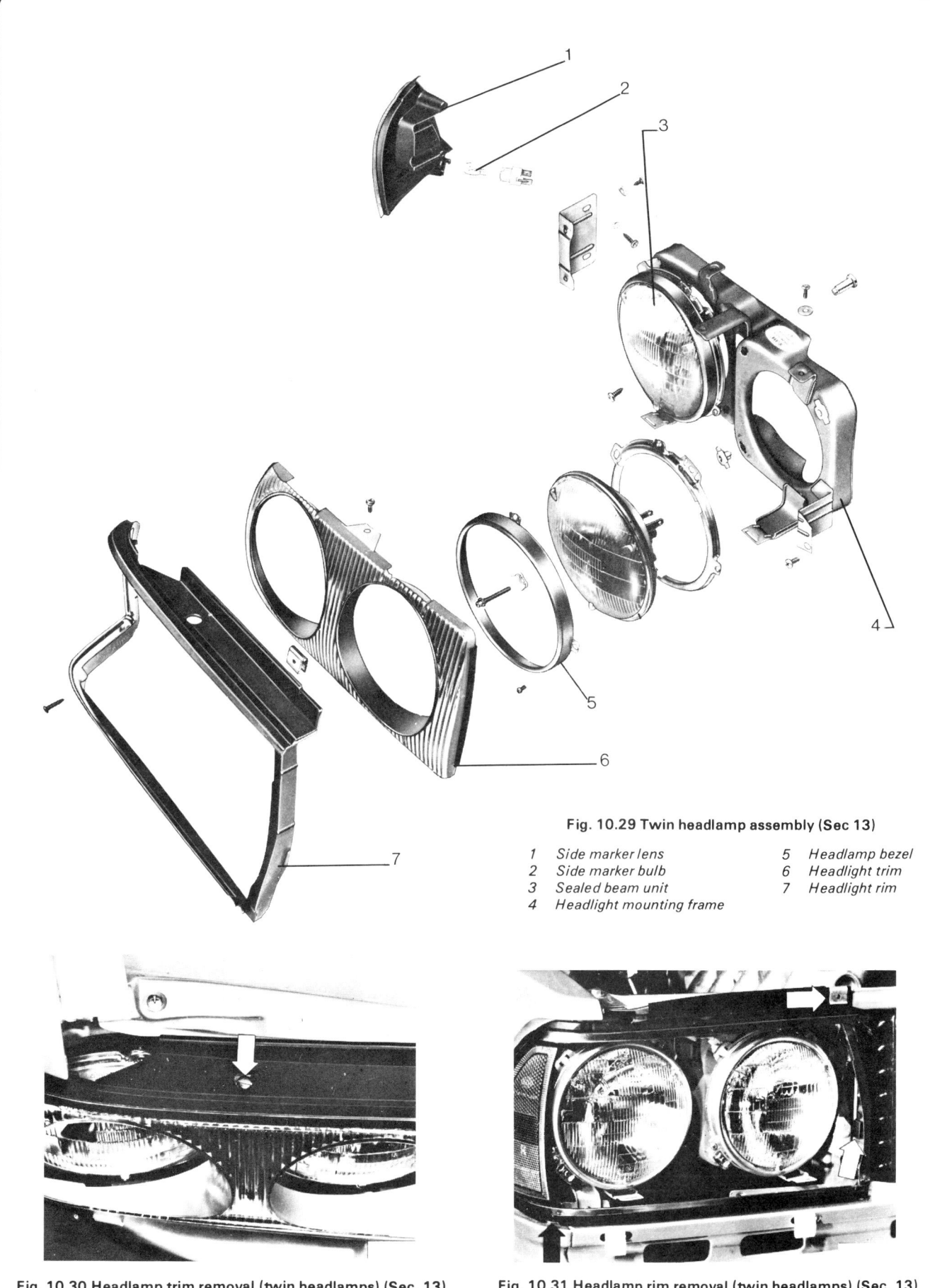

Fig. 10.29 Twin headlamp assembly (Sec 13)

1 Side marker lens
2 Side marker bulb
3 Sealed beam unit
4 Headlight mounting frame

5 Headlamp bezel
6 Headlight trim
7 Headlight rim

Fig. 10.30 Headlamp trim removal (twin headlamps) (Sec. 13)

Fig. 10.31 Headlamp rim removal (twin headlamps) (Sec. 13)

Fig. 10.32 Headlamp mounting frame screws (twin headlamps) (Sec. 13)

7   Take the sealed beam unit out of its support ring and pull the connector off the back.

8   To remove the complete headlight assembly, disconnect the plugs from each of the headlights and from the side marker light. Remove the two screws from the top and the two from the bottom of the headlight mounting frame (Fig. 10.32), and remove the frame with the headlight units in position on it.

9   If the headlight mounting frame is removed, the setting of the headlight beams will need to be checked after the frame has been refitted.

14 Rear light cluster – removing and refitting

1   The position of the bulbs within the cluster is different on the Audi 100 and the Audi 5000 (see Figs. 10.33 and 10.34), but the units are generally similar.

2   From inside the boot push up the cover over the cable entry to the light cluster and remove the cover.

3   Disconnect the multi-point plug.

4   Push in the clips at the two ends of the bulb holder and remove the bulb holder (photo).

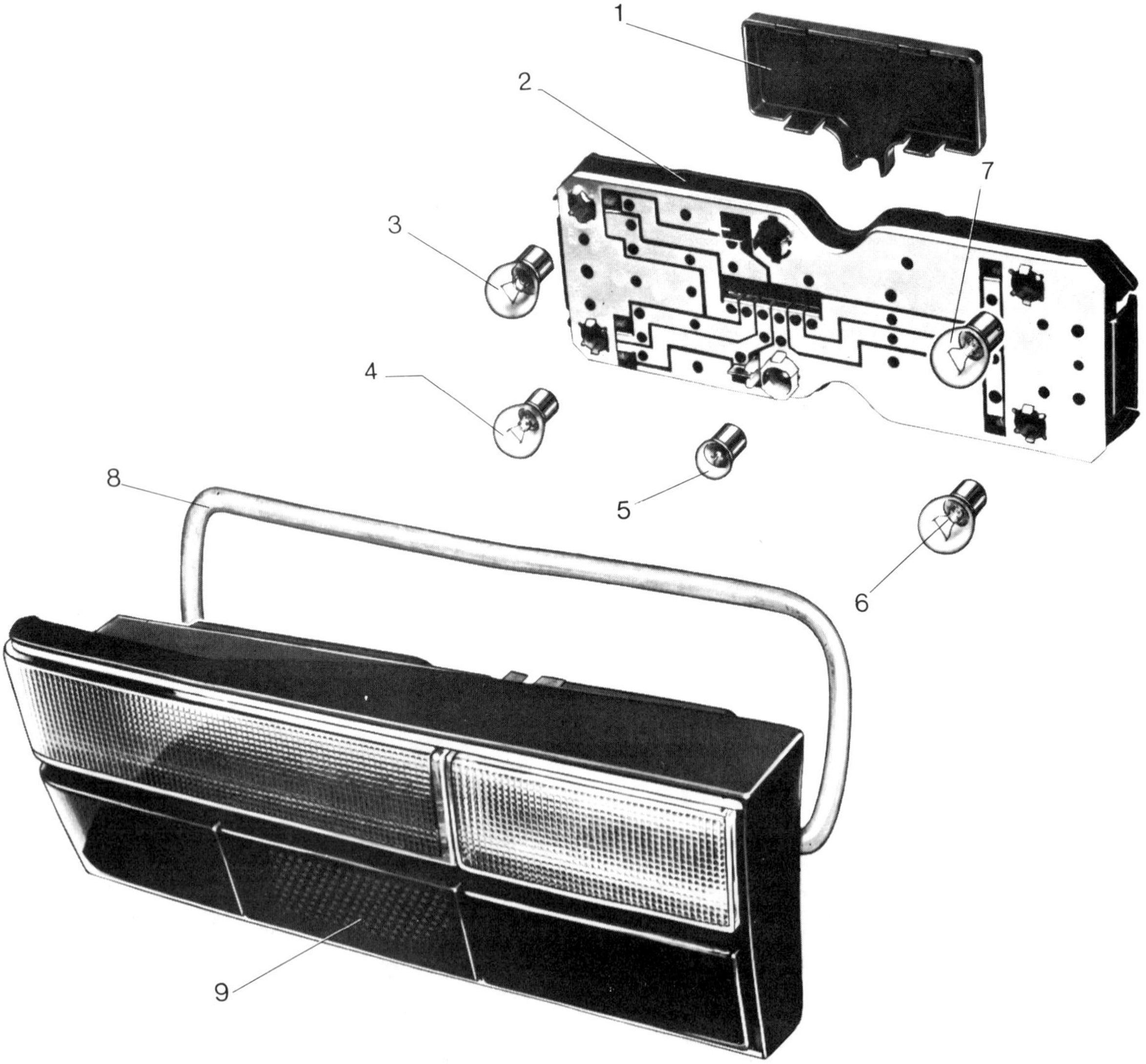

Fig. 10.33 Rear light cluster (Audi 100) (Sec. 14)

1 Cover	4 Brake light	6 High intensity rear light	8 Gasket
2 Bulb holder	5 Tail light	7 Reversing light	9 Lens
3 Turn indicator			

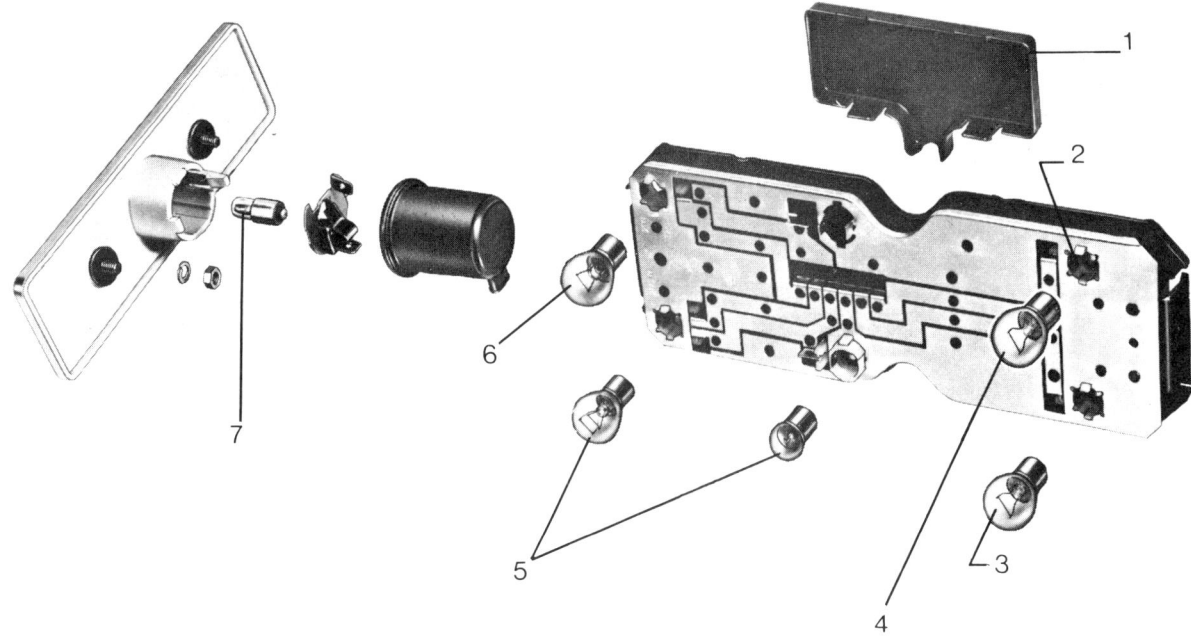

Fig. 10.34 Rear light cluster (Audi 5000) (Sec. 14)

1	Cover	3	Reversing light	5	Tail light	7	Side marker
2	Bulb holder	4	Brake light	6	Turn indicator		

14.4 Rear light cluster bulb holder

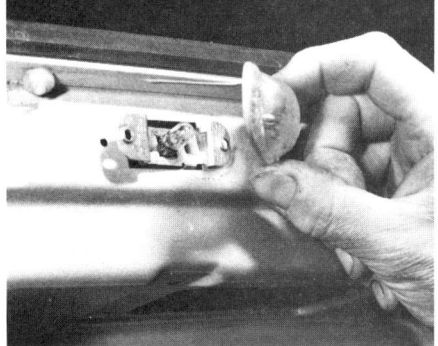

15.2 Number plate light

16.1 Position of relay fuse panel

5 Remove the six nuts and washers securing the lens. Push out the lens, taking care not to damage the gasket and peel off the gasket.
6 Use a new gasket when refitting the lens and take care to tighten the nuts evenly to avoid damaging the lens.

15 Number plate lights – removing and refitting

1 The number plate lights are recessed into the bottom edge of the boot lid.
2 Remove the two screws from the lens, remove the light assembly and separate the lens and the lampholder (photo).
3 Check that the assembly has been watertight and if not, clean off all corrosion.
4 Use a new gasket when refitting the lens.

16 Fuses and relays

1 All the principal circuits are separately fused and many of the individual items of electrical equipment have switching relays. Relays and fuses are mounted on a panel at the side of the plenum chamber in the engine compartment (photo).
2 It is unlikely that a fuse will blow unless there is a fault and the fault must be found and cured before a new fuse is fitted.
3 Never fit a fuse of greater rating than that given in Fig. 10.35

because this may permit overloading and damage to the wiring harness and may result in a fire.
4 All relays are of the plug in type. Relays cannot be repaired and if one is suspect, it should be removed and taken to an auto electrical workshop for testing (Fig. 10.36).

17 Bulbs – renewal

Headlamps – sealed beam
1 The inner sealed beam units are for high beam only and have one filament. The outer units are for high and low beams and have two filaments.
2 Remove the screw which is accessible between the two headlamps when the bonnet is raised and remove the headlight trim by swinging it forward.
3 Remove the three screws which retain the lamp bezel. These three screws are equally spaced round the bezel and should not be confused with the beam adjustment screws which have springs on them.
4 Take the sealed beam unit out of its support ring and pull the connector off the back.
5 Push the connector on to the pins of the new unit and fit the unit so that the three lugs on the glass engage in the slots in the support ring. Fit the bezel and refit the grille.
6 If the unit is renewed in this way and no other parts were disturbed, it should not be necessary to adjust the headlamp beam setting.

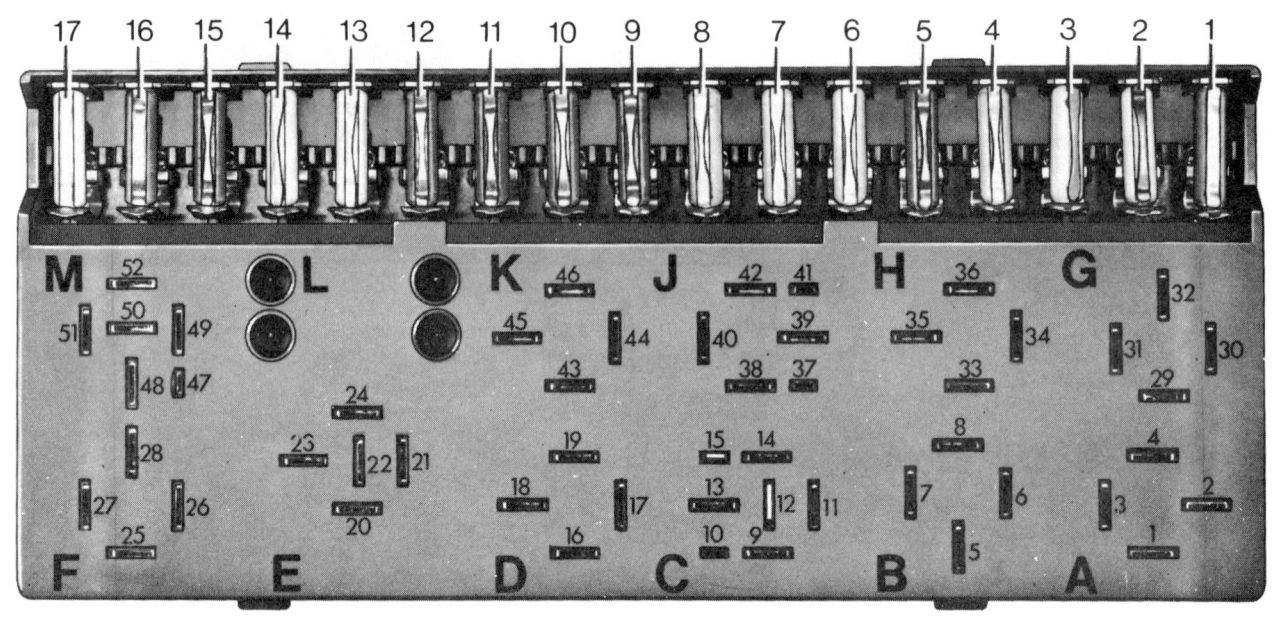

Fig. 10.35 Fuse and relay positions (Sec. 16)

Fuses:

1	Air conditioner and blower	25 amps
2	Foglights	8 amps
3	High beam headlight, LH	8 amps
4	High beam headlight, RH	8 amps
5	Electric fuel pump	16 amps
6	Side light, RH	8 amps
7	Side light, LH	8 amps
8	Glove compartment light, licence plate lights, instrument illumination	8 amps
9	Horn, instrument cluster, blower (2-speed)	16 amps
10	Radiator fan	25 amps
11	Brake lights	16 amps
12	Cigar lighter, radio, clock interior light	16 amps
13	Low beam headlight, RH	8 amps
14	Low beam headlight, LH	8 amps
15	Reversing lights, wiper motor	16 amps
16	Heater rear window	25 amps
17	Turn signals	8 amps

Relays:

A Relay, air conditioner and blower, or fresh air blower
B Auxiliary relay terminal 75
C Cruise control, or electric windows
D Horn relay
E Relay, headlight cleaners
F Not used
G Relay, foglights
H Relay, automatic gearbox
J Relay, fuel pump
K Relay, radiator fan
L Provision for 4 spare fuses
M Wipe/wash intermittent relay

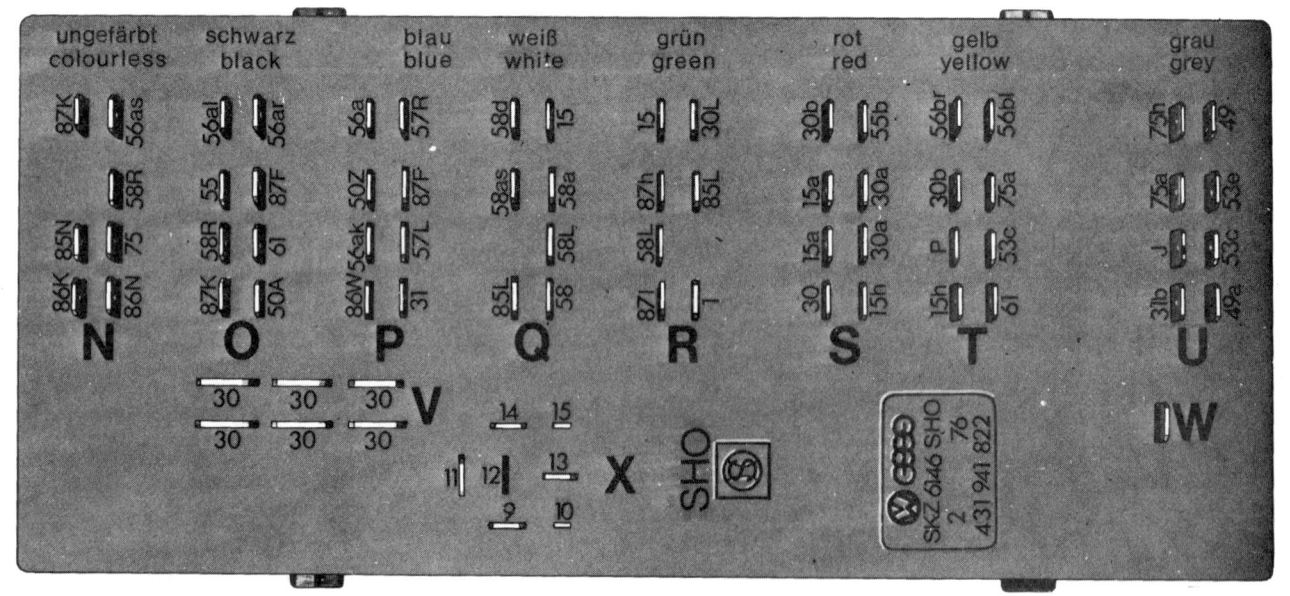

Fig. 10.36 Harness connections at rear of relay plate (Sec. 16)

N Instrument panel harness
O Front harness
P Instrument panel harness
Q Instrument panel harness
R Front harness
S Instrument panel harness
T Front harness
U Instrument panel harness
V Single plug (terminal 30)
X Power windows
W Connection for turn signal indicator light (for trailer operation)

Fig. 10.37 Headlamp trim retaining screw (arrowed) (Sec. 17)

Fig. 10.38 Removing the headlamp trim (Sec. 17)

Fig. 10.39 Headlamp bezel screws (arrowed) (Sec. 17)

Headlamps – semi-sealed beam

7　Switch off the headlights before changing a bulb and do not touch the glass of the bulb, because finger marks cause marking of the glass and loss of light output, also reduced life when the bulb gets hot.

8　Lift the bonnet, turn the plastic cap on the back of the headlight to the left and remove the cap (photo).

9　Disconnect the 3-pin plug, then press the retaining ring towards the reflector, turn it to the left and remove it (photo).

10　Remove the defective bulb from the reflector (photo) and replace it with one of the same type, ensuring that the flange on the bulb engages properly in the hole in the reflector.

11　Press the retaining ring against the reflector and turn it to the right as far as it will go.

12　Connect the 3-pin plug and then press on the plastic cap and turn

it to the right. The cap should be fitted so that the marking *Oben* is at the top.

Sidelights – single headlight models

13　The sidelight is part of the headlamp assembly and requires the removal of the cap, 3-pin plug and retaining ring as described in paragraphs 8 and 9 (photo).

14　Remove the sidelight bulb by pressing it in and turning to the left to release its bayonet fitting, then replace it by a bulb of the same type and rating.

Sidelights – twin headlight models

15　The sidelight is incorporated with the front turn indicator by using a double filament bulb.

16　Remove the two cross-head screws from the lens and carefully prise out the lens. Press the bulb in gently and turn it to the left to release its bayonet fitting.

17　Fit a new bulb of the same type and rating. Because of the asymmetrical arrangement of the pins the new bulb can only be fitted the correct way round.

18　Check that the gasket is in good condition and properly in position before refitting the lens. Tighten the screws evenly and do not overtighten them because this may crack the lens.

Rear lights cluster

19　Remove the bulb holder as described in Section 14, paragraphs 1 to 4. Remove the bulb by pressing it in gently and turning to the left to release it from its bayonet fitting.

20　Fit a new bulb of the same type and rating and refit the bulb holder and multi-pin plug.

21　The position of the various bulbs in the cluster is shown in Figs. 10.33 and 10.34.

Front turn indicators

22　*Single headlamp models*. The turn indicator is located outboard of

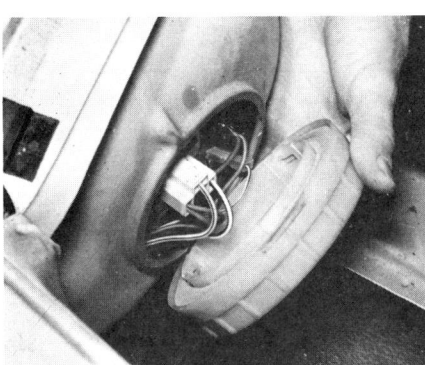

17.8 Removing the cap from the rear of the headlight

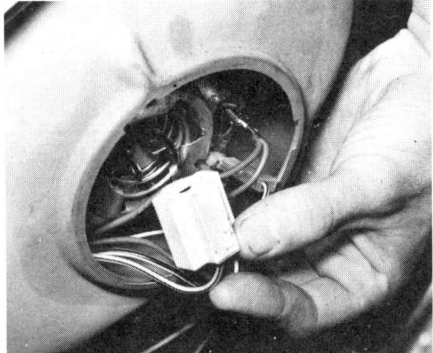

17.9 Disconnecting the headlight bulb 3-pin plug

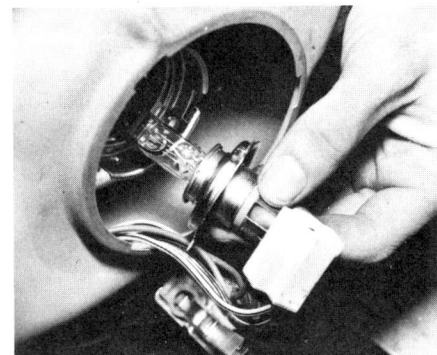

17.10 Removing the headlight bulb

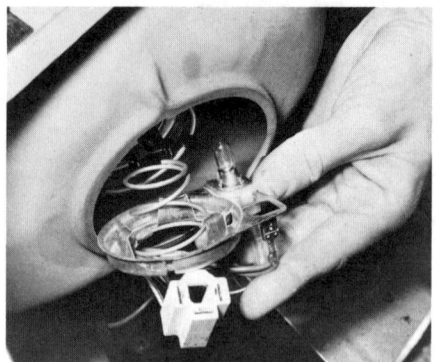

17.13 Removing the sidelight (single headlamp assembly)

17.23 Front turn indicator (single headlamp models)

18.2 Position of windscreen wiper motor (behind battery)

19.2 Windscreen wiper arm nut

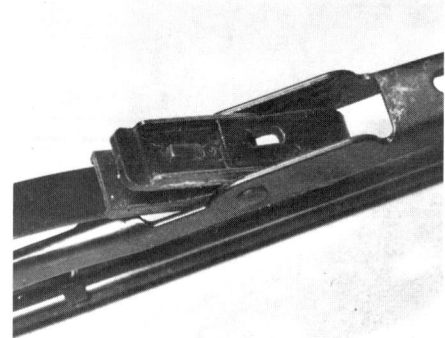

20.2 Windscreen wiper blade retaining clip

the headlamp and the unit is accessible when the bonnet is raised.

23 Pull back the rubber sleeve over the lamp holder assembly. Press in the clips at the top and bottom of the lampholder and withdraw it (photo).

24 Press the bulb into the holder and turn it to the left to release it from its bayonet fitting.

25 Fit a new bulb of the same type and rating, refit the bulb holder and slide the rubber sleeve into its original position.

26 *Twin headlamp models* The front turn signal is incorporated with the sidelight and renewing the bulb is as described in paragraphs 15 to 18 of this Section.

Number plate light

27 There are two number plate lights, fitted symmetrically on each side of the boot lock.

28 Unscrew and remove the two cross-head screws from the lens and remove the lens.

29 Press the bulb in and turn it to the left to release it from its bayonet fitting then fit a new bulb of the same type and rating.

30 Fit the lens and tighten the screws, but do not overtighten the screws because this may crack the lens.

Interior light

31 Insert a screwdriver under the lamp housing at the opposite end to the switch and press in the spring clip so that the assembly can be withdrawn.

32 Remove the festoon bulb from between the two spring contacts and fit a new bulb of the same type and rating.

33 Refit the light assembly by inserting the switch end first and then pressing in the other end until the spring clip engages.

Side marker lights

34 *Front.* Open the bonnet lid and pull the bulb holder out of its socket.

35 Press the bulb in and turn it to the left to release it from its bayonet fitting.

36 Fit a new bulb of the same type and rating and refit the bulb holder into its socket.

37 *Rear.* The method of renewing a side marker bulb is similar to that described for the number plate bulb in paragraphs 28 to 30.

18 Windscreen wiper motor – removing and refitting

1 Disconnect the battery leads.

2 Remove the battery retaining clamp and lift the battery out to give better access to the windscreen wiper motor (photo).

3 Disconnect the windscreen wiper motor from the wiring harness.

4 Remove the nut from the crank and draw the crank off the motor spindle.

5 Remove the three bolts holding the motor to the wiper frame and withdraw the motor from beneath the frame.

6 When refitting the motor, bolt it on to the wiper frame and reconnect it to the wiring harness. Fit the battery and connect the battery leads, then switch the wiper motor on and run the motor for at least two revolutions before switching *off*. This will ensure that the motor stops in its parked position.

7 Set the windscreen wiper blades to their parked position, connect the crank to the motor spindle, then screw on the nut.

19 Windscreen wiper arms – removing and refitting

1 Ensure that the blades are in their parked position.

2 Prise the plastic cover off the spindle nut and unscrew the nut (photo).

3 Pull the arm off the spindle.

4 When refitting the arms, hold them in their parked position when fitting them on to the spindle.

20 Windscreen wiper blades – removing and refitting

1 Lift the blade from the screen and swing the arm outwards away from the screen until it is in its service position.

2   Press in the spring clip on the blade assembly so that the protrusion on it is disengaged from the hole in the wiper arm and then pull the blade off (photo).

3   Fit the replacement blade, taking care to ensure that the protrusion on the clip is properly locked into the hole in the wiper arm.

21   Windscreen wiper linkage – removing and refitting

1   Remove the windscreen wiper arms, as described in Section 19.

2   Open the bonnet, remove the cover over the plenum chamber and

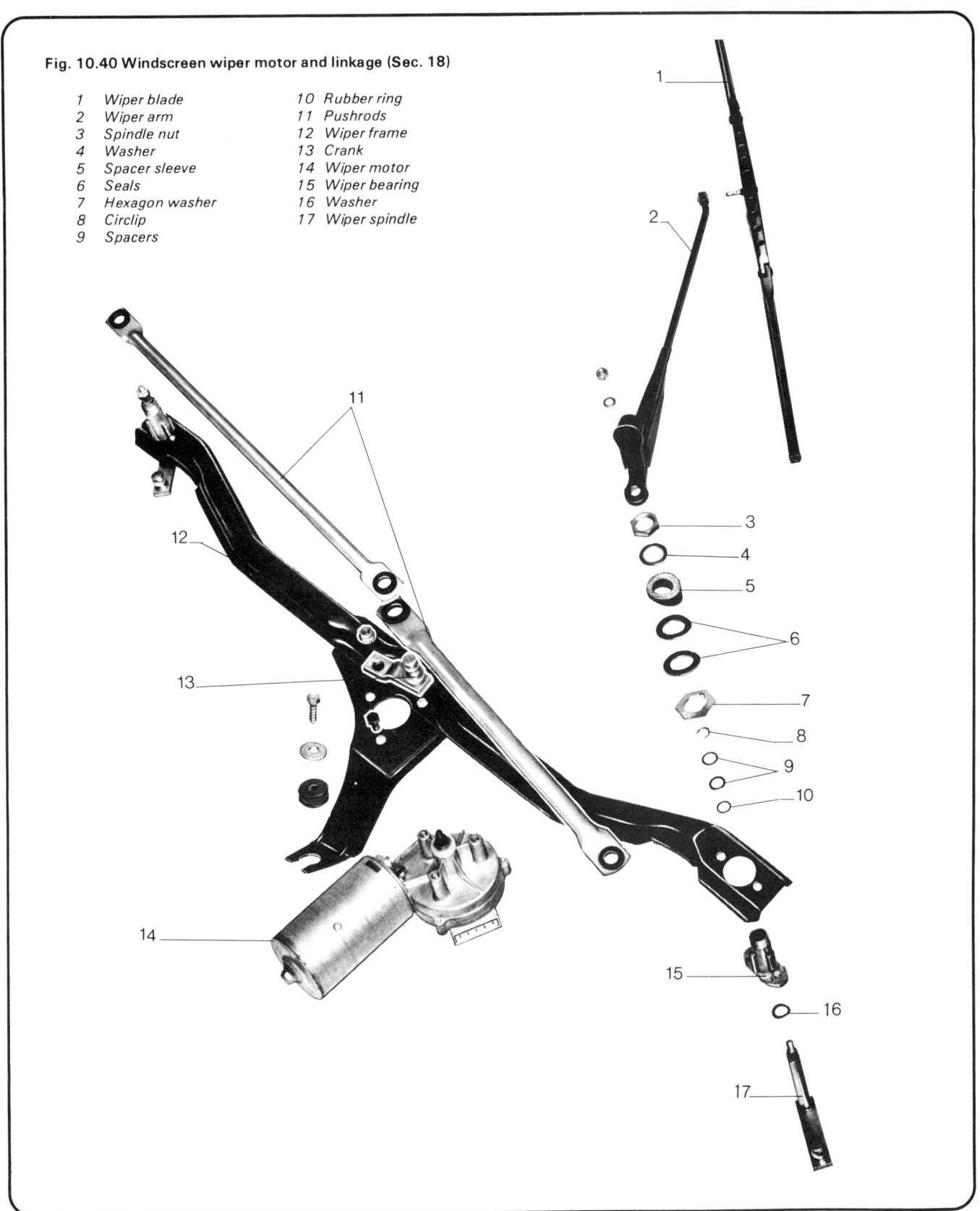

Fig. 10.40 Windscreen wiper motor and linkage (Sec. 18)

1	Wiper blade	10	Rubber ring
2	Wiper arm	11	Pushrods
3	Spindle nut	12	Wiper frame
4	Washer	13	Crank
5	Spacer sleeve	14	Wiper motor
6	Seals	15	Wiper bearing
7	Hexagon washer	16	Washer
8	Circlip	17	Wiper spindle
9	Spacers		

21.5 Windscreen wiper spindle nut

remove the battery.
3   Disconnect the windscreen wiper motor from the wiring harness.
4   Remove the bolt and washer from the rubber bush holding the wiper frame.
5   Remove the nut, washer, spacer sleeve and seal from each of the wiper spindles (photo), push the spindles down through the body panel and withdraw the wiper motor and linkage from the plenum chamber.
6   Remove the seal and washer from each of the wiper spindle bearings.
7   When refitting the linkage, fit new seals and ensure that the spacer sleeves are turned so that they fit the spindle bearings properly.

22 Windscreen wiper linkage – dismantling and servicing

1   Remove the wiper linkage from the vehicle and remove the motor from the linkage.
2   Prise the two pushrods off the crank arm and their respective wiper spindles.
3   Remove the circlip from the wiper spindle and take off the two spacers and the rubber ring.
4   Push the wiper spindle out of its bearing and take the washer off the spindle.
5   If the wiper bearings are worn and require renewal, saw, or file off the cast rivets which secure them to the wiper frame and then knock the bearings out of the frame.
6   Fit the new bearings and clinch, or hammer over the cast rivets to secure the bearing to the frame.
7   When reassembling the linkage, lubricate the wiper spindles and the balljoints with molybdenum disulphide grease. Ensure that all washers and spacers are refitted the same way as they were before dismantling.

23 Windscreen washer – removing, refitting and adjusting

1   Disconnect the battery leads.
2   Note the terminals to which the two pump wires are connected and remove the wires.
3   Pull the plastic pipe off the pump and lift the reservoir and pump out of the bracket.
4   Empty out the contents of the reservoir and then pull the pump out of the rubber bush in the reservoir. The pump cannot be repaired and if defective must be replaced by a new pump.
5   It is important that the electrical connections to the pump are correct if the pump is to operate properly. To check the connections, remove the wire from the negative terminal and connect the pump negative terminal to chassis earth. If the pump operates when the switch is pressed, the wire connected to the positive terminal is correct and the wire to the negative terminal can be re-connected.
6   If the jets require cleaning, do not use a needle or piece of wire

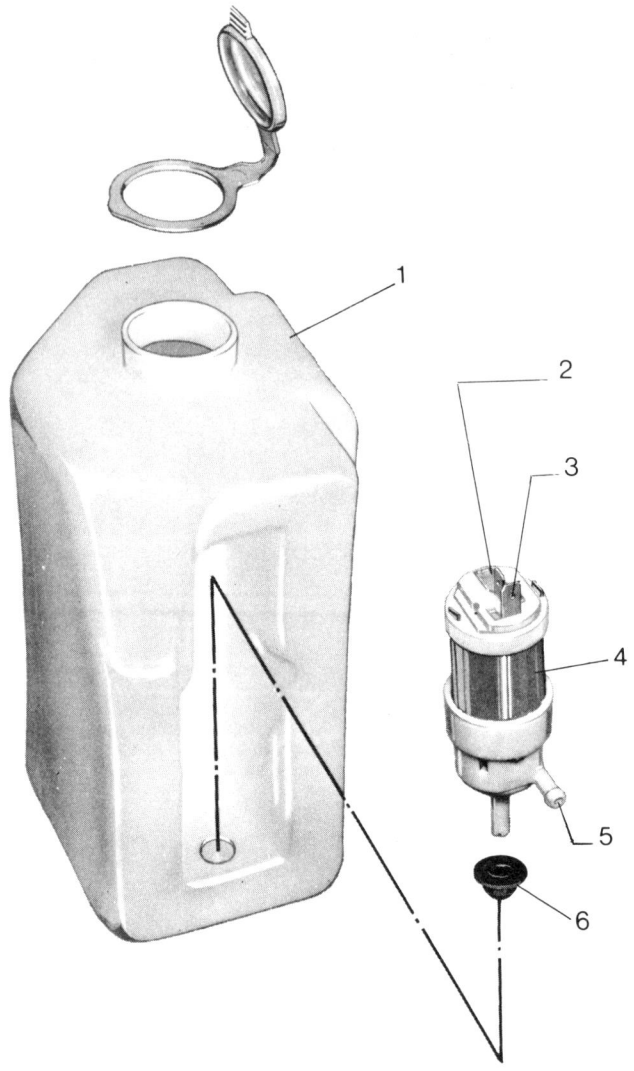

Fig. 10.41 Windscreen washer pump and reservoir (Sec. 23)

1 Reservoir	4 Pump assembly
2 Positive terminal	5 Pump outlet
3 Negative terminal	6 Rubber bush

because this will damage the jets. Jets can be cleaned without damage by using a brush bristle, or a piece of nylon line.
7   Use an approved screen cleaning fluid in the washer, because this will remove traffic film from the screen and will prevent the washer liquid from freezing.
8   To operate most effectively, the jets should be adjusted to give the spray patterns shown in Figs. 10.42 and 10.43.

24 Headlamp washer – removing, refitting and adjusting

1   Disconnect the battery leads.
2   Note the terminals to which the two pump wires are connected and remove the wires.
3   Release the clamp on the hose connected to the pump and pull the hose off.
4   Remove the screw securing the reservoir to the engine compartment (photo) and lift out the reservoir.
5   Empty the contents of the reservoir and then pull the pump out of the rubber bush in the reservoir. The pump cannot be repaired and if defective must be replaced by a new pump.
6   The washer system works at high pressure, and pressure valves are fitted to the jet mountings. It is therefore important that only high pressure reinforced hose and not plastic hose is used in the system

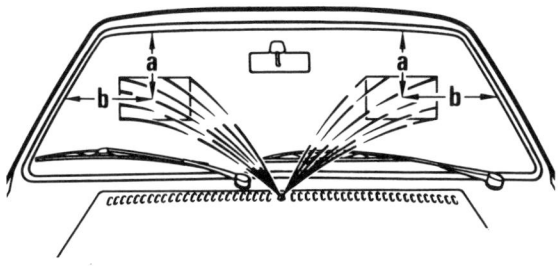

Fig. 10.42 Spray jet pattern (early models) (Sec. 23)

a 150 mm   *b* 400 mm

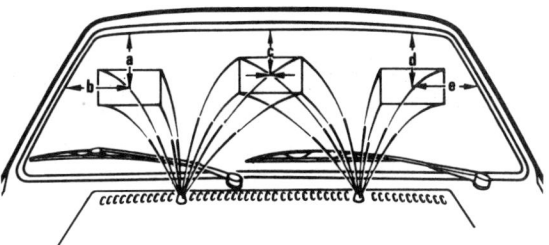

Fig. 10.43 Spray jet (later models) (Sec. 23)

a	260 mm	*d*	160 mm
b	220 mm	*e*	220 mm
c	120 mm		

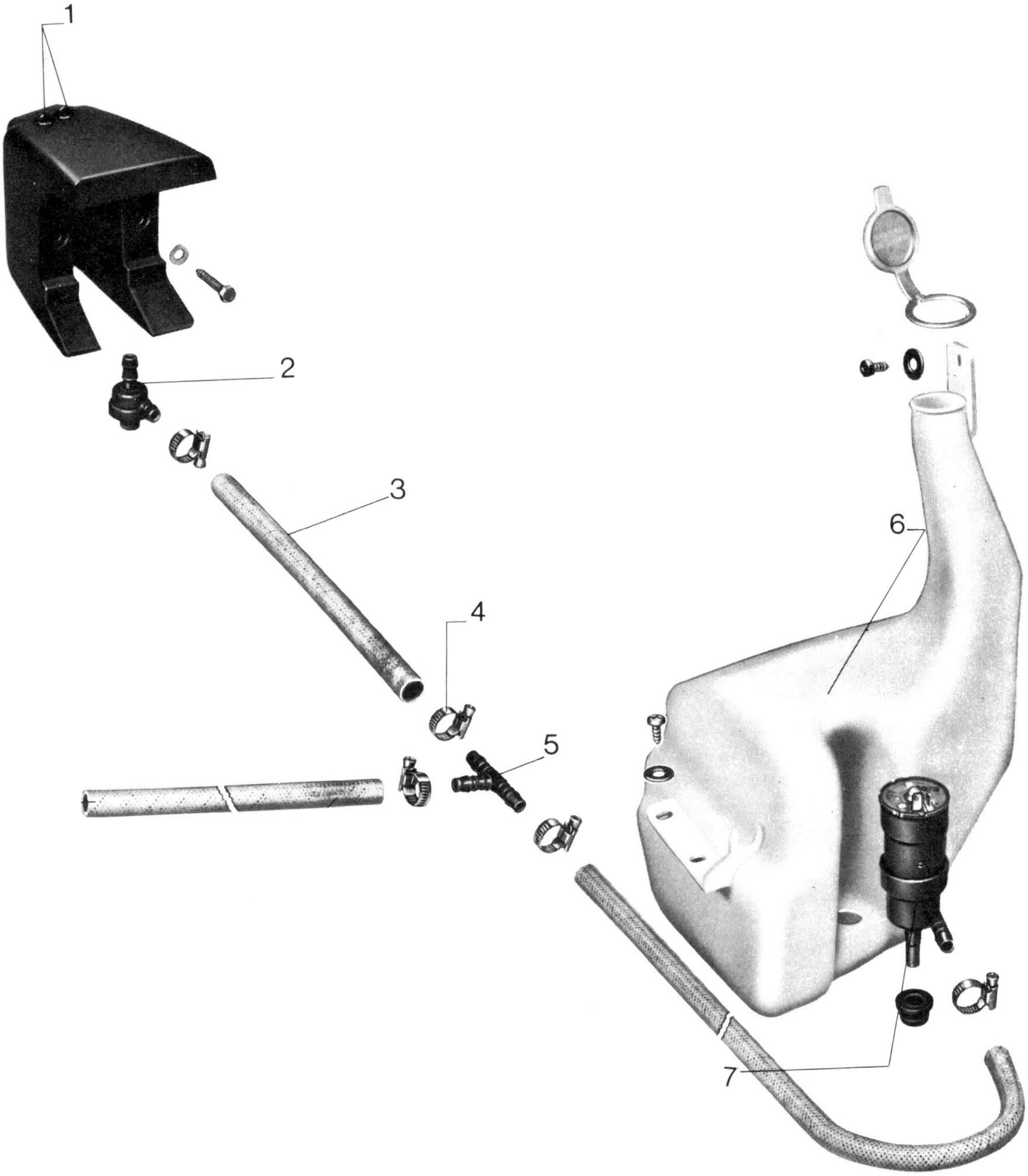

Fig. 10.44 Headlamp washer components (Sec. 24)

1	Jets	3	Reinforced hose	5	Connector	7	Pump assembly
2	Pressure valve	4	Hose clip	6	Reservoir		

24.4 Headlamp washer reservoir position (arrowed)

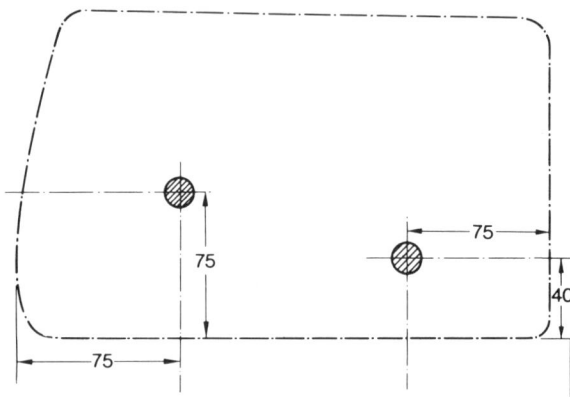

Fig. 10.45 Spray jet pattern – left-hand headlight (Sec. 24)

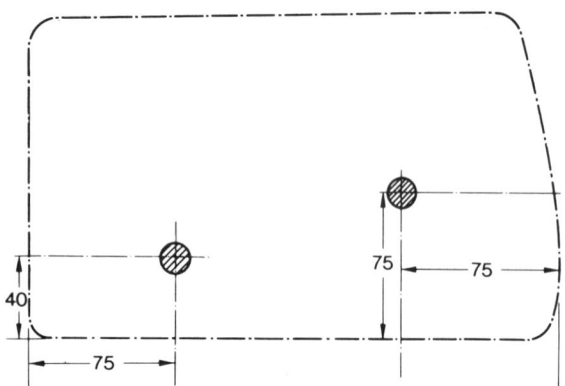

Fig. 10.46 Spray jet pattern – right-hand headlight (Sec. 24)

and that the hose clips are tightened adequately.

7   To remove the pressure valves, remove the two screws which secure the jet mountings to the bumper and take the jet mounting off. Disconnect the hose from the pressure valve and prise the pressure valve out, using a screwdriver. Lubricate the spigot of the pressure valve with petroleum jelly before prising it back into its mounting.

8   Correct aiming of the jets is shown in Figs. 10.45 and 10.46, but it is difficult to adjust the jets without the special tool which fits into them.

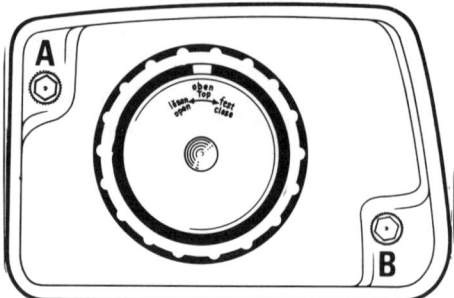

Fig. 10.47 Headlamp beam adjustment (single headlamps)
(Sec. 25)

A   Height adjustment   B   Lateral adjustment

Fig. 10.48 Headlamp beam adjustment (twin headlamps)
(Sec. 25)

A   Height adjustment   B   Lateral adjustment

25   Headlights – beam adjustment

1   To set the headlights correctly so that they meet legal requirements, optical beam setting equipment is required.

2   If the headlamp units have been removed, or if they are obviously well out of alignment they may be adjusted as a temporary measure until the car can be taken to a garage for precise beam alignment.

Single headlamp models

3   Behind the headlamp there is a knurled knob at the upper inner and lower outer corners of the assembly (Fig. 10.47). Beam aiming of the headlamps is achieved by turning these screws.

Twin headlamp models

4   The beam adjustment screws are diagonally opposite each other on the front of the headlamp (Fig. 10.48). To adjust the screws it is necessary to remove the headlight trim as described in Section 13 paragraph 5.

26   Horns

1   Two tone horns are fitted and they are mounted immediately in front of the front wheel (photo).

2   The horns may be of either Spartan, or Klaxon manufacture and there are slightly different fixings for the two types as shown in Figs. 10.49 and 10.50.

3   In the event of the horns not working, check that fuses S9 and S11 have not blown and check the horn relay by substituting another one.

4   If no electrical fault can be found, check the distance between the steering wheel and the steering column is correct (Chapter 11, Section 10), because this is necessary for proper operation of the horn switch.

26.1 Horn position

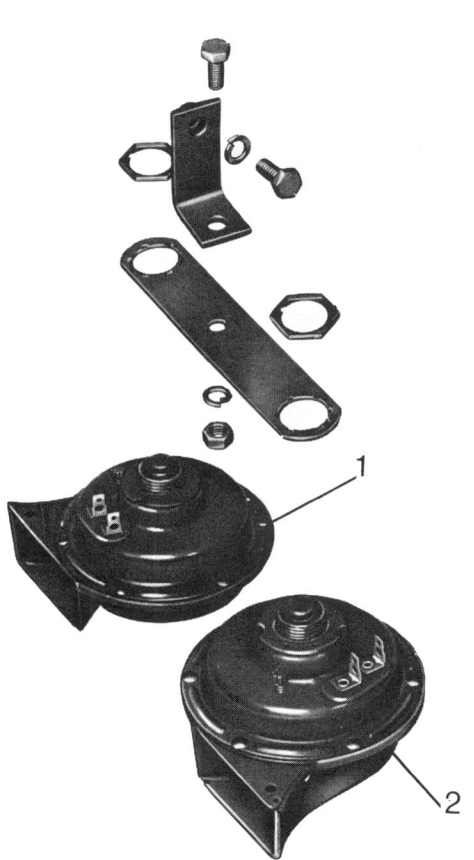

Fig. 10.49 Horns and bracket (Sparton) (Sec. 26)

1   High tone horn   *2   Low tone horn*

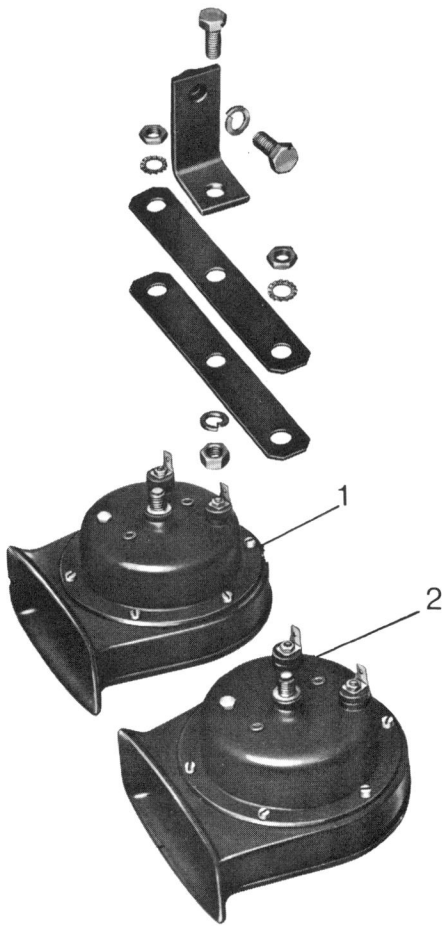

Fig. 10.50 Horns and bracket (Klaxon) (Sec. 26)

1   High tone horn   *2   Low tone horn*

27 Installing additional electrical equipment

1   Before fitting any additional electrical equipment, consult an Audi dealer. There are many approved accessories, but care is needed to ensure that cabling and fuses are not overloaded.

2   When fitting radios and tape players always consult a specialist because some additional suppressors may be required.

3   If any additional wiring is required, make certain that the cables are of the correct size for the load being connected. Whenever possible route the cables along existing cable routes and tape the additional cables to the existing wiring harness. Make sure that the cables cannot chafe against any metalwork and if it is necessary to take a cable through a panel, fit a grommet to the hole.

28 Fault diagnosis – electrical system

Symptom	Reason(s)

Starter

Fails to turn engine

Battery discharged, or defective
Battery terminals loose, or dirty
Starter motor solenoid faulty
Starter motor defective
Starter motor lead, or earthing strap loose

Turns engine slowly

Battery discharged, or defective
Battery terminals loose, or dirty
Starter solenoid faulty

Spins, but does not turn engine

Starter motor clutch defective or stuck

Noisy on engagement

Worn pinion
Loose mounting bolts

Battery

Does not hold charge

Battery defective
Electrolyte level low
Alternator drivebelt slipping
Alternator, or regulator defective

Ignition light stays on

Broken alternator drivebelt
Alternator, or regulator defective

Horn

Operates all the time

Horn push, or relay stuck
Horn cable earthed

Fails to operate

Blown fuse
Defective relay
Incorrect steering column adjustment
Defective horn

Sounds intermittently

Intermittent wiring fault such as dirty connection
Defective horn
Defective relay

Lights

Give poor illumination

Dirty contact, or corroded earth connection
Defective alternator, or regulator

Wipers

Motor fails to work

Blown fuse
Defective relay
Switch, or wiring fault
Worn brushes
Defective motor

Works slowly, or erratically

Excessive load, caused by worn linkage, or lack of lubrication
Worn, or dirty brushes

Key to Fig. 10.51 Wiring diagram for Audi 100, 100L and 100GL, (see pages 242 and 243)

Designation			in current track
A	–	Battery	10
B	–	Starter	5–8
C	–	Alternator	3
C 1	–	Voltage regulator	4
D	–	Ignition/starter switch	24
E 1	–	Light switch	26–29
E 2	–	Turn signal switch	29–31
E 3	–	Hazard light switch	36–39
E 4	–	Headlight dip switch and flasher	25
E 9	–	Switch for blower (upper lever)	75–76
E 13	–	Switch for blower (lower lever)	77
E 15	–	Switch for heated rear window with symbol	62
E 20	–	Regulator for instrument illumination	74
E 22	–	Wiper switch for intermittent operation	40–42
E 23	–	Switch for foglights and tail foglight	66, 67
F	–	Brake light switch	48
F 1	–	Oil pressure switch	53
F 2	–	Door contact switch, front, left	83
F 3	–	Door contact switch, front, right	84
F 4	–	Reversing light switch	37
F 9	–	Switch for handbrake indicator light	55
F 18	–	Thermo switch for radiator fan	44a
F 26	–	Thermo switch for automatic choke	16
F 34	–	Switch for brake fluid level warning light	56
G	–	Sender unit for fuel gauge	58
G 1	–	Fuel gauge	58
G 2	–	Sender unit for temperature gauge	59
G 3	–	Temperature gauge	59
G 5	–	Rev counter	60
G 7	–	Adaptor for workshop TDC sensor	33, 34
H	–	Horn control	52
H 2	–	Two-tone horn	50–52
J 2	–	Turn signal/hazard light flasher unit	34–36
J 4	–	Relay for two-tone horn	48–51
J 5	–	Relay for foglights	67–69
J 6	–	Voltage stabilizer	57
J 13	–	Blower relay	2, 3
J 26	–	Radiator fan relay	44,44a
J 31	–	Intermittent wipe-wash relay	40–42
J 59	–	Auxiliary relay	58,59
K 1	–	Highbeam indicator light	71
K 2	–	Alternator charge indicator light	54
K 3	–	Oil pressure indicator light	53
K 5	–	Turn signal indicator light	55
K 6	–	Hazard light indicator light	64
K 10	–	Heated rear window indicator light (instrument cluster)	63
K 13	–	Tail foglight indicator light	65
K 14	–	Handbrake indicator light	56
K 30	–	Indicator light for foglights and tail foglight	68
L 1	–	Twin filament bulb, left headlight	18, 19
L 2	–	Twin filament bulb, right headlight	20, 21
L 10	–	Bulb for instrument illumination	72
L 15	–	Ashtray light bulb	79
L 20	–	Tail foglight bulb	65
L 21	–	Heater control light bulb	74
L 22	–	Foglight bulb, left	69
L 23	–	Foglight bulb, right	70
L 28	–	Cigar lighter light bulb	79
L 29	–	Bulb, engine compartment illumination (with switch)	47
M 1	–	Sidelight bulb, left	23
M 2	–	Tail light bulb, right	45
M 3	–	Sidelight bulb, right	22
M 4	–	Tail light bulb, left	46

Designation			in current track
M 5	–	Tur signal bulb, front, left	27
M 6	–	Turn signal bulb, rear, left	31
M 7	–	Turn signal bulb, front, right	29
M 8	–	Turn signal bulb, rear, right	30
M 9	–	Brake light bulb, left	48
M 10	–	Brake light bulb, right	49
M 16	–	Reversing light bulb, left	37
M 17	–	Reversing light bulb, right	39
N	–	Ignition coil	13, 14
N 1	–	Carburettor/automatic choke	16
N 3	–	Bypass air cutoff valve	17
N 6	–	Series resistance lead	13, 14
N 23	–	Series resistance, blower	77
N 24	–	Series resistance, blower	76
O	–	Distributor	12–14
P	–	Spark plug connectors	12–14
Q	–	Spark plugs	12–14
R	–	Radio	80,81
S1, S2, S3, S4, S6, S7, S9, S10, S11, S12, S13, S14, S15, S16, S17		Fuses in relay plate with fuse holder	
T 1	–	Connector, single-pole (plenum chamber, left)	
T 1a	–	Connector, single-pole (luggage compartment, left)	
T 1b	–	Connector, single-pole (engine compartment, left)	
T 1c	–	Connector, single-pole (engine compartment, right)	
T 2	–	Connector, two-pole (behind dashboard)	
T 2a	–	Connector, two-pole (below left front seat)	
T 2b	–	Connector, two-pole (behind dashboard)	
T 2c	–	Connector, two-pole (luggage compartment, centre)	
T 2d	–	Connector, two-pole (instrument panel harness/slip ring connection)	
T 3	–	Connector, three-pole (behind dashboard)	
T 3a	–	Connector, three-pole (behind dashboard)	
T 7	–	Connector, seven-pole (behind dashboard)	
T 10/	–	Connector, ten-pole (instrument cluster)	
T 12/	–	Connector, twelve-pole (instrument cluster)	
T 12	–	Connector, twelve-pole (behind dashboard)	
T 20	–	Central socket	42
U 1	–	Cigar lighter	81
V	–	Windscreen wiper motor	40,41
V 2	–	Blower	76
V 5	–	Windscreen washer pump	43
V 7	–	Radiator fan	44
W 6	–	Glove compartment light	84
W 7	–	Interior light	82
X	–	Number plate light	85, 86
Y	–	Clock	70
Z 1	–	Heated rear window	62

①	–	Earthing strap, battery/body
⑦	–	Earthing strap, engine/alternator
⑧	–	Earthing point behind dashboard
⑨	–	Earthing point in engine compartment, front, left
⑩	–	Earthing point in engine compartment, front, right
⑪	–	Earthing point in luggage compartment
⑫	–	Earthing point at central socket
⑬	–	Earthing point in plenum chamber

Where wires end in numbered circles, the circles mark the connections of the test circuit leads which go directly to the connections of the central socket (T 20). The numbers in the circles correspond with the connections in the central socket.

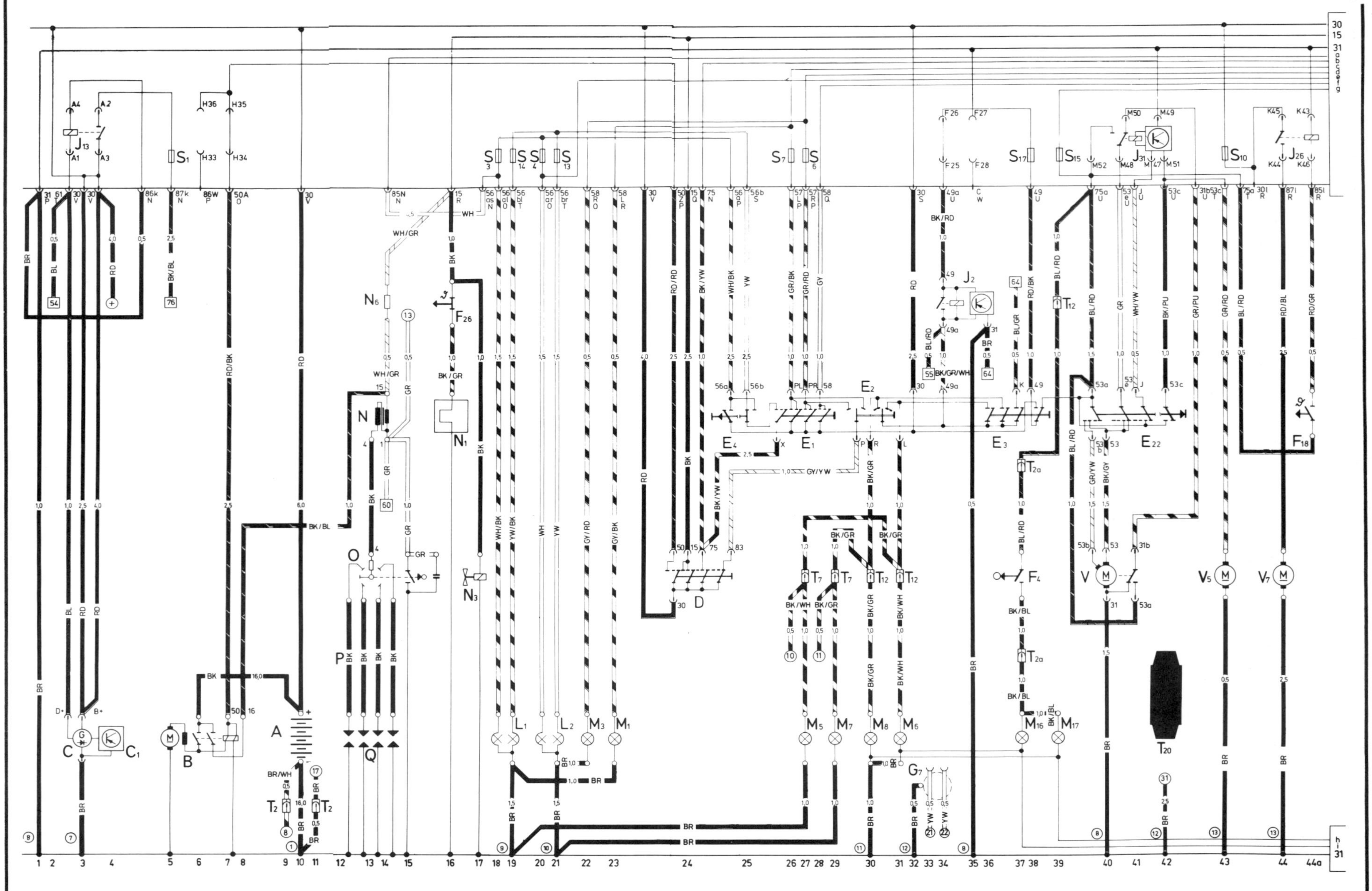

Fig. 10.51 Wiring diagram for Audi 100, 100L and 100GL (see page 241 for 'Key')

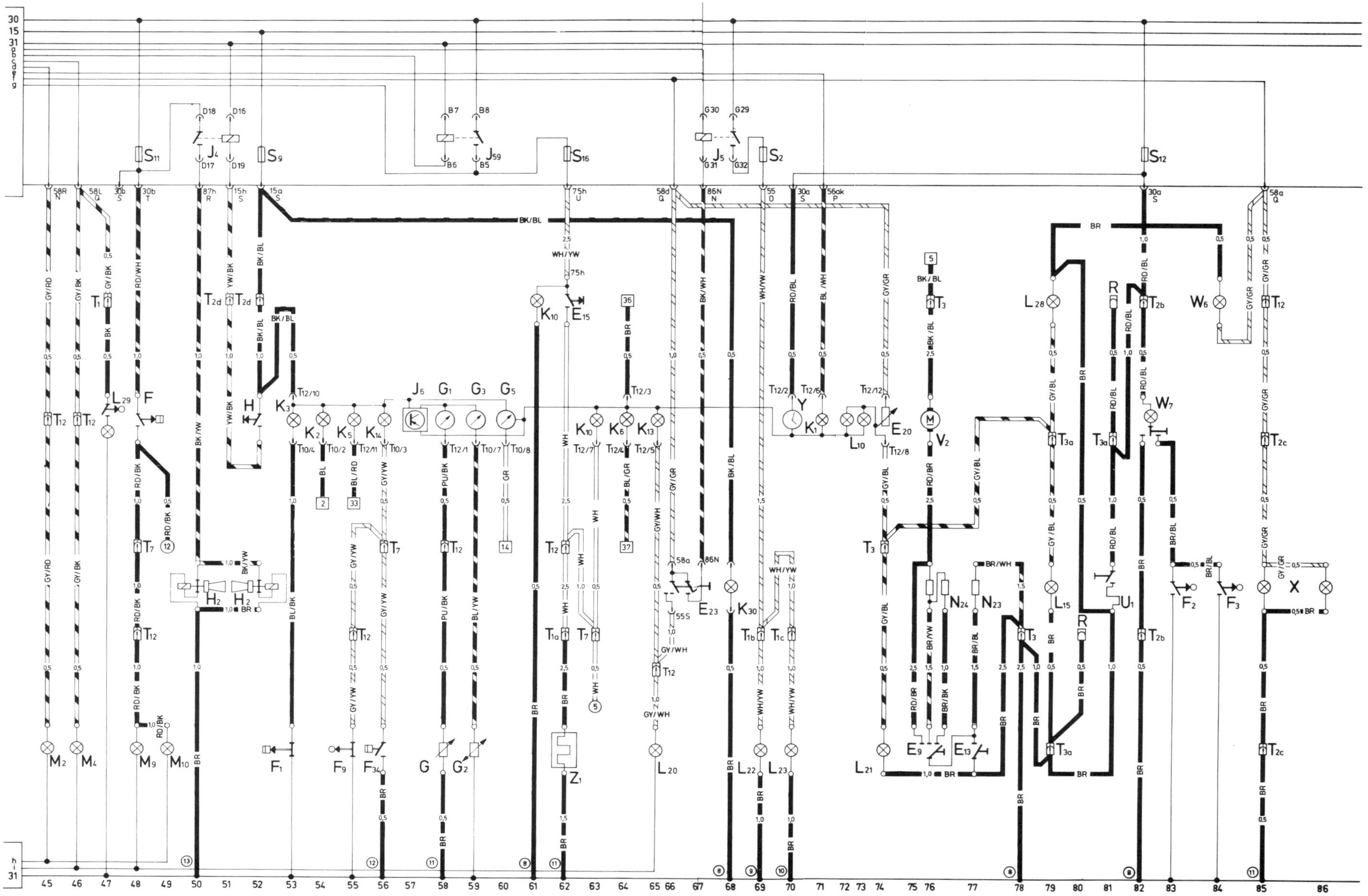

Fig. 10.51 Wiring diagram for Audi 100, 100L and 100GL (see page 241 for 'Key')

244

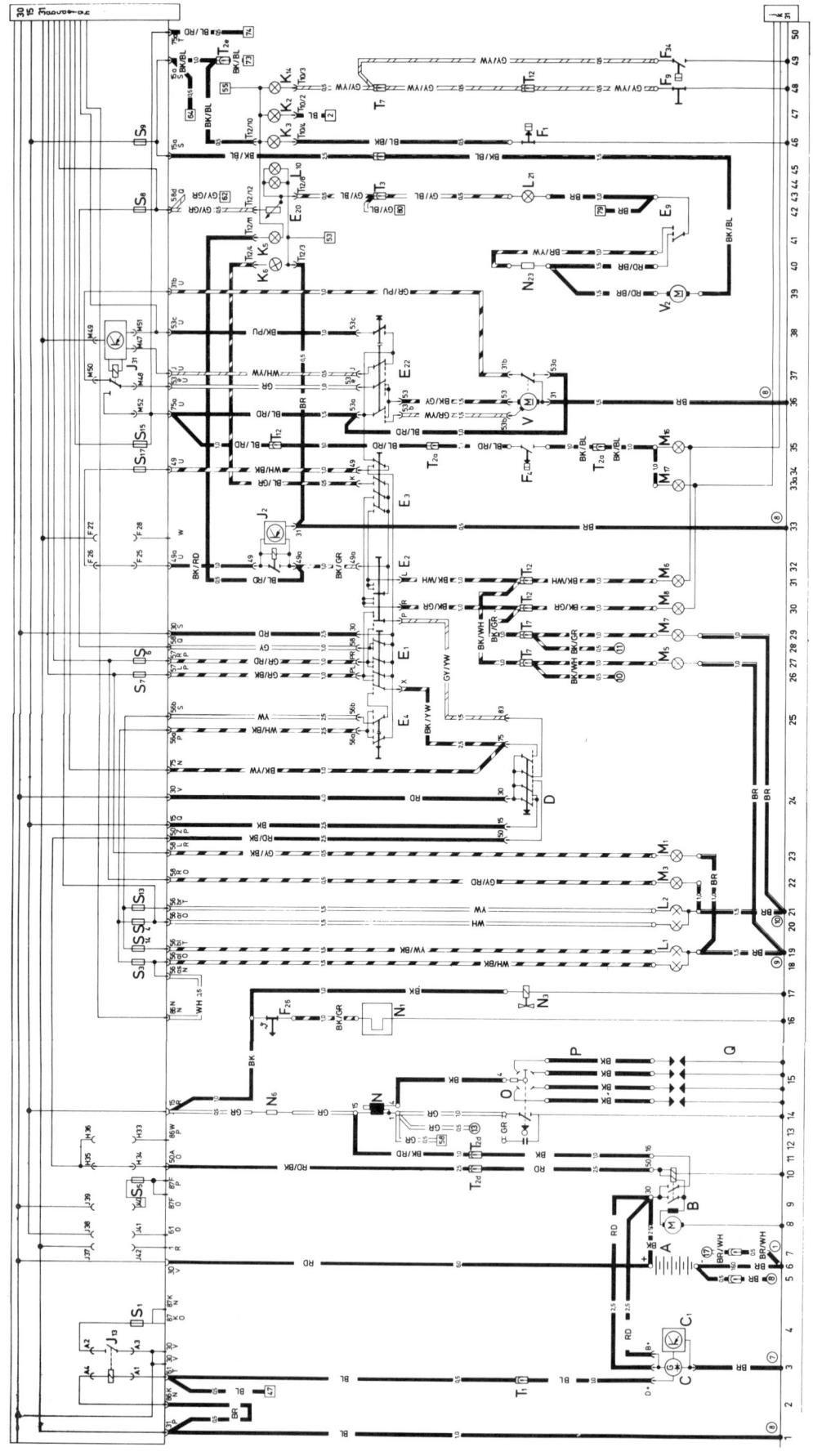

Fig. 10.52 Wiring diagram for Audi 100S, 100LS and 100GLS (see page 246 for 'Key')

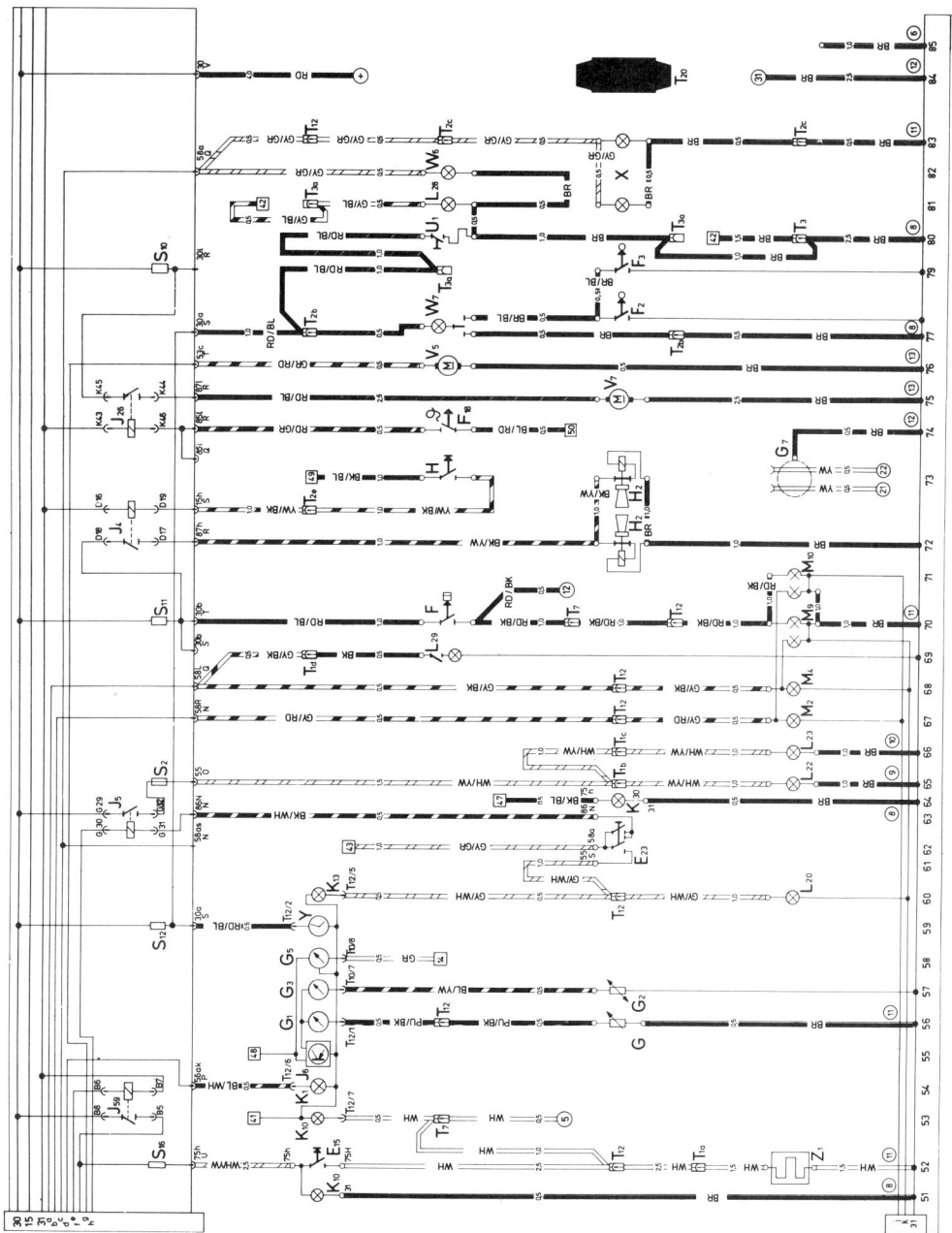

Fig. 10.52 Wiring diagram for Audi 100S, 100LS and 100 GLS (see page 246 for 'Key')

Key to Fig. 10.52 Wiring diagram for Audi 100S, 100LS and 100GLS (see pages 244 and 245)

Designation			in current track
A	–	Battery	5–7
B	–	Starter	8–11
C	–	Alternator	
C 1	–	Voltage regulator	4
D	–	Ignition/starter switch	26–29
E 2	–	Turn signal switch	30–32
E 3	–	Hazard light switch	33a, 34
E 4	–	Headlight dip switch and flasher	25
E 9	–	Blower switch	41
E 15	–	Switch for heated rear window with symbol illumination (K 10)	52
E 20	–	Control for instrument cluster illumination	42
E 22	–	Wiper switch for intermittent operation	36–38
E 23	–	Switch for foglights and tail foglight	61–63
F	–	Brake light switch	70
F 1	–	Oil pressure switch	46
F 2	–	Door contact switch, front, left	79
F 3	–	Door contact switch, front, right	79
F 4	–	Reversing light switch	35
F 9	–	Handbrake indicator light switch	48
F 18	–	Thermo switch for radiator fan	74
F 26	–	Thermo switch for automatic choke	16
F 34	–	Brake fluid level warning light switch	49
G	–	Sender unit for fuel gauge	56
G 1	–	Fuel gauge	56
G 2	–	Sender unit for coolant temperature gauge	57
G 3	–	Coolant temperature gauge	57
G 5	–	Rev counter	58
G 7	–	Adaptor for workshop TDC sensor	73, 74
H	–	Horn control	73
H 2	–	Two-tone horn	71–73
J 2	–	Turn signal/hazard light flasher unit	32, 33
J 4	–	Relay for two-tone horn	72
J 5	–	Foglight relay	63, 64
J 6	–	Voltage stabilizer	55
J 13	–	Blower relay	3, 4
J 26	–	Relay for radiator fan	74, 75
J 31	–	Intermittent wipe-wash relay	36–38
J 59	–	Auxiliary relay	53, 54
K 1	–	High beam indicator light	54
K 2	–	Alternator charge indicator light	47
K 3	–	Oil pressure indicator light	46
K 5	–	Turn signal indicator light	41
K 6	–	Hazard light indicator light	40
K 10	–	Heated rear window indicator light (instrument cluster)	53
K 13	–	Tail foglight indicator light	60
K 14	–	Handbrake indicator light	48
K 30	–	Indicator light for foglights and tail foglight	64
L 1	–	Twin filament bulb, left headlight	18, 19
L 2	–	Twin filament bulb, right headlight	20, 21
L 10	–	Bulb for instrument cluster illumination	44, 45
L 20	–	Tail foglight bulb	60
L 21	–	Heater control light bulb	43
L 22	–	Foglight bulb, left	65
L 23	–	Foglight bulb, right	66
L 28	–	Cigar lighter light bulb	81
L 29	–	Bulb, engine compartment illumination (with switch)	69
M 1	–	Sidelight bulb, left	23
M 2	–	Tail light bulb, right	67
M 3	–	Sidelight bulb, right	22
M 4	–	Tail light bulb, left	68
M 5	–	Turn signal bulb, front, left	27

Designation			in current track
M 6	–	Turn signal bulb, rear, left	31
M 7	–	Turn signal bulb, front, right	29
M 8	–	Turn signal bulb, rear, right	30
M 9	–	Brake light bulb, left	70
M 10	–	Brake light bulb, right	71
M 16	–	Reversing light, bulb, left	35
M 17	–	Reversing light bulb, right	33a
N	–	Ignition coil	14
N 1	–	Automatic choke (carburetter)	16
N 3	–	Bypass air cutoff valve	17
N 6	–	Series resistance	14
N 23	–	Series resistance for blower	40
O	–	Distributor	15
P	–	Spark plug connectors	15
Q	–	Spark plugs	15
S1 to S17 inclusive – Fuses in relay plate with fuse holder			
T 1	–	Connector, single-pole (engine compartment, front, right)	
T 1a	–	Connector, single-pole (luggage compartment, left)	
T 1b	–	Connector, single-pole (engine compartment, left)	
T1c	–	Connector, single-pole (engine compartment, right)	
T 1d	–	Connector, single-pole (plenum chamber, left)	
T 2a	–	Connector, two-pole (below left front seat)	
T 2b	–	Connector, two-pole (behind dashboard)	
T 2c	–	Connector, two-pole (luggage compartment, centre)	
T 2d	–	Connector, two-pole (engine compartment, front, right)	
T 2e	–	Connector, two-pole (instrument panel harness/slip ring connection)	
T 3	–	Connector, three-pole (behind dashboard)	
T 3a	–	Connector, three-pole (behind dashboard)	
T 7	–	Connector, seven-pole (behind dashboard)	
T 10/	–	Connector, ten-pole (instrument cluster)	
T 12/	–	Connector, twelve-pole (instrument cluster)	
T 12	–	Connector, twelve-pole (behind dashboard)	
T 20	–	Central socket	84
U 1	–	Cigar lighter	80
V	–	Wiper motor	36–37
V 2	–	Blower	39
V 5	–	Windscreen washer pump	76
V 7	–	Radiator fan	75
W 6	–	Glove compartment light	82
W 7	–	Interior light	77
X	–	Number plate light	81, 83
Y	–	Clock	59
Z 1	–	Heated rear window	52

①	–	Earthing strap, battery/body
⑥	–	Earthing strap, body/engine support
⑦	–	Earthing strap, engine/alternator
⑧	–	Earthing point behind dashboard
⑨	–	Earthing point in engine compartment, front, left
⑩	–	Earthing point in engine compartment, front, right
⑪	–	Earthing point in luggage compartment
⑫	–	Earthing point on central socket
⑬	–	Earthing point in plenum chamber

Where wires end in numbered circles, the circles mark the connections of the test circuit leads which go directly to the connections of the central socket (T 20). The numbers in the circles correspond with the connections in the central socket.

Key to Fig. 10.53 Wiring diagram for Audi 100 5E, 100 L 5E and 100 GL 5E (see pages 248 and 249)

Designation		in current track
A	– Battery	9
B	– Starter	5–8
C	– Alternator	1, 2
C 1	– Voltage regulator	3
D	– Ignition/starter switch	29–32
E 1	– Light switch	35–37
E 2	– Turn signal switch	38–40
E 3	– Hazard light switch	42–44
E 4	– Headlight dip switch and flasher	32–34
E 9	– Blower switch (control lever)	63–67
E 13	– Blower switch (OFF button)	71
E 15	– Switch for heated rear window with symbol illumination	88
E 20	– Regulator for instrument cluster illumination	70
E 22	– Wiper switch for intermittent operation	46–52
E 23	– Switch for foglights and tail foglight with symbol illumination	90–92
E 49	– Blower switch, intermediate speed	68–70
E 50	– Defroster switch	68
F 1	– Oil pressure switch	82
F 2	– Door contact switch, front, left	78
F 3	– Door contact switch, front, right	79
F 4	– Reversing light switch	45
F 9	– Handbrake indicator light switch	80
F 18	– Thermo switch for radiator fan	56
F 21	– Brake pressure switch 1	60
F 22	– Brake pressure switch 2	59
F 26	– Thermo switch for cold start circuit	4
F 34	– Brake fluid level warning light switch	81
G	– Sender unit for fuel gauge	84
G 1	– Fuel gauge	84
G 2	– Sender unit for temperature gauge	83
G 3	– Temperature gauge	83
G 5	– Rev counter	85
G 6	– Electric fuel pump	22
H	– Horn control	62
H 2	– Two-tone horn	61–63
J 2	– Turn signal/hazard light flasher unit	39–41
J 4	– Relay, two-tone horn	61–63
J 5	– Foglight relay	91–94
J 6	– Voltage stabilizer	85
J 13	– Blower relay	3–5
J 17	– Fuel pump relay	17–21
J 31	– Intermittent wipe/wash relay	47–52
J 59	– Auxiliary relay	86–88
K 1	– High beam indicator light	67
K 2	– Alternator charge indicator light	1
K 3	– Oil pressure indicator light	82
K 5	– Turn signal indicator light	81
K 6	– Hazard light indicator light	79
K 10	– Heated rear window indicator light	86
K 13	– Tail foglight indicator light (not for Switzerland and Finland)	87
K 14	– Handbrake indicator light	80
K 17	– Symbol illumination for foglight and tail foglight switch	92
L 1	– Twin filament bulb, left headlight	23, 24
L 2	– Twin filament bulb, right headlight	25, 26
L 10	– Bulb for instrument cluster illumination	71, 72
L 20	– Tail foglight bulb (not for Switzerland and Finland)	90
L 21	– Bulb for heater control illumination	71
L 22	– Foglight bulb, left	93
L 23	– Foglight bulb, right	95
L 28	– Cigar lighter light bulb	73
L 29	– Bulb, engine compartment light with switch	58
M 1	– Sidelight bulb, left	28
M 2	– Tail light bulb, right	53
M 3	– Sidelight bulb, right	27
M 4	– Tail light bulb, left	54

Designation		in current track
M 5	– Front turn signal bulb, left	36
M 6	– Rear turn signal bulb, left	40
M 7	– Front turn signal bulb, right	37
M 8	– Rear turn signal bulb, right	38
M 9	– Brake light bulb, left	59
M 10	– Brake light bulb, right	60
M 16	– Reversing light bulb, left	45
M 17	– Reversing light bulb, right	43
N	– Ignition coil	12–14
N 6	– Series resistance lead	11
N 9	– Warm-up regulator	20
N 17	– Cold start valve	6
N 21	– Auxiliary air regulator	20
N 23	– Series resistance, blower	68
N 24	– Series resistance, blower	64
N 41	– Transistorized ignition control unit	13–18
O	– Distributor	12–16
P	– Spark plug connectors	12–16
Q	– Spark plugs	12–16
S1 to S17 inclusive	– Fuses in relay plate with fuse holder	
T 1	– Connector, single-pole (engine compartment, right)	
T 1a	– Connector, single-pole (near ignition coil)	
T 1b	– Connector, single-pole (behind dashboard)	
T 1c	– Connector, single-pole (engine compartment, front, left)	
T 1d	– Connector, single-pole (engine compartment, front, right)	
T 2	– Connector, two-pole (engine compartment, right)	
T 2a	– Connector, two-pole (below rear seat)	
T 2b	– Connector, two-pole (below left front seat)	
T 2c	– Connector, two-pole (instrument panel harness/slip ring connection)	
T 2d	– Connector, two-pole (below hatrack)	
T 2e	– Connector, two-pole (behind dashboard)	
T 3	– Connector, three-pole (behind dashboard)	
T 3a	– Connector, three-pole (behind dashboard – connection for centre console harness)	
T 7	– Connector, seven-pole (behind dashboard)	
T 10/	– Connector, ten-pole (instrument cluster)	
T 12/	– Connector, twelve-pole (instrument cluster)	
T 12	– Connector, twelve-pole (behind dashboard)	
U 1	– Cigar lighter	74
V	– Windscreen wiper motor	46–50
V 2	– Blower	64
V 5	– Windscreen washer pump	20
V 7	– Radiator fan	56
W	– Interior light	77
W 6	– Glove compartment light	73
X	– Number plate light	73, 75
Y	– Clock	68
Z 1	– Heated rear window	88

①	– Earthing strap, battery/body
⑦	– Earthing strap, engine/alternator
⑧	– Earthing point behind dashboard
⑨	– Earthing point in engine compartment, front, left
⑩	– Earthing point in engine compartment, front, right
⑪	– Earthing point in luggage compartment
⑭	– Earthing point, below rear seat
⑮	– Earthing point, left wheelhousing
⑯	– Earthing point, hatrack

*On vehicles for Sweden, Switzerland, Norway, Holland and Denmark foglight relay (J5) is connected directly to headlight dip switch and flasher switch (E4), terminal 56, via contact N 85 N on relay plate

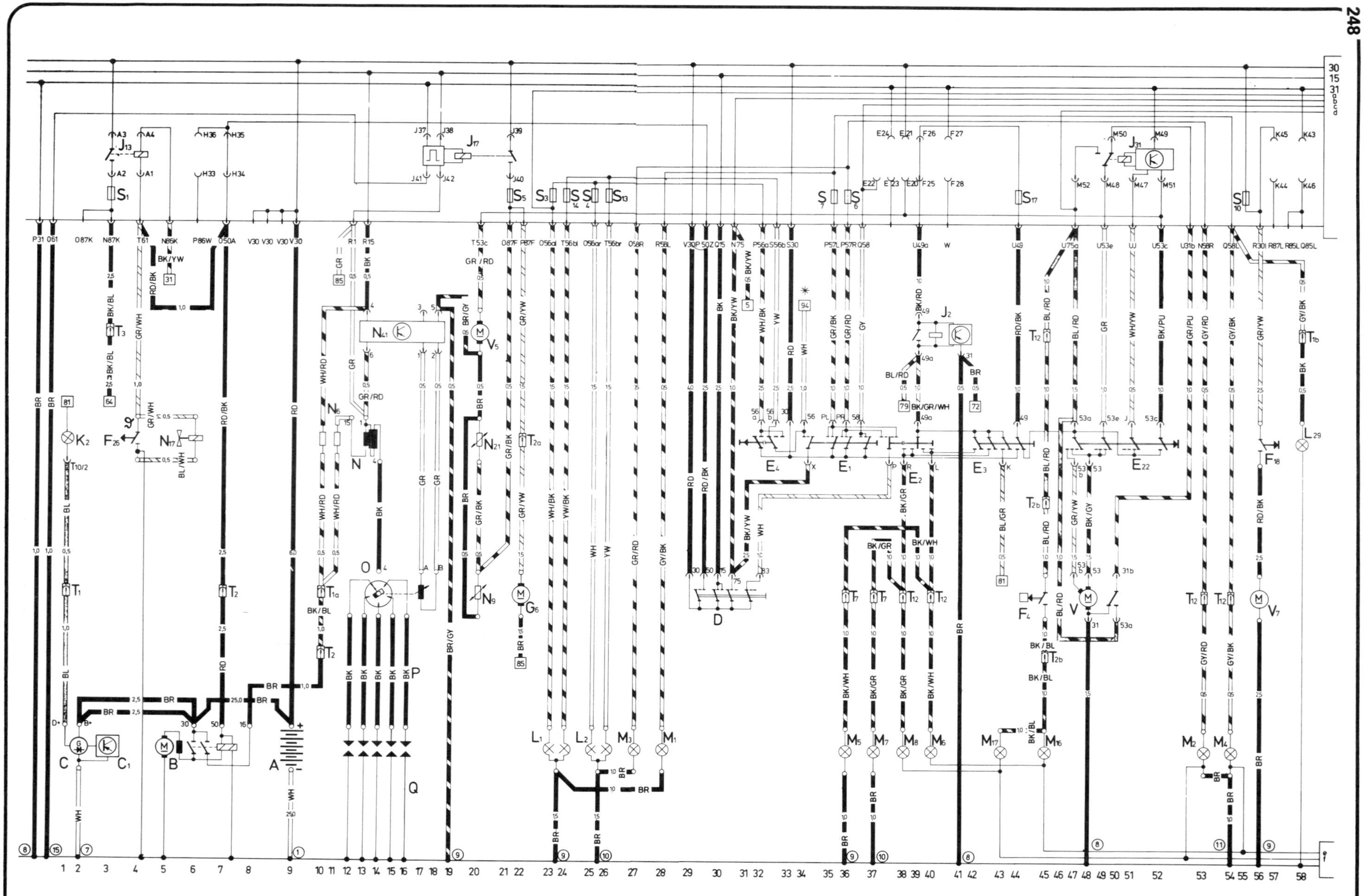

Fig. 10.53 Wiring diagram 100 5E, 100 L 5E and 100 GL 5E (see page 247 for 'Key')

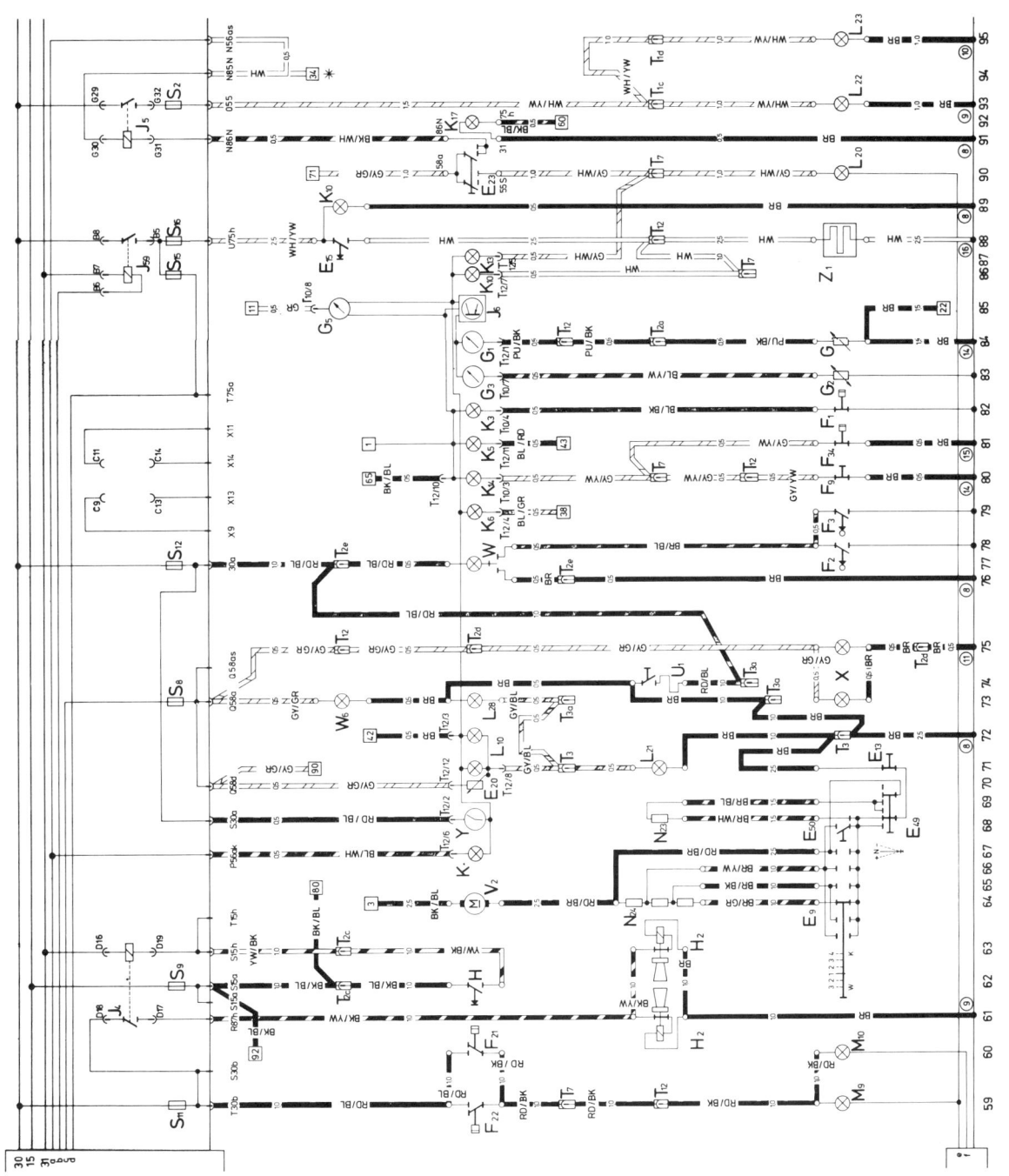

Fig. 10.53 Wiring diagram for 100 5E, 100 L 5E and 100 GL 5E (see page 247 for 'Key')

Chapter 11 Front suspension, steering and driveshafts

Contents

Specifications

Steering

Steering type .... Rack-and-pinion, with, or without power assistance

Wear limits:
Permissible steering play .... Nil
Permissible play at tie-rod ends .... Nil

Steering wheel turns from lock-to-lock:
Manual steering .... 4·69
Power assisted steering .... 3·76

Overall steering ratio:
Manual steering .... 22·9
Power assisted steering .... 18·4

Power steering system:
Pump maximum pressure (5 seconds duration) .... 68 to 82 kg/cm² (967 to 1166 lbf/in²)
System operating pressure .... 68 to 82 kg/cm² (967 to 1166 lbf/in²)
Fluid specification .... Dexron ATF
Steering system fluid capacity .... 0·8 litres, 1·4 Imp pt, 1·7 US pt

Wheel size:
Steel rims .... 5½J x 14
Aluminium rims .... 6J x 14

Tyres:
Standard .... 165 SR 14
                                                    185/70 HR 14 (fuel injection models)
Optional .... 185/70 HR 14

Steering geometry:
Castor .... 0° 30' to 0° 50' negative
Total toe-in .... 1·0 mm ± 0·5 mm (0·039 ± 0·020 in)
Camber:
    Normal .... 1° negative to 0°
    Bad road version .... 0° 40' to 1° negative
Max. difference in camber between left and right .... 0° 30'

Suspension

Type .... Coil springs with double acting hydraulic shock absorbers

Spring identification:

1·6 litre engine	2 white stripes
2·0 litre engine	2 yellow stripes
2·2 litre engine	2 brown stripes

Packing ring thickness:

Standard	8·5 mm (0·335 in)
Alternative (to level the suspension)	14·5 mm (0·571 in) or 20·5 mm (0·807 in)

Driveshaft

Type	Double constant velocity joint

Length:

Model year	Right	Left
1·6 litre manual 1977	588·0 mm (23·15 in)	549·5 mm (21·63 in)
1·6 litre automatic 1977	549·5 mm (21·63 in)	607·3 mm (23·90 in)
1·6 litre manual 1978 on	582·7 mm (22·94 in)	544·2 mm (21·43 in)
1·6 litre automatic 1978 on	544·2 mm (21·43 in)	602·0 mm (23·70 in)
2·0/2·2 litre manual 1977 on	553·9 mm (21·81 in)	553·9 mm (21·81 in)
2·0/2·2 litre automatic 1977 on	532·1 mm (20·95 in)	585·8 mm (23·06 in)

Torque wrench settings

	Nm	lbf ft
Suspension strut-to-body	25	18
Suspension strut mounting-to-piston rod	60	44
Suspension strut screw cap	180	130
Tie-rod-to-suspension strut	60	44
Tie-rod-to-steering gear	60	44
Caliper-to-wheel bearing housing	115	83
Suspension joint-to-wheel bearing housing	64	47
Wheel hub-to-driveshaft	280	202
Driveshaft-to-flange	45	33
Track control rod-to-subframe	85	62
Subframe-to-body	110	80
Anti-roll bar-to-subframe	105	76
Anti-roll bar-to-track control arm	110	80
Wheel bolts	110	80
Flange tube to steering gear:		
Manual steering	20	15
Power steering	30	22
Column outer tube flange-to-body	10	7
Steering wheel-to-steering column	50	36
Steering gear-to-body	25	18
Steering damper attachment bolts	40	29
Steering damper bracket-to-steering gear	60	44
Locknut on tie-rod	45	33

1 General description

The front suspension is of the independent strut type with coil springs and telescopic double-acting hydraulic dampers (photo). The front suspension units are mounted on a subframe and if the engine is supported from above, the subframe and complete suspension may be removed as an assembly.

The upper end of the suspension strut fits into a dished plate which is attached to a turret incorporated into the wheel arch. The plate has slotted holes which permit adjustment of the wheel camber.

The lower end of the suspension strut is mounted on the wheel bearing housing via an axial bearing to allow steering movement. Track control arms, mounted on the subframe at their inner end through a bonded rubber bush, are attached to the wheel bearing housing by a balljoint. Fore-and-aft location of the front suspension is provided by an anti-roll bar which braces the track control arms to the subframe (photo).

The front wheels are driven by shafts which incorporate two constant velocity joints capable of accommodating the axial and angular movement of the road wheels and engine drive flanges under all driving conditions.

The steering system is of rack-and-pinion type, accommodated in an oil-tight housing. It comprises a rack, having teeth which engage with a pinion carried on a short shaft, the tip of which is splined and to which is fitted the lower steering tube. A steering damper is fitted. The steering tube incorporates a pin joint, so that the steering column collapses and minimises injury to the driver in the event of a collision.

1.1 Front suspension strut and coil spring

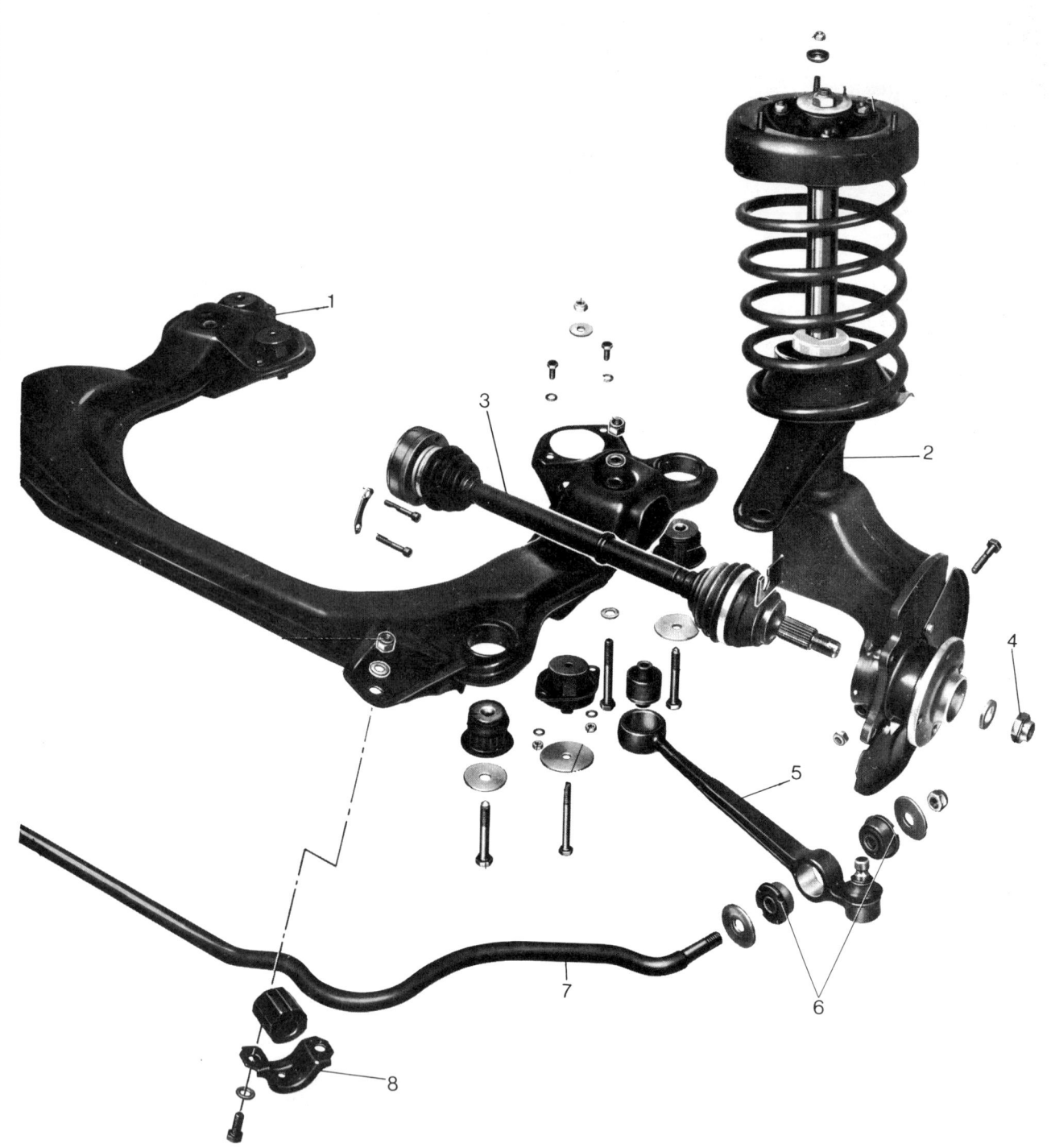

Fig. 11.1 Front suspension components (Sec 1)

1 Subframe	3 Driveshaft	5 Track control arm	7 Anti-roll bar
2 Suspension strut assembly	4 Hub nut	6 Track control arm bushes	8 Anti-roll bar bracket

1.3 Anti-roll bar and track control arm

2 Suspension strut assembly – removing and refitting

1   Remove the hub cap.

2   Unscrew the driveshaft nut. This is tightened to a very high torque and no attempt to loosen it must be made unless the full weight of the car is on the road wheels.

3   Loosen the four bolts securing the road wheel.

4   Jack the car and support the body securely on stands, or wood blocks.

5   Remove the road wheel.

6   Remove the two bolts from each of the brackets securing the anti-roll bar to the subframe and remove the brackets.

7   Remove the two bolts securing the brake caliper, remove the brake disc and tie the brake caliper assembly to the car body.

8   Remove the nut from the tie-rod balljoint, and press the tie-rod end out of the steering arm, which is incorporated in the wheel bearing housing.

9   Remove the clamp-bolt from the track control joint (Fig. 11.3) and lever the joint out of the wheel bearing housing. When levering out the joint be careful not to damage the rubber boots on the driveshaft or on the track control joint.

10 Using a hub puller, press the driveshaft out of the wheel hub.

11 Support the suspension strut assembly from below and then remove the three nuts which attach the top of the strut to the wheel arch turret (Fig. 11.7).

Fig. 11.2 Anti-roll bar bracket and bolts (Sec 2)

Fig. 11.3 Brake caliper and control arm clamp-bolts (Sec 2)

Fig. 11.4 Levering off the track control arm joint (Sec 2)

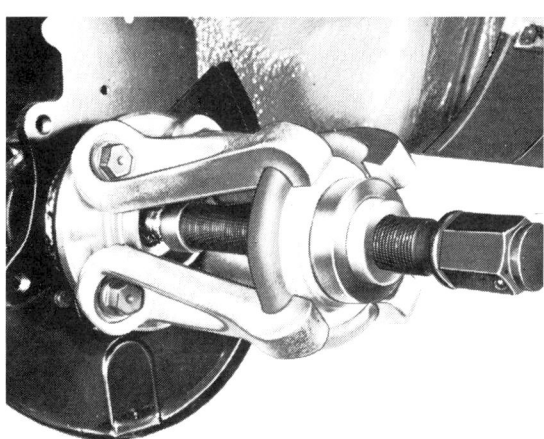

Fig. 11.5 Pressing out the driveshaft (Sec 2)

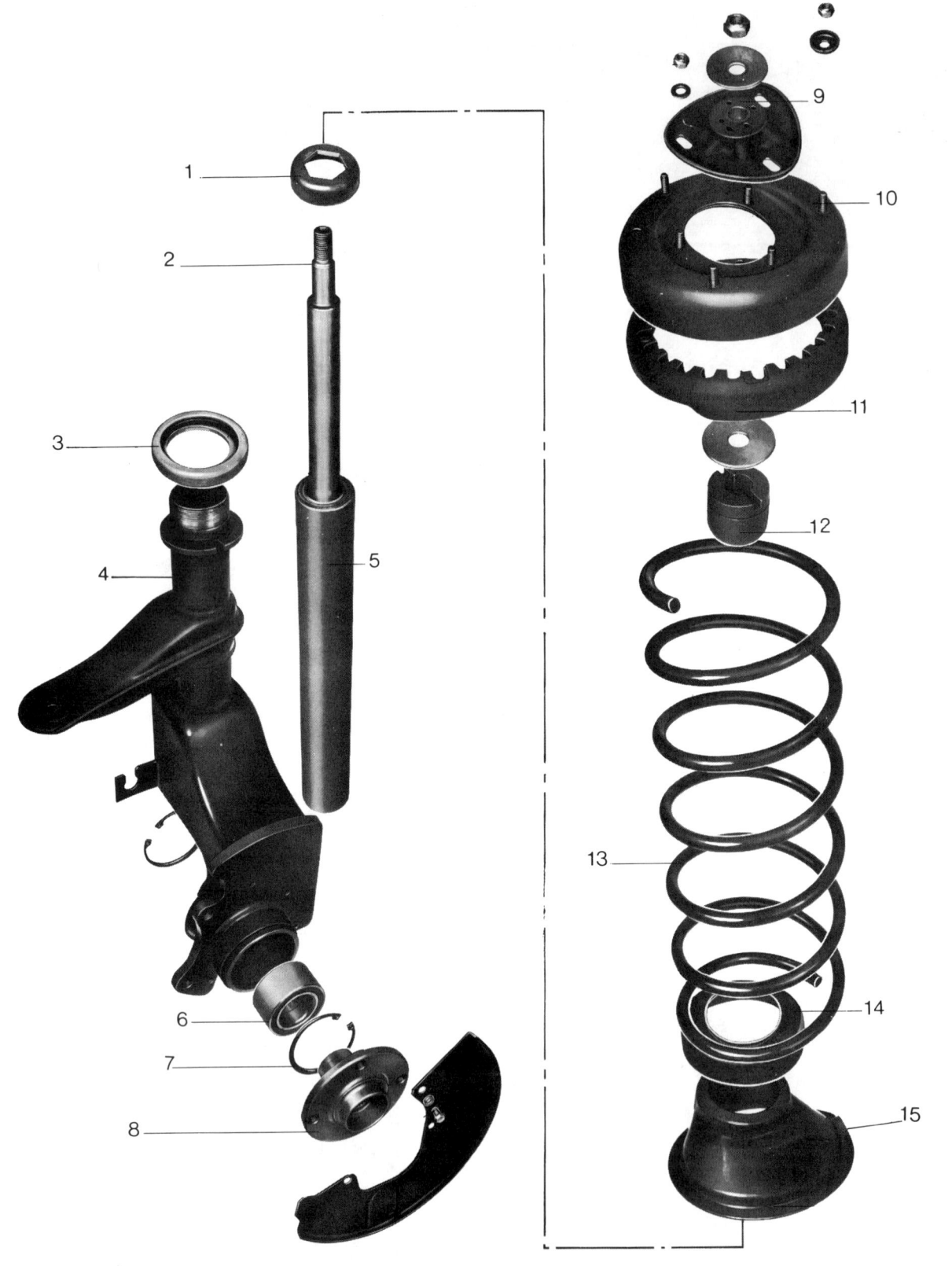

Fig. 11.6 Suspension strut assembly (Sec 2)

1 Screw cap	5 Shock absorber	9 Spring strut mounting	13 Coil spring
2 Piston rod	6 Wheel bearing	10 Upper spring retainer	14 Cover
3 Axial bearing	7 Circlip	11 Packing ring	15 Lower spring retainer
4 Suspension strut	8 Wheel hub	12 Bump stop	

Fig. 11.7 Suspension strut nuts (arrowed) (Sec 2)

Do not disturb the other nuts (camber adjustment)

Fig. 11.9 Position of axial bearing on front strut (Sec 3)

12 Remove the strut assembly, pulling it clear of the driveshaft.
13 Before refitting the suspension strut clean the splines of the driveshaft to remove oil, grease and traces of locking compound. Apply locking compound D6 around the splines in a band about 5 mm (0·20 in) wide at the end of the shaft and then fit the driveshaft to the hub.
14 The hub nut must be tightened to a higher than usual torque wrench setting (given in Specifications). If a suitable torque wrench is not available, tighten the nut firmly and then take the car to a garage for the nut to be tightened properly.

3 Suspension strut – dismantling and reassembly

1 Do not attempt to dismantle the suspension strut unless a spring compressor has been fitted. If you have no special compressor, take the strut to a garage for dismantling.
2 If a spring compressor is available, the strut may be dismantled without removing it from the car and the principal steps are the same as the following which describes how to dismantle the strut after removing it.
3 With the spring compressor in place on the spring clamp the wheel bearing housing in a vice.
4 Compress the spring until the upper spring retainer is free of tension, then remove the nut and washer from the top of the piston.
5 Pull off the upper spring retainer with the spring strut mounting attached to it. Do not loosen the nuts securing the spring strut mounting, because this will disturb the wheel camber setting.
6 With the spring compressor still in place on the spring, remove the

Fig. 11.8 Area to be covered with locking compound (arrowed) (Sec 2)

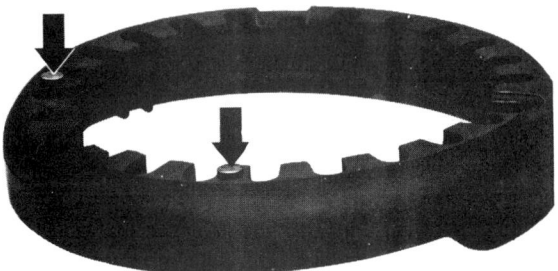

Fig. 11.10 Front strut packing ring locating pegs (Sec 3)

spring from the strut and remove the cover and lower spring retainer.
7 Unscrew and remove the screw cap which retains the shock absorber in the suspension strut and pull out the shock absorber.
8 With the shock absorber removed, examine it for oil leaks and obvious signs of damage. Hold the shock absorber vertically and check its operation by pulling the piston rod out fully, then push it in fully by hand several times. Resistance should be even and the movement smooth over the entire stroke. If a shock absorber has not been in use for a long time, it may require pumping up and down several times before it becomes effective.
9 If there has been excessive leakage of oil from the shock absorber it may be ineffective on the rebound stroke, but if there is only a slight oil seepage, it may be refitted.
10 Clean out the bore of the suspension strut before fitting the shock absorber, so that the shock absorber slides in easily. Do not drive the shock absorber into the strut.
11 Fit the axial bearing so that its peg engages in the notch in the suspension strut (Fig. 11.9).
12 Fit the lower cover so that the marking on it faces outwards.
13 When fitting the packing ring to the upper spring retainer, locate the projections on the ring (Fig. 11.10) into the holes in the spring retainer. If a new packing ring is being fitted, note that the top of the ring has either one, or two small projections on its underside (Fig. 11.11). These denote different thickness of ring and the new ring should be of the same thickness as the old one unless the spring has been changed or there is a difference in ride height between the right and left-hand side of the suspension.
14 Fit the bump stop and the washer to the piston rod before fitting the spring, packing ring and upper spring retainer.

4 Hub bearing – removing and refitting

1 Removing and refitting the wheel bearing requires a press.
2 Remove the suspension strut assembly as described in Section 2.
3 Press out the wheel hub, to which the bearing inner race is attached. The inner race can then be removed with a commercial bearing puller.
4 Remove the circlip retaining the wheel bearing and press the bearing out.

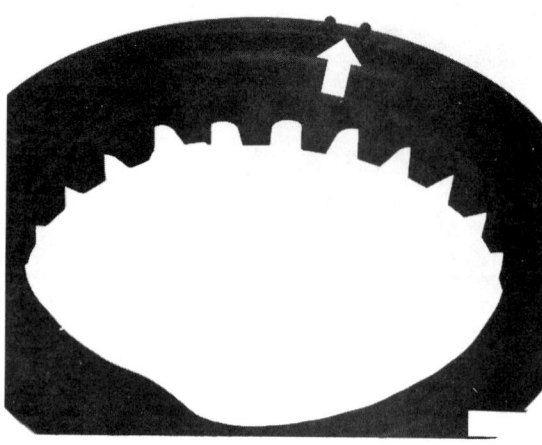

**Fig. 11.11 Front strut packing ring identification projections
(Sec 3)**

6.6 Driveshaft guardplate

6.7 Driveshaft inner coupling bolts

5   Before pressing in a new bearing, smear the bearing seat with
general purpose grease. Press it in until it is in contact with the inner
circlip and then fit the outer circlip.

5   Anti-roll bar – removing and refitting

1   If the anti-roll bar is distorted, or damaged, it must not be
straightened, but a new one must be fitted.
2   Remove the two bolts from each of the two brackets which secure
the anti-roll bar to the subframe and remove the brackets.
3   Remove the nut and washer from each end of the anti-roll bar.
4   Bounce the front suspension up and down with the vehicle standing on its wheels, at the same time pulling the anti-roll bar out of the
bushes on the track control arms.
5   Refitting is the reverse of removal and the front suspension should
be bounced up and down while inserting the anti-roll bar into the
bushes of the track control arms.

6   Driveshafts – removing and refitting

1   Remove the hub cap.
2   Unscrew the driveshaft nut. This is tightened to a very high torque
and no attempt to loosen it must be made unless the full weight of the
car is on the road wheels.
3   Loosen the four bolts securing the road wheel.
4   Jack the car and support the car securely on stands, or wood
blocks.
5   Remove the road wheel.
6   Remove the driveshaft guard plate from the right-hand side of the
gearbox (photo).
7   Using a socket wrench, remove the bolts from the inner driveshaft
coupling (photo) and separate the driveshaft from the gearbox drive
flange.
8   Using a hub puller, press the driveshaft out of the wheel hub.
9   Guide the flanged end of the driveshaft over the gearbox and pull
the splined end clear of the wheel bearing housing.
10   Clean the splines of the driveshaft to remove oil, grease and traces
of locking compound.
11   Refitting the shaft is a reversal of the removal operations, but
before fitting the shaft to the hub, apply locking compound D6 around
the splines in a band about 5 mm (0·20 in) wide at the end of the
shaft.
12   The hub nut must be tightened to the torque wrench setting given
in Specifications. If a suitable torque wrench is not available, tighten
the nut firmly (with the car standing on its wheels), and then take the
car to a garage for the nut to be tightened properly.
13   If the car has automatic transmission the driveshaft cannot be
removed without removing the two brackets which clamp the anti-roll
bar to the subframe and separating the track control arm joint to the
suspension strut (Section 2, Paragraph 9). The suspension strut can
then be swung outwards, permitting the driveshaft to be removed.

7   Driveshafts – dismantling and reassembly

1   With the driveshaft removed as described in the preceding
Section, remove the two clamps on the rubber boot at the inner end of
the shaft and pull the boot down the shaft and off the coupling.
2   Remove the circlip from the end of the shaft and press the shaft
out of the coupling.
3   Remove the two clamps from the outer joint boot and pull the
boot down the shaft and off the coupling.
4   Open the circlip securing the joint assembly to the shaft (Fig.
11.13) and by using a copper drift against the coupling hub, drive the
coupling off the shaft.
5   Before starting to dismantle the outer joint, mark the position of
the hub in relation to the cage and housing. Because the parts are
hardened this mark will either have to be done with a grinding stone,
or with paint.
6   Swivel the hub and cage and take out the balls one at a time.
7   Turn the cage until the two rectangular openings (Fig. 11.15) align
with the housing and then remove the cage and hub.
8   Turn the hub until one segment can be pushed into one of the
rectangular openings in the cage (Fig. 11.16) and then swivel the hub

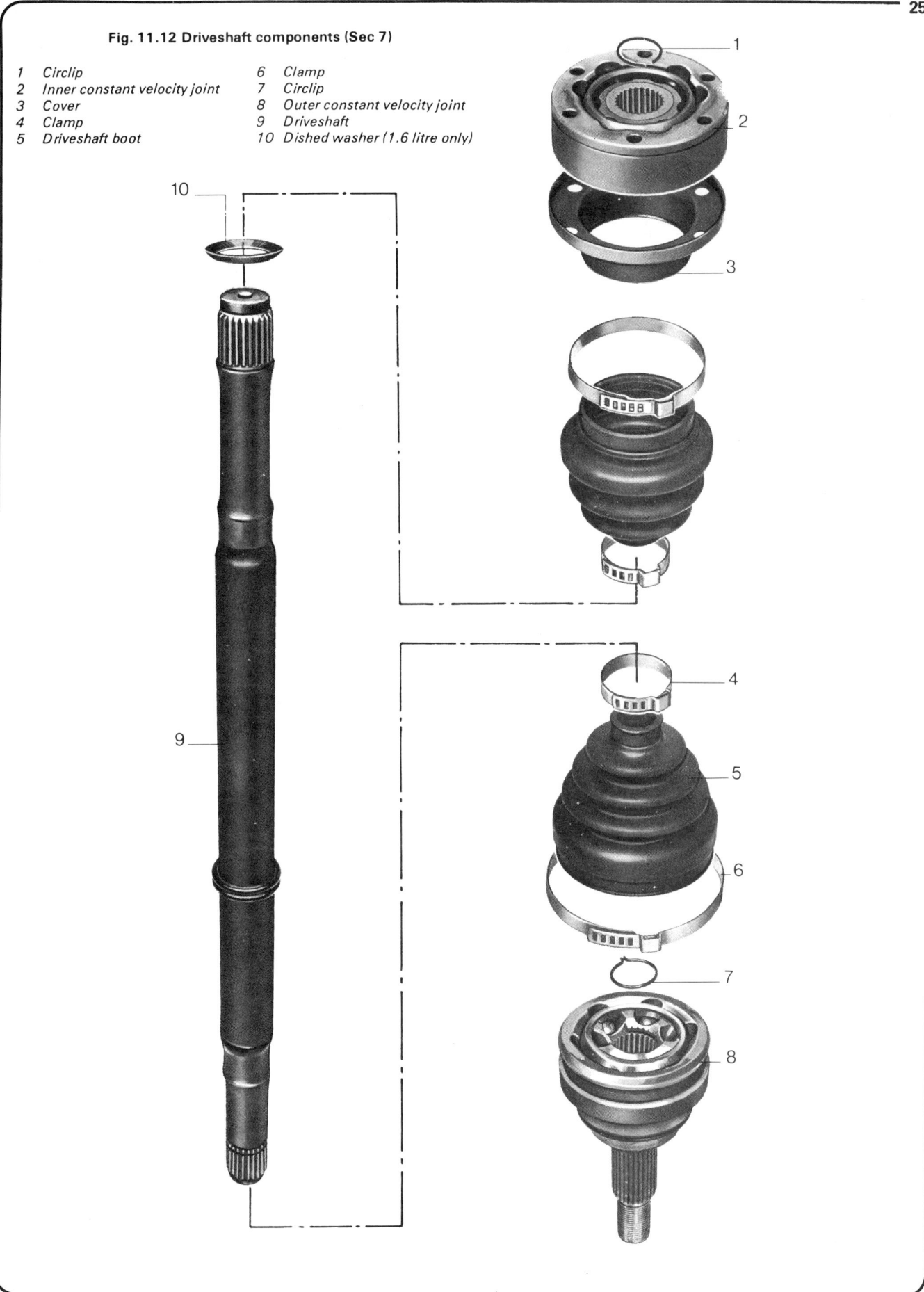

Fig. 11.12 Driveshaft components (Sec 7)

1 Circlip
2 Inner constant velocity joint
3 Cover
4 Clamp
5 Driveshaft boot
6 Clamp
7 Circlip
8 Outer constant velocity joint
9 Driveshaft
10 Dished washer (1.6 litre only)

Fig. 11.13 Removing the outer driveshaft joint (Sec 7)

A – Circlip   B – Hub

Fig. 11.15 Align rectangular slots (arrowed) with housing (Sec 7)

Fig. 11.14 Removing the balls from the outer constant velocity joint (Sec 7)

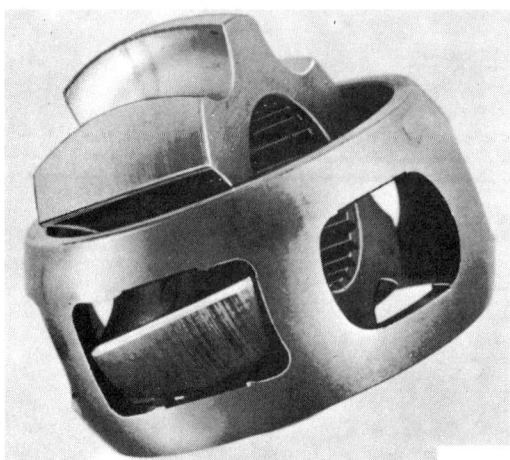

Fig. 11.16 Removing the hub from the cage (Sec 7)

Fig. 11.17 Removing the hub and cage from the inner constant velocity joint (Sec 7)

out of the cage.

9   The parts of the joint make up a matched set and no individual parts can be replaced.

10 If there is excessive play in the joint which is noticeable when changing from acceleration to overrun, or vice versa, a new joint must be fitted but do not replace a joint just because the parts have been polished by wear and the track of the balls is clearly visible. If a new joint is required for a 1·6 litre model earlier than 1978, the joint is different from that of the 2·0 and 2·2 litre models and can only be obtained as a complete shaft assembly.

11 When reassembling a joint, clean off all the old grease and use new circlips, rubber boots and clips. Use only the special coupling grease recommended by Audi for packing the joints.

12 Press half a sachet of grease (45 gms, 1·6 ozs) into the joint and then fit the cage and hub into the housing, ensuring that it will be possible to line up the mating marks of the hub, cage, and housing after the balls have been inserted.

13 Press the balls into the hub from alternate sides and when all six have been inserted check that the mating marks on the hub, cage and housing are aligned.

14 Fit a new circlip into the groove in the hub and finally squeeze the remainder of the grease into the joint.

15 The inner joint is dismantled in a similar way. Pivot the hub and cage and press them out of the housing as shown in Fig. 11.17.

16 Press the balls out of the cage.

17 When reassembling the joint, press half of the charge of grease into each side of the joint.

18 If a new driveshaft is being fitted, make sure that the new one is the same length as the old one. The right-hand and left-hand shafts are of different length and there are variations in length with model, year of manufacture and whether a manual, or automatic transmission is fitted (see Specifications).

19 It is advisable to fit new rubber boots to the shaft because a defective boot will soon lead to the need to fit a new joint due to wear caused by grit entering the joint.

20 Fit the boots to the shaft and put any residual grease into the boots.

21 Press the inner coupling on to the end of the shaft and secure it with a new circlip.

22 On the 1·6 litre model ensure that the dished washer is fitted to the inner end of the shaft before the coupling is fitted. The concave side of the washer should face the coupling.

23 Use a soft-faced hammer to drive the outer joint on to the shaft until the circlip engages in the groove in the shaft.

24 Fit new clamps to each end of the rubber boots, tighten them and crimp them.

8 Wheels and tyres

1 There are options on the size of wheels and tyres fitted, as shown in Specifications.

2 It is important to note that the wheel bolts for steel rims are shorter than those for light alloy rims and the correct bolt length must be fitted.

3 If long bolts are used with steel rims, the bolts will protrude into the rear brakes and damage them.

4 If short bolts are used with light alloy rims, there is a danger of the wheels becoming loose.

9 Steering wheel – removing and refitting

1 Pull off the horn pad and disconnect the two horn wires by pulling the connections out of the steering wheel hub (Fig. 11.19).

2 Unscrew the steering wheel nut and remove the nut and washer.

3 Pull the steering wheel off the splines of the steering column. If the wheel is stuck, do not thump it but use a suitable extractor, otherwise the column may be damaged.

4 When refitting the steering wheel, ensure that the car wheels are in the straight ahead position and that the turn signal switch is in its centre position.

5 Fit the steering wheel with the tongue for the cancelling mechanism to the left and ensure that the lower edge of the horn bar is horizontal.

10 Steering column – removing and refitting

1 Disconnect the battery leads.

2 Remove the steering wheel.

3 Insert a screwdriver through the hole in the steering column switch shroud (Fig. 11.20) and undo the switch assembly clamp. Disconnect the plugs connecting the switch wiring and lift off the switch assembly.

4 Loosen the clamp securing the flange tube to the steering pinion and pull off the flange tube to separate it from the steering column.

5 Remove the two bolts securing the flange at the base of the steering column outer tube to the car floor.

6 Remove the trim from beneath the steering column, to give access to the two bolts which hold the steering lock bracket to the body. This bracket is fitted with bolts having heads which shear off when tightened and the bolts have to be drilled out with an 8.5 mm (0.335 in) drill. When the bolt heads have been drilled away and the bracket taken off, the shanks of the bolts can be removed with a pair of pliers.

7 Pull out the steering column and steering column outer tube assembly.

8 When refitting the steering column, use new shear bolts to attach the steering column lock and ensure that the hole in the steering column outer tube aligns with the locking peg of the lock mechanism.

9 Clamp the steering column joint (Fig. 11.21) so that the two parts are tight against each other and then adjust the position of the flange tube on the steering pinion spindle so that the projection of the steering column from the top of the outer tube is as Fig. 11.22.

10 When fitting the steering column switch housing, adjust the clearance between the face of the switch housing and the back of the steering wheel so that there is a gap of about 3 mm (0.12 in).

11 After making the adjustment, tighten the clamp on the flange tube.

11 Tie-rods – removing and refitting

1 The tie-rods transfer the movement of the steering rack to the steering arm on the suspension strut. If the balljoints become worn, the complete tie-rod must be renewed.

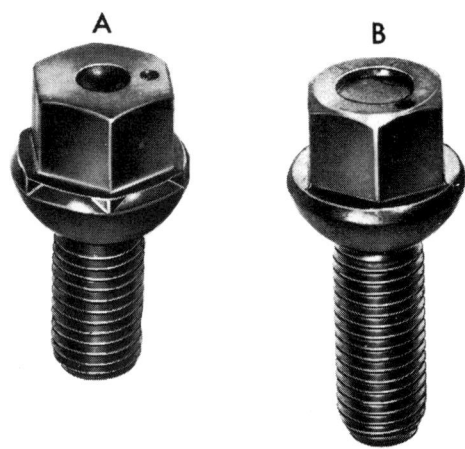

Fig. 11.18 Wheel bolt markings (Sec 8)

A Short bolt for steel wheels
B Larger bolt for aluminium wheels

2 The right-hand tie-rod is a single piece and the left-hand tie-rod consists of two end pieces, joined by a threaded sleeve so that the length of the rod and hence the toe-in of the front wheels can be adjusted (Fig. 11.23).

3 Remove the nut from the tie-rod end and use an extractor or knuckle breaker to press the tie-rod end out of the steering arm.

4 Bend back the tabs of the lockplate which covers the inner end of the tie-rods. Remove one bolt, extract the tie-rod and re-insert the bolt. Remove the second bolt and extract the other tie-rod. If both bolts are removed at the same time, it is difficutlt to align the holes in the rubber boot with the threaded holes in the rack to re-insert the bolts.

5 If renewing the tie-rod end of the adjustable tie-rod, measure the distance between the two ends before screwing the old tie-rod end out and then screw in the new one to the same dimension, otherwise the amount of toe-in will be changed.

6 When refitting the tie-rods, use a new lockplate for the bolts securing the tie-rod ends to the steering rack. Always check the front wheel alignment after any part of the steering system has been disturbed (see Section 22).

12 Steering gear – removing and refitting

1 The steering gear cannot be dismantled and if defective must be renewed as a complete assembly.

2 Remove the tie-rod ends from the rack, as described in the previous Section.

3 Remove the bolt securing the steering damper to the tie-rod bracket (manual steering only).

4 Loosen the clamp on the flange tube connection to the pinion and pull the flange tube off the pinion spindle.

5 Remove the two bolts securing the pinion side of the rack assembly to the engine compartment.

6 Remove the through-bolt which secures the other end of the steering rack to the bracket in the engine compartment and take out the rack assembly.

7 When refitting the flange tube, ensure that the coupling between the flange tube and the steering column is fully engaged (Fig. 11.21).

13 Steering play – adjustment

1 The depth of engagement between the rack and the pinion may be adjusted and this should be done if the steering rattles, or feels excessively loose.

2 Loosen the locknut (Figs. 11.24 or 11.25) and with an Allen key inserted in the socket-head screw, screw the adjusting screw in, until it is felt to touch the thrust plate.

3 While holding the adjusting screw stationary, tighten the locknut.

4 Test the steering to see that it is not too stiff and readjust if necessary.

Fig. 11.19 Steering column components (Sec 9)

1 Horn pad
2 Steering wheel
3 Steering column switch assembly
4 Bearing
5 Steering wheel nut
6 Steering lock
7 Steering column outer tube
8 Bearing flange
9 Steering column
10 Flange tube
11 Bush
12 Clamp

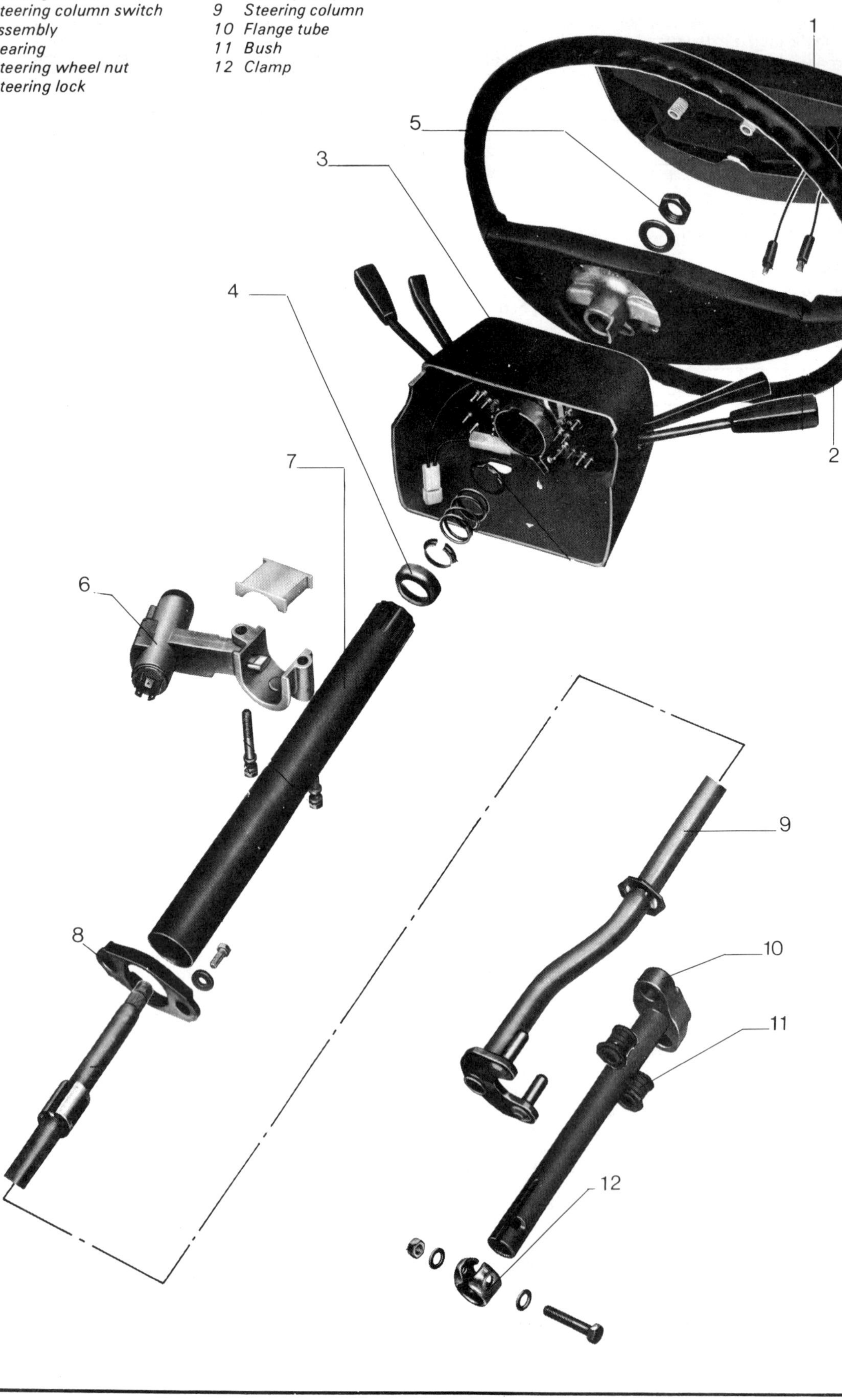

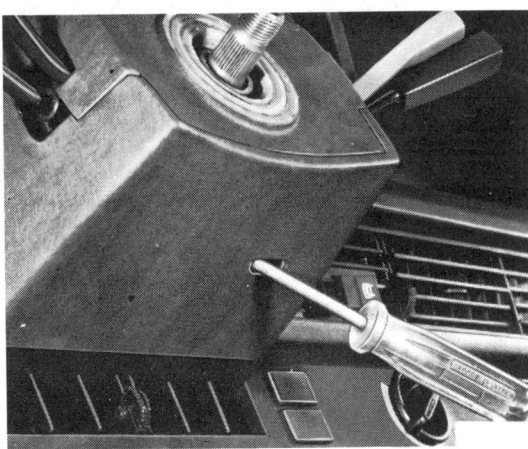

Fig. 11.20 Removing the steering column switch assembly (Sec 10)

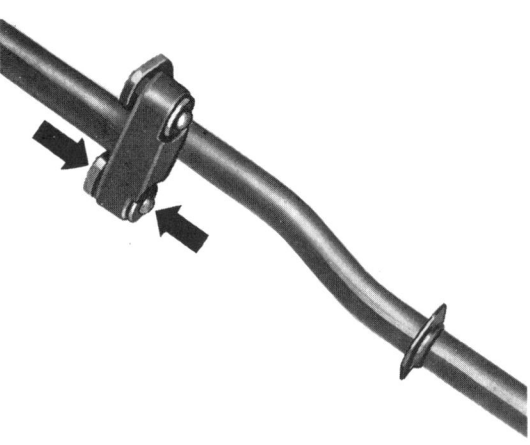

Fig. 11.21 Push steering column joint as far as stop (Sec 10)

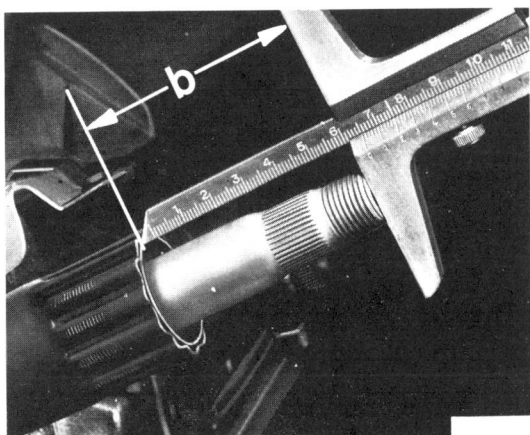

Fig. 11.22 Correct position for steering column (Sec 10)

Projection b = 65 mm (2.56 in)

5   On models with power steering, the adjustment of steering play is similar, but the adjustment must be made with the engine running.

14 Power steering – general

1   Because of the greater weight on the front wheels of the larger engines and the use of radial tyres, the steering effort required, particularly at low speeds tends to be rather high.
2   To counteract this, some models are fitted with power assisted steering, which consists of an engine driven hydraulic pump (photo), a pinion box which incorporates a hydraulic valve and a special rack assembly which has hydraulic pistons to assist its movement.
3   Removal of the steering gear is similar to that for the manual steering gear described in Section 12, except that it is also necessary to disconnect the two hydraulic pipes from the pinion housing before the rack assembly can be removed.
4   Dismantling and overhaul of the assembly by the home mechanic is not recommended, but an exploded view is shown in Fig. 11.26 for interest.

15 Power steering – renewing filter

1   If any component in the steering system is renewed, or if the fluid in the steering system is changed, a new filter should be fitted.
2   The filter is fitted in the bottom of the fluid reservoir and can be renewed as follows.
3   Remove the reservoir cover and pull the lockwasher and spring off the central bolt.
4   Lift off the filter cover and take out the filter.
5   Fit a new filter and sealing ring.

16 Power steering system – draining and refilling

1   Disconnect the feed hose from the steering fluid reservoir and drain the reservoir (photo).
2   Disconnect the return hose from the reservoir and put its open end into a jar. Turn the steering wheel from lock-to-lock to expel as much fluid as possible.
3   Discard the fluid which has been drained off.
4   After fitting a new filter, ensure that all hoses are in place and their clips tightened and then fill the system with fresh fluid of the approved specification.
5   Fill the reservoir to the top with fluid and then start the engine and switch off as soon as it fires, repeating the starting and stopping sequence several times which will cause fluid to be drawn into the system quickly.
6   Watch the level of fluid and keep adding fluid so that the reservoir is never sucked dry. When the fluid ceases to drop as a result of the start/stop sequence, start the engine and allow it to run at idling speed.
7   Turn the steering from lock-to-lock several times, before careful not to leave the wheels on full lock because this will cause the pressure in the system to build up.
8   Watch the level of fluid in the reservoir and add fluid if necessary to keep the level at the *MAX* mark.
9   When the level stops falling and no more air bubbles appear in the reservoir, switch the engine off and fit the reservoir cap. The level of fluid will rise slightly when the engine is switched off, but the rise should not exceed 10 mm (0.39 in).
10 Metal fluid reservoirs have a single level mark. Plastic fluid reservoirs have a *MIN* and *MAX* mark.

17 Power steering system – checking for leaks

1   With the engine running, turn the steering to full lock on one side and hold it in this position to allow maximum pressure to build up in the system.
2   With the steering still at full lock, check all joints and unions for signs of leaks and tighten if necessary.
3   Turn the wheel to full lock on the other side and again check for leaks.

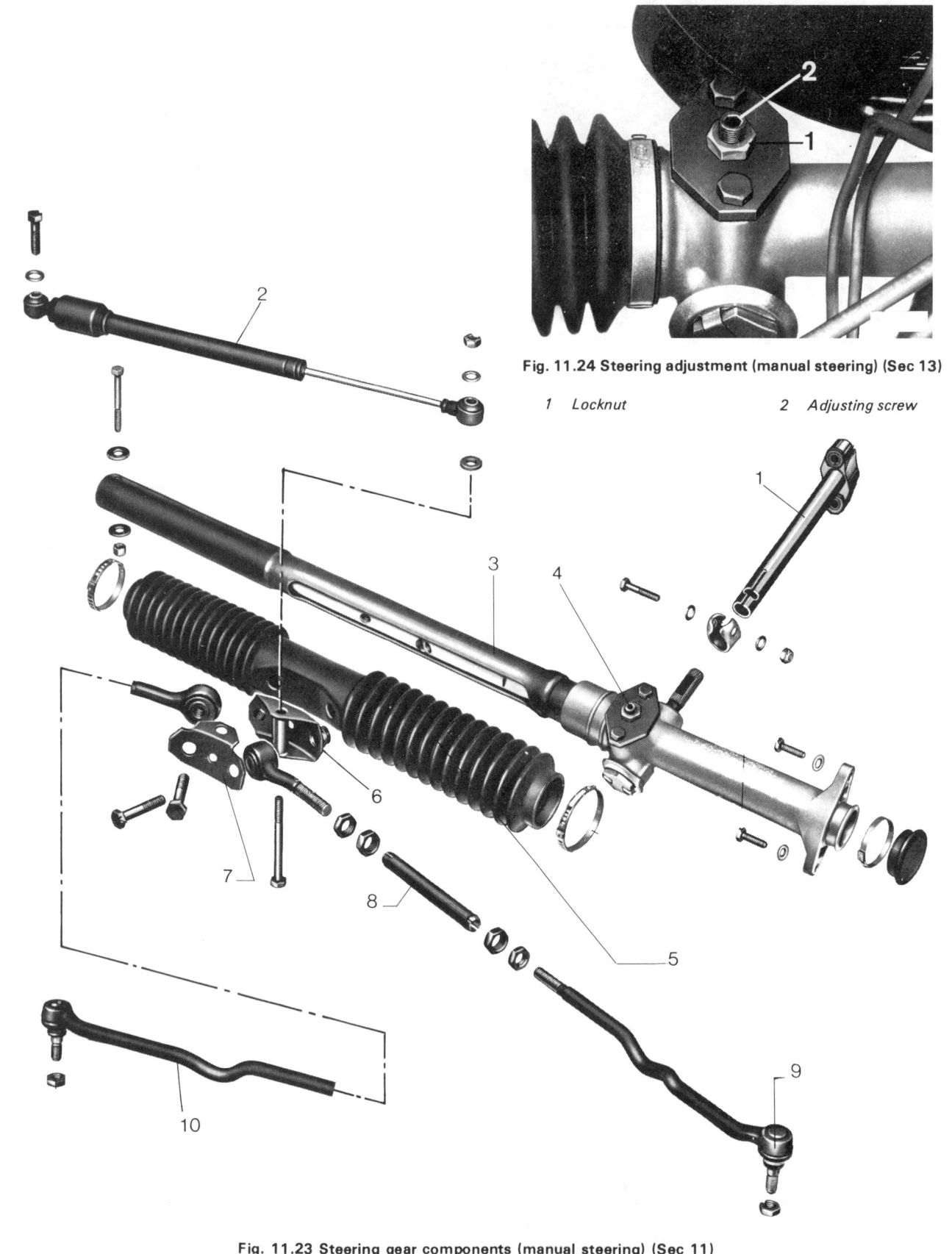

Fig. 11.24 Steering adjustment (manual steering) (Sec 13)

1	Locknut	2	Adjusting screw

Fig. 11.23 Steering gear components (manual steering) (Sec 11)

1	Flange tube	4	Adjusting screw	7	Lockplate	9	Tie-rod end
2	Steering damper	5	Rubber boot	8	Threaded sleeve	10	Tie-rod
3	Steering rack assembly	6	Tie-rod bracket				

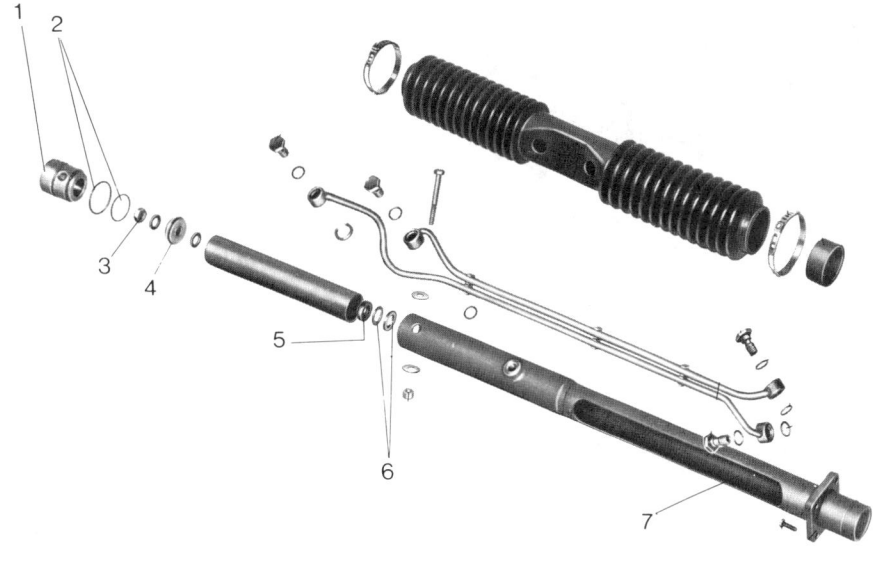

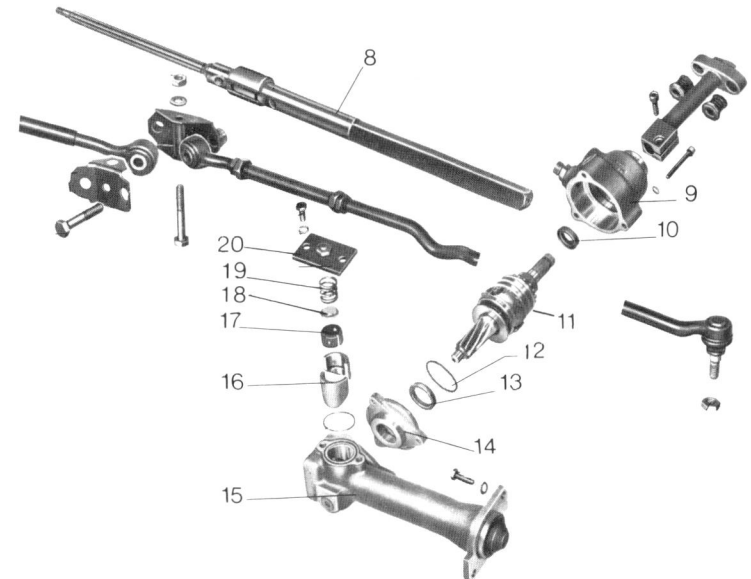

Fig. 11.26 Steering gear components (power steering) (Sec 14)

1	End housing	11	Spool and pinion assembly
2	Seals	12	O-ring
3	Nut	13	Seal
4	Piston	14	Intermediate cover
5	Seal	15	End housing
6	Shims	16	Thrust piece
7	Steering housing	17	Spring sleeve
8	Rack	18	Thrust plate
9	Valve housing	19	Spring
10	Seal	20	Adjusting screw

Fig. 11.25 Steering adjustment (power steering) (Sec 13)

1	Locknut	2	Adjusting screw

14.2 Power steering pump (2.2 litre)

16.1 Power steering fluid reservoir (plastic type)

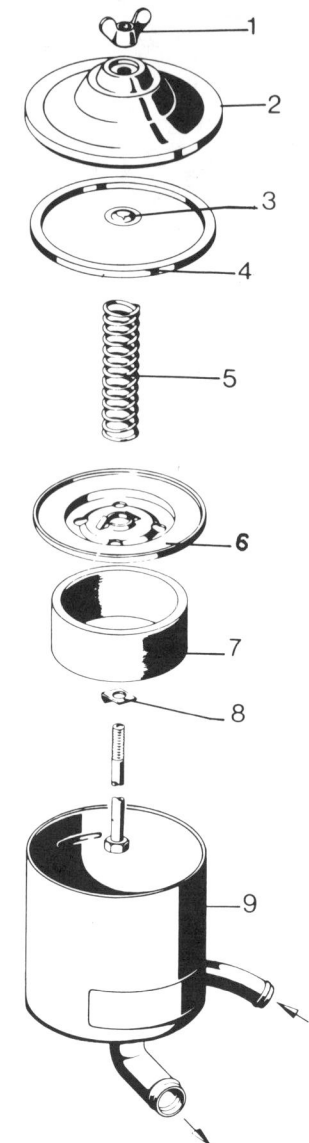

Fig. 11.27 Power steering filter and reservoir (metal type)
(Sec 15)

1	Wing nut	6	Filter cover
2	Cover	7	Filter
3	Lockwasher	8	Retaining spring
4	Seal	9	Reservoir body
5	Spring		

18 Power steering pump – repair

1   If the pump shaft, or bearing is worn, a new pump must be fitted, but if the seal is leaking, or if the pressure relief valve is defective, a new part may be fitted.
2   To fit a new seal on pre-mid 1977 models, loosen the pulley mounting nut and remove the pump from the vehicle.
3   Remove the pulley and the Woodruff key and prise out the old seal with a screwdriver (Fig. 11.28).
4   Fill the groove of the new seal with multipurpose grease and drive the seal in until its front face is 2.6 to 3 mm (0.10 to 0.12 in) below the rim of the casting (Fig. 11.30).
5   On the later model pump, a circlip is visible when the pulley is removed (Fig. 11.32).
6   To fit a new seal in this case, screw the nut on to the spindle, grip the nut in a soft-jawed vice and knock the pump off the shaft using a soft-faced hammer (Fig. 11.33).
7   Remove the inner circlip (Fig. 11.34) and hook out the seal.

Fig. 11.28 Prising out the seal from power steering pump (early models) (Sec 18)

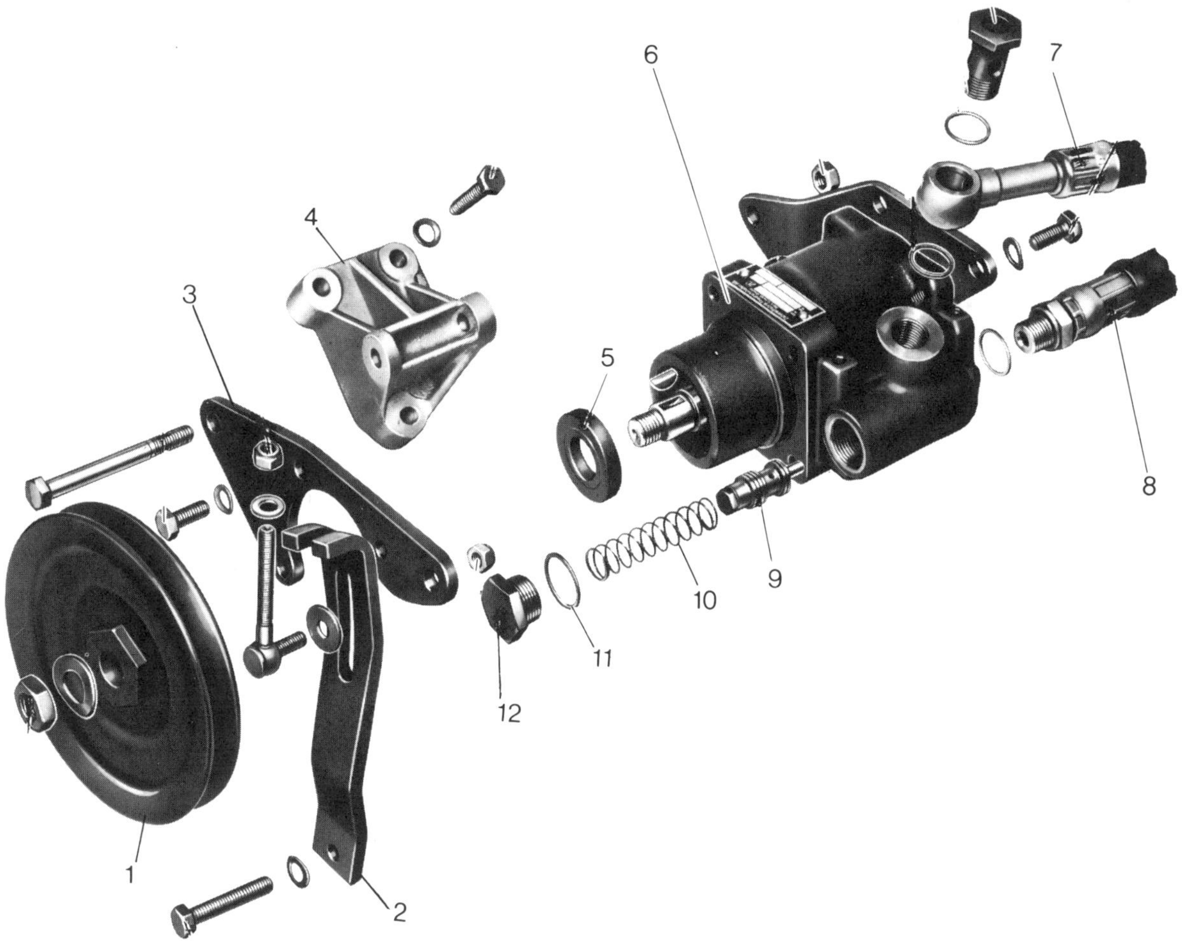

Fig. 11.29 Power steering pump (2.2 litre) (Sec 18)

1	Pulley	4	Mounting bracket
2	Adjuster	5	Seal
3	Front plate	6	Pump assembly

7	Inlet hose	10	Valve spring
8	Outlet hose	11	Seal
9	Pressure valve	12	Plug

Fig. 11.30 Correct fitting of seal to power steering pump (Sec 18)

a = 2.6 to 3 mm (0.102 to 0.12 in)

8   Fill the groove of the new seal with multipurpose grease and drive the seal on to its seat with the lettering on the seal uppermost. When driving the seal in, be careful not to damage the splines of the pump shaft and rotor.

9   Fit the circlip, the shaft assembly and the second circlip. Finally fit the Woodruff key, the pulley and the shaft nut.

19 Power steering pump – belt fitting and adjustment

1   There are three different locations of the pump and two different belt tensions depending upon pump position and engine size.

2.0 litre engine – pump in lower position
2   If the pump is fitted as in Fig. 11.35, belt tension is adjusted by loosening the two bolts 1, and the locknut 2 then turning the bolt 3 until thumb pressure at the mid-point of the belt between the pulleys gives a deflection of 20 mm (0.79 in).
3   When the tension is correct, hold the bolt 3 stationary while the locknut is tightened and then tighten the two fixing bolts.
4   To remove or fit a drivebelt, it is first necessary to remove the shell of the front engine support.

2.0 litre engine – pump in upper position
5   If the pump is fitted as in Fig. 11.36, belt tensioning is achieved by loosening the two nuts (arrowed) and moving the pump with a lever.
6   The belt deflection on adjustment, and the method of changing the belt are the same as when the pump is in the lower position.

2.2 litre engine
7   Adjust belt tension by releasing the clamping nuts 1 in Fig. 11.37 and turning the adjuster nut 2.
8   Correct tension is when thumb pressure at the mid-point of the span will deflect the belt 10 mm (0.39 in).
9   Before renewing the steering pump drivebelt, the alternator drivebelt must be removed. On models fitted with air conditioning, the compressor drivebelt also has to be removed.

Fig. 11.31 Power steering pump (later models) (Sec 18)

1   Outer circlip   3   Inner circlip
2   Spindle and bearing   4   Seal

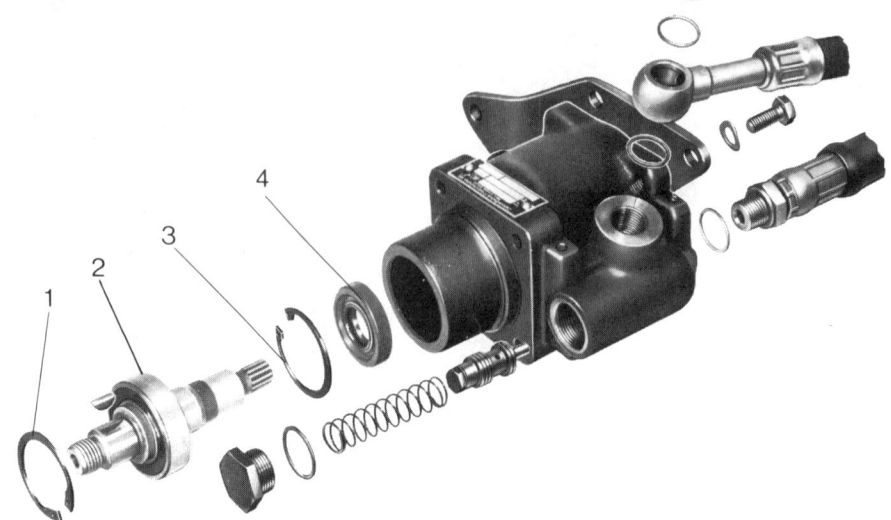

Fig. 11.32 Remove the circlip from power steering pump (Sec 18)

Fig. 11.33 Method of removing power steering pump from shaft (Sec 18)

Fig. 11.34 Inner circlip (power steering pump) (Sec 18)

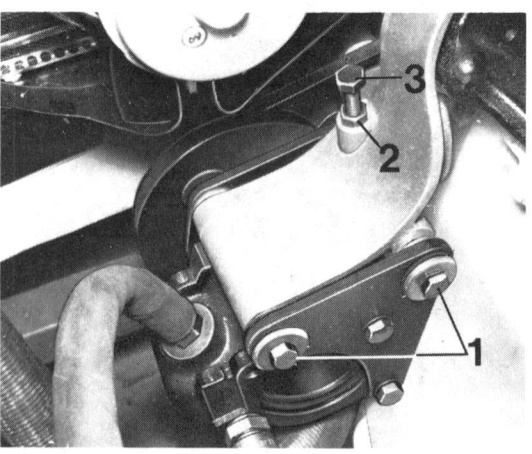

Fig. 11.35 Power steering pump (2.0 litre, lower position) (Sec 19)

1   Clamping bolts   3   Adjusting bolt
2   Locknut

Fig. 11.36 Power steering pumps (2.0 litre, upper position) (Sec 19)

Clamping nuts (arrowed)

Fig. 11.37 Power steering pump (2.2 litre) (Sec 19)

1   Clamping nuts   *2   Adjuster*

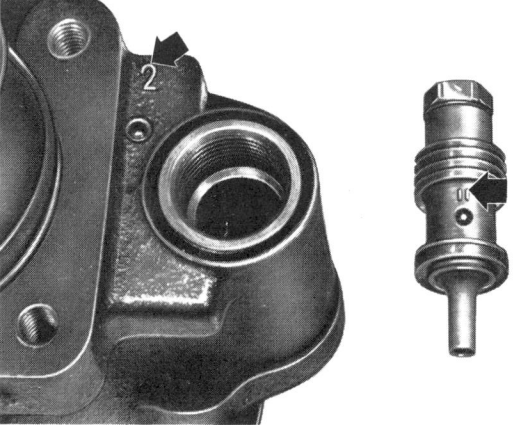

Fig. 11.38 Pressure valve tolerance marks (power steering pump) (Sec 20)

20 Power steering pump – pressure valve renewal

1   Checking of the pump and system pressure requires special equipment, but if it is suspected that pressure is too low, it is worth looking at the pressure control valve on the pump.
2   Remove the hexagon plug on the front of the pump and take off the sealing washer.
3   Extract the spring and the valve plunger.
4   Check that the spring is not damaged, that the holes in the valve piston are clear and that the piston moves freely in the bore in the housing.
5   If the piston is worn, or damaged, a new one can be fitted, but it must be of the same tolerance group as the one which is removed. The tolerance group is a figure stamped on the front of the pump casting adjacent to the valve bore. This figure should be the same as the number of marks on the valve stem (Fig. 11.38).

21 Steering damper – removing and refitting

1   A steering damper is fitted to models which do not have power steering and it is connected between the tie-rod bracket and the side of the engine compartment.
2   Repair of the steering damper is not possible. If the steering is sensitive to road shocks, remove the damper and check its operation. The damper is attached by a bolt at each end.
3   Test the damper by moving the piston in and out by hand, over the whole range of its travel. If the movement is not smooth and with a uniform resistance, fit a new damper.

22 Steering angles and front wheel alignment

1   Steering angles and front wheel alignment are critical to ensure good roadholding and a slow rate of tyre wear.
2   Before considering the steering angles check that the tyres are correctly inflated, that the front wheels are not buckled and that the steering linkage is not worn.
3   Steering and front wheel alignment angles and settings consist of four factors:

Camber, which is the angle at which the front wheels are set from the vertical when viewed from the front of the car. Camber is positive when the wheels are inclined outward at the top from the vertical.
Castor is the angle between the steering axis and a vertical line when viewed from each side of the car. Castor is positive when the steering axis is inclined rearward.
Steering axis inclination is the angle when viewed from the front of the car between the vertical and an imaginary line drawn between the upper and lower suspension strut swivels.
Front wheel alignment (tracking) is the relative position to each other of the front roadwheels. This may be parallel or the front of the wheels may toe-in or toe-out according to Specification.

4   Castor is set in production and cannot be altered.
5   Camber is adjustable by slackening the suspension strut top mounting nuts and moving the strut within the limits of the elongated mounting plate holes. Without the special gauges, adjustment should not be attempted but left to your dealer.
6   Front wheel alignment can be checked and adjusted if the steering and front roadwheels are first centralised (straight ahead position).
7   Obtain or make a front wheel alignment gauge. One may be easily made from tubing, cranked to clear the sump, having an adjustable setscrew and locknut at one end.
8   Using the gauge, measure the distance between the edges of the two inner wheel rims at hub height at the rear of the roadwheels.
9   Move the car backwards and forwards so that the roadwheels turn through 180° (half a turn) and again using the gauge, measure the distance between the edges of the two inner wheel rims at the front of the roadwheels.
10   The difference in the measurements should be within the tolerance given in Specifications.
11   Where this is not the case, release the locknuts on the adjuster sleeve which is located towards one end of the tie-rod and then turn the sleeve. Turn the sleeve only $\frac{1}{4}$ turn at a time before rechecking the front wheel alignment.

12 When the correct setting has been obtained, tighten the locknuts making sure that the tie-rod balljoints are correctly aligned in the centre of their arcs of travel.

13 It is recommended that the threaded part of the tie-rod sleeve adjuster is kept covered with grease to prevent rust and corrosion causing the threads to seize.

14 If after adjustment, the steering wheel spokes are no longer horizontal when the front roadwheels are in the straight ahead position then the steering wheel must be removed (see Section 9) and repositioned.

23 Fault diagnosis – front suspension, steering and driveshafts

Symptom	Reason(s)
Steering wheel needs considerable movement before road wheels turn	Play between pinion and rack Worn tie-rod joints
Vehicle difficult to steer and with a tendency to wander	Play between pinion and rack Worn tie-rod joints Incorrect wheel alignment
Steering stiff	Power steering not working (if fitted) Tyre pressures incorrect Steering adjustment too tight Incorrect wheel alignment
Wheel wobble and vibration	Roadwheels buckled Tyres not balanced Wear in suspension and steering Steering damper ineffective
Power steering noisy	Dirty filter in fluid reservoir Loose unions on inlet side, allowing air to be sucked in Fluid level too low
Excessive pitching and rolling when cornering	Defective shock absorbers
Knocking noise when moving off with wheels turned	Worn driveshaft couplings

Chapter 12 Bodywork and fittings

Contents

1 General description

1   The body is of unit construction, welded to a frame/floor assembly. It is treated with zinc phosphate and primed by electrocoating to give good corrosion resistance and the underside and wheel arches are coated with PVC to give protection against flying stones.

2   A special anti-corrosion treatment is applied to the body cavities and the engine bonnet panels are treated to give extra protection.

3   The body has been aerodynamically designed to give low drag and a novel feature of body design gives a high degree of protection against impact. This protection is achieved by incorporating square section tubes into each side of the body at the front and the rear. On impact these tubes crumple into accordian pleats absorbing a large amount of the impact energy.

4   There are three basic body styles, the 2-door and 4-door saloons and the 5-door Avant. There is a range of trim options and a choice of refinements such as sun roof, central door locking, air conditioning and cruise control.

2 Maintenance – bodywork and underframe

1   The general condition of a car's bodywork is the one thing which significantly affects its value. Maintenance is easy, but needs to be regular. Neglect, particularly after minor damage, can lead quickly to further deterioration and costly repair bills. It is important also to keep watch on those parts of the car not immediately visible, for example the underframe, inside the wheel arches and the lower part of the engine compartment.

2   The basic maintenance routine for the bodywork is washing, preferably with a lot of water, from a hose. This will remove all the loose solids which may have adhered to the car. It is important to wash these off in a way which prevents them from scratching the surface. The wheel arches and underframe need washing in the same way to remove accumulated dirt, which retains moisture and tends to encourage rust. The best time to do this is in wet weather when the dirt is soft and once the large accumulations have been removed, the underframe should be inspected.

3   Periodically it is a good idea to have the whole of the underframe of the car and the engine compartment steam cleaned so that it is easy to see what repairs are necessary. Steam cleaning is available at some of the larger garages and will remove the accumulation of thick oily grime which tends to form around parts of the engine, gearbox and differential. If steam cleaning is not available easily, there are proprietary grease solvents which can be brushed or sprayed on so that the grime can then be washed off with a hose.

4   After washing paintwork, wipe off the water with a chamois leather to leave a clean, unspotted finish and occasionally give a coat of clear wax polish to give added protection from rain and pollutants in the air. If the paintwork has become dull, use a cleaner polisher to restore the shine and if the colour has lost all its lustre, use a colour restoring polish. These are mildly abrasive but can be used occasionally on a car which has deteriorated because of neglect.

5   Always check that the door and body shell drain holes and pipes are clear so that water can drain out.

6   If windscreens still retain a smeary film after cleaning, add a small quantity of ammonia to the water, or use a proprietary screen cleaning fluid. If the glass is slightly scratched, it can be polished with metal polish, but wax polish, or any body polish containing silicones, must not be used on the windscreen because it will damage the wiper blades.

7   Bright parts should be cleaned in the same way as paintwork, using only water and a chamois leather. Wax polish will give added protection, but abrasive polishes should be avoided.

3 Maintenance – upholstery and carpets

1   Mats and carpets should be brushed, or vacuum cleaned regularly to keep them free from grit. If they are badly stained, remove them from the car for scrubbing, or sponging, but make sure that they are completely dry before refitting. Seats and interior trim panels can be kept clean by regular wiping with a damp cloth. If they become stained, use an upholstery shampoo, or some mild detergent and a soft brush. The head lining should also be cleaned regularly using the same method as used for the seats and trim.

2   When using liquid cleaners inside the car, do not make the surfaces any wetter than is necessary. Excessive moisture can soak in at the seams to cause staining, unpleasant odours, or even rotting of the padding. If the interior gets wet accidentally, remove the carpets and anything else which can be taken out easily and dry them outside the car. Do not put any form of heater inside the car for drying it out. Leave the car in the sun with the windows partially open.

This sequence of photographs deals with the repair of the dent and paintwork damage shown in this photo. The procedure will be similar for the repair of a hole. It should be noted that the procedures given here are simplified — more explicit instructions will be found in the text

In the case of a dent the first job — after removing surrounding trim — is to hammer out the dent where access is possible. This will minimise filling. Here, the large dent having been hammered out, the damaged area is being made slightly concave

Now all paint must be removed from the damaged area, by rubbing with coarse abrasive paper. Alternatively, a wire brush or abrasive pad can be used in a power drill. Where the repair area meets good paintwork, the edge of the paintwork should be 'feathered', using a finer grade of abrasive paper

In the case of a hole caused by rusting, all damaged sheet-metal should be cut away before proceeding to this stage. Here, the damaged area is being treated with rust remover and inhibitor before being filled

Mix the body filler according to its manufacturer's instructions. In the case of corrosion damage, it will be necessary to block off any large holes before filling — this can be done with zinc gauze or aluminium tape. Make sure the area is absolutely clean before...

...applying the filler. Filler should be applied with a flexible applicator, as shown, for best results; the wooden spatula being used for confined areas. Apply thin layers of filler at 20-minute intervals, until the surface of the filler is slightly proud of the surrounding bodywork

Initial shaping can be done with a Surform plane or Dread-nought file. Then, using progressively finer grades of wet-and-dry paper, wrapped around a sanding block, and copious amounts of clean water, rub down the filler until really smooth and flat. Again, feather the edges of adjoining paintwork

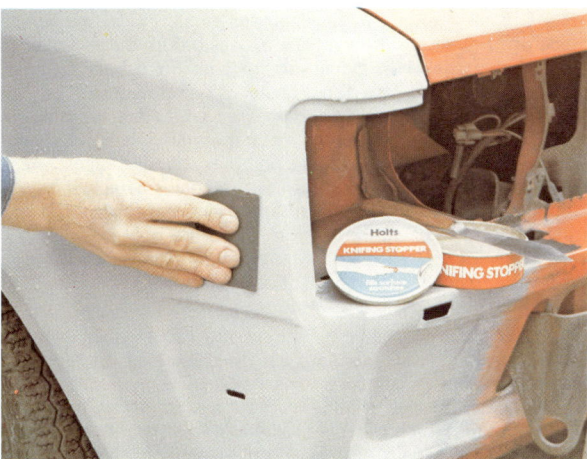

Again, using plenty of water, rub down the primer with a fine grade of wet-and-dry paper (400 grade is probably best) until it is really smooth and well blended into the surrounding paintwork. Any remaining imperfections can now be filled by carefully applied knifing stopper paste

The top coat can now be applied. When working out of doors, pick a dry, warm and wind-free day. Ensure surrounding areas are protected from over-spray. Agitate the aerosol thoroughly, then spray the centre of the repair area, working outwards with a circular motion. Apply the paint as several thin coats

The whole repair area can now be sprayed or brush-painted with primer. If spraying, ensure adjoining areas are protected from over-spray. Note that at least one inch of the surrounding sound paintwork should be coated with primer. Primer has a 'thick' consistency, so will fill small imperfections

When the stopper has hardened, rub down the repair area again before applying the final coat of primer. Before rubbing down this last coat of primer, ensure the repair area is blemish-free – use more stopper if necessary. To ensure that the surface of the primer is really smooth use some finishing compound

After a period of about two weeks, which the paint needs to harden fully, the surface of the repaired area can be 'cut' with a mild cutting compound prior to wax polishing. When carrying out bodywork repairs, remember that the quality of the finished job is proportional to the time and effort expended

4   Maintenance – PVC coverings

Water and a mild soap is all that is required to remove dirt from PVC. If the dirt is ingrained, use a soft brush to clean out the grain, but do not use detergents, caustic soaps or solvent cleaners because these may do irreparable damage. If soap and water are not adequate, ask for advice on approved proprietary cleaners at an Audi garage.

5   Minor body damage – repair

See photo sequence on pages 270 and 271

Repair of minor scratches

If the scratch is superficial and does not penetrate to bare metal, repair is very simple. Rub the area of the scratch lightly with a paint renovator, or a very fine cutting paste to remove loose paint from the scratch and to clear the surrounding bodywork area of wax polish. Rinse the area with clean water and allow time for it to dry thoroughly.

Apply touch-up paint to the scratch using a thin paint brush and when one layer has dried, apply another layer on top until the scratch has been filled to the level of the surrounding paint. Allow the new paint at least two weeks to harden and then blend the new paint into the surrounding paintwork by rubbing the area with paint renovator, or fine cutting paste. Finally, apply wax polish to the touched-up area.

A paint patch may be used as an alternative to painting out a scratch. Use the same method of preparation and then pick a patch of sufficient size to cover the scratch completely. Press the patch against the scratched area and burnish the backing paper until the paint has adhered to the car and the backing paper has become detached. Polish the touched-up area to blend the patch into the surrounding paintwork.

If the scratch has penetrated through the paint to the metal of the bodywork, a different repair technique is necessary. If there is any rusting, carefully scrape away any loose rust and then apply a rust inhibiting paint or liquid to prevent further rusting. Using a non-metallic applicator, fill the scratch to paintwork level with filler paste. If a cellulose based stopper is used, the filler can be lightly wiped with a piece of rag moistened with thinners to remove excess filler before it hardens. If any epoxy filler is used, allow it to harden and rub the surface down with wet and dry paper until the area is smooth. Paint the treated area as described earlier in the Section.

Repair of dents

When the car has sustained a deep dent, it is preferable to try and remove as much as possible of the dent before doing any filling. Unless it is a shallow dent which can be sprung out completely, there is little point in trying to restore the original shape entirely because the surrounding metal may have stretched so that it cannot be reshaped to its original contour. It is better to bring the level of the dent to a point about $\frac{1}{8}$ in (3.2 mm) below the level of the surrounding bodywork and then make good with filler.

If the underside of the dent is accessible, it can be hammered out carefully from behind using a wooden mallet or a soft-headed hammer. While doing this hold a block of hardwood or a second mallet on the other side of the metal to absorb the impact from the blows and prevent the metal from being belled out.

When the dent is in a section of the bodywork which is inaccessible from behind, drill small diameter holes through the metal of the dented areas, screw long self-tapping screws into the holes far enough to take a good grip and pull the dent out by pulling on the screw heads with a pair of pliers.

The next stage of the repair is the removal of the paint from the damaged area and from about an inch (25.4 mm) into the surrounding undamaged area. This is done most easily with a power drill having a wire brush, or abrasive disc, but it is just as effective to rub down by hand, using abrasive paper. Score the clean bare metal with a screwdriver, or scriber to give a good key for the filler paste. Alternatively, drill small holes in the area to be filled to give a key for the filler. To complete the repair, refer to the Section on filling and spraying.

Repair of rust holes and gashes

Remove all the paint from the area to be repaired and about an

inch (25.4 mm) into the surrounding undamaged area of bodywork as when repairing a dent. With the paint removed, the severity of the corrosion will be revealed and a decision can be made on whether to attempt a repair, or fit a new panel. Body panels are not particularly expensive and there are many workshops which will do any necessary welding for a reasonable price. Alternatively, there are companies who specialise in supplying body panels which can be fitted over the existing one.

Remove all fittings from the affected area, except any which are necessary as a guide to the original shape of the damaged bodywork. Using a hacksaw blade, or tin snips, cut away all the badly corroded metal and then hammer the edges of the hole inwards to create a slight depression for the filler paste.

Wire brush the area round the hole to remove any loose rust and then treat the bare metal with rust inhibitor, or an anti-rust paint. If the back of the panel under repair is accessible, treat it also with rust inhibitor.

Before filling can be done, it will be necessary to cover the hole in some way and this is usually done by using one of the following methods.

Zinc gauze is probably the best material to use for a large hole. Cut a piece big enough to overlap the edges of the hole and fix it on the opposite side of the panel to the surface to be filled. The gauze can be fixed in place by putting several blobs of filler paste around its edges.

Aluminium tape can be used for small, or narrow holes. Pull a piece off the roll and trim off the excess before placing over the hole. With some tapes it is necessary to peel off a backing strip before applying the tape. Use the handle of a screwdriver, or something similar to burnish the edges and ensure that it adheres firmly.

Polyurethane foam is the best material when the hole is in a section of bodywork which has a complex shape, such as where the sill panel joins the rear wheel arch. The material is usually in two different containers and should be mixed and used in accordance with the instructions on the pack. Pour the mix into the hole and hold a piece of card over the hole until the polyurethane has stopped expanding. When the foam hardens, cut it back to a level just below that of the surrounding bodywork.

Filling and spraying

Before using this Section, see the Sections on repair of minor scratches, dents, rust holes and gashes.

A variety of types of body filler are available, but, in general those which contain a tube of resin hardener and a tin of filler paste are best for this type of repair. A wide, flexible plastic, or nylon applicator will be found invaluable for imparting a smooth and well contoured finish to the surface of the filler. Mix a small quantity of filler at a time, because it sets rapidly. Use the hardener sparingly and follow the instructions carefully.

Using the applicator, apply the filler paste to the prepared area and then draw the applicator across the surface of the filler to level it and achieve the correct contour. As soon as an approximate contour is achieved, stop working the filler and allow it to harden. If working is continued, there is a tendency for the filler to become sticky enough to be picked up by the applicator. Build up the filler until it is just proud of the surrounding bodywork by adding thin layers at intervals of about twenty minutes.

When the filler is completely hard, remove the excess with a file and then rub it down to a smooth, correctly contoured finish using successively finer grades of abrasive paper, starting with 40 grade and finishing with 400 grade wet-and-dry paper. Wrap the paper round a block of wood, or cork, otherwise the surface of the filler will not be rubbed flat and when using wet paper for the final stages, dip the paper in water periodically to rinse it. This will ensure that at the final stage, the filler has a very smooth finish.

When rubbing down has been completed the repaired area should be surrounded by an area of bare, polished metal which should in turn be surrounded by a finely feathered edge of good paintwork. Rinse the repaired area with clean water until all the dust produced by rubbing down has been removed and then allow it time to dry completely.

Spray the whole repair area with a light coat of primer. This will show up any imperfections in the surface of the filler and these should then be made good with body stopper, or filler before rubbing down again. Repeat this repair and spray procedure until the surface of the filler and the feathered edge of good paintwork are perfect because the final finish achieved depends on the finish achieved in the earlier stages. Clean the repair area with clean water and allow it to dry completely.

Spraying can now be done and this should be carried out in a warm, draughtless and dust-free atmosphere. If spraying indoors, first spray water on to the floor to lay the dust. If working in the open, it is worth waiting for the right weather before attempting to spray. If possible, spray a complete panel and mask off the surrounding panels so that if there is any slight mis-match of colour it is less obvious. Mask all body fittings and other bright parts, using masking tape and several thicknesses of newspaper.

If using an aerosol spray can, agitate it thoroughly and read the instructions carefully. Practice spraying on to a piece of glass, or an old tin and do not attempt the repair area until you have mastered the technique of spraying. The tendencies which must be avoided are to have the spray nozzle too close to the work and to spray too heavy a coat.

Build up a thick coating of paint by spraying several light coats and allowing each one to dry before applying the next. Rub the surface of the primer coat down with the wet 400 grade paper until the paint surface is perfectly smooth, rinsing the paper periodically as when rubbing down the filler. After rubbing down the primer, rinse it and allow the area to dry thoroughly.

Spray the top coat, using the same procedure of building it up from several light coats. Start spraying in the centre of the repair area and work outwards, using a circular motion until the repair area and about two inches (50.8 mm) into the original paintwork has been covered. When the paint has had time to dry, remove all the masking material.

Leave the paint at least two weeks to harden and then use paint renovator, or a mildly abrasive polish to blend the new paint into the surrounding area. Finally, apply a coat of wax polish.

6 Major body damage – repair

1 Major subframe and body repair work cannot be done successfully by the home mechanic. Work of this nature should be entrusted to a competent body repair specialist who should have the necessary jigs, welding and hydraulic equipment, as well as skilled panel beaters to achieve a satisfactory repair.

2 If the damage is severe, it is vital that the chassis is aligned correctly on completion of the repair. Less severe damage may also have resulted in chassis distortion, although it may not be obvious. It is recommended that for anything other than superficial damage, the body alignment is checked by an Audi agent when repairs have been completed.

7 Door rattles – tracing and rectification

1 The most common cause of door rattles is a striker plate which is worn, loose, or misaligned, but other causes may be

  (a) *Loose door handles, window winder handles, door hinges, or door stays*
  (b) *Loose, worn or misaligned door lock components*
  (c) *Loose, or worn remote control mechanism*
  (d) *Loose window glass*

2 If the striker catch is worn, as a result of door rattles, fit a new striker before adjusting the door.
3 If door hinges are worn significantly, new hinges should be fitted.

8 Front door trim panel – removing and refitting

1 Unscrew and remove the lock knob.
2 Note the position of the window winder handle (window closed) and prise out the trim from the centre of the window winder handle and remove the retaining screw. Remove the screw and pull off the handle.
3 Prise out the finger plate from the door remote control lever (photo), remove the screw then exposed and take out the escutcheon (photo).
4 Remove the plugs which cover the screws of the door pull (photo), take out the screws and remove the door pull.
5 Prise out the trim panel from the centre of the door (photo).
6 Remove the screw from the centre of the outer trim and the screw from the overtaking mirror (photo), if fitted.

8.3a Removing a door lock remote control lever finger plate

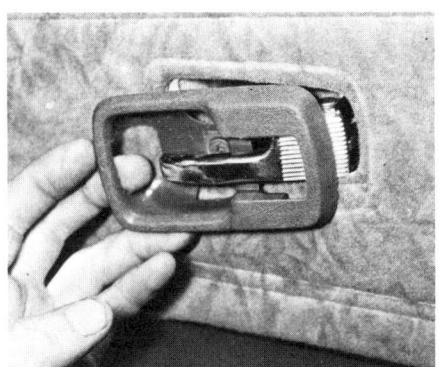
8.3b Removing door lock remote control escutcheon plate

8.4 Door pull with screw cover plugs removed

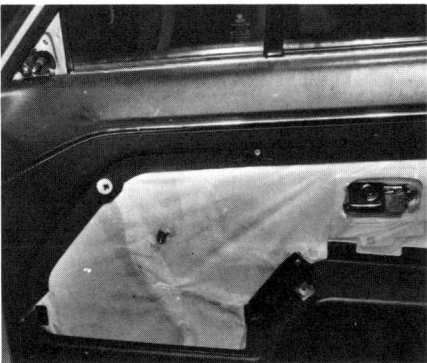
8.5 Door with trim panel removed

8.6 Door mirror interior screw cover plate

7   Prise and lift off the trim panel and peel off the waterproof membrane.

8   Before refitting the trim, fit the waterproof membrane and take care to ensure that it is sealed all the way round.

9   When fitting the trim, ensure that the clips on the trim are aligned so that they enter the plastic inserts on the door panel then strike the trim with the flat of the hand to snap the clips into their inserts.

10   Refit the window winder handle in its original (window closed) position and fit the lock knob, remote control lever and door pull.

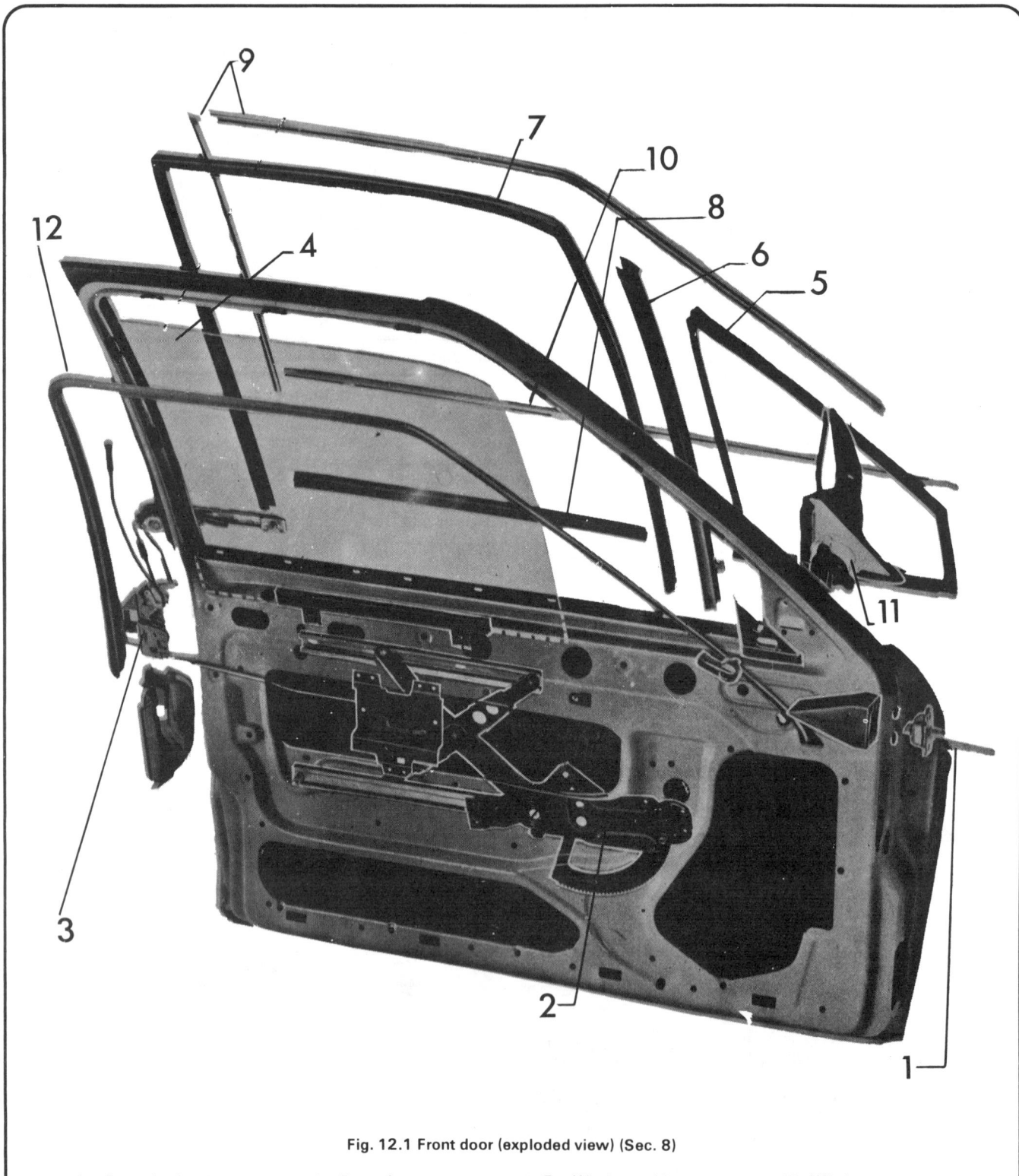

Fig. 12.1 Front door (exploded view) (Sec. 8)

1 Door check rod	4 Door glass	7 Window guide	10 Window recess strip
2 Window regulator	5 Quarter light	8 Outer window seal	11 Exterior mirror
3 Lock	6 Front guide rail	9 Sealing strips	12 Inner strip

9 Front door lock – removing and refitting

1   Remove the door trim as described in the previous Section.
2   Remove the two screws from the polythene cover over the lock mechanism.
3   Remove the three screws from the inner door mechanism, unhook the lock rod and remove the door mechanism (photo).
4   Remove the three screws which secure the door lock to the edge of the door and unhook the two rods from the external door handle mechanism. Remove the door lock with the control rods attached.
5   Remove the screws which secure the external door handle mechanism to the door (photos). On some models the door handle is held on by a single screw. Later models have a second screw under the trim plate of the outer door handle (photo).
6   Refitting is the reverse of removal, but after refitting the lock mechanism, check the operation of the door catch and the lock from both inside and outside the car before refitting the door trim.

10 Rear door trim – removing and refitting

1   The method of removing the rear door trim (photo) is similar to that for the front door trim described in Section 8, except that the inner trim has only a single screw to be removed before the trim is prised off.

11 Rear door lock – removing and refitting

1   The method of removing the rear door lock is similar to that described for the front door in Section 9, except that there is only one control rod between the external door handle and the lock; and the internal locking rod is attached to a bellcrank instead of being attached to the lock directly.

12 Doors – removing and refitting

1   Remove the door trim as described previously.
2   If the same door is being refitted, mark round the hinges on the door, using a pencil or a fine tipped ball point pen. This simplifies realignment of the door.
3   Remove the circlip from the pin in the door check link and tap out the pin. Fit the pin and circlip back into the clevis to prevent their being lost.
4   With an assistant supporting the weight of the door, or with the bottom of the door propped, remove the screws from the hinges and take the door off.
5   Refitting is the reverse of removal. If the same door is refitted, screw the screws in until they are just tight and line the hinges up with the marks made prior to removal. If using a different door, screw the hinge screws in until they are just tight, close the door and push it into the position which aligns its edge with the body contour. Move the door up or down or sideways as necessary to give an even gap between the edge of the door and the body pillars. When door alignment is correct, tighten the hinge screws fully. If necessary, adjust the striker as described in the following Section.

13 Door striker – adjustment

1   Mark round the door striker (photo) with a pencil, or a fine ball point pen.
2   Fit a spanner to the hexagon on the striker and unscrew the striker about one turn so that the striker moves when tapped with a soft-headed hammer.
3   Tap the striker towards the inside of the car if the door rattles, or towards the outside of the car if the door fits too tightly, but be careful to keep the striker in the same horizontal line, unless it also requires vertical adjustment. Only move the striker a small amount at a time and the actual amount moved can be checked by reference to the

9.3 Door lock remote control mechanism fixing screws

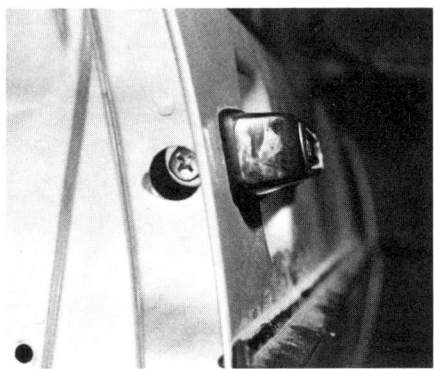

9.5a Door exterior handle fixing screw

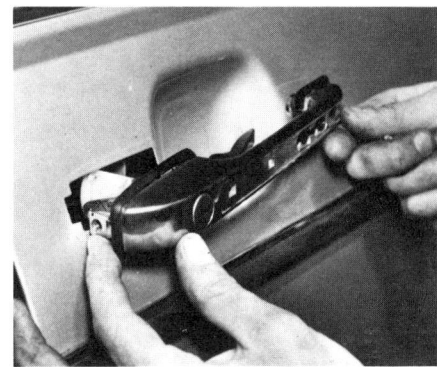

9.5b Removing door exterior handle

9.5c Door exterior handle second fixing screw (trim insert removed) fitted to some models

10.1 Rear door trim panel

13.1 Rear door striker

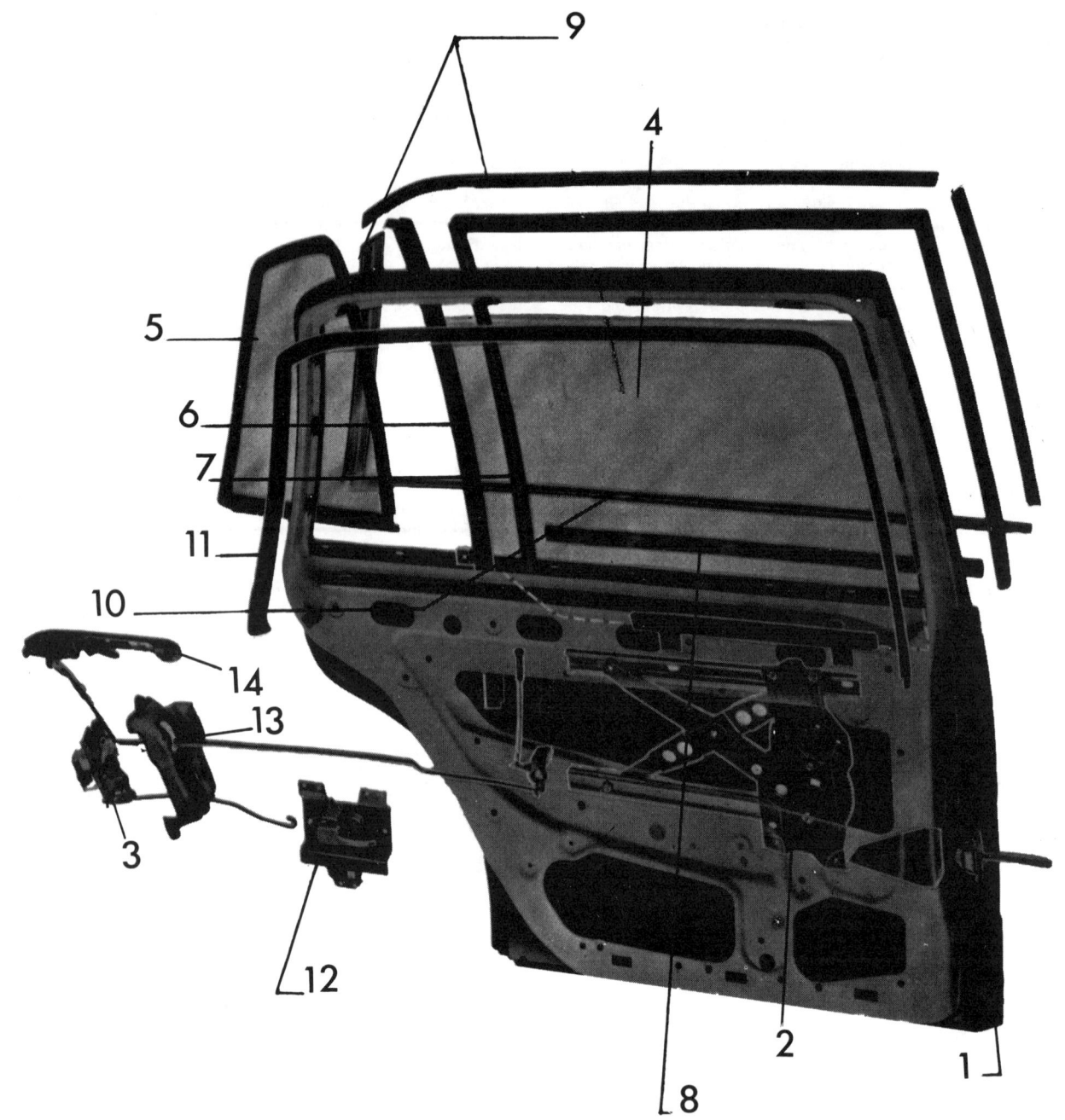

Fig. 12.2 Rear door (exploded view) (Sec. 10)

1 Door check rod	4 Door glass	7 Window guide	10 Window recess strip
2 Window regulator	5 Quarter light	8 Window recess eal	11 Inner strip
3 Lock	6 Rear guide rail	9 Sealing strips	12 Door lock remote control mechanism

pencil mark made before the striker was loosened.

4   When a position has been found in which the door closes firmly, but without difficulty, tighten the striker.

14 Bonnet lid – removing and refitting

1   Raise the lid and support it on its stay.

2   To minimise the risk of damaging the car paintwork, it is advisable to seek the services of an assistant so that there is one person on each side of the car.

3   Disconnect the snap connector to the bonnet light and pull off the pipe to the windscreen washer jet.

4   Mark round the hinges with a pencil, or a fine ball point pen to facilitate positioning the bonnet when it is refitted.

5   Support the bonnet and remove the two nuts and washers from each side, then lift the bonnet off.

6   Refitting is the reverse of removal. The nuts should be partially tightened initially and the hinges lined up with the scribed marks made before removal. After positioning the bonnet, tighten the nuts.

7   Any adjustment of the bonnet lock which may be necessary to provide smooth, positive closure can be carried out at the cable

adjusters under the bonnet. Never adjust the cable so that it is under tension in the released position.

15 Windscreen – removing and refitting

1 The windscreen and rear window are directly bonded to the metalwork and the removal and fitting of this glass should be left to your Audi dealer or a specialist glass replacement company.

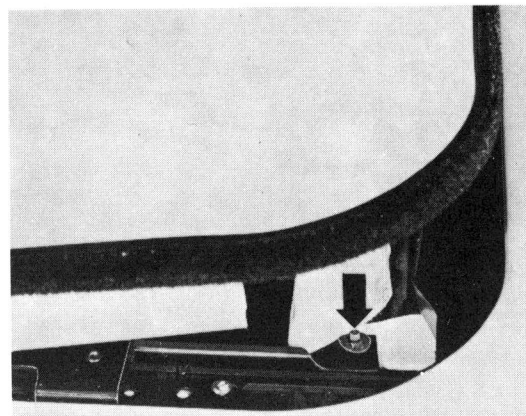

Fig. 12.3 Sunroof trim clamping washer (Sec. 16)

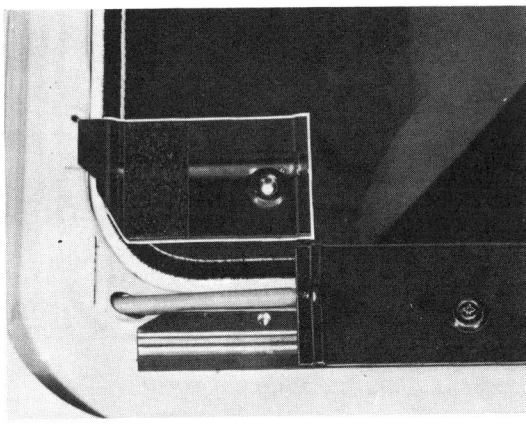

Fig. 12.5 Sunroof front guide cover (Sec. 16)

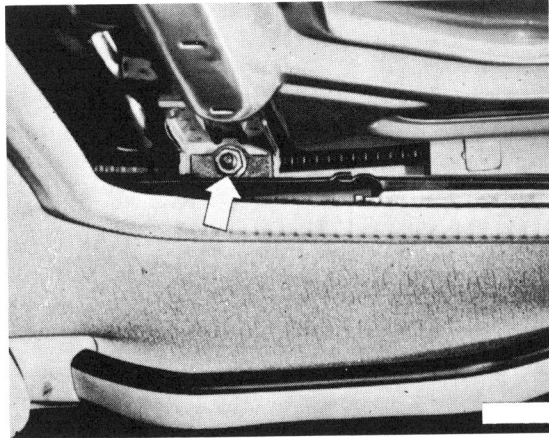

Fig. 12.7 Sunroof front height adjusting nut (Sec. 16)

16 Sunroof – removing and refitting

1 Raise the sunroof.
2 Release the clips at the front of the sunroof trim and unscrew the bolt and clamping washer from the back, then lift out the trim.
3 Close the sunroof, detach the front of the trim and slide it back.
4 Remove the cover for the front guide. Remove the screws at the rear and lift out the sunroof lid.
5 Refitting is the reverse of removal, but note that the sunroof trim can only be pushed forward, or backwards when the roof is closed.
6 Adjust the height of the sunroof by means of the screws and elongated holes at the rear of the lid and by the height adjusting nuts at the front of the lid.
7 If a power operated sunroof is fitted, the motor can be removed in the following way.
8 Disconnect the battery and unscrew and remove the sun visor brackets.
9 Detach the cover from the electric motor.
10 Disconnect the electrical connector from the sliding roof switch.

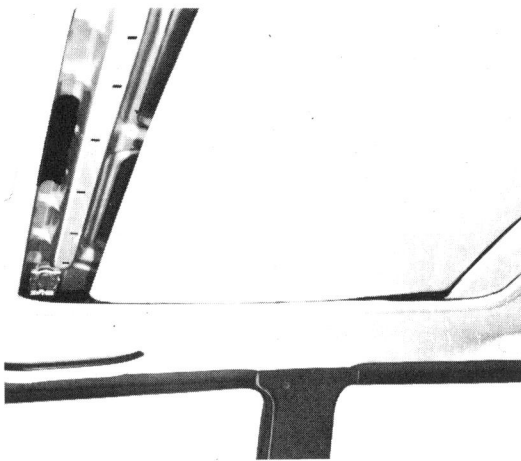

Fig. 12.4 Pushing back the roof trim (Sec. 16)

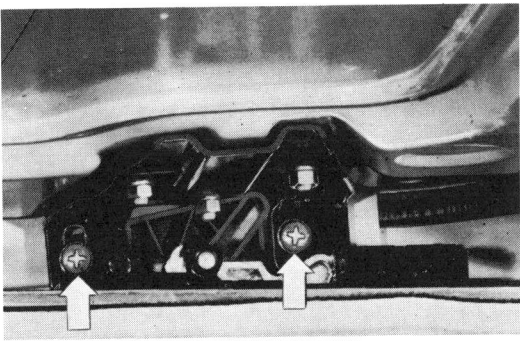

Fig. 12.6 Sunroof rear screws with adjusting slots (Sec. 16)

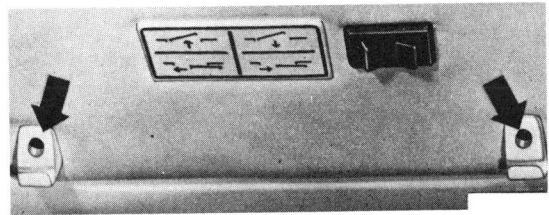

Fig. 12.8 Sun visor brackets (Sec 16)

Fig. 12.9 Sunroof motor mounting plate screws (Sec 16)

Fig. 12.10 Sunroof (power operated) pinion tooth alignment (Sec 16)

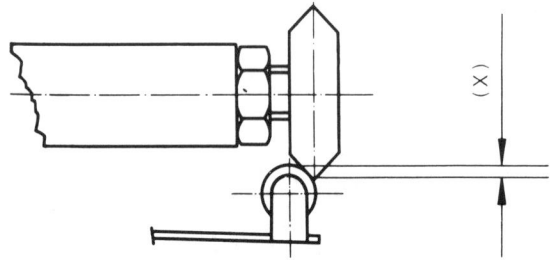

Fig. 12.11 Sunroof (power operated) control pin setting (Sec 16)

$x = 1.0$ to 1.5 mm (0.039 to 0.059 in)

11 Loosen the mounting plate screws (arrowed in Fig. 12.9) and withdraw the electric motor complete with the gear mechanism.
12 When refitting the motor/gear assembly refer to Fig. 12.10, and check that the switch control rod is in alignment with the centre of the pinion (arrow A). If correct, one tooth of the pinion must be fully engaged with the drivegear (arrow B).
13 Adjust the control pin so that dimension (X) corresponds with the cut-in point of the switch. (See Fig. 12.11).
14 Refit the sun visor brackets and reconnect the battery.

17 Instrument cluster – removing and refitting

1 Disconnect the battery then prise out the two wood grain trim panels, to reveal the top fixing screws of the instrument cluster shroud.
2 Remove the two screws beneath the shroud and take off the shroud.

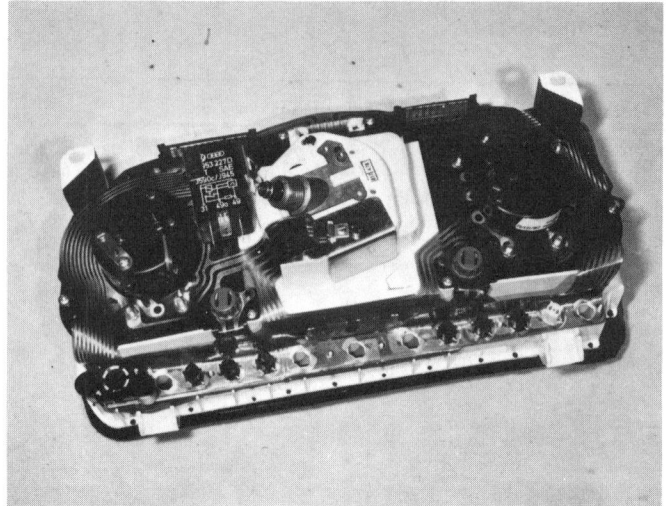

17.4 Rear view of instrument cluster showing speedometer and wiring harness connections

3 Remove the two screws from the top of the instrument cluster and pull the cluster forward.
4 Disconnect the speedometer cable from the instrument and disconnect the multi-plug connections from the wiring harness (photo).
5 Carefully remove the instrument cluster assembly.
6 When refitting the cluster, ensure that the speedometer cable is pushed through into the engine compartment, so that the cable is not kinked, or strained. Also make sure that the electrical cables are positioned so that they are not pinched, or strained when the cluster is screwed into place.

18 Console and parcel shelf – removing and refitting

1 Unscrew and remove the gear lever knob.
2 Remove the auxiliary instrument panel screws and pull the panel out (photo) to reveal the rear fixing screw of the console.
3 Remove the screws from the brackets on the side of the console, which attach the console to the parcel shelf.
4 Prise off the cover plate at the rear end of the console and remove the screw beneath it, then lift out the console (photo).
5 Remove the screw from each end of the parcel shelf, and the three screws which secure the top of the parcel shelf and lift the shelf out (photo).
6 Refitting is the reverse of removal.

19 Central door lock system

1 On certain models, a vacuum operated central door lock system is fitted.
2 Any fault in the system is most likely to be caused by a leak in one of the vacuum hoses due to chafing. Once these have been checked out, inspect the vacuum chamber and the non-return (check valve).
3 If only one door lock fails to operate correctly then the control valve or individual actuators should be removed for testing when connected to an independent vacuum source.
4 The location of the individual components are shown in the illustrations (Fig. 12.12 and 12.13).
5 When fitting a check valve, make sure that the black coloured side of the valve is towards the vacuum source.

20 Power operated windows

1 Certain models are equipped with power (electric) operated windows which can be raised or lowered when the ignition is switched on.
2 If a fault develops, first check that the system fuse has not blown.

18.2 Auxiliary instrument panel removed

18.4 Centre console removed showing gear lever assembly

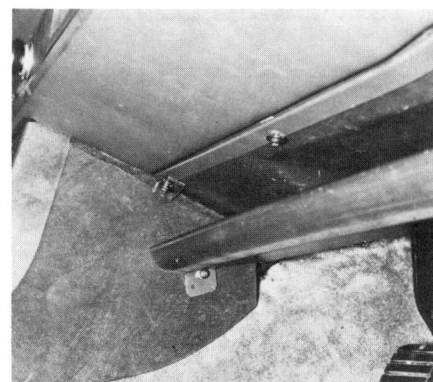

18.5 Parcels shelf fixing screws and dashboard lower cover

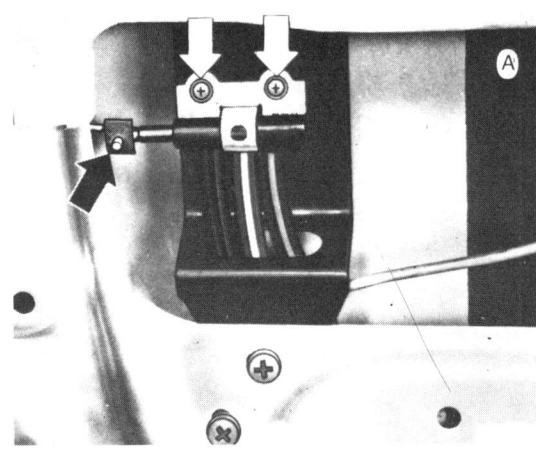

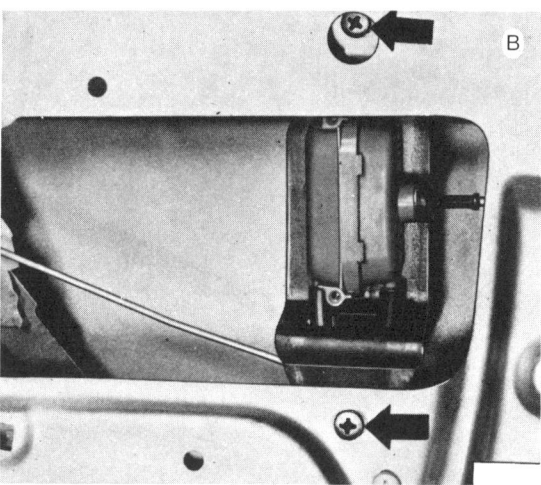

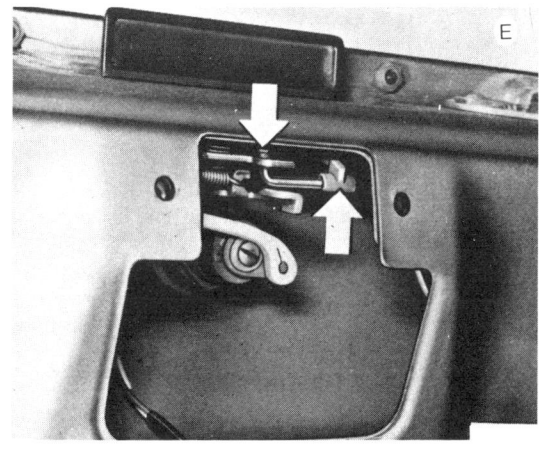

Fig. 12.12 Actuator mounting screws for centralised system door locks (Sec 19)

A Left front door control valve
B Right front door actuator
C Luggage boot lid actuator
D Rear door actuator
E Luggage boot lid actuator linkage rod

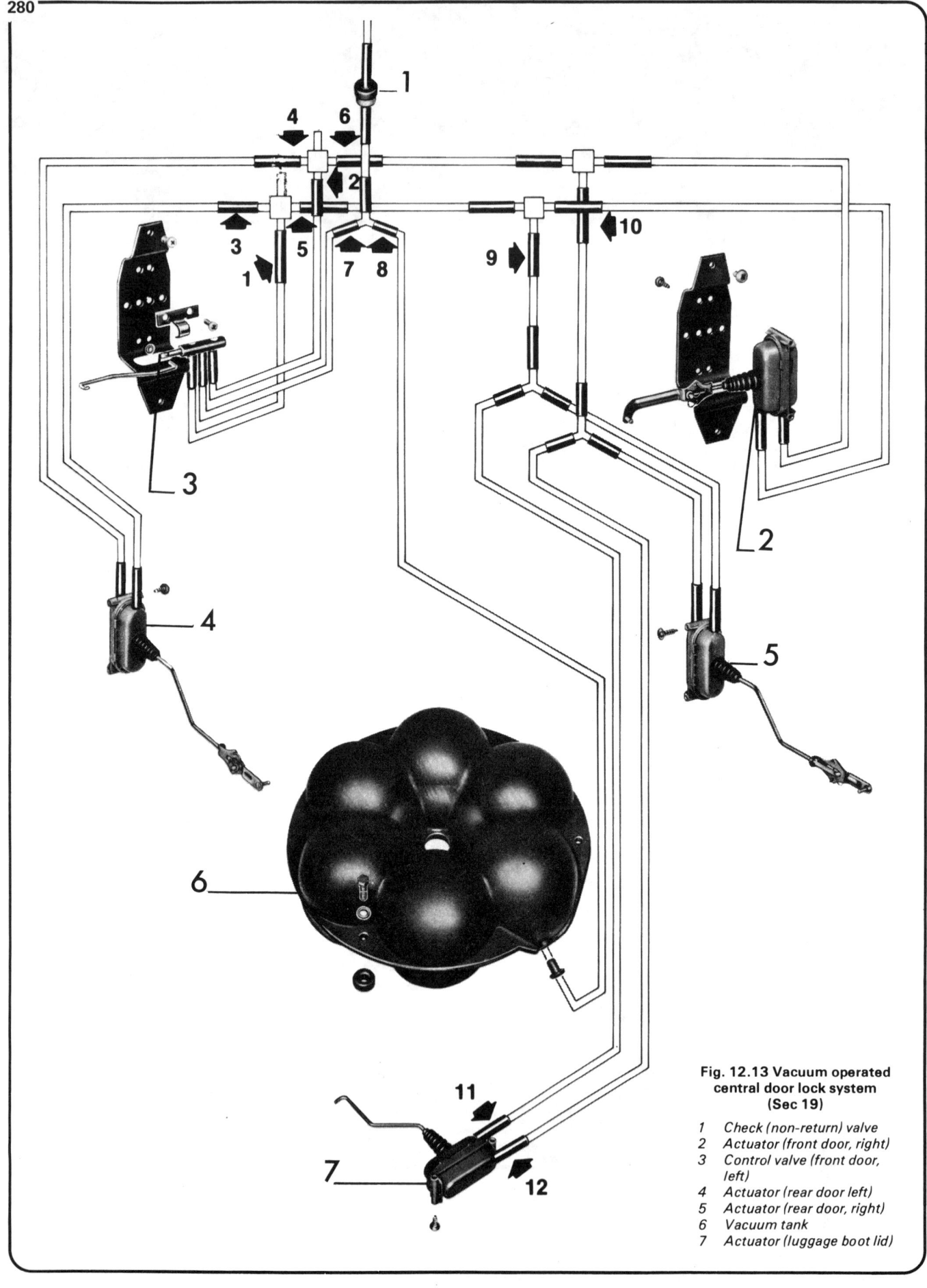

Fig. 12.13 Vacuum operated
central door lock system
(Sec 19)

1   Check (non-return) valve
2   Actuator (front door, right)
3   Control valve (front door,
    left)
4   Actuator (rear door left)
5   Actuator (rear door, right)
6   Vacuum tank
7   Actuator (luggage boot lid)

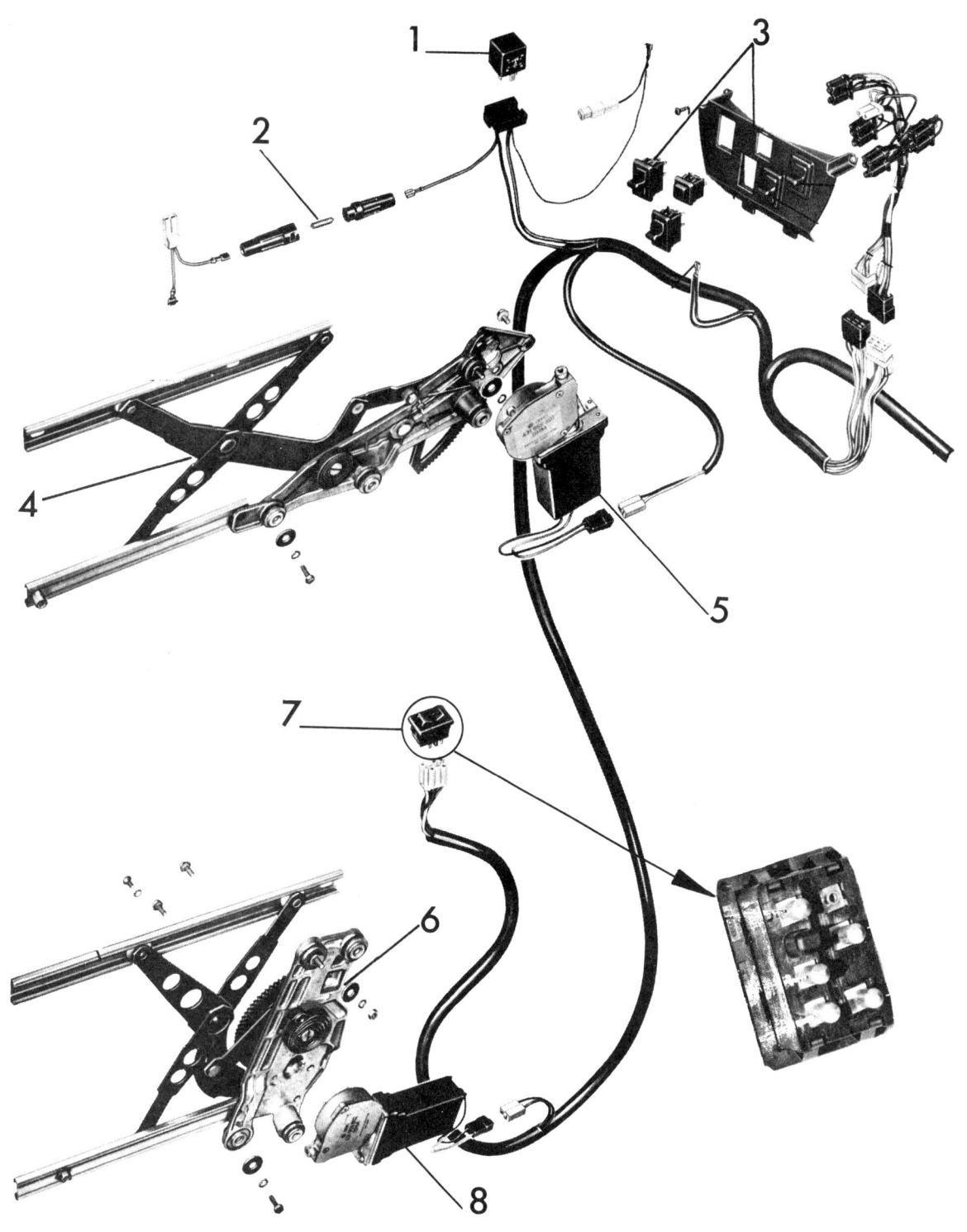

Fig. 12.14 Power operated window system (Sec 20)

1	Motor relay	4	Regulator assembly (front door)	6	Regulator assembly (rear door)	7	Rear door switch
2	In-line fuse					8	Electric motor (rear door)
3	Switch control assembly	5	Electric motor (front door)				

3 Access to the driving motors and electrical connections is gained by removing the door interior trim panels as described in Section 8.

21 Heater (cars without air conditioning) – removal and installation

1 Disconnect the battery.
2 Either drain the cooling system or pinch the heater hoses with suitable clamps, as near to the heater matrix as possible and then disconnect the hoses from the heater.
3 Working both within the engine compartment and under the instrument panel, identify all electrical leads, control cables and vacuum hoses and disconnect them from the heater assembly and the control panel.
4 Under the instrument panel, disconnect the demister ducts from the heater body.
5 Working within the engine compartment, disconnect the heater mounting strap. Cut round the adhesive seal which seals the heater assembly to the body aperture.
6 Lift the heater from its location and as it is withdrawn, unclip any wiring harness and release the cable grommets which may still be in position.
7 Installation is a reversal of removal, but re-seal the heater to the body aperture and top-up the cooling system (Chapter 2) on completion.

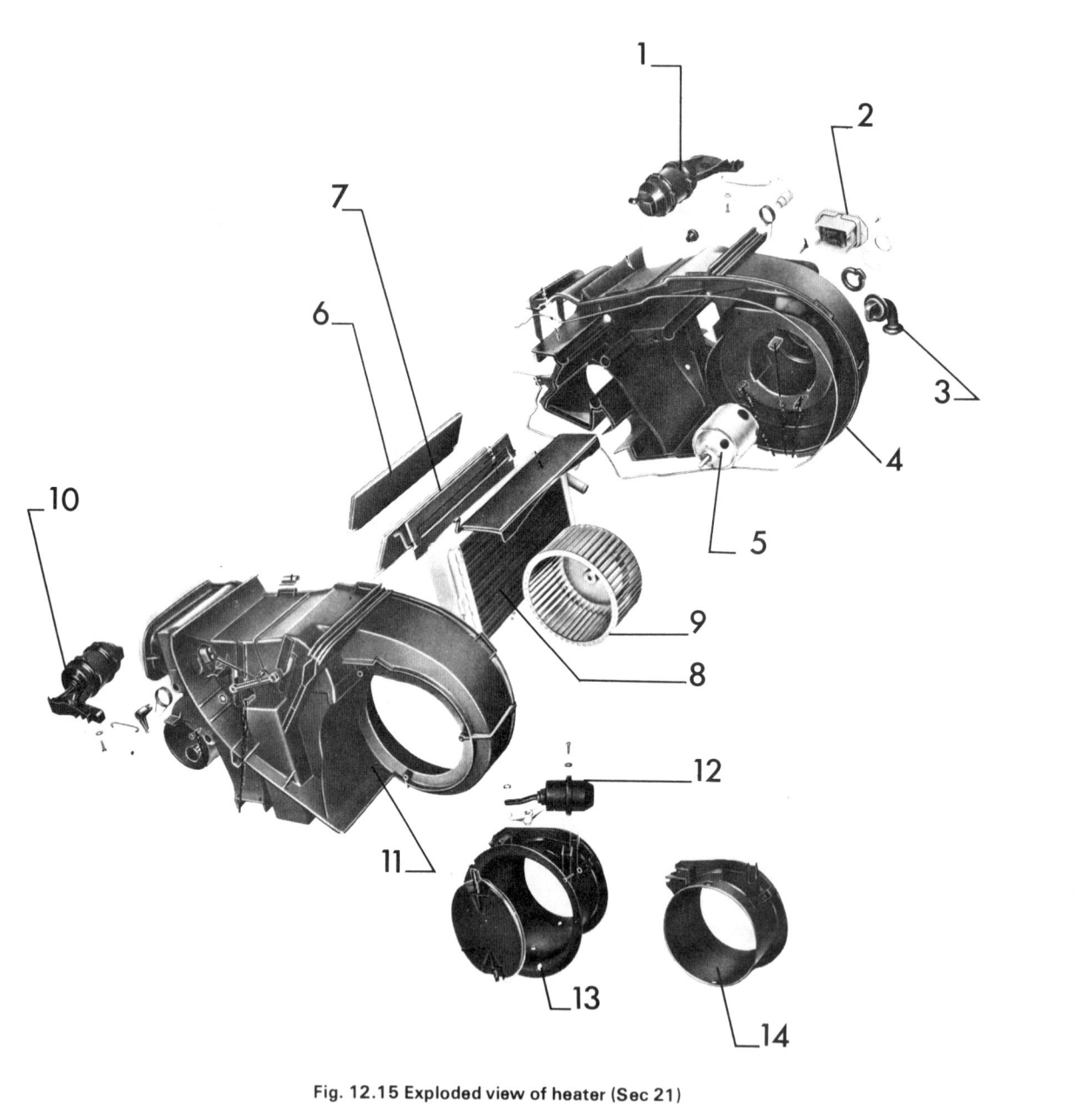

Fig. 12.15 Exploded view of heater (Sec 21)

1	*Vacuum unit (footwell/ demister flap)*	*5*	*Motor*	*9*	*Fan*
2	*Resistor*	*6*	*Air distribution flap*	*10*	*Vacuum unit (air vent flap)*
3	*Vent*	*7*	*Footwell/demister flap*	*11*	*Left-hand half casing*
4	*Right-hand half casing*	*8*	*Matrix (heat exchanger)*	*12*	*Vacuum unit (cut-off flap)*

13 Intake duct and cut-off flap
14 Air conditioner intake duct (cars with air conditioner only)

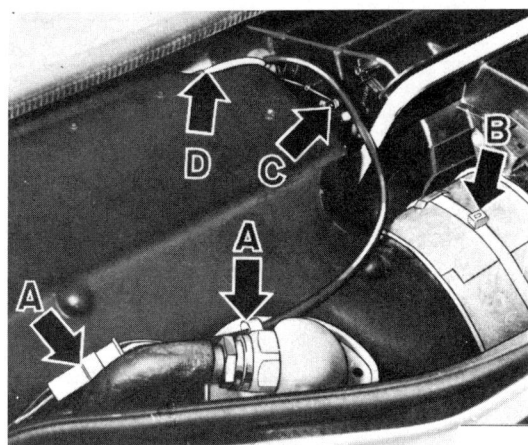

Fig. 12.16 Thermostat connector plug (air conditioner) (Sec 22)

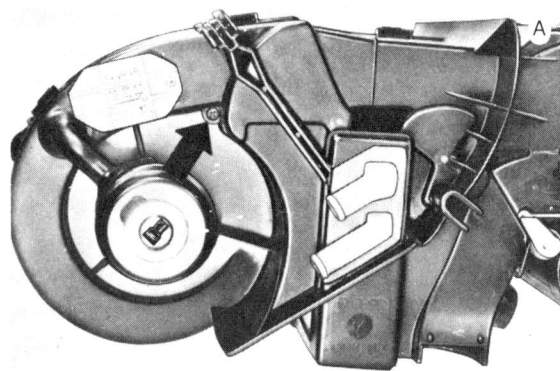

Fig. 12.18A Heater casing screw right-hand side (Sec 23)

Fig. 12.17 Mounting screws at evaporator housing (Sec 22)

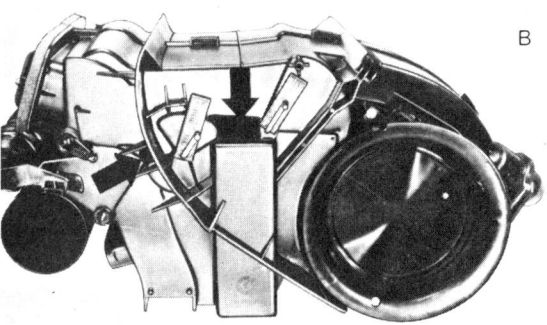

Fig. 12.18B Heater casing screws, left-hand side (Sec 23)

Fig. 12.19 Heater control cable cover plate (Sec 24)

22 Heater (cars with air conditioning) – removal and installation

1   The operations are very similar to those described in the preceding Section except that the following additional items must be disconnected:

   (a) Electrical lead for thermostat
   (b) Evaporator/heater clamping strap
   (c) Mounting screws from evaporator housing

2   Withdraw the heater assembly at the same time supporting the evaporator. Do not disconnect any of the air conditioner refrigerant lines during the foregoing operations.
3   Installation is a reversal of removal but seal the air conditioner intake duct to the heater casing.

23 Heater – dismantling and reassembly

1   With the heater removed from the car, drain out any remaining coolant from the matrix.
2   To gain access to the motor or matrix, separate the two halves of the heater casing. To do this, prise off the spring clips and extract the screws, one from the right-hand side and two from the left.
3   The motor/fan and the matrix can now be removed, also the vacuum units and resistor if required.
4   If the matrix is leaking, it is recommended that a new one is obtained rather than an attempt made to repair the old one.
5   Reassembly is a reversal of dismantling. Use a strip of self-adhesive foam to insulate the matrix from the heater casing and when the two halves of the casing are assembled, seal round the edge of the matrix with silicone rubber compound.

24 Heater control panel – removal and refitting

1   The heater control panel is accessible after pulling off the control lever knobs and withdrawing the escutcheon plate (Fig. 12.21).
2   Unscrew and remove the upper and lower mounting screws from the control assembly and lower it.
3   The various vacuum hoses can be detached as necessary but identify their position first.
4   Access to the temperature control cable is obtained by extracting the screws and removing the cover from the control lever housing (Figs. 12.19 and 12.20).
5   Disconnect the cable by unclipping it and sliding its hooked end from the sliding member.
6   When reassembling, insert the temperature control outer cable as far as it will go and fit its retaining clip having first connected the inner cable to the sliding member. Now move the control lever as far as it will go to the left (Cold) and connect the outer cable to the heater casing with its clip and the inner cable to the heater flap valve.

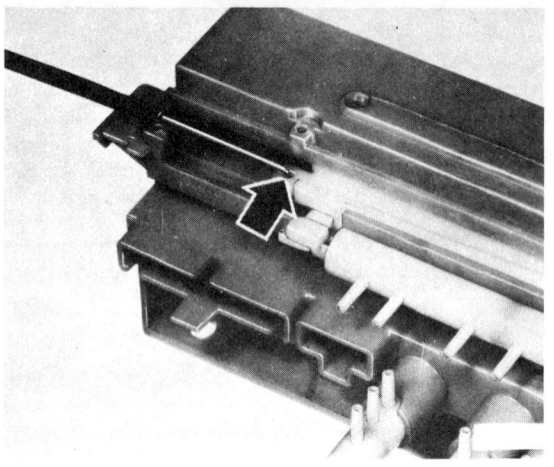

Fig. 12.20 Heater temperature control cable attachment to sliding member (Sec 24)

25 Air conditioner – description and maintenance

1   The air conditioner fitted to some models (2.0 and 2.2 litre engine) operates and is controlled in conjunction with the heater assembly and fresh air ventilation system.

2   Regularly check the condenser for clogging with flies or dirt. Hose clean with water or compressed air.

3   Regularly check the tension of the compressor drivebelt. The belt deflection should be about 10 mm (0.39 in) at the centre point of its longest run. If adjustment is required, release the compressor mounting nuts and turn the nut on the adjuster eyebolt as necessary.

4   In winter when the unit is not in use, run it for a few minutes to keep the compressor in good order.

26 Air conditioner – precautions

1   Never disconnect any part of the air conditioner refrigeration circuit unless the system has been discharged by your Audi dealer or a qualified refrigeration engineer.

2   Where the compressor or condenser obstruct other mechanical operations such as engine removal, then it is permissible to unbolt their mountings and move them to the limit of their flexible hose

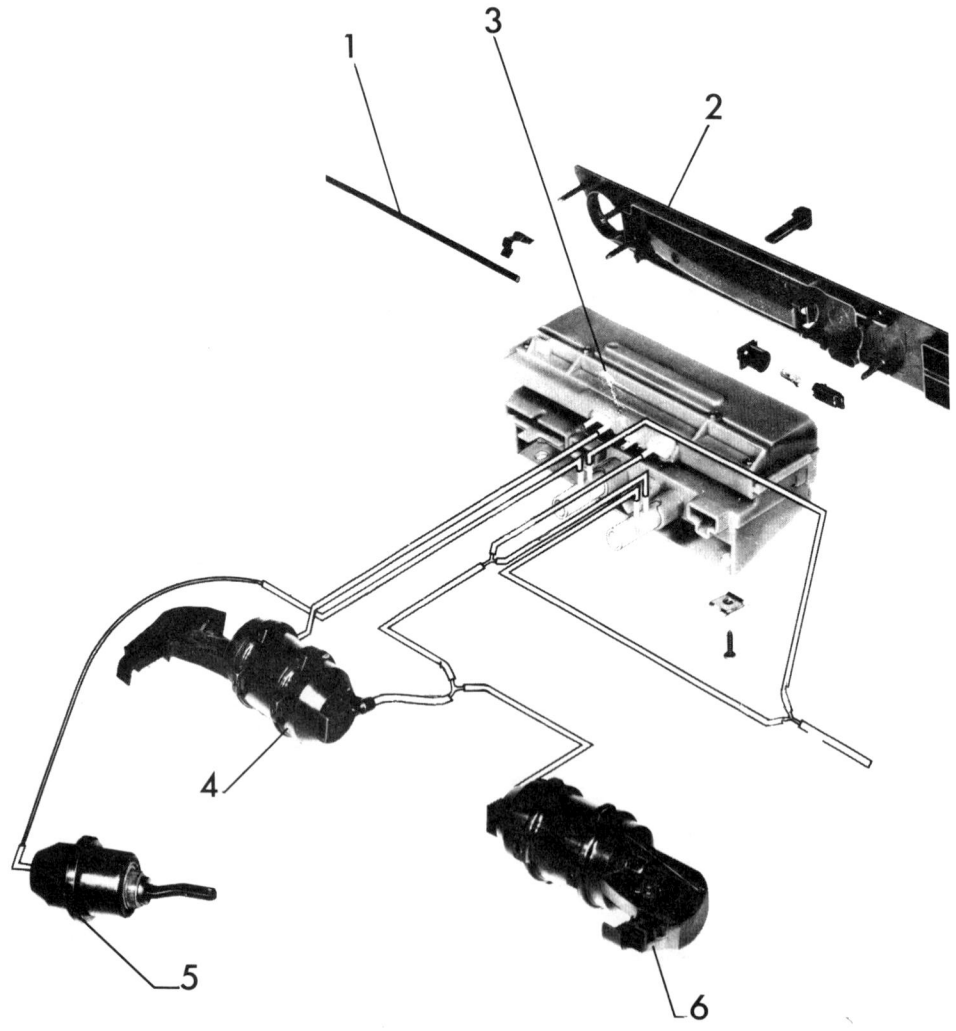

Fig. 12.21 Heater control panel (car without air conditioning) (Sec 24)

1 Temperature control cable	4 Vacuum unit (distribution	6 Vacuum unit (footwell/
2 Control panel escutcheon	flap)	demister flap)
3 Control panel assembly	5 Vacuum unit (cut-off flap)	

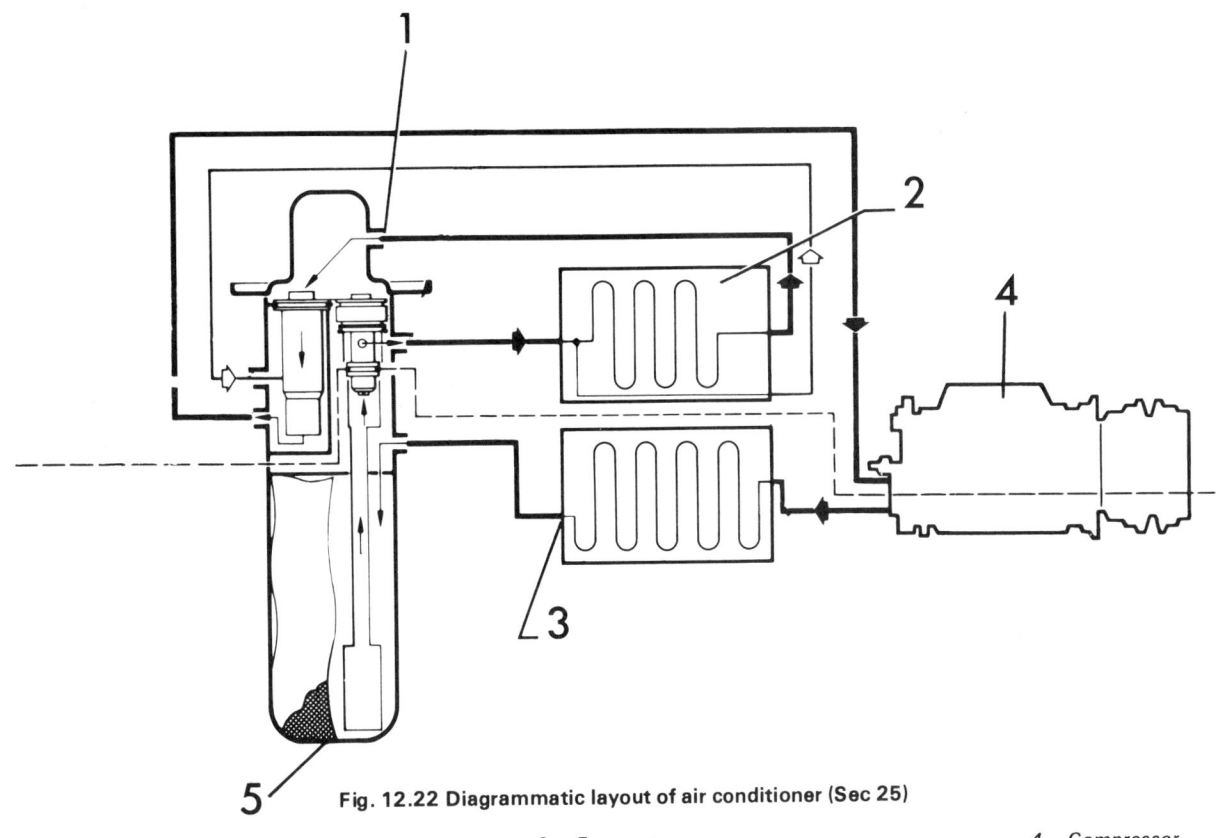

Fig. 12.22 Diagrammatic layout of air conditioner (Sec 25)

1 Valves in receiver (VIR) assembly	2 Evaporator 3 Condenser	4 Compressor 5 Receiver/drier

deflection but not to disconnect the hoses. If there is still insufficient room to carry out the required work then the system must be discharged before disconnecting and removing the assemblies.

3   The system will of course have to be recharged on completion.

27 Air conditioner – removal and refitting

1   Have the system discharged (evacuated) of refrigerant by your Audi dealer or a qualified refrigeration engineer before carrying out the operations marked *

Controls
2   Remove the upper section of the centre console, the glove compartment and the dashboard lower cover.
3   Disconnect the battery, remove the two mounting screws from the lower surface of the control assembly and pull it towards you and downward.

Vacuum unit (fresh air flap)
4   Extract the two screws and remove the by-pass flap from under the dashboard. By reaching through the by-pass opening, disconnect the vacuum unit from the fresh air flap. Turn the vacuum unit through 90° and remove it.

Compressor *
5   Disconnect the hoses from the compressor. Release the mounting bolts and turn the adjuster eyebolt nut until the drivebelt can be slipped off the pulley and withdrawn (Fig. 12.24).
6   Unbolt the compressor mounting brackets and withdraw the compressor.

Evaporator and valves-in-receiver (VIR) assembly *
7   Extract the four screws located one behind each corner of the by-pass flap (do not remove the by-pass air flap) (Fig. 12.25).
8   Working within the plenum chamber under the bonnet, loosen the water drain hose retainer and push the drain hose into the chamber.

Fig. 12.23 Removing air conditioner controls (Sec 27)

9   Disconnect the vacuum unit hose at the thermostat leads within the plenum chamber.
10 Disconnect the refrigerant hoses from the condenser and the compressor. Plug the open pipes.
11 Detach the evaporator/VIR assembly from its sealing gasket, turn it and remove from the centre part of the plenum chamber.

Condenser *
12 The condenser is mounted ahead of the engine. To remove it, disconnect the connecting pipelines and plug the open ends. Unbolt and remove the condenser.
13 Refitting of the components is the reverse of removal but observe

Fig. 12.24 Air conditioner compressor and mountings (Sec 27)

| 1 | Support bracket | 2 | Pulley/clutch assembly | 3 | Compressor | 4 | Adjuster bolt | 5 | End bracket |

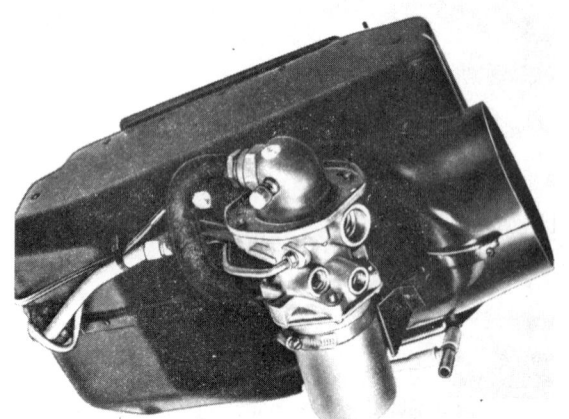

Fig. 12.25 Air conditioner evaporator/VIR assembly (Sec 27)

the following points.

    (a) The evaporator and VIR assembly can only be installed as a combined unit
    (b) Have the complete system checked over before it is professionally re-charged with refrigerant

28 Air conditioner switches and relays

1   Several switches and relays are incorporated in the air conditioning system as protection and safety devices. Failure or faulty operation can normally only be overcome by substitution of a new component. Those marked * cannot be removed until the system has been discharged.

Superheat switch

2   Located in the compressor, it cuts off power if refrigeration circuit is overheated by causing the superheat fuse to blow.

Fig. 12.26A Air conditioner superheat switch (Sec 28)

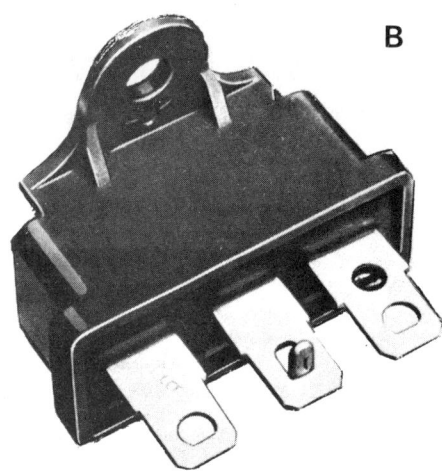

Fig. 12.26B Air conditioner superheat fuse (Sec 28)

Fig. 12.27 Air conditioner high pressure switch (Sec 28)

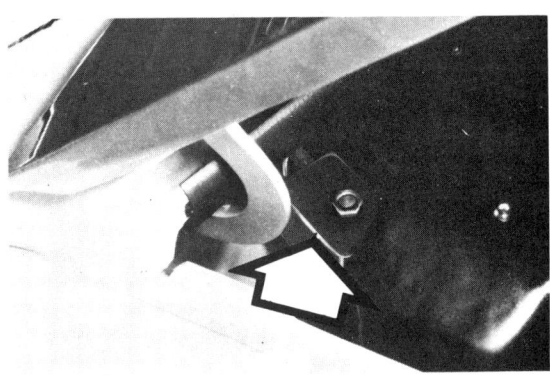

Fig. 12.28 Air conditioner air temperature switch (Sec 28)

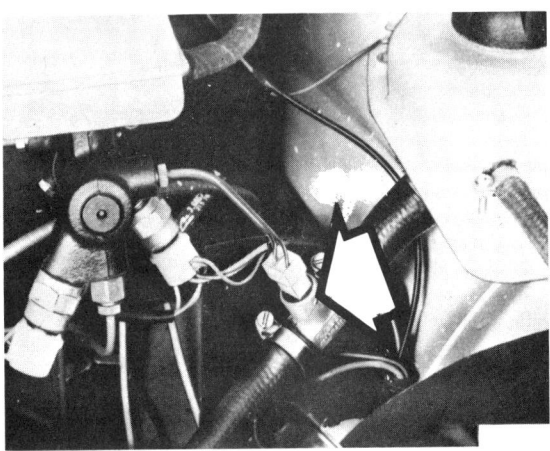

Fig. 12.29 Air conditioner coolant overheat switch (Sec 28)

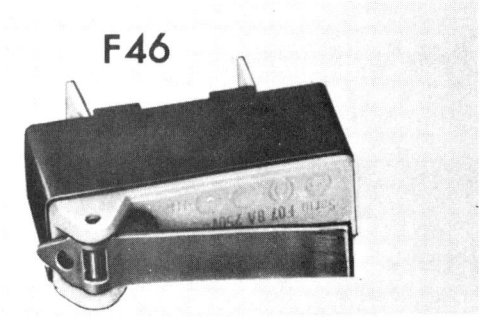

Fig. 12.30 Air conditioner compressor cut-out switch (Sec 28)

reengages at ambient temperatures above this level.

Coolant (overheat) switch
5   Also controls engagement and disengagement of compressor clutch dependent upon coolant temperature. Disengages at temperatures in excess of 120°C (248°F). Engages at 106°C (223°F) and below.

Compressor cut-out switch
6   Fitted to cars equipped with automatic transmission only, the switch operates the delay relay to disengage compressor clutch for six seconds.

Fuse panel relays
7   These control the various circuits as shown in Fig. 12.31.

High pressure switch *
3   Operates condenser cooling fan to switch on at 14 bar (199 lb/in^2) and off at 12 bar (170 lb/in^2).

Air temperature switch
4   Controls engagement and disengagement of compressor clutch. Disengages at 5°C (41°F) and lower ambient temperatures and

Fig. 12.31 Air conditioner fuse/relay arrangement (Sec 28)

J13   Fresh air fan relay
J59   Compressor cut-out relay
J69   Radiator cooling fan relay

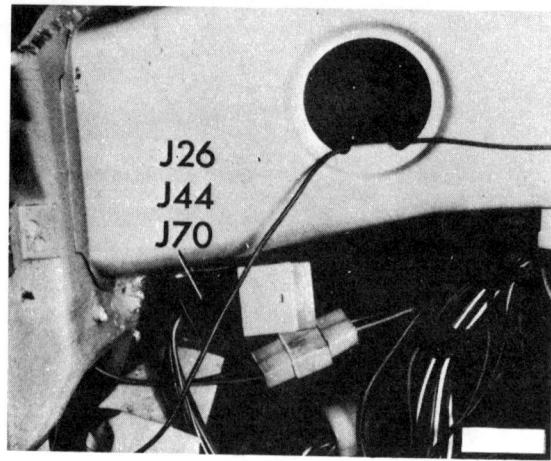

Fig. 12.32 Air conditioner under dashboard relays (Sec 28)

J26   Radiator cooling fan relay
J44   Compressor clutch relay
J70   Delay relay (automatic transmission only)

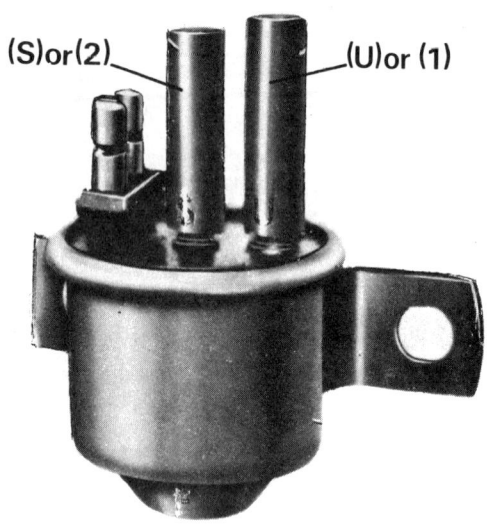

Fig. 12.33 Air conditioner idle two-way valve (Sec 28)

S or 2 to vacuum line
U or 1 to distributor vacuum unit

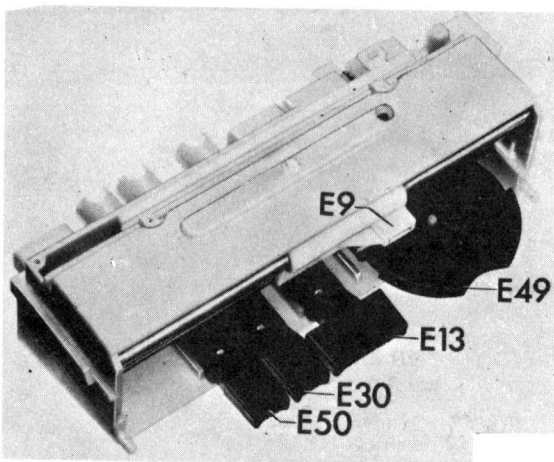

Fig. 12.34 Air conditioner control panel electrical connections (Sec 28)

E9   Fresh air fan
E13   Heater/air conditioner
E30   Air conditioner (ECON)
E49   Fresh air fan speed control
E50   Demister

Under dashboard relays
8   The location and purpose of these relays is shown in Fig. 12.32.

Idle two-way valve
9   Installed to offset the drag of the air conditioner compressor by increasing the engine idle speed.

Control panel electrical connections
10   These are to the rear of the air conditioner control panel and are shown in Fig. 12.34. On cars operating in Canada, the control assembly is electrical and operates various micro-switches.

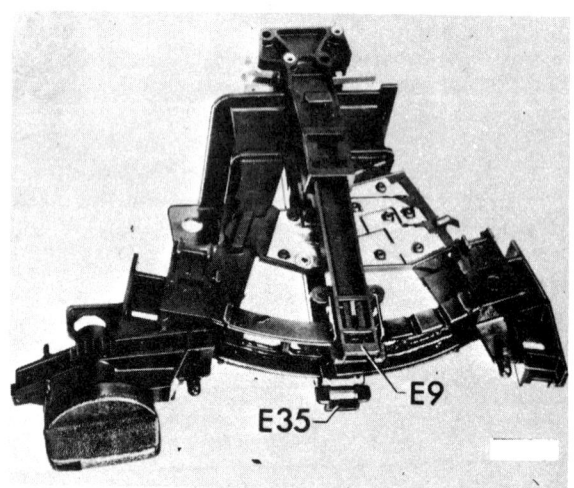

Fig. 12.35 Air conditioner control assembly (Canada) (Sec 28)

E9   Fresh air fan switch
E35   Air conditioner switch

29 Dashboard – removal and refitting

1   Disconnect the battery.
2   Remove the instrument cluster as described in Section 17.
3   Remove the steering wheel as described in Chapter 11.
4   Remove the centre console by extracting the fixing screws, removing the gear lever knob and sliding the assembly with rubber gaiter off the gear lever. Disconnect the leads from the radio as it is withdrawn. Refer to Section 18 if supplementary instruments are fitted.

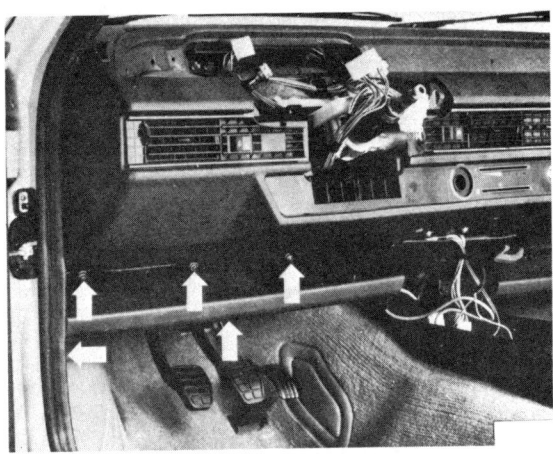

Fig. 12.36 Parcel shelf screws (Sec 29)

Fig. 12.37 Dashboard fixing screws (Sec 29)

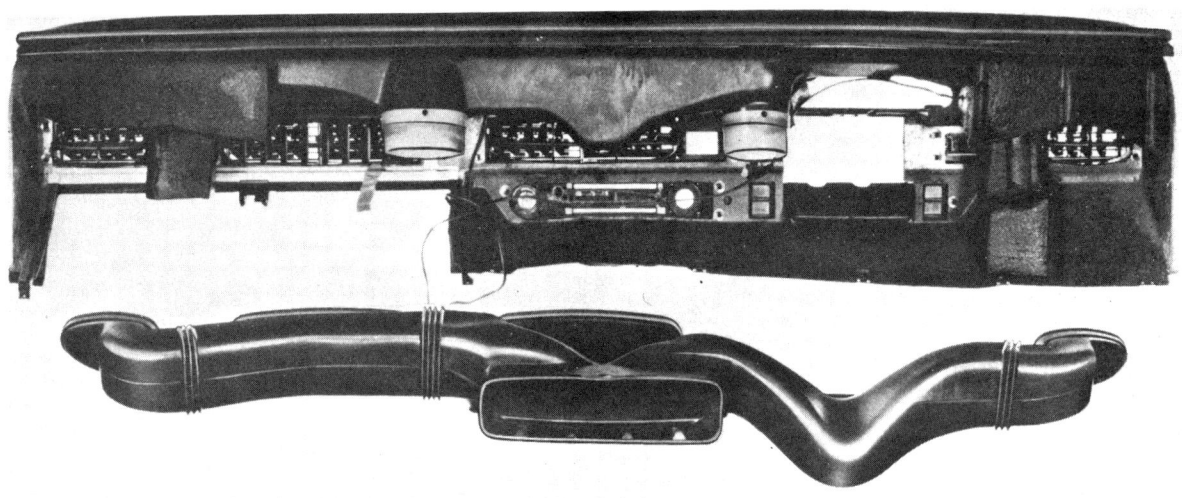

Fig. 12.38 Rear view of dashboard showing air duct assembly (Sec 29)

5   Remove or disconnect the heater (or air conditioner) control assembly as described earlier in this Chapter.
6   Extract the parcel shelf screws and release the insulation material.
7   Extract the dashboard fixing screws (arrowed in Fig. 12.37).
8   Remove the heated rear window switch.
9   Disconnect the fresh air ducting.
10 Disconnect the wiring for the glove compartment lamp and the heater control illumination.

11 Withdraw the dashboard carefully making sure that all wires have been disconnected.
12 From the reverse side of the dashboard, the instrument panel support, the air duct assembly and the air duct outlets can be detached if required. The radio speaker cover grilles are also accessible.
13 Refitting is a reversal of removal but before installing the dashboard, make sure that the anti-rattle felt strips are stuck correctly in position.

Metric conversion tables

Inches	Decimals	Millimetres
1/64	0.015625	0.3969
1/32	0.03125	0.7937
3/64	0.046875	1.1906
1/16	0.0625	1.5875
5/64	0.078125	1.9844
3/32	0.09375	2.3812
7/64	0.109375	2.7781
1/8	0.125	3.1750
9/64	0.140625	3.5719
5/32	0.15625	3.9687
11/64	0.171875	4.3656
3/16	0.1875	4.7625
13/64	0.203125	5.1594
7/32	0.21875	5.5562
15/64	0.234375	5.9531
1/4	0.25	6.3500
17/64	0.265625	6.7469
9/32	0.28125	7.1437
19/64	0.296875	7.5406
5/16	0.3125	7.9375
21/64	0.328125	8.3344
11/32	0.34375	8.7312
23/64	0.359375	9.1281
3/8	0.375	9.5250
25/64	0.390625	9.9219
13/32	0.40625	10.3187
27/64	0.421875	10.7156
7/16	0.4375	11.1125
29/64	0.453125	11.5094
15/32	0.46875	11.9062
31/64	0.484375	12.3031
1/2	0.5	12.7000
33/64	0.515625	13.0969
17/32	0.53125	13.4937
35/64	0.546875	13.8906
9/16	0.5625	14.2875
37/64	0.578125	14.6844
19/32	0.59375	15.0812
39/64	0.609375	15.4781
5/8	0.625	15.8750
41/64	0.640625	16.2719
21/32	0.65625	16.6687
43/64	0.671875	17.0656
11/16	0.6875	17.4625
45/64	0.703125	17.8594
23/32	0.71875	18.2562
47/64	0.734375	18.6531
3/4	0.75	19.0500
49/64	0.765625	19.4469
25/32	0.78125	19.8437
51/64	0.796875	20.2406
13/16	0.8125	20.6375
53/64	0.828125	21.0344
27/32	0.84375	21.4312
55/64	0.859375	21.8281
7/8	0.875	22.2250
57/64	0.890625	22.6219
29/32	0.90625	23.0187
59/64	0.921875	23.4156
15/16	0.9375	23.8125
61/64	0.953125	24.2094
31/32	0.96875	24.6062
63/64	0.984375	25.0031

Millimetres to Inches

mm	Inches
0.01	0.00039
0.02	0.00079
0.03	0.00118
0.04	0.00157
0.05	0.00197
0.06	0.00236
0.07	0.00276
0.08	0.00315
0.09	0.00354
0.1	0.00394
0.2	0.00787
0.3	0.01181
0.4	0.01575
0.5	0.01969
0.6	0.02362
0.7	0.02756
0.8	0.03150
0.9	0.03543
1	0.03937
2	0.07874
3	0.11811
4	0.15748
5	0.19685
6	0.23622
7	0.27559
8	0.31496
9	0.35433
10	0.39370
11	0.43307
12	0.47244
13	0.51181
14	0.55118
15	0.59055
16	0.62992
17	0.66929
18	0.70866
19	0.74803
20	0.78740
21	0.82677
22	0.86614
23	0.09551
24	0.94488
25	0.98425
26	1.02362
27	1.06299
28	1.10236
29	1.14173
30	1.18110
31	1.22047
32	1.25984
33	1.29921
34	1.33858
35	1.37795
36	1.41732
37	1.4567
38	1.4961
39	1.5354
40	1.5748
41	1.6142
42	1.6535
43	1.6929
44	1.7323
45	1.7717

Inches to Millimetres

Inches	mm
0.001	0.0254
0.002	0.0508
0.003	0.0762
0.004	0.1016
0.005	0.1270
0.006	0.1524
0.007	0.1778
0.008	0.2032
0.009	0.2286
0.01	0.254
0.02	0.508
0.03	0.762
0.04	1.016
0.05	1.270
0.06	1.524
0.07	1.778
0.08	2.032
0.09	2.286
0.1	2.54
0.2	5.08
0.3	7.62
0.4	10.16
0.5	12.70
0.6	15.24
0.7	17.78
0.8	20.32
0.9	22.86
1	25.4
2	50.8
3	76.2
4	101.6
5	127.0
6	152.4
7	177.8
8	203.2
9	228.6
10	254.0
11	279.4
12	304.8
13	330.2
14	355.6
15	381.0
16	406.4
17	431.8
18	457.2
19	482.6
20	508.0
21	533.4
22	558.8
23	584.2
24	609.6
25	635.0
26	660.4
27	685.8
28	711.2
29	736.6
30	762.0
31	787.4
32	812.8
33	838.2
34	863.6
35	889.0
36	914.4

1   Imperial gallon = 8 Imp pints = 1.20 US gallons = 277.42 cu in = 4.54 litres

1   US gallon = 4 US quarts = 0.83 Imp gallon = 231 cu in = 3.78 litres

1   Litre = 0.21 Imp gallon = 0.26 US gallon = 61.02 cu in = 1000 cc

Miles to Kilometres		Kilometres to Miles	
1	1.61	1	0.62
2	3.22	2	1.24
3	4.83	3	1.86
4	6.44	4	2.49
5	8.05	5	3.11
6	9.66	6	3.73
7	11.27	7	4.35
8	12.88	8	4.97
9	14.48	9	5.59
10	16.09	10	6.21
20	32.19	20	12.43
30	48.28	30	18.64
40	64.37	40	24.85
50	80.47	50	31.07
60	96.56	60	37.28
70	112.65	70	43.50
80	128.75	80	49.71
90	144.84	90	55.92
100	160.93	100	62.14

lbf ft to kgf m		kgf m to lbf ft		lbf/in^2 to kgf/cm^2		kgf/cm^2 to lbf/in^2	
1	0.138	1	7.233	1	0.07	1	14.22
2	0.276	2	14.466	2	0.14	2	28.50
3	0.414	3	21.699	3	0.21	3	42.67
4	0.553	4	28.932	4	0.28	4	56.89
5	0.691	5	36.165	5	0.35	5	71.12
6	0.829	6	43.398	6	0.42	6	85.34
7	0.967	7	50.631	7	0.49	7	99.56
8	1.106	8	57.864	8	0.56	8	113.79
9	1.244	9	65.097	9	0.63	9	128.00
10	1.382	10	72.330	10	0.70	10	142.23
20	2.765	20	144.660	20	1.41	20	284.47
30	4.147	30	216.990	30	2.11	30	426.70

Index

Printed by
Haynes Publishing Group
Sparkford Yeovil Somerset
England